LEEDS UNITED
INTERNATIONALS
FOR CLUB AND COUNTRY

Martin Jarred

LEEDS UNITED
INTERNATIONALS
FOR CLUB AND COUNTRY

First published in Great Britain in 2009 by The Breedon Books Publishing
Company Limited, Breedon House, 3 The Parker Centre, Derby, DE21 4SZ

This paperback edition published in Great Britain in 2014 by DB Publishing,
an imprint of JMD Media Ltd

ISBN 978-1-78091-397-1

Printed and bound in the UK by Copytech (UK) Ltd Peterborough

Contents

Acknowledgements

THE idea for this book came while I was collaborating on *The Who's Who of Leeds United* with Malcolm Macdonald. It seemed a natural progression to delve deeper into the international careers of the 100-plus Leeds players – City and United – to have represented their country. Malcolm and I have worked together on several Leeds books for Breedon since 1986, and this one is the first I have done 'solo'. While taking a breather, Malcolm has very kindly proofread this book. We hope to have an updated version of *Leeds United: A Complete Record* published by Breedon in the near future.

Others who have helped provide gems of information and material include, in no particular order: Paul Dews, head of media at Leeds United; Barry Hugman; the family of Aubrey Powell; Glenda Dines, of the Irish FA; statisticians Paul Clayton (Charlton Athletic), Dave Smith (Leicester City) and Yaniv Bleicher (Israel); David Barber at the FA, *The Press*, York, for many of the photographs; staff at Leeds City Library; the Revd Jane Craske of Lidgett Park Methodist Church for information on the late Eric Stephenson; and Steve Caron and staff at Breedon Publishing.

Finally, thanks to my wife, Jenny, for her patience and understanding while I have been toiling for endless hours on my laptop surrounded by a mountain of books, newspapers, cuttings, programmes and reams of paper.

It is impossible to do a book such as this without referring to countless others for assistance. Among the main ones I have consulted are:

England Football Fact Book Cris Freddi

An English Internationalists' Who's Who and *Who's Who of Scottish Internationalists 1872–1986* Douglas Lamming

Scotland The Team Andrew Ward

Who's Who of Welsh International Soccer Players Gareth M. Davies and Ian Garland

The Complete Who's Who of Irish International Football 1945–98 Stephen McGarrigle

Ireland On The Ball Donal Cullen

The Guinness Book of World Soccer Guy Oliver

Leeds United Book of Football Nos 1, 2 and 3

Rothmans and Sky Sports Yearbooks

Feet First Stanley Matthews

Bobby Collins: The Wee Barra David Saffer

Peter Lorimer: Leeds and Scotland Hero Peter Lorimer and Phil Rostron

King John: The True Story of John Charles, Leeds United Legend Richard Coomber

Bremner! The Legend of Billy Bremner Bernard Bale

Marching On Together Eddie Gray

Madiba's Boys Graeme Freidman

Careless Hands: The Forgotten Truth of Gary Sprake Stuart Sprake and Tim Johnson

Leeds United Official Handbooks

Preface

FANS always feel a sense of pride when one of their club's players earns full international honours. When someone they watch week in, week out, gets to pull on their country's shirt and play at the highest level it adds something to the club's stature. It is something to be celebrated.

That is certainly the case at Leeds United, where visitors who go through the entrance to the West Stand at Elland Road are greeted by a huge panel bearing the names of those at the club who have achieved international status. Nearby are framed England and Scotland shirts donated to the club by two of its most famous sons, World Cup winner Jack Charlton and Scotland captain Billy Bremner.

Leeds United Internationals: For Club and Country tells the international stories of all the Leeds players, both United and City, in alphabetical name order. It covers the men who have formed the bedrock of their national team and the one-cap wonders. It includes those who have been on international duty while on loan at Elland Road, and also takes a brief look at those who were capped before and after their time at Leeds. There is also a section on managers and backroom staff, international matches at Elland Road and full international appearance records.

Research has thrown up some unusual stories and events. For example, how many Leeds fans could recall that United's all-time record goalscorer, Peter Lorimer, once scored an own-goal against England? Collating all the information and statistics has taken years. The occasional fact has not been found – usually attendances, which are a bit of a minefield anyway – but very little is missing from the whole picture. The websites of various countries' Football Associations have certainly helped speed up research, but even they can throw up anomalies which require further checking.

In the main text, appearances are often referred to as caps. Although caps were often distributed in seasons, with the year and opposition embroidered on the headwear, the term cap has been used in this book to signify an international appearance.

Though international matches continued throughout the war, the wartime matches of 1939–45 and the 1946 Victory internationals were not recognised as full internationals, and, therefore, those appearances are not included in the total number of caps won; however, details of such games involving Leeds players are recorded in the International Appearances section which is laid out in country order.

Leeds United and Leeds City have provided some top-class players to the international arena over the years. Hopefully, this book will provide a little more insight into what they got up to when they represented their country.

Martin Jarred
July 2009

Leeds United Internationals

MARK AIZLEWOOD
(Wales 1986–94)

Midfield/Defender

Born: Newport, Monmouthshire, 1 October 1959.
Caps: Charlton Athletic 4, Leeds United 9, Bradford City 4, Bristol City 21, Cardiff City 1. Total: 39

PASSIONATE patriot Mark Aizlewood was every inch a Welshman, right down to his boot studs. Of his 39 caps, nine were won during a 16-month spell at Elland Road. His influence in Welsh football stretched beyond the field, as he has served his country as a coach and administrator. He became his home-town club Newport County's youngest player at the age of 16 years and 179 days, having to have permission from his headmaster to make his debut against Darlington in March 1976.

The Aizlewood family lived just a few hundred yards from County's Somerton Park ground, and his brother Steve, older by seven years, had also made his debut for Newport at 16. Mark, who played for Wales Schools and captained his country at youth level, had turned down big guns Arsenal to play for Newport.

The teenager could play either in midfield or defence, and at 18 became County's record sale when he moved to Luton in April 1978 for £50,000. He was already a Wales Under-23 cap when he went to Kenilworth Road, where he continued to develop. After four years with the Hatters he switched to Charlton, making his debut against Leeds at Elland Road on 6 November 1982 when United were beaten 2–1, the Addicks' winner coming from another Welsh hero, Carl Harris, the former Leeds favourite.

Aizlewood was initially used as a full-back by Charlton, but it was only when he reverted to midfield or defence, where he had shone as a youngster, that he was truly appreciated by Charlton's fans. He was their Player of the Year in 1985 and 1986, skippering the club to Division One in 1985–86. He was surprisingly overlooked by the Welsh selectors until, at the age of 26, he made his full debut against Saudi Arabia when he came on as substitute for David Williams – later a first-team coach at Elland Road – in a friendly on 15 February 1986.

Aizlewood started all of Charlton's First Division games the following season until Billy Bremner persuaded him to drop down a division and join United's promotion push. When the £200,000 deal went through on 5 February 1987, Aizlewood was already the proud possessor of four full caps. He made his Leeds debut two days later in a 0–0 draw at Sheffield United and made his home bow the following week in a 2–2 draw with Charlton before winning his fifth cap – his first as a Leeds player – in a goalless draw in a friendly against Russia at Swansea.

Bremner's squad were fighting on two fronts, battling for promotion and pushing ahead in the FA Cup. Aizlewood was Cup-tied and so was a spectator when United lost their semi-final thriller against Coventry at Hillsborough. But his presence as midfield anchorman in League games gave the talented John Sheridan licence to push forward.

United missed out on promotion, finishing fourth, and went into the Play-offs where they squeezed past Oldham to set up a Play-off Final against Aizlewood's old club, Charlton, who had finished 19th in Division One. After two nerve-shredding games it ended 1–1 on aggregate, and in the replay at Birmingham's St Andrew's ground it was heartbreak for Aizlewood and Leeds. Sheridan's late free-kick prised open the promotion door in extra-time, but it was slammed shut as two late Charlton goals condemned United to another season in Division Two and preserved Athletic's First Division status. Leeds skipper Brendan Ormsby was badly injured in that Final game, and Bremner named Aizlewood as United's captain in Ormsby's prolonged absence when the new campaign got underway.

Mark Aizlewood.

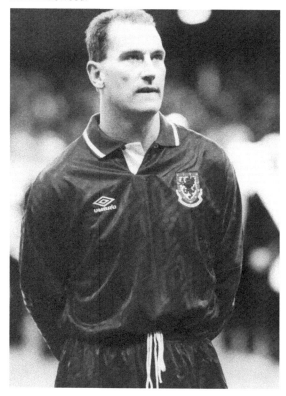

Aizlewood (left) tussles with Germany's Jürgen Klinsmann.

A month into the 1987–88 season Aizlewood played his part in Wales's 1–0 win against group leaders Denmark in a European Championship qualifier at Cardiff, coming on for the last 20 minutes to enable the Welsh to successfully defend Mark Hughes's 19th-minute goal. Three days later Aizlewood was injured in a 2–0 home defeat at the hands of Hull and was out of action until the end of February. During that time Wales lost in Denmark and Czechoslovakia, failing to qualify for the European Championship Finals, the 2–0 defeat in Prague being Mike England's last game in charge of the Red Dragons.

After David Williams was in charge in a caretaker role for a match against Yugoslavia in March 1988, former Leeds star Terry Yorath was appointed as Wales boss the following month and included Aizlewood in his first selection – a 4–1 defeat in Sweden. Aizlewood also started June friendlies in Malta and Italy, which were won 3–2 and 1–0 respectively, and was looking an integral part of Yorath's side.

Leeds had finished the season a disappointing seventh, and when the Whites made a poor start to 1988–89 Bremner was sacked and Howard Wilkinson, the Sheffield Wednesday boss, installed as manager. With Ormsby still laid low with a career-threatening injury, Aizlewood continued to wear the skipper's armband for United and played his first World Cup qualifying game in September when the battling Welsh lost 1–0 in Holland. Neville

Southall produced a sensational display to keep the multi-talented Dutch at bay until Ruud Gullit scored the only goal of the game late on. It was a bitter blow, but qualification was always going to be tough for the Welsh with West Germany and Finland also in the group.

There was further disappointment for Aizlewood as the season – and his time at Leeds – drew to a close. On May Day Bank Holiday he was taking some criticism for his performance from the sparse crowd that turned up at Elland Road for the visit of Walsall. Aizlewood netted the only goal of the game and thrust two fingers up to the boo-boys in the Kop as part of his goal celebrations. Wilkinson stripped the Welsh star of the captaincy and suspended him for the rest of the season. He never played for Leeds again.

Aizlewood's next competitive action was in front of a feverish Ninian Park crowd where Wales's World Cup qualification hopes virtually ended, despite holding the Germans to a 0–0 draw. It was Aizlewood's ninth cap as a Leeds player – and his last. Inevitably, after the Walsall incident he left the club in the summer, joining neighbours Bradford City for a season. He became a Wales regular under Yorath, winning further Wales appearances while at Bristol City and Cardiff, taking his tally to 39, the last coming in a 2–0 win over Cyprus in 1994.

A competitive, strong, forceful character, Aizlewood remained in Wales to play and coach the likes of Welsh League sides Aberystwyth, Merthyr, Newport, Carmarthen and Cwmbran Town. He also did plenty of media work, in which he was not afraid to air controversial views and, despite ruffling a few feathers among Welsh football's hierarchy, he was appointed technical director of the Welsh Under-16 side in 2003 and was assistant to Ian Rush in helping develop the Under-17s.

When Rush was appointed manager at Chester, he made Aizlewood his assistant. Aizlewood was axed in April 2005 and Rush stepped down in protest. A highly rated coach, and a big believer in progressing the game in Wales, Aizlewood was then appointed director of the FA of Wales Trust, an organisation dedicated to developing youngsters through a coaching network.

EIRIK BAKKE
(Norway 1999–2005)
Midfield
Born: Sogndal, 13 September 1977.
Caps: Sogndal 2, Leeds United 24. Total: 26

EIRIK BAKKE timed his move to Leeds United perfectly. The Norwegian Under-21 captain had just sampled his first taste of full international football when David O'Leary swooped for the midfielder in summer 1999. 'He's one for the future', said O'Leary of his £1.5 million capture after beating off Chelsea and Rosenborg for his signature. The 6ft 2in Bakke made such rapid progress that he figured in all Norway's games in the European Championships the following year, with his form at club level in the Premiership hotbed making his international selection claims impossible to ignore.

Throughout his teens Bakke played for his home-town club, Sogndal, representing Norway at various levels, including 34 games for the Under-21s. Although Sogndal were in the Norwegian Second Division and the Scandinavians boasted a strong squad at international level, young Bakke won his first full cap as an 80th-minute substitute in a 1–0 friendly win in Israel and four months later won his second cap when he came on during the 6–0 thrashing of Jamaica in Oslo – Tore Andre Flo scoring the first two goals.

O'Leary's gamble paid off, with Bakke's strength and driving runs in midfield earning the admiration of the Elland Road faithful, who were enjoying a golden period as Leeds started to make their mark in European competition. After just one season at Elland Road, where he had become a regular starter in the second half of the campaign as David Batty was injured, Bakke played himself into his country's Euro 2000 squad. The Norwegians had reached the Finals for the first time in their history and were unbeaten in competitive matches for a year. Featuring Bakke and six other Premiership players, they made a brilliant start by beating the highly fancied Spanish 1–0 in Rotterdam.

Defeat to Yugoslavia followed, and Bakke was on the bench for the final game against underdogs Slovenia, knowing that victory would put Norway into the quarter-finals. Norway were over-cautious, with Bakke coming on after an hour for striker John Carew as coach Nils Johan Semb seemed happy to settle for the 0–0 draw his men achieved. Most of the Norway squad were still on the pitch as news filtered through that Yugoslavia were beating Spain 3–2. But joy turned to despair as the Spaniards fought back to win in injury time, denying Bakke and Norway a place in the last eight.

Despite criticism of his tactics, Semb kept his job and Bakke remained a big part of his plans as Norway chased a place in the 2002 World Cup. It was to be a poor qualifying campaign for the Norwegians, who managed just two victories from their 10 games in Group Five – against Wales and Armenia – with Bakke featuring in only four of the games. But there was consolation at Elland Road as Bakke was an integral part of the Whites squad that stormed to the semi-finals of the Champions League and finished fourth in the Premiership. Bakke missed three months of the 2001–02 season through injury as both Leeds and Norway suffered stop-start seasons. United dropped a place in the Premiership and were knocked out of the UEFA Cup by PSV Eindhoven.

Gradually news of United's over-spending to fund the new-found glory days began to leak out of Elland Road,

Eirik Bakke on the ball.

and the club's bright new future turned into a dark nightmare. Star players started leaving as costs were cut at Elland Road, and the Whites slid to 15th in 2002–03. One consolation for Bakke was the improved form Norway had shown in the Euro 2004 qualifiers. He was an established part of the international squad, which was now under the guidance of the former Nottingham Forest player Age Hareide.

Qualification for the Finals developed into a two-horse race between Norway and Denmark, but at the end of the season Bakke was struggling with a chronic knee injury. At the end of the 2002–03 campaign Norway had a friendly against Finland ahead of two crucial qualifiers against Denmark and Romania. They were desperate to include Bakke, but United provided medical evidence that the midfielder was not fit to play. However, Norway did not heed United's warning, and he figured in all three games. Norway lost in Copenhagen, were held at home by Romania and missed automatic qualification.

Bakke reported back to Elland Road having suffered further knee ligament damage while on international duty, and Leeds made noises about compensation from the Norwegian FA, although nothing came of it. The Norwegian gamble had backfired. Bakke missed the vast majority of 2003–04, including the Euro qualification Play-off matches against Spain, who won both legs easily. Bakke went to the US for specialist treatment but found himself back at square one when he snapped cruciate ligaments and damaged his cartilage in a United friendly against Swedish part-timers Pitea in July 2004. He was out of action for another year, and when he returned cash-strapped Leeds had been relegated and his international career was all but over. He did come off the bench to face Switzerland in a friendly in August 2005, but was a shadow of his former self.

Leeds, anxious to slash their wage bill, loaned him to Aston Villa, where O'Leary was in charge, and eventually he returned to his homeland with Brann Bergen, where he gradually rediscovered some of his old magic.

PETER BARNES

(England 1977–82)

Winger

Born: Rugeley, Manchester, 10 June 1957.
Caps: Manchester City 14, West Bromwich Albion 6, Leeds United 2. Total: 22
Goals: 4

WINGER Peter Barnes sped across football's firmament like a comet, but by the time he arrived at Leeds his international career was suffering from burn-out. At £930,000 Barnes was United's record signing in August 1981 and the man that manager Allan Clarke believed would unlock First Division defences. He was 24 and already had 20 England caps, with the promise of many more to come, but it did not work out that way for either club or country. He struggled in United's relegation side and added just two more international appearances – both as a substitute – to his tally. One of England's brightest stars simply faded away.

Barnes burst onto the scene with devastating effect at Manchester City, playing in the England Youth team that won the Mini-World Cup in 1975 in Switzerland when the young Lions beat Finland 1–0 in the Final. He made his City debut against Luton the same year and scored in the Maine Road club's 2–1 League Cup Final triumph over Newcastle in 1976, being named Young Player of the Year a few months later.

Already established at Under-21 level, he made his full England debut as a 20-year-old in a World Cup qualifier against Italy at Wembley on 16 November 1977. He was one of three new caps – Steve Coppell and Bob Latchford were the others – in a game that England had to win and then live in the vain hope that Luxembourg would beat the Italians to send England to the Finals in Argentina. England

got the first bit right, Barnes sparkling in a 2–0 win over the Azzurri. His mazy dribbling and speed was a constant menace to the Italian defence, but inevitably Enzo Bearzot's side went on to defeat Luxembourg to end hopes of an England miracle.

The Italian game had been the third and final match of Ron Greenwood's temporary spell in charge. The former West Ham man had stepped into the breach following former Leeds boss Don Revie's controversial decision to quit the England job to take charge of the United Arab Emirates. The super display against Italy earned Greenwood the FA's blessing to carry on as Revie's full-time replacement, and Barnes became an integral part of his plans.

The blond-haired flier became an established England player alongside United teammate Trevor Cherry, with gifted midfield clubmate Tony Currie occasionally keeping them company. Barnes scored four England goals – all of them in victories. The first two came against Wales and Hungary, then he sank a super 20-yard half-volley equaliser against Scotland as England pushed on to win 3–1 and netted with a rare diving header in a 3–0 European Championship qualifying triumph against Bulgaria in Sofia.

Barnes was hot property and after England's 1979 summer tour left Manchester City for West Brom for £650,000 – a record for both clubs. However, his left wing berth in the England team, which had looked secure for a couple of seasons, was coming under threat from two

Peter Barnes.

rising stars – Laurie Cunningham and Tony Woodcock. Barnes replaced Cunningham at the Hawthorns after his England rival moved to Spanish giants Real Madrid, while Woodcock, who was also making great strides at Nottingham Forest under the guidance of one-time Leeds boss Brian Clough, also moved abroad with German club FC Cologne.

Woodcock's ability to link up with Forest clubmate Trevor Francis on the international stage was giving him the edge over Barnes, who missed five successive England games, including victories over Northern Ireland and Bulgaria, which wrapped up qualification for the European Championships. With Greenwood pondering his squad for the Finals in Italy, he re-called Barnes for the Home International at Wrexham with the Euro Finals less than a month away. England gave an abject display, crashing 4–1 as they lost in Wales for the first time since 1955. Barnes was dropped and did not make it to the European Championships. He had enjoyed a fine season with West Brom, finishing as top scorer, but even after England failed to make much progress in Euro 1980 he did not start as England began their World Cup qualifying campaign the following season.

Greenwood did give Barnes a chance to show what he could do in a friendly against Brazil at Wembley at the end of the 1980–81 season, and this time the winger took his chance with a superb display as red-shirted England were unlucky to lose 1–0. Barnes had forced his way back into the England frame and retained his place for a 0–0 home draw with Wales. Greenwood's England were finding goals hard to come by, and a nasty shock was lurking round the corner as they lost 2–1 in Switzerland, a result which put World Cup qualification in peril. Barnes came on in Basel as England sought to break down the Swiss defence, but the stunning loss meant that qualification hopes were no longer in their hands. The following week England, without Barnes, put on a superb display to win 3–1 in Hungary to end a poor run of six matches without a win and give themselves an outside chance of reaching the Finals.

Barnes's career was at a crossroads when Leeds came calling. After two productive seasons at West Brom, he joined Clarke's Leeds, his final game for Albion being a 0–0 draw at Elland Road. In some ways life had come full circle for Barnes. When he was 13 he was among a bunch of promising youngsters from the Manchester area that went to Elland Road for training. But, not surprisingly, he was taken on by Manchester City, where his father, Ken, a former Maine Road player, was chief scout. Unfortunately for both Barnes and the Whites his spell at Elland Road did not work out. Too often he was on the fringes of the action, but his pedigree ensured a place in Greenwood's squad as they resumed their World Cup qualifying campaign in Norway.

It was another disastrous night as England slumped 2–1, Barnes coming on for Glenn Hoddle in the second half in a bid to provide hapless England with more width, but the Scandinavians held on to record a famous victory. England got lucky. Other countries took points off each other, and two months later England beat group winners Hungary at Wembley to finish second, which was enough to book a slot in the 1982 World Cup Finals in Spain. Barnes, however, was to miss out on a major tournament yet again. After a disappointing season which saw Leeds relegated, he made his final England appearance as an 82nd-minute substitute in a 2–0 friendly win over Holland at the end of the season.

Still 24, an age at which many international careers have not even started, Barnes's England days were over. He did make it onto the plane to Spain – but not as part of the World Cup squad. Second Division football with Leeds was not an option, so he was loaned to Seville club Real Betis. That was the start of a nomadic career that saw him play for clubs in Australia, Portugal, Malta, Norway and Wales, via both Manchester clubs, Coventry, Bolton, Sunderland and Stockport.

An undoubted talent, Barnes was probably one who played too much, too young. Leeds fans certainly did not see the best of him, but for a while he twinkled on the flanks for England.

DAVID BATTY
(England 1991–99)
Midfield
Born: Leeds, 2 December 1968.
Caps: Leeds United 14, Blackburn Rovers 3, Newcastle United 20, Leeds United 5. Total: 42

MILLIONS looked on in horror as David Batty missed the decisive penalty that saw England tumble out of the 1998 World Cup. But it was Manchester United's David Beckham – not Leeds-born Batty – who shouldered much of the blame for England's quarter-final exit against Argentina. England had fallen behind after just five minutes in St Etienne to a Gabriel Batistuta penalty. But the Three Lions came roaring back with an Alan Shearer penalty and a superb solo goal from 19-year-old Michael Owen.

A free-flowing game levelled up when Javier Zanetti struck home Juan Sebastian Veron's free-kick just before half-time. A minute after the break Beckham was red-carded by Danish referee Kim Milton Nielson for flicking a foot out at Diego Simeone. Ten-man England kept the South Americans at bay for the rest of regulation time and all of extra-time to take the game to penalties. Hernan Crespo and Paul Ince missed the third and fourth spot-kicks and, with Argentina going first, it was at the sudden death stage when Batty struck the 10th penalty, which Carlos Roa saved. Had Beckham still been on the pitch then he would unquestionably have been one of England's designated penalty takers.

David Batty.

When Batty stepped up to the mark more than a few eyebrows were raised by Leeds fans. The midfield dynamo had a reputation for finding it difficult to hit the back of the net. In over 300 appearances for the Whites he had netted just four goals, and two of those came as a teenager early in his career. 'Shoot' became a regular terrace cry at Leeds virtually every time Batty received the ball anywhere within the opposition half. But it was typical of the man that he volunteered to take on such a high-pressure kick – he never shirked a challenge in his life. He later revealed that he had never taken a penalty in his career.

Batty, whose dreaded miss came as a Newcastle player, was afforded cult hero status at Elland Road. The Allerton Grange School youngster came up through the ranks at Leeds and was given his senior United debut against Swindon in November 1987 when he was just 18. The baby-faced assassin was a superb ball-winner, and his passing was always crisp and accurate. Magnificent displays in the white shirt of Leeds were soon transferred to the white of England at Under-21 level. His eye-catching performances pushed him to the brink of full honours when he was named as a stand-by player for the squad that travelled to Dublin to take on the Republic of Ireland in a European Championship qualifier.

It was not long before 'Batts' became a regular central midfielder in the senior England side under Graham Taylor

and won the first of his 42 senior caps as a substitute for Dennis Wise, who became United's boss 15 years later, in a 3–1 win against the USSR at Wembley on 21 May 1991 in the England Challenge Cup competition. Four days later he made his first start, against Argentina, and gave a great display in the centre of the park. The 2–2 draw was enough to give England the trophy, and his excellent performance earned Batty a place on the plane Down Under and to the Far East, where England took on Australia, New Zealand and Malaysia.

Batty went from strength to strength. At Leeds he was a member of a superb all-international quartet alongside Gordon Strachan (Scotland), Gary McAllister (Scotland) and Gary Speed (Wales) as the Whites swept to the 1991–92 First Division title after lifting the Second Division crown two years earlier. Batty's stock rose still further when he wore the captain's armband as England B won 1–0 against Czechoslovakia B on 24 March 1992. The Leeds midfield terrier was now an integral part of the international scene and helped England qualify for the 1992 European Championship Finals in Sweden. Batty did not figure in the disappointing 0–0 opener against Denmark, who only went through to the Finals after the late withdrawal of the expelled Yugoslavian team. He came in for Arsenal's Paul Merson in the next game, against France, which also finished 0–0.

Right-back had been a problem area for England in both games, with Manchester City's Keith Curle and Andy Sinton (Queen's Park Rangers), neither recognised right-backs, filling that position in the first two games. For the crunch game against hosts Sweden it was Batty's turn, and he made a pretty good fist of it, playing a part in the build-up to David Platt's goal, which gave England the lead. But the Swedes equalised with a Jan Eriksson header, before rising star Tomas Brolin struck a superb winner past goalkeeper Chris Woods with a shot on the run. Brolin was at the peak of his powers, but was a shadow of his former self when he signed for Leeds three years later.

England's next task was to qualify for the 1994 World Cup, but Batty was not a regular in the qualifiers and they badly missed his snap as they were held at Wembley by Norway and Holland, drew in Poland and crashed to defeat in Norway. He did figure in the US Cup in summer 1993, but the next time he pulled on an England shirt he was a Blackburn Rovers player. United followers were stunned in September 1993 when their local hero was transferred to big-spending Rovers for £2.75 million. The man who fans thought was the nearest in midfield dynamism to the legendary Billy Bremner was sacrificed to raise cash for Howard Wilkinson to rebuild his team.

Terry Venables had replaced the under-fire Taylor as England's manager and in his first match in charge, a Wembley friendly against Denmark, he brought Batty on for England's new midfield superstar, Paul Gascoigne, his former Under-21 roommate. In many of his England

Argentina goalkeeper Carlos Roa celebrates as David Batty contemplates his 1998 World Cup penalty shoot-out miss.

appearances Batty acted as Gascoigne's 'minder', winning the ball to provide the skilful Geordie with possession to weave his magic.

England were Euro '96 hosts, so did not need to qualify, but Batty missed out on a string of friendly matches because of a broken foot, which ruled him out of all but five matches of Blackburn's Premiership-winning 1994–95 season. He was back in the midfield cockpit at Ewood Park at the start of the following season, but his fracture had left him out of the England picture. A few months after a much-publicised on-pitch bust-up with fellow England international Graeme Le Saux in a Champions League game against Spartak Moscow, Batty put in a transfer request and joined Kevin Keegan's Newcastle United for £3.75 million in March 1996.

Although Batty rediscovered his top form with the Magpies, it was not enough to secure him a place in Euro

Polish players surround stricken teammate Radoslav Michaelski as referee Gunter Benko brandishes a red card for David Batty.

'96, in which Venables's squad reached the semi-finals before bowing to the inevitable penalty shoot-out defeat against old foes Germany. However, he earned a recall from new England boss Glenn Hoddle for the World Cup qualifiers, coming on as a late substitute in a 3–0 victory which saw David Beckham win his first senior cap. Batty gave a superb display in a 0–0 draw against Italy in Rome in October 1997, which clinched England's place in the Finals – a match regarded by Batty as one of the most important of his entire career.

Unlike Gascoigne, Batty made Hoddle's final 22 for France '98 and started the group games against Tunisia and Romania. He made way for rising talent Beckham for the next game, a victory against Colombia in which the Manchester United man scored with a trademark free-kick. That saw England through against old foes Argentina. Once again Batty started on the bench, but came on midway through the first period of extra-time for an exhausted Darren Anderton as the match moved relentlessly towards the penalty shoot-out in which he was to have the defining role. Despite his miss, Batty remained mentally strong and Hoddle had no hesitation in keeping him in the squad as England launched their Euro 2000 campaign.

Hoddle was eventually replaced by Batty's old boss at Newcastle, Kevin Keegan, a big fan of Batty's huge desire for work and determination to win. By the time Keegan had been handed the England job, 30-year-old Batty had returned to Leeds in a £4.4 million transfer to link up with David O'Leary's rising young United team. Batty picked up a rib injury on his second Leeds debut, against Coventry, and was ruled out for 15 games, but he still had a role to play for England, although Keegan's men were unable to turn their campaign around and secure an automatic place in the Euro 2000 Finals. Their last game of the qualifying campaign in Poland ended 0–0, which forced England into a Play-off against Scotland. However, Batty would not line up against the Scots because of suspension, as he was sent off six minutes from the end of the stalemate in Poland. His ill-timed tackle on Radoslav Michaelski drew a straight red card and was to prove his final act as an England player.

England got past the Scots to make Euro 2000, but Batty was struck down by an Achilles injury two months after his dismissal in Poland and was out of action for a year. Although his England career had ended in anti-climax, he did make a successful comeback with Leeds in 2001–02; however, the Whites were sliding towards financial disaster, and Batty found himself in a team that could not kick the losing habit. He retired at the end of the 2003–04 Premiership relegation season as one of the most popular players to pull on a Leeds shirt. His midfield qualities saw him serve under four England managers – Taylor, Venables, Hoddle and Keegan – testimony to his great consistency.

WILLIE BELL

(Scotland 1966)

Full-back

Born: Johnstone, Renfrewshire, 3 September 1937.

Caps: Leeds United 2

TOUGH competitor Willie Bell tussled with a couple of all-time international greats in his two appearances for Scotland – Pelé and Eusebio. Consistent Willie was rewarded for his excellent displays at left-back for Leeds by featuring in two games at Hampden Park in summer 1966 against opponents who were warming up for the following month's World Cup.

First up were Portugal, who featured the outstanding Eusebio. Bell was called up for the game by manager John Prentice, the former Hearts, Rangers and Falkirk player, who was in charge at Clyde. Prentice's first game in charge was a 4–3 home defeat against England when Celtic's Tommy Gemmell made his debut in the number-three shirt. The following month the Scots were thumped 3–0 by Holland, with Rangers' David Provan at left-back, so Bell became the third different player to fill that troublesome position in as many matches.

The Portugese, who won with a 72nd-minute goal by Jose Torres, were a class act with Eusebio, who was to have such an impact on the World Cup, steering his side to the semi-finals, proving a real handful for the Scottish defence.

Willie Bell.

Willie Bell, back row, left, with Leeds United's tartan army from the mid-1960s: Jim Storrie, Billy Bremner and (front) Tommy Henderson and Bobby Collins.

Bell however, who linked up well with Billy Bremner, did well enough to retain his place for the following Saturday's first-ever meeting between Scotland and Brazil.

A packed Hampden Park went wild in the first minute when Steve Chalmers converted Jim Baxter's pass to put Scotland ahead, but Brazil, with the planet's greatest player, Pelé, in their attack, drew level after a quarter of an hour through Servilio, and that was how it finished. For Bell it had been a fantastic experience to pit his wits and his strength against the likes of star forwards Pelé and Eusebio. He had acquitted himself well, but by the time Scotland were next in action, against Wales, in October Prentice had been replaced by Kilmarnock manager Malcolm MacDonald. The new man at the helm was a former Celtic player, and it was to his old club that he turned to recall Gemmell for the Wales game. Gemmell took his opportunity and became the regular left-back for the next four years.

Those two outings were not Bell's only taste of international football, however, as he was also capped at amateur level. He was a 17-year-old playing for Neilston Juniors when Stoke City asked him to turn pro. Bell turned the Potters down as he was still serving his engineering apprenticeship. He then joined the famous Glasgow amateur club, Queens Park, who played their home games at Hampden, and his performances at centre-half earned him amateur caps against England and Ireland.

Bell had completed his apprenticeship when Leeds came calling, and he agreed to switch to Elland Road as a professional in July 1960. He found it a struggle at first, and it was only when Don Revie converted him to left-back that Bell's career really took off. Bell was sceptical about his positional switch at first, but he stuck with it and proved one of United's most consistent performers in the 1964 Second Division title-winning team and played in the FA Cup Final against Liverpool the following year. His strong tackling and excellent distribution marked him out as one of the top defenders in the First Division, and he earned his reward when he returned to his old surroundings at Hampden to face Portugal and Brazil.

Bell continued to be the regular left-back in 1966–67, but the emergence of Terry Cooper saw him move to Leicester for £45,000 in September 1967 after nearly 250 games for the Whites. He later played for Brighton before being appointed coach at Birmingham, where Freddie Goodwin, his old Leeds teammate, was manager. Bell later stepped up to be boss at St Andrews and had a brief spell in charge at Lincoln before going to the United States to join a religious group in Colorado called the Campus Crusade for Christ. Bell coached football at Liberty University in Virginia before returning to England to set up a Christian Prison Ministry called 'Within the Walls'.

LEE BOWYER

(England 2002)

Midfield

Born: Canning Town, London, 3 January 1977.
Caps: Leeds United 1

CONTROVERSY shadowed Lee Bowyer throughout his career, and had he avoided trouble he could well have earned more than his solitary England cap. He had already built a reputation as being a bit of a hothead when Howard Wilkinson signed the 19-year-old for Leeds in July 1996 from Charlton Athletic for £2.8 million – a record fee for a British teenager – on a five-year contract.

Bowyer had been brought up on the tough Teviot estate in Tower Hamlets, East London, and joined Charlton, where he soon won England youth caps. The wiry teenager had endless energy, nifty skills and an eye for goal. Young Bowyer was certainly no physical giant, but his competitive nature and spiky temperament meant he could handle himself on the pitch against stronger, more experienced players. Charlton fans certainly thought he was the real deal, but the first of his well-publicised conflicts with authority emerged in March 1995 when he tested positive for cannabis and was banned by Charlton for eight weeks and dropped from the England Under-18 side. He had only played four Division One games for the Addicks, but he bounced back the following season with a string of superb displays and gained his first England Under-21 cap as a substitute in a 2–2 draw against Norway on 10 October 1995.

By the end of his first full season the attacking midfielder had 14 club goals to his name. Nearly every Premiership club in London was linked with Bowyer, but they were all beaten to the punch by Wilkinson, who was not put off by the player's poor disciplinary record, which had seen him amass 48 penalty points in his maiden season. The Leeds boss said: 'This boy has exceptional talent. He

can pass, score goals and he can run' – all attributes he displayed on his Leeds debut, a 3–3 draw at Derby. But within three weeks Wilkinson was sacked after eight years in charge of the Whites following a 4–0 home defeat against Manchester United – a match that saw Bowyer leave the action after a freak injury. The ball struck the midfielder in the face, causing bleeding behind the eye and prompting Bowyer to have an operation on his retina.

Bowyer was out for two months, and when he returned to action George Graham was in charge. The former Arsenal double-winning manager initially curtailed Bowyer's foraging runs, but remained a big fan of the young midfielder, despite more unwanted headlines outside the game. In early December Bowyer was fined £4,500 after throwing chairs across a McDonalds restaurant after drinking with friends. Once more Bowyer emerged from an off-field drama a stronger player and was named United's 1998–99 Player of the Year after David O'Leary had taken over as manager from Tottenham-bound Graham. He was also short-listed for the PFA Young Player of the Year award, which was eventually won by Arsenal's Nicolas Anelka.

Bowyer's improvement on the pitch also went hand-in-hand with trouble on and off it. In 1999–2000 he was fined by the FA for becoming the first Premiership player to amass 14 yellow cards, but that was the least of his troubles. Together with teammates Jonathan Woodgate and Tony Hackworth, and two friends of Woodgate, Bowyer was charged with assaulting student Sarfraz Najeib in January 2000 after a night out at a Leeds nightclub. In addition, centre-back Michael Duberry was charged with perverting the course of justice. All denied the charges and reserve-team striker Hackworth was soon cleared of any involvement when the trial eventually started 12 months later.

That left Bowyer, Woodgate and Duberry, plus Woodgate's pals, in the dock. The two Leeds stars were among the brightest in the country and pushing hard for full England recognition. But the FA announced that neither would be considered for international duty until the court case was resolved, much to the disgust of United chairman Peter Ridsdale, who felt that the adage of innocent until proven guilty should apply. Woodgate, who was labouring with injury during the case, clearly struggled with being in the media spotlight as the evidence unfolded before the nation. Bowyer, on the other hand, used football as a release and took his game to a higher plane as Leeds finished third in the Premiership in 2000 to clinch a place in the Champions League. The spectre of the attack still hung over Bowyer and Woodgate, however, as the trial was abandoned in April – after nearly three months – as the jury considered their verdict, because of a predjudicial article published by a Sunday newspaper.

Despite being unable to get to United's Thorp Arch training centre because of the court case, Bowyer was unstoppable on the pitch as Leeds, the new darlings of the

Premiership, powered their way to the Champions League semi-finals. But for the FA ban the Leeds midfielder would have walked into Sven-Goran Eriksson's England squad, who were qualifying for the World Cup Finals in Japan and Korea. He was the joint leading scorer in the Champions League, which included dramatic late winners at Elland Road against AC Milan and Anderlecht in the group stages, but missed the semi-final second leg at Valencia after being banned by UEFA on the eve of the game for an alleged stamp on Juan Sanchez in the goalless first leg, even though match referee Pierluigi Collina had seen nothing wrong with the incident. Without Bowyer Leeds lost 3–0, and the only compensation for the midfielder was winning the club's Player of the Year trophy again.

In October the new trial began, and after two months Bowyer was cleared of all charges but was demonised by the tabloids. Duberry was also acquitted of a charge of perverting the course of justice. Bowyer's clean slate at Leeds soon became scratched as United fined him four weeks wages for breaking drinking regulations. He refused to pay and was transfer-listed, but although the dispute was resolved after a few days his relations with Ridsdale were at an all-time low.

The soap opera continued in the summer, with Bowyer confirming he would not sign a new contract with Leeds, and a £9 million move to Liverpool looked to be in the bag until the deal collapsed over personal terms. Against all the

odds Bowyer was back at Leeds for the start of the 2002–03 season and, despite being unable to recapture his best form, that elusive first England cap finally came his way in September 2002. He started a friendly against Portugal at Villa Park which finished 1–1, setting up the goal for Leeds teammate Alan Smith.

Bowyer, who made 12 Under-21 appearances, was replaced after 62 minutes by Trevor Sinclair. It was his only game for the full national side, and within a few months he had played his 264th and final game for Leeds before joining West Ham, the club he had supported as a child, on a six-month contract for just £100,000. He could not help keep the Hammers up and moved to Newcastle in the summer, where, in between bouts of injury, he began to look more like the Bowyer of old. In 2004–05 he was sent off three times, including a red card for a much publicised on-pitch confrontation with teammate Kieron Dyer, which precipitated a £250,000 return to West Ham in June 2006. He has since joined Birmingham City.

Wearing the Three Lions shirt for just over an hour in a friendly game was poor reward for a player who, for a time, was among the best midfielders on the Continent. Had the FA not imposed their international ban, Bowyer could well have established himself in England's World Cup squad. Although he was ultimately proved innocent, the Sarfraz Najeib court case had a massive impact on Bowyer's international career.

Lee Bowyer.

BRAVO, RAUL
(Spain 2002–04)
Defender
Born: Gandia, Valencia, 14 April 1981.
Caps: Real Madrid 13, *Leeds United 1. Total: 14
*While on loan from Real Madrid

WHEN word got out that Terry Venables had used his Spanish contacts to sign Raul on loan from Real Madrid, Leeds fans could hardly believe their ears. In fact El Tel, the former Barcelona coach, had not recruited ace marksman Raul, but his lesser-known 21-year-old teammate Raul Bravo, a left-back. Recruits of quality were sorely needed at Elland Road as financially-crippled United were already on the slippery slope towards Premiership relegation.

On the final day of the January 2003 transfer window the young Spaniard agreed to move to England for the remainder of the season in an effort to secure a regular place in the Real side. His path to the Real first team was blocked by Brazilian superstar Roberto Carlos, who still had a couple of years to run on his contract with Madrid, so Bravo knew he needed regular first-team football to press his claims at his parent club. He had been with Real since he was a boy and represented his country at Under-16 and Under-17 level before making his first-team debut in the Madrid derby against Atletico on 6 October 2001.

Raul Bravo.

probably a great relief when he returned to Spain for a European Championship qualifier against Armenia. The Leeds loanee played the full game in Amilvia in which goals by Diego Tristan, Helguera and Joaquin gave Spain a 3–0 win. He was soon back home permanently, as his ill-fated loan with Leeds came to an end.

Reid kept United up, only for them to go down the following season in a whirlpool of debt. Meanwhile, Raul Bravo's career was on the upturn. He played impressively in all three of Spain's Euro 2004 Finals games in Portugal and went on to play more regularly for Real Madrid, either at left-back or centre-back, before a £1.2 million move to Greek side Olympiacos in July 2007, having a brief spell back in Spain on loan with Numancia in January 2009.

BILLY BREMNER
(Scotland 1965–75)
Midfield
Born: Stirling, Stirlingshire, 9 December 1942.
Died: Doncaster, 7 December 1997.
Caps: Leeds United 54

IT WAS only a matter of time before born leader of men Billy Bremner captained his country. The third most capped Leeds United player of all time, Bremner's 54 appearances for Scotland included 39 as captain. He was one of the stars of the 1974 World Cup, his display against Brazil having observers from around the globe purring in admiration. The all-action Scot, who had just led United to their second Championship triumph, was at the peak of his considerable powers, yet within 14 months he was controversially banished by the Scottish FA. It was a shattering and premature end to a marvellous international career that had spanned 10 years.

Bremner was already one of the stars of the Scotland Boys team when Leeds chairman Harry Reynolds persuaded the youngster to reject the overtures of Arsenal, Chelsea and Celtic to join modest Second Division United. He made his debut as a 17-year-old in a 3–1 win at Chelsea on 23 January 1960, on the right wing. His inside partner that day was experienced England international Don Revie – it was the start of a relationship that was to transform the Elland Road club.

After overcoming a yearning to return to Scotland, Bremner was a key component in Revie's squad that won the Second Division title in 1964. His fiery temper often got him into trouble with referees, but Revie's decision to appoint the flaming midfield ball of energy as his captain was a masterstroke. Bremner was able to channel his aggression in a more responsible manner, and his iron will-to-win forged United together. International honours came Bremner's way before he was able to lift club trophies as Leeds so often finished runners-up on their return to top-flight domestic football.

Although he was effectively a Real Madrid reserve-team player, Bravo was a fully-fledged full international, and only illness prevented him from facing Germany in Mallorca the month before he arrived at Elland Road. That would have been his seventh full cap, so on the face of it Venables appeared to have pulled of a bit of a coup by getting someone with Raul Bravo's pedigree. Unfortunately, it did not turn out that way. He made a winning debut at home to West Ham but was on the losing Leeds side in his next four games. Six days after the third of those defeats – a 3–2 home loss to Middlesbrough – it was announced on the Stock Exchange that Venables's eight-month reign as manager was over and Peter Reid became caretaker boss for the remainder of the season.

Raul Bravo started Reid's first game in charge but did not finish it. He was hauled off at half-time after enduring a nightmare 45 minutes at Liverpool in which he was caught out of position time and time again. The Reds went on to win 3–1, and poor Bravo did not feature in the United first team again. His dream of regular first-team football with Leeds had lasted just five games, and it was

Billy Bremner.

A month after helping Leeds to the Second Division title, Bremner made his Under-23 debut in a 2–0 win against France in Nantes. He was on the scoresheet in a 3–0 win over Wales in December 1964 and figured in a 0–0 draw with England the following February. The Scottish selectors did not need to see any more – young Bremner was ready for the big international stage, and on 8 May 1965 he made his senior debut in a goalless draw against Spain at Hampden Park at the age of 22. The Scots' manager was Ian McColl, but within a couple of weeks he was axed ahead of two World Cup qualifying games in Poland and Finland. Appointed as his temporary successor was Jock Stein, who was making a big impact at Celtic and later had a brief spell in charge at Elland Road.

Stein, although an admirer of Bremner's skills, opted for experience for the two vital away qualifiers and left Bremner out. The Leeds midfield tyro did, however, start the return game against the Poles at a packed Hampden, and the Scots knew that victory would go a long way to securing their place in the 1966 Finals in England. Billy McNeill gave Scotland the lead, but Poland scored twice in the last six minutes to snatch an unlikely 2–1 win. That result effectively meant that Scotland had to beat Group Eight leaders Italy twice to make the Finals. Bremner was in both clashes with the Azzurri and tasted vastly differing fortunes. John Greig's late piledriver gave the ecstatic Scots a 1–0 win at Hampden, but four weeks later an injury-ravaged side crashed 3–0 in Naples – a result which triggered Stein's resignation.

Although the big man's international managerial career was over – for the time being at least – wee Bremner's days as the midfield fulcrum for the Scots were just beginning. Scotland's only consolation for not reaching the Finals was to see Italy's humiliation at the hands of North Korea at Middlesbrough. The relatively unknown John Prentice replaced Stein as part-time boss and selected Bremner for his first game in charge – a 4–3 defeat in Glasgow against England just a few months before Alf Ramsey's 'Wingless Wonders' lifted the greatest prize in football – the World Cup.

That England defeat had taken on extra significance. The flagging Home Internationals had been given more bite as the competition for the next two seasons was acting as the qualifying rounds for the 1968 European Championship Finals. The Hampden loss was obviously damaging to Scotland's Euro prospects, but, for many Scots based with clubs south of the border, England's thrilling extra-time World Cup Final victory over West Germany at Wembley was even harder to take, although a tartan glory day was just round the corner.

By the time Scotland resumed their Euro campaign against Wales at Ninian Park, Kilmarnock boss Malcolm MacDonald was at the helm. Football was hardly relevant in the principality, however, as the previous day a mountain of coal slag had slid and buried the village school at Aberfan, killing 144 people – 116 of them children. Black armbands were worn by both sides, but even the partnership of Bremner and the mercurial Jim Baxter in midfield for the Scots could not lift the subdued atmosphere, and the match ended as a 1–1 draw.

The following month Bremner and the Scots scraped past Northern Ireland 2–1 at Hampden, and MacDonald's brief spell in charge came to an end with the appointment of Bobby Brown as Scotland's first full-time boss. The new man's first game in charge proved to be one of the highlights of Bremner's international career as Scotland defeated the world champions 3–2 at Wembley. 'Bremner and Baxter were magnificent,' said Brown, who went like-for-like with Ramsey's 4–3–3 system and brought England's 19-game unbeaten run to an end.

Matches were coming thick and fast for Bremner at both club and international level, and confirmation that he had really arrived on the European stage came when he skippered the Scots for the first time in a 1–0 win in Denmark. Bremner said later: 'It made me feel deeply proud and confident. I promised myself that I would do my best to follow in the footsteps of all those great Scotland captains who had gone before me.' He certainly lived up to those words. Leading by example, he scored the 75th-minute winner – his first senior international goal – in a 2–1 World Cup qualifier against Austria in Glasgow.

Captain Billy Bremner is chaired by his Scotland teammates after leading his team to victory against Czechoslovakia and qualifying for the 1974 World Cup Finals.

Scotland's bid to reach the World Cup Finals in Mexico was up and running, with Bremner the heartbeat of both Leeds and Scotland. The little red-headed maestro was ever-present as United won their first-ever Championship in 1968–69 and his national team achieved a thumping 5–0 World Cup qualifying victory in Cyprus – all the goals coming in the first half. West Germany held the Scots 1–1 at Hampden, but a crushing 8–0 home win over the Cypriots left Scotland well placed with seven points from four games, although they knew progress would hinge on difficult trips to West Germany and Austria.

Before those key games were played, the Home Internationals were held at the end of the season for the first time, and Bremner featured in them all, scoring in a 5–3 thriller against Wales. After a 1–1 draw against Northern Ireland in front of just 7,483 fans at Hampden, England routed the Scots 4–1 at Wembley in the first televised live game between the two old enemies. Of more significance was that West Germany beat Austria the same evening.

Bremner, who had already lifted the Championship, Fairs Cup and League Cup with Leeds, was confident Scotland could beat the Germans in Hamburg, and they made a dream start with a goal from Celtic wing wizard Jimmy Johnstone. Bremner and Tommy Gemmell both hit the woodwork with the score at 1–1, but the Germans won 3–2, Gemmell being sent off near the end, to kill off the Tartan Army's hopes of a trip to Mexico.

The 1969–70 season was a shattering season for Bremner as Leeds finished League runners-up, were beaten FA Cup Finalists and were defeated by Celtic in the European Cup semi-finals. The skipper was named Footballer of the Year, but did not feature in any of the end-of-season Home Internationals as he was still chasing, fruitlessly, honours with United.

Bremner, in fact, missed six successive internationals as availability became an issue between club and country, and when he did return for a 0–0 draw with Wales in May 1971 Newcastle's Bobby Moncur, who had led the Scots in Bremner's absence, kept the captain's armband. With

Bremner out of the side the Scots were not the same outfit. They had scored just three goals in their last 12 games and Bremner had featured in just three of those matches.

Brown lost his job, and Tommy Docherty was placed in temporary charge and immediately galvanised the Scots. Bremner was back as leader for the Doc's debut – a 2–1 home win against Portugal, which included a goal for Derby's John O'Hare, who was later taken to Elland Road by Brian Clough. O'Hare also got the only goal, which saw off Belgium in Aberdeen, and Docherty was confirmed as manager. His predecessors chose the squad in conjunction with a selection committee, but former Chelsea chief Docherty, an outspoken character, was given a free rein.

After failing to qualify for the 1972 European Championships, Scotland's eyes were firmly fixed on reaching the 1974 World Cup Finals, and they found themselves in a three-country group with Czechoslovakia and Denmark. Bremner, revitalised by Docherty's appointment, had Leeds teammate Peter Lorimer for company as he drove his men to back-to-back victories over the part-time Danes – 4–1 in Copenhagen and 2–0 at Hampden. It was now a straight fight between Scotland and the Czechs, who were then surprisingly held 1–1 by the Danes, which meant that if the Scots beat the Czechs in Glasgow they would reach the World Cup Finals for the first time since 1958. They would have to do it without the inspirational Docherty, however, who had quit to become manager at Manchester United, with Willie Ormond taking charge of the national team. Ormond's reign got off to an embarrassing start as his Bremner-led side crashed 5–0 at a frozen Hampden against England in a game that celebrated the centenary of the Scottish FA.

Scotland went into the big game against the Czechs on the back of four successive defeats against Northern Ireland, England, Switzerland and Brazil – and they did not make the best of starts against the Czechs, as a 34th-minute long-range shot from Zdenek Nehoda beat goalkeeper Ally Hunter. But Bremner was at his best, driving his men forward against the massed defensive ranks of the visitors, and before the interval Scotland were level with a Jim Holton header. With 11 minutes remaining, a Bremner shot hit a post then rolled along the goalline before it was partially cleared to Willie Morgan, who knocked the ball in for Bremner's Leeds teammate Joe Jordan to head the winning goal. Bremner and his teammates carried Ormond aloft around Hampden as the 100,000 crowd went crazy – Scotland had reached the World Cup Finals for the first time in 16 years.

Bremner missed the academic return match, which Czechoslovakia won 1–0, with an ankle injury. But the big news that night was England's failure to beat Poland at Wembley, which saw Sir Alf's men tumble out of the competition. Two friendlies were arranged with West Germany, one of the big favourites to become world

champions, Bremner having a 77th-minute penalty saved by Sepp Maier in a 1–1 draw at Hampden. The Leeds skipper, an ever-present as United swept to the 1973–74 title, missed the 2–1 defeat in Frankfurt, but figured in all the build-up games as Scotland prepared for the World Cup Finals.

The last of those matches was a scrappy 2–1 win in Norway, but the aftermath of the game could have ended Bremner's involvement in the World Cup. Unable to sleep, he and Celtic winger Jimmy Johnstone broke the team curfew and were drinking in an Oslo bar when they were discovered by Ormond. The two players were ordered to their rooms by the SFA doctor. Some sections of the Press called for the duo to be sent home, but Ormond knew he could ill-afford to lose his players and, after a severe reprimand, they were allowed to remain with the squad.

Bremner was one of five Leeds players in the Scotland squad – Peter Lorimer, Joe Jordan, David Harvey and Gordon McQueen being the others – that found itself in a group with Brazil, Yugoslavia and little-known African side Zaire. Goals by Lorimer and Jordan gave cautious Scotland a 2–0 win against Zaire, but that result was put in perspective when Zaire were thrashed 9–0 by Yuogoslavia. Inevitably Scotland started as underdogs against world champions Brazil and were on the back foot in the opening stages, but Bremner, in his 50th international, seized control of the midfield and gave a magnificent display, which was heralded by the world's media, including the

One of Billy Bremner's Scotland shirts, framed and hung in Elland Road's reception area.

on-looking Pelé. Bremner came within a whisker of breaking the deadlock late on when the ball came off his shins and went an inch wide of the post with goalkeeper Leao stranded.

It was Brazil's second 0–0 draw, having being held by Yugoslavia in their opening game, so assuming they beat Zaire by at least three clear goals, Scotland needed to beat the Slavs. Brazil were only 1–0 up against the Africans at half-time so the Scots, who were locked at 0–0 with the Slavs, still had hope. Bremner's men salvaged a 1–1 draw thanks to a late Jordan goal, but Brazil sneaked through 3–0, the decisive last goal coming 11 minutes from the end through a goalkeeping error. Scotland, the only unbeaten side in the 1974 Finals, were on their way home.

With his place assured in the SFA's Hall of Fame after reaching the 50-cap mark, 31-year-old Bremner looked an integral part of the Scottish set-up for years to come. In his first match after the Finals he scored in a 2–1 European Championship qualifying defeat against Spain in Glasgow. His appetite for the game showed no signs of diminishing, but there was trouble at club level when Bremner and Liverpool's Kevin Keegan were sent off in the Charity Shield clash at Wembley – Brian Clough's first game in charge during his brief spell at United. Both players received hefty bans, and by the time Bremner returned from suspension in November 1975 Clough had been replaced by Jimmy Armfield.

Leeds's priority was the European Cup, and they battled all the way through to the Final against Bayern Munich in Paris. That meant Bremner was unavailable for five Scotland games towards the end of the season, and his return to international action the following September saw his Scotland career come screeching to a halt. Scotland needed to beat Denmark in Copenhagen to keep their European qualification hopes alive, and they managed it with a solitary goal from Joe Harper. But three days after the game newspaper reports revealed that Bremner, Harper, his Aberdeen colleague Arthur Graham – later to sparkle on the wing for Leeds – Pat McCluskey and Willie Young had got into trouble in a nightclub over non-payment of a bill.

Scottish FA officials held a special meeting and came down hard on the five players, banning them from playing for Scotland for life. The actual details of the affair have been riddled with inconsistencies, with the Scottish PFA revealing that Graham was not even involved. But he, Bremner and the rest never got the opportunity to put their case to the Scottish FA. Bremner, who maintained that it was 'all a storm in a teacup', was also reprimanded by Leeds, who warned him as to his future conduct.

It was a painful and humiliating end to Bremner's international career. He was the most senior of the players involved, but felt he had been judged on hearsay and exaggeration. Although bitterly upset, he said little publically about the matter, but confided in close friends that he thought the whole business had been blown out of all proportion by the media and that had forced the Scottish FA to act. The suspension on the players was lifted in July 1977, but by then Leeds hero Bremner had moved on to Hull City after 587 League appearances for the Whites, and his best playing days were long gone.

Management followed at Doncaster Rovers before returning to Elland Road in October 1985 for a three-year spell as manager, during which his passion for the club burned as fiercely as ever. He could not bring the glory days back to Leeds, and after a second stint as Doncaster's manager he slipped out of the full-time game. Two days before his 55th birthday he died in Doncaster Royal Infirmary of pneumonia – Leeds had lost a legend and Scotland a national hero. His memory lives on at Leeds with the dynamic Bremner statue – the meeting point for so many fans – and Billy's Bar in the South Stand. Bremner was a man of the people and would no doubt have beamed with pride at such tributes.

BROWNE, BOBBY

(Northern Ireland 1935–38)
Wing-half
Born: Derry, County Londonderry, 9 February 1912.
Died: 1994.
Caps: Leeds United 6

BOBBY BROWNE'S full international career with Northern Ireland took off immediately after he signed for Leeds. The ink was barely dry on his Elland Road contract when he was named in the team to face England at Windsor Park on 19 October 1935. The 23-year-old wing-half was signed by manager Billy Hampson for £1,500 and 10 days later made his international bow in a 3–1 defeat in a Home International encounter.

Browne had much to thank former Leeds City forward Billy Gillespie for. As a youngster he grew up with the Gaelic code of football, but preferred the association game and had figured for Maleven and Clooney Rovers before joining Irish League side Derry City, where Gillespie was manager. The precocious Browne was a part-timer, splitting his job as a joiner with playing. He proved adept with both his hands at work and his feet at play. Encouraged by Gillespie, he earned a regular place in the Derry team with whom he won the North-West Senior Cup and earned his big breakthrough in 1935.

On 25 September he was in the Irish League side that earned a shock 2–1 win at Blackpool over a Football League side containing the likes of Frank Swift and Raich Carter. It was a result that caught the eye, and Browne's performance also saw watching scouts among the 26,000 at Bloomfield Road scribbling positive comments in their notebooks about the tidy young half-back's display. Hampson was the quickest to act, persuading Browne to

Bobby Browne (centre) and Northern Ireland teammate Jim Twomey (left) are congratulated on their selection to face England in 1938 by their Leeds teammates.

go to Elland Road, striking the deal on 9 October. Browne was absent for United's first division home game against West Brom three days later when a Jack Milburn penalty salvaged a point for the Peacocks in a 1–1 draw.

The following Saturday – as Leeds were involved in another 1–1 game, this time at Middlesbrough, Browne was back in Northern Ireland making his senior international debut against England at Windsor Park. The game went according to form, with the visitors running out 3–1 winners, but Browne and Co. pushed them hard for an hour, and only goals by Manchester City duo Fred Tilson (66 and 69 minutes) and Eric Brook (85 minutes) saw England home.

Browne's taste for life at the top of the football tree continued the following Saturday when he made his Football League debut for Leeds, replacing the doughty Cyril Hornby at left-half. The new man enjoyed a great start with his new club as Aston Villa were dispatched 4–2 at Elland Road with forward George Brown getting a couple of the goals. Browne was playing regularly for United, who felt they were able to sell his predecessor, Hornby, to Sunderland in February 1936. The following month he figured in a 3–2 Home Championship win over Wales in Belfast and finished the season with 29 games under his belt for Leeds, who completed the campaign in a comfortable mid-table position. He missed the next three internationals, with his left-half spot going to Chelsea's Billy Mitchell, but was back in a green jersey to face England in Belfast in October 1937. However, it was an all-too-familiar result, with Chelsea centre-forward George Mills scoring a hat-trick on his debut for the visitors in a 5–1 win.

Browne was in good form in 1937–38 and was playing more regularly in the United team that finished ninth in Division One. He picked up a fourth cap in the latter part of the season when a lone goal from Joe Bambrick saw

Wales beaten in Belfast. The Leeds man kept his international place for the next Irish match against Scotland, who emerged triumphant in Belfast thanks to goals by Jimmy Delaney and Tommy Walker. The following month Ireland gathered at Manchester to take on England. The Maine Road dressing room had a familiar feel to it for Browne as he had Leeds teammates Jim Twomey and Davy Cochrane, making his debut, for company. However, they were upstaged by Willie Hall's five goals, which swept England to a 7–0 win and ended the international careers of Twomey and Browne.

During the war, Browne became an army PT staff sergeant and guested for Watford while he was stationed in Colchester. He only played a handful of games for United and also turned out for Derry City when he was posted back to Ulster. Browne was back at Elland Road for the disastrous first post-war season when an ageing United squad were relegated, a massive 15 points from safety after losing 20 of their 21 away games. Inevitably there was a huge clearout, and Browne moved to York City, then

Bobby Browne.

becoming Yorkshire League Thorne Colliery's player-manager. In August 1954 he was appointed Halifax Town's coach and had a brief spell as caretaker manager after his former Leeds teammate Gerry Henry resigned.

Browne was a dogged, hard-working defensive half-back, who notched up 110 League appearances for United without scoring a goal, but rubbed shoulders with some of the top players of the day in his half-dozen international games.

JACOB BURNS

(Australia 2000– to date)

Midfield

Born: Sydney, New South Wales, 21 January 1978.
Caps: Leeds United 2, Wisla Kracow 3, Unirea Urziceni 15. Total: 10

JACOB BURNS played a small part in Australia's football revolution. For years, the game Down Under was low down in the pecking order of Aussie sport, but as the Millennium approached more and more Australians sought to test themselves in the lucrative European market.

Burns was a graduate of the heralded Westfield Sports High School – Australia's first such establishment. Fellow Westfield students Harry Kewell, Jamie McMaster and Shane Cansdell-Sheriff all became United recruits. While Burns was a regular starter at Westfield, Kewell was sometimes left on the bench – a position which was to change dramatically at Elland Road. McMaster did make United's first team and Cansdell-Sheriff, although failing to make the breakthrough at Leeds, emerged as captain at Tranmere Rovers after a spell in Danish football.

Burns played for Sydney United and was recruited by Leeds from Paramatta Power for £250,000, giving up the chance to play in the 2000 Olympics with the Aussies' Olyroos to have a crack at Premiership football. The switch to England was too good an opportunity to miss, as it could open the door for Burns to become a full international player, particularly as the Australian national team were playing more and more games in Europe. Initially it proved a struggle for the feisty fetch-and-carry midfielder to get himself in United's first-team shop window. He did not even make the bench in the first few games, but with injuries to David O'Leary's squad piling up he got his first start in a 3–1 win over Charlton. That was the start of a sprinkling of first team games, including a few outings in the high-profile Champions League. He had started five games for United when he was drafted in to Frank Farina's injury-riddled squad for a friendly against Scotland at Hampden Park.

Among the non-starters for the Aussies were the dazzling Kewell, who had joined Leeds several years earlier straight from Westfield Academy, and new Leeds signing Mark Viduka, whose famous four-goal salvo had sunk Liverpool at Elland Road 11 days before the Scotland match. Despite their weakened side, the Aussies, with Burns on the bench, cruised to a 2–0 win. Brett Emerton netted the opener, and immediately after David Zdrillic's 66th-minute header made it 2–0 Farina sent on Burns for Danny Tiatto to partner Paul Okon, then of Middlesbrough, but later to join Leeds, in midfield.

Jacob Burns.

Burns returned to Leeds, where the treatment room was clearing, and the newly-capped Aussie found himself confined to the bench again. The Australian Football Federation was anxiously trying to arrange a friendly in winter 2001, and finally Colombia agreed to play them in Bogata in February. Farina inquired about Burns's availability and O'Leary, with David Batty back in the United engine room, felt able to release Burns for the trip to South America. Despite his commitment, the long haul did not further Burns's international career. The Green and Golds lost 3–2 – after trailing 3–0 – and he did not play another full international for over six years.

Five weeks after the Colombia defeat, the Aussies opened their World Cup qualifying campaign without their European-based stars, whose seasons were coming to a climax. They were not missed. On 9 April the home-based Aussies set a new World Cup record by thrashing Tonga 22–0 at Coffs Harbour. Hayden Foxe, later to have a spell in Leeds's disastrous 2006–07 season, played in that game but was missing two days later when the Australians beat American Samoa 31–0 on the same ground, Archie Thompson, of Marconi Stallions, scored a record 13 goals in a World Cup game.

While his teammates had well and truly got the show on the road, Burns found himself stuck in neutral at Leeds. It was the era of Peter Ridsdale's big spending, and as the United squad got bigger and better Burns's chance of an international recall got slimmer. Injuries did not help, and Burns did not start a Leeds senior game in 2001–02 and managed just a couple of starts the following season.

After a short spell with Dutch club Feyenoord, Burns linked up with Barnsley and in February 2006 joined Polish champions Wisla Krakow, where his fine displays saw him recalled for the national team for games against Denmark, China and Nigeria. His club coach was former Chelsea man Dan Petrescu, whom he followed to Romania to play under him at Unirea Urziceni. Burns's form and attitude impressed Aussie manager Pim Veerbek, who used the former Leeds man in four matches during 2008, the last in a 4–0 World Cup qualifying win against Qatar.

STEPHEN CALDWELL

(Scotland 2001–06)
Central-defender
Born: Stirling, Stirlingshire, 12 September 1979.
Caps: Newcastle United 4, Sunderland 5, *Leeds United 1. Total: 9
*While on loan from Sunderland

AS LEEDS slid to their sixth successive defeat – a 3–0 home humiliation to Middlesbrough in January 2004 – caretaker manager Eddie Gray turned to Scottish international Stephen Caldwell to plug the gap in United's defence. The Stirling-born player had been out of favour at

Stephen Caldwell.

Newcastle and jumped at the chance of regular first-team football, even though it was in a side bound for relegation from the Premiership. The switch certainly did not do his international career any harm, as he added another Scotland cap to his collection during his stay with the Whites. After a 2–0 defeat at Aston Villa on his debut, an improved Leeds then thumped Wolves 4–1 at Elland Road, with Caldwell at centre-back. The following week he lined up for Scotland in a friendly against Wales for his third international cap.

The 23-year-old had made his Scotland debut as a substitute in a 1–1 draw with Poland in Bydgoszcz in a World Cup qualifier and on 12 February 2003 figured in a

2–0 defeat against the Republic of Ireland at Hampden Park. Craig Brown's side failed to qualify for the World Cup Finals, so the door was open for fringe players like Caldwell to make his mark.

The defender's hopes of making a big impression in Cardiff were wrecked as an experimental Scottish side lost 4–0, Robert Earnshaw scoring a hat-trick for Wales, for whom former Leeds star Gary Speed – a teammate of Caldwell's at Newcastle – was making his 80th international appearance. It was a bad night for the Scots, who could not cope with the pace of the Welsh attack, but Caldwell returned to Leeds and played regularly in what was a lost cause for financially-crippled United. When relegation was confirmed by a 4–1 defeat at Bolton, Caldwell was recalled by injury-hit Newcastle and figured in their final three games of the season.

Caldwell played 13 Premiership games for United, of which four were won, three drawn and five lost – stats which would have seen United stay up if they had been replicated over a season. Caldwell even had the satisfaction of scoring in one of the victories, netting an early opener in a 2–1 victory at Blackburn. When he left Elland Road his career was very much at a crossroads, both on the domestic and international scene. At the end of the season he won his fourth cap in a 4–1 friendly romp over Trinidad and Tobago at Hampden when he replaced his younger brother, Gary, one of the scorers, in the 80th minute.

Stephen left Newcastle for Sunderland in the summer and scored the winner in the victory over Leicester that clinched the Black Cats' promotion from the Championship. He took his number of international caps to nine before leaving Sunderland for Burnley in a £400,000 deal in January 2007 and was appointed skipper of the Clarets. Earlier in his career with Newcastle he won four Under-21 caps and also had loan spells with Blackpool and Bradford City. Brother Gary, who had been at Newcastle at the same time as Stephen, went on to become an established full international with Hibernian and Celtic, taking his number of caps beyond the 30 mark.

ERIC CANTONA
(France 1987–95)
Forward
Born: Marseille, Bouche-du-Rhone, 24 May 1966.
Caps: Auxerre 5, Montpellier 8, Marseilles 7, Leeds United 9, Manchester United 16. Total: 45
Goals: 20

CONTROVERSIAL, charismatic and classy Eric Cantona revived his career with title-winning Leeds United. No stranger to clashes with authority at national and international level, the French forward made a major impact during his nine-month stay at Elland Road. He helped United become League champions and was a huge hero with the fans until his shock departure to arch-rivals Manchester United, with whom he enjoyed outstanding success and popularity.

Cantona made his French League debut as a 17-year-old for Auxerre in a 4–0 win against Nancy on 5 November 1983 – and it was not long before the fireworks were exploding. He earned his first full cap at the age of 21, marking his debut with a goal in a 2–1 defeat against West Germany in Berlin, but in the same year he was fined for punching an Auxerre teammate. Despite his fiery temperament there was no questioning his skill, and he was a member of the French side that won the 1988 Under-21 European Championship and he moved to Marseille for a French-record fee of 22 million francs. The switch did little to soothe Cantona's angst, as he was dropped from the national team and in a post-match television interview referred to the French manager Henri Michel – the man who had given him his international debut – as a 'bag of shit'. The French Football Federation immediately banned Cantona from all international matches, but it was not long before the same organisation axed Michel after France failed to qualify for the 1990 World Cup.

Michel Platini, a big fan of Cantona, was put in charge, and he recalled him to the French squad. By this time Cantona had been loaned out by Marseille to Bordeaux and Montpellier, having another dressing room bust-up at the latter, with whom he won the French Cup. Recalled by Marseille, he helped his home-town team to the 1991 title but did not get on with coach Raymond Goethals and was transferred to Nimes. During this period of instability the mercurial Cantona had become a regular in the French team under Platini's guidance, but it all blew up in December 1991 when he threw the ball at a referee during a Nimes game. He was banned for a month at an FFF hearing, at which Cantona told each member of the committee they were an 'idiot'. The ban was increased to three months. A furious Cantona soon announced his retirement from football at the age of 25. At the time he had played 20 times for his country, scoring a dozen goals, and was a talent the national team could ill afford to lose.

French coach Platini knew Cantona was regarded as damaged goods in his own country, but the stylish player was an instrumental part of his team. He persuaded Cantona to make a comeback and in January 1992 he went to England for a trial with Sheffield Wednesday, but when the Owls were slow to follow up on their interest in the player Leeds boss Howard Wilkinson stepped in to snatch Cantona from under his old club's noses. Leeds and Manchester United were locked in a titanic struggle for the Division One title, and the addition of Cantona to his squad unquestionably gave Wilkinson the edge over his title rival Alex Ferguson.

Although not a regular starter, Cantona added impetus to the Whites' title charge and provided fans with

Eric Cantona.

moments of sublime skill. After Leeds wrapped up the title and Cantona announced his love of the Leeds fans during the title celebrations in the city centre, Wilkinson finalised a £900,000 deal with Nimes. The following season Cantona scored a hat-trick at Wembley in the 4–3 Charity Shield victory over Liverpool and hit an early season Premiership treble in a 5–0 rout of Tottenham at Elland Road.

On the surface everything looked fine, particularly as Cantona was blossoming in the French side under Platini's guidance. He played nine times for France during his time at Elland Road, the first being a friendly at Wembley when England won 2–0 with goals from Alan Shearer and Gary Lineker. After friendlies against Belgium, Switzerland and Holland, the new Leeds star Cantona headed to Sweden for the 1992 European Championships. France had won all eight of their qualifying games, winning a group that contained Spain and Czechoslovakia by an impressive nine points. With Cantona in dazzling form, it was not surprising that France were the favourites to win the European title. They opened with a 1–1 draw in Stockholm against hosts Sweden, Cantona's strike partner Jean-Pierre Papin scoring a 58th-minute equaliser for Les Bleus.

Four days later France slugged out a 0–0 draw in Malmo with an England side bereft of key players like Paul Gascoigne, John Barnes and Mark Wright. The final group games saw France take on Denmark, with England tackling

Sweden. The French were widely expected to see off the Danes, who had only been entered in the Finals as late replacements for Yugoslavia, which was being ripped apart by war.

The Danes had been second best in drawing 0–0 with England and losing 1–0 to Sweden, but found their form against an off-key French side, winning 2–1 to qualify for the semi-finals with Sweden, who beat England by the same score, future Leeds player Tomas Brolin getting the hosts' late winner. Denmark went on to capture the hearts of the Continent by beating Holland on penalties in the semi-final and defeating Germany 2–0 in the Final.

France coach Platini quit, but that did not appear to affect Cantona on his return to Leeds, as the champions lifted the Charity Shield and opened with successive home wins in the Premiership. Cantona followed his hat-trick against Spurs with a couple of goals in a 2–2 draw at Oldham the following week. But United's away form was causing Wilkinson some concern, and a 3–0 European Cup defeat in Stuttgart on 16 September saw Cantona limp off. He was never quite the same player for Leeds after that game, and rumours were rife of a split with the manager, particularly after he was omitted from the side which lost at Queen's Park Rangers on 24 October – just 10 days after scoring in a 2–0 World Cup qualifier against Austria in Paris.

A thumping 4–0 defeat at Manchester City and a Football League Cup exit at Watford prompted Wilkinson to seek new blood. Wilko contacted Manchester United manager Alex Ferguson about the availability of former Leeds right-back Denis Irwin. Fergie said 'no deal' but, in turn, asked about the availability of Cantona. Although Cantona's Leeds form may have dipped, he was still a force for France, scoring in a 2–1 World Cup qualifier victory over Finland in Paris on 14 November. A fortnight later he was a Manchester United player. The trans-Pennine clubs thrashed out a £1.2 million transfer. For Cantona it was a dream move, as he won four Premiership titles, including two League and FA Cup doubles, with the Red Devils. Leeds fans were angered by the sale of their talismanic French ace, who became the centrifugal force in Manchester United's dominance of the Premiership in the 1990s. Ferguson seemed able to handle Cantona's temperament well and even managed to keep him on the rails after the controversial player received a nine-month worldwide playing ban and a sentence of community service after attacking a spectator with a 'kung-fu' style kick following his red card at Crystal Palace on 25 January 1995.

Despite Cantona's presence and the many talents of those around him, France failed to qualify for the 1994 World Cup Finals under Gerard Houllier after a disastrous 2–1 home defeat to Bulgaria in the key qualifying game. Houllier quit, and Aime Jacquet was installed as French coach and appointed Cantona as captain, a position he held until the infamous Selhurst Park attack. By the time Cantona had served his ban and was available to return to the international fold, Jaquet had built the French side around Cantona's successor as playmaker and skipper, Zinedine Zidane, who was backed up by rising stars Patrick Viera and Thierry Henry.

France, quite simply, no longer needed Cantona, and he finished his international career with 20 goals in 45 appearances, the last coming a week before that ill-fated Crystal Palace game. He would undoubtedly have played much more for his country, but for his spats with authority. After football he pursued a career as a writer and film actor, as well as managing the French beach soccer national team.

JEFF CHANDLER
(Republic of Ireland 1979)
Winger
Born: Hammersmith, London, 19 June 1959.
Caps: Leeds United 2

Jeff Chandler.

JEFF Chandler's switch to Elland Road paid instant dividends as he made his full Republic of Ireland debut with just one United reserve game under his belt. The box-of-tricks winger was still only 20 when he moved from Third Division Blackpool to First Division Leeds for £100,000 in September 1979. His rise through the ranks at Bloomfield Road had been rapid after his sports master, Dave Johnston, son of Tangerines' legend Harry Johnston, recommended Chandler to his dad's old club. The former West London Boys star earned rave reviews after breaking into the Blackpool first team and won his first Republic Under-21 cap in a 1–1 draw against Poland in Dublin – just a week before his transfer to Leeds.

Although born in Hammersmith and the possessor of a strong London accent, Chandler qualified for the Republic as his mother was born in Southern Ireland. He was regarded by Leeds boss Jimmy Adamson as one for the future and two days after signing featured in the reserves' 2–1 victory against Bolton. Chandler had barely had time to get to know his new teammates before he was jetting out to Prague with the full Republic squad for a friendly against Czechoslovakia. Former Leeds midfield hero Johnny Giles was the Irish boss and took the opportunity to check out some of his younger fringe players against the European champions. It was certainly an experimental Irish line up, with David O'Leary's brother Pierce (Shamrock Rovers), John Devine (Arsenal), Fran O'Brien (Philadelphia Fury) and Terry Donovan (Aston Villa) all making their first starts. Not surprisingly, the Irish spent most of the game chasing shadows and despite a spirited effort were beaten 4–1. Chandler became the fifth Irish debutant on the night when he came on for Gillingham's Damien Richardson with seven minutes remaining.

Three days later Chandler was back on the bench – this time for the Leeds first team at Elland Road – and came on for Paul Madeley, who was making his 500th League appearance, for his United debut in a 2–1 defeat against Manchester City. Chandler had to wait until 27 October before his first Leeds start – a 2–1 win at Southampton. It was United's first away victory of the season, and Chandler had double cause for celebration as he made his first start for the Republic two days later.

Unusually, a friendly had been arranged against the United States at Dalymount Park on a Monday night. It was a fairly inexperienced Irish side, and they found themselves a goal down against the Americans. Alan Kelly, who was in charge in the absence of manager Giles, reshuffled the side at half-time, bringing on Paddy Mulligan for his 50th cap and pushing Newcastle's Mick Martin into midfield at the expense of Chandler. Although the States went 2–0 up, the Irish fought back with three goals in the space of five minutes to earn a face-saving 3–2 victory. But for young Chandler it was the end of the international road – 53 minutes spread over two games. He also found himself back in the reserves at Leeds, although he marked his comeback to senior action with United's goal in a 2–1 defeat at Tottenham in March. He figured in the Leeds side for the rest of the campaign, which ended with United in 11th place.

The following season Chandler did not really progress, and in October 1981 he moved to Bolton for £40,000. He made over 150 appearances for the Trotters before helping Derby County move up from Division Three to Division One in successive seasons. A second spell at Bolton saw him recover from a nine-month lay-off with a snapped cruciate ligament in his left knee to play at Wembley in the 1989 Sherpa Van Trophy Final 4–1 victory against Torquay, in which he scored with a deflected shot.

A knee injury at his final club, Cardiff, brought a premature end to his career in 1990, and he started life selling advertising and double glazing before becoming a residential social worker in Blackpool. He is now a youth justice worker in Preston and a fully qualified counsellor, helping get youngsters with criminal convictions to get their lives back on track. Chandler's time on the international stage may have been brief, but it remains the highlight of his career.

JOHN CHARLES

(Wales 1950–65)

Centre-forward / Centre-half
Born: Cwmbwrla, Swansea, 27 December 1931.
Died: Wakefield, 21 February 2004.
Caps: Leeds United 23, Juventus 11, Leeds United 1, Cardiff City 3. Total: 38
Goals: 15

FOR many, John Charles was Leeds United's greatest player, a tag that is certainly not open to debate with anyone from Wales. His influence was so great that the Leeds team of the 1950s was dubbed 'Charles United'. The muscular giant from Swansea could lay claim to be both the club's best centre-half and centre-foward, such was his impact at Elland Road, but his fame stretched beyond the shores of the British Isles, as he was revered in Italian football with Juventus and was a colossus for his beloved Wales.

John Charles.

Charles was spotted playing in the juniors with his home-town team Swansea by United's scout in South Wales, Jack Pickard, and Leeds boss Major Frank Buckley persuaded the youngster to move up to Yorkshire. Buckley was a high-profile manager with a reputation for developing young talent, and his gift of the gab helped lure Charles to Elland Road. Swansea's loss was United's huge gain. Buckley was never shy of giving young players a go, so when regular number five Tom Holley was injured he gave 17-year-old centre-half Charles his chance in a friendly against Queen of the South on Easter Tuesday, 19 April 1949. He totally blotted out Billy Houliston, who had been one of the heroes of Scotland's 3–1 win at Wembley 10 days earlier, in a 0–0 draw. A star had been born. Charles was so good that he kept his place for the remaining two League games of the season, against Cardiff and Queen's Park Rangers.

Awesome in the air and powerful in the tackle, Charles could pass accurately, long and short, had instant ball control, could dribble at speed and possessed a sledgehammer shot – all married to an ice cool temperament. Buckley's prediction that Charles would soon play for Wales quickly came true – on 8 March 1950, aged 18 years 71 days, he became the youngest player to represent his country, a record that stood for 42 years until it was broken by Manchester United winger Ryan Giggs. It has since been lowered further by Ryan Green (Wolves) and Lewis Nyatanga (Derby).

The difference between shining for a moderate Second Division side like Leeds and handling international football quickly became apparent for the teenage Charles. His debut game was against Ireland at Wrexham with Charles lining up alongside boyhood heroes like Trevor Ford and Ronnie Burgess. Wales had thumped Belgium 5–1 in their previous game but the Welsh selectors, keen to look at new blood, made five changes for the Ireland game. The introduction of Charles was one of them and, for once, he played like a teenager – nervous and unsure – in a 0–0 draw.

Charles was an ever-present in 1949–50 as United finished fifth in Division Two and reached the FA Cup sixth round, but he had to wait until May 1951 for his second game in a Welsh jersey. Like the first, it was also at Wrexham, and once again Charles did not live up to his club form. The game was against Switzerland and was one of a series of games played as part of the Festival of Britain. Wales roared into a 3–0 lead, but canny Swiss forward Fredy Bickel, the man Charles was marking, dropped deeper into midfield. It was a tactic young Charles had not encountered before and saw the Swiss get hold of the final 20 minutes, leaving the Welsh happy to hang on 3–2 winners.

Charles was mixing playing with doing his National Service with the 12th Lancers at Catterick, and consequently he missed several games in 1950–51. He

John Charles scores one of his two goals against England at Wembley in 1954.

missed a large chunk of the following campaign after undergoing knee surgery. By this time Charles had played a handful of games as an emergency centre-forward, and in October 1952 Major Buckley opted to switch the Welsh prodigy to centre-forward on a permanent basis. The move was a stunning success as he smashed in 26 goals in 28 League games from his new berth, prompting a recall to the national side before the end of the season.

This time there was no sign of nerves as Big John rattled in a couple of goals in a 3–2 victory against Northern Ireland in Belfast. Although Wales were heavily beaten by France and Yugoslavia on their continental tour in May, Charles had arrived as an international player. His first appearance against England came on 10 October 1953 in Cardiff when Wales were condemned to a bitterly unlucky 4–1 defeat, with all England's goals coming after left-back Alf Sherwood suffered concussion. Charles, still only 21, was superb and had a hand in Ivor Allchurch's 22nd-minute goal, which gave the principality a deserved lead. Sherwood went off about 10 minutes later, and by the time he returned as a token left-winger England were 3–1 up.

Despite the Three Lions's victory, all the talk was about Charles's brilliant performance in attack, and the following month he rattled in a couple of goals at Hampden Park as Wales drew 3–3 with Scotland. He was reproducing his stunning goalscoring form with Leeds for his country. In 1953–54 Charles netted a club record 42 goals in 39

League games, but was switched back to defence by Major Buckley's managerial successor, Raich Carter, early on the following season as United were conceding too many goals.

Wales suffered a case of déjà vu when Charles made his Wembley debut in November 1954. He scored twice – the second a blistering ground shot from distance past Ray Wood – but a hat-trick from Chelsea's Roy Bentley saved the day for England after injuries to Welsh stars Ray Daniel and Derek Sullivan. The following April unstoppable Big John scored his only international hat-trick as Northern Ireland were beaten 3–2 in Belfast, a match in which his brother Mel made his Wales debut at right-half.

Big John rises to plant a header past Tommy Younger, later to play with Leeds, during a 2–2 draw at Ninian Park in October 1956.

John got on the scoresheet in the next game – but at the wrong end. Back at centre-half, he headed into his own net, but it did not prevent Wales beating an ageing England 2–1 in Cardiff – their first victory over the English for 17 years. He totally mastered Nat Lofthouse and had cemented his place on the world stage. Inevitably there was much speculation about Charles's future at Leeds, who were still bobbing along in the old Second Division, but the Elland Road directors were keen to hang on to their skipper and prized asset as long as possible.

Charles hankered after First Division football and finally earned it when United gained promotion in 1956, a season in which Charles rattled in 29 goals. In the final couple of months of the season Carter cleverly switched Charles from number nine to inside-right. It meant the big Welshman saw more of the ball and was a greater influence on matches. Critics who expected him to be less influential in the top flight were well wide of the mark, as Big John netted 38 goals in 40 Division One games. By this time he had also skippered Wales, leading his men out for the first time on 10 April 1957. Although the game was a relatively uneventful 0–0 draw with Northern Ireland, it was to prove a turning point in Charles's career.

On the day of the game Leeds announced that they would not sell Charles to another English club, but would not stand in his way if one of the big clubs on the Continent came in for him. There had already been rumours that Italian giants Juventus had been trailing Charles for many months, and an interested spectator at the goalless draw in Belfast was 22-year-old Umberto Agnelli, a member of the mega-rich family that owned the Fiat car company and controlled the Juventus club.

Soon after the match, United and relegation-threatened Juventus thrashed out a £65,000 world-record transfer fee for Charles in the Queen's Hotel in the heart of Leeds. Although the transfer did not take long to sort out, Charles's personal terms took considerably longer before it was a 'done deal' involving a £10,000 signing on fee over the two-year period of his first contract. Charles flew to Turin, passed his medical and returned to Yorkshire for his swansong game, a 3–1 triumph over Sunderland at Elland Road in which Charles scored twice to sign off in typical style.

Juventus did stay up and prospered with Charles at the hub of their team. In five years in Italy he won three Championships, two Italian Cups, was voted Italian Footballer of the Year and represented the Italian League. But the move to Italy did impact on his international career. He was not always available for his country and only played 11 times for Wales as a Juventus player; however, this did include the 1958 World Cup in Sweden. It was the only time that all four Home nations reached the Finals, but in Wales's case it was, amazingly, as the representatives of the Asia-Africa group.

The Home International Championship had previously been used to determine who would make the World Cup

Wales skipper John Charles shakes hands with his East German counterpart Schoen before their World Cup qualifier in Leipzig in 1956.

Finals, but for 1958 the UK sides were all split into European groups. England, Scotland and Northern Ireland all topped their groups to qualify, but Wales missed out by finishing second to Czechoslovakia. The Welsh were handed a lifeline, however, when Israel won the Asia-Africa qualifying competition without playing a game after their opponents Turkey, Indonesia, Egypt and Sudan all refused to play them.

FIFA ruled that no country, other than the holders and hosts, should reach the Finals without playing. All the runners-up from the other qualifying groups went into a draw to determine who would face the Israelis in a two-match Play-off, with a place in Sweden at stake. Wales won both games 2–0, Charles playing in the second game at Cardiff on the day of the Manchester United Munich Air Disaster. The Welsh team manager was Jimmy Murphy, who was Matt Busby's assistant, and so he missed that ill-fated flight after a European Cup tie at Red Star Belgrade.

In those days there was no FIFA rule that gave countries priority over clubs, and the FA of Wales were slow to ask Juventus for Charles's release for the Finals in Sweden. Juventus wanted him to stay behind and play in the Italian Cup, and even when they did agree to let him go the Italian FA refused him permission to travel because of a lack of notice. Eventually, common sense prevailed and the red tape was unravelled, and Charles arrived in Sweden just four days before their opening game against Hungary, who

John Charles (right) attempts to block a cross by Hungary's Laszlo Budai during the 1958 World Cup.

Swansea, Queen's Park Rangers and Oxford, while John's son, Terry, played rugby union for Cardiff and Wales B. John Charles died aged 73 on 21 February 2004. After his funeral at Leeds Parish Church the procession headed to Elland Road, scene of some of his greatest games, where thousands gathered inside to say farewell to a football genius.

JACK CHARLTON

(England 1965–70)

Centre-half

Born: Ashington, Northumberland, 8 May 1935.
Caps: Leeds United 34
Goals: 6

were a shadow of the side beaten by Germany in the 1954 Final. The Magyars closely marked Charles – sometimes literally – but could not stop the big man from heading in a Cliff Jones cross to earn the Welsh a 1–1 draw.

Dull 1–1 and 0–0 draws with Mexico and Sweden in Solna followed to earn Wales a Play-off with Hungary, who had belatedly found their form to beat Mexico 4–0. Hungary were red-hot favourites and went ahead but Wales, shaking off the opposition's rough tactics, stormed back to win 2–1. Referee Nikolai Latychev finally dismissed Ferenc Sipos, but not until Charles, sporting four stitches in an eye wound sustained against Sweden, had been kicked from pillar to post. Victory came at a cost as the injured Charles missed the quarter-final against Brazil – the most important game in his country's history. The brave Welsh gave their all, only to lose to a toe-poke shot from 17-year-old Pelé, which deflected past goalkeeper Jack Kelsey.

After 108 goals with Juventus and a movie star lifestyle British footballers of the 1950s could only dream of, 'Il Gigante Buono' – the Gentle Giant – returned to West Yorkshire at the age of 31. Leeds were back in Division Two, but still managed to raise £53,000 to re-sign Charles in August 1962. The pressure was on him to carry Don Revie's emerging young squad back to the top flight, but Charles was not fully fit and after 11 games and three goals he returned to Italy in a £70,000 deal with Roma. His 91 days back at Elland Road included an outing at centre-half for Wales in a 3–2 defeat against Scotland in which he scored his final goal for his country.

Charles's second stint in Italy was injury-hit, and he joined Cardiff City and played three more times for Wales, taking his international tally to 38 – a figure that would have been considerably more had he remained in Britain. Never booked or sent off in his League career, he was later player-manager with non-League Hereford, managed Merthyr Tydfil and did some coaching at Swansea and had several, not altogether successful, business ventures.

Sport was clearly in the Charles's genes. As well as brother Mel, his nephew Jeremy also played for Wales,

LEEDS fans burst with pride that one of their men, Jack Charlton, was a key figure in the greatest day in English football. Alf Ramsey's World Cup-winning team of 1966 was drawn from eight clubs, centre-half Jack representing the Elland Roaders on that magical day against West Germany in late July. Big Jack was certainly a late developer on the international scene, gaining his first cap a month before his 30th birthday when he played in a 2–2 draw with Scotland in April 1965.

Club form demanded that Charlton joined his more famous younger brother Bobby, the Manchester United hero, in the England set-up as Ramsey prepared for the World Cup. The brothers were from an Ashington mining family in the football-mad North East and were part of the famous Milburn clan. Their uncles George, Jack and Jim Milburn had been tough full-backs with Leeds, another uncle, Stan, played for Chesterfield and Jack and Bobby's mother's cousin was the legendary Newcastle centre-forward Jackie Milburn. While Jack Charlton inherited the defensive qualities of the family, brother Bobby followed the path of 'Wor Jackie' by banging in goals left, right and centre.

Bobby was recruited by Manchester United as a youngster while brother Jack gave up his mining job and applied to join the police. His uncle, Jim Milburn, recommended Jack, then playing for Ashington YMCA, to the top brass at Elland Road and the skinny youngster impressed sufficiently in a trial game to be offered an apprenticeship and turn professional in May 1952, making his debut in a 1–1 draw at Doncaster Rovers in the final Division Two game of the 1952–53 season as a 17-year-old. He did not become a regular for a couple more years after completing his National Service with the Royal Horse Guards and played 34 consecutive League games as United won promotion to Division One in 1956.

Despite occasional clashes with the Elland Road hierarchy, Big Jack's performances in the top flight did not go unnoticed, and he represented the Football League against the League of Ireland at Elland Road in October

Jack Charlton hobbles off after England's 3–2 defeat against Scotland at Wembley in 1967.

1957. Charlton was one of the few bright spots in United's 1959–60 relegation season, and when teammate Don Revie, with whom Charlton had his fair share of disagreements as a player, took over as player-manager it seemed the big centre-half could be on his way. Leeds seemed set to sell their big centre-half, who was becoming disillusioned with the lack of progress the club was making, but he remained at Elland Road despite interest from other clubs and became one of the senior players in the Revie revolution.

Charlton's stock rose as Leeds stormed to the Division Two title and came heart-breakingly close to the League and FA Cup double on the return to the top flight. As the race for the Championship with Manchester United was gathering pace, Jack made his international debut in a dramatic Home International game with Scotland at Wembley. Also making their England debuts that day were Nobby Stiles, the Manchester United wing-half, and Chelsea forward Barry Bridges.

Torrential London rain gave way to bright sunshine before the start, and England certainly shone in the early stages as goals by Bobby Charlton and Jimmy Greaves gave them a 2–0 advantage. But a terrible error by goalkeeper Gordon Banks gifted a goal to Denis Law before Ray Wilson went off just before half-time with a strained side muscle. It was in the era before substitutes, and just after

the interval England were effectively reduced to nine men as Johnny Byrne was hobbling with ligament damage. With Bobby Charlton dropping back to emergency left-back, under-strength England looked there for the taking, but Jack, Bobby Moore and Stiles performed heroics in defence to restrict Scotland to an Ian St John equaliser on the hour. The point had been good enough to earn England another Home Championship title, but it also showed Ramsey that the older Charlton was up to the task of international football.

Although Leeds missed out on the title on goal difference and were beaten in the FA Cup Final by Liverpool in extra-time, Jack had the compensation of playing in all four of England's summer games. With him at the heart of the defence, England looked extremely solid as they beat Hungary 1–0, drew 1–1 in Yugoslavia, lost 1–0 in West Germany and won 2–1 in Sweden.

Charlton was particularly eye-catching in Nuremburg alongside the cool Bobby Moore in a game which saw Leeds forward Mick Jones make his international debut. The commanding centre-back had grabbed his England opportunity, and it was abundantly clear that he would be the first-choice number five for the World Cup Finals, playing in 14 successive internationals from his debut. One of the features of Jack's play was the amount of goals he scored for Leeds and England. On United's return to the top division he weighed in with a remarkable nine League goals in 39 games and translated those kinds of stats to the England set-up. Many of his goals came from corners, as he had perfected the technique of standing in front of the goalkeeper and using his 6ft-plus frame to create havoc. Oddly, his first international goal did not come via that route. England were 2–0 up in Finland on the opening game of their Scandanavian tour ahead of the World Cup when he joined the attack in the last minute, shot from an acute angle and the ball went in off the boot of Timo Kautonen.

Big Jack (centre) looks on as his club skipper Billy Bremner just fails to get on the end of a cross for Scotland.

Little and large…Jack Charlton (England) wins this aerial battle with Leeds colleague Billy Bremner (Scotland).

Charlton was rested for the next game against Norway and replaced by Wolves's Ron Flowers, whose poor fourth-minute back pass gave Harald Sunde a simple goal. But a sharp-shooting performance by Jimmy Greaves, whose four-goal haul saw England cruise home 6–1, completed a spectacular recovery. Charlton was back in the side four days later for the game in Denmark and got on the scoresheet again by heading in Alan Ball's cross after John Connelly had over-hit his corner. By this time England were playing a 4–4–2 formation without wingers, and their last test before the Finals came in Poland, where a Bobby Charlton goal earned an impressive 1–0 victory. Brother Jack and Bobby Moore were once more in superb form at the back for England, who went into the World Cup in magnificent shape.

Big Jack played in every England game, all at Wembley, in the Finals which began with a dull 0–0 draw against Uruguay, a nervy 2–0 win against Mexico followed by a 2–0 victory against France in which 'the Giraffe's' header set up the opener for Roger Hunt. The quarter-final will always be remembered for the dismissal of Argentina captain Antonio Rattin, who refused to accept German referee Rudi Kreitlein's decision to send him off 10 minutes before the interval. He had been one of three South Americans cautioned in a stormy match, but it took seven minutes for him to leave the field of play as players and officials jostled on the pitch. At one stage a mass walk-off of the entire Argentina team looked likely, but eventually order was restored and the game, such as it was, resumed.

Two more Argentines were added to the referee's notebook in the second period, as were the Charlton brothers, as England threatened to let frustration get the better of them. Mercifully, England conjured a superb winner 13 minutes from the end when Geoff Hurst's glancing header sent a magnificent cross from his West Ham colleague Martin Peters ripping past goalkeeper Antonio Roma. England had stood up to heavy punishment dished out by Argentina to book a semi-final place against a Eusebio-inspired Portugal, the tournament's most entertaining team. An all-European showdown for a place in the Final was a wonderful spectacle, which did much to erase the foul taste of the Argentina debacle.

Stylish England led 2–0, with both goals from Bobby Charlton, while at the other end brother Jack did a magnificent job in dealing with 6ft 4in dangerman Jose Torres. But eight minutes were still on the clock when Torres escaped his Leeds marker and sent a header goalwards, and Jack Charlton's hand kept the ball out. Up stepped Eusebio to ram home the penalty, and Portugal poured forward in search of an equaliser. Somehow England hung on to face West Germany in the Final.

If England's semi-final had been action-packed with drama and tension, then it was surpassed by the Final on Saturday 30 July 1966. Helmut Haller gave the Germans an early lead, but the advantage was wiped out inside six minutes by a Hurst header. Red-shirted England came close to taking the lead when Bobby Charlton rapped an upright with a 20-yarder. In the 77th minute England got their noses in front as Peters swept in a loose ball to send the vast majority of a noisy Wembley crowd wild with delight. England had one hand on the trophy as the game entered the final seconds of injury time, but Big Jack, who had been a rock at the back, was harshly penalised for a foul on Sigi Held. There was barely time to take the free-kick, which Lothar Emmerich smacked against England's defensive wall. The ball rebounded to Held, whose miscued shot found its way to a lurking Wolfgang Weber, whose outstretched foot sent the ball past the despairing Banks from six yards.

But that last-gasp drama was topped in extra-time by one of the most famous goals in football. England looked the more likely to score again on an energy-sapping pitch, and in Ball they had a non-stop midfield dynamo. Just before half-time of extra-time the little man from Blackpool sent in a centre which Hurst collected. He swiveled and crashed the ball against the underside of the bar and down before it was cleared by Weber. Millions around the globe held their breath as referee Gottfried Dienst went to Azerbaijani linesman Tofik Bakhramov, whose nod of the head prompted the Swiss whistler to signal a goal. The Germans protested bitterly that the whole of the ball had not crossed the line, and even today no one can say for sure that it was a genuine goal.

There was no doubting England's fourth, however, with just seconds remaining as Hurst latched on to Moore's magnificent long pass and thumped the ball past goalkeeper Hans Tilkowski to become the only man to score a hat-trick in a World Cup Final. Dienst's shrill whistle signalled the end of the game and triggered extraordinary scenes. An exhausted Jack collapsed on to the pitch as he raced to congratulate brother Bobby, who wept tears of joy. The roar as Moore hoisted aloft the Jules Rimet Trophy was deafening and the nation, taking their cue from Stiles's victory jig, partied in style. England have never had a day like it since.

The Charltons were not the first brothers to win the World Cup – Fritz and Ottmar Walter had achieved the

Jack Charlton has the ball plucked off his head by Wales and Leeds 'keeper Gary Sprake.

feat in 1954 when Germany beat Hungary 3–2 in Switzerland – but it was a remarkable family achievement. England paraded the trophy and fielded their World Cup-winning XI in their next game – a 2–0 win in Belfast against Northern Ireland as the Home Championships doubled up as qualifiers for the 1968 European Championships. Leeds man Charlton then scored England's final goal in a 5–1 Wembley victory over Wales, heading in a Hurst centre. He also scored in his next international – against Scotland – but it was the men from north of the border who became the first side to beat the world champions with a dramatic 3–2 success at Wembley.

Charlton broke a toe in a tackle on Bobby Lennox early on and was forced to hobble along as a makeshift winger, later switching to centre-forward. Scotland, who featured Charlton's club colleague Billy Bremner in their side, cashed in on England's misfortune. The hungry Scots led with a Law goal, and Lennox made it 2–0 with 10 minutes left. But somehow the hobbling Charlton managed to poke the ball in to reduce the arrears, only for Jim McCalliog to immediately restore the Tartan Army's two-goal advantage, before Hurst headed a late consolation for England, who lost for the first time in 19 games and left themselves plenty to do if they were to progress in the European Championships. Ultimately Ramsey's team did go through to the last eight as Scotland were surprisingly beaten by Northern Ireland.

Charlton missed the rest of Leeds's season through injury. United had been pushing hard for silverware, both at home and on the Continent in the Fairs Cup, only to fall short on all fronts. The consolation for Big Jack was being named the 1967 Footballer of the Year, and the following season United finally gained some tangible reward for their efforts as they beat Arsenal 1–0 in a feisty League Cup Final which saw Jack simply unbeatable in the air.

Jack could certainly look after himself on a football pitch and was now one of Europe's most experienced defenders, having gained a vast array of knowledge through his England and Fairs Cup games. This would be needed as England took on Spain in the European Championship quarter-finals over two legs. England edged the first game at Wembley 1–0, with Jack winning the 85th-minute free-kick which led to sibling Bobby driving home the only goal. Injury ruled Charlton out of the rematch, in which club teammate Norman Hunter scored the winner in Madrid. Everton's Brian Labone had done well in Charlton's absence, but could do little to prevent England losing 1–0 to Yugoslavia in their semi-final in the Italian city of Florence. England eased past the USSR in Rome's Olympic Stadium to take third place.

Charlton, now 33, began the 1968–69 season in fine style. His tactic of standing on the goalline at corners paid dividends once again as it paved the way for Mick Jones to score the only goal of the delayed two-leg Fairs Cup Final against Hungarian outfit Ferencvaros; however, his England

slot was now held by Labone for friendlies against Romania and Bulgaria before Charlton returned for another friendly against Romania at Wembley in January 1969. Once again his ploy at corners paid off as he headed in England's goal, only to be penalised for handball 15 minutes from the end and for Florea Dumitrache to equalise from the spot.

Charlton had a magnificent season for Leeds, who conceded just 26 goals on their way to their first title. The big Geordie missed just one League game and, despite being in the autumn of his career, still had a key part to play for United and England, for whom he headed the only goal in a friendly against Portugal at Wembley in December 1969. In 1970 Leeds finished runners-up, were European Cup semi-finalists and were beaten in extra-time by Chelsea in the FA Cup Final replay after Charlton had headed Revie's side ahead in the first game at Wembley, which finished 2–2.

The new decade had seen the younger Labone supplant veteran Jack in the England side, but he was still selected for the 1970 World Cup in Mexico, where he won his final cap at the ripe old age of 35 in a crucial 1–0 Group win against Czechoslovakia on the day United teammate Allan Clarke marked the start of his England career with the only goal from the penalty spot. Charlton had played 35 times for England in a five-year period, scoring six times, and was only on the losing side twice. Those impressive statistics confirmed that even well into his 30s he was

One of Jack Charlton's England shirts framed in the Elland Road reception area.

among the world's best defenders and never let his country down. The end of his international career certainly did not signal the end of the road with Leeds, with Charlton missing just one domestic game in 1970–71 as Leeds finished Division One runners-up again. He continued to defy Father Time for another season as he returned to his second home, Wembley, as Arsenal won the Centenary FA Cup Final in 1972 two days before his 37th birthday, as Leeds went within a whisker of the double.

With Paul Madeley and newcomer Gordon McQueen challenging for the famous number-five shirt at Elland Road, Charlton's club appearances became more sporadic, and when he limped off injured in a 3–1 defeat at Southampton on 28 April 1973 it was the end of a glittering 21-year career with Leeds. He played 770 first-team games for United – 629 of them in the League – both club records that are likely to stand forever. However, another chapter in the old warrior's illustrious career was just about to start, as he entered football management. (See Leeds International Managers.)

TREVOR CHERRY
(England 1976–80)
Defender / Midfield
Born: Huddersfield, 23 February 1948.
Caps: Leeds United 27

NOT many men can claim to have led England to a win at the Sydney Cricket Ground, but Trevor Cherry can. While touring English cricket captains have often come unstuck at the SCG, Leeds defender Cherry skippered the Three Lions to victory there in 1980 on the only occasion he led his country. It was a tremendous honour for a player who had been the only non-international first teamer when he joined Don Revie's glittering squad from neighbours Huddersfield in a £100,000 transfer in summer 1972.

The match, played to mark the Australian FA's centenary, saw Cherry become only the second Leeds player to lead out an England side after Willis Edwards. It was the first football meeting between the two sporting rivals but, coming just a couple of weeks before the start of the European Championships in Italy, was probably regarded more as an inconvenience by England's administrators. Manager Ron Greenwood was certainly not taking any risks as he took a shadow squad on the long haul Down Under and gave starting debuts to Ipswich Town duo Terry Butcher and Russell Osman, David Armstrong of Middlesbrough and Arsenal's Alan Sunderland, who was replaced by another debutant, Brighton forward Peter Ward. The Aussies were one of the weaker playing nations in those days, but Cherry had to lead by example with some excellent defending to keep them at bay before England's youthful midfield took a firm grip and went 2–0 up inside 24 minutes with goals from

Glenn Hoddle and Paul Mariner. Australia never gave up and were rewarded two minutes from the end with a consolation goal from London-born Gary Cole, a schoolmaster by profession.

None of the England squad figured in England's opening Group Two game against Belgium in Turin 12 days later. The match was marred by terrace trouble, which prompted Italian police to use tear gas to quell the skirmishing after Jan Ceulemans cancelled out Ray Wilkins's brilliant opener for England. Play was suspended for 10 minutes to allow the gas to clear, but neither side really threatened after the resumption and the game ended 1–1. A 1–0 defeat to hosts Italy meant England had to beat Spain to have an outside chance of qualifying for the third-place Final. Cherry came on for Viv Anderson in this game and, although they won 2–1, Belgium's unexpected goalless draw with Italy scuppered England's hopes of progress. It proved to be Cherry's 27th and final cap for England, who immediately started rebuilding in an attempt to qualify for the 1982 World Cup, by which time the popular and reliable Leeds star would be 34.

Cherry was a rising star with his home-town club Huddersfield before his switch to Elland Road. Playing at left-half, he had a fine defensive partnership with Roy Ellam as the Terriers won the Second Division title in 1970. Two years later both men joined Leeds, where Cherry's career flourished while the more experienced Ellam struggled to shift the evergreen Jack Charlton from the United starting

Trevor Cherry.

line up. Cherry could fill a variety of roles in defence and was a solid anchorman in midfield, where his crisp tackling and consistent passing were a key feature. He won a League Championship medal in his second season with Leeds, and played the the European Cup-Winners' Cup Final defeat against AC Milan in Salonika the following campaign, but missed out on the 1975 European Cup Final loss against Bayern Munich in Paris. However, compensation lay just round the corner as Don Revie, the man who had signed him from Huddersfield, was in charge of England's fortunes. The former Leeds boss called up Cherry for his international debut in the FA of Wales centenary game at Wrexham's compact Racecourse Ground.

Revie sent out an experimental side with six players – Cherry, Phil Neal (Liverpool), Mike Doyle (Manchester City), Phil Thompson (Liverpool), Phil Boyer (Norwich) and Ray Kennedy (Liverpool) all making their first starts. Peter Taylor (Crystal Palace) and Dave Clement (Queen's Park Rangers) also both came on as substitutes to earn their first caps. England, led by Kevin Keegan for the first time, won 2–1 with goals from new men Kennedy and Taylor. Cherry, at right-back, put in a solid display and tasted more competitive action when he came on as a substitute at Hampden Park in the final Home International of the season; however, he was helpless as a rare Ray Clemence error handed the Scots a 2–1 victory.

Cherry then flew out with the England squad to take part in the United States Bicentennial Tournament and was in the starting line up against Brazil in the Coliseum Stadium, Los Angeles. The South Americans snatched the only goal late on through replacement Roberto. Cherry occupied a midfield role against the Brazilians and took up the same position in his next international match, a World Cup qualifier in Finland, in which England cruised to a 4–1 win, and almost added a fifth goal late on, but his shot came back off a post.

The versatile Cherry then popped up at left-back in a 1–1 friendly draw with the Republic of Ireland at Wembley. One of the criticisms of Revie's international tenure was his failure to find a settled side, and once again he shuffled his pack for the big World Cup qualifier against Italy in Rome. Cherry was back in midfield for the Olympic Stadium clash, but England were outplayed and slumped to a 2–0 defeat as Giancarlo Antognoni and Roberto Bettega struck in the 36th and 77th minutes respectively. Among the Italian stars in Rome was AC Milan's Fabio Capello, a future England manager. The atmosphere was more sedate in Cherry's next outing as a much-changed England rolled over Luxembourg 5–0 in another World Cup qualifier, with the Leeds man hardly tested at left-back.

Cherry was an ever-present for Leeds in 1976–77 when United's new-look side finished in mid-table. Although most of his games that term had been in midfield, he was deployed by Revie at right-back in the

2–1 Home Championship victory against Northern Ireland at Windsor Park. In the summer England headed to South America for a gruelling three-match tour against Brazil, Argentina and Uruguay, with Cherry figuring in all the games. While Italy remained in Europe to strengthen their grip on England's World Cup qualification group with a 3–0 win over Finland, England faced the mighty Brazilians in the Maracana. Cherry, at left-back, gave probably his best display in an England shirt as he helped keep the likes of Zico and Rivelino off the scoresheet in a 0–0 draw.

If Cherry was walking on air at that stage, he was brought down to earth, literally, in the Argentina game in Buenos Aires. It was the two countries' first meeting since their explosive encounter in the 1966 World Cup, and the 60,000 crowd were howling for blood, only to be silenced after three minutes when Stuart Pearson flicked in the opener. The volume was back on full blast 12 minutes later when Daniel Bertoni curled a free-kick past Ray Clemence, but England held firm and the game was dying out when Cherry found himself at the centre of an extraordinary incident 10 minutes from the end. He put in a routine tackle on Bertoni near the touchline, and as he moved away Bertoni swung a punch, knocking out two of Cherry's front teeth. Uruguayan referee Ramon Barreto sought the advice of his linesman and showed the red card to Bertoni before also sending off an astonished Cherry.

The game petered out to a draw, and Revie observed: 'Cherry was the unluckiest player in the world to be sent off.' The Leeds man was only the third England player to be dismissed, following Alan Mullery (versus Yugoslavia, 1968) and Alan Ball (versus Poland, 1973), although several have since followed them down the tunnel, including Leeds duo David Batty and Alan Smith.

It speaks volumes about Cherry's courage and South American dental practice that Cherry turned out against Uruguay in a 0–0 draw just three days later. England had completed a tour of South America unbeaten for the first time, but Revie controversially walked away from his job in the summer and the FA appointed Ron Greenwood in temporary charge. The former West Ham boss was given three games to prove his worth, and Cherry figured in all of them in defence – a dull 0–0 friendly with Switzerland, a stumbling 2–0 World Cup qualifying win in Luxembourg and a vibrant victory over group leaders Italy at Wembley.

Despite the 2–0 triumph over the Azzurri, with goals from Kevin Keegan and Trevor Brooking, Italy knew they had only to beat Luxembourg in their final game to go through on goal difference – and that miracle did not happen as Italy beat the minnows 3–0 to book a ticket to the Finals in Argentina. Such was the praise England received for their victory over the Italians, that Greenwood was put in charge on a permanent basis. Cherry remained an integral part of the England set-up, but suffered a major blow in England's 3–1 win against Wales at Ninian Park on 13 May 1978.

Everton forward Bob Latchford had headed England into an early lead when Cherry fell awkwardly in the 16th minute and went off with a broken collarbone. He missed the next five internationals before making his comeback at Wembley at the end of November in a 1–0 friendly win against Czechoslovakia. Cherry occupied the left-back berth, and his full-back partner was Nottingham Forest's debut man Viv Anderson, who thus became the first black footballer to be capped at senior level for England.

Cherry also had the satisfaction of tasting victory over Argentina, the side against whom he had been ridiculously sent off in 1977. He came on for Phil Neal in a match laced with sublime skill and, for many, the first glimpse of 19-year-old Maradona, who made a series of magnificent high-speed dribbles that left Wembley gasping. Despite the teenager's brilliance, a confident England emerged deserved 3–1 winners.

Cherry played in all three end-of-season Home Internationals and rounded off a fine season with the ultimate honour of leading his country against Australia in what was to prove his penultimate England appearance. Cherry was captain at Elland Road by now and was named United's Player of the Year for 1980–81. Although Leeds were relegated the following season, he turned out for them in Division Two before joining Bradford City as player-manager. A wonderful servant for Leeds over a 10-year period which saw him easily top 400 appearances, he tasted success at Valley Parade, leading the club up to Division Two for the first time since 1937.

ALLAN CLARKE

(England 1970–76)

Forward

Born: Short Heath, near Willenhall, Staffordshire, 31 July 1946.

Caps: Leeds United 19

Goals: 10

ICE-COOL striker Allan Clarke showed nerves of steel on his England debut in the lung-sapping humid heat of Mexico. Never short of confidence, the Leeds marksman slotted home the only goal of the game against Czechoslovakia to seal England's place in the 1970 World Cup quarter-finals. It was the first of 10 goals from 19 international appearances for the slim Midland-born forward, who hailed from a family with a rich football pedigree. Brothers Wayne, Frank, Derek and Kelvin all played League football.

Wayne, the youngest, was an England Schools and Youth international who scored goals for Wolves, Birmingham, Everton, Leicester, Manchester City, Shrewsbury and Stoke; Frank, the oldest of the clan, was even more prolific with Shrewsbury, Ipswich, Queen's Park Rangers and Carlisle, while Derek figured in attack for Walsall, Wolves,

Oxford, Leyton Orient and Carlisle. Kelvin, the only defender among the brood, played a handful of games with Walsall.

Allan was the pick of the bunch and, like Kelvin and Derek, started his career at his local club, Walsall, where his sharpness in front of goal prompted a £35,000 transfer to Fulham. He continued to score at will for the Cottagers – 45 League goals in just over two years – and made five England Under-23 appearances before Leicester splashed out a club record £150,000 to take him to Filbert Street. He was Man of the Match in their 1–0 FA Cup Final defeat against Manchester City in 1968, a game that turned out to be his last with the Foxes as Don Revie paid a British record £165,000 for a man he believed would add more firepower to his attack. It was to prove money well spent.

Clarke was an England player in waiting, having added another Under-23 appearance while at Leicester, and had already outscored the likes of Geoff Hurst and Jimmy Greaves with three goals in his two Football League representative matches in games against the Scottish League and the Belgian League. Leeds had just been crowned champions for the first time in their history, but Clarke went straight into the side, scoring on his debut in an impressive 3–1 win against Spurs. He ended the season with 26 goals for Leeds, making his inclusion in the World Cup squad a formality. He was the only member of the 22-strong party yet to make a full England appearance, and did not get a run out in the pre-tournament victories over Colombia or Ecuador, but did play in two games classed as B internationals against Colombia and an Ecuador XI.

On their way to Mexico, England had a stopover back in the Colombian capital Bogota, where skipper Bobby Moore was held by police after he allegedly stole a bracelet from the jewellery shop where England had stayed the previous week. The allegations were absurd, and Ramsey was convinced his captain had been set up. World champions England were regarded with suspicion in South America, where the feeling was that they had only won the 1966 tournament through dubious refereeing decisions and home advantage at Wembley. The Moore incident threatened to undermine Ramsey's plans, and it took four

Ice cool debut man Allan Clarke strokes the ball past Czechoslovakia goalkeeper Ivo Viktor to give England victory in the 1970 World Cup Finals.

Allan Clarke.

days of diplomacy to obtain Moore's release on bail. In the event, he had no case to answer.

England opened in the sweltering heat of Guadalajara against Romania and Geoff Hurst, who netted the last goal of the 1966 World Cup, scored the first in the 1970 version with a 70th-minute winner. Brazil, who crushed Czechoslovakia 4–1 in their opening game, were next up for England in a genuine blockbuster of a game. Brazil won 1–0 courtesy of Jairziho's goal, but Ramsey's men merited a draw in a high-class encounter. Brazil then beat Romania 3–2, leaving England needing to avoid defeat against the Czechs to qualify for the last eight. Ramsey opted to rest several of his star names for the expected quarter-final clash and give his fringe players a chance.

England took the field in a pale blue strip to avoid a colour clash and turned in an equally pallid performance. Clarke, in for Manchester City's Francis Lee, seized his opportunity more than most in a tedious match, which only came to life four minutes after the interval when Ladislav Kuna slipped while attempting to tackle Colin Bell in the area and brushed the ball with his hand. French referee Roger Machin pointed to the spot, and Clarke calmly stroked the ball wide of Ivo Viktor for a poor game's only goal.

Ramsey recalled his big guns for the quarter-final – a rematch of the 1966 Final against West Germany – and they looked on course for victory when they went 2–0 up, but the dogged Germans hit back to win 3–2 in extra-time to gain revenge for their historic Wembley defeat. Ramsey began his rebuilding programme in November with a friendly against an in-form East German side at Wembley. Clarke was paired up front with Hurst and Lee in a new-look England attack, and it paid off with a fluent attacking performance against a team who had won their last four matches. The impressive Clarke put the icing on the cake of a 3–1 victory with the final goal, superbly converting Lee's pass.

'Sniffer' had made a fine start to his England career, and it was to continue as England were unbeaten in his first 10 appearances. Qualifying for the 1972 European Championships was England's main objective, and Clarke

was on target again with a penalty as Malta were despatched 5–0 beneath the Twin Towers – although he also put a spot-kick well wide in the same match.

Three days later the Leeds striker put on his boots for his first Home International and snaffled the only goal in Belfast to sink Northern Ireland, who felt aggrieved with the result. Not only did their fans think there had been a handball by Lee in the build-up to the goal, but they also believed the charismatic George Best had a goal wrongly disallowed.

Injury saw Clarke miss a couple of autumn internationals and he found himself behind Tottenham's Martin Chivers in the international pecking order by the time Ramsey's men took on old foes West Germany in the European Championship quarter-final first leg at Wembley. From Clarke's point of view it was not a bad game to miss as Germany won 3–1. Before the second leg in Berlin – which ended goalless with Clarke again absent – the Leeds forward was basking in Wembley glory, having netted the superb diving header that saw United beat Arsenal 1–0 to lift the 1972 FA Cup for the only time in club's history.

Clarke had added subtlety to his play and was more than an out-and-out finisher, but he had to wait until February 1973 for his next England game. He certainly returned with a bang as Ramsey's boys completely outplayed Scotland on a hard Hampden pitch covered with a dusting of snow. The game against the Auld Enemy was to launch the Scottish FA's centenary celebrations, but England gate-crashed the party with a 5–0 romp in Bobby Moore's 100th England appearance. Clarke's link-up play with Southampton's Mick Channon was magnificent, and the Leeds sharpshooter helped himself to a couple of well-taken goals.

Despite the disappointment of failing to retain the FA Cup in the 1973 Final against Second Division Sunderland, Clarke continued to shine for England, orchestrating some

'Sniffer' Allan Clarke lifts the ball over East German goalkeeper Jurgen Kroy in England's 3–1 win at Wembley in 1970.

dazzling moves in a 3–0 thumping of Wales before cracking the equaliser in a 1–1 friendly draw with Czechoslovakia in Prague. That set England up for their crucial World Cup qualifier in Poland, but the England midfield failed to provide Clarke and Chivers with a decent chance in a 2–0 loss. It was a disastrous game for England, with Moore making a rare error to gift the Poles their second goal and Alan Ball sent off for violent conduct.

A month before the rematch at Wembley, England, with Clarke in peerless form, filled their boots by crushing Austria 7–0. The Leeds poacher scored his best goal for England in this rout. Taking a pass from Sheffield United's Tony Currie – a future Leeds player – on the half hour, he dummied Robert Sara before turning inside to clip a left-foot shot into the far corner. He snapped up his second on the stroke of half-time and came within a whisker of his hat-trick when his shot was kicked on to a post by a defender and Channon knocked in the loose ball. If anything, England created more chances against Poland, but as every fan of the Three Lions knows, they could only manage a 1–1 draw in October 1973 and failed to make it to the World Cup Finals.

England battered the Poles in front of a disbelieving 100,000 Wembley crowd who could not believe their eyes as inspired goalkeeper Jan Tomaszewski kept rampant England at bay with a succession of saves, some by accident, others by design. Just before the hour the visitors broke out of defence to score through Jan Domarski, but England, needing to win to qualify, continued to pound the Poles and were soon level. Clarke had already had a goal disallowed when Martin Peters was pushed in the box, and the Leeds striker, showing admirable calm on a night of unremitting tension, sent Tomaszewski the wrong way with his penalty kick. But the floodgates did not open in the remaining half hour or so, and England were out. It was Clarke's last international goal, and like his first one it had come from the spot.

The following April Sir Alf was sacked as England team manager and Clarke, who gained a Championship medal with Leeds at the end of the season, did not feature in any of temporary England manager Joe Mercer's seven games in charge. Former United boss Don Revie was the man entrusted with reviving England's fortunes, but Clarke only played sporadically for his old chief and made his final international appearance as a substitute in a 1–1 European Championship qualifier with Portugal in Lisbon on 19 November 1975.

Sniffer left Leeds to be Barnsley's player-manager in 1978 with an excellent scoring record for the Whites – 110 goals in 270 starts and 43 goals in other competitions.

Always one to back his own ability, he returned to Elland Road as manager in October 1980, but, curiously considering his own scoring record, was in charge of a side who found goal-scoring difficult and was axed after the club's relegation to the Second Division in 1982.

He then had spells in charge of Scunthorpe, Barnsley (again) and Lincoln before quitting the game, but like many from the Revie era he is a regular visitor to Elland Road on matchdays.

DAVID COCHRANE
(Northern Ireland 1938–49)
Winger
Born: Portadown, Co. Armagh, 14 August 1920.
Died: Leeds, June 2000
Caps: Leeds United 12

BOY star Davy Cochrane was just 18 when he won his first cap for Northern Ireland – and it turned out to be a bitter sweet day for the teenager. The little right winger beamed with pride when he learned of his call up for the clash with England on 16 November 1938 at Old Trafford, but a dashing England ruined the day with a crushing 7–0 win, Willie Hall scoring five of the goals.

That match signalled the end of the Irish careers of Cochrane's Leeds teammates Jim Twomey and Bobby Browne, but the selectors stood by young Cochrane, who retained his place for the following game, against Wales in March. Ireland lost 3–1 in what was to be the final international before the outbreak of World War Two. The hostilities undoubtedly cost young Davy a stack of caps, and after a handful of wartime games for Leeds he returned to his native Portadown in 1940 to play regularly as a guest in the Northern Regional League.

Cochrane was a small man, standing just 5ft 4in, but had built a big reputation in the Irish League with Portadown before his pre-war switch to Elland Road. His dad had been an inside-right with Linfield, and Cochrane junior proved an early student of the game, playing for Portadown's reserves at 15, and turned professional five days after his 16th birthday to become one of the province's youngest-ever professional players. He was only 17 when he netted 14 Irish League and Cup goals in 13 games, and that prompted several League clubs to send scouts across the Irish Sea to watch the boy star in action. After Portadown's Gold Cup semi-final replay with Derry City in January 1937, Leeds took a £2,000 gamble on the youngster. Scouts from Elland Road decided that, despite his size, he could cope with the rough and tumble of the English game.

When he first arrived at Elland Road some of the players joked that he should have been a jockey not a footballer, but he got his head down in United's reserves and found the Central League a good arena to add muscle to his clever ball skills and blistering pace. He made his Leeds debut in a 2–0 home defeat against Derby on 26 March 1938 and forced his way into the United team on a more regular basis the following season, prompting the Irish selectors to pick him against England when he was just 18 years and three months old. Cochrane was the first

David Cochrane.

regarded as the closest thing to internationals. The Northern Regional League played several times, and Cochrane was an integral part of the set-up, scoring in a crushing 8–3 win over the Irish League at Dalymount Park, Dublin, in front of 36,000 fans. The boot was on the other foot the following season when Cochrane, now with Shamrock, played for the Irish League against the NRL. In all he played eight times for the NRL and had four games for the Irish League, netting four times for the Northern Irish. After spending the 1945–46 campaign back at Shamrock, he returned to his full-time employers at Leeds. Although he was still only 26, he found himself surrounded by ageing teammates, and Leeds finished bottom of Division One, a massive 15 points from survival.

Despite the club's poor showing, Cochrane was a shoe-in for his third full cap, which came against England in the Home Championship. Deprived of top-class football for so long, a record 57,000 squeezed into Windsor Park, scene of many of Cochrane's most dazzling displays for Linfield, to see Northern Ireland take on England in the first full international since 1939. So many supporters were in the ground that they spilled on to the pitch, but good-natured order was restored before the kick-off, and the match was able to start. England soon made up for lost time, Raich Carter, a future Leeds manager, scoring in the first minute. The visitors ended up runaway 7–2 winners, and in the two games against England Cochrane had seen the opposition score 14 goals.

The Irish selectors made sweeping changes for the next match, against Scotland, and Cochrane was one of only four players to keep his place as a revamped Irish side deservedly drew 0–0 at Hampden. Cochrane and Co. finished the Home Championship in style with a 2–1 win over Wales in Belfast, as the Leeds winger tasted a rare victory in what had been a dreadful season for his club.

The Leeds board got rid of a large chunk of their squad and named former England international Willis Edwards as the man to replace Billy Hampson, who had resigned as manager. Although Leeds only had a moderate season in Division Two, relegation did not put Cochrane's international place under threat. While Leeds were losing 3–3 at West Brom on 4 October 1947, little Davy was turning on the style for his country, who beat Scotland 2–0, with both goals coming from Wolves's Sammy Smyth, a last-minute replacement for Peter Doherty.

The following month Cochrane was in the side that halted England's run of 12 successive victories over Northern Ireland when the teams drew 2–2 at Goodison Park. But the Irish left it late to check England's record, Huddersfield Town hero Doherty scoring with a spectacular diving header in the final seconds. Cochrane played in a 2–0 loss against Wales and missed the next international against England, who resumed normal service with a 6–2 win, but was back in the side to face

Leeds United winger to play for his country and up to the suspension of the Football League had two international caps to his name and just over 30 senior Leeds games under his belt.

For many observers Cochrane was at his peak back in Ireland during the war period. He helped Portadown finish Northern Regional League runners-up in 1941 just before the club was forced to temporarily fold. He then spent a season in Dublin with Shamrock Rovers before returning north with Linfield, whose Windsor Park home was to become the scene of several of Cochrane's international matches. He was an absolute inspiration at Linfield, scoring 50 goals in one season and helping the club to two Wartime League titles, two Irish Cup Final appearances and a Gold Cup Final victory.

Despite the suspension of international football, representative games were still played, and these were

Scotland in November 1948 when two Dave Walsh goals in the opening five minutes stunned the Tartan Army. But the Scots hit back to snatch victory, Billy Houliston heading home a last-minute winner. Cochrane's international career was on the downturn as Ireland lost to Wales again before being crushed 8–2 by Scotland on 1 October 1949, East Fife's Henry Morris scoring a hat-trick in his only full international appearance.

Worse was to follow for Cochrane and the Irish the following month. They were slaughtered 9–2 in the persistent drizzle at Maine Road by England, whose Jack Rowley (Manchester United) helped himself to four goals. It was Ireland's biggest defeat since they had lost 11–0 to the same opponents in 1901. Cochrane never pulled on the green shirt of Ireland again and, still aged only 30, stunned Northern Ireland and Leeds United fans alike when he announced his retirement from football in October 1950. Cochrane was out of the Leeds team at the time, but he still had plenty to offer, and explained: 'I always wanted to finish at the top.' He settled down to run a newsagents business in Beeston, not far from Elland Road, for many years and died in the city in June 2000, aged 79.

BOBBY COLLINS

(Scotland 1950–65)

Midfield
Born: Govanhill, Glasgow, 16 February 1931.
Caps: Celtic 22, Everton 6, Leeds United 3. Total: 31
Goals: 10

MIDFIELD maestro Bobby Collins's brilliant form with Leeds United earned an amazing recall to the Scotland side after an absence of six years. The diminutive Elland Road skipper began his international career in 1950 as a dashing Celtic winger and ended it as an astute veteran midfielder with Leeds 15 years later. It was a remarkable transformation considering that many critics felt his career was on the slide when he left First Division Everton in 1962 for a Leeds side fighting to avoid the drop into Division Three.

Collins had been a great player but was already 31, had not represented his country for three years, and had lost that yard of pace which had been a feature of his early days at Celtic. He still believed he had something to offer at Goodison and took some persuading to join a club at the bottom of Division Two. The £22,500 fee Leeds paid for the wee man seemed way over the top, but it proved a masterstroke as the first model of the Revie machine was built around the canny promptings of his new crafty inside-forward. Two days later, on 10 March 1962, Collins made his debut at Swansea, scoring the opener in a 2–0 win. Slowly but surely, the Peacocks nudged away from the drop zone and guaranteed their safety with a 3–0 victory at Newcastle on the final afternoon of the season.

It had been a narrow escape, and Leeds did not start the following campaign too brightly either – even with the returning legend John Charles back in the team after his glorious reign in Italy with Juventus. Collins was playing well enough and showed a will to win every time he stepped on to the field, but as United lost 2–1 at home to Bury in early September, Revie took drastic action. The next game, at Swansea, saw him hand debuts to rookies Paul Reaney, Norman Hunter and Rod Johnson, while bringing in teenager goalkeeper Gary Sprake for only his second start. It was a huge risk, but it proved to be a watershed game for Leeds United as they won with goals from Johnson and another up-and-coming young player, Billy Bremner. Collins played with his head while the enthusiastic new breed ran the legs off the Welsh side.

Harnessing Collins's skills with the exuberance of youth was now the way forward for Revie, who saw his side shoot up the table. Although they finished short of promotion, the building blocks were in place and United, with Collins as skipper, started 1963–64 as one of the promotion favourites and did not disappoint as they finished the season as champions – the first time they had won the division in 40 years. Revie hailed Collins as 'my best buy ever' at the time, adding 'he is one of the all-time greats'. But their work together was only just starting, as the emerging Leeds team, hungry for more glory, took the First Division by storm. One of the keys to their success was an unquenchable team spirit. They never knew when they were beaten – even in training, when England versus Scotland five-a-side games produced some bone-jarring challenges until trainer Les Cocker put a stop to the matches. Collins probably did not realise it, but he would soon be renewing his rivalry with the English in a real game.

Despite standing not much more than 5ft 3in in his stocking feet, the stocky Collins could still look after himself in the top division as he led United to the brink of an astonishing double. He was in inspirational form throughout the season, spraying inch-perfect passes around the park, and was particularly adept at feeding South African wing wizard Albert Johanneson. Leeds went on to finish as runners-up to Manchester United and were beaten by Liverpool in the FA Cup Final, but Collins's contribution to a magnificent season had not gone unnoticed, and he became the first Scot to be named Footballer of the Year in England.

Just after Leeds edged out Manchester United in their FA Cup semi-final replay to reach their first Final, Collins earned a deserved recall to the Scotland team at the age of 34. Scotland had been hunting for a player to replace Tottenham's gifted inside-forward John White, who had tragically died the year before, aged 27, when he was struck by lightning on a golf course. Despite his advancing years, Collins was playing better than ever and was seen as a key man for the big showdown with England at Wembley.

Bobby Collins (left) in action for Scotland against Spain at Hampden Park in 1965.

But things did not go according to plan for Ian McColl, whose side were 2–0 down inside 35 minutes. Denis Law pulled a goal back just before half-time with a dipping 30-yarder that deceived Gordon Banks and thus became Scotland's highest-ever goalscorer. Injuries to Ray Wilson and Johnny Byrne helped Scotland's cause, and Ian St John headed in the equaliser. Despite the dominance of Collins and Co., Scotland could not break down England's dogged rearguard, and it finished all-square at 2–2.

Collins led Leeds out at the Twin Towers three weeks later in the FA Cup Final, in which a header from his Scottish teammate St John broke Leeds's hearts in extra-time and took the Cup back to Anfield. Collins barely had time to digest that 2–1 Wembley defeat before he lined up with debut boy Billy Bremner for Scotland at a windswept Hampden in a friendly against Spain. Friendly was the wrong word, as a fractious match ended goalless with referee Kevin Howley sending off Severino Reija of Spain.

Scotland were blessed with a good squad in the mid-1960s and were hopeful of reaching the World Cup Finals, which were being staged across the border. They were in a group with Italy, Finland and Poland, the game in the pouring rain of Chorzow proving to be Collins's 31st and final appearance for his country. But there was a shock in store for Scotland supporters as the squad prepared for the

trip to Eastern Europe. The Scottish FA replaced McColl as manager with Celtic boss Jock Stein, a former teammate of Collins when he was with the Hoops, on a temporary basis. Poland took a 50th-minute lead through Roman Lentner, but Scotland earned a draw through Law 12 minutes from time. After such a long gruelling season with Leeds, Collins was rested for the game in Finland four days later, Stein continuing his successful start at international level with a 2–1 win.

Collins recharged his batteries for the rest of the summer, but was soon back in the groove with Leeds, who had started the new campaign well. They were also playing in Europe for the first time and had made a flying start by beating Italian side Torino 2–1 in the first leg at Elland Road. The second leg in Turin finished goalless, but Collins did not hear the final whistle. He was on his way to hospital after a brutal tackle by full-back Fabritzio Poletti just after half-time.

Wrapped in Revie's raincoat, Collins, accompanied by fellow Scot Willie Bell, was taken to the nearby Maria Vittoria Hospital which, due to its close proximity to the mountains, specialised in treating fractures. Professor Carlo Re carried out surgery on Collins's thigh, which had been shattered by the impact of the tackle. He inserted a 15-inch pin and told the veteran he would be able to play again, but deep down Collins knew it was the end of his top-flight football career. Remarkably, however, Collins fought his way back to make Professor Re's prediction true, making his return in the final game of the season at Old Trafford, eight months after his horrific injury.

Although Collins started the 1966–67 season in the Leeds starting line up, Johnny Giles took over his mantle as the midfield creator, having been successfully converted from a winger during Collins's enforced absence. In February 1967 he joined Bury, then had a stint back in Scotland with Morton before working as a player-coach in Australia. On his return to England he was in demand as a coach and worked for several clubs, including a spell back at Elland Road in 1976. He also managed Huddersfield and Barnsley before opting out of the game he had served so well since his early days at Celtic, where he started in 1948.

The Glasgow-born youngster was dubbed the 'Wee Barra' by Bhoys supporters, who loved Collins's energy and ballwork on the flank. He was a genuine legend at Parkhead, winning a Scottish League title in 1954, two Scottish Cups and two Scottish League Cups, as well as representing the Scottish League a remarkable 16 times. He made his Scotland debut on 21 October 1950 against Wales in a 3–1 win in Cardiff, then was an integral part of Scotland's 6–1 hammering of Northern Ireland at Hampden.

Collins's third international game of the year saw Austria become the first side to beat any of the British nations on their own soil with a 1–0 win on a frozen Hampden pitch. After this, Collins found himself out in the cold with Scotland's selectors for four years, but stormed back with a peerless display in Belgrade against Yugoslavia in 1955 and became a regular for the next four years.

That included playing in the 1958 World Cup Finals in Sweden, in which he scored one of his 10 international goals in the 3–2 defeat against Paraguay. He continued to represent his country after joining Everton in a big-money move later that year, but thought his career at the highest level had come to an end after a 1–0 defeat in Portugal in 1959. However, his passion for the game, fuelled by his sheer determination, ensured a romantic swansong while he was at Leeds – who knows how long he could have played at the highest level had he not been so terribly injured in Turin?

TERRY COOPER
(England 1969–74)
Left-back
Born: Brotherton, near Castleford, 12 July 1944.
Caps: Leeds United 20.

ONE of the finest sights during the Don Revie era was Terry Cooper's mesmerising white boots dancing down the flanks. The Castleford-born star and his full-back partner Paul Reaney were among the first overlapping full-backs in the English game. Both had been converted from wingers and were masters of their art, backing up the men in front of them and firing crosses into the box. Cooper was hailed as the best left-back on the planet after his displays in the searing Mexican heat in the 1970 World Cup. As temperatures soared, England's players were sweating off an average of 10lb in weight in each game, prompting manager Alf Ramsey to juggle his squad. Cooper, Bobby Moore and Alan Mullery were the only three men to play every minute of all four of England's games. Playing conditions were in stark contrast to what Cooper and Co. usually faced in the course of an English season, but the Leeds man took it all in his stride in the same way he took on his opponents.

Unlike many of the young players who broke through in Revie's squad in the 1960s, he was not an overnight sensation and at one stage looked as though he would be leaving Elland Road because of a lack of opportunities. Cooper first came to the Leeds public's attention as a 19-year-old left winger when he played as a second-half substitute against Juventus at Elland Road on 8 April 1964 in a game arranged as part of John Charles's transfer to the Italian giants. Three days later he was a surprise inclusion for a vital game at Swansea, where victory could see United clinch promotion. The teenager was in for the injured Albert Johanneson and was not overawed as United swept to a 3–0 victory at Vetch Field to guarantee their return to Division One – not a bad way in which to make your debut.

Games were more forthcoming, but still sporadic, in the next couple of years, as Cooper alternated between left-wing and left-back, but he did talk about a possible transfer as he wanted more regular football. Revie persuaded him to stay at Elland Road, and the departure of Scottish international Willie Bell to Leicester in September 1967 saw Cooper installed as United's regular number three. There was no looking back after that. It was his goal against Arsenal in the League Cup Final that gave United their first triumph at Wembley in March 1968.

Cooper's willingness to join the attack and supply dangerous crosses made him an eye-catching player, but his fitness, speed and positional sense saw him tame many a tricky winger. It was like having two players rolled into one, and it did not take long for the international selectors to sit up and take notice. He had already played for Young England in their annual match against England when he was called into Alf Ramsey's squad for the Wembley friendly against Bulgaria on 11 December 1968. Injury forced him to withdraw, and his place went to Arsenal's Bob McNab, who retained his place for the following month's friendly against Romania. Both matches ended 1–1, but Cooper's first full international was just round the corner.

As holders, England did not have to qualify for the 1970 World Cup, so Ramsey was able to experiment in a series

Terry Cooper, watched by Martin Peters, clears for England during their epic clash with Brazil in the 1970 World Cup Finals.

England were looking strong, and competition for places in the national side was red-hot, so Cooper may have fretted about his place in the World Cup squad when injury ruled him out of the next internationals against Holland and Portugal. Liverpool's rising star Emlyn Hughes started both games at left-back, but Cooper was back for the first international of 1970 – a rather dull 0–0 draw with Holland – and gave an excellent display in Brussels as England beat Belgium in February.

On the club front Leeds were pushing hard for a League, FA Cup and European cup treble. Matches were coming thick and fast for Leeds and their England players were in danger of burning out before the end of the season. No Leeds player featured in the Home Internationals, but four of them – Cooper, Jack Charlton, Norman Hunter and Allan Clarke – were in the 28-man squad which headed to South America for warm-up games against Ecuador and Colombia before starting the defence of their trophy. The squad was reduced to 22 for the tournament and the quartet of Leeds stars were all included. Significantly, Cooper, the holder of eight caps, was given squad number three, a clear indicator that he was Ramsey's first choice. He repaid that faith handsomely and, showing no ill effects from a draining, and ultimately honourless, season with the Whites, proved one of the stars of the World Cup with his surging runs and sharp tackling.

England opened with a 1–0 victory over Romania before a mega-match with favourites Brazil played in the midday heat of Guadalajara. A magnificent game, which featured an astonishing save by Gordon Banks from Pelé's downward header, lived up to expectation, and England were unlucky to go down to Jairzinho's 60th-minute goal.

A spluttering 1–0 win against Czechoslovakia, courtesy of Clarke's penalty, sealed England's place in the quarter-final, where they took on old foes West Germany in Leon. England were without inspirational goalkeeper Banks, a victim of food poisoning, but took the lead after just half an hour when Cooper won the ball, fed Alan Mullery, who exchanged passes with Francis Lee and Newton before firing past Sepp Maier.

Cooper had totally subdued the dangerous Reinhard Libuda, who had been in top form in the group stages, and England looked home and dry when Martin Peters squeezed in a second goal shortly after half-time. Germany replaced Libuda with another flying winger, Jurgen Grabowski, who soon began to test Cooper, who was starting to feel the heat. Ramsey was on the verge of making a substitution when Bonetti failed to deal with Franz Beckenbauer's tame shot and Helmut Schoen's side were back in it with 20 minutes remaining.

Ramsey went ahead with his change, withdrawing Bobby Charlton, who was making his record 106th full international appearance, and sending on Colin Bell, who went close to regaining England's two-goal advantage. Cooper now had his hands full with Grabowski, so Ramsey

of friendlies in the build-up to the tournament proper. If you got into the England side you needed to make a early impression, and Cooper certainly did that. He had already had plenty of European football experience and was a member of the Leeds side which won the 1968 Fairs Cup, giving a tremendous defensive display against Ferencvaros in the second leg in Hungary.

Cooper's England debut was a spectacular one against France in March 1969, in which he formed a devastating partnership on the left with clubmate Mike O'Grady, who scored the opening goal in a 5–0 rout of Les Bleus. World Cup hero Geoff Hurst went on to score a hat-trick – his first since the 1966 World Cup Final – and the match saw two other milestones. The West Ham forward's first goal was the 200th for England at Wembley, and the victory was England's 100th against foreign opposition. Cooper was on a high and, after winning the League title, earned rave reviews for his end-of-season performances against Wales and Scotland to book his place on England's dress rehearsal tour of South America as preparation for the World Cup.

In the rarified atmosphere of the Azteca Stadium, Cooper again caught the eye in a 0–0 draw with Mexico, but was disappointed to miss out on selection for the remaining two games against Uruguay and Brazil as Blackburn's Keith Newton was switched from right-back to left-back to enable Tommy Wright of Everton to get some match action.

put on his Leeds colleague Hunter to help out. But seconds later Germany were level as veteran forward Uwe Seeler's looping back header caught Chelsea 'keeper Bonetti in no man's land.

The force was now with a revitalised German side, and five minutes into extra-time Grabowski went round Cooper and centred deep to create confusion in the heart of England's defence, where poacher Gerd Muller volleyed home the winner from close range. England, losing a two-goal lead for the first time in Ramsey's tenure, were out after being in control for the vast majority of the match.

The 1970 World Cup signalled the end of the international careers of the Charlton brothers, but Cooper continued to thrive in an England shirt as the Three Lions began their European Championship campaign. The dashing Leeds defender played against Switzerland (twice) and Malta as England moved steadily towards the quarter-finals. But disaster struck on 8 April 1972, when Cooper broke a leg in a routine 3–0 League win at Stoke. He missed the European Championship quarter-final elimination at the hands of West Germany and the FA Cup Final triumph over Arsenal, and did not feature for Leeds at all in 1972–73.

The fracture was a bad one, and when Cooper managed only one League start in the Championship-winning 1973–74 campaign there were genuine fears for his future. But he got his head down, worked hard and was in Brian Clough's starting line up for the opening game of 1974–75. Don Revie was now in charge of England and recalled Cooper for his second game in charge, a European Championship qualifier against Portugal at Wembley on 20 November. It was Cooper's first England game for two years, but the comeback lasted just 24 minutes as he limped off after a challenge to be replaced by Derby's Colin Todd. It was the last time England fans saw him, and Cooper was to play just once more for United – in a 1–0 win at Middlesbrough in February – before joining the Teessiders the following month in a £50,000 deal.

Cooper played 20 times for England and started about 340 games for Leeds in 13 years at Elland Road, during which time he provided United fans with some wonderful memories – notably his League Cup Wembley winner in 1968. He later played and managed both Bristol clubs, Doncaster Rovers, Birmingham City and Exeter before working as Southampton's scout overseas. His son, Mark, played at Bristol City, Exeter, Birmingham, Fulham, Huddersfield and Wycombe.

WILF COPPING
(England 1933–39)
Wing-half
Born: Barnsley, Yorkshire, 17 August 1909.
Died: Southend, Essex, June 1980.
Caps: Leeds United 6, Arsenal 13, Leeds United 1. Total: 20

Wilf Copping.

A STRAW poll among current Leeds fans would probably have Norman Hunter as the hardest player to pull on a United shirt – but those with longer memories would probably give Wilf Copping that dubious distinction. 'Iron Man' Wilf went out of his way to look menacing on the pitch and intimidate the opposition. But behind the tough guy image was a footballer of great quality who won 20 England caps and was never sent off or cautioned in a career spanning 340 League games.

After playing for Dearne Valley Old Boys, his local club, Barnsley, rejected Copping as a teenager, so the former Houghton Council School pupil followed many men in south Yorkshire by working down the pit – a gruelling job which may well have helped shape his footballing future. He was playing for Middlecliffe Rovers when he was spotted by Leeds, who took him on in March 1929, and he initially cut his teeth in the professional game in the Central League. With regular left-half George Reed ruled out of the start of the 1930–31 season with a damaged knee, manager Dick Ray reckoned the 21-year-old left-half was ready for his League debut – a 2–2 home draw with Portsmouth.

Copping played in every League game that season, improving with every match, but despite their all-star half-back line of Willis Edwards, Ernie Hart and Copping, Leeds were relegated. With such a classy trio at their disposal it was no surprise that United came straight back up, as runners-up to Wolves. Back in the First Division, Copping was outstanding and gave the country's best forwards a tough time with his uncompromising approach. 'The first man into the tackle never gets hurt,' was his much-quoted motto. But after spending the season battering the opposition, differences were put to one side as Copping and Leeds teammate Billy Furness were chosen for their England debuts in Rome. The match ended 1–1 and proved to be Furness's only game, but Copping impressed and became an automatic choice. From Rome, England moved on to Berne, where they walloped Switzerland 4–0 with two goals each from Cliff Bastin and Jimmy Richardson.

Tales of Copping's macho image were the stuff of legends. One story has it that he once broke his nose in a League game, reset it himself, and played on. A study of portrait pictures of Wilf in the 1930s does reveal a flattened boxer's nose, so perhaps he did not do such a good repair job. He also never shaved before a match, and the blue stubble on his 'Desperate Dan' chin added to the impression of menace. But it was not all bravado. Copping could pass the ball with pinpoint accuracy, was powerful in the air, possessed a powerful throw-in and could, of course, tackle like no man in the country.

In 1933–34 England beat Ireland 3–0 but lost to Wales, who retained the Home Championship. The Welsh result rendered the England versus Scotland game at Wembley in April meaningless, but England defeated the spirited Scots 3–0 with a first-half goal by Bastin, a 25-yarder from Eric Brook and a Jack Bowers header past Jakey Jackson, the Chelsea reserve goalkeeper, who later became a golf professional in Canada and played in the 1950 Open at Troon. Sandwiched between the Wales and Ireland games was a 4–1 victory against Switzerland at White Hart Lane.

Copping missed the summer tour games in Hungary and Czechoslovakia, but had other things on his mind as he was on the verge of completing a transfer from Elland Road to Arsenal. The Gunners had just retained their First Division title and their manager Herbert Chapman, the former Leeds City boss, made no secret of the fact that he wanted Copping to replace veteran Welsh international Bob John at Highbury. Leeds were struggling financially and had opened talks with Arsenal when Chapman died of pneumonia, but an £8,000 deal was concluded by his successor, George Allison, in June 1934.

While Leeds struggled without Copping at the back, Arsenal powered on towards their third successive title with their new signing enjoying life in London. Copping's first England appearance as an Arsenal player was one of the most notorious games ever played: 'The Battle of Highbury' against Italy. The England selectors picked an unprecedented seven Arsenal players for the game against the world champions. Five Gunners were originally named in the team, but when skipper Tommy Cooper and Fred Tilson dropped out, George Male and Ted Drake came in.

Italy were reportedly on big financial bonuses promised by Fascist leader Mussolini if they won. They were certainly fired up from the start, when Swedish referee Otto Olsson awarded England a penalty, which Eric Brook saw saved by Carlo Ceresoli. Shortly afterwards, Juventus hard man Luisito Monti broke a toe in a challenge which England saw as legitimate and the Italians unfair. Tackles and elbows were flying about all over the place, with Copping relishing the battle with his two-footed tackles and brutal shoulder charges. In between the rough stuff, Stanley Matthews, in only his second international, crossed for Brook to head in, and the same player doubled England's lead with a free-kick.

Eddie Hapgood, captaining England for the first time, had his nose broken, prompting a fraças. Monti limped off after another challenge and England had made it 3–0 inside 15 breathless minutes with a goal by Drake, who then had to limp from the fray with a gashed leg.

It was brutal stuff, and Copping had to be at his defensive best in the second period after two goals from Guiseppe Meazza put the result in doubt. England weathered the storm to hang on, but the press were unanimous in their verdict on the game – it was a disgrace. One reporter even signed his match report 'by Our War Correspondent'.

The England dressing room certainly represented a field hospital after the game, with Hapgood and Brook, who finished with his arm in a sling, requiring hospital treatment. Copping, typically, emerged unscathed, apart from a few bruises, but was to be laid low by injury later

Iron man Wilf Copping relaxes in a foam bath after another afternoon's battle.

in the season. Arsenal were at Everton in March when Gunners goalie Frank Moss injured a shoulder and was replaced by Hapgood. Copping then severely damaged a knee, but battled on to help Arsenal to a 2–0 win, although he then missed the last nine games of the campaign.

Copping won another title with Arsenal in 1938, having picked up an FA Cup-winners' medal two years earlier, but was about to end his five-year stay at Highbury. Sensing war was in the air, he wanted to move back North with his family before joining the Army and got his wish by returning to Elland Road in March 1939.

Leeds were struggling to stay in Division One, but Copping's presence in defence saw them improve considerably, including a 4–2 win against Arsenal on his first game back in front of the Elland Road fans. Yet to reach 30, he was still a class act and travelled with England to face Romania in his 20th and final international at the end of the season.

While Lord Rosebery's horse *Blue Peter* was winning the Derby in great style, England cantered home in Bucharest. An early goal by Len Goulden, of West Ham, and a header by Charlton's Don Welsh reduced the 50,000 crowd – the biggest at that time ever to see a football match in Romania – to near silence. The match was the last recognised international for more than seven years and inevitably signalled the end of many England careers, Copping's included.

Copping served in North Africa during the war, reaching the rank of Company Sergeant Major. He played football for the Army and still turned out for Leeds when he could before retiring in 1942. He trained the Army team in Germany at the end of the war and developed his coaching skills with Royal Beerschot in Antwerp before a brief spell as the Belgian national team coach. In summer 1946 he returned to England to become Southend's trainer and later held similar positions with Bristol City and Coventry before ending his 30-year career in football.

He settled at Prittlewell, near Southend, and took a job at Ford's plant in Dagenham until retiring in August 1972. Wilf died eight years later, but the Football League ensured his name would never been forgotten by including him on their list of 100 League Legends to mark the League's centenary in 1998.

TONY CURRIE

(England 1972–79)

Midfield

Born: Edgware, London, 1 January 1950.
Caps: Sheffield United 7, Leeds United 10. Total: 17
Goals: 3

BACK-page headline writers certainly thought Tony Currie was hot stuff. The gifted midfielder won 10 of his 17 England caps while at Elland Road, moving the short

Tony Currie.

distance up the M1 from Sheffield United, where he attained God-like status. Despite a moderate goals return for Leeds, he was an attacking midfield player of great flair who enjoyed some magical moments in his international career.

After leaving Whitefield Secondary School in Cricklewood, he was on Queen's Park Rangers's books but was released and picked up on trial by Chelsea, who also reckoned he would not make the grade. Currie ended up joining Watford as an amateur, signing a professional contract in May 1957. He made a sensational start to his career, scoring twice on his debut against Bristol Rovers. He was soon called up to the England Youth team and in his 17 League starts for the Hornets scored nine goals, including two hat-tricks.

Sheffield United moved in with a £26,500 bid. Watford agreed to sell the player, but only after they were knocked out of the FA Cup. Ironically, it was the Blades that put the Vicarage Road side out of the competition, and the transfer went through. Currie was an overnight sensation at Bramall Lane, scoring on his debut in a 3–2 victory over Spurs, and he was to spend the next eight years dazzling and entertaining at the Lane.

England Under-23 and Football League honours paved the way for his first full cap against Northern Ireland in

Alan Curtis (left) and Brian Greenhoff adorn the cover of *Shoot* magazine.

for Wales in a friendly against the Republic of Ireland a month later in his first international as a Leeds player.

With fellow Welsh stars Brian Flynn, Carl Harris and Byron Stevenson in the Leeds squad, Curtis looked to have settled in well to his new surroundings and scored his first Elland Road goal in a 1–1 draw with Liverpool on 15 September, then scored United's fastest-ever European goal, coming after just 20 seconds against Maltese minnows Valetta in the UEFA Cup. But, despite scoring the Welsh consolation in a 5–1 mauling by West Germany in Cologne a fortnight later, Curtis was to score only one more Leeds goal that season. It came at Southampton on 27 October, where the game seemed to be heading for a 1–1 draw before the Welsh striker scored a magnificent late solo goal to earn Adamson's men their first away win of the campaign. It was a classic mesmerising run from Curtis, who then went 10 League games – and an international against Turkey – without finding the net before his season ended on Boxing Day. He sustained a bad knee injury and watched from the sidelines as Elland Road turned into a melting pot of anger. Fans, growing restless for past glories, were unhappy with Adamson's tactics and the team performances. A mid-table showing of 11th was below par for many supporters, and for the sidelined Curtis it must have been frustrating not to be able to show that he was worth his big fee.

Curtis did start the 1980–81 season, but Leeds lost six of their opening seven games and Adamson quit, opening the door for old Leeds hero Allan Clarke to return to the club as manager. Curtis scored just once under Clarke's management – the winner against Everton on 11 October – but seven days later pulled on a Leeds shirt for the final time in a 2–1 defeat at Wolves. With nagging doubts about his long-term fitness, Leeds cut their losses in December and sold Curtis back to Swansea for a cut price of £165,000. Inevitably he scored the winner on his second debut for the Swans, knocking in an early penalty to beat Watford.

Curtis's signing gave Swansea the impetus they needed to gain promotion, and by a delicious irony their opening First Division fixture was against Leeds at the Vetch. United were crushed 5–1, with Bob Latchford scoring a hat-trick for the Welsh, but Curtis scored the pick of the bunch, a superb curling shot, to complete United's humiliation. Curtis continued to torment First Division defences as Swansea headed the table right through to March, and he was back performing at his best in the national side. However, financial problems at Vetch Field led to an exodus of star names – Curtis among them. He was sold to Southampton for just £80,000 in November 1983, was loaned to Stoke, then joined Cardiff before returning to his 'home' at Swansea in October 1989 to see out his career.

After playing Welsh League football, Curtis was appointed Swansea's Football in the Community officer, then stepped up to youth coach in 1996 and had a couple of years as assistant manager before becoming the club's head of youth development. In December 2004 he linked up with his old Swansea strike partner Toshack once again. New Welsh boss Toshack overhauled the national side's coaching set-up, bringing in Brian Flynn as manager of the Under-21, Under-19 and Under-17 sides, with Curtis and Liverpool legend Joey Jones as his assistants.

During his short time at Leeds he managed just six goals in 35 starts and represented Wales six times, scoring twice. In all he played for Wales 35 times, also scoring six goals, but his time at Leeds – although punctuated by some highlights – is generally regarded as a blip in an impressive career that spanned more than 600 games for club and country and provided 122 goals.

WILBUR CUSH

(Northern Ireland 1950–61)
Wing-half/Centre-half
Born: Lurgan, Co. Armagh, 10 June 1928.
Died: Lurgan, Co. Armagh, 25 July 1981.
Caps: Glenavon 8, Leeds United 15, Portadown 3. Total: 26
Goals: 6

LITTLE Billy Cush was an immense player for Northern Ireland. Within weeks of joining Leeds United his goals sent the green-shirted Irish to their first World Cup Finals

Wilbur Cush, fourth from left, lines up for Northern Ireland in the 1958 World Cup Finals ahead of their key game against Czechoslovakia.

in 1958, and the minnows from the province became the surprise package in Sweden, reaching the quarter-finals.

Cush was only a small man, standing 5ft 5in, but was never intimidated by larger opponents and was a real terrier all around the pitch. After leaving Carrisk School he played for Lurgan Boys' Club and Shankhill YMCA before joining Glenavon as a 19-year-old in 1947. He spent more than a decade in the Irish League, collecting a stack of honours in the 1950s. Equally effective in either midfield or defence, Cush helped Lurgan-based Glenavon to their first-ever Irish League title in 1952 and the Irish Cup double in 1957. The men from Mourneview Park also won the Irish Gold Cup in 1954 and 1956 and the Ulster Cup in 1955.

The stocky Cush was particularly effective when buzzing around in midfield and won his first cap at left-half against England on 7 October 1950 at Windsor Park. Although England emerged 4–1 winners, Cush was in sparkling form on a cold drizzly afternoon as the home side dominated the opening half-hour without having a goal to show for it. England's superior attack took advantage, but Cush's display guaranteed he kept his place for the game against Scotland in Glasgow.

Irish defensive weaknesses were exposed at Hampden Park, where John McPhail scored twice in the opening quarter of an hour before amateur star Kevin McGarry, a fully qualified doctor, pulled a goal back. The second half belonged to Billy Steel, who netted four times to see the Scots ease home 6–1. It was a chastening experience for Cush, who did not represent his country again for another three years. He had lost his place to Frank McCourt, but was back to take on Scotland again in October 1953 in a World Cup qualifier. The match in Belfast went according

to form, with Charlie Fleming, the East Fife forward, scoring twice to take the visitors to a 3–1 victory.

It was the same scoreline at Goodison Park as England booked their place in the Finals to be held in Switzerland the following June. Cush linked up well with Danny Blanchflower in that game, but it was not enough to prevent the axe from falling on the Glenavon man once again. All four of his international games had ended in defeat, with the opposition piling in 16 goals. His exile from the national side lasted four years and two months, returning to the team at inside-left as the Irish began their World Cup qualifying campaign with a 1–1 draw in Portugal. Italy were favourites in the three-team group, and the next stop for the Irish was in the Olympic Stadium where, with the diminutive Cush at centre-half, they gave an heroic display in a 1–0 defeat, Fiorentina's Sergio Cerrato striking in the third minute.

Peter Doherty's team returned to Belfast the following week and kept their qualification hopes alive by beating Portugal 3–0. Cush had been the top man in Ireland that season and was named Ulster Player of the Year, an honour that no doubt helped pave the way for his £7,000 move to Elland Road in November 1957. United's Irish scout Matt Willis had watched Cush several times and persuaded the club to sign the 28-year-old. It was a great piece of business, as he never shirked a tackle in his 18 months at Elland Road. Cush had bags of experience, playing a remarkable 23 times for the Irish League in addition to his eight full international games. He quickly adapted to the tempo of the English First Division before crossing back over the Irish Sea a few weeks later for what was billed as the big World Cup qualification showdown with Italy, who had been beaten 3–0 in Portugal. But with match referee

Wilbur Cush.

brutal challenges that sent a feverish 53,000 Windsor Park crowd mad. Alcides Ghiggia's 24th-minute goal was cancelled out three minutes later by Cush's first international goal. In between the niggle and fierce fouling, Italy regained the lead through Miguel Montuori, only for Cush to square matters once again.

Stand-in referee Tommy Mitchell gradually lost control of proceedings in the second half, but an horrendous foul by right-half Guiseppe Chiapella on Billy McAdams saw the Italian sent off in the 83rd minute. The match ended 2–2, but Mitchell's final blast on the whistle was only the signal for more aggro, as a large group of angry fans spilled on to the pitch to confront the Italian players. Centre-half Rino Ferrario swung out at a couple of aggressors before being felled to the ground, where he held his head in his hands for protection. Celtic star Bertie Peacock went to the aid of young centre-forward Gastone Bean to extract him from another ugly situation. Windsor Park was seething, and it was only the belated arrival of the baton-charging Royal Ulster Constabulary that tempers cooled and some kind of normality was achieved.

The game sent shockwaves through the world of football, with questions being asked by MPs at Stormont and in the Italian Senate, but the IFA seem to have escaped censure. Italy went on to gain revenge over Portugal with a 3–0 win in Milan to set up a winner-takes-all rematch in Belfast on 15 January 1958. This time referee Zsolt, who was manager of the Budapest Opera House, was in charge of the potentially fiery fixture, but it did not produce the brutality of their previous meeting.

It was a glorious afternoon for Irish football as Jimmy McIlroy put them ahead on 13 minutes, and United's new man Cush wrote his name into his country's folklore by adding what proved to be a match-winning second before half-time. Dino Da Costa, the Roma winger, did pull a goal back, but the Irish maintained control, and any hope the Italians had vanished when Ghiggia was sent off with more than 20 minutes remaining. For Ghiggia it had been a spectacular fall from grace, as he had scored the winning goal for Uruguay against Brazil in the 1950 Final before taking Italian citizenship.

The 2–1 win earned Northern Ireland their first ticket to the World Cup Finals, which, for the first time, would not feature Italy. Nor would Ireland's centre-half from Manchester United, Jackie Blanchflower, be there. Although he survived the Munich Air Disaster barely a month after the euphoria of qualification, he had to retire because of injuries sustained in the crash. The drama was not over, however, as the fixtures for the Finals included two games scheduled to be played on Sundays, and the Irish FA had a rule which forbade players to turn out on the Sabbath.

The issue opened up a big debate in Ulster, and some religious groups rallied to call for the country's withdrawal from the competition. For a while that seemed a genuine

Istvan Zsolt stranded by dense fog at London Airport, the Italians would not accept another FIFA appointment and refused to play the game as a World Cup match.

With a big crowd expected, it was too late to call the game off, so it went ahead as a 'friendly', but it was anything but friendly and became known as 'the Battle of Belfast'. For whatever reason, a keyed-up Italy put in some possibility, but the Irish FA opted to ignore their own rule and their team headed to Sweden. Leeds, with their skipper Cush alternating between right-half and left-half, finished the season in a moderate 17th place, but while his teammates put their feet up during the summer the little Irish hero was preparing for the biggest stage of his career.

Northern Ireland manager Peter Doherty had moulded a fine side, but no one gave them a hope of qualifying from Pool One, which included holders West Germany, Argentina and Czechoslovakia. The Irish made their bow on Sunday 8 June in Halstad against an accomplished Czechoslovakian side, and once more the diminutive figure of Cush rose to the occasion. He headed in the only goal on 20 minutes and then worked like a Trojan with skipper Danny Blanchflower to keep the Czechs at bay. The group was split wide open when Argentina, beaten 3–1 in their opener by West Germany, defeated the Irish by the same score. A 2–2 draw between Czechoslovakia and the Germans meant Ireland had to beat the 1954 winners in Malmo, and they got within 10 minutes of achieving that dream as two goals from Peter McParland put them in the driving seat, only for Uwe Seeler to grab an 80th-minute leveller to ensure Germany's progress.

News filtered through that Czechoslovakia had thrashed Argentina 6–1 to finish joint second with Ireland on three points. It was in the days before goal difference, so the two group runners-up went head-to-head in a Play-off for a place in the quarters. The in-form Czechs seemed to warrant their favourites' tag by taking the lead through Zedenek Zican on 19 minutes, but Cush's determination set up the equaliser for McParland, who scored the winner 10 minutes from the end of extra-time.

The heroic, but weary, Irish then had an arduous eight-hour coach journey from Malmo to Norkopping to take on France, with key players nursing injuries. The walking wounded included goalkeeper Harry Gregg and Tom Casey, who had started his career at Elland Road. It was a game too far for Cush and his green-shirted colleagues, as the tournament's shooting star, Juste Fontaine, scored twice in a 4–0 win.

Cush resumed domestic duty at Leeds at the start of the 1958–59 season and returned to Belfast as a national hero when Ireland's World Cup heroes were given a rousing welcome at a rain-battered Windsor Park for the eagerly-awaited Home Championship clash with England. Once again the Irish rose to the occasion and came desperately close to beating England on Irish soil for the first time since 1927. They led three times – with Cush collecting a Blanchflower pass to blast in the opener after 30 minutes – and hit the woodwork twice, but England fought back each time to level the match.

Cush remained in Ireland to get married on the Monday after the England game and was soon on his international travels again, netting a goal in Madrid where Spain romped home 6–2 in a friendly. He then played a key role as Ireland's fighting spirit came to the fore again at Hampden Park, where they hit back from 2–0 down to draw 2–2.

Although Cush was now a fixture in the Irish side, Leeds were struggling to make an impact in Division One, and when Don Revie arrived in November 1958 Cush stepped aside as club captain in favour of the former England inside-forward. Leeds finished the season in the relative comfort of 15th place, but the 1959–60 relegation season was to prove Cush's last at Elland Road. His form had dipped and Ireland were looking to inject new blood into their squad, so a return to the Irish League at the age of 32 seemed to be the logical step. He joined Portadown and rediscovered his old drive, winning back a place in the Irish side for the World Cup qualifiers in Greece and West Germany.

The match in Athens was an ill-tempered affair, the Greeks winning 2–1, but Cush signed off his international career with a 2–0 win in the return match in front of his adoring Belfast public on 17 October 1961. He certainly went out with a bang. He laid out a Greek opponent who had spat in his face and calmly walked away. The referee arrived at the scene and promptly sent off Manchester United's Jimmy Nicholson, who just happened to be standing near the action.

Cush returned to Glenavon in November 1966 and continued to play in the Irish League past his 40th birthday. He then briefly coached at Glenavon before working as a butcher. Fulsome tributes were paid to him when he died in July 1981. At Leeds he was a tireless player with a huge appetite for work and a love of the crunching tackle, while in Ireland's football history he is regarded as one of their most underrated players.

OLIVIER DACOURT

(France 2001–04)

Midfield

Born: Montreuil-sous-Bois, Paris, 25 September 1971.

Caps: *Leeds United 5, AS Roma 16. Total: 21

*1 appearance while on loan at AS Roma

Goals: 1

LEEDS UNITED played a huge role in launching the international career of French midfielder Olivier Dacourt. His pulsating displays in the Whites' engine room saw him break into the World Cup-holders' multi-talented squad in 2002. Dacourt had a sparkling record with Les Bleus. In the 21 matches in which he was involved 15 were won, three drawn and just two lost, and those statistics included a sequence of 13 successive victories.

After playing with junior club Thorvars, Dacourt joined Racing Club Strasbourg when he was still only 17 and worked his way through their youth system into the first team, winning Under-21 honours and playing in the side

Olivier Dacourt.

Dacourt certainly had an eventful time in his only season at Goodison Park, picking up 11 cautions and a red card – which came against Leeds – in a disappointing campaign for the Merseysiders. Everton fans liked his aggressive approach, but his relationship with them turned sour as he criticised the club for a lack of ambition, and when the club revealed it was in financial difficulties it was no surprise when he returned to France to join Lens for £6.5 million.

Within a year Dacourt was back in the Premiership as a Leeds player, signed for a club record £7.2 million in July 2000. The bait for the Frenchman, apart from handsome wages, was Champions League football and the promise that more top signings were coming in. David O'Leary had put together a vibrant young side who had finished third in the Premiership, and Dacourt was seen as the man to knit them together. His Leeds debut was a 2–0 victory at Elland Road against his old club Everton, against whom he scored one of only three goals that season in the drawn return game at Goodison in February 2001. But it was in Europe that Leeds and Dacourt were making headlines. After a weakened United team were slaughtered 4–0 in Barcelona, they powered through a group containing AC Milan and Turkish side Besiktas to move into the second phase of the competition, where they saw off Real Madrid, Lazio and Anderlecht.

Leeds were living the dream, and Dacourt's astute passing, snappy tackling and classy midfield twists and turns were an integral part of the adventure. He was in peerless mood as Deportivo La Coruña were crushed 3–0 at Elland Road to pave the way to a semi-final with another top Spanish side, Valencia. The battle for a place in the Final proved just a step too far for Leeds, but Dacourt had developed into one of Europe's top midfielders, and it was inevitable that French manager Roger Lemerre took him to the Far East to take part in the Confederations Cup.

France, blessed with a star-studded talented squad, were World and European champions. To break into a side containing superstars of the calibre of Zinedine Zidane, Patrick Viera, Thierry Henry, Robert Pires, Emmanuel Petit, Claude Makelele and Vincent Candela you had to be some player. But Dacourt had earned his place and became the second man, after Eric Cantona, to be capped by France as a Leeds player when he replaced Pires near the end of a 5–0 thumping of South Korea.

The roles were reversed a couple of days later when Dacourt made his first start and was replaced by the Arsenal man as France slipped to a surprise 1–0 defeat to Australia. Dacourt also featured as a replacement against Mexico in the tournament, but his arrival on the international stage could not earn him a place in the 2000 World Cup squad, even though Zidane was injured. In the event, it was probably a good competition to miss, as holders France lost 1–0 to Senegal, were held 0–0 by Uruguay and beaten 2–0 by Denmark to finish bottom of

that reached the quarter-finals of the Olympic tournament in Australia in 1996. He was one of the stars of Strasbourg's fine run in the 1997–98 UEFA Cup, which exposed him to a wider audience, and continental clubs were keen to take advantage of the Bosman ruling and cast their recruitment net beyond their own borders.

In the first leg Strasbourg beat Walter Smith's Rangers 2–1, home and away, to set up a meeting with mighty Liverpool. The French underdogs stunned the Reds by winning 3–0 in Stade de la Meinau and hung on to go through 3–2 on aggregate. Amazingly, Strasbourg beat Inter Milan 2–0 in the next round, only for the Italian giants to turn the tie around in the San Siro to advance to the quarter-finals. It was not long before Strasbourg were fielding inquiries for their midfield dynamo, with Bordeaux and Everton at the head of the queue. Dacourt had made a lasting impression on ex-Rangers boss Smith, now in charge at Everton, and the Goodison outfit emerged as the highest bidders, with a £4 million offer seeing him join the Toffees in August 1998 after 127 French League games with Strasbourg.

Group A without scoring a goal. Inevitably, Lemerre lost his job and his replacement Jacques Santini set about building a side for the defence of Les Bleus' European title. Dacourt was very much in his plans but suffered an injury-hit 2001–02 season, including a shoulder injury which ruled him out for a couple of months.

Rumours started to circulate about a possible move to Juventus, but Dacourt was still at Elland Road as the 2002–03 season kicked off under a new manager, Terry Venables, the former England coach. O'Leary had paid the price for failing to qualify for the Champions League, and Venables was installed in July 2002. However, Leeds had severely overstretched themselves financially and, much to Venables's chagrin, it was not long before the sale of their star names began. Niggling injuries saw Dacourt in and out of the side, but he earned his first appearance for the new national team manager Lemerre as a substitute in a 4–0 win in Malta on 16 October.

Dacourt did not see eye-to-eye with Venables, however, and criticised Leeds's moderate start to the season. With Leeds's debts mounting, he became an obvious candidate for departure. After a proposed £10 million move to Lazio stalled, the French star was loaned to Roma until the end of the season, when the clubs concluded a permanent £4 million transfer. During this loan period Dacourt figured in a 5–0 victory over Egypt in the Stade de France, a match which saw defender Marcel Desailly make a record 104th appearance for France (which has since advanced to 116, although that has now been surpassed by Lilian Thuram's amazing 142 games).

As Leeds imploded, Dacourt flourished in the Eternal City with a series of dominant displays which helped them reach the Italian Cup Final, where they were beaten by AC Milan. Santini was quite a fan of Dacourt, and he was a regular in the Confederations Cup matches staged in France in summer 2003 and went on to play his part in the team's qualification for the European Championships. His most telling contribution came in Slovenia, where France, leading 1–0, were rocked by the dismissal of Claude Makelele in the 71st minute. Santini shuffled his line up, sending on Dacourt for striker David Trezeguet, and after just three minutes on the pitch he scored his only goal in French tricolours to confirm a priceless victory.

Dacourt played in the Finals, although if you blinked you would have missed his contribution, in France's 2–1 group win over luckless England in Lisbon. Frank Lampard's goal looked as though it was going to give the Three Lions a roaring start when Zidane smashed in a last-minute equaliser then rammed in a penalty in the third minute of injury time to break English hearts. Dacourt came on for the final few seconds as the French ran the clock down to claim a sensational victory.

France eventually went out to winners Greece, and Santini was replaced by Raymond Domench, who only gave Dacourt a couple of opportunities before turning to younger players. His last appearance for his country was in a 2–0 World Cup qualifying win in Cyprus. Dacourt moved to Inter Milan, but after a fine start he badly damaged his left knee and was on the sidelines for the second half of the 2007–08 season. He was not in new manager Jose Mourinho's plans for the following Serie A term, returning to the Premiership with Fulham.

TONY DORIGO
(England 1989–93)
Full-back
Born: Melbourne, Victoria, Australia, 31 December 1965.
Caps: Chelsea 6, Leeds United 9. Total: 15

PIONEER Tony Dorigo was the first Australian-born player to represent England in a full international. He was certainly a class act in his six years at Elland Road and was named United's Player of the Year in the 1991–92 title-winning season, by which time he had established himself in the England squad.

Born in Melbourne of Italian parents, he was a promising teenager when he wrote to a string of clubs in England asking for a trial. Aston Villa were one of the few clubs to reply and their courtesy was rewarded as they took the young Aussie on in July 1983. He made his debut as a substitute in the final game of the 1983–84 season against Ipswich and within a couple of years was a Villa regular, breaking into the England Under-21 team before a £475,000 transfer to Chelsea, where he took his Under-21 caps total to 11. He helped the Stamford Bridge club win the Second Division in 1988–89 and scored the winning goal in the Zenith Data Systems Final against Middlesbrough in 1990.

Dorigo was a neat and tidy player, quick, with a strong left foot, and was remarkably consistent. Such attributes saw him play in an England B tour of Europe, taking in Switzerland, Iceland and Norway, in 1989. He was then elevated to full international status, coming on for Nottingham Forest's Stuart Pearce in a friendly against Yugoslavia on 13 December 1989 as the scramble for World Cup places began. Dorigo was one of five substitutes used by manager Bobby Robson – the first time England had used such a large number.

Pearce was clearly the first choice for the left-back berth, but Dorigo was on the plane for Italia '90 as back-up for the uncompromising and passionate Forest defender. England battled through to the semi-finals where they lost to West Germany in a penalty shootout, poor Pearce missing one of the spot-kicks on a night of unremitting drama. Dorigo was given his first England start by Robson in the third-fourth Play-off against hosts Italy and enjoyed a fine 90 minutes, providing the cross for David Platt to head in England's goal in a 2–1 defeat in Bari.

Tony Dorigo.

It was Robson's last game as England boss, and his successor, Graham Taylor, stuck by the rock-solid Pearce but fleetingly used Dorigo, who was on the brink of a move to Elland Road. Leeds had enjoyed a magnificent return to the top flight, finishing fourth, but manager Howard Wilkinson was acutely aware of the need for a left-back. Glynn Snodin, Mike Whitlow, Chris Kamara and Peter Haddock had all played in that position in 1991–92, without any of them nailing a regular place.

With Dorigo looking for a change after four years at Chelsea, Wilkinson snapped him up in a £1.3 million deal. He was a brilliant signing, linking superbly on the left with rising star Gary Speed, and missed only four League games as United won the Championship for the third time in the club's history.

Dorigo oozed class and composure and was hailed as the best Leeds left-back since Terry Cooper, but breaking into the England team on a regular basis was more difficult. Pearce, regarded by Wilkinson as the best left-back in Europe, continued to be remarkably consistent for his country, and Dorigo had to be patient for his international opportunities.

After scoring his first Leeds goal in a 3–0 demolition of Manchester City at Elland Road on 7 September 1991,

Dorigo reported for England duty and was handed a rare start against the new unified German team at Wembley. The German jinx continued as a goal by Karl-Heinze Reidle in injury time of the first half condemned Graham Taylor to his first defeat as England manager in his 13th game in charge. Taylor's top priority was qualification for the European Championships, and Pearce was brought back for the games against Turkey and Poland before Dorigo got another England outing, coming off the bench for a friendly against Czechoslovakia in Prague. The Leeds man did not enjoy the best of evenings, with both he and goalkeeper David Seaman culpable for the Czechs' second goal, before Everton defender Martin Keown scored a rare goal to salvage a 2–2 draw.

At the end of the season, which saw Leeds become the last team to win the old Division One title before the start of the Premiership era, Dorigo played the full 90 minutes in successive games as England won 1–0 in Hungary and drew 1–1 with Brazil at Wembley. He was a member of the squad for the European Championships in Sweden but did not get a game as England crashed out disappointingly in a group containing Denmark, France and the hosts.

The affable Aussie began the new season in fine style, scoring one of the goals on a sunny Wembley afternoon as champions United beat FA Cup-winners Liverpool 4–3. New Leeds hero Eric Cantona, the French international, took centre stage that day with a complete hat-trick – left and right-foot shots and a header. Dorigo's next game under the Twin Towers was against minnows San Marino in February 1993 because skipper Pearce was injured. David Platt, playing in Italy with Juventus, marked his first game as England captain with four goals – and missed a penalty – as England won 6–0. Dorigo spent much of the night supplementing the attack and came close to scoring his first international goal several times in a low-key World Cup qualifier.

The 1992–93 season was an anti-climax for Leeds, who failed to win a single away game in the defence of their crown and made early exits from the European, FA and Football League Cups. Dorigo maintained his high level of performance throughout and was rewarded with his 12th England cap at the end of the campaign as England eked out a valuable World Cup qualification point in Poland. Despite the useful 1–1 draw, manager Taylor opted for a different system in Oslo the following Wednesday, playing a back-three formation including central defenders Gary Pallister (Manchester United), Des Walker (Nottingham Forest) and Tony Adams (Arsenal). Dorigo was one of four players from the Poland game to miss out, but the new tactical plan was a disaster as Norway won 2–0. The result meant England probably had to win their three remaining group fixtures and hope others would slip up, otherwise they would not make the Finals in the United States.

England barely had time to digest their parlous position when they flew across the Atlantic to take part in the US

Cup – a trip that was supposed to help them acclimatise before the real thing the following year. The Norway defeat had severely damaged morale, and it plunged still deeper as England, with Dorigo at left-back, gave a dire display in a humiliating 2–0 defeat against the cock-a-hoop Americans in Boston. The shambles came almost 43 years to the day after England lost 1–0 to the US in the 1950 World Cup – a scoreline regarded as one of the greatest shocks in world football.

Some pride was restored with a 1–1 draw with Brazil in Washington, but Dorigo gave way to Queen's Park Rangers's Andy Sinton for the final match of the competition – a 2–1 loss to Germany in Detroit. England kept their faint World Cup qualification hopes alive by beating Poland 3–0, but the end effectively came as England lost 2–0 in Rotterdam in Dorigo's final international appearance.

Relations between Taylor and the media had become strained as England's hopes of taking part in the Finals faded month by month, and they clashed once more over his team selection for the do-or-die game with the Dutch. Sheffield Wednesday's Carlton Palmer, shortly to join Leeds, was chosen as the replacement for the suspended Paul Gascoigne, while Paul Merson got the nod over Arsenal colleague Ian Wright, despite being behind him in the Highbury pecking order. As England suffered a rotten Rotterdam night, Norway booked their berth in the Finals by winning 3–0 in Poland. The following month Holland won in Poland to take the other spot from Group Two, making England's 7–1 win against San Marino academic.

Dorigo's career at Leeds also ended in disappointment as his last two seasons were blighted by injury, and after spending a year on loan with Torino in Italy he joined Derby in October 1998 before ending his playing days with Stoke.

Wonderfully consistent for the Whites, he was never able to get an extended run in the England team because of the excellence of Stuart Pearce. In most other eras Dorigo might have doubled his tally of caps. But 15 full international appearances, seven more with England B and 11 games at Under-21 level represents a healthy total for a young Aussie who had the bottle to fly halfway round the world as a teenager to pursue his dream of being a professional footballer.

JONATHAN DOUGLAS

(Republic of Ireland 2004–07)

Midfield

Born: Monaghan, Co. Monaghan, 22 November 1981.
Caps: Blackburn Rovers 3, Leeds United 5. Total 8

SHEER hard graft paved the way for Jonathan Douglas to earn his international spurs with the Republic of Ireland. He overcame a career-threatening injury with Blackburn

Jonathan Douglas.

Rovers, where he won his first three full caps as a substitute, before playing on a more regular basis under Steve Staunton in Eire's ill-fated 2008 European Championships qualifying campaign. The paths of midfielder Douglas and his former Ireland boss Staunton were soon to cross again when Staunton was named assistant to Gary McAllister at Elland Road in February 2008 – four months after being axed as national team boss.

Douglas began as a kid with Clones Town, where his father John and uncle Norman had played, before graduating to Monaghan United, with whom he made his League of Ireland debut at 16. He was making his way up the Irish football ladder when family tragedy struck in 1997 – his brother, Jeffery, who was having trials with Luton Town, died in a car crash. It was a loss that spurred Jonathan on to do his best on the pitch in times of adversity. Resisting the temptation to join one of the bigger clubs, he stayed with Monaghan and was a member of the Ireland squad that won the European Under-16 Championship in 1998.

Inevitably that crop of Irish talent attracted the interest of some big clubs, with Celtic one of the first to check him out. In the end the Hoops opted to recruit Liam Miller, another of the Irish Under-16s, instead of Douglas. Ironically, both went on to play together as loanees with Leeds United six years later. Douglas had played for Celtic in a pre-season friendly against Blackburn, who liked what they saw of the midfielder and followed up their interest after Celtic dropped theirs. A Blackburn fan, Douglas jumped at the opportunity to become a trainee with the Ewood Park club, but his career was almost over before it started. The Eire youth international ruptured his cruciate ligament in April 2001, but he fought back through the pain barrier to earn his Rovers debut the following year as a substitute in a 1–0 FA Cup fifth-round defeat at Middlesbrough, whose 87th-minute winner was scored by Ugo Ehiogu, who later played on loan at Leeds.

Eire Under-21 honours followed, and he was loaned to Chesterfield towards the end of 2002–03, scoring the goal at Blackpool on the final day of the season which preserved the Spireites' status. Ironically it was the Tangerines who took him on loan at the start of the following season, only for him to be recalled to Ewood Park to enjoy a decent run in the first team as a left-sided wide player. His senior international debut came in April 2004 against Poland, and the following month he was a substitute in a 3–0 defeat against Nigeria, but could not secure a regular Rovers first-team spot and went out on loan again, this time to Gillingham.

At the start of 2005–06 Douglas began a season-long loan with Kevin Blackwell's Leeds and immediately impressed with his tackling, spirit and work-rate to create space for fellow loanee and Republic teammate Liam Miller's more intricate skills. The partnership helped push United all the way to the Championship Play-off Final at Cardiff's Millennium Stadium, where the Whites slumped to a 3–0 defeat. His form had not gone unnoticed by Eire manager Staunton, who rewarded Douglas by selecting him for a friendly against Holland in Dublin on 16 August 2006, in which he came on at half-time in a 4–0 defeat. At the end of that month he joined Leeds permanently on a three-year deal, but United suffered a poor start and Blackwell was replaced by former England and Chelsea man Dennis Wise in October.

Douglas barely had time to adjust to Wise's tactics before he was called up for the Republic's Euro 2008 qualifiers against Cyprus and the Czech Republic. The game in Nicosia offered Douglas little respite from a trot of bad results, as he came on in the 83rd minute with the Republic already 5–2 down and a man short following the dismissal of Richard Dunne. That is the way it stayed, and not surprisingly there were changes for the Czech game in Dublin four days later.

Douglas was handed his first start and had an outstanding game alongside Everton's Lee Carsley as the Irish rekindled their qualification hopes with a 1–0 victory. However, he did not retain his place for the next game against San Marino, as Staunton opted for a more attacking line up, although he came on as a sub in a 5–0 win which featured a hat-trick from former Leeds striker Robbie Keane in the last match on the old Lansdowne Road pitch, scene of many famous games.

Douglas also played in the historic first football game ever at Croke Park – a bastion of Gaelic sports – on 24 March 2007 when Wales were beaten 1–0 in a Euro qualifier. By this time Douglas had replaced Kevin Nicholls as United's captain after Nicholls requested a move back to former club Luton. But despite driving his team on with typical determination, Leeds slid into League One, Douglas missing the last five games of the season after receiving his 15th yellow card of the campaign in a last-gasp defeat at Colchester.

If relegation was not bad enough, Leeds went into administration and were then docked 15 points at the start

Jonathan Douglas.

of 2007–08, but Douglas remained with the Whites, who rolled up their sleeves and reeled off seven successive victories from the start of the season. Douglas missed the fifth match when a 2–0 triumph over Hartlepool took them on to zero points, as he was on duty with the Irish, coming on as a sub again in time to see Slovakia's Mark Cech snatch a 2–2 draw in Bratislava.

Leeds's form dipped after Douglas sustained a bad leg injury at Walsall in December, and by the time he returned to action against the same opponents three months later Wise had left for a lucrative post at Newcastle. Old Leeds hero McAllister was running the team with Staunton, who had been axed by the Republic after a poor showing in the European qualifiers. With skipper Douglas back in harness, Leeds finished the season strongly to battle to a Wembley Play-off Final with Yorkshire neighbours Doncaster Rovers – a fantastic achievement considering the 15-point handicap. But Donny won 1–0 to book their place in the Championship, while United contemplated another season in League One.

Transfer talk linked Douglas with a move to Burnley, and speculation that he was on his way increased still further when he was overlooked by McAllister at the start of 2008–09, but the midfielder got back in the side and played regularly, taking his appearance tally over 100 for the Whites before moving on to Swindon Town in summer 2009.

HARRY DUGGAN
(Ireland 1929–35 and Republic of Ireland 1927–37)
Winger
Born: Dublin, 8 June 1903.
Died: Leeds, September 1968.
Caps (Ireland): Leeds United 8
Caps (Republic of Ireland): Leeds United 4, Newport County 1. Total: 5
Goals (Republic of Ireland): 1

DUAL international Harry Duggan was one of Leeds United's star turns in the inter-war years as patience finally paid off. A swift and busy right winger plucked from Irish junior club Richmond United, he made nearly 200 appearances in Leeds colours, scoring 49 goals.

After leaving school the young Dubliner started out as an apprentice stonemason, but it was on the football pitch that he was to shape his career. In 1924–25 he rattled in 49 goals for Richmond in the FAI Intermediate League, and that was enough to convince Arthur Fairclough to sign him for Leeds. It was a calculated gamble as United were in need of a younger player to understudy former England international Bobby Turnbull, and, eventually, replace him.

After a season in the reserves, Duggan made his Leeds debut in a 4–2 triumph at Anfield on 2 October 1926 when Tom Jennings scored all four United goals in a First Division fixture. Although he only made eight starts in the First Division that season, he was called up by the Dublin-based FA of Ireland for the Irish Free State's first-ever home international at Lansdowne Road, on 23 April 1927.

The Irish Free State was created following political division in Ireland in 1922 and lasted until 1937 when the country declared independence under the name Eire. After a referendum it became the Republic of Ireland in 1949, but the Belfast-based Irish FA exercised its right as a member of the game's International Board to field teams under the name Ireland and to select players, like Duggan, from the south. That is why the Leeds winger and some of his contemporaries ended up playing for both Ireland and the Irish Free State, although IFS matches usually come under the Republic heading in football books.

The Free State's first-ever international was a 3–0 defeat in Turin against Italy, with all the Irish players drawn from Irish clubs. The side was skippered by Shelbourne's Mick Foley, the former Leeds City player, while Shamrock Rovers players Bob Fullam and John Joe Flood, both formerly on the Elland Road payroll, also played. Thirteen months later Italy sent a B team to Dublin for the Lansdowne Road opener, Fullam scoring the historic first Irish goal before the Italians shot back to win 2–1. Back in England on the same afternoon Leeds were losing 4–1 at Tottenham, a result that confirmed their relegation.

United bounced back as runners-up to Manchester City the following season, and Duggan had to be content with reserve-team football as Turnbull continued to produce the goods on the right flank. At this stage, Duggan was getting more international football than he was action in the Leeds first team. He was picked for his first Ireland game against England in Belfast on 19 October 1929, England easing home 3–0 with Middlesbrough's George Camsell netting twice.

After playing in the Free State's 3–1 win in Belgium at the end of the 1929–30 season, he was called upon by the IFA for another Home Championship showdown with England in October 1930 when Ireland were thumped 5–1 at Bramall Lane. He also featured in a 3–2 loss against Wales at Wrexham at the end of the season. Duggan was 27 by now and was still playing more for United's reserves than the first team, despite Leeds suffering another relegation. But, at long last, his breakthrough at club level came in 1931–32 as United finished second in Division Two a couple of points behind Wolves. With the evergreen Turnbull now virtually out of the picture, Duggan was appointed captain and played 35 League games that season. He continued to give full-backs a hard time on United's

Harry Duggan.

H. DUGGAN

return to Division One and faced England again when a goal from Sheffield United's Bobby Barclay edged out the plucky Irish at Blackpool.

Duggan had to wait 12 months before the chance of revenge – and his next cap – when he lined up against Wilf Copping and Co. in Belfast. Although Duggan was firmly established in the Leeds side, the outcome against England was the same, as goals by Eric Brook, Tom Grosvenor and Jack Bowers condemned the Irish to a 3–0 defeat. Duggan had played five times for Ireland, four of them against England, and lost the lot. But he finally broke his international duck against Scotland on 20 October 1934. He had been having a few games for Leeds at centre-forward with some success, including both goals that won the West Riding derby against Huddersfield. But for the Scotland game he was back on the right wing and saw his goalkeeper Elisha Scott save a penalty and goals from Davy Martin and Jackie Coulter, a national roller-skating champion, give the Belfast crowd plenty to cheer about. Bob McPhail pulled one back, but the Irish hung on for only their second victory over Scotland in 46 matches.

Duggan was also restored to his wing berth by new Leeds manager Billy Hampson, who had been brought in to revive a team who were in danger of relegation once more. Crowds had dipped, and only just over 9,000 were at Elland Road to see United slug out a 1–1 draw with Wolves just before Duggan joined the Irish squad for their game at Wrexham against Wales, which ended in a comfortable 3–1 home win. United did pull their season round and avoid the drop, Duggan finishing as second top scorer behind Arthur Hydes, with nine goals. Duggan went into his final international for Ireland on a real high. He had scored his first and only Leeds hat-trick in the 7–2 rout of Sheffield Wednesday on 9 November 1935, four days before facing Scotland at Tynecastle in Edinburgh when Dally Duncan scored in the dying seconds to deny the Irish a Home Championship point.

Leeds finished in a comfortable 11th place in the First Division, but Duggan missed the final game of the season against Arsenal as he had been called up by the Free State for their game in Hungary the following day, his first outing for the team in six years. They drew 3–3 in Belfast then took on Rhineland in an unofficial international in Cologne, losing 4–1. At least Duggan ended the summer in good spirits, setting up plenty of chances in a 5–1 romp against Luxembourg.

Duggan played in the opening game of 1936–37, a 3–2 home defeat against Chelsea, but it proved to be his last in an old gold-and-blue shirt. In October he was transferred to Newport County for £1,500 and skippered the Welsh side to the Division Three (South) title in 1938–39, as well as playing his final, and most important, international. Ireland took on Norway in Dublin in a World Cup qualifier on 7 November 1937 in a match they had to win to go through to the 1938 Finals in France. Ireland had lost 3–2 in Oslo the previous month, and with the aggregate winners progressing to the Finals there was a frenzied atmosphere inside Dalymount Park, which exploded after 10 minutes when Duggan headed on for Jimmy Dunne to score.

Norway kept their cool and by the 50th minute had taken a 3–1 lead. Kevin O'Flanaghan pulled a goal back, and with two minutes to go Duggan fired in the equaliser to see the game end 3–3. Athough the Scandinavians held on, the goal was virtually Duggan's last kick in international football at the age of 34 – quite a way to sign off.

Duggan took on duties as an ARP warden in South Wales before returning to Leeds in March 1940 and began working for a firm of glass merchants.

WILLIS EDWARDS
(England 1926–1929)
Half-back
Born: Newton, near Alfreton, Derbyshire, 28 April 1903.
Died: Leeds, 27 September 1988.
Caps: Leeds United 16

WILLIS Edwards, the first Leeds United player to be picked for England, was one of the club's all-time greats. Hugely respected, he spent 35 years at Elland Road as a player, manager and trainer and had the honour of captaining his country five times.

It was a red letter day for the city of Leeds when Edwards stepped on to the Crystal Palace pitch on 1 March 1926 for his England debut. United had been a League club for less than seven years following the expulsion of Leeds City and, after gaining promotion from Division Two in 1924, were battling with the cream of English football in the top flight. Edwards was not even with the club when United went up to Division One, but within 12 months of his United debut was making his first start for England at the age of 22. It was an amazing ascent up football's ladder and had started with his home village team Newton Rangers in north-east Derbyshire when he left school and began work at the local pit.

The young miner was spared a life underground by his football skills, which attracted the attention of Blackburn Rovers in 1922. But, as he was on his way to Ewood Park, he was intercepted by his local club, Chesterfield, who successfully persuaded him to stay closer to home. The Spireites signed him for £10 and put the teenager on a wage of 30 shillings a week. He made his debut against Hartlepool in front of 6,000 fans at Saltergate on 7 April 1923, and it was not long before scouts were checking out the little Chesterfield wing-half.

Among them was former Sheffield United and England player Ernest 'Nudger' Needham, who reported back to the Blades that Edwards was too small to make it in the higher divisions. Leeds, struggling in Division One, had no such qualms and snapped him up for £1,500 in March

Willis Edwards.

Willis Edwards, captain of England, with the ball at his feet, before the 2–1 victory against Ireland at Goodison Park in October 1928.

1925 shortly after Chesterfield had thumped Durham City 6–0 in a Division Three (North) encounter.

Edwards and Russell Wainscoat, a new signing from Middlesbrough, who also went on to play for England, made their Leeds debuts together at Newcastle. The pair played in the final nine games of the season as relegation was successfully staved off, and Edwards took to playing in the First Division like a duck to water. With the redoubtable centre-half Ernie Hart at his side, Edwards was able to express himself. He had magnificent ball control and could pass the leather as well as anyone in the country. Despite being relatively short – 5ft 8in – he had a great spring, and very few forwards could get the better of him in the air. He featured in an England trial game against The Rest at Newcastle and impressed enough to earn that precious first full cap, having played only 40 games in the First Division.

The local press, who had campaigned for his selection, were ecstatic when Edwards became the 500th player to be capped by England, but the local hero's international debut turned sour as Wales won 3–1, Swansea's Jack Fowler getting a couple of the goals. Edwards retained his place for the next match against Scotland at Old Trafford in front of 49,429, swelled by an estimated 10,000 Scottish fans. It was the 50th meeting between the old rivals, and it was the Scots, unbeaten against the Auld Enemy since 1920, who scored the only goal when a shot from Huddersfield Town's Alex Jackson went in off a post after 36 minutes. It was enough to give Scotland the Home International title and left England clutching the wooden spoon. Two home games and two defeats – Edwards's international career had not got off to a good start.

Despite those losses, Edwards was still highly regarded by the selection committee and won his third cap in

October 1926 in a 3–3 draw with Ireland at Anfield, when Sunderland goalkeeper Albert McInroy, who had a spell with Leeds much later in his career, won his only cap. Edwards's next international, against Wales, also finished 3–3 and was significant for the emergence of 20-year-old Everton forward Dixie Dean, who marked his debut with a couple of goals. His speed and power in the air added a sharpness to the England attack, which now faced the defensive might of Scotland at Hampden Park.

The Scots had a superb side in the 1920s and were hunting their sixth Home Championship title in seven years when they took on England on 2 April 1927, having not conceded a goal for seven matches. That sequence looked set to continue when England lost centre-half Jack Hill with an eye injury and Alan Morton put Scotland ahead. Hill returned to the fray on the left wing with a heavily bandaged head as England reshuffled and snatched victory with two Dean goals.

Edwards finally tasted victory in his fifth England start and was soon to enjoy more success as he played in all three of England's summer tour matches in Europe. New star Dean scored hat-tricks as Belgium and Luxembourg were swept aside 9–1 and 5–2 respectively and hit two more in the 6–0 thumping of France. But while Edwards was enjoying himself on the Continent, his club were rebuilding after suffering relegation. Despite 35 goals in 41 games from Tom Jennings, the United defence endured a torrid time, and not even Edwards's brilliance could keep them up.

The big questions were – would Edwards stay, and would the England selectors pick a Second Division player? The answer to the first was yes, while injury put the answer to the second on hold. Leeds and Edwards were soon involved in the promotion race, and the wing half was playing as well as ever and, following his recovery from injury, fully merited his recall against Scotland at Wembley. He had missed games against Ireland and Wales, but came through a couple of trial games at West Bromwich and Middlesbrough successfully. Edwards was in the Football League side that thrashed the Scottish League 6–2 at Ibrox and was relishing the prospect of tackling the Scots in the Empire Stadium three weeks later.

Both the Ireland and Wales games had been lost in Edwards's absence, and the Scotland game went with form in spectacular fashion, with the men in navy blue putting on a stunning performance to win 5–1. They were dubbed 'the Wembley Wizards' and simply took England apart in front of the future King George VI. The nippy little Scottish forwards skimmed across the greasy surface and took England apart. Even the majestic Edwards could not keep up with the tartan terrors in what was only the second international held at the stadium, which had opened in 1924.

As a well-beaten England trooped off at least Edwards got to hear that United had coped well without him in a 4–0 home win over Blackpool which took them a step nearer promotion, which finally came as runners-up to Manchester City.

Once again Edwards figured in both May friendlies abroad – a 5–1 win in France and a 3–1 success against Belgium – and was in dominating mood for Leeds, who returned to the First Division with a bang. Dick Ray's team had won eight and drawn two of their opening 13 League games when Edwards was named captain of his country for the first time. He proudly led England out at Swansea on a doubly historic day for United. As the match kicked off, centre-half Ernie Hart was at Edwards's side, making his debut, so two Leeds men were in an England side together for the first time.

Edwards made a successful start to his captaincy, with Joe Hulme scoring twice in a 3–2 win, but it was in the days before club fixtures were postponed because of international call-ups, and on the same afternoon a weakened United slumped 2–0 at Elland Road to Sheffield Wednesday. The new England skipper was hoping to go for revenge against Scotland at Hampden Park, where victory would see England win the Home Championship, but his hopes were blown away with the last kick of the game when Aberdeen's Alec Cheyne scored direct from a corner.

United ended the season in a solid 13th place, and the Edwards-Hart tandem were in harness for a comfortable 3–0 win against Ireland on 19 October 1929. While the dynamic duo were strutting their stuff in Belfast, United were racking up a seventh straight League win by beating Birmingham at Elland Road. Football life seemed as though it could not get better for Willis Edwards – but it did in his final international as England clobbered Wales 6–0 at Stamford Bridge, with George Camsell of Middlesbrough scoring a hat-trick.

Leeds had finished the 1929–30 season in fifth place, their highest position to date, and introduced a star in the making after the summer break – Wilf Copping. The famous half-back line of Edwards-Hart-Copping played together for the first time on the opening day of the 1930–31 season, a 2–2 draw at Portsmouth. Between them they only missed eight games, but Leeds went down, failing to find any semblance of form on the road and winning only two away games. By now Edwards had lost his England place to Sheffield Wednesday's Alf Strange, a remarkably consistent performer who played in 20 of the next 21 internationals. The Leeds skipper was left to concentrate on his club football, and with the Holy Trinity of Edwards, Hart and Copping as their base Leeds bounced back to the First Division at the first time of asking.

Gradually time caught up with Edwards, who started to turn out less frequently for Leeds. He was being groomed for a backroom job. A wonderful clubman, his career stretched into wartime when he played a handful of games in emergencies. He became assistant to trainer Bob Roxburgh with responsibility for the reserves and in April

1947 replaced Billy Hampson as manager. He faced a huge task in revamping an ageing squad and, although he lowered the average age of the team and improved their fitness, Leeds flirted with relegation to Division Three (North). Although they avoided the drop, he moved back to his old job as assistant trainer when Frank Buckley was appointed manager.

Edwards stayed at Elland Road a further 10 years before ending a remarkable 35-year association with the club, and the last few years of his working life were spent employed in a jam factory. The Leeds legend had played 444 times for the club, captained England in the last five of his 16 internationals, represented the Football League on 11 occasions and taken part in eight England trial matches, yet was never sent off or cautioned. That spoke volumes about a man who ranks among the best Elland Road has ever seen.

GYLFI EINARSSON
(Iceland 2000–06)
Midfield
Born: Reykjavik, 27 October 1978.
Caps: Fylkir 1, Lillestrom 15, Leeds United 8. Total: 24
Goals: 1

EVEN playing for a country that has never qualified for a major international football tournament has its rewards, as Gylfi Einarsson discovered just months before he joined Leeds United. Iceland, which is closer to Greenland than mainland Europe, only has a population of slightly more than 300,000 – more than half the city of Leeds. Yet they were nearly all celebrating after a sensational 2–0 victory over Italy in Reykjavik when Einarsson scored his only goal for the national team. That moment of glory was in stark contrast to the injury-hit time the midfielder spent on the Elland Road payroll after his long-awaited transfer finally went through.

Einarsson was born in the Icelandic capital and first made his mark in football with Fylkir, a small club in Reykjavik. He made his international debut as a 21-year-old when he came on as a substitute in a 5–0 friendly win over Malta, which featured a hat-trick by Helgi Sigurdusson, a striker with Greek club Panathinaikos. Most of the Icelandic squad were with clubs beyond the shores of Iceland, as the standard of the island's main League, which plays its fixtures in the summer because of the extreme cold and lack of light in winter, was not high. It was not long before Einarsson was joining the exodus when he signed for Norwegian club Lillestrom shortly after making his international bow. His next outing with the national side certainly saw a change in climate as he flew to India with the Icelandic squad, taking part in the Millennium Super Soccer Cup, playing in the 3–0 win against the hosts, then playing in the heat of Calcutta as the Europeans lost to Chile 2–0.

Gylfi Einarsson.

Although Einarsson had a reputation as an attacking midfielder, he played for his country at full-back against Lithuania, Estonia and Finland before a clutch of substitute appearances in his more favoured position in the middle of the field. When he started a friendly against Italy on 18 August 2004 he seized the moment. Eidur Gudjohnson, the Chelsea striker, stunned the Azzurri with a 17th-minute goal, and three minutes later Einarsson swooped to make it 2–0 and send the record 20,204 inside the Laugardalsvollur wild with delight. Despite the likes of Gennaro Gattuso, Gianluca Zambrotta, Allessandro Nesta, Marco Materazzi and Luca Toni, the Italians could not break through a well-organised defence, and Iceland held on to record one of their most famous victories.

While Einarsson was the toast of his country, financially crippled Leeds United were just starting life in the Championship after their relegation. The once-mighty Whites no longer had a scouting network that covered the Continent because they could not afford it, and it was a Leeds supporter who told the club that Einarsson's contract with Lillestrom would soon be up.

Einarsson, shortlisted for the Norwegian Player of the Year award after scoring 19 goals from midfield, featured in World Cup qualifiers against Bulgaria, Hungary, Malta and Sweden. He would become a free agent after his contract expired on 30 November, but Leeds were not favourites to sign him as he had lined up a trial with Cardiff City, while Wigan, Burnley and Coventry were also interested. The Bluebirds opted not to take him on, and after a trial at Elland Road he signed a pre-contract agreement in November to join the Whites.

Because of UEFA regulations, Einarsson could not link up with Leeds until the reopening of the transfer window in January and spent the whole of December in limbo. Even when he started training with his new club he had his training disrupted because of food poisoning, which saw him lose half a stone in a week. He was given squad number 16, and on New Year's Day he came on as a substitute in a 2–0 loss to Crewe at Elland Road. In only his second Championship start he showed travelling Leeds fans his prowess in the air by heading the winner at Burnley, whose Frank Sinclair was later sent off for kicking out at the new signing.

Despite that promising start, Einarsson was out of the United team when he reported for World Cup qualifying duty with Iceland the following month. He was in the side which lost 4–0 in Croatia and then drew 0–0 in Padova in a friendly with Italy. Games against Hungary, South Africa and the return against Croatia followed. Einarsson's hopes that he would get a decent run in the United side in 2005–06 failed to materialise, however, mainly due to a succession of injuries. In September a dislocated finger saw him playing in a cast, but he started Iceland's October friendly in Poland ahead of the islanders' 3–1 World Cup qualifying defeat against Sweden in Stockholm. But at Leeds he was still struggling to make an impact, and his stop-start career at Elland Road was not helped when he received a straight red card at Blackburn for a foul on Robbie Savage in a Carling Cup tie.

After his suspension it proved to be his final first team outing of the season for Leeds after dislocating a shoulder in a reserve game against Birmingham City, and he was still in the reserves when he made his last international appearance – facing a Caribbean team in London! Trinidad & Tobago had qualified for the World Cup Finals, where they would be in England's group, and arranged a friendly for their European-based players against Iceland at Queen's Park Rangers's Loftus Road ground on 28 February 2006. Einarsson came on for Eidur Gudjohnson in a 2–0 defeat against the Soca Warriors, whose veteran Dwight Yorke scored both goals, the second a cheekily-chipped penalty.

With Leeds going well, there was no way Einarsson was able to get back in the United team, and he was very much on the fringes as United missed out on promotion by losing to Watford in the Play-off Final at Cardiff. It was to get worse for the Icelander, as an operation to remove floating bone from his hip in September 2006 ruled him out for several months. He managed a smattering of substitute appearances under Dennis Wise, but when United's relegation to League One was confirmed Einarsson's

contract was terminated. Barnsley and Millwall both had a look at him, but he resurfaced in Norwegian football again when he joined champions Brann Bergen in January 2008, hoping to resurrect his career at both club and international level.

RIO FERDINAND
(England 1997 – to date)
Defender
Born: Peckham, London, 7 November 1978.
Caps: West Ham United 10, Leeds United 17, Manchester United 46. Total: 73
Goals: 3

CLASSY defender Rio Ferdinand became the world's most expensive defender when he joined Leeds from West Ham for £18 million. Already an England international, he grew in stature at Elland Road before the club's finances dictated he be sold to cross-Pennine rivals Manchester United for another record-breaking transfer for a defender, thought to be around £29.1 million.

After gambling on a Champions League qualification, which they did not achieve, the Whites were plunged into money troubles, taking the club to the brink of collapse. Virtually all of their top names were sold in a fire sale in January 2003 – but Ferdinand had already left by then, and at least Leeds appeared to get a decent price for a man regarded as one of the world's best defenders. He hardly put a foot wrong in his two seasons at Elland Road, but with his employers reportedly £77 million in the red, his sale after the 2002 World Cup was inevitable.

Leeds boss David O'Leary, a top defender in his day, had long admired the cultured Ferdinand's play at West Ham, where he had a meteoric rise to the top. He made his debut in the final game of the 1995–96 season and was only eight days past his 19th birthday when he made his England debut as a substitute in a friendly against Cameroon on 15 November 1997. That made him the youngest defender to play for England, a record since broken by Manchester City's Micah Richards.

Ferdinand was still only 20 when he was picked for the 1998 initial World Cup squad, but was omitted from the final party by manager Glenn Hoddle after being charged with drink driving; however, the quality of Ferdinand's play meant that future England appearances were inevitable, and he had represented his country 10 times before he joined Leeds in November 2000. He was handed the number-29 shirt in a Leeds squad which, although they had not found their form in the Premiership, took the Champions League by storm. United's high-profile acquisition made his first European appearance for Leeds in a 2–1 win against Anderlecht in the third match of the second phase of the competition. Ferdinand quickly showed he could handle the big stage, enjoying a fantastic

Rio Ferdinand.

night in the quarter-final first leg against Deportivo La Coruña when he led the team for the first time in the absence of Lucas Radebe and headed in his first goal in Leeds colours to seal a tremendous 3–0 triumph. It was also his first goal for four years.

Leeds went out to Valencia in the semi-finals but, with Ferdinand at the heart of the defence, the Whites had managed to turn their season around with eight wins from their last nine League games to just miss out on another Champions League season. The games were coming thick and fast for Ferdinand as he was a regular in Sven-Goran Eriksson's squad battling for a place in the 2002 World Cup Finals. Qualification had been put in doubt by an early qualifying defeat against Germany at Wembley when Kevin Keegan was in charge. Significantly, Ferdinand missed that game and a 0–0 draw in Finland that left England with just one point from a possible six. But Eriksson, recruited by the FA on a massive salary, got England back on track, with Ferdinand one of the first names down on his teamsheet.

Successive victories against Finland, Albania and Greece were followed by a never-to-be-forgotten 5–1 England victory in Munich against Germany, which changed the dynamic of group. Michael Owen's stunning hat-trick earned England their first win on German soil since 1965. But Ferdinand, and the rest of the nation, were put through agony in the final match of the group on 6 October 2001. England and Germany were level on 16 points each, with Sven's men holding the upper hand because of goal difference. England were taking on Greece at Old Trafford while Germany hosted Finland in Gelsenkirchen.

Both the favourites suffered badly from nerves, with Germany held to a goalless draw, but England were in even deeper trouble. They trailed 2–1 in the dying seconds until David Beckham stepped up to fire in a stunning 25-yard free-kick to pinch the point that sent England to the Finals and condemned Germany to a place in the Play-offs. Ferdinand, his Leeds teammate Danny Mills and England gave a good account of themselves in South Korea and Japan.

After opening with a 1–1 draw with Sweden, Beckham's penalty beat Argentina in one of the most eagerly anticipated games of the competition, and England guaranteed their passage into the second round with a 0–0 draw with Nigeria. Unpredictable Denmark stood between England and a place in the last eight, but it was all over by half-time as Ferdinand got his first goal for his country after just five minutes, and further goals by Owen and Emile Heskey tied up an easy win before the interval.

When Owen put England ahead against an off-colour Brazil, hopes of a semi-final spot soared, but the South Americans fought back to break England hearts and went on to win the trophy by beating Germany, who had finished runners-up in England's qualification group but reached the Finals after beating Ukraine in a Play-off. On the day of the Final in Yokohama, where two Ronaldo goals ended Germany's challenge, Leeds announced that former England boss Terry Venables was to be their new manager.

Failure to achieve Champions League qualification had cost O'Leary his job after Leeds, skippered throughout the season by Ferdinand, had topped the table going into 2002. United had anticipated battling it out in the lucrative Champions League in 2002–03 and had budgeted accordingly, so had to dramatically reassess their finances. The bottom line was that their huge outlay on the likes of Ferdinand, Mark Viduka, Olivier Dacourt, Robbie Fowler, Seth Johnson and others had left United financially crippled.

Speculation was rife that star names would have to go, and one of the first to depart was Ferdinand, whose calm defensive work had been a feature of his 20-month stay at Elland Road. He had excellent ball skills for a centre-back and always seemed to be in the right place at the right time because he read the game so well – qualities that had not gone unnoticed by Manchester United supremo Sir Alex Ferguson. His switch to Old Trafford inevitably did not go down well with Leeds fans, and it signalled the decline of the Whites, who were swamped by club-threatening cash troubles.

For Ferdinand, though, it turned out to be a dream move. He signed a five-year deal and went on to win the Premier League title in his first season and has since won it in 2007, 2008 and 2009. He led the Red Devils to a

Champions League Final victory over Chelsea in 2008 and has gained winners' medals in the 2006 and 2009 Carling Cups. But life at Old Trafford has not been without a hitch.

In 2003 he failed to attend a drugs test, claiming he had forgotten to take it because he was preoccupied with moving house and had gone shopping. An FA Disciplinary Committee announced in January 2004 that they had banned Ferdinand from all football and fined him £50,000. That meant he missed the rest of Manchester United's season – in which they won the FA Cup – and England's European Championship Finals matches. His place in the England team was taken by Chelsea's John Terry, but Ferdinand returned to international action in a 2–0 victory against Wales on 9 October 2004 and went on to captain England for the first time in a friendly against France on 26 March 2008. He has led the national team on several occasions since, scoring as he skippered a 5–1 World Cup qualifying win against Kazakhstan, but the job was given to his centre-back partner Terry on a permanent basis by current England coach Fabio Capello.

Barring injury, Ferdinand could well achieve 100 caps for England, for whom he has been extremely consistent, and his professional life is a far cry from his younger days, when he won a scholarship to attend the Central School of Ballet in London when he was 11 years old. No doubt four years there helped his poise and balance, but football was his first love. He played as an attacking midfielder for local club Eltham Town and had trials with several League sides in London and beyond before settling on West Ham, who launched him on an outstanding career.

Ferdinand's brother Anton, an England Under-21 international, also played for West Ham before joining Sunderland, and their cousin Les won 17 full caps while with Queen's Park Rangers, Newcastle and Spurs.

PETER FITZGERALD
(Republic of Ireland 1960–61)
Forward
Born: Waterford, 17 June 1937.
Caps: Leeds United 3, Chester 2. Total: 5
Goals: 2

ALTHOUGH his games were few and far between in his only season with Leeds, Peter Fitzgerald briefly hit the headlines with the Republic of Ireland. The centre-forward managed only a handful of games for United and failed to find the back of the net, yet was the toast of his country with a double-goal salvo in only his second international appearance.

Although his 11-month spell at Leeds was a disappointment, it was a vastly different story at his native Waterford, where he was a member of a famous Munster footballing family. Brothers Jack, Denny, Tom, Ned and

Peter Fitzgerald, standing far right on back row, in a Republic of Ireland team ahead of a game against Czechoslovakia in 1961. A young Johnny Giles is in the middle of the front row.

Paul all played for Waterford, and their father was an international selector. Right-half Jack, a former milkman, played twice for Eire against Holland in 1955 and 1956, about four years before brother Peter won his international spurs. Peter scored 17 League of Ireland goals for Waterford in 1958–59 and was also on target

Peter Fitzgerald.

Programme from the Republic of Ireland versus Norway game, in which Peter Fitzgerald scored twice.

when they lost in the Irish Cup Final that season. Bigger things beckoned, and he joined Sparta Rotterdam, the Dutch League's oldest side, for the start of 1959–60. He stayed in the Netherlands for a year before becoming part of Jack Taylor's rebuilding programme at Elland Road.

Leeds had been relegated to Division Two, and manager Taylor brought in plenty of new faces, including £7,000 purchase Fitzgerald, who made his debut on the opening day of the new campaign, a 2–0 defeat at Liverpool. But he immediately lost his place to another Irishman, Noel Peyton, and found himself out of the first-team reckoning. Fitzgerald still had just the one Leeds appearance to his name when he was picked for his international debut against Wales at Dalymount Park on 28 September 1960. The Republic had an eight-game unbeaten run at home, but the Welsh emerged victorious, 3–2, on their first visit to Dublin.

Fitzgerald played at centre-forward, with clubmate Peyton at inside-left and Manchester United youngster Johnny Giles, later to have such a major influence at Elland Road, at inside-right. Fitzgerald was still scratching around in the Leeds reserves when he won his second cap and had his day in the international spotlight. The Irish took on Norway in a Sunday friendly on 6 November and found

themselves a goal down to Harald Hennum's second-minute strike. Fionan Fagan levelled to set the stage for Fitzgerald's afternoon of glory.

The Leeds man was on the spot after Fagan drew a save from Asborn Hansen and knocked in a first-time shot to give Ireland the lead. Fitzgerald continued to be a threat throughout the game and wrapped up victory two minutes from the end when he was set up by Giles. Despite this eye-catching performance, he failed to breakthrough at Elland Road and was overlooked by Ireland for the first of back-to-back World Cup qualifying games against Scotland.

At Hampden Park the dominant Scots won 4–1, and Fitzgerald was recalled for the rematch four days later. But before Eire could get any foothold in the game, Alex Young of Everton scored two early goals and then set up Ralph Brand four minutes from time to complete a routine 3–0 victory. It was Fitzgerald's third and final appearance for Ireland as a Leeds player, and he moved on to Chester City in July 1961.

Despite dropping into Division Four, Fitzgerald played two more World Cup qualifiers against Czechoslovakia, but he and the rest of the Irish team were jeered as they crashed 3–1 in Dublin then suffered a 7–1 humiliation in Prague. Although Chester had to seek re-election in both Fitzgerald's seasons at Sealand Road, City fans remember him with some fondness before his return to Waterford in September 1963. The following month he was in the League of Ireland side that beat the Football League 2–1, the first of four LoI representative games. The last came at Boothferry Park, Hull, when a Football League side containing Jack Charlton and Norman Hunter romped to a 5–0 win against the part-timers.

Fitzgerald won a League of Ireland Championship medal in 1966 before going on to manage his home-town club. His international and Leeds career was certainly a curious one, as borne out by the stats – just eight starts for United and three for the Republic.

BRIAN FLYNN

(Wales 1974–84)
Midfield
Born: Port Talbot, 12 October 1955.
Caps: Burnley 21, Leeds United 32, Burnley 13. Total: 66
Goals: 7

GOOD things come in small packages. And at 5ft 3in they do not come much smaller – or better – than Brian Flynn. A Wales regular for 10 years, he formed a splendid midfield partnership with Tony Currie at Elland Road in the immediate post-Revie period. He was already firmly established in the Welsh side when he arrived at Leeds for £175,000 from Burnley, where he had been idolised by the Clarets supporters. It was not long before United fans were adopting the popular Manfred Mann song *Mighty Quinn* to belt out 'Come on without, come on within, you ain't seen nothing like the mighty Flynn.' He zipped around the pitch with great endeavour, but also possessed instant ball control and could provide his strikers with a defence-splitting pass. He and the more flamboyant Currie dovetailed superbly at times, even though Leeds were unable to recapture past glories.

A Welsh Schools international, Flynn originally looked bound for Cardiff City. He played for Afan Lido and Neath Boys, but when the Bluebirds got in a tangle over schoolboy forms Burnley stepped in to sign him as an apprentice in 1971. Three years later he made his First Division debut against Arsenal, and nine months after that he made his first appearance for the senior Welsh side, at the age of 19, when he came on as a substitute against Luxembourg at Swansea in a European Championship game. Leeds man Terry Yorath got one of the goals in a 5–0 win. After another sub's outing in the return leg, he made his first full start against Scotland, scoring in a 2–2 draw at Ninian Park. The goal was his first in senior football as Flynn had yet to find the back of the net for his club. He was one of the stars of the 1975 Home Championships and from then on became a regular fixture in the Wales engine room, featuring in a famous Welsh win at Wembley in May 1977.

Burnley's relegation to Division Two made Flynn a prime target for many clubs, with Leeds winning the race. His switch to Leeds in November 1977 saw him link up with his old Burnley pal Ray Hankin, and it was not long before the little Welsh wizard was setting up goals for the striker, who finished the season with 20 League goals. Flynn's Leeds debut was a 2–2 home draw with Norwich – a match which saw Peter Lorimer net his 150th League goal for the Whites.

Matches were coming thick and fast for Flynn, whose first appearance for Wales as a Leeds player was a World Cup qualifying defeat in Czechoslovakia, when Zdenek Nehoda scored the only goal of the game. Wales did not have too long to dwell on their failure to qualify for the 1978 World Cup Finals, for the draw for the 1980 European Championships had pitched them in with West Germany, Turkey and Malta. For a while it looked as though the battling Welsh would pull off a major surprise and top the group. They opened up with a crushing 7–0 win over Malta at Wrexham, with Flynn among the scorers. It equalled Wales's biggest margin of victory in the 20th century, and Chester's Ian Edwards scored four of the goals to equal Mel Charles's all-time best against Northern Ireland in 1962.

Wales then beat Turkey 1–0 and were sitting pretty at the top of the group after Germany struggled to draws in both Malta and Turkey. The stage was set for a big showdown with Germany at Wrexham's compact Racecourse Ground, with Wales knowing victory would

Brian Flynn.

put them in control of the group. But Wales were without the injured Flynn and goals by Herbert Zimmermann and Klaus Fischer saw Germany home to split the group wide open.

Flynn was back for the three end-of-season Home Internationals and was on the scoresheet again in a 2–0 Euro victory in Malta in early summer, which left Wales two points ahead of Germany. That capped a fine season for the little Welsh star, who had helped lift Leeds, under new manager Jimmy Adamson, back into the UEFA Cup by finishing fifth.

Flynn was joined at Elland Road by Welsh international teammate Alan Curtis at the start of 1979–80 after the striker's big money move from Swansea. But Leeds, now without Currie, made a disappointing start to the campaign and the Welsh boys were to find no relief when they travelled to Cologne for their key qualification game in October.

Victory would virtually put Wales through to the Finals in Italy, but that was never on the cards as Germany powered into a 4–0 half-time lead, the game finishing 5–1 with Curtis getting the consolation. It was the heaviest defeat since Mike Smith had taken over as manager of the Welsh side. The following month the Welsh dream was over as they lost 1–0 in Turkey while Germany pulled away at the top of the group by defeating the Turks and Malta in their final two fixtures. United had also struggled in 1979–80 with fans, used to success under Revie, becoming increasingly restless at the lack of success and entertainment, but for Flynn at least there was the consolation of a rousing 4–1 Wales triumph over England at Wrexham at the end of the campaign – their first victory over England since 1955.

World Cup qualification was now the main international focus, and Wales got off to a flyer with a 4–0 win in Iceland, Flynn notching a rare penalty. He also scored the opener as Turkey were thumped by the same score at Cardiff on 15 October 1980. Successive 1–0 victories at home against Czechoslovakia and in Turkey gave the Welsh maximum points after four games. A month before that victory in Ankara, Flynn had scored his first away goal for Leeds in the League, coming in a famous victory at Old Trafford. Leeds, now under the guidance of Allan Clarke, had been battered by Manchester United, but Flynn showed typical energy to pop up in the box to get on the end of a cross from fellow Welsh international Carl Harris to score a late winner. Flynn and Harris were in tandem for Wales at the end of the season in their Group Three World Cup qualifier against the USSR at Wrexham, but could not break down a tough Soviet defence in a goalless draw.

The 1981–82 season was a bad one for Leeds and Flynn. United did not start the season well, particularly away from home, and Wales, with Flynn battling away in midfield, lost 2–0 in Czechoslovakia, who had now emerged as the biggest threat to the Soviet Union at the top of the group. An ankle injury ruled him out for a large part of the season, and in his absence Leeds slid towards relegation and Wales out of the World Cup reckoning, with a damaging 2–2 home draw with Iceland.

Flynn did manage to play for Wales in Tbilisi on 18 November 1981, when the USSR powered to the top of the group in front of 80,000 fans. The Soviets then drew 1–1 in Czechoslovakia, a result which put both countries into the Finals and eliminated Wales. But the little dynamo was struggling with niggling injuries and in March 1982 rejoined Burnley on loan. He played his final international as a Leeds player in a 1–0 European Championship qualifying win against Norway on 22 September 1982 and went back to Burnley in a £60,000 move a couple of months later. His time at Leeds did not bring the silverware he had hoped for, but Flynn rarely had a bad game in any of his 178 matches in a Leeds shirt and had the honour of captaining his country.

Back at Burnley, Flynn stretched his appearance tally for Wales to 66, his last outing coming in 1984 against Israel, to ensure his standing as one of the principality's all-time greats. After seeing out his playing career with Doncaster, Cardiff, Bury and Limerick he had a stint working with Burnley's Football in the Community scheme before joining Wrexham as assistant manager to Dixie McNeil in 1988.

When McNeil quit, Flynn took over, donning his boots once more as player-manager. Initially it was a struggle, as the Red Dragons finished bottom of the League in 1990–91, but the following season he masterminded one of the greatest FA Cup shocks of all time when his team beat champions Arsenal. Mickey Thomas, who later had a short spell at Leeds, scored the winner with a scorching free-kick. Wrexham's faith in Flynn was well-placed, and he steered them up to the Second Division in 1992–93. He was with the north Wales club 12 years and did a similar job when he took over at Swansea in 2002, with the club on the brink of going out of business. He was appointed by John Toshack to oversee the development of the Welsh international Youth and Under-21 set up in December 2004 and soon produced some impressive results to ensure that his country's future looks positive.

ROBBIE FOWLER

(England 1996–2002)
Striker
Born: Liverpool, 9 April 1975.
Caps: Liverpool 22, Leeds United 4. Total: 26
Goals: 7

MASTER poacher Robbie Fowler saw out his England career with Leeds United – including a fleeting appearance in the 2002 World Cup. He was only a fringe player in Sven-Goran Eriksson's squad, but proved he had not lost the scoring knack, which served him so well throughout his career with Liverpool, where he rattled in goals at will.

Leeds supporters only got a small taste of Fowler's predatory skills, but the player Reds fans dubbed 'God' ranks as one of the most popular players ever seen at Anfield. He had been with the club since a Toxteth schoolboy and signed as a YTS trainee in 1991, turning pro the following year. He made goalscoring look effortless. Simply give him a chance, and he would take it.

After helping the England Under-18s win the 1993 European Championship, he made a scoring Liverpool senior debut in a 3–1 first-round Coca-Cola Cup success at Fulham and netted all five goals in the return leg a couple of weeks later. A Premiership hat-trick against Southampton and an England Under-21 debut against San Marino, in which he scored after just three minutes, confirmed his arrival as a star striker. Voted the PFA Young Player of the Year in 1995 and 1996, he won a League Cup-winners' medal and also scored the fastest Premiership hat-trick – four minutes 33 seconds – against Arsenal. The goal machine netted four times against Middlesbrough on

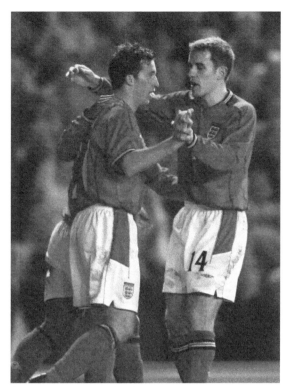

Striker Robbie Fowler (left) is congratulated by his England teammate Phil Neville after scoring against Italy at Elland Road in 2002.

article, and in those early games in a Leeds shirt it was easy to see why. He was always aware of what was going on around him on a football pitch, cherished possession and came alive in the penalty area, where he was capable of producing something out of nothing.

With the World Cup on the horizon, Fowler was keen to be on the plane to Japan, although with Owen, Emile Heskey, Teddy Sheringham, Nick Barmby, Andy Cole and Darius Vassell also in Eriksson's thoughts, Fowler could not guarantee his place in the final squad. He had figured in the qualifiers, scoring a wonderful late solo goal against Albania to seal a 2–0 win at Newcastle, and was in the starting line up which snatched a last-gasp 2–2 draw with Greece to secure England's place in the Finals.

A host of friendlies followed in which Eriksson checked out a variety of new faces up front, including Kevin Phillips and Bolton's Michael Ricketts, later to surface as a Leeds player. With Wembley being rebuilt, England matches were spread around the country, and Elland Road hosted one of the friendlies, against Italy, on 27 March 2002. It was the first England game to be played at the stadium since Sweden were the visitors in 1995, when the FA tested out facilities at the ground before the staging of Euro '96.

Leeds goalkeeper Nigel Martyn and right-back Danny Mills both started against Italy, and Fowler was one of an amazing nine half-time substitutions. He put England ahead on 63 minutes with a typically cool piece of finishing. But the Elland Road crowd were disappointed as Vincenzo Montella equalised and then hit the winner from the penalty spot in the last minute.

A similar exercise against Paraguay followed when Fowler received a warm welcome from the Anfield crowd when replacing his former Liverpool colleague Owen, who had opened the scoring in an easy 4–0 win. Fowler earned his place in the squad for the Finals, but at Elland Road financial storm clouds were gathering after the club announced a £13.8 million loss, sparking the inevitable speculation that some star names would have to be sold.

Fowler gained his 25th England cap in the last World Cup warm-up game against Cameroon, when he came on for Vassell and got on the end of a Wes Brown free-kick to head a last-minute equaliser. Once again he had proved his worth, but Eriksson plumped for the Owen-Heskey partnership in the group games, and Fowler's only taste of action was as a half-time sub for Owen with England already 3–0 up and a place in the quarter-finals guaranteed. It was his last outing as an England player. The last four had been as a Leeds player and all as a substitute. Fowler finished with seven goals from his 26 England games, a modest return for a player who found scoring so easy in the Premiership.

Fowler returned to the Far East for United's pre-season tour, but aggravated a hip injury and did not return to action until December 2002, by which time Rio Ferdinand, Robbie Keane and Olivier Dacourt had been

14 December 1996, which meant he had reached 100 Liverpool goals one game quicker than Ian Rush, another Liverpool legend who also featured for Leeds.

Fowler's first full England cap came as a substitute against Bulgaria on 27 March 1996, but a knee ligament injury saw him miss the 1998 World Cup. During his absence fellow Liverpool striker Michael Owen shot to prominence, and there was an inevitable debate about whether the pair would fit in together. Fowler was in Liverpool's treble Cup-winning teams of 2000–01, when they lifted the FA Cup, League Cup and UEFA Cup – skippering the side which beat Birmingham in the League Cup and coming on as a substitute in the other two against Arsenal and Deportivo Alaves. His relations with manager Gerard Houllier were strained, and his appearances were becoming increasingly intermittent. After scoring a hat-trick against Leicester in October 2001 he was dropped for the next match.

With rumours of a training ground bust-up doing the rounds, Leeds seized the moment to sign the deadly Liverpool finisher just a month after his Leicester treble. The fee was £11 million, and he soon started to justify the transfer, scoring a hat-trick in a 3–0 win at Bolton in his sixth Premiership start for the Whites. Despite only playing half the season with Leeds, he finished as top scorer with a dozen goals as David O'Leary's side qualified for the UEFA Cup. O'Leary described Fowler as the finished off-loaded as Leeds sought to ease their financial burden. Fowler only managed a handful of appearances as fitness worries persisted and after 15 goals in just 31 appearances for Leeds he was transferred to Manchester City for £3 million – yet desperate Leeds continued to pay a proportion of his wages as part of the deal.

Fowler battled hard to find fitness and form at City and did score his 150th Premiership goal before a surprise return to Liverpool on a free transfer. He proceeded to overhaul Kenny Dalglish as Liverpool's all-time top scorer, scoring 183 goals in 369 appearances in his two spells with the club. He then joined Cardiff City in July 2007 and linked up with another old Leeds favourite, Jimmy-Floyd Hasselbaink, in attack. But his long-standing hip problem resurfaced again and at the end of 2008–09 he went to Blackburn on a pay-as-you play basis, before being released in December 2008. He now plays in Australia.

BILLY FURNESS
(England 1933)
Inside-left
Born: New Washington, Co. Durham, 8 June 1909.
Died: Norwich, Norfolk, 29 August 1980.
Caps: Leeds United 1

MEETING the Pope and a Fascist dictator was all part of Billy Furness's England tour of duty. The Leeds inside-forward had been an ever present in the 1932–33 season, and his consistent displays caught the attention of the England selectors, who named him and club colleague Wilf Copping for the two-match tour of Italy and Switzerland. The pair lined up for their international debuts against Italy in the Stadio del Partido Nacional Facista in Rome in front of the country's leader, Benito Mussolini.

For Furness it completed a five-year rise from the pits of County Durham to football's top table. He worked as a colliery clerk and played for Washington Colliery, then Usworth Colliery, who received £50 when he joined Leeds as a 19-year-old in August 1928. Furness was an absolute bargain. He made his Leeds debut against Middlesbrough on 30 November 1929, but it was not until the following season that he became a United regular. He was one of the leading lights of United's promotion season in 1931–32, scoring in eight successive Division Two games between 17 October and 5 December. His combination with his Geordie friend, left-winger Tom Cochrane, was irresistible at times, and the pair continued to be a dangerous combination as United finished eighth in the First Division.

Furness's reward was an England call-up for a trip into the unknown. England had never played either Italy or Switzerland, so there was great interest in the tour. Sir Frederick Wall, secretary of the FA, addressing the press immediately before the party's departure on the boat train from London's Victoria Station, said: 'Naturally, I expect England to win.' His optimism was fairly well placed as England had a good record against continental opposition and boasted a strong squad, which included the likes of Arsenal duo Eddie Hapgood and Cliff Bastin, Birmingham goalkeeper Harry Hibbs and the two Leeds lads Furness and Copping. Originally three Elland Roaders were due to make the trip, but centre-half Ernie Hart was ruled out by suspension, so Everton's Tom White took his place.

Excitement had been building in Italy before England's arrival for the big game. The country had undergone a huge political change, with Mussolini sweeping the Fascists to power in 1922 with the March to Rome by his Black Shirts, an armed squad of war veterans. The game was seen as a symbolic clash between the old democratic order of England and the thrusting totalitarian state which Mussolini had created.

Before the kick-off the English players had lined up in front of Mussolini's special tribune in the stands and gave the naval salute to the Italian leader. The PNF Stadium was shaking as 50,000 boomed out 'Duce, Duce, Duce' – 'Leader, Leader, Leader' – in reverence to their dictator. Elland Road on a Saturday afternoon must have seemed a long way away.

England trainer Larry Edwards, who was attached to Derby County, revealed that he had devised a special diet for the players to help them cope with the heat they

Billy Furness.

Billy Furness, sixth from the right, lines up with a dapper England squad at London's Victoria Station before heading off to Italy in 1933.

expected to face in Rome, although he declined to say exactly what the diet consisted of. But it was rain, rather than sun, that was a problem for goalkeeper Hibbs early in the game. After just four minutes he slipped on the wet turf and let a shot from Giovanni Ferrari slip under his body. England kept their heads and on 23 minutes equalised through Bastin, and that is how it stayed until the end. In retrospect it was a good result for England as Italy were crowned world champions the following year.

It had been a clash of political and football ideologies, with the Rome crowd not taking a liking to the tackling of the excellent Copping, who snuffed out the Italian right wing. Furness, by all accounts, had a quiet game. The following day the England party were invited to a reception, and each shook hands with Mussolini before the group had an audience with the Pope, Pius XI, before taking a train to Milan for the onward journey to Berne.

It was to be Furness's only England appearance – an experience shared by centre-half White, who pulled a muscle during the game and was replaced for the Switzerland game by Chelsea's Peter O'Dowd. Furness reported back to Elland Road for the new season in peak fitness. He was still only 24 and enjoyed another sparkling campaign in 1933–34, missing just one game and scoring eight goals, two of them coming in the club's biggest League victory, an 8–0 crushing of Leicester on 7 April.

With Bastin now installed as an inside-forward by England, there was no way back into the international scene for Furness, who continued to churn out top-quality club performances for Leeds. After 233 League appearances and 62 goals, he was transferred to Norwich City in summer 1937 for £2,500. Ironically, it was against the Canaries that Furness had fractured a collarbone in a fourth-round FA Cup defeat in 1935. He played for Norwich before and after the war, hanging up his boots one short of a century of appearances for the East Anglians. By this time he had already qualified as a coach for the Norfolk County FA and had gone into business as an electrical masseur.

Norwich employed him as assistant trainer, then head trainer until 1955 when he took on the role of physiotherapist. In 2003 he was inducted into the Norwich City Hall of Fame, but it was with Leeds United that he enjoyed his best playing days, which led to his sole England cap.

JOHNNY GILES
(Republic of Ireland 1959–79)
Midfield
Born: Cabra, Dublin, 6 January 1940.
Caps: Manchester United 11, Leeds United 32, West Bromwich Albion 7, Shamrock Rovers 9. Total: 59
Goals: 5

JOHNNY Giles is the greatest Republic of Ireland player ever – and that's official. He was chosen by the Football Association of Ireland as their top man for the UEFA Jubilee Awards in November 2003. Very few would argue with the FAI's choice, as the Leeds United midfield maestro had a massive influence on his country's fortunes for the best part of 25 years as a player, then manager.

Giles's partnership with Billy Bremner was the best midfield combination ever seen at Elland Road and was at the core of the glittering Don Revie era. No player in Leeds colours has passed the ball better than Giles. In Ireland, it is said that he only had two passes – fantastic and brilliant. Right foot, or left, it did not matter, he could manipulate the ball to go exactly where he wanted. But there was more to his game than precision passing. His awareness and reading of a game were unparalleled, he packed a punch in his shot and could get his foot in to tackle when required.

They were talents that Manchester United let slip through their fingers after letting him join Leeds for £33,000 in August 1963. Red Devils boss Sir Matt Busby is reckoned to have said it was the biggest mistake of his managerial career letting Giles leave Old Trafford.

Johnny Giles.

Giles's dad, Christy 'Dicky' Giles, had played for Bohemians and managed Drumcondra, and clearly young Johnny inherited his football talent at an early age. He shone with a succession of junior clubs in Dublin, including Stella Maris and Home Farm, a club that had a great reputation for bringing on top Irish youngsters.

Manchester United snapped him up on amateur forms as a 15-year-old for just a tenner, and schoolboy international Giles turned pro on his 17th birthday. A broken leg temporarily delayed his progress, but he made his First Division debut in September 1959, three days after Busby's men thrashed Leeds 6–0 at Old Trafford. But it was a harrowing first outing for Giles, as Tottenham won 5–1 on Manchester's own patch.

Giles could play either on the right wing or at inside-right, and by the end of the season was getting more game time, breaking into the full Irish team at 19 and becoming his country's youngest marksman by scoring just 16 minutes into his debut as the Republic fought back from 2–0 down to defeat Sweden 3–2 at Dalymount Park. He quickly cemented his place at club and international level and gained an FA Cup-winners medal in 1963 after a 3–1 win against Leicester City. However, that Wembley appearance was his last for the red half of Manchester, who surprisingly sold Giles to Leeds shortly after the start of the new season. He made an instant impact on his debut against Bury at Elland Road, twinkling on the right wing in a 3–0 victory, and was to play a key role in helping Don Revie's side to the Second Division title. He had been at Elland Road for just over three weeks when he pulled on the green shirt of Ireland for the 12th time in a battling 0–0 draw against Austria in Vienna's Prater Stadium. It was a priceless European Championship qualification point and Giles was at the heart of the Republic's 3–2 victory against the Austrians in Dublin the following month when Noel Cantwell's last-minute penalty winner sparked a pitch invasion.

The quarter-finals paired Eire with Spain, who totally outclassed the Irish 5–1 in the mud of Seville in the first leg before completing a 7–1 aggregate victory with a couple of headers from Barcelona's Pedro Zaballa.

The Saturday after the Republic's second-leg defeat Giles was on target as Leeds won 3–0 at Swansea to clinch promotion. It was just the start of a wonderful 12 years for Giles with the Whites. The skilful United winger continued to rack up appearances for his country as Leeds took the First Division by storm, with their skill, determination and unquenchable team spirit pushing them to the brink of a League and FA Cup double. Ultimately they were to lose the title to Giles's former club on goal average and missed out on the Cup as Liverpool emerged from extra-time 2–1 winners.

Giles had little time to feel sorry for himself. Just four days after that Wembley disappointment he was lining up against Spain again in Dublin. This time it was a World Cup qualifier, and this time Ireland gained revenge for their European Championship hammering with a 1–0 win.

A draw in Spain would be good enough to earn the Irish a place in the 1966 World Cup Finals in England, but it went according to the formbook with a 4–1 Spanish victory, but only after Giles had set up Blackburn's Andy McEvoy for the opening goal to rattle the Spanish.

Aggregate scores did not count in World Cup qualifiers so the two countries met again in a Play-off. Both London and Paris were on the table as proposed neutral venues, but the FAI, who were short of money, accepted Spain's proposal that the Irish would get the gate receipts if the match was played in the French capital. The game went ahead at the Colombes Stadium, with about 30,000 travelling Spaniards making it a virtual home game for their side. Giles had another influential match, but was unable to stop Jose Ufarte scoring the only goal 11 minutes from the end.

Giles was to cross swords with several members of the Spanish team again as United faced Valencia and Real Zaragoza in their first venture into the Inter Cities Fairs Cup. That competition brought about a major sea-change in Giles's career, as United's veteran play-maker Bobby Collins broke a thigh in the first round against Torino, prompting Revie to move Giles in from the wing to a more central role. The Irish star was a revelation in his new role alongside the dynamic Bremner as the pair seized control of matches from the first whistle, with Giles able to unfold his complete repertoire of incisive passing. United were battling away on all fronts, both in Europe and at home, so for the likes of international regulars like Giles the workload was immense over the course of a season.

Spain and Giles's Ireland seemed permanently intertwined as the next European Championship draw put the two countries together with Czechoslovakia and Turkey in Group One.

The old sparring partners slugged out a dull goalless draw in Dublin before Giles celebrated his 25th appearance for his country by beating Turkey 2–1 at Dalymount Park on 16 November 1966. Giles was absent for the 2–0 defeat in Spain, but was back for the away game against Turkey in Ankara, which the Turks won to virtually end Ireland's qualification hopes.

Giles missed both defeats against Czechoslovakia and injury ruled him out of almost the first half of the 1967–68 season, but he soon got back into his stride, helping United lift the League Cup by beating Arsenal 1–0. The Republic had struggled in Giles's absence, but he was back in the midfield cockpit as they began their next World Cup qualifying campaign with a home game against Denmark.

Johnny Giles, in his final Republic of Ireland appearance as a Leeds United player, can only look on as Rudi Elsener cracks in a 1975 European Championship qualifying winner for Switzerland in Berne.

The game kicked off nearly 30 minutes behind schedule because of thick fog, but Scottish referee Willie Syme called it off six minutes after the interval because he could not see his linesmen. It was 1–1 at the time, Giles having got the Irish goal from the penalty spot.

By the time the game was replayed 10 months later, Giles was the proud possessor of a League Championship medal. Leeds had been virtually untouchable in 1968–89, losing only two of their 42 games, and clinched the title with a tense 0–0 draw at Liverpool, their nearest challengers, on Monday 28 April.

Two nights later Elland Road was packed to the rafters to welcome the new champions, who did not disappoint, Giles scoring the only goal against Nottingham Forest with a brilliant shot. In the course of a magnificent season United had beaten or equalled nine club records – most points (67), most home points (39), most wins (27), most home wins (18), fewest defeats (two, both away, another record), unbeaten at home, 26 goals conceded with only nine at home. Defeats against the Danes, Czechoslovakia and Hungary brought a swift end to Ireland's World Cup qualification hopes, but Giles was about the most experienced player in the squad and led his country for the first time in a 2–1 friendly defeat in Poland on 6 May 1970.

Giles was to skipper the Republic 30 times, and his elevation to leadership provided some consolation after a season in which Leeds finished League runners-up, beaten FA Cup Finalists and European Cup semi-finalists. Ireland, managed by Mick Meagan, had some good players but often struggled when Giles was not around to knit them together. Injury saw him miss four successive internationals – none of which were won – but he returned to lead the men in green out against Italy for a European Championship qualifier in Dublin at the end of a season that had seen Leeds finally lift the FA Cup.

Despite an improved Irish performance they went down 2–1, but Giles did taste success against the Italians in the summer as United won their second Fairs Cup by beating Juventus. The two-leg Final against the Turin side meant Giles missed the Euro games against Austria in which Ireland were thrashed 4–1 at home and 6–0 away, stretching their winless run to 19 games. The sequence was finally broken in that summer's Brazilian Independence Cup competition – which Giles missed – with victory against Iran.

Giles started 1972–73 in superb form as Leeds, given more licence to express themselves than in recent years, produced some magnificent football. He translated that form to the national team in a famous 2–1 World Cup qualifying victory against France in Dublin – the first Irish home win in six years.

Eight days after playing in the Leeds side beaten by surprise packet Sunderland in the 1973 FA Cup Final, Giles and Ireland did well to restrict the other big guns in their group, USSR, to a 1–0 win in Moscow. They then headed to France where, despite missing Giles from their line up, the Emerald Isle men gained their first away point in the World Cup with a 1–1 draw.

That was manager Liam Tuohy's last game in charge, and his long-term replacement was the experienced Giles, who took on the mantle of player-manager. He was in charge for the first time on 21 October 1973 against Poland, and injury meant he watched from the sidelines as his men gave him a winning 1–0 start to his managerial career.

Giles missed a large part of United's 1973–74 title-winning season, which signalled the England-bound Don Revie's departure. Giles was tipped as his successor in many quarters, but Brian Clough was the surprise appointment by the Elland Road board. It proved a mistake and after 44 days Clough and Leeds parted company, with Bolton manager Jimmy Armfield installed as the new boss.

Giles was 34 and, although less mobile than he was, could still pass the ball to perfection and played his part in United's run to the European Cup Final. The 2–0 defeat to Bayern Munich in Paris was his last game as a Leeds United player, but it was clear he still had a lot to offer the game, not least the Republic of Ireland, for whom his final appearance as a Leeds player was in a 1–0 away defeat against Switzerland – a result which virtually killed off the Irish hopes of making the European Championship Finals.

Giles played 515 League, Cup and European games for Leeds, scoring 115 goals – many struck with unerring accuracy from the penalty spot. While the chapter of his fabulous career with Leeds had come to an end, the Johnny Giles story was far from over, as his great influence on his country's fortunes grew even stronger (see International Managers). He had success with West Brom and Shamrock Rovers before playing and coaching in the United States and Canada.

Football certainly runs in the Giles blood. His sons, Michael and Chris, have both played for Shamrock Rovers and he is the brother-in-law of World Cup winner Nobby Stiles, with whom he played at Manchester United. Nobby's son John played for his uncle Johnny at Shamrock Rovers before joining Leeds as a midfielder.

ARTHUR GRAHAM
(Scotland 1977–81)
Winger
Born: Castlemilk, Glasgow, 26 October 1952.
Caps: Leeds United 11
Goals: 2

POPULAR winger Arthur Graham lit up the left flank for Leeds United to belatedly earn a place in the Scottish team. He had thought that day would never come, as he had been banned for life from international football by the

Scottish FA after an infamous incident in Copenhagen in 1975 which ended Leeds skipper Billy Bremner's days with his country.

Three days after Scotland won in Denmark, the FA suspended Graham, his Aberdeen teammate Joe Harper, Bremner, Willie Young and Pat McCluskey after trouble in a Copenhagen nightclub. The actual facts of the case have never been fully explained and although Graham, who had yet to make his debut for Scotland, and Harper were innocent bystanders and were not called by the Scottish FA to give their side of the story, the ban stood.

Graham broke into the first team at Pittodrie as a 17-year-old shortly after joining from Junior club Cambuslang Rangers and, despite having played only five League games, started the 1970 Scottish Cup Final against Celtic. The bold gamble by Dons manager Eddie Turnbull paid big dividends as Graham set up two of the goals in a 3–1 triumph.

Graham was an overnight sensation, and his dazzling wing play soon paved the way for Scottish Youth honours before he came on as a substitute for the Scottish League at Middlesbrough on 15 March 1972, when a couple of Tony Currie goals gave the Football League a 3–2 victory. Graham made his first Under-23 appearance against England on his home ground at Aberdeen in December 1974. The English proved far too strong, winning 3–0, but Graham's next representative action saw Scotland beat Sweden and Romania, both 2–1.

His skill was not just confined to patrolling the touchline; he could cut in and shoot to devastating effect. Ever present in 1974–75 when he was top scorer, a full international call-up came when he was included in the party to travel to Denmark for what turned out to be a nightmare trip.

Back on the domestic scene, Graham won a Scottish League Cup-winners' medal in 1977, when Aberdeen beat Celtic 2–1 in the Final. After more than 200 appearances for Aberdeen, he joined Leeds for £125,000 in July 1977, and at around the same time the Scottish FA lifted the ban on the 'Copenhagen Five'. He was soon feeding in crosses from the left flank for muscular strikers Joe Jordan and Ray Hankin, who started piling in the goals.

At long last he made his full international debut when he came on for Maurice Johnston in a 1–0 defeat in East Germany on 7 September after just four First Division games. Leeds fans were delighted with his dribbling skills, but those who travelled to Birmingham City on 14 January 1978 were hailing his finishing skills too as he scored one of the quickest hat-tricks in the club's history – six minutes – in a 3–0 win.

Scotland qualified for the World Cup Finals, but Graham did not make the trip to Argentina, where Ally MacLeod's men under-performed. It was only after Jock Stein replaced MacLeod that the international door opened again for winger Graham. He made his first start in a 3–2 European Championship qualifying victory against Norway at Hampden Park on 25 October 1978, when Archie Gemmill's late penalty snatched victory.

Injury ruled Graham out of the following month's trip to Portugal, when the Scots went down to a lone Alberto goal, but Graham was back for the Home Internationals, netting his first senior international goal when he scored the only goal against Northern Ireland at Hampden Park with 14 minutes remaining. The games against Wales and England ended in 3–0 and 3–1 defeats, but Graham had done well enough to keep his place for a high-profile friendly against world champions Argentina. For many Europeans it was their first glimpse of a teenager called

Arthur Graham.

Maradona, who was to set the football world alight. Graham's first sight of the squat 18-year-old Argentinos Juniors star was in the tunnel, when he mistakenly thought he was the Argentina mascot.

Once they were on the pitch the Scot had to revise his opinion as Maradona ran the game from start to finish. After just over half an hour he drew gasps of amazement from the Hampden Park crowd when he raced from the edge of his own penalty area to the other end of the pitch to set up Albert Luque. Maradona's close control and speed left Scottish defenders trailing in his wake before he calmly slotted in his first international goal on 70 minutes.

Maradona-inspired Argentina were in command at 3–0 when Leeds man Graham showed what he could do by scoring Scotland's consolation five minutes from the end. After the game Graham and Maradona swapped shirts, and the Argentine's shirt ended up in a plastic bag in Graham's garage for years before he cleaned it up and offered it to the Hampden Museum. Football life came full circle, for Maradona was to return to Hampden 20 years later for his first game in charge as Argentina's coach and once more emerged victorious with a 1–0 win.

Five days after the historic Argentina match Graham switched from the left flank to the right against Norway to accommodate Nottingham Forest's John Robertson, who was among the scorers in a 4–0 romp in Oslo. It was a great finale to a fine season for Graham, who missed only two League games as United finished in ninth place in Division One and reached the League Cup semi-finals. He continued to twinkle on the left for Leeds, who lifted themselves up to fifth in 1978–79 and featured in another Football League semi-final – a case of nearly, but not quite for Jimmy Adamson's side. It was a similar story for Graham, who had lost his Scottish left wing berth to Robertson, but the pair were both included in the 1–1 European Championship home draw with Austria on 17 October 1979. It was to be another 17 months before his next – and last – game for Scotland, when Wales beat the Tartan Army 2–0 at Swansea in a match which saw former Leeds striker Joe Jordan sent off.

Graham was one of the few players to play consistently in the 1981–82 relegation season and the following Second Division campaign before a surprise move back into the top flight with Manchester United, just a couple of months short of his 31st birthday. Leeds banked £45,000 for a player who had given them top-quality service for six years, in which he played 260 games, scoring 47 goals.

Graham enjoyed a couple of seasons at Old Trafford before joining former Leeds teammate Trevor Cherry at Bradford City in June 1985, taking over as reserve and junior coach when he retired in February 1987. He even had a brief spell as caretaker manager following the dismissal of Terry Dolan in January 1989. He then coached at Halifax Town, ran a physiotherapy business and worked at the Leeds United Academy at Thorp Arch.

Arthur was not the only footballer in the Graham clan. His brother Tommy enjoyed a decent career as a midfielder with Motherwell, Aston Villa, Barnsley, Halifax, Doncaster and Scarborough; Jimmy figured with Bradford City and Rochdale, and David turned out for Queen's Park in Scotland.

EDDIE GRAY
(Scotland 1969–76)
Winger
Born: Holyrood, Glasgow, 17 January 1948.
Caps: Leeds United 12
Goals: 3

JUST 12 caps for Scotland was poor reward for Eddie Gray's fantastic football skills. It would have been many, many more but for injuries and his own club's hunger for glory. With the Whites invariably involved in the chase for silverware on all fronts, Gray became a victim of Leeds United's success as he played in an era in which clubs were not obliged to release players for international duty.

While Scotland would have dearly loved to have had Gray's skills on their left flank more often, he was required for Cup and European action by Leeds, the club who had fought tooth and nail to sign him as a kid. His performances for Glasgow Schools and the Scottish Under-15 side soon had clubs clamouring for his signature. No fewer than 35 teams, including champions Everton, Manchester United, Tottenham, Chelsea, Arsenal and Scottish giants Celtic wanted the precocious young talent on their books. Yet he chose unfashionable Second Division outfit Leeds because he was immediately struck by its family spirit and manager Don Revie's plans for the future when he visited Elland Road with his parents.

Leeds's top scout in Scotland, John Barr, a former Partick Thistle and Queen's Park Rangers defender, was the first to recognise Gray's outstanding talent, and the youngster signed for United as an amateur in 1962 when he was still at school. He arrived at Elland Road with fellow Glasgow Schools player Jimmy Lumsden, Gray's lifelong pal, for the start of an enduring association with the Whites.

Within a year Gray suffered an injury to his left thigh in a reserve game against Sheffield Wednesday and was out of action for 14 months after an operation. So it must have been doubly satisfying for him when he marked his first-team debut as a 17-year-old against the Owls with a goal from 25 yards in a 3–0 win on New Year's Day 1966. Immediately Gray caught the eye with his dribbling and tight control as he skimmed across the surface of a heavy Elland Road pitch. A star was born. It was not long before the first club versus country fixture conflict reared its head. Gray had been picked for the Scottish Youth team, but had to pull out as he was making his Inter-Cities Fairs

Cup debut in the semi-final first leg against Real Zaragoza in Spain.

Gray's football education continued with a couple of goals on his Scotland Under-23 debut in a 6–0 rout of Wales at Wrexham in November 1966 and he was a key figure in the 3–1 victory against England Under-23s at Newcastle three months later. At this stage Gray was playing a more midfield role as the left wing slot for Leeds was held by the lightning quick Albert Johanneson, but 1967–68 proved a breakthrough season for Gray as he moved out to the flank and occupied that position when Leeds won the League Cup by beating Arsenal 1–0.

By the time Gray returned to Wembley the following year for his full international debut against England, Leeds had won the Division One title and the Fairs Cup. It was the first time that an England versus Scotland clash had been televised live, and so Gray's debut display had an audience of millions rather than the 89,902 inside Wembley.

The world champions put on a wonderful performance which the Scots, led by Gray's club captain Billy Bremner, could not live with. The two Leeds men were the pick of a Scottish side beaten 4–1, and the promising Gray had the satisfaction of supplying the cross which Colin Stein planted past Gordon Banks, who was winning his 50th England cap. On the same evening Scotland's hopes of qualifying for the World Cup Finals received a hammer blow as group rivals West Germany beat Austria to severely undermine the Tartan Army's chances of a trip to Mexico.

A week after the England defeat Gray pulled on the dark blue jersey again as Scotland rekindled their World Cup hopes by crushing Cyprus 8–0 at Hampden Park. Gray opened the floodgates with the first goal and Stein helped himself to four goals as Scotland ran up their biggest margin of victory since 1901. However, the scoreline was put into perspective the following Wednesday when Germany hammered the hapless islanders 12–0, to run up a record World Cup score. That meant Scotland's qualification for the Finals depended on the outcome of their final two group games in Germany and Austria.

The key match was in Hamburg where Scotland, unbeaten against Germany in six matches, looked capable of earning the victory they needed. Gray helped give Scotland a flying start when goalkeeper Sepp Maier saved his 25-yard shot, and little Celtic wizard Jimmy Johnstone put in the rebound.

Defender Klaus Fitchel equalised, Bremner and Tommy Gemmell both hit the woodwork and Gerd Muller's header put Germany 2–1 up. The Scots refused to lie down and Alan Gilzean headed them level just after an hour to set up a thrilling finish to the game. But it was Germany who secured victory 11 minutes from the end with Reinhard Libuda's goal to break Scottish hearts. To rub salt into the Scots' wounds full-back Gemmell was sent off by Swiss referee Gilbert Droz near the end.

The result meant that Scotland's game in Vienna on Bonfire Night was immaterial, but it did feature three Leeds players – Gray, Bremner and Peter Lorimer, who made his international debut as a substitute for Wolves striker Hugh Curran. Austria won 2–0, Helmut Redl netting both goals.

For many, Gray was at his peak in 1970 as Leeds were scrapping to land an historic treble of European Cup, League and FA Cup. Fighting on three fronts led to a crippling fixture pile up – not helped by three epic FA Cup semi-final encounters with Manchester United – as the season reached its climax. Matters were not helped by an earlier-than-normal scheduled end to the campaign to accommodate England's preparations for the World Cup.

Leeds ultimately fell behind Everton in the closing stages of the title race and the game was already up when Don Revie fielded an understrength side for the visit of Burnley a week before the FA Cup Final against Chelsea. The Leeds public, knowing that it would be mainly a reserve side, stayed away in droves, but the absent thousands missed a couple of stunning Gray goals. Only 24,691 were in Elland Road to witness two of the greatest goals to grace the famous old stadium.

The winner was an amazing solo effort as a series of feints, tricks and flicks manoeuvred Gray from the left goalline into a shooting position, from which he sent the ball hurtling past goalkeeper Peter Mellor with his right foot. But the player himself reckons his opening goal against the Clarets gave him most satisfaction, instantly controlling the ball under pressure 35 yards from goal and chipping the ball to perfection over the head of Mellor, who had strayed off his line.

Gray took that kind of mesmerising magic in his boots to Wembley the following Saturday where, despite tormenting Chelsea defender David Webb mercilessly with his trickery in another brilliant display, Leeds were held to a 2–2 draw. When the replay at Bolton's Burnden Park came round 18 days later Chelsea designated the rugged Ron 'Chopper' Harris to take care of Gray and, irony of ironies, Webb headed the winner in extra-time.

Leeds ended an arduous campaign empty-handed and with the Home Internationals played over a week in April none of their players were available for the tournament.

Although Leeds made a blazing start to the 1970–71 season, it was a frustrating time for Gray, who pulled a muscle in a 2–0 derby win over Huddersfield and was out for a month. Three games into his return he fractured an ankle and spent a week in hospital before hobbling around on crutches for a further 10 weeks, making his comeback in the controversial 2–1 home defeat against West Brom which handed the initiative in the title race to Arsenal. The decision by referee Ray Tinkler to allow the Baggies' second goal – which was offside – sparked a pitch invasion which led to United having to play their opening four games of the following season away from Elland Road.

There was more pain to follow for Gray as a long-standing shoulder injury came to the fore. It popped out in a League game against Southampton and trainer Les Cocker was able to work it back into the socket, but it was clear that Gray was going to need an operation in the summer to solve the problem.

In the meantime he nursed his way through games, including the Home Championship match against Northern Ireland. Heavy rain on top of a dusty pitch made the Hampden surface treacherous, and the Leeds winger hurt his shoulder once more as he slipped when avoiding a tackle

from George Best. A similar thing happened again in Turin in the summer when the first leg of the Fairs Cup Final against Juventus had to be abandoned because of torrential rain, ruling Gray out of the replay and second leg, in which Leeds went on to lift the trophy for a second time.

Gray did not resume action until October, but saw out the season without any further mishap and won a coveted FA Cup-winners' medal. He also got back into the Scotland team, which was now under the guidance of Tommy Docherty, who, when he was Chelsea's manager, had been one of the men desperate to sign Gray as a kid.

The Leeds winger was in the Doc's team to face Belgium in Aberdeen in the last European Championship

Eddie Gray has another international defender spellbound.

qualifying game. Scotland, who could not qualify, won 1–0 in a match which signalled the start of Kenny Dalglish's illustrious international career when he came on for Alex Cropley. Gray figured in a friendly against Holland in Amsterdam the following month when the Dutch snatched a 2–1 victory through Barrie Hulsoff in the 87th minute. George Graham, later to manage Leeds, hit Scotland's goal. But it was to be Gray's last appearance for his country for four years – a period covering 40 international games, including the 1974 World Cup Finals. The thigh injury that had plagued him since he was a teenager returned to haunt him and his games for Leeds became more infrequent.

Just a few weeks into United's 1973–74 title-winning season Gray went under the knife again, and although he was still only 26 his future was on the line when Brian Clough took over as Revie's successor. In his first team meeting with the squad Clough said that if Gray was a racehorse he would have been shot long ago. Gray had not long to run on his contract and was steeling himself for the worst, but Clough's controversial reign only lasted 44 days and his replacement, Jimmy Armfield, offered Gray new hope.

Gray had virtually given up the game, but Armfield asked him to help with coaching the club's juniors, which developed into playing reserve games with them. It went so well that Gray made a comeback in a third-round FA Cup tie against Cardiff, scoring the opening goal in a 4–1 win. With confidence restored, he regained his place on the left wing with his younger brother, Frank, playing behind him at left-back. Although both missed out in the starting line up for the European Cup Final against Bayern Munich in Paris, the sibling combination continued to thrive as United finished fifth in 1975–76.

Gray senior made a triumphant return to the Scottish ranks on 6 May 1976, heading in Joe Jordan's cross for the final goal as Wales were beaten 3–1 at Hampden Park. The Scots were on a roll and Gray savoured a 2–1 win against England which wrapped up the home title.

The following September Gray was on target for his country again as the Scots crushed Finland 6–0 at Hampden to stretch their unbeaten run to nine games, and he made his farewell appearance for Scotland a couple of months later in a World Cup group game against Wales, in which Dalglish's backheeled effort went in off visiting defender Ian Evans for the only goal of the game.

Gray was still not 30, but after Ally MacLeod took over as Scotland's manager from Willie Ormond in May 1977 it was the end of the international road for Gray. United's purchase of Arthur Graham, an out-and-out left winger, put Gray's place at Leeds under threat, but he was such a good player that Armfield, and his successor Jimmy Adamson, were able to accommodate the likeable Scot in the United team.

Gray and Paul Madeley were now the senior pros in the Leeds squad, which inevitably could not scale their heights

of the Revie era. As United went into decline, Gray was switched to left-back by new manager Allan Clarke to shore up a struggling defence, but for all his experience Gray could not prevent Leeds sliding into Division Two in 1982.

Clarke lost his job, and the Leeds board turned to Gray to get them back up. United were short of money, and player-manager Gray dipped into the junior ranks to bring through exciting new talent like John Sheridan, Scott Sellars, Denis Irwin and Tommy Wright. Gray ended his Leeds playing career – in which he was never sent off or booked – in May 1984, but was sacked on 11 October 1985, thus ending 22 years with the club.

His dismissal caused a furore, but Gray, who was awarded the MBE the same year, bowed out quietly, had a short spell with non-League Whitby Town, coached Middlesbrough's reserves and juniors and managed Rochdale and Hull before returning to Leeds as a coach in March 1995.

Gray stepped up to be David O'Leary's assistant in May 2003 and filled the manager's post once again for a six-month period when United were in turmoil. Star names were leaving in droves, and so were managers as O'Leary, Terry Venables and Peter Reid went in quick succession as United sank deeper into the mire on and off the field.

Gray, the only man to managed the club twice, could not save them from relegation and left the club, but maintained a watching brief over his beloved Leeds United as a summariser for Radio Leeds. When the BBC lost the rights to live radio broadcast of Leeds matches, Gray moved to the club's official radio station, Yorkshire Radio, as a matchday analyser. No one could be better placed to pass judgement on Leeds United than a man whose one-club playing career encompassed 579 games and 69 goals, as well as an unblemished disciplinary record.

Gray is unquestionably one of the most popular and skilful players to pull on a white shirt. In his pomp he was a sight to behold for Leeds and Scotland fans. He would approach an opposition full-back, shoulders hunched, arms thrust out to perfect his balance, and drift past his marker with a twitch of his body or a change of pace or a piece of unfathomable ballwork or a combination of the lot. He was simply unforgettable.

FRANK GRAY
(Scotland 1976–83)

Full-back / Midfield
Born: Castlemilk, Glasgow, 27 October 1954.
Caps: Leeds United 7, Nottingham Forest 7, Leeds United 18. Total 32
Goals: 1

ALTHOUGH often overshadowed by older brother Eddie at Elland Road, Frank forged a much more productive international career. In many ways his early days mirrored that of his star sibling, with a raft of clubs chasing his signature as a kid, the decision to join Leeds United, a goal on his full debut and Under-23 caps which were followed by the elevation to full international status. But while Eddie remained a one-club man, Frank won a European Cup medal under Brian Clough at Nottingham Forest before returning to Leeds for a second spell. He won 25 of his 32 Scottish caps as a United player and featured in the 1982 World Cup after making the left-back position his own.

Gray junior represented Glasgow and Scotland Schools, trained with Glasgow Celtic and even served as a ball-boy at Parkhead. Although the Hoops were hopeful that young Gray would stay in Scotland, he opted to follow his brother to Elland Road, signing apprentice forms in May 1970 and turning pro the following year.

A supreme athlete, it was not long before he was knocking on the first-team door, coming on as a sub in a 2–0 defeat at Leicester in February 1973. But the outcome on his full debut was far happier, as he rattled in United's third goal in a 4–0 demolition of Crystal Palace on 21 April in front of a delighted Elland Road crowd, who instantly knew they had another Gray gem in their hands. Although he was in the injury-hit United line up that sank to a controversial defeat against AC Milan in the European Cup-winners' Cup Final, Gray only had a handful of senior games to his name when he won his first Under-23 cap against England at Newcastle.

He was a skilful left-sided midfielder, highly mobile, possessor of an excellent range of passing skills and was decent in the air. But with the likes of Billy Bremner and Johnny Giles running matters in the middle of the park, Gray had to be patient. An injury to Terry Cooper prompted Leeds boss Jimmy Armfield to try Gray at left-back in the 1974 Boxing Day game against Burnley. Although United were held 2–2, Gray took to his new role like a duck to water. With Gray senior returning to the side after injury, the brothers provided an excellent left-flank partnership, and Frank got the nod over Trevor Cherry to wear the number-three shirt in the European Cup Final against Bayern Munich in Paris.

The old Revie team was being disbanded, but Gray, along with fellow young Scots Joe Jordan and Gordon McQueen, was seen as crucial to the development of the new-look Leeds. Gray was a League ever-present when Leeds finished fifth in 1975–76 and, after a string of excellent displays which helped Scotland reach the quarter-finals of the Under-23 European Championship, it was a question of when, rather than if, he would gain his full international spurs. His chance came on 7 April 1976 when eight of Willie Ormond's 18-strong party pulled out of the friendly against Switzerland at Hampden Park. Gray was one of five new caps that secured a 1–0 win in front of only 15,531 fans, thanks to Willie Pettigrew's strike after

just 90 seconds. The only downside for Gray was that he did not make his debut alongside brother Eddie, who was one of those who withdrew.

While injuries were to blight Eddie's career, the consistent Frank stayed clear of the treatment table and missed only one game in both the 1976–77 and 1977–78 seasons, but it was insufficient to earn a ticket to Argentina for the World Cup Finals. Scotland boss Ally MacLeod preferred Willie Donachie, Martin Buchan, Sandy Jardine and Tom Forsyth to 23-year-old Gray. Scotland lost 3–1 to Peru when Donachie was suspended and were held to an embarrassing 1–1 draw by Iran before restoring some pride with a 3–2 victory against Holland. MacLeod used three different left-backs in the tournament, so it was clear the position was up for grabs. The much-criticised Scotland manager quit after the first post-World Cup game, a 3–2 defeat in Austria.

In stepped Jock Stein, who quit his job as Leeds United manager after just 44 days – the same time-span as Brian Clough's ill-fated reign at Elland Road – to take charge of Scotland. Stein's appointment may have been bad news for Leeds, but it reopened the door to international football for Gray, who was to become a regular under his former club boss.

Gray played in Stein's first game in charge, a thrilling 3–2 win over Norway at Hampden on 25 October 1978, 28 months after his first Scotland appearance. All 11 players who pulled on the Scottish shirt that night were with English clubs. The Leeds left-back then played in a 1–0 European Championship qualifying defeat in Portugal

Frank Gray.

and all three Home Internationals at the end of the season, also coming on on in Argentina's Maradona-inspired 3–1 win at Hampden.

With Leeds struggling on the financial front, the Elland Road board accepted a record £475,000 bid from Nottingham Forest, managed by the incomparable Brian Clough, for Gray in the summer. The player probably needed a new challenge and responded in style at the City Ground, but tasted defeat in a third successive Final when Forest lost 1–0 to Wolves in the League Cup at Wembley. He did not have to wait long to win his first medal, however, as he played at left-back in the Forest side which beat Hamburg in the European Cup Final, thus becoming the first player to appear in the Final for two different English clubs. He also played in the European Super Cup Final when Clough's men defeated Barcelona.

After two seasons in Nottingham, Gray was brought back to Leeds by manager Allan Clarke for £300,000 in May 1981, the deal going through just after he played in Scotland's 2–0 loss against Wales in Swansea. He then played in the 2–0 win against Northern Ireland before enjoying a sweet victory at Wembley against the Auld Enemy, courtesy of John Robertson's 64th-minute penalty. Despite the victory, the Home Internationals did not reach a conclusion as England and Wales refused to play in Belfast because of security concerns.

Gray had continued to feature for Scotland when at Forest and was a key man in their bid to reach the World Cup Finals in a group containing Sweden, Northern Ireland, Israel and Portugal. The Scots took a huge stride towards their goal with a 2–0 home win over Sweden and then took the point they required to qualify in a hard-fought goalless draw with Northern Ireland.

Although Gray had the World Cup Finals to look forward to, the future was looking bleak for Leeds United. They were struggling to score goals and were involved in a bitter relegation scrap by the time Gray netted his only goal for Scotland – from the penalty spot – in a 2–1 win against Holland in a Glasgow friendly on 23 March 1982.

United's relegation was confirmed two months later, but Gray had no time to dwell on that as he headed to Spain to confront Brazil, New Zealand and the Soviet Union in group six. The Scots kicked off with a 5–2 win over the Kiwis in Malaga, but despite taking the lead through David Narey's superbly struck shot, Brazil fought back impressively in 90-degree heat to win 4–1, Eder's chip over goalkeeper Alan Rough being the pick of the goals. With the Soviets beating New Zealand 3–0, Gray and his Scottish colleagues knew their goal difference was not good enough and they would have to win their final group game.

Joe Jordan put Scotland ahead, but Aleksandr Chivadze levelled on the hour, and a mix-up between Alan Hansen and Willie Miller six minutes from the end enabled Ramaz Shengelia to race through to put the Soviets 2–1 up.

Souness's late goal rescued a draw, but it was not enough and Scotland were eliminated on goal difference for the second tournament running. When Gray reported for training at the start of 1982–83 season his brother Eddie was in charge as player-manager. Although he had dropped into Division Two, Frank kept his place in the Scotland side.

Hampden Park was undergoing reconstruction work, and the capacity was temporarily cut to 57,000 for the first post-World Cup game, a European qualifier against East Germany. Scotland showed no ill-effects from their summer disappointment and played well to win 2–0 in driving rain and high winds.

A 2–0 defeat against Switzerland on a mudbath pitch in Berne was a setback, but worse was to follow for Scotland – and Gray in particular. Jock Stein's men twice took the lead in Brussels with great goals from Kenny Dalglish, but each time Belgium hit back to level through Erwin Vandenbergh and West Ham's François Van Der Elst. In the second half Van Der Elst put his team ahead, but 12 minutes from the end Walter Meeuws fouled Souness in the penalty area. Gray saw his penalty kick saved by Jean-Marie Pfaff, who denied Scotland a point and extended Belgium's undefeated home run to 17 games.

After successive away defeats Scotland needed to get their qualification plans back on track against Switzerland at Hampden. They trailed 2–0 after an hour and were glad of a point thanks to strikes from John Wark and new Celtic star Charlie Nicholas.

Gray was in the side that won 2–0 in Cardiff – Scotland's first win in Wales for a decade – and lost to goals by Bryan Robson and Gordon Cowans at Wembley. The Scots then headed for a three-game series against Canada in June. Gray missed out on the first match, a 2–0 win on an artificial surface in Vancouver, and the last, when two goals from namesake Andy Gray earned victory in Toronto.

In between, Gray made his final international appearance in a curious game in Edmonton. Goals from Nicholas, Souness and defender Richard Gough saw the Scots to an easy 3–0 win, but confusion reigned when referee Roland Fusco blew for half-time after only 41 minutes.

Gray stuck with Leeds for another season in the Second Division, but after 405 appearances and 35 goals in two spells with the Whites he was sold by his brother to Sunderland for a much-needed £100,000. He spent four seasons at Roker, helping the Black Cats to the Division Three Championship before going to Darlington as player-coach, then manager, pushing his League career appearance tally to nearly 650. After a period in Bahrain with the Al Manannah club, he managed Farnborough, Grays Athletic, Woking and Basingstoke Town.

Frank's son, Andy, also played with Leeds, Nottingham Forest and Sunderland, as well as winning a couple of Scottish caps and figuring in big-money moves to Sheffield United, Burnley and Charlton. His nephew Stuart, Eddie's son, played for Celtic, Morton, Reading and Rushden, while Eddie's other son, Nick, was also on Leeds's books. The Gray clan have certainly served Leeds with great honour.

BRIAN GREENHOFF
(England 1976–80)
Midfield/defender
Born: Barnsley, 24 April 1953.
Caps: Manchester United 17, Leeds United 1. Total: 18

BRIAN GREENHOFF flew halfway round the world to play just two minutes of football for England. It was his only cap as a Leeds United player, coming in a friendly at the Sydney Cricket Ground to celebrate the centenary of the Australian FA. An England side shorn of its star names was skippered by Greenhoff's captain at Elland Road, Trevor Cherry, and beat the Socceroos 2–1 in the first football meeting between the two countries. It was looking like a wasted 21,000-mile return trip for Greenhoff before manager Ron Greenwood sent him on to replace midfielder Bryan Robson in the 88th minute. Not surprisingly, it earns him the dubious distinction of being the player with the shortest international career while at Leeds. For Greenhoff it was his 18th and final cap, the rest being won while he was at Manchester United, the club he joined as a boy.

While he was at Old Trafford, his older brother Jimmy was forcing his way into the Leeds team. Both Greenhoffs had played for Barnsley and Yorkshire Schools and, with their striking fair hair, were similar in looks, but they did different jobs on the pitch. While bustling Jimmy was a clever and tricky forward, the calmer Brian occupied either a defensive or midfield role with his more modest skills.

While Jimmy was helping Leeds to beat Arsenal in the Football League Cup Final in 1968, Brian was on the sidelines acting as a 14-year-old Wembley ball-boy. However, he was to return to the Twin Towers several times as a player, with both Manchester United and England.

Brian made his Manchester United debut against Ipswich on 8 September 1973, was soon elevated to England Under-23 status and won his first England cap in a 1–0 win against Wales at Cardiff on 8 May 1976, retaining his place for the 4–0 win over Northern Ireland at Wembley three days later. He was all smiles coming off the pitch after the Irish game – a sharp contrast to the previous week when he trudged off in tears after Southampton's shock FA Cup Final victory against the Red Devils.

By the time he played in the following year's Cup Final – a victory that denied Liverpool the double – he had become a regular with Don Revie's England. His early games were as a central defender, but his fifth cap saw him

Brian Greenhoff.

deployed as a holding midfielder in a crucial World Cup qualifier in Rome. It proved a disastrous tactic as England were outclassed, with Greenhoff suffering more than most. After the 2–0 defeat he went off with an arm injury in a friendly against Holland, but was back for the Home Internationals in a central defensive role alongside Manchester City's Dave Watson.

After Revie quit England, Greenwood showed less faith in the Manchester United utility player who joined Leeds for £350,000 in August 1979. His time at Elland Road was not a happy one. There was considerable unrest on the terraces as fans became disillusioned with the lack of success, with manager Jimmy Adamson bearing the brunt of their ire. New signing Greenhoff struggled to provide the goods as he was beset by a succession of injury problems, although he did manage to make that long-haul trek Down Under for his last, brief, hurrah with England. His only goal for Leeds was a real cracker, smashing the ball past Peter Shilton to defeat Nottingham Forest in December 1980, but that was a rare moment of delight for injury-hit Greenhoff, who struggled to live up to his big fee.

With Leeds heading for relegation, Greenhoff went to play in Hong Kong on loan and eventually joined Rochdale shortly after brother Jimmy was appointed manager at Spotland. For many, Jimmy, who also had a successful spell at Old Trafford, was the better of the two brothers, but he did not win an England cap. Injury forced Brian to call it a day in March 1984 and he's since run a pub in Rochdale and a snooker centre in Manchester, worked as a rep for a sports goods manufacturer and run a restaurant on the island of Menorca.

Leeds fans did not see Greenhoff at his best, with just 78 appearances spread over a four-year period at a time when the club was in decline. And if you blinked you would have missed him in his only outing for England as a Whites player.

ALF-INGE HAALAND
(Norway 1994–2001)
Midfield/Defender
Born: Stavanger, Rogaland, 23 November 1972.
Full-back/Midfield
Caps: Nottingham Forest 23, Leeds United 10, Manchester City 1. Total: 34

AFTER playing a major role in unbeaten Norway's qualification programme, Alfie Haaland suffered the crushing disappointment of missing the 1998 World Cup Finals. The Leeds United player had featured in six of the eight games as Norway topped a difficult group six in style, but he surprisingly did not make Egil Olsen's squad of 22 for France, particularly as he could play in both defence and midfield.

Haaland kicked off his club career with Bryne and represented his country at youth level as a central defender

against Italy in May 1990. He won 29 caps at Under-21 level, scoring three goals against Malaysia, San Marino and England, the latter coming in a 2–0 Norwegian victory at Peterborough in October 1992. He was keen to progress his career in England and had trials with Nottingham Forest in January 1994, which paved the way for a £250,000 move. It was not long before Haaland won his first full cap, in a goalless draw with Costa Rica in San Diego as Norway prepared for the World Cup Finals in the United States later that year.

Haaland's second cap was as a substitute against England at Wembley, again in the heart of the defence, when he blunted the threat of Alan Shearer and Peter Beardsley in another goalless draw. Forest's new man had only managed three games in their Second Division promotion season, but had played himself into Norway's World Cup squad. He played in the 1–0 win against Mexico and the 1–0 defeat against Italy, but was missing for the 0–0 draw which saw Norway eliminated, paying a harsh price for their defensive tactics.

A revitalised Forest finished third in their first season back in the top flight and reached the quarter-finals of the UEFA Cup, going out to eventual winners Bayern Munich. But despite Haaland enjoying an excellent season, they were relegated in 1997 and George Graham stepped in with a transfer deadline day offer. A transfer tribunal settled the fee at £1.6 million. United had acquired a versatile seasoned international with 23 caps to his name who developed a cult following at Elland Road as fans loved the way he went about his business on the pitch: tough, uncompromising, but willing to do any job his manager asked of him. He settled into a central midfield role and came up with several important goals, including two against Blackburn Rovers in March, the second a thumping 35-yard drive. Leeds finished fifth in the Premiership and Haaland was looking forward to the World Cup only to be left out of the squad, a decision that caused plenty of comment back home in Norway.

Graham's decision to move him into midfield looked as though it impacted on Haaland's international career. Norway preferred to use him as a defender, primarily as a right-back, and his first two internationals as a Leeds player were as a late substitute for United teammate Gunnar Halle, who started as the right-back in the qualifying victories against Finland and Switzerland.

Haaland did get the nod for the full-back berth for a high-profile friendly with France in Marseille on 28 February 1998, which saw Norway come within seconds of a famous scalp. Liverpool's Vegard Heggem put the visitors 3–2 up in the 89th minute, but Zinedine Zidane preserved home pride with an equaliser two minutes into injury time.

Haaland was back on bench duty for a friendly in Brussels the following month and saw about 20 minutes of action in defence, while Halle enjoyed the full 90 minutes

Alf-Inge Haaland.

another barrier to the first team. Leeds were flying in the Premiership, which they led at Christmas before ending up in third place, and Haaland did not fit in with O'Leary's plans. A move was inevitable, and United banked a handsome profit when Haaland joined Manchester City for £2.5 million in the summer. Joe Royle named Haaland as captain, and he soon became as popular with City as he had been at Leeds. But his career was effectively brought to a shattering end in one of the Premiership's most notorious incidents – Roy Keane's infamous revenge 'tackle'. Put Haaland's name into Google and it throws up literally dozens of stories about the fateful Manchester derby on 21 April 2001, which ended with Haaland flat out on the Old Trafford turf.

The feud between the two players had its roots in a typical abrasive Leeds United versus Manchester United clash at Elland Road three-and-a-half years earlier. Keane went to tackle Haaland, but only succeeded in injuring his own cruciate ligament. As Keane lay on the ground Haaland bent over the prostrate Irishman and initially implied that he had dived. On seeing it was an actual injury, Haaland felt it was justice for his reckless tackle.

Keane's season was over, but resentment over what had been said boiled for years, and the Manchester United firebrand exacted full retribution in what he admitted in his autobiography was a premeditated act. Keane's studs went into Haaland's right kneecap, he bent over Haaland, said a few choice words and, without waiting for referee David Elleray to brandish his red card, he walked off. Keane received a three-match ban and a £5,000 fine.

Amazingly, Haaland started City's next game, against West Ham, but had to go off and was never to complete a game again. Although his right knee caught the blow, the impact did more damage to his cartilage and knee on his standing leg. After three operations and two unsuccessful years of rehabilitation, Haaland had to finish.

The sting in the tail came with the publication of Keane's autobiography, in which he admitted wanting to hurt Haaland. The FA found Keane guilty of bringing the game into disrepute, suspended him for five matches and hit him with a £150,000 fine. Haaland and Manchester City considered taking legal action, but to date nothing has come of it. The Norwegian was a tough opponent on the pitch, picking up 11 yellow cards in Leeds's 1998–99 season, but his disciplinary record at international level was impeccable – not a single booking in his 32 Norway appearances.

of the 2–2 draw with Belgium. A fortnight before Norway's World Cup opener against Morocco, Olsen had lined up a friendly against another North African side, Saudi Arabia. But the Norway boss learned little in what turned out to be a farce as Mohammed Al-Daeya and Mohammed Al-Khlawi were sent off inside the first 10 minutes and Norway romped home 6–0. Haaland, who played the full 90 minutes at right-back, was barely tested defensively.

Haaland did not make the Finals, but Halle did, although even he did not get a start as Henning Berg and Stig-Inge Bjornebye were preferred at full-back by Olsen. Norway, who did boast a strong squad, went out in the second round to Italy, and that spelled the end of Olsen's reign. A managerial change was also underway at Elland Road, with Graham moving to take over at Tottenham and his assistant, David O'Leary, moving into the Leeds hot seat.

Just after Graham's departure, new Norway coach Nils Semb recalled Haaland, who played in both October European Championship qualifiers – a 2–1 win against Slovenia in Ljubljana and a disappointing 2–2 home draw with Albania in what was his 30th game for his country. O'Leary, like Graham, utilised Haaland in a variety of positions, but niggling injuries and suspensions led to a stop-start 1998–99 season, although he did gain his last cap as a Leeds player in a 1–1 draw in Egypt in November.

The emergence of another Norwegian, Eirik Bakke, at Elland Road saw Haaland slip down the midfield pecking order in 1999–00, while the arrival of Danny Mills proved

GUNNAR HALLE
(Norway 1987–99)
Right-back / Midfield
Born: Larvik, Vestfold, 11 August 1965.
Caps: Lillestrom 27, Oldham Athletic 25, Leeds United 11, Bradford City 1. Total: 64
Goals: 5

Gunnar Halle.

ASK any Whites fan to draw up a list of players who have turned out for Leeds United and who have scored a World Cup hat-trick then it is a fair bet that the name of Gunnar Halle would not appear on it. The Norwegian made nearly all his 54 international appearances in defence or in an anchor role in midfield, but he did net a treble for his country – about five years before he landed at Elland Road.

It came in quite an historic match, as it was San Marino's first-ever World Cup qualification game, but Norway's 10–0 hammering of the minnows immediately cast doubt over the wisdom of allowing the Sammerrenise to enter the tournament. The people of Oslo certainly voted with their feet, as only 6,511 bothered to turn up at the Ullevaal Stadium on 9 September 1992 to witness a one-sided farce that featured Halle's hat-trick. He was with Oldham Athletic at the time and struck in the sixth, 53rd and 70th minutes to write his name in the international record books. The result proved the springboard to Norway's qualification for the 1994 Finals in the United States, while poor San Marino have yet to register a victory in a competitive match. Their only success was a 1–0 friendly win over fellow minnows Liechtenstein in April 2004.

Halle went on to play in the Finals and, briefly, again four years later in France when he was a Leeds player. Although he was generally regarded as a solid player in English football, his displays for Norway, usually at right-back,

earned him rave reviews in his homeland. As a teenager he attended the elite sports programme at Bjerke Viderengaende School based in Oslo and began his football career with local teams Nesjar and Larvik Turn. In 1985 he joined Norwegian Premier League club Lillestrom, helping them win the League title in 1986 and 1989. His first international saw a 4–0 defeat against Bulgaria in Sofia on 14 November 1987, and the following year he featured in the Norwegian Olympic team run by Tord Grip, who later became assistant to England manager Sven-Goran Eriksson.

Halle made great strides as a right-back and played in World Cup qualifying games against France, Cyprus and Yugoslavia, but the Norwegians failed to make it to Italia '90. Halle was one of the first of the Viking invasion of England in the 1990s and undoubtedly helped pave the way for other Norwegian players to follow him. Standards were much higher in England, and when Joe Royle made Lillestrom a £280,000 offer in February 1991, Halle took the opportunity to join Oldham Athletic. Royle had secured a player with bags of experience – 27 full caps – and the Norwegian slotted in effortlessly on the right of the defence as the Latics stormed to the Second Division title. He stayed at Boundary Park for four seasons, and even though the club were relegated he was still very much involved with the Norwegian national team.

Under manager Egil Olsen, Norway had developed a reputation for being difficult to beat, and their ability to grind out results saw them drive remorselessly towards the 1994 World Cup Finals in the US. After the spectacular start against San Marino, which featured Halle's hat-trick, Olsen knew the games against England and Holland would be the key to qualification. Halle played in a surprise win against the Dutch and was in the side that drew at Wembley – results which gave Norway a great chance of qualification. Belief grew when Halle and his colleagues sank England 2–0 in Oslo, and a 3–0 win in Poznan on 13 October 1993 secured Norway's first appearance in the Finals since 1938.

Halle was included in the squad that flew to the States, their startling run of results having lifted them to second in FIFA's world rankings. These were dizzy heights for Norway, who made a flying start with a 1–0 win over Mexico, thanks to Kjetil Rekdal's long-range 85th-minute screamer. Halle came on for Mini Jakobsen at half-time, his usual right-back spot occupied by Nottingham Forest's Alf-Inge Haaland, later to become a teammate at Leeds. A disappointing 1–0 defeat to 10-man Italy and a goalless draw with the Republic of Ireland saw the Norwegians on the plane home, leaving the thoughtful Olsen to plan his strategy for the European Championships.

Halle and Haaland both remained in Olsen's plans, Halle scoring his fifth Norway goal in a 7–0 thumping of Estonia in February 1995. But it was his consistency at club level that continued to attract the attention of Leeds boss Howard Wilkinson.

United were rebuilding after winning the First Division in 1992, and a £400,000 fee was agreed for the 31-year-old in September 1996. But before everything was signed, sealed and delivered, Wilkinson was sacked, putting the transfer on ice. George Graham took over and two months later resurrected the deal that made Halle a Leeds player. The new manager was quick to use Halle's versatility right across the backline and also played him in a midfield holding role.

Neat and tidy in possession, he soon won over Elland Road sceptics and regained his place in the national team towards the end of the 1996–97 season. Halle made his first Norway appearance for more than two years when he won his 53rd cap in a 1–1 World Cup qualifying draw with Finland in Oslo. The following month Halle lined up against Brazil in the Ullevaal Stadium as Norway claimed a notable scalp with a 4–2 win – two of the goals coming from young Brann striker Tore Andre Flo, who was to play in Leeds's colours a decade later.

Halle's move to Elland Road had unquestionably raised his profile back in Norway, and he was once more an integral part of Olsen's squad. A 4–0 win in Finland clinched a place in the Finals with two games to spare, and Norway ended up as unbeaten group three winners, having conceded just two goals in their eight games.

The veteran Halle played in the remaining 1–0 and 5–0 victories, against Azerbaijan and Switzerland respectively, with performances that effectively guaranteed his place in Olsen's squad for the Finals in France. The big surprise was that he was not joined by Leeds clubmate Haaland.

Norway improved on their showing four years earlier by getting through the group stages. They opened with a 2–2 draw with Morocco, then finished all-square with Scotland at 1–1 before claiming one of the most famous victories in their history. Trailing 1–0 to Brazil with eight minutes left, Tore Andre Flo equalised then won the penalty which enabled Rekdal to hit the winner two minutes from the end. Norway stayed in Marseille for the second round, but a Christian Vieri strike saw Italy knock out the Norwegians, just as they had in 1994. Halle watched all these games from the bench – only getting on for the last eight minutes of the Scotland match in Bordeaux. Approaching his 33rd birthday, Halle could well be forgiven for thinking his international career was over, but even though he was struggling to hold down a first-team place at Leeds, he played in a 2–0 European Championship qualifying victory against Greece in Athens.

At the end of the season he made his 11th – and last – international appearance as a Leeds player in a 6–0 romp against Jamaica in Oslo. The following month he joined United's neighbours Bradford City in a £200,000 move, making his international farewell in a 1–0 win against Lithuania in August 1999. After a brief loan spell with Wolves, Halle returned to Norway to finish his playing career with Lillestrom before being appointed player-coach with Third Division side Aurskog/Finstadbru in 2004. He then worked as assistant coach at Lillestrom and Viking under former Manchester City striker Uwe Rosler, before being appointed assistant manager of Lyn Oslo.

CARL HARRIS
(Wales 1976–82)
Right-winger
Born: Neath, 3 November 1956.
Caps: Leeds United 24
Goals: 1

JET-HEELED winger Carl Harris was fast-tracked into the Wales team at 19. The teenager had only made two League starts for Leeds United before lining up against England at Wrexham in a game to mark the FA of Wales's centenary. It was a rapid rise to international football for a teenager who had turned his back on the professional game because he was homesick for Wales. It was only United's dogged determination that persuaded young Harris to stick at the full-time game – a move which was to bear fruit for both player and club.

Harris's ball skills first surfaced at Cwrtsart Secondary School and earned him a place in the Neath Schools squad, followed by Welsh Schools recognition. He seemed set to follow Brian Flynn, another former Neath Schools player, to Burnley, but was rejected after trials. Leeds stepped in after a recommendation from their veteran Wales scout Jack Pickard and took the speedy winger on trial, but after only a week at Elland Road the homesick Harris returned to South Wales to work in a factory and play junior football. United had liked what they saw during his brief stay in Yorkshire, tracked him down and persuaded him to return to Elland Road. Harris thought it over, agreed, and after serving his apprenticeship turned professional when he was 17.

Leeds boss Jimmy Armfield monitored Harris's progress in the reserves and, after a sub appearance in the European Cup against Hungarian side Ujpest Doza, the youngster got his First Division chance in the final home game of the 1974–75 season when he replaced Johnny Giles against Ipswich and scored the winner. It was Irish star Giles's final League appearances for the Whites, so as the door closed on one United international's League days with Leeds it opened for another. The following week Harris made his first start, wearing the number-nine shirt in a 1–1 draw at Wolves just a couple of days after United's 1–1 draw in Barcelona booked them a place in the European Cup Final. Harris had only added a handful of appearances from the bench to that sole start when, just a few days after his 19th birthday, he was included in the Welsh squad to face Austria in a key European Championship encounter. He did not play, but his blistering pace and ability to take on defenders had been recognised by his country's top brass.

Carl Harris.

A Wales Youth-team regular, he had already represented the Under-23 side against Scotland when he lined up at Goodison Park against Everton on 20 March 1976 for his second League start. A goal in a 3–1 victory – a shot which bounced in off the bar – added to his career impetus. When Derby's Leighton James withdrew from the Wales squad for the prestigious friendly against Don Revie's England the following Wednesday, starlet Harris was given his chance. Both teams were experimental, but it was Harris who made the most impression, with his dangerous runs and a couple of stinging shots, which tested goalkeeper Ray Clemence.

On his return to Leeds he played in all the remaining games that season and added a second Welsh cap when he started at Hampden Park. Clubmate Eddie Gray got on the scoresheet in a 3–1 win. After such a brilliant finale to the season, it was surprising that Harris did not play more regularly in 1976–77, particularly as more players from the Revie era were leaving. But he did not feature on the official first-team squad photo, and although he came on to score in the opening day home draw with West Brom, who had Johnny Giles in their line up, he still found it difficult to break into the Leeds first team.

That was still the case when he gained his third cap in December 1977. Controversially, Wales boss Mike Smith dropped John Toshack and John Mahoney for the trip to Dortmund to take on world champions West Germany. Although it was a friendly, the two countries had been put in the same qualification group for the European

Championships, so it was seen as a bold move by Smith. Klaus Fischer gave Germany a second-half lead, but the determined Welsh gained a draw thanks to a goal from Norwich's David Jones.

With Harris not figuring in the first team, United gave him the thumbs up for the long trek to Tehran to play in Wales's 1–0 friendly win against Iran in April, and although he was still nowhere near a Leeds regular, he played in all three end-of-season Home Internationals. Although on the fringes at Elland Road, he played in eight consecutive internationals, including European Championship games against Malta, Turkey and West Germany. Malta were crushed 7–0 and a goal from PSV Eindhoven striker Nick Deacy saw off Turkey, but the Welsh fell short against West Germany at Wrexham as the West Germans won 2–0. With his moustache making him an instantly recognisable figure, Harris was certainly the 'Tash with the dash'. He was capable of carving open the best defences, but consistency was not his strong suit. He had enjoyed his most productive season in terms of Leeds appearances in 1978–79, but did not feature in the Home Internationals; however, he contributed to Wales's 2–0 win in Malta in June, which saw the principality move two points clear of West Germany in the table. The Welsh subsequently lost in Germany and Turkey – both games Harris missed – and failed to qualify for the Finals in Italy.

The Turkish game in Izmir was an explosive affair in which Harris's clubmate Byron Stevenson was sent off, and there were fears of another brutal battle when the countries found themselves in the same World Cup qualification group, along with Czechoslovakia, Iceland and the Soviet Union. Wales eased to a 4–0 win in Iceland in June 1980, Harris coming on for Gordon Davies to get their campaign off to a flying start. Harris then led the Turkish defence a merry dance as Wales gained revenge for their Euro defeat in Izmir with another 4–0 victory at Ninian Park.

Wales and Harris were on a roll in 1980–81. The pacy winger was United's top scorer with 10 League goals in a season in which Leeds only managed 39 in the First Division. The Welshman's goals were priceless for a struggling Leeds team, particularly at Elland Road, with his strikes against Manchester City, Brighton, Norwich and Sunderland earning vital 1–0 wins.

United were finding victories difficult to come by, but Wales were hitting the back of the net regularly, as Harris appeared in 11 consecutive games for his country, form that saw Arsenal inquire about his availability. Wales made it maximum points from three European Championship games when they edged out the Czechs at Cardiff, Harris coming on for match-winner David Giles. The roles were reversed in Ankara four months later when Giles replaced Harris after the Leeds winger's only goal for his country earned a priceless 1–0 win against Turkey.

Wales were sitting pretty in Europe and took their form into the Home Championships, where two Ian Walsh goals saw off Scotland at Swansea. That was Wales's sixth successive win and Harris had played in them all. The sequence was halted by a goalless stalemate at Wembley, although Harris gave England full-back Kenny Sansom plenty to think about and sent in a couple of superb crosses that almost broke the deadlock.

Wales had put themselves in a position to win the Championship, but both the FA of Wales and England declined to play in Northern Ireland because of security fears amid political unrest so the tournament was not completed for the first time in its history and was declared null and void at a meeting of the Home Associations on 13 June.

By then Wales had picked up another European Championship point when they were held 0–0 by Russia, but it was clear the group was going to be a straight fight between the Welsh, Soviets and Czechs for the two qualification places. Wales lost 2–0 in Prague, but the real damage was done by Iceland in Swansea on 14 October 1982, when the islanders literally dimmed Welsh hopes. The match was hit by a floodlight failure and Wales, who led through Robbie James, had to settle for a 2–2 draw as Asegir Sigurvinsson scored twice for Iceland.

A deflated Wales, without the absent Harris, lost 3–0 in Russia, who then drew in Czechoslovakia 11 days later – a result which saw Wales miss out on qualification on goal difference. Failure to beat Iceland at Vetch Field had been the principality's downfall. Harris made his final appearance for Wales when he came on for Leeds teammate Brian Flynn against England at Cardiff, a Trevor Francis strike giving the English a narrow win.

After United's relegation in 1981–82 they needed money, so it was no surprise when they accepted a £100,000 offer from Charlton Athletic for Harris, whose 176 appearances for Leeds included 40 as a substitute. Ever-present at the Valley in his first season, he began to struggle with a succession of injuries and was released on a free transfer in August 1985.

A return to Leeds looked a possibility when he had a run out in United's reserves, but he was not taken on and joined Bury. He then had trials with Swansea, Cardiff and Airdrie before Eddie Gray signed him for Rochdale. Harris finished his career at Exeter City where another old Leeds hero, Terry Cooper, was the manager. After finishing with full-time football, he played Welsh League football with Briton Ferry, having a spell as player-manager and general manager. Harris later ran a removals business, quite fitting for a winger who could really shift for Leeds and Wales.

ERNIE HART

(England 1928–34)

Centre-half
Born: Overseal, Derbyshire, 3 January 1902.
Died: Leeds, 21 July 1954
Caps: Leeds United 8

Ernie Hart.

IT IS hard to imagine these days that a red card in a County Cup game would see a player dropped by England. But that is exactly what happed to Leeds United's Ernie Hart in the 1930s, when the football authorities took a hardline stance over the centre-half's dismissal in a West Riding Cup game against Bradford City.

Hart had already played for England five times and was the current stopper, having figured in the most recent internationals against Austria and Scotland, when he ran into trouble in the local Final against Huddersfield Town on 26 April 1933. The game was played at Valley Parade, home of Bradford City, and the Terriers won 1–0 with a disputed penalty by Reg Mountford. United skipper Hart was sent off for a few choice words directed at Bradford referee J.E. Mellor, who had given the spot-kick for pushing.

Although it was Hart's only misdemeanor in 13 years with the Elland Road club, the West Riding FA were unhappy that the Final of their own competition, which was only watched by 2,700 people, had been besmirched. England man or not, they made an example of the Leeds skipper at a disciplinary meeting the following Tuesday. He was suspended from 2–6 May and from 26 August–17 September the following season – a total of seven games.

134,170 People see Scotland beat England.

Superior play beats the Sasscnach at Glasgow.

England's Ernie Hart (left) and goalkeeper Harry Hobbs see a shot by Scotland's Jimmy McGrory drift wide during the 1933 international at Hampden Park, which attracted a massive crowd.

Players were not paid during periods of suspension in those days. The ban would also cost Hart £32 in wages, but he was to lose something money could not buy – his place in the England team. In his absence Leeds lost their final game of the season 5–0 at Bolton on 6 May, but the West Riding FA ban had left the door open for Hart to go on England's tour to Italy and Switzerland, for which he had been selected along with Leeds teammates Wilf Copping and Billy Furness, the following week.

In true sledgehammer to crack a nut style, the FA announced the day after the West Riding FA disciplinary meeting that they would not be taking Hart to the Continent. It would take the United defender nearly a year to get back into the national team. The Leeds public were furious with Hart's treatment at the hands of football's top brass. He had become a firm favourite at Elland Road since joining the re-formed United club from Doncaster junior side Woodlands Wesleyans.

The Derbyshire-born former miner was to become a rock at the heart of the Leeds defence after making his debut a month after his 19th birthday at Stockport County. He only missed one game in 1922–23 and helped United win the Second Division title the following year. Hart's excellent displays enabled United to successfully stave off relegation for a couple of years, but injury restricted him to just five League games in 1926–27, and it was no coincidence that the club dropped into the Second Division.

After temporarily losing his place to former Scottish international Tom Townsley, Hart came back stronger than ever as United went up at the first attempt. Not only was he solid in the tackle and in the air, but his passing out of defence was also spot on. He also liked to push forward whenever he could to provide United with another option in their play. United made a great start to 1928–29, and

the FA began to check out Hart, picking him alongside United colleague and England captain Willis Edwards for the Football League versus Scottish League game at Villa Park on 7 November. The England boys won 2–1 in what was effectively an international trial, and the United duo teamed up again 10 days later for Hart's England debut – a 3–2 win against Wales in Swansea. It was the first time that two men from the Elland Road club had played in an England international together.

In summer 1929 Hart and United colleague Bobby Turnbull were in the FA tour party that travelled to Rhodesia and South Africa to play a series of games, including three Test matches, against South Africa. They were not regarded as full internationals, but Hart played in all three games, which were won by England, scoring in the first match, a 3–2 win at Durban's Kingsmead Stadium.

Hart had formed an outstanding partnership at Elland Road with Edwards. Although Hart was the older of the Leeds pair, Edwards, in possession of the England captaincy, was regarded as the more senior player. The combination played for the Football League in September 1929 when the Irish League part-timers were crushed 7-2 at Goodison Park, Birmingham's Joe Bradford getting five of the goals. Not surprisingly, Bradford was in the England team to face Ireland the following month – but so were the Leeds duo, who shone in a 3–0 win in Belfast. In their absence Leeds beat Birmingham 1–0 at Elland Road, a goal from former England international Bobby Turnbull giving United a seventh straight League win.

League games were not postponed because of international call-ups in those days, and the same applied to Football League representative matches. Leeds had made a superb start to the season and showed no sign of weakness a fortnight after the Belfast clash when Hart and Edwards played in the Football League against the Scottish League at Ibrox. While they tasted a defeat, rampant Leeds, complete with stand-ins, thumped Grimsby 6–0. Leeds were looking like title contenders, but lost their next five League games to blow any hope of winning a first Division One Championship. They had to settle for fifth place – the club's best-ever showing in its 10 years as a League club.

Hart had settled in well with England alongside captain Edwards, confirming the solidity of their partnership with a 6–0 beating of Wales at Stamford Bridge, but by the end of the season the selectors had disbanded the Leeds combination in preference of Maurice Webster (Middlesbrough) and Alf Strange (Sheffield Wednesday). Edwards, who had led England in his last five internationals, was never to play for his country again.

Hart must also have thought he would never pull on a white shirt adorned by the crest of Three Lions again as Leeds were relegated in 1930–31. As in previous years, they bounced back at the first attempt, and after an absence of 14 internationals he was picked to face the mighty Austrians at Stamford Bridge.

The game was eagerly anticipated as Austria, unbeaten in 14 games, were regarded as the Continent's best side. Dubbed the 'Wunderteam' and coached by an Englishman, Jimmy Hogan, and Hugo Meisl, the secretary of the Austrian FA, their tactics and skills were said to be further advanced than any of their contemporaries. Their superb unbeaten run had included an 8–2 humiliation of Hungary in Vienna, but England, with just two defeats in 16 games, were no mugs either. It was an intriguing clash of styles between the neat passing of the Alpine side, whom many thought to be the first to play 'Total Football' promoted by the Dutch several decades later, and the more robust approach of England.

Each member of the Austrian team possessed a deft touch and were supreme masters of the ball, none more so than their captain Matthias Sindelar, who would be in direct opposition to Hart. The United defender was expecting a challenging afternoon against the slimline centre-forward Sindelar, nicknamed 'Man of Paper' for his uncanny knack of slipping through defences, and he got it.

The Austrians had breathtaking ball skills and, with Sindelar dropping into midfield, produced some scintillating football. All they lacked was the sort of cutting edge shown by Blackpool's Jimmy Hampson, who netted twice in the opening 26 minutes. Austria, continued to dominate and pulled a goal back through Karl Zischek shortly after half-time. It was all Austria with only the crossbar preventing an equaliser from Walter Nausch, before Eric Houghton of Aston Villa cracked home a free-kick off an Austrian player to make it 3–1.

The sylph-like Sinderlar got his inevitable goal before Sammy Crooks crashed in England's fourth very much against the run of play. Wacker Vienna's Zischek set up a tense last five minutes from close range, but to the relief of the crowd England held out and Austria, despite all their brilliance, had failed to become the first side from mainland Europe to win on English soil.

The match was hailed as the finest ever seen on these shores, and Hart retained his place to face Scotland and the mighty Hampden Roar. The noise from the record 134,170 crowd was deafening as the Auld Enemy locked horns in Glasgow, two goals from Jimmy McGrory swaying the game the Scots' way. Just as Hart looked set for a long run in the England team the West Riding Cup incident set back his international career a year, but his return to the national side saw England gain revenge over the Scots with a comfortable 3–0 Wembley win that signalled the debut of 20-year-old inside-forward Raich Carter, who managed Leeds in the 1950s. It was probably Hart's best performance for England as he subdued the considerable threat of dangerman Hughie Gallacher. The attendance of 92,963 was a then record for an England international, with the match being played in front of the Duke of York, later King George VI.

Hart went on England's European summer tour and played in both games against Hungary and Czechoslovakia, each ending in 2–1 Danubian defeats on hard, grassless pitches. The Czechs, in particular, looked a good side, with their short passing getting behind Hart and his defenders.

Czechoslovakia, like England, had managed a recent victory over Austria, so the game between the two sides was eagerly anticipated. Although Manchester City's Fred Tilson gave England the lead, goals by Oldrich Nejedly and Antonin Puc gave the home side a deserved win. It was England's fourth defeat against foreign opposition, and while they went back to the drawing board the impressive Czechs went on to lose in extra-time to Italy in the 1934 World Cup Final.

Hart was 32 and free to concentrate on his club football with Leeds, staying two more years at Elland Road and taking his total of United appearances to 472 before joining Mansfield Town in August 1936. A couple of years later he was appointed manager at Tunbridge Wells and did a bit of scouting for Coventry, but his main interests now lay outside football. With his savings he bought a bus and launched a coach and haulage business in Doncaster called the Beehive Bus Company. It later became Wilfreda Beehive, whose coaches have been a regular sight in the Elland Road coach park over the years. Hart, who gained three promotions with United, was only 52 when he died in Leeds General Infirmary on 21 July 1954 after a long illness.

IAN HARTE
(Republic of Ireland 1996–2007)
Left-back
Born: Drogheda, Co. Louth, 31 August 1977.
Caps: Leeds United 56, Levante 8. Total: 64
Goals: 11

FREE-KICK specialist Ian Harte helped propel the Republic of Ireland to two World Cups with his dead-ball skills. When the Leeds United defender lined up a shot around the edge of the penalty box it spelled danger for the opposition. His left foot curled in some vital goals for the Republic when he played many games with his uncle, Gary Kelly, an Elland Road teammate and fellow full-back.

Harte followed a well-trodden path from the Emerald Isle to English football. He played regularly for Ireland's Under-16 side before joining Leeds as an apprentice from St Kevin's Boys. He could play in a variety of roles, with coaches at Elland Road trying him out up front, in defence, at wing-back and on the left side of midfield. Eire Under-18 caps soon followed, and Howard Wilkinson gave Harte his first senior run-out as an 18-year-old in the Coca-Cola Cup quarter-final against Reading on 10 January 1996, when he replaced Phil Masinga for the last few minutes and occupied a place in the attack. His uncle Gary, himself only 21, was already on the pitch.

Ian Harte moves in to tackle Portugal's Rui Costa.

It proved to be a major breakthrough and the start of a rapid rise to full international status after skippering the Republic's Under-21s against Norway and Russia. By the time Harte reported for training ahead of the 1996–97 season he had represented his country four times at senior level, yet had made only two starts as a Leeds first-teamer in the left wing-back position. New Republic boss Mick McCarthy was keen to check out all the new talent at his disposal early in his reign. In his fourth game in charge, Harte became the 10th new player to be capped by McCarthy when he came on as a half-time replacement for former United full-back Terry Phelan, in a 2–2 draw with Croatia at Lansdowne Road in June 1996.

McCarthy liked what he saw in that 45 minutes and put him in from the start of the next friendly against Holland in Rotterdam at centre-back, where he was tested by the likes of Denis Bergkamp. Another mature display meant McCarthy had no hesitation in taking Harte on the Republic's summer trip across the Atlantic to take part in the United States Cup. It was a rebuilding process for the Irish as they had failed to make the Finals of Euro '96 in England, and Harte was quick to grab his opportunity in what was a surprisingly competitive tournament played in sweltering heat.

After sitting out a 2–1 loss to the hosts in Boston, Harte played in a bruising 2–2 draw with Mexico in the Giants Stadium, New Jersey, where the Irish had Liam Daish and Niall Quinn sent off and manager McCarthy dismissed to the stands. It was much calmer against Bolivia, and Harte scored his first international goal with a near-post header from a corner in a 3–0 victory just before half-time.

Despite his heroics in the US, Harte was only on the bench for Leeds for the season's opener at Derby, coming on for Brian Deane to score a 20-yarder in a 3–3 thriller. By the end of the month he had added his second international goal as the Republic steamrollered Liechtenstein in Eschen to get their World Cup qualifying campaign off to a good start. The following Wednesday the new rising Irish star's amazing start continued as he scored the only goal as United saw off Blackburn Rovers.

It had been a whirlwind few months for Harte, but the storm blew out a bit after Wilkinson was sacked after eight years in charge and George Graham took over. Harte's Premiership appearances became more limited, but he was regarded by McCarthy as a key man for Ireland and played in all their internationals that season, in a variety of positions. Ireland's results were mixed as they chased runaway group leaders Romania, who made it six wins out of six by beating the Republic 1–0 at the end of April with an Adrian Illie goal. The match was the first international in which the uncle and nephew combination of Harte and Kelly started together. Back in Dublin the following month, the two Leeds lads played against Liechtenstein as Ireland notched a second successive 5–0 win against the minnows, 19-year-old Watford striker David Connelly becoming his country's youngest hat-trick man.

Graham's recruitment of Gunnar Halle and former Scottish international David Robertson made it harder for Harte to get into the Leeds first team, but he continued to do his bit for Ireland, who finished runners-up to Romania and went into a Play-off with Belgium for a place in the Finals. Former Leeds defender Denis Irwin gave Ireland the perfect start in Dublin with a goal after just eight minutes, but Belgium equalised on the half-hour through Luc Nilis and, but for an outstanding display by Shay Given, would have made the second leg in Brussels a formality. But it only prolonged the agony for Harte and his teammates as Nilis scored the winner in Belgium after Ray Houghton had levelled the aggregate scores at 2–2.

Harte had an outstanding Premiership season in 1998–99 as Leeds finished fourth under new manager

David O'Leary to recapture a place in the UEFA Cup. Although he had settled in at left-back at Elland Road, he did not figure in any of Ireland's European Championship qualifiers, his only international action coming in a dominant 2–0 success against Paraguay in a Dublin friendly.

Irwin and Steve Staunton, later to manage Ireland and assist Gary McAllister at Leeds, shared left-back duties for Eire, and that scenario continued in the second half of the qualification campaign. He only made two appearances as a substitute in the eight-game programme in group eight, replacing his uncle Gary in Zagreb, where Davor Suker's injury-time winner dealt the Republic a shattering blow. He then came on just after Staunton had spared Ireland's blushes with a 74th-minute free-kick winner in Malta.

That victory in Valetta had kept Ireland's hopes of topping the group alive, but Harte did not feature in the crucial final fixture when victory in Macedonia, coupled with a Yugoslav defeat in Croatia, would put them through. Once more the luck of the Irish did not materialise. While Croatia and Yugoslavia drew 2–2, Ireland were leading 1–0 in Skopje when Macedonian's Goran Stavrevski equalised with 12 seconds of added-on-time remaining.

For the second successive major tournament Ireland faced the nerve-shredding Play-offs, but Harte sat out both tension-riddled games with Turkey. A late penalty earned the Turks a 1–1 draw in Dublin, and they put up the shutters in Bursa as a goalless draw saw the Irish eliminated on the away goals rule. Harte's only international start that season came on 23 February 2000 in a friendly against the Czech Republic, scoring in a 3–2 victory. But at Leeds he was in prime form, scoring six times in the Premiership – four of them penalties – as his deadball skills and crosses from the left saw United qualify for the Champions League in third place. He topped that in 2000–01 with seven Premiership goals and missed only one game in United's fantastic run to the Champions League semi-finals. Harte's recall to the Irish team was inevitable, and he played in all eight European Championship qualification games, thumping home penalties against minnows Cyprus and Andorra.

The Republic announced their intentions in their opening group game when they attacked Holland in Amsterdam, building up a 2–0 lead inside 64 minutes before having to settle for a draw. A point in Portugal and a routine win against Estonia got the Republic off to a flying start, rubbing home their advantage with away wins against Cyprus and Andorra when Harte tucked away his penalties.

On the day Leeds paid £12 million Inter Milan for Irish striker Robbie Keane, Andorra took a shock lead in Dublin, but Ireland hit back to win 3–1. A home draw with Portugal and a 2–0 win against Estonia on a difficult pitch in Tallin saw Ireland finish the season on top of Group Two. The big showdown with Holland in Dublin on 1 September 2001 would be the make or break of Irish hopes. While England were powering to an historic 5–1 win against Germany in Munich, Harte and the battling Irish sank group favourites 1–0 with a Jason McAteer goal, despite playing a third of the game with 10 men following the dismissal of Gary Kelly. It left the Dutch requiring a miracle to reach the World Cup Finals, leaving Portugal and the Republic to contest top spot. When the last games were played Ireland needed a cricket score against Cyprus or to pray that Estonia could pull off an unlikely win in Lisbon.

Harte got Ireland off to a flier with a third-minute strike, and Niall Quinn marked his 35th birthday by heading his record 21st goal for the Republic, but the men in green had to settle for a 4–0 win. Meanwhile, Portugal thumped Estonia 5–0 to win the group on goal difference, leaving Ireland to face Iran, the Asian runners-up in a Play-off with a place in the Finals at stake. Ireland had home advantage first, and goals by Leeds duo Harte and Robbie Keane earned them a useful, if not conclusive, advantage to take to Tehran the following Thursday. Harte got the show on the road two minutes before the break when he fired in a penalty kick after McAteer was brought down by Rahman Rezaei, then shortly into the second half Keane volleyed in the second.

Ireland held their nerve in front of 110,000 fans five days later, when Iran could only manage one goal, 30 seconds from the final whistle, to earn a place in the Finals for the first time in eight years. McCarthy's men played four friendlies as preparation for the Finals in Japan and Korea. Harte played in them all, and the full-back continued his impressive strike rate for his country with a goal in a 3–0 success against Denmark. But McCarthy's plans were left in tatters when skipper Roy Keane, the Manchester United midfielder, had a training ground bust-up and told the manager he wanted to go home. He then reversed that decision, only to be sent home by McCarthy after launching an abusive tirade on the Republic boss.

Ireland were in danger of imploding a week before they had kicked a ball in anger, but they pulled themselves round and Matt Holland's equaliser earned them a draw with Cameroon in their opening fixture. Harte was suffering from a toe injury and came off before the end, but was fit enough to face Germany in the next match when Aston Villa's Staunton became the first Irishman to win 100 caps. It was a dramatic game, with Leeds striker Robbie Keane scoring in the second minute of injury time to earn Ireland a point.

McCarthy's men eased past Saudi Arabia to move into a second-round meeting with highly fancied Spain. Yet again it was a dramatic match, with Harte at the centre of affairs. Fernando Morientes put Spain ahead, but Ireland were handed the opportunity to equalise in the 62nd minute when Damien Duff was tripped. Up stepped Harte, but the man who was so deadly from the spot for his country saw his shot saved by Real Madrid's Iker Casillas, and Kevin

Kilbane put the rebound wide. Casillas was Spain's second-choice 'keeper and only got his chance because Santiago Canizares had to withdraw from the tournament because of a freak accident.

A weary Harte was withdrawn eight minutes from time as McCarthy went for broke and sent on striker Connelly. The Leeds man watched agonisingly from the bench as the match reached the 90th minute, when Fernando Hierro pulled Niall Quinn's shirt. Most of the Irish bench could not watch as Harte's Elland Road colleague, Keane, slotted in the resulting penalty to send the game into extra-time. With no more goals in additional time, the place in the quarter-finals was settled by spot-kicks. Holland, Connelly and Kilbane all failed to find the net, and Spain went through 3–2 on penalties.

On their return to Elland Road, Irish trio Harte, Keane and Kelly found they were playing for a new manager – ex-England coach Terry Venables, who had replaced David O'Leary, one of Ireland's legendary players. But failure to make the Champions League again had put a massive strain on United's finances, leading to the sale of top players, Keane among them. The mood at Elland Road was one of foreboding, and it was much the same for Ireland fans as their team made a disastrous start to their European Championship campaign, losing to Russia and Switzerland, then struggling to beat Georgia and Albania, the latter also holding the Irish to a goalless draw in Tirana.

Harte's post-World Cup form had dipped, and he was replaced in the national side by Manchester United's John O'Shea and temporarily lost his first-team place at Leeds, before coming back strongly at the end of the season to help United pull clear from relegation. It was only a temporary stay of execution for Leeds, who went down in 2003–04, with Harte in and out of the side. The Republic failed to qualify for the Euro Finals in Portugal, but Harte did find himself back in demand at international level.

The Irish FA arranged no fewer than 10 friendlies during the season as they looked to rebuild, and Harte made his 50th appearance for his country when he came off the bench to help his side come from behind to defeat Australia 2–1 in Dublin. He also added another goal to his impressive tally when the Czech Republic's 20-game unbeaten run was ended by Robbie Keane's last-gasp goal in Dublin on 31 March 2004, which gave Ireland a 2–1 triumph.

Harte, whose superb displays in the Champions League sparked rumours of moves to either Barcelona or AC Milan, did move to the Continent in July 2004 when he joined newly promoted Levante and scored their first goal in La Liga for 41 years in a 1–1 draw with Real Sociedad. Fans dubbed him 'the Bull', but he missed the second half of the season with an ankle injury, and the newcomers were relegated. The club were promoted at the first attempt with Harte in sparkling form.

Harte believed his move to Spain had seen him frozen out of the Irish team, which was being picked by

McCarthy's successor Brian Kerr, a claim denied by the new boss. Harte was eventually chosen during Kerr's brief reign, playing – and scoring – against Israel and the Faroe Islands. He was also chosen by Steve Staunton for his first game in charge – a 3–0 win against Sweden in March 2006 – and played his final game for Ireland 11 months later in San Marino. But injuries were beginning to take their toll and Harte, never the quickest player out of the blocks, was released by Levante in 2007 and joined former Irish teammate Roy Keane at Sunderland. After a year he was released, had trials with Mick McCarthy's Wolves, played a reserve game with Sheffield United, trialled with Charlton and Norwegian club Valerenga and briefly played for Blackpool before joining Carlisle. His top-flight career may have come to a premature end, but he spent some glorious years with Leeds and Ireland, his 11 goals putting him in the all-time Irish top 10 goalscorers list – quite an achievement for a defender.

DAVID HARVEY
(Scotland 1972–76)
Goalkeeper
Born: Leeds, 7 February 1948.
Caps: Leeds United 16

IN SUMMER 1974 Leeds United goalkeeper David Harvey was on top of the world. He was named as the planet's number one after his displays for Scotland in the World Cup. Patience had certainly been a virtue for the Leeds-born player, who waited in the shadow of Welsh international Gary Sprake for the best part of eight years before becoming a United regular towards the end of the 1971–72 season.

Born in Leeds to a Scottish father and an English mother, Harvey attended Foxwood School and was an automatic choice for Leeds City Boys. A week after his 17th birthday he turned pro with United and made his debut in a weakened Leeds side in a Football League Cup third-round tie against West Brom in October 1965, Albion winning 4–2. His League debut came towards the end of that season and again ended in a home defeat as Fulham won 1–0. It was back to a long apprenticeship with the reserves in the Central League, as Sprake held the first-team place in his hands.

Harvey was called up to fill in when Sprake was injured – which was not often – and did not get to play in any of the high-profile games during the early part of the Revie era. That changed when Sprake was injured in the second leg of the European Cup semi-final against Celtic in 1970. The Hoops had been good value for their 1–0 win at Elland Road and forced home their advantage in the second installment of the 'Battle of Britain' in front of a passionate 136,505 Hampden Park crowd – the biggest attendance of any tie in the competition. Celtic held a 2–1 aggregate lead

David Harvey, third left on back row, takes his place in Scotland's 1974 World Cup squad photograph. Also included are Leeds United colleagues Gordon McQueen (far left, back row); Joe Jordan (seventh from left, middle row); Peter Lorimer (far right, middle row) and Billy Bremner (fourth from left, front row).

when Sprake went off after a collision with John Hughes, and the first time Harvey touched the ball was to pick it out of the net after being beaten by Bobby Murdoch's 15-yard drive.

Sprake had not recovered in time to play in the FA Cup replay against Chelsea a fortnight later, when the Blues ruined Harvey's big night with a 2–1 victory in extra-time. It was back to reserve-team duty for most of 1970–71, but his big breakthrough came the following season when he did well in Sprake's absence towards the end of the season, keeping his place for United's FA Cup Final triumph against Arsenal.

Harvey was the regular first choice the following season, and his stirring displays saw him opt to play for Scotland, the country of his father's birth, making his international debut in a World Cup qualifier against Denmark. He kept a clean sheet, and goals by Kenny Dalglish and Harvey's clubmate Peter Lorimer saw Scotland home. Lorimer was also sent off and Willie Morgan missed a penalty. It was also Tommy Docherty's last game in charge of Scotland, so it was an eventful start for the Leeds goalkeeper.

New manager Willie Ormond tried Bobby Clark (Aberdeen), Peter McCloy (Rangers) and Ally Hunter (Celtic) as Scotland qualified for the World Cup, before finally settling on Harvey's skills between the posts. The Scots had already booked their place in the Finals when Harvey played in the final group fixture, giving another fine display against Czechoslovakia in Bratislava when Dukla Prague's Zdenek Nehoda scored the only goal from the penalty spot.

Sprake had moved on to Birmingham, so Harvey had was the undisputed number one at Elland Road, playing in all United's record unbeaten 29-match start to the 1973–74 Championship-winning season. He played in all three Home Internationals, conceding just one goal to Northern Ireland, and again looked secure in a 2–1

Leeds United goalkeeper David Harvey lines up for a Scotland team photograph ahead of the 1974 World Cup Finals opener against Zaire. Back row, left to right: David Harvey, Jim Holton, Joe Jordan, Danny McGrain, John Blackley. Front row: Kenny Dalglish, Sandy Jardine, Peter Lorimer, Billy Bremner, David Hay, Denis Law.

friendly defeat in Brussels where Raoul Lambert netted a controversial late penalty winner.

Scotland had a strong squad, boosted by the presence of five Leeds players – Harvey, Billy Bremner, Peter Lorimer, Joe Jordan and Gordon McQueen – as they headed to Germany for the World Cup Finals. Only McQueen was absent from Ormond's starting line up when they opened their campaign against unknown African team Zaire. The Scots led 2–0 with goals from Lorimer and Jordan when the Dortmund floodlights failed. The teams gathered in the centre circle while an electrician restored power to the lights, but Scotland's concentration had been broken and although Lorimer hit the bar, Harvey made some fine saves to keep a clean sheet. He expected to be busier against Brazil and so it proved, making a great stop from Rivelino's 30-yard free-kick as the holders made a blazing start to the game. But Scotland held firm for a deserved goalless draw to set up a nerve-shredding game against Yugoslavia, who had drawn with Brazil and caned Zaire 9–0.

Scotland knew they probably needed to win and were unlucky to fall behind to an 81st-minute goal by Stanislav Karasi, of Red Star Belgarde. They did not give up, and Jordan struck the equaliser, leaving Scotland's fate in the hands of Zaire. The African minnows were expected to be gobbled up by Brazil, who needed to win by a three-goal margin to go through. Zaire looked like doing the Tartan Army a favour until they conceded a late goal to a Valdomiro shot which crept under goalkeeper

Kazadi's body to give the South American team the required 3–0 win.

Harvey's immaculate handling and shot-stopping were the among the highlights of Scotland's showing and earned him the 'best goalkeeper' of the tournament tag. The Scottish party received a great welcome from 10,000 fans as they landed back at Abbotsinch Airport, and they knew the squad was strong enough to make the Euro Finals in two years time. The feel-good factor was carried into the new season, with Harvey having little to do at Hampden as East Germany were swept aside in a friendly by goals from Dalglish, Tommy Hutchinson (penalty) and Kenny Burns, who had a spell with Leeds later in his career.

The Scots started their bid for the European Finals by taking on Spain in back-to-back games. Despite Bremner's early goal, they slipped to a 2–1 defeat in Glasgow where Quini scored twice, the winner a shot that Harvey should have saved. It was probably the first mistake that he had made in his 12 internationals. The rematch with Spain in Valencia in February 1975 saw a vastly improved Scottish performance in a hostile environment. Jordan's head gave Scotland an early lead, but Spain grabbed a 65th-minute equaliser when Belgian referee Alfred Delacourt awarded them a penalty for handball by Martin Buchan on the line. But just as Harvey thought he would be facing a penalty, the referee changed his mind and awarded the goal.

After helping United to a 0–0 draw at Derby the following Saturday, Harvey shut out battling non-Leaguers

Wimbledon as Leeds edged their fourth-round replay 1–0 at Selhurst Park, but at the peak of his powers Harvey was involved in a road accident. The injuries he sustained saw him miss the last 13 League games of the season and the European Cup Final as David Stewart took his place between the posts. Harvey recovered to recapture his place in the Leeds team at the start of 1975–76 season and returned to Scotland's ranks for the vital double header against Denmark.

Scotland needed to win both games to keep their European qualification hopes alive. Harvey kept another clean sheet as Scotland won in Copenhagen with a Joe Harper goal and had little to do at Hampden as three unanswered second-half goals gave Scotland a 3–1 victory. It was Harvey's last start for Scotland as he was usurped by the impressive Partick Thistle 'keeper Alan Rough, whom the Leeds man came on for in a 6–0 friendly cakewalk against a poor Finland side. Harvey only let in 10 goals in 16 internationals, and two of those were penalties,

statistics that suggest he should have been picked more often for Scotland.

Within a few months Harvey lost his place in the Leeds team to Stewart, who went on to win a Scottish cap, and for the next couple of years the pair contested the goalkeeping jersey as United struggled to recapture past glories. With the emergence of John Lukic, Stewart moved on to West Brom, and Harvey followed him out of Elland Road when he joined Canadian side Vancouver Whitecaps for £40,000 in March 1979.

Another road accident put him on the sidelines once again, and he returned to Leeds, now playing in the Second Division, in March 1983 at the age of 35. A local lad, who was always popular with Leeds fans because of his great loyalty, he went on to total 350 League games in his two spells with United – a tidy tally considering he also made about 200 Central League appearances for the Whites. He later played for Partick, Bradford City and Carlisle, as well as having a spell as player-manager at Whitby Town and turning out for his local club, Harrogate Town.

Harvey reputedly had a harder shot than Peter Lorimer, but when it was put to the test at Wembley it was not accurate. The 1974 Charity Shield was Brian Clough's first game in charge of the champions and ended 1–1 in ordinary time. Liverpool won the penalty shootout 6–5 when Harvey blasted his kick over the bar and Ian Callaghan netted the winning kick.

After hanging up his gloves Harvey ran a pub, delivered fruit and vegetables to hotels and worked as a postman before leaving his home in Harrogate to move to a farmhouse and smallholding on the Scottish island of Sanday in the Orkneys. He delivered the goods for Leeds and Scotland during his football career, and now his work includes collecting the mail from the local ferry and delivering it to the islanders.

As the national anthems are played at the 1974 World Cup Finals, David Harvey stands to attention next to his skipper Billy Bremner.

JIMMY-FLOYD HASSELBAINK
(Holland 1998–2002)
Striker
Born: Paramaribo, Surinam, 27 March 1972.
Caps: Leeds United 5, Atletico Madrid 3, Chelsea 15.
Total: 23
Goals: 9

PROLIFIC scoring in the Premiership with Leeds United fired Jimmy-Floyd Hasselbaink into Holland's 1998 World Cup squad. His sledgehammer shooting brought him 22 goals in his maiden season at Elland Road after being picked up for a bargain £2 million from Portuguese football by George Graham, who beat off competition from Benfica, Sporting Lisbon, Werder Bremen and Real Zaragoza.

Although Holland had an embarrassment of attacking riches with the likes of Dennis Bergkamp, Ruud van

Jimmy-Floyd Hasselbaink (left) battles for possession with Scotland's Paul Ritchie.

Nistelrooy, Marc Overmars, Patrick Kluivert, Pierre van Hooijdonk and Roy Mackaay at their disposal, he was called up by Guus Hiddink. Hasslebaink was one of the few men to play for Holland without playing in the top Dutch League, the Eredivise, but carved out a decent international career considering the star names that were battling for places up front for the Orangjie.

Hasselbaink was born in Surinam, previously known as Dutch Guyana, in South America, but his family moved to Holland when he was just five. He launched his career with Telstar before joining AZ Alkmaar in 1991. They released him after three modest seasons, and he drifted into Dutch non-League football before trying his hand in Portugal with Campomaiorense in August 1995. He hit a dozen goals in his first season and moved to Boavista, scoring 20 goals in 29 League games and helping them beat Benfica 3–2 in the 1997 Portuguese Cup Final.

Graham had already laid the defensive foundations at Elland Road and was on the look-out for someone to give the team a cutting edge. A trip to Portugal sparked rumours that Leeds were going to sign Jardel, Porto's leading goalscorer, but instead he came back with Hasselbaink, who was virtually unknown in England.

Many were intrigued by this unknown striker's exotic-sounding name. He was actually named Jerrel Hasselbaink, but because the Portuguese could not pronounce it properly he changed it to Jimmy-Floyd. Leeds fans were certainly soon chanting his name. He announced himself with a debut goal against Arsenal in a 1–1 draw and quickly established himself as a favourite with the Elland Road faithful with his blockbusting shooting, as United finished in fifth place in the Premiership.

Hiddink was finalising his plans for the World Cup and decided to have a look at Hasselbaink, giving him a run-out in a pre-tournament friendly against Swiss club Lausanne Sport. He scored in a 4–1 win and made his international debut three days later when he replaced Overmars after an hour of a goalless draw against Cameroon in Arnhem. The Leeds striker then came on against Paraguay in Eindhoven and scored in the 71st minute as the Dutch came from a goal down to cruise home 5–1. His first international start against Nigeria in Amsterdam also saw him score a goal in another 5–1 victory.

Hiddink was impressed not only by Hasselbaink's shooting skills, but also by his strength and surprising speed. He offered Holland something a bit different to the silky skills of Bergkamp and got the nod over the Arsenal man, who was still returning to fitness, in Holland's opening Group E game against neighbours Belgium in the Stade de France.

It was a frustrating game for Hasselbaink and the Dutch. After failing to find a way through the Belgian defence, the Leeds striker was taken off and replaced by Bergkamp, but eight minutes from the end Patrick Kluivert was sent off by charismatic Italian referee Pierluigi Collina and Holland had to settle for a 0–0 draw.

Kluivert was banned for the next game against South Korea, but Hiddink went with the Bergkamp-Overmars combination in a comfortable 5–0 victory. Holland's superior goal difference meant a draw against Mexico in St Etienne would see them through to the next stage. Holland were 2–0 up at half-time, but Mexico had pulled a goal back by the time Hasslebaink replaced Bergkamp for the final 10 minutes – just long enough to see Luis Hernandez equalise for the Mexicans. Hasslebaink did not feature again as the business end of the tournament approached. Edgar Davids hit an injury-time winner against Yugoslavia in the second round and Bergkamp scored a last-minute wonder goal to eliminate Argentina, but the Dutch's fine run ended when they lost on penalties to Brazil in the semi-finals.

Hasselbaink returned to Leeds a better player for his World Cup experience, and his 18 Premiership goals outgunned anyone else as United finished fourth in 1998–99, but despite his scoring exploits he was not required by Holland's new manager Frank Rijkaard. United offered Hasslebaink a contract that would have made him the best-paid player in the Premiership, but he turned it down. In stark contrast to what would happen in years to come, Leeds refused to budge and Hasselbaink requested a transfer.

Amid some acrimony, Hasselbaink was sold to Spanish club Atletico Madrid for £12 million – earning Leeds a big profit. He continued to score prolifically, but his 24 goals could not save his new team from relegation, and another move was inevitable, returning to the Premiership with big spending Chelsea for £15 million. While in La Liga he earned a recall to the Dutch squad from Rijkaard and was also retained by Louis Van Gall, making an eventful return to Spain in a friendly in Seville. He scored in a 2–1 Dutch win but was also sent off, with his marker Fernando Hierro.

Hasselbaink was a storming success at Chelsea, forming an excellent partnership with Icelandic international Eidur Gudjohnsen and finishing the Premiership's top scorer in 2000–01. At international level, the Blues' striker played in several World Cup qualification games, including the 1–0 defeat in Dublin which effectively knocked the Dutch out. He did not make Dick Advocaat's squad for the 2004 European Championships in Portugal and announced his retirement from international football shortly afterwards, at the age of 33. He then joined Middlesbrough, playing in the UEFA Cup Final in which they lost 4–0 to Seville, before a season at Charlton. In August 2007 he linked up with former Leeds chairman Peter Ridsdale at Cardiff and helped the Bluebirds reach their first FA Cup Final for 81 years. He started at Wembley, but Portsmouth's 1–0 win ensured that the only winners' medal Hasselbaink ever gained was with Boavista back in 1997.

DAVID HEALY
(Northern Ireland 2000–09)
Striker
Born: Killyleagh, Co. Down, 5 August 1979.
Caps: Manchester United 7, Preston North End 32, Leeds United 17, Fulham 9, Sunderland 9. Total: 74
Goals: 35

UNFORTUNATELY David Healy could not translate his fantastic scoring record for Northern Ireland to Leeds United. Worshipped by the Windsor Park faithful, his record-breaking scoring exploits made him a true legend, while his strike rate at Elland Road was only modest. A genuine penalty-box predator, he was not helped by being stuck out on the right wing in many of his Leeds games, but it was frustrating for United fans to see him score for his country with remarkable regularity. His goal-every-other-game record for a relatively small footballing nation is astonishing, and some of his greatest nights in a green shirt were as a Leeds United player.

Healy was initially picked up as a teenager by Manchester United's scouting system and made his

Northern Ireland Under-21 debut in November 1998 when he came off the bench to equalise in a 1–1 draw with Moldova. His B international debut – a 1–0 defeat to Wales – came the following year and was rapidly followed by scoring twice in a 3–1 win against the multi-talented French Under-21 side. All this came before he had played a senior game for the Red Devils.

Just before he was loaned out to Port Vale, Healy made his full international debut as a 20-year-old against Luxembourg, scoring twice in a 3–1 win. The striker had scored five times in seven games for Northern Ireland when he was sold to Preston North End in December 2000 for £1.5 million – an amazing fee for a player who had yet to make a Premiership start. The pick of his international goals in the early stages of his career had been a blistering 40-yard rocket past former Manchester United teammate Peter Schmeichel in a World Cup qualifying draw with Denmark.

Although popular at Preston, Healy was finding goals hard to come by at both club and international level when he was loaned out to Norwich in 2003, but on his return to Deepdale his Northern Ireland career suddenly took off. He ended a drought of 14 games without a goal by scoring in a friendly against Norway in February 2004. Although the Irish lost 4–1, it was their first goal in 13 matches,

David Healy.

Northern Ireland scoring sensation David Healy smashes in the winner against England in 2005.

coming after an incredible 1,298 minutes of football. It was former Wimbledon man Lawrie Sanchez's first game in charge after taking over from Sammy McIlroy, and the following month Healy hit the winner in Estonia before boosting his goal tally on a morale-boosting summer tour of the West Indies. His brace in a 3–0 win against Trinidad and Tobago saw him overhaul Colin Clarke's record of 13 goals.

The Irish were looking a better unit under Sanchez as they prepared for their World Cup qualifiers against England, Poland, Wales, Austria and Azerbajian in group six, but they got off to a bad start when they were outclassed by Poland 3–0 at Windsor Park. Pride was restored the following Wednesday in a fiery and controversial encounter against Wales in the Millennium Stadium. It took Italian referee Domenica Messina just eight minutes to brandish red cards to Robbie Savage and Ireland's Michael Hughes after the pair had clashed. Two minutes later Jeff Whitley fired the visitors ahead, and in the 21st minute Healy pounced on a mistake to put the Ulstermen 2–0 up – but the joy lasted just seconds. Amid wild celebrations, he kicked over a corner flag and pumped his arms in celebration in front of the Welsh fans, only to turn round to find the referee showing him two yellow cards.

The nine men of Ireland managed to hang on for a point but missed the sharpness of the suspended Healy in a 0–0 draw in Azerbaijan. The ban brought to an end the striker's run of 38 consecutive international appearances. He bounced back with a goal in Belfast as Ireland shared six goals with an Austrian side featuring former Leeds defender Martin Hiden. A fortnight later Healy moved to Elland Road after 44 goals in 139 appearances for Preston. His quality soon surfaced, and he returned to Deepdale to score a double in an impressive 4–2 Leeds victory to form an instant bond with United supporters.

Leeds, rebuilding in the Championship after relegation, did well to finish 14th with a squad hastily put together by Kevin Blackwell. United's revival continued in 2005–06 as Healy finished joint-top scorer with Rob Hulse to help the

Whites to the Play-off Final at the Millennium Stadium. Leeds ultimately came up short against Watford, losing 3–0, but Healy had already made himself a hero on the international stage earlier in the season.

Despite Healy's goals, Northern Ireland had only won one of their opening seven qualifying games – labouring to a 2–0 win against Azerbaijan in Belfast, the second goal being a late penalty fired in by former Leeds reserve Warren Feeney. With no hope of qualification, Northern Ireland were expected to crumble when Sven-Goran Eriksson's Premiership all stars came calling. But the Swede's 4–5–1 formation was brought crashing down by Healy's 74th-minute angled drive, which ripped past ex-Leeds 'keeper Paul Robinson. It had been just reward for a spirited Irish performance as England failed to come to terms with their opponents' sheer determination and a baying Windsor Park crowd. Irish fans rose to a man as Healy was substituted two minutes from time after securing his country one of their most famous victories.

It was an historic result – Ireland's first win against England for 33 years and their first in Belfast against the English since 1927. Despite putting the skids under England, Healy received a rapturous reception on his return to Elland Road, scoring twice in a 3–3 draw with Brighton. England did go on to qualify while the Irish lost their remaining games to Wales and Austria, but Healy's position as a national icon was secure. He captained Northern Ireland for the first time against Finland in his 50th game, celebrating a 2–1 victory with his 20th international goal; however, he could not translate his international goalscoring prowess to club level, although he was not helped by playing many games on the right wing rather than being the focal point of the attack.

It was not long before Healy's next international milestone came along – a hat-trick against Spain in a stunning 3–2 victory – the first treble at Windsor Park since George Best in 1971. The Leeds striker was to enjoy an unforgettable European Championship campaign, netting the winner against Latvia before another hat-trick, this time against Liechtenstein, made him the first man to score two separate hat-tricks for Northern Ireland. In his next outing, on 28 March 2007 against Sweden, he scored both goals to send the Scandinavians packing 2–1.

While Ireland were dreaming of qualification, Leeds fans were having nightmares about relegation. Those worst fears became a reality as United slid into League One, a drop that would inevitably see the departure of prized asset Healy.

After 31 Leeds goals in 110 games Healy linked up with former Northern Ireland boss Lawrie Sanchez at Fulham in a £1.5 million transfer. He scored after 50 seconds of his debut against Arsenal, and netted in his second game against Bolton, but the goals and the Cottagers' results dried up and Sanchez was sacked. New boss Roy Hodgson hardly played him, but he continued to pile in the goals for Northern

Ireland, the winner against Denmark being his 13th in the qualifying series, beating the previous best by Croatia's Davor Suker. Dubbed 'Sir David' by Irish fans, his exploits were officially recognised when he became an MBE.

After one season and just four Premiership goals with Fulham, he joined Sunderland on a three-year deal in August 2008 and now has his sights set on 50 goals for his country. That would be a remarkable feat for a man playing for a largely unsuccessful international side.

MARTIN HIDEN

(Austria 1998–2008)

Defender

Born: Stainz, Styria, 11 March 1972.
Caps: Leeds United 7, Austria Vienna 14, Rapid Vienna 27, Austria Karnten 2
Total: 50
Goals: 1

MARTIN HIDEN'S move to Leeds United finally pushed the door open to the Austrian national team. Persistence by George Graham landed the 24-year-old defender, who immediately gained his first international call-up. Hiden was uncapped when he arrived at Elland Road, although he had spent some time training with the Austrian squad in Bordeaux during the winter break. It was during that mid-season split in the Austrian League that the wily Graham made his move for the Rapid Vienna man. He had only seen him play on video tape and had been impressed by his ability to fill a variety of defensive positions – an asset that was required in what was a tight-knit Whites squad.

The United boss thought he would have to wait until the Austrian League restarted before flying to the Continent to run the rule over the player himself. But he received a tip-off that Rapid had fixed up a friendly against a Russian club in Dubai as part of their warm-up for the start of the new season. He took a mid week flight from Heathrow, liked what he saw, and struck a £1.5 million deal with Rapid to make Hiden the first Austrian outfield player to feature in the Premiership.

Hiden's debut came in a 1–0 home defeat at the hands of Southampton, but he quickly settled into the side and after his fifth game in United colours – a thumping 5–0 win at Derby – made his international debut at centre-back in a 3–2 loss to Hungary in Vienna on 25 March 1998. That was one of several friendlies Austrian coach Herbert Prohaska had set up ahead of the World Cup Finals in France, where the Austrians had been drawn in Group B with Italy, Chile and Cameroon.

Hiden started the next game against the US at right-back and looked out of sorts as the States won 3–0 in Vienna. The penultimate warm-up game saw Hiden on the bench against Tunisia, but he did get on for Wolfgang Feiersinger in the second half of a 2–1 victory. The Leeds utility defender had done enough to earn a place in the World Cup squad, but was omitted from the final pre-tournament game, a 6–0 breeze against Liechtenstein, and did not play in the Finals as Prohaska preferred the more experienced Feiersinger at centre-back and Peter Schottel at right-back.

Austria drew with Cameroon and Chile, but lost 2–1 to Italy. Oddly, all the Austrian goals were scored in injury time, as Anton Polster salvaged a point against the Africans in Toulouse, while sub Ivica Vastic denied Chile victory in St Etienne. Goals by Christian Vieri and Roberto Baggio put the Azzurri ahead before Andreas Hertzog's 92nd-minute consolation.

Hiden showed no ill effects from the disappointment of not getting any World Cup action when he resumed Premiership action with Leeds complete with orange dyed hair. He looked increasingly assured as United only conceded one goal in their opening seven matches, which included the return of UEFA Cup football with a 1–0 victory over Portuguese side Maritimo. Austria's main focus was now the Euro 2000 qualifiers, and they had a relatively gentle introduction to their group games with ties against Israel, Cyprus and San Marino before squaring up to favourites Spain.

Hiden was a late substitute for Schottel in a disappointing 1–1 draw with the Israelis, who had defender David Amsalem, recently signed by Terry Venables for Crystal Palace, sent off. Prohaska reacted to that disappointment by giving Hiden his first competitive start in the October internationals. Austria made heavy weather of beating Cyprus, who had Demetis Ioannu dismissed. They eventually emerged victorious with second-half goals from Harald Cerny (2) and Hannes Reinmayr. Hiden had helped Austria keep a rare clean sheet and scored his first – and only – international goal in the next match when he netted after 69 minutes of the 4–1 win in Liechtenstein.

Things were looking up for Hiden. He was now established in the Austrian team and was a regular for Leeds

Austria's Martin Hiden stretches to block a pass from England's David Beckham.

in the Premiership, but it all turned sour one Sunday late in November at Old Trafford. Leeds, now under the stewardship of David O'Leary, headed to Manchester United in fifth place but lost 3–2 to a Nicky Butt goal 13 minutes from the end. But it was even worse for Hiden, as his studs got caught in the recently relaid Old Trafford turf and damaged his knee ligaments, ruling him out for the rest of the season. He did not start a Premiership match for Leeds again.

In the summer O'Leary bought Danny Mills from Charlton and, with Gary Kelly still around, the right-back position in which Hiden had done so well was a no-go area for the Austrian. He managed just one appearance as a substitute in 1999–00 and returned to his homeland in a cut-price £500,000 deal with Austria Vienna, with his dreams of making it in English football largely unfulfilled. In his absence from the national team, Austria had some horrendous results, losing 5–0 to Israel and 7–0 to Spain, and failed to reach the European Championship Finals.

Reconstruction of the Austrian team was undertaken by new coach Otto Baric, who was glad to welcome back Hiden's defensive steel in a 5–1 win against Iran in September 2000. He went on to reach a half century of caps for his country, reaching the milestone in Euro 2008 when he played, at the age of 35, in a 1–0 defeat for the hosts in Vienna against old rivals Germany, who won with a fierce free-kick from Chelsea's Michael Ballack. An excellent reader of the game, he was a strong tackler with a good temperament who generally avoided bookings, but he did see red against Holland in 2002 when he collected a second booking in a 3–0 defeat from referee Pierluigi Collina.

Graham's judgement was spot on. Hiden became one of his country's best post-war defenders, captaining Austria twice in 2007 and winning lots of honours. He spent three seasons with Austria Vienna, winning his second Austrian League title, having won his first as a youngster with Salzburg in 1995. He joined Rapid Vienna in 2003 and won further Championships in 2005 and 2008 before joining Austria Karnten.

Despite that dreadful cruciate injury while with Leeds, he has enjoyed a long and fruitful career, including two Champions League campaigns 11 years apart – with Salzburg in 1994–95 and Rapid in 2005–06.

DAVID HOPKIN
(Scotland 1997–99)
Midfield
Born: Greenock, Renfrewshire, 21 August 1970.
Caps: Crystal Palace 2, Leeds United 5. Total 7
Goals: 2

HOPES that big-money signing David Hopkin would advance his career with both Leeds United and Scotland sadly failed to materialise. George Graham believed the midfielder had the all-round qualities to drive the club

David Hopkin.

forward and added him to the Elland Road roster in summer 1997. The new £3.25 million record signing from Crystal Palace was named United's skipper, but his first season in Yorkshire was blighted by injury, illness, suspension and family bereavement. He did have his moments, for both club and country, but did not fulfil his maximum potential, mainly because of bad luck with injuries.

Hopkin first caught Graham's eye when Crystal Palace played Leeds in the FA Cup, and he was impressed with his strength, passing ability, sharp tackling and desire to command the midfield. The former Morton and Chelsea man underscored Graham's view by curling in a magnificent 25-yard last-gasp Play-off Final winner at Wembley against Sheffield United to take Palace into the Premiership. His 17 goals from midfield for the Selhurst Park club saw him break into the Scotland team shortly after that Wembley wonder-goal, making his international debut in a 3–2 victory in Malta before starting a World Cup qualifier in Minsk against Belarus. A penalty from Gary McAllister earned the Scots a hard-fought victory from a tough group four victory.

Hopkin was a player on the up. He was poised to play in the Premiership, had just won his international spurs and was a man in demand. Although Palace fought to keep the 26-year-old, Leeds and Sheffield Wednesday were keen to sign him, the Whites winning the race against their Yorkshire rivals. A month after his arrival, Hopkin was included in Craig Brown's Scotland squad for the return game against Belarus in Aberdeen – a match put back a day to Sunday because of the funeral of Diana, the Princess of Wales. A half-time replacement for former Leeds hero Gary McAllister, who was then at Coventry, Hopkin was to make an immediate impact, scoring from close range just nine minutes after coming on. That certainly boosted his confidence, and he took the game by the scruff of the neck, wrapping up a 4–1 victory with a fine solo goal two minutes from time. The Leeds man took command of the ball, skipped past three tackles to get into the box and tucked home a fine shot to bring the Pittodrie crowd to its feet.

The victory put Scotland back on top of their group and they were looking a good bet for France '98. Hopkin reaffirmed his form by scoring what turned out to be the winner the following week in an amazing 4–3 victory at leaders Blackburn, where all the goals came in the opening 33 minutes. Although Graham had built a reputation for putting together dour sides, United were providing some rich entertainment, and Hopkin was in the team that fought back from being 3–0 down to beat Derby 4–3 at Elland Road in November before joining up with the Scotland squad for a friendly in France. He only played a couple of minutes in the 2–1 defeat in St Etienne when he came on for Gordon Durie in a game that signalled the end of McAllister's international career. Knee ligament damage was to rule the former Leeds skipper out of the World Cup Finals, and at that stage Hopkin looked set to be part of Brown's World Cup plans.

Over the second part of the season, however, Hopkin suffered from injuries, including one to an eye in a reserve game against Birmingham in another seven-goal thriller, this time United losing 4–3. The greater loss was Hopkin's, for although he managed a few Premiership games as a substitute at the end of the season it had come too late to force his way back into the World Cup reckoning.

That fragmented first season as a Leeds player saw Hopkin lose the captaincy to Lucas Radebe, but the Scot enjoyed a fine 1998–99 season as United finished fourth in the Premiership. He forced his way back into the Scotland set-up, completing his first full 90 minutes for his country in a European Championship defeat at the hands of the Czech Republic at Parkhead at the end of March. It was

David Hopkin, front row, third from right, in a Scotland squad picture taken at Troon.

Scotland's first home defeat for 12 years and left the Czechs eight points clear at the top of the group. It was a damaging result for the Tartan Army, as Estonia had also leapfrogged them into second place by defeating Lithuania. Prospects for qualification were slim, and although the Czech Republic fully deserved their 2–1 victory their opening goal looked suspect. Hopkin made a clean challenge on Vladimir Smicer to win the ball on the edge of the Scottish box, only for the referee to give a free-kick which resulted in Jan Scuchoparek heading in the opener off Leicester's Matt Elliott.

Smicer added a second in the 35th minute, and although Eoin Jess pulled a goal back after Hopkin's long throw caused confusion in the Czech area, the Scots could not find a second goal. Hopkin was probably fortunate to miss the next couple of games – an embarrassing 1–1 draw with the Faroe Islands, who netted an injury-time equaliser after Elliott's first half dismissal, and a 3–2 loss in Prague where a goal from the giant Jan Koller completed a fine Czech fightback after being 2–0 down. The result saw the Czech Republic qualify leaving Scotland to scrap for a Play-off place at best.

Hopkin started 1999–2000 alongside David Batty and Lee Bowyer in midfield, and the trio looked a good combination for a United squad who were making great strides under David O'Leary. Yet it was at right-back that Hopkin was to play his next game for Scotland. The Scots had been decimated by injury for their trip to war-ravaged Sarajevo to take on their main rivals for a Play-off place, Bosnia Herzegovina, and the Leeds midfielder was pressed into service as an emergency defender. He helped Scotland to their first away win in three years as goals from Don Hutchison and Billy Dodds secured a 2–1 win, which was greeted with wild celebration by the travelling Tartan Army of supporters, whose numbers had been swelled by members of the Royal Highland Fusiliers, who were part of the city's peace-keeping mission.

Two days after United's victory at Watford sent them to the top of the Premiership, Hopkin played in the 1–0 win against the Bosnians at Ibrox, which guaranteed a Play-off place against England with a European Championship Finals place up for grabs. It was to be his last appearance for Scotland, and he only played a handful more games for Leeds as United emerged as title contenders.

Hopkin did net a first-minute goal at Hillsborough as the Whites thumped the Owls 3–0 in his final game in a Leeds shirt before joining Premiership rookies Bradford City for £2.5 million in the summer. Once again he was badly hit by injuries, and the Paraders cut their losses by selling Hopkin to his old club, Palace, in March. He ended his second spell at Selhurst Park by returning home to his first Scottish League club, Morton, where he went on to take a coaching role. He then ran a newsagents in Greenock, a life far removed from the days when he was back-page news with Leeds United and Scotland.

NORMAN HUNTER

(England 1965–74)

Defender

Born: Eighton Banks, Co. Durham, 24 October 1943.

Caps: Leeds United 28

Goals: 2

FOREVER linked with England's World Cup exit at the hands of Poland in 1973, that game has overshadowed Norman Hunter's England career. Yet Hunter was an outstanding defender for Leeds and, but for the presence of the legendary Bobby Moore, would have won a lot more than his total of 28 caps.

Sir Alf Ramsey certainly recognised the hard-tackling Hunter's talents and was fortunate to have two such excellent players at his disposal. Indeed, the England manager would often accommodate Hunter in a different role to the left-half position that West Ham golden boy Moore had made his own. About half of Hunter's caps were won with Moore in the side, so it was not always a case of the Leeds man only playing when the England skipper was not available.

Behind the 'Norman Bites Yer Legs' image was a player of remarkable consistency, who figured in all the major triumphs of Don Revie's reign at Elland Road. The former electrician's apprentice could certainly make the sparks fly with his tackling, but his magical left foot could also deliver passes to perfection, and his understanding of match play could not be bettered.

After making his debut in a 2–0 win at Swansea in September 1962 in Division Two, Hunter immediately cemented his place in the first team. A Leeds teamsheet without Hunter at number six was a rare sight indeed as he was an ever-present in no fewer than five seasons. A flurry of representative games – three for the Under-23s and three for the Football League – paved the way for his elevation to full international status. He was selected as reserve for the England side to take on Hungary, but had to withdraw because of a knee injury he sustained in the 1965 FA Cup Final defeat against Liverpool.

When he made his first full international appearance Hunter created a bit of history, becoming the first England player to make his debut as a substitute. Although a friendly, the game in Madrid's Bernabeu Stadium was significant as it heralded a change in tactics to Ramsey's 'Wingless Wonders'. It was the first time that Ramsey dispensed with out-and-out wingers, and he caught the Spanish on the hop with their full-backs bemused as they had no one to mark. England swept into an early lead through Arsenal's Joe Baker, who limped off with a pulled leg muscle on the half hour, allowing Hunter to come on. England continued their domination and the only surprise was that they could only add one more goal, from Liverpool forward Roger Hunt.

With the World Cup Finals only seven months away, it was the perfect time for Hunter to stake his claim, although at that early stage in his career the 22-year-old probably knew that, barring injury to Moore, his chances of appearing in the Finals were slim.

As the build-up for July continued, Hunter played against West Germany – with Moore at right-half – Yugoslavia and Finland. With United colleague Jack Charlton at centre-half, Hunter was on familiar territory, and the pair were both included in Ramsey's final squad of 22 for the Finals. While Charlton played in every game in the tournament, Hunter, who was handed the number-18 jersey, did not get on to play alongside his Leeds clubmate and was on the bench when Moore hoisted aloft the Jules Rimet Trophy.

For 41 years all Hunter had to show for his contribution was the tracksuit he wore while watching the drama unfold

Norman Hunter on the ball.

from the England bench. None of the reserves ever received a medal until FIFA president Sepp Blatter announced in November 2007 that all non-playing members of winning squads between 1930 and 1974 would be given medals. Before 1978 only players featuring in the Final received them. Together with the rest of the reserves, Hunter finally got his medal in June 2009 from Prime Minister Gordon Brown at 10 Downing Street.

Hunter's next game for England was as a defensive midfielder in a 1–0 win against Austria in Vienna, coming after he had missed the last 14 internationals. Patient Hunter had to play a waiting game, but 1968 saw him collect League Cup and Fairs Cup-winners' medals, and also scored the first of his two England goals. It came in the second leg of the European Nations Cup quarter-final against holders Spain in Madrid, scene of his England debut two years earlier. This time the stakes were much higher, as England were seeking to add the Euro crown to their world title.

The first leg at Wembley had produced just one goal, struck home with typical power by Bobby Charlton, so the tie was still in the balance when England faced the Spaniards in front of a volatile 120,000 crowd. England soaked up early Spanish pressure, and shortly after half-time a loose pass by Hunter was picked off by Spain, whose Francisco Gento set up Real Madrid teammate Amancio Amaro to smash the ball past Peter Bonetti. England levelled six minutes later with a Martin Peters header to silence the vast crowd. As time ticked on, England's defence held firm, and with eight minutes remaining Hunter atoned for his earlier error when he fired a Roger Hunt cross past goalkeeper Salvador Sadurni. It was a famous win, and Hunter retained his place for the 3–1 friendly win over Sweden at Wembley.

England had lost only two of their last 40 internationals, but they looked a jaded outfit as they slipped to a disappointing 1–0 defeat in Hanover when Franz Beckenbauer's deflected shot gave Germany their first win against England in 12 games. Four days later, England lost to a young emerging Yugoslavia side in an ugly European Nations semi-final in Italy. Cautious Ramsey put Hunter in a packed five-man midfield, and the match deteriorated into a succession of free-kicks as the Yugoslavia players rolled around after nearly every England tackle. Neither side looked like, or deserved to, break the deadlock in a game of constant niggle. It was left to Red Star Belgrade winger Dragan Dzajic to put the Florence crowd out of their misery when he hammered the ball high past Gordon Banks. To add to the depression Alan Mullery became the first player to be sent off while playing for England, who were playing their 424th official international, when he retaliated after being hacked down by Dobrioje Trivic.

Ramsey stood by Hunter for the third-fourth Play-off game against Russia in Rome, in which a revitalised England won 2–0. Hunter was a rock alongside Jack Charlton as United won the Division One title in 1968–69. The duo played together for England when Romania made their first visit to Wembley in January and drew 1–1, and again in an exciting 2–1 victory over Wales at the end of the season.

Hunter was still playing second fiddle to Moore, but was included in the 1970 World Cup party for Mexico, along with United teammates Terry Cooper, Jack Charlton and Allan Clarke. The Leeds quartet had endured a gruelling round of matches as they unsuccessfully chased a League, FA Cup and European Cup treble, and would have to dig deep to find extra reserves of energy to cope with the stifling heat of Mexico. Although Hunter did not figure in any of the senior warm-up games, he did play in a couple of B internationals in Colombia and Ecuador.

At one stage it looked as though Hunter would be required for the opening game against Romania after Moore was detained by the authorities for allegedly stealing a gold bracelet from the hotel shop in the Colombian capital of Bogata where England had been staying. The England captain denied any knowledge of the matter, and despite the lack of evidence was held for four days before his release. No further action was taken over what the England party felt had been a set-up to disrupt their plans. England beat Romania and Czechoslovakia in their group games with a narrow defeat against Brazil in between, before taking on old rivals West Germany in the quarter-finals.

Ramsey's men had the game in Leon firmly under control, holding a 2–0 lead with 22 minutes remaining. With England wearing their red shirts it looked like 1966 all over again, but there was a nasty sting in the tail. Beckenbauer pulled a goal back, and in the 80th minute Ramsey replaced Martin Peters with Hunter to shore up the 2–1 advantage, but within seconds Uwe Seeler's looping header drifted over Bonetti and the game went into extra-time. Fatigue was creeping through the England ranks, and ace goal poacher Gerd Muller completed the comeback to break England hearts. The 40 minutes Hunter spent on the pitch in the Guanajuato Stadium was his only taste of World Cup action, despite being in both 1966 and 1970 squads.

Hunter was still part of Ramsey's plans as he partnered new cap Roy McFarland in defence when England opened their European Championship bid with a 1–0 win in Malta, the Leeds man setting up the only goal for Peters.

Hunter was outstanding as Leeds won the Fairs Cup for a second time by beating Juventus on the away goals ruling, and clocked up yet another ever-present League season in 1971–72 as United won the FA Cup. That joyous afternoon at Wembley was in sharp contrast to Hunter's experience at the Twin Towers the previous week, when impressive West Germany swept to a 3–1 European Championship quarter-final victory in a game marked by uncharacteristic errors by skipper Moore on a wet pitch. Hunter was given a midfield role in the second leg in the Olympic Stadium, Berlin, a physical game ending in a 0–0 stalemate.

Norman Hunter has the tools of his tackling trade – his feet – sharpened for action as he relaxes during the 1970 World Cup.

For the first time Huter played in all three Home Internationals at the end of the season, playing as midfield destroyer in an impressive 3–0 demolition of Wales, slotting back into central defence in a shock 1–0 loss to Northern Ireland and switching back to midfield in a bruising 1–0 victory at Hampden Park. England had been paired with Wales and Poland in the fight for 1974 World Cup qualification, a task which Ramsey's squad should have found straightforward. But from the outset the four-game shootout proved troublesome.

The short trip to Cardiff's Ninian Park in November 1972 gave Ramsey a 1–0 win to mark his 100th game in charge. Wales, who drew on a fair sprinkling of players from the lower divisions, made life even more uncomfortable at Wembley 10 weeks later. Sluggish England were slow out of the blocks, and Wales deserved their lead from Liverpool forward John Toshack. England were huffing and puffing until Hunter struck with a bolt from the blue. Just four minutes of the half remained when he tore onto a half-clearance 25 yards out without checking his stride and sent it whistling into the top corner of clubmate Gary Sprake's net.

It finished 1–1, so qualification would now depend on the double header with the Poles, but before those came round Hunter and Leeds were to suffer Cup Final agony in duplicate. They were shocked by Sunderland in the FA Cup Final and a suspension and injury-hit Leeds squad headed to Greece to play AC Milan in the European Cup-winners' Cup Final in Salonika. The Italians won with an early controversial deflected free-kick by Luciano Chiarugi, but that was only half the story on a storm-battered night. Greek referee Christos Michas allowed Milan fouls to go unpunished, while United's challenges produced inevitable free-kicks for the opposition. Three strong Leeds penalty claims were rejected, and any United attack was generally halted by a foul. In the final minute Hunter was powering through midfield when he was chopped down from behind by Gianni Rivera. Hunter retaliated, tussled with Riccardo Sogliano and the pair were sent off. The Greek Federation were so embarrassed that they later suspended Michas, but never commented on why his performance had been so inept.

Hunter's mood darkened further the following month as England lost 2–0 in Poland and had midfield dynamo Alan Ball dismissed in the closing stages for violent conduct. Hunter did not play in the Slaski Stadium but came on in the next game, a 2–1 win in Russia, and did not put a foot wrong as England slaughtered Austria 7–0 to warm up for the big showdown with Poland on 17 October 1973.

The maths were simple: England needed to win, yet the Football League refused to postpone the League games on Saturday involving the England players. An expectant Wembley was packed to the rafters, and Ramsey's men seized control from the outset as the game flowed one way – towards the Polish goalmouth. England battered the visitors, whose goal led a charmed life and their goalkeeper Jan Tomaszewski – dubbed a 'clown' in the pre-match build-up – pulled off a series of outstanding saves with all parts of his body.

Luckless England pounded away but somehow had not found a way through by half-time. The fans got right behind the white-shirted men of England with fantastic vocal backing, but were silenced on the hour when Poland broke away and scored. Hunter, in for Moore, failed to clear a routine ball out of the Polish defence near the Royal Box

Norman Hunter is consoled by non-playing captain Bobby Moore (left) and trainer Harold Shepherdson after England's World Cup exit at the hands of Poland at Wembley in 1973.

touchline, Grezgorz Lato won the ball, raced on past the exposed England defence and laid the ball inside, where Jan Domarski's low shot flew under the goalkeeper Peter Shilton's dive.

Six minutes later England were level when Adam Musial pushed Martin Peters, and star Leeds striker Allan Clarke calmly despatched the resulting penalty. Time was still on England's side, but despite a ferocious barrage the floodgates would not open. With one last throw of the dice Ramsey sent on Leeds-born Derby forward Kevin Hector for Martin Chivers. In the final minute United's Tony Currie sent England's 23rd corner into the Polish box, and Hector was first to the ball, but his goal-bound header was cleared off the line. It was an agonising end to an equally agonising night, and no one felt the pain more acutely than a distraught Hunter, who left the pitch, head bowed, the weight of the world on his shoulders, consoled by Moore and trainer Harold Shepherdson.

For months Hunter was vilified by opposition fans whenever Leeds were playing away, but he did not let the Polish experience destroy his form. He was once again ever-present as Leeds won the 1973–74 title in great style. To cap it all, Hunter won the first PFA Player of the Year award – his fellow professionals recognising his outstanding defensive talent. Many predicted that the Poland defeat would see the end of Hunter's international career, particularly as Ramsey was sacked shortly afterwards. But he was included in caretaker manager Joe Mercer's squad for the Home Internationals, coming in the 1–0 win against Northern Ireland and starting in England's 2–0 defeat against Scotland.

Hunter was not part of the summer tour of Eastern Europe; however, the appointment of Don Revie as England chief saw Hunter handed his final international appearance in his former manager's first game in charge. Both were able to celebrate as England got their European Championship qualifying campaign off to a flying start with a 3–0 win against Czechoslovakia.

Days later Hunter had cartilage removed and was out of action for nearly four months but, indestructible as ever, he bounced back to help United reach the European Cup Final, where they lost to Bayern Munich in Paris. After 726 Leeds appearances Hunter joined Bristol City in October 1976, then moved to Barnsley where he worked under Allan Clarke as player-coach. When 'Sniffer' became Leeds boss, Hunter took over the managerial reins at Oakwell, taking the Tykes up to Division Two. After Barnsley started to slide, Hunter was sacked. He worked as Johnny Giles's assistant at West Brom for a spell then was in charge of Rotherham for a short period.

Hunter returned to Elland Road when he was offered a coaching job by Billy Bremner, but lost it in October 1988 when Howard Wilkinson took charge. He was then assistant to another Leeds old boy, Terry Yorath, for a year before moving out of the game. He became a summariser with BBC Radio Leeds in 1993, which took him back to his spiritual home, Elland Road.

Hunter forged an unbreakable bond with the Leeds fans, who adored his unquenchable commitment. That popularity may not have extended to his England career, but when he got the call to arms to serve his country he always answered. Revie sometimes took a dim view of his all-action defender joining up with Ramsey's England, but Hunter said he would never pull out of an England squad – just like he never pulled out of a challenge.

MATTHEW JONES

(Wales 1999–2003)

Midfield
Born: Llanelli, Camarthenshire, 1 September 1980.
Caps: Leeds United 5, Leicester City 8. Total: 13

INJURY wrecked the promising international career of Matthew Jones at the age of 23.

The midfielder had come through the ranks at Elland Road and graduated to the full Welsh team before being sold to Leicester for a big fee. But his football world came crashing down when he was forced to retire in summer 2004 after a succession of injuries. He had recovered from ruptured knee ligaments in 2002 but a prolapsed disc in his spine forced him to take his surgeon's advice and retire from the game.

Former United goalkeeper Glan Letheren recommended the Llanelli-born youngster to the Whites, and he joined United's Youth Academy. A Welsh Youth international, he was a member of Leeds's FA Youth Cup-winning side in 1997, winning the first of his seven Under-21 caps in a 1–0 defeat against Belgium. The Youth Cup side were an outstanding crop, featuring future internationals Paul Robinson, Alan Maybury, Harry Kewell, Jonathan Woodgate, Stephen McPhail and Jones, who scored one of the goals in the 3–1 aggregate victory in the Final against Crystal Palace.

Matthew Jones.

The 1998–99 season saw Jones make his senior breakthrough. He was given his chance in a thumping 5–1 win at Portsmouth in the FA Cup fourth round when he came on for Danny Granville. A few days later he made his full debut in United's 2–1 win at West Ham in the Premiership. He was still only 18 when he was called up for Wales B against Scotland and finished the season with a handful more starts as United finished an excellent campaign in fourth place.

Jones made quite an impression with his snappy tackling in midfield, and John Toshack had no qualms about moving the teenager up to full international status. The Welsh had already failed to qualify from group one for the European Championship Finals, and Jones won his first senior cap when he came on for John Oster, who was to have a spell on loan with Leeds, in the later stages of a 2–0 defeat against Switzerland at Wrexham. He made his first full international start in a friendly in the warm climes of Qatar in February 2000 when he partnered former Leeds favourite Gary Speed in midfield. A 10th-minute goal from Charlton's John Robinson gave Wales victory in Doha.

Leeds were flying in the Premiership, and Jones found it hard to break into central midfield with David Batty, Eirik Bakke and Lee Bowyer ahead of him in David O'Leary's pecking order, but he never let O'Leary down whenever he played. The man-marking job he did on Italian star Francesco Totti in United's 0–0 away draw with Roma was probably his best display in a Leeds shirt as he continued to gain valuable experience in the UEFA Cup.

The rookie found himself part of a little bit of football history when he lined up against multi-talented Brazil on 23 May when the first major international played in an enclosed dome took place at Cardiff. It was one of the first football matches played at the Millennium Stadium, and a capacity 72,500 crowd saw the South American giants win 3–0, with goals from Elber, Cafu and Rivaldo coming in a golden 10-minute spell in the second half.

Wales were also on the receiving end of a 3–0 defeat in Portugal in the summer, when Jones found himself up against Figo, who opened the scoring in the friendly in Chaves. With Frenchman Olivier Dacourt added to the Elland Road roster, there were fewer opportunities for Jones to break into the Leeds first team, but he did figure in a fine Wales display in a goalless draw with Poland in October before leaving Elland Road for Leicester for £3 million a couple of months later. His time with the Foxes was riddled with injuries, but he did figure in Wales's disappointing World Cup qualifying campaign, having a few games as a full-back. In January 2002 he sustained a knee ligament injury against Liverpool after a tackle by Gary McAllister. Jones was out for more than a year, but a big injury crisis forced Leicester to rush him back. He did so well that he was recalled into the Welsh squad, but his career was to end in a massive anti-climax. He had only played 50 League games in seven years with Leeds and Leicester when he made his last appearance. It was to come in a 13th – and unlucky – appearance for Wales on 27 May 2003 against the US in San Jose.

Wales went into the game on the back of a 10-game unbeaten run, but Mark Hughes's side were on the back foot from the moment Jones fouled Jovan Kirovski and Landon Donovan slotted in from the spot. Jones was yellow-carded for the challenge and received his second – and marching orders – just after the interval for a foul on Bobby Convey. Wales went on to lose 3–0 and Jones was never to play full-time football again. He was released by Leicester and underwent several operations on his back to salvage his career. Eventually he had to quit in 2004 and has since worked in the sports media before coming out of retirement in 2007 to play for his home-town club in the Welsh Premier League. His career may have only been short, but Jones certainly packed plenty into it at the top level, with internationals for Wales and Champions League football with Leeds.

MICK JONES
(England 1965–70)

Forward

Born: Rhodesia, near Worksop, Nottinghamshire, 24 April 1945.

Caps: Sheffield United 2, Leeds United 1. Total: 3

WHY Mick Jones never partnered Allan Clarke in the England team has long been a mystery for Leeds United fans. The pair had a near-telepathic understanding of each other's game, yet the combination was never tried at international level. While Clarke was the surgical rapier, Jones was the broadsword, cutting his way through defences by sheer strength. If any goal epitomised their play it was the Centenary FA Cup-winner against Arsenal in 1972.

Jones's persistence forced his way past left-back Bob McNab and crossed to perfection into the box, where the deadly Clarke's header took the Cup back to Elland Road for the one and only time in the club's history. It was also typical of the hard-grafting Jones that as the game was near the end he should strive to get a second goal. He tried to beat goalkeeper Geoff Barnett from a tight angle, but as he fell to the turf he put out his left arm and dislocated his elbow.

After the team received their winners' medals and collected the Cup, Jones discovered substitute Mick Bates had his medal, but the stricken striker was determined to meet the Queen. Aided by Norman Hunter, he gingerly climbed the steps to the Royal Box and received the gentlest of handshakes from the guest of honour before being stretchered off to the dressing rooms.

The all-action centre-forward received a wonderful ovation from the Leeds fans at the tunnel end, but it was not just the Elland Road faithful who appreciated his will to win. In his only England appearance as a Leeds player he received a standing ovation after being surprisingly substituted against Holland at Wembley by World Cup hero Geoff Hurst. Ironically, Jones had a head start on Hurst in the build up to the 1966 tournament after his rapid rise through the ranks at Sheffield United.

As a football-mad youngster, Jones scored 14 goals in a game for Priory Secondary Modern School, Worksop, and played for Dinnington Miners' Welfare while working in a

Mick Jones was among seven Leeds United players named in the provisional squad for the 1970 World Cup. From left to right, Terry Cooper, Paul Reaney, Mick Jones, Norman Hunter, Paul Madeley, Allan Clarke and Jack Charlton.

cycle factory. He was invited to train with Sheffield United's juniors and in March 1961 joined the groundstaff, signing pro forms the following week.

Goals flowed in the juniors and reserves and Jones made his debut in a 1–1 draw at Manchester United on 20 April 1963. Within 18 months he won the first of his nine Under-23 caps when he scored the opener in a 5–0 victory against Romania at Coventry. Leeds's own rising star, defender Norman Hunter, was also in the side that night.

Jones's progress had been rapid, and with the World Cup a little over a year away he was included in England's 1965 post-season tour of Yugoslavia, West Germany and Sweden. It was clear World Cup places were up for grabs, and Jones did well on his debut as England won 1–0 in Nuremburg, having a hand in Terry Paine's goal which earned England their third successive win against West Germany. He had only just turned 20 and retained his place in a 2–1 win against Sweden in Gothenburg, but by his own admission did not have the best of games.

At this stage West Ham's Hurst had yet to play for England as Ramsey tried out Leeds's Alan Peacock, Barry Bridges (Chelsea) and Joe Baker (Arsenal) after finally turning to the Hammer in a 1–0 friendly win against West Germany in February 1966...the rest is history. More Under-23 caps followed for Jones, and although he was named in the initial World Cup squad of 28 he missed out to Hurst, Roger Hunt and Jimmy Greaves when it was whittled down to 22.

Jones's final Under-23 cap came in May 1967 when he partnered Allan Clarke, then with Fulham, for the first time. Although neither found the net, England saw off Austria 3–0 with a fine all-round display. While Sheffield United were going well in Division One, further north ambitious Leeds were among Europe's elite. Don Revie needed more firepower in his attack, and Jones fitted the bill, so in September 1967 the respective chairmen thrashed out a £100,000 transfer – a record for both clubs.

It took Jones a few months to settle at Elland Road as he struggled with an ankle injury and sat out the League Cup Final victory against Arsenal as he was Cup-tied. But once fully fit he soon showed what he could do, scoring the goal against Ferencvaros which saw United lift the Fairs Cup. Jones had always been an aerial threat, but the coaching he received at Elland Road improved his groundwork and made him into a more complete forward. He was top scorer in 1968–69 when United won their first Division One Championship, but it was the purchase of Allan Clarke in the summer that enabled Revie to put together one of the world's best striking partnerships.

In 1969–70, while Leeds were chasing the League, FA Cup and European Cup treble, Jones earned an England recall after a three-year absence. It came against the skilful Dutch and was expected to give Ramsey some pointers towards the World Cup in Mexico. In a poor 0–0 draw the lively Jones was one of the few shining lights for England,

and the Wembley crowd howled their disapproval when he was replaced by Hurst with 15 minutes remaining. The Leeds man received a fine ovation from the crowd as he put on his tracksuit, but he was never to wear the Three Lions crest again.

There was further disappointment as United ended the season empty-handed, although it looked as though Jones's 82nd-minute strike would win the FA Cup, only for Ian Hutchinson to snatch Chelsea a 2–2 draw. Jones also fired Leeds ahead in the replay, but the Londoners fought back to win 2–1 in extra-time. The deadly duo of Jones and Clarke each scored 26 goals in 1969–70, but only Clarke went to Mexico in the summer, although his strike partner was named in the initial group of 40 players.

Despite a scoring drought the following season, Jones helped United win the Fairs Cup a second time by seeing off the challenge of Juventus in a tight two-leg Final, and the following year his heroics saw Leeds land the FA Cup.

After double Cup Final anguish against Sunderland and AC Milan, Jones and United bounced back to win the title in 1973–74 with considerable flair. But there was a price to pay for Jones, as a knee injury sustained in training got worse, and he played several games to help Leeds over the finishing line ahead of challengers Liverpool when he was not fully fit. He was named United's Player of the Year and in the summer underwent a series of tests on his damaged knee before an exploratory operation revealed bone under the kneecap had flaked away. At the age of 28 Jones's career was over, and he announced his retirement in October 1975. The non-stop running by a chaser of lost causes had finally taken its toll on one of the most unselfish players ever to don a Leeds shirt.

JOE JORDAN
(Scotland 1973–82)
Striker
Born: Carluke, Lanarkshire, 15 December 1951.
Caps: Leeds United 27, Manchester United 20, AC Milan 5. Total: 52
Goals: 11

BRAVEHEART striker Joe Jordan scored some of the most important goals in Scotland's international history. Although he was never a prolific scorer, the fearsome forward netted some priceless gems for his country as they qualified for the 1974 and 1978 World Cups. He was a wonderful successor to Mick Jones as the target man in the Leeds United attack, with his strength and bravery ensuring opposition defenders never got a moment's rest. He worked in an architect's office before becoming a footballer, and old Leeds hero Bobby Collins was the first man to map out Jordan's future in the game. Wee Bobby was manager of Morton, where the raw-boned teenager Jordan was making his name in the Scottish League.

Collins tipped United off about his 18-year-old centre-forward, and a £15,000 transfer went through in October 1970. Cappielow Park in Greenock and Elland Road were worlds apart on the football scale, and young Jordan had to bide his time before getting his first-team chance. He was gradually blooded by Revie in 1971–72, having made his first appearance as a substitute in a UEFA Cup match the previous season against Vitoria Setubal, of Portugal.

Jordan's first senior goal for Leeds came in a 2–1 defeat in Barcelona on 22 September 1971 in a match between Fairs Cup holders Leeds and the first winners of the trophy to decide who should keep it before the advent of new silverware for the UEFA Cup. Jordan was still not a first-team regular by any stretch of the imagination when he won his first Scottish cap at the end of 1972–73. He was often used a substitute by Revie, so it was a familiar scenario when he replaced Lou Macari at Wembley, where England shaded a 1–0 win against the injury-hit Scots with a Martin Peters header.

Jordan was up and running on the international scene and, after coming off the bench against Switzerland in Berne, made his first start in a centenary celebration game against Brazil at Hampden Park, the world champions winning 1–0 with a Derek Johnstone own-goal. But for Scotland the main quest was World Cup qualification, which received a massive boost when main rivals Czechoslovakia were held 1–1 by Denmark. It meant Scotland would go through to the Finals if they could beat the Czechs in Glasgow the following September.

On a night of huge tension in front of an expectant 100,000 Hampden crowd, super-sub Jordan was the hero of the hour. With Colin Stein and Derek Johnstone out through injury, Jordan earned a place on the bench and watched his teammates pour forward in the opening stages. But the visitors silenced the massed ranks at Mount Florida when Zdenek Nehoda's hopeful shot evaded goalkeeper Ally Hunter. But centre-half Jim Holton powered in a headed equaliser before half-time, and that aerial weakness in the heart of the Czech defence proved the key to victory. Cometh the hour, cometh the man, and Jordan was sent on to replace Kenny Dalglish and within 10 minutes headed in Willie Morgan's cross after Billy Bremner's shot hit a post. Scotland had a new national hero as they qualified for the Finals for the first time in 16 years.

Jordan was now playing, and scoring, more often for Leeds, who swept to the First Division title, and his stock with the Tartan Army rose still further as his shot crashed in off defender Mike Pejic after only four minutes to give Scotland the lead against England, a Colin Todd own-goal completing a 2–0 win. The Leeds forward was a fearsome sight when he was in full flow and earned the nickname 'Jaws' because of his toothless grin, which usually appeared after he had despatched the ball into the net. His third international goal came in a 2–1 win against Norway in Oslo, and Willie Ormond's team headed to the Finals in

Joe Jordan.

Germany in great heart. African minnows Zaire were beaten 2–0 in the opening group game, with Jordan's head setting up the first goal for clubmate Peter Lorimer before nodding in the second.

After a 0–0 draw with Brazil, Scotland were held 1–1 by Yugoslavia in Frankfurt, where Jordan scored a last-minute equaliser. Although they were unbeaten, Scotland went home having being pipped by Brazil's marginally better goal difference. Jordan was firmly established in the Scotland set-up and in the hearts of the fans, who were looking forward to the European Championship qualifiers with Spain, Romania and Denmark.

The Leeds striker missed a penalty in a 3–0 victory against East Germany in a friendly and was in the side which lost 2–1 to Spain in Glasgow. The Scots got back in the hunt with a 1–1 draw in Valencia courtesy of a Jordan header.

Jordan was earning rave reviews, particularly for his performances in the European Cup, and after the Final defeat at the hands of Bayern Munich the German side made a million-mark bid for him in the summer. United and Scotland were not able to call on Jordan at the start of 1975–76 after he damaged stomach muscles on the club's pre-season tour of France and Germany. After that cleared up he suffered an ankle injury and did not start for the Whites until the following February.

Back to full fitness, he played in all three Home Internationals at the end of the season as Scotland swept aside Northern Ireland, Wales and England. Scotland had

Fearsome Joe 'Jaws' Jordan put the bite on many an international opponent. Here he celebrates another goal for Scotland.

failed to qualify for the European Championships in Jordan's enforced absence, but had regained their form and started their bid to qualify for the World Cup Finals with a trip to Prague. Despite going into the game on the back of an unbeaten nine-game run, Scotland lost 2–0 and had Andy Gray sent off.

Scotland got back on track in their three-team group by beating Wales and grabbing a 3–1 home win against Czechoslovakia, in which a fulminating Jordan header paved the way for a 3–1 victory. The result meant the all-British tie between Wales and Scotland would determine who would he heading to Argentina for the Finals. Because

Cardiff's Ninian Park 10,000 crowd safety limit simply could not house the expected attendance, the FA of Wales forfeited ground advantage and chose Anfield, home of Liverpool, to stage the match.

Just over 50,000 supporters – the vast majority wearing Scottish favours – turned the ground into a mini-Hampden. Scotland dominated but could not find a way through the Wales defence until 11 minutes from time when Jordan and Dave Jones leapt to contest a long throw in the Welsh box. A hand, which looked like Jordan's, touched the ball, but French referee Roger Wurtz awarded a penalty, despite strong protests from the Welsh. After the furore died down Don Masson despatched the spot-kick, and three minutes from the end Dalglish marked his 50th cap by heading in the second on his home ground. It was Jordan's last appearance as a Leeds player as he joined cross-Pennine rivals Manchester United for a record fee of £350,000 in January 1978.

That summer Scotland failed up to live up to the hype generated by manager Ally McLeod, losing to Peru and being held by Iran before restoring some pride – although they failed to go any further in the tournament – by beating Holland 3–2. Jordan netted in the 3–1 loss to Peru.

Jordan played more than 100 games for Manchester United before joining AC Milan for £325,000. He was still with the Italian giants when another header in a key match against Sweden sent Scotland on the way to a 2–0 win and virtual World Cup qualification. A few months earlier he had been sent off after an incident in a 2–0 defeat by Wales in Swansea which left Terry Boyle with a broken nose and a missing tooth. He created a record by becoming the first Scottish player to score in three World Cup Finals when he netted in a 2–2 draw with the USSR in Malaga in his final international appearance. He later played for Verona and then returned to England with Southampton and Bristol City, becoming manager of the latter. He also managed Hearts, Stoke and Bristol City (again), before coaching appointments with Huddersfield, Southampton, Portsmouth and Tottenham.

TRESOR KANDOL
(DR Congo 2008– to date)
Striker
Born: Banga, 30 August 1981.
Caps: *Leeds United 1
*On loan to Millwall

SOMERSAULTING striker Tresor Kandol clawed his way out of non-League football to play for his country. The Leeds United forward made his debut for DR Congo in a friendly against Gabon in Paris in 2008 as national team coach Patrice Neveu checked on a number of European-based players ahead of the World Cup qualifiers. Kandol's road to the top was sometimes a rocky one as he strove to

emulate his cousin, Lomana Lua Lua, with whom he shares the same goal celebration.

Born in the city of Banga when the country was known as Zaire, Kandol came to England as a youngster and his football skills saw him taken on as a trainee with Luton Town, making his League debut for the Hatters in 1999. Coaches at Kenilworth Road were convinced he would make it to the top, but he was released as a 20-year-old and had short unsuccessful stays with Cambridge United and Bournemouth before dropping into non-League football with Thurrock and Dagenham & Redbridge, among others. His goals with Dagenham saw him loaned to Darlington before a £50,000 move to Barnet, where he helped preserve the Bees' League status in 2006. He also served a short prison sentence that year for driving offences, but a batch of goals, including a hat-trick against Rochdale, prompted Dennis Wise to pay £200,000 to take the striker to Elland Road in January 2007 after an initial loan spell.

Leeds fans saw his trademark somersault and flip goal celebration just eight minutes into his home debut against Barnsley, but he could not stop United's relegation from the Championship. Kandol's striking partnership with Jermaine Beckford was one of the main reasons United won their opening seven League One games to quickly wipe out the club's 15-point deduction from the start of the season. Kandol's power in the air made him a particular threat to opposition defences. His exploits came to the attention of DR Congo, who, as Zaire, were the first black African team to qualify for the World Cup Finals in 1974. The Leopards were now looking to put a squad together to mount a serious challenge for the 2010 Finals in South Africa.

Several of their players, like Kandol, were based in Europe, so coach Neveu held a training camp in Paris in March 2008, which Kandol attended. Two back-to-back

Tresor Kandol.

games were also arranged, the first a 0–0 draw with Gabon at the Stade du Docteur Pieyre in the northern Parisian suburb of Aubervilliers on 25 March. The following day the Congo party were in action in Nanterre in another part of the French capital and drew 1–1 with Algeria, but Kandol did not play in either match.

The Leeds striker did well enough to be called into the squad for the World Cup opener against Egypt in June, but did not feature in the 1–0 defeat in Cairo. He finally got his chance in another friendly in France, against Togo in August 2008, as Congo came from behind to win 2–1 in Dreux thanks to a 68th-minute penalty from Lomana Lua Lua. Kandol was injured in that game and was dropped from 20-man squad for the next qualifier against Malawi, along with captain Shabani Nonda.

By this time Kandol was on loan with Millwall, making a spectacular start to his Lions' career with a goal after just 13 seconds on his debut during a 4–3 home loss to Oldham. He did well at the Den but after his loan spell was up was loaned out to another London club, Charlton. In addition to Lomana Lua Lua, Kandol's other younger cousins Kazenga Lua Lua (Newcastle) and Yala Bolaise (Plymouth and Barnet) have also played League football.

ROBBIE KEANE

(Republic of Ireland 1998– to date)

Striker

Born: Tallaght, Dublin, 8 July 1980.
Caps: Wolverhampton Wanderers 9, Coventry City 9, Inter Milan 4, Leeds United 13 (including 3 while on loan from Inter Milan), Tottenham Hotspur 46, Liverpool 4, Tottenham Hotspur 5. Total: 90
Goals: 39

THE Republic of Ireland's greatest marksman, Robbie Keane, is unquestionably one of his country's all-time greats. He left Leeds United shortly after the 2002 World Cup Finals, where his eye-catching displays elevated his status on the global stage. He scored three goals in four games in the tournament, but hopes that he would continue that rich vein of form at Elland Road did not come to fruition as he joined the exodus from Leeds before the start of the new season.

A boy star, Keane has made a huge impact on the international scene. He was part of the squads which won the Under-16 and Under-18 European Championships under the guidance of Brian Kerr and quickly built on that pedigree at club level. He played with South Dublin schools team Crumlin United and at 15 joined Wolves, where he turned pro, making his senior debut with two goals against Norwich in August 1997. The following March he made his first senior appearance for the Republic against the Czech Republic, and the razor-sharp youngster netted his first goal against Malta later that year.

Robbie Keane.

Keane finished 1998–99 as Wolves's top scorer, and inevitably attracted the attention of larger clubs, but the big guns were beaten to the punch by Coventry City, whose £6 million bid – a British record for a teenager – was accepted by the hard-up Molineux club. It was good financial business by the Sky Blues, who sold him on to Italian giants Inter Milan after a season for £13 million. Marcello Lippi was a big fan of Keane's, but he was sacked soon after the Irish star arrived at the San Siro and Lippi's successor, Marco Tardelli, hardly played him.

It was another Irishman, Leeds boss David O'Leary, who rescued Keane from his Milan misery. In December 2000 he arrived at Elland Road on loan and made an instant impact, with nine goals from just 12 Premiership starts as United finished in fourth place.

At the end of the season Keane's £12 million transfer went through, but he struggled for goals and the arrival of Robbie Fowler saw him largely confined to bit-part appearances from the bench. With Mark Viduka and Alan Smith also on the payroll, Keane was finding it hard to win a regular shirt at Leeds, but that was not the case with Ireland. He played in seven of their 10 qualification games in group two, which contained Portugal, Holland, Estonia, Cyprus and whipping boys Andorra. It was clear from the outset that the biggest threat to Ireland would come from the Dutch and Portugese, against whom Mick McCarthy's team would open their campaign.

Keane scored his only goal in the group stages as the Republic drew 2–2 in Amsterdam – after leading 2–0. A draw in Lisbon, followed by the expected victories against the smaller nations, put Ireland in with a great chance of qualification. Only a late Luis Figo goal in Dublin denied Ireland victory, but in September 2001 they beat Holland 1–0, despite Keane's United teammate Gary Kelly being sent off. That result virtually finished off the Dutch, and the Republic went on to finish second behind Portugal on goal difference. That put McCarthy's side into a Play-off with Asian runners-up Iran for a place in the Finals.

Ireland had home advantage first, and five minutes after Leeds colleague Ian Harte put the Emerald Islanders ahead from the spot Keane made it 2–0 – a scoreline they defended well in Tehran, restricting Iran to just one goal in injury time, to go to the Finals 2–1 on aggregate. Keane warmed up for the tournament with goals in friendly victories against Denmark and Russia, but Irish hopes were rocked when skipper Roy Keane was sent home for his behaviour a week before the Republic's opening game against Cameroon. The Irish showed they certainly did not lack spirit without the Manchester United star as they came from behind to draw 1–1 with dangerous African side Cameroon and only the woodwork denied Robbie Keane a late winner.

While Roy Keane was giving the tabloids plenty to write about, the squad he had left behind in the Far East, and his namesake in particular, were making their own headlines. Their second game was against Germany, who went in front with a Miroslav Klose header on 18 minutes. That looked like being the final outcome, as Oliver Kahn's saves kept the battling green shirts at bay until the last minute, when the effervescent Keane got on the end of a Niall Quinn flick and calmly clipped the ball over the German 'keeper for a priceless and deserved point.

Ireland and their vast army of supporters knew victory over a Saudi Arabia side already thumped 8–0 by Germany and beaten 1–0 by Cameroon would put them into the second round. It was Keane who sent them on their way to a 3–0 win by hooking in a seventh-minute volley and set up a meeting with Spain in the South Korean city of Suwon. The Spanish, eternal World Cup under-achievers, were hot favourites and lived up to that billing when Fernando Morientes put them ahead after only eight minutes. But the half-time introduction of veteran Niall Quinn revitalised Ireland, who took the game to the Spaniards, with Damien Duff causing all sorts of problems on the wing. When the Blackburn man was tripped in the box just after the hour, Leeds man Harte, usually so deadly from the spot, had his penalty saved by Iker Casillas.

Undaunted Ireland continued to pour forward, and just when it looked as though they were going to run out of time, Quinn was fouled in the box and Swedish referee Anders Fisk had no hesitation in pointing to the spot again.

This time Keane stepped up and struck the ball past Casillas to send the game into extra-time.

McCarthy's men were agonisingly close to winning the match in the extra period, but the match was settled by penalties. Keane converted the first, but misses by Matt Holland, David Connelly and Kevin Kilbane left the Irish broken-hearted. Back home, the people of Ireland were proud of their team's efforts and 100,000 fans welcomed them home in Dublin – but there was to be no homecoming for Keane at Elland Road.

Leeds United were in financial free-fall, and with Keane's value having risen on the back of a wonderful World Cup rumours of his exit soon became fact when he joined Tottenham for £7 million. The bubbly striker became a bit of an institution at White Hart Lane, winning Spurs' Player of the Year three times, scoring 100 goals for the club and helping them win the Football League Cup in 2008. He continued to lead from the front for the Republic of Ireland and, following Steve Staunton's appointment as manager, was named skipper.

Adored by Irish fans, Keane scored a hat-trick against San Marino in the final game at Lansdowne Road before the move to Croke Park. After an ill-fated £19 million move to Liverpool, he returned to Tottenham just six months later and was installed as captain. Nine days after his return he played his 86th full international, scoring both goals against Georgia at Croke Park to boost the Republic's chances of reached the 2010 World Cup Finals in South Africa. If Keane keeps scoring they should make it – they have never lost a game in which he has scored, apart from that 2002 game against Spain when they were beaten on penalties. His strike against Nigeria at Craven Cottage took him to 39 goals, having overhauled the previous best of 21 by Niall Quinn long ago and, barring injury, he could well reach the double landmark of 100 appearances and 50 goals for his country in the years to come.

GARY KELLY
(Republic of Ireland 1994–2002)
Right-back
Born: Drogheda, Co. Louth, 9 July 1974.
Caps: Leeds United 51
Goals: 2

GARY KELLY moved rapidly through the gears to become a World Cup star with the Republic of Ireland. He came from nowhere to earn a place in Jack Charlton's squad for the 1994 Finals thanks to a tactical switch by Leeds boss Howard Wilkinson. Young Kelly arrived at Elland Road in July 1991 as a striker from Dublin junior club Home Farm. He was a sharp little player with an excellent touch, but United's coaches reckoned he was not cut out to be a forward and preferred to utilise his speed on the right-wing.

After just 15 minutes of reserve-team football the youngster made his first-team debut as a 17-year-old, coming off the bench to replace Carl Shutt for the final 15 minutes of a League Cup tie against Scunthorpe on 8 October 1991. The Under-18 international then returned to junior and reserve team football to learn his trade, winning the first of his five Under-21 caps a year later against Spain.

Indeed, apart from a couple more first-team sub appearances, many Leeds fans heard little of his progress behind the scenes until he was the surprise name on the teamsheet on the opening day of the 1993–94 season at Manchester City. Even more surprising was to find him playing at full-back. United drew 1–1 with a late goal by new signing Brian Deane, but it was the classy display of young Kelly on his full debut which got the Whites faithful talking. He looked a natural right-back, and Wilkinson's decision to change the teenager's position was a brilliant and enduring success.

Kelly did not anticipate a long run in the first team, but he was simply too good to drop. And it did not take others long to appreciate how well he was playing. After just 14 Premiership games he was included in the Republic of Ireland squad for the first time, watching from the bench as they drew 1–1 in Belfast to earn the point they needed to qualify for the World Cup Finals in the US. It was not long before Republic boss Jack Charlton gave Kelly his first start, a goalless draw with Russia in which the teenager showed maturity beyond his years. Ireland had discovered a young player who could challenge Denis Irwin, the former Leeds player, for the right-back spot.

Kelly had an outstanding ever-present season and played in several Irish warm-up games, including outstanding wins in Holland and Germany ahead of the trip to the States. The German victory saw him come on as a substitute for Irwin in Hanover, with the Republic leading through Tony Cascarino's first-half header. There was no question of Kelly being overawed and he was soon joining in an attacking move. Picking up the ball on the right he cut in and hit a shot with his left foot, which deflected past goalkeeper Bodo Illgner to seal victory and end Germany's six-year unbeaten home run.

Ireland took their form to the World Cup, Ray Houghton's early goal giving Charlton's team a fantastic 1–0 win against Italy in New York, but the group was split wide open when Mexico beat Ireland 2–1. Big Jack had opted for Irwin's greater experience in those games but brought in Kelly for the crunch game against Norway after Irwin had received cautions in the opening two games.

While Kelly and Co. fought out a 0–0 draw, Italy were held 1–1 by Mexico, leaving all the teams on four points and level on goal difference. The South Americans were deemed group winners having scored more goals, while the Irish got the nod over Italy, after finishing with identical records, on the basis of their win against the

Gary Kelly in action against Andorra.

Azzurri in the Giants Stadium. Kelly kept his place for the second-round game against Holland, in which the Dutch avenged their pre-tournament defeat in Amsterdam with a 2–0 victory in Orlando with first-half goals from Dennis Bergkamp and Wim Jonk.

Holland were to inflict more damage on the Republic the following year. Kelly had played in all 10 Euro '96 qualification games as Ireland finished runners-up to Portugal in group seven. That put them in a Play-off against Holland, who had surprisingly been pipped for the group five leadership by the Czech Republic. The one-off game was staged at Anfield, home of Liverpool, where two goals from teenage striker Patrick Kluivert killed off Irish hopes of joining the Finals party in England the following summer. The match was also the last in the wonderful 10-year managerial reign of former Leeds hero Jack Charlton.

Big Jack, aged 60, may have been going into retirement, but he left Ireland with a crop of players they could be proud of, including the remarkably consistent Kelly, who at the age of 21 was already a seasoned international. From his Premiership debut he had a run of 118 successive games for Leeds, and that was only ended as the five-day international rule was invoked ahead of the Play-off with Holland.

Ireland's new boss Mick McCarthy initially preferred the Irwin-Jeff Kenna full-back combination, and Kelly did not play a full international during 1996. His form had dipped slightly, but picked up when Leeds boss George

Graham made him captain in the absence of David Hopkin and switched him to a more advanced midfield role. He broke his club scoring duck that year, netting the opener in a 2–0 victory at Southampton, which ended a long sequence of away games without a win. A couple of months later he scored his second – and last – Premiership goal as United triumphed 2–0 at West Ham in January 1997.

Ireland's World Cup hopes once again hinged on the Play-offs, and Kelly played in both legs against Belgium to decide who would go to France '98. Eire went out 3–2 on aggregate, but Kelly had regained his place in the national team and played in post-season friendlies against the Czech Republic, Argentina and Mexico.

The 1998–99 season was a complete write-off as Kelly missed the entire campaign suffering from shin splints. It was not until September 1999 that he was able to pull on that white number-two shirt for Leeds, starting in a 3–2 victory against Newcastle at Elland Road, and became an automatic choice once more. Because of the injury he had only played fleetingly in the Euro 2000 qualifiers, which again ended in Play-off misery for the Republic of Ireland, losing on away goals to Turkey. However, a revitalised Kelly was back helping steer the Republic to another place in the World Cup Finals while playing his part in United's run to the Champions League semi-finals. He scored his second international goal in a 4–0 win in Cyprus to keep Ireland up with group two, rivals but was sent off in the 1–0 win against Holland in Dublin. He made late appearances from the bench in the Play-offs against Iran, which saw Eire win 2–1 on aggregate, and Kelly was back in the World Cup Finals. He started all their games in Japan and South Korea as Ireland came through a group containing Germany, Cameroon and Saudi Arabia to face Spain in the second round. The Spanish match was an epic, with the brave Irish losing in a penalty shootout in what was Kelly's landmark 50th appearance for his country.

The Drogheda-born player pulled on the green shirt just twice more before announcing, at the age of 29, the end of his international career in September 2003. He said the decision was made to prolong his career at Leeds, and he went on to become only the 10th United player to make more than 500 appearances for the club, reaching the milestone in a 2–1 victory against Luton at Elland Road on 25 February 2006.

In all that time he only scored four goals, the last coming a month before the Luton game – a thunderous long-range piledriver against Wigan, which took the FA Cup tie to penalties. It was his only goal at Elland Road and his first for three years since netting a quick free-kick in a 2–1 FA Cup win at Crystal Palace. His scoring record was quite a contrast to his nephew Ian Harte, his Leeds and Ireland full-back partner, who was a real dead-ball specialist.

The loyal one-club man was awarded a testimonial match in May 2002, played against Celtic, and he donated the proceeds to several cancer charities, in dedication to his sister Mandy, who died from the disease in 1998. True to his word he saw out his career with Leeds, even after relegation from the Premiership, and he then returned to live in Ireland, the nation he had served so proudly on football fields around the world.

HARRY KEWELL
(Australia 1996– to date)
Striker / winger
Born: Smithfield, New South Wales, 22 September 1978.
Caps: Leeds United 13, Liverpool 23, Galatasaray 5. Total: 41
Goals: 13

AUSTRALIA'S golden boy Harry Kewell found himself at the centre of an on-going club-versus-country row during his seven years at Leeds United. Regarded as the best footballer to come out of Oz, he played just 13 times for the Socceroos during his seven and a half years at Elland Road. Soccer Australia were frustrated by United's refusal to release him for internationals, sparking a war of words between the Australian football body and the Whites.

Kewell was a wonderfully gifted player who had come through the ranks of the New South Wales Soccer Academy, so it was no surprise that the Aussies wanted to call on his talents. However, United argued that they were his employers, and it was simply not practical to release the player to travel halfway round the world for what were, sometimes, just friendly internationals.

A student of Westfield Sports High School, Kewell played for youth side Marconi Stallions and was invited for a four-week trial at Leeds when he was just 15. He arrived at Elland Road with future Socceroo teammate Brett Emerton and, although United wanted to keep both young Aussies, Leeds were only able to take on Kewell because his father Rod was English, so he satisfied visa requirements.

Kewell signed in December 1995 and could not have had a better mentor than Howard Wilkinson, the Leeds boss, who had an outstanding crop of youngsters on his hands. Initially, Kewell was either a full-back or wing-back, and after just two Premiership appearances he made his full international debut as a 17-year-old in a friendly against Chile towards the end of 1995–96. The Socceroos had Joe Spitieri sent off after half an hour and lost 3–0. Kewell also turned out against Saudi Arabia in Riyadh the following October in what was Eddie Thomson's last game as Australia coach.

At this stage of his career Kewell was still only a fringe player at Elland Road, and the club were happy to let him go to Tahiti in January 1997 to take part in a series of World Youth Cup qualification games against Fiji and New Zealand. The young Aussie was among a crop of outstanding up-and-coming talent at Elland Road, and it was no surprise when they won the FA Youth Cup in 1997.

Harry Kewell, the 'Wizard of Oz', in action against England at Upton Park in 2003.

Kewell's high-speed dribbling skills marked him out as a star of the future, and it was not long before he broke into the Leeds senior side on a regular basis, which was to precipitate the club-versus-country bust-up. United had no problem in releasing him for Australia's crucial World Cup double-header against Iran, which would determine who would go through to the Finals. Kewell scored in front of a massive 128,000 crowd in Tehran where the Aussies, now coached by Terry Venables, drew 1–1.

A goalless draw or a win in Melbourne the following week would put the Green and Golds through. Kewell sent the MCG into raptures with a goal on 32 minutes, and Tony Vidmar made it 2–0 three minutes after the break. Venables's side were just 20 minutes away from their first appearance in the Finals since 1974 when Karin Bagheri and Khoadadad Azizi struck twice in five minutes to snatch the big prize on away goals.

No sooner had Kewell returned to Leeds, who were making steady progress under George Graham, than the Aussies were demanding his release for the Confederations Cup in the Middle East. Graham was furious. He had no quibble with international calls for important competitive matches, but felt nations were not showing enough courtesy towards clubs by continually asking for players like Kewell, and, in the case of South Africa, Lucas Radebe.

Leeds had to bow to Australia's request, and Kewell faced Saudi Arabia, Uruguay and Brazil in the Confederations Cup. He hit the golden-goal winner against Uruguay to set up a Final meeting with Brazil, against whom Mark Viduka was sent off early on. The Samba stars took full advantage, winning 6–0 to inflict Australia's heaviest defeat in 40 years. The rift between Leeds and Soccer Australia had been opened, and Kewell did not represent his country again for nearly three years, until he helped Australia to a 3–0 win in Hungary to give Frank Farina his first victory as the Socceroos' coach.

The Aussies certainly did not need top European stars like Kewell and Mark Viduka to overcome the likes of Fiji, American Samoa and Tonga in Oceania group games as they looked towards the 2002 World Cup. Soccer Australia had complied with a FIFA request that European-based players were not be chosen for such games. With Leeds established in European competitions and having genuine Premiership aspirations, Kewell was left to concentrate on his club commitments.

'Harry Cool' was named the PFA Young Player of the Year in 1999–2000 when United reached the semi-finals of the UEFA Cup, the Aussie being red-carded in the highly-charged second leg against Galatasaray which followed the death of two Leeds supporters prior to the game in Turkey.

Kewell was given a more attacking role by David O'Leary and responded to the challenge with some dazzling displays and an increased goal output, many of them spectacular efforts. The 21-year-old's stunning strike, which knocked out Fabio Capello's Roma in March 2000, showed why both Milan clubs and Lazio had inquired about his availability.

While Leeds tore up the formbook by qualifying for the second phase of the Champions League, Kewell was sidelined by injury and did not start a match in the competition until the 3–2 defeat at Real Madrid in March 2001. To the delight of Aussie fans both Kewell and his Leeds clubmate Mark Viduka were available for the World Cup Play-offs against Uruguay in November 2001 to determine who would go through to the Finals.

Despite grumblings from European clubs, Kewell, Viduka and other Euro stars played against France in a 1–1 draw in Melbourne as a warm up to the crunch game against Uruguay. The Leeds duo were paired up front against the South Americans, who lost to a late Kevin Muscat penalty, although they easily overturned the deficit in Montevideo five days later, winning 3–0.

With Australia failing to reach the Finals again they went into semi-hibernation in 2002, playing only Oceania Nations Cup games against Vanuatu, New Caledonia, Fiji, Tahiti and New Zealand, for which their big names were not required. When the Aussies were able to put out their main side they looked a decent outfit, as England discovered in Kewell's last international appearance as a Leeds player. He took Sven-Goran Eriksson's squad apart in a famous Socceroos 3–1 victory at Upton Park, weighing in with a fine solo goal on 42 minutes.

As Leeds's financial difficulties became apparent, Kewell was among the early departures, joining Liverpool for a cut-price £5 million. The move was acrimonious as it involved a row over his agent's cut of the transfer fee. Injuries that had blighted the last year or so of his time at Leeds were also to dog his time at Anfield, where he won 2005 Champions League and 2006 FA Cup-winners medals, despite limping off in both games. He also achieved his dream of playing in the World Cup Finals. Once again the Green and Golds faced Uruguay in a Play-off and this time Australia, under the guidance of Guus Hiddink, went through after a penalty shootout.

Kewell played in the opening 3–1 win in the Finals against Japan, when all the Australian goals came in the last six minutes, came on in the 2–0 defeat against Brazil and scored the equaliser against Croatia which put them into the second phase against Italy, a 1–0 defeat which he missed with a foot injury. He hardly played at all in 2006–07, although he came on in the Champions League Final defeat against AC Milan in Athens. He moved to Galatasaray on a two-year deal in July 2008 – a transfer which provoked strong criticism from some Leeds fans, given that he was a United player when two Whites supporters were knifed to death ahead of the 2000 UEFA Cup semi-final in Istanbul.

Since his move to Turkey he has captained his country, but once again suffered from injury after a bright start with his new club. Kewell may have upset Leeds followers since his departure from Elland Road, but he provided some magical memories as a United player. As for Aussie fans, they know the treble winner of the Oceania Player of the Year award is the best footballing talent they have ever produced.

NEIL KILKENNY

(Australia 2006– to date)
Midfield
Born: Enfield, London, 19 December 1985.
Caps: Birmingham City 1, Leeds United 1. Total: 2

NEIL KILKENNY found himself up against some of the world's best midfielders as he strove for Olympic glory with Australia. The Leeds United pass-master was a member of the Under-23 team which represented Australia in the 2008 Olympics in China. He missed the opening four games of the Whites' League One programme as a result, but the tournament was all part of Kilkenny's learning curve. He was on the bench as the Aussies drew 1–1 with Serbia in their first game, but was brought in to face Argentina for the second match. He found himself tussling with players of the calibre of Lionel Messi (Barcelona), Juan Riquelme (Boca Juniors) and Liverpool's Javier Mascherano in the stifling heat of Shanghai. Kilkenny and the Aussies lost to a goal from Ezequiel Lavezzi on 77 minutes, but were not disgraced. It was back on bench duty for Kilkenny for the decisive game against Ivory Coast, which the boys from Down Under needed to win to progress, but they went down to the only goal from Chelsea's Saloman Kalou.

Although born in London, Kilkenny was raised in Brisbane and played with junior club Coalstars in Queensland before returning to England to join Arsenal's Academy. After failing to make the grade at Highbury, he joined Birmingham City as a 19-year-old and was loaned out to Oldham to gain experience. Back at St Andrew's, he made an eventful full Premiership debut against Liverpool, having an excellent match, only to be sent off seven minutes from the end for handling the ball on the line, enabling the Reds to grab a 2–2 draw from the resulting penalty.

Kilkenny was eligible to play for England, Ireland or Australia, but pledged himself to the latter just before the 2006 World Cup and was called up by Socceroos boss Guus Hiddink to train with the senior squad prior to the tournament. His reward for his commitment was a first cap, coming on as a late substitute against Liechtenstein in the German city of Ulm.

After failing to earn a regular place in Birmingham's team, Kilkenny returned to Boundary Park for a second loan spell and, just four days after helping the Latics win at Elland Road, signed a three-and-a-half year deal with Leeds in a £150,000 transfer. He helped Leeds reach the Play-off Final against Doncaster – the club Leeds beat to his signature – at Wembley. Rovers won 1–0, but while the United squad had a deserved summer break, Kilkenny flew to Australia to join the 33-man pre-Olympic training camp.

Soccer Australia used their Under-23 side to qualify for the Olympics and Kilkenny had played his part in helping the squad make it to the Beijing Games. There was an added bonus for the Leeds midfielder as he was one of several of the Olympic team to get a run in a dead World

Neil Kilkenny, second from right, helps the Australian squad prepare for the 2008 Olympic Games tournament.

Cup rubber against China at Sydney's ANZ Stadium. The Aussies had already qualified and the Chinese were out of the running, but the Asian side took the spoils with a blistering 20-yard shot from Sun Xiang. Kilkenny replaced Mile Jedinak for the final 11 minutes to win his second cap.

The real business was the Olympics, though, and Kilkenny made the final 18-man squad and featured in five warm-up games, including the first international football match at any level in the Northern Territories when the Olyroos lost 4–3 to Chile in Darwin. The quality of the opposition in China, particularly gold medallists Argentina, proved too much for the Australians and Kilkenny returned to Leeds and went straight into the side for a fine 4–0 League Cup win against Crystal Palace. But after Gary McAllister was replaced as manager by Simon Grayson, Kilkenny initially found himself out of the first-team picture, although a strong finish to 2008–09 rekindled his international aspirations.

RADOSTIN KISHISHEV

(Bulgaria 1996–2007)
Full-back/Midfield
Born: Burgas, 30 July 1974.
Caps: Neftochimik, Bursapor, Litex, Charlton Athletic 40, *Leeds United 1, Leicester City 4. Total: 78
* On loan from Leicester City

VETERAN defender Radostin Kishishev returned to the scene of one of Bulgaria's milestone games when he joined Leeds United on loan. He was an up-and-coming youngster when Bulgaria made their first appearance in the European Championships at Elland Road in Euro '96. The defender had been a regular at Youth and Under-21 level before breaking into Ditimar Penev's squad just before the tournament and won his seventh cap as Bulgaria drew 1–1 with Spain in that opening game in Leeds. He was booked in that game, received a yellow card as Bulgaria won 1–0 at Newcastle and did not play in the 3–1 defeat in France which eliminated the Balkan side.

Fast forward 11 years, and Kishishev returned to Elland Road on loan from Charlton and was still a fixture in the national side. A couple of weeks after joining United's battle for survival in the Championship, he was in action for Bulgaria when they were held 0–0 by Albania in Sofia in a European Championship qualifier. Despite solid displays in midfield by Kish, Leeds were relegated and he returned to the Valley, joining Leicester in June 2007 on a free transfer. He did not get much of a look-in with the Foxes and jumped at the chance to join Leeds on loan again, shortly after making his 78th international appearance, in which he scored an own-goal in a 1–1 draw in Albania, which effectively ended Bulgaria's hopes of reaching the European Championships Finals. He did not seem fully match-fit in his second spell with Leeds and,

Radostin Kishishev attempts a tackle for Bulgaria against Wales's Joe Ledley.

after the departure of Dennis Wise, he was deemed surplus to requirements and returned to his parent club.

In January 2009 he went back to his homeland and signed for Litex Lovech for a second time. He began his career in Bulgaria playing in the top division as a teenager with one of his local clubs, Chernomoretz Burgas. He was transferred to neighbours Neftochimik in summer 1994 when Chernomoretz were relegated and Neftochimik, simultaneously, were promoted. He made his international debut the following year against Hungary in a tournament in Malaysia, although there is some debate as to whether this was classified as a full international.

After Euro '96 he became a regular in the Bulgarian side, playing in all three of their matches in the 1998 World Cup Finals in France at right-back. After a year in Turkey with Bursapor he joined Litex, winning the Bulgarian League title twice before pitching up at Charlton in summer 2000. Addicks boss Alan Curbishley used Kishishev in both midfield and at right-back, and he continued to represent his country, although he fell out with national team boss Plamen Markov in May 2003 after being surprisingly overlooked for the captaincy after the retirement of Krassimir Balakov. Kishishev announced that he would not play for Bulgaria again – even though they had a key qualifier against Belgium a fortnight later.

Markov's men did qualify for the Finals, and Kishishev did a U-turn and offered to play for his country again, but he was not included in Markov's 23-man squad for the Euro Finals in Portugal. When legendary striker Hristo Stoichkov took over as Bulgaria's boss he brought Kishishev straight back into the fold, picking him for a friendly against the Republic of Ireland in Dublin which ended 1–1. Subsequently, Kishishev played in World Cup qualifiers and skippered his country, but gave up the captain's armband after a spat with the fiery Stoichkov. Solid and reliable at full-back, Kishishev was also noted for the huge amount of hard graft he did in midfield, attributes which have left him in the top 10 list of appearances for Bulgaria.

EDDIE LEWIS

(United States of America 1996–2008)

Midfield/Left-back

Born: Cerritos, California, 17 May 1974.
Caps: San Jose Clash 20, Fulham 23, Preston North End 21, Leeds United 8, Derby County 9, Los Angeles Galaxy 1. Total: 82
Goals: 10

EDDIE LEWIS ranks as one of the United States's best football exports. He was certainly a class act in his two seasons at Elland Road, in what were tough times for Leeds United, playing in the 2006 World Cup. The Californian began with UCLA Bruins as a teenage striker, stepping up to Major League Soccer with San Jose Clash in 1996, quickly earning his first cap in a 4–1 defeat to Peru.

A switch to the left side of midfield paid big dividends for the energetic Lewis, who was an ever-present in 1998 and made his second international appearance in a 0–0 draw with Australia at his home-team stadium in San Jose. His delivery from the left provided lots of goals at club and international level, and Lewis became a regular in Bruce Arena's improving American team before signing for Fulham in March 2000 for £1.3 million. The winger struggled to adapt to the pace of the English game and only made one start as Fulham won the First Division title in 2001. But he still retained his place in the US side, helping them to the World Cup Finals, where they knocked out the highly-fancied Portugal team in the group stages.

Lewis played in the second-round game against Mexico in Jeonju, where his perfectly flighted cross was headed in by Landon Donovan to seal a 2–0 win and set up a quarter-final meeting with Germany. Lewis played the full 90 minutes against the Germans, who were somewhat flattered by their 1–0 victory courtesy of Michael Ballack's goal.

Shortly into the new season he moved to Preston for £500,000 after gaining the appropriate work permit and quickly became popular with the Deepdale fans with a string of fine performances. His last game for Preston was in the 2005 Championship Play-off Final at the Millennium Stadium, in which the Lilywhites lost 1–0 to West Ham. Having missed out on the Premiership, Lewis turned down a new contract and joined Leeds.

Consistent, busy and deadly from set-pieces, Lewis scored some crucial curling free-kicks, none so vital as the one which rescued a 1–1 home draw in the Play-off semi-final against his old club, Preston. Leeds completed the job, winning the second leg 2–0, but lost 3–0 in the Final against Watford. Lewis had little time to digest that disappointment before heading to Germany for the World Cup Finals. Once again he had played his part in qualification and skippered the States back on his old stamping ground at San Jose against Costa Rica shortly

Eddie Lewis (far right) celebrates with Landon Donovan and goalkeeper Brad Friedel after the USA's 2–0 win against Mexico in the 2002 World Cup.

after a 2–0 win against Mexico ensured the US reached their fifth successive Finals.

Arena's side, with Lewis at left-back, made a poor start, losing 3–0 to the Czech Republic. He was dropped for the second match against Italy which saw three players sent off. Daniele de Rossi was dismissed for elbowing, but the Americans' numerical advantage did not last long, as Pablo Mastroeni was ordered off, followed early in the second half by Eddie Pope. However, the Italians could not make the most of their extra man in the remaining 43 minutes and the nine men from the States held on for a fine 1–1 draw. The point kept their hopes alive, and the red cards saw Lewis return to his more favoured left-wing role for the vital game against Ghana in Nuremburg. This time the States did not do themselves justice and returned home after a 2–1 defeat.

After his extended summer schedule, Lewis was subject to a bid from Wolves, which was rejected, and he spent the season flitting between midfield and defence on the left as Leeds struggled to find the winning formula.

Eddie Lewis moves in but cannot prevent Tomas Rosicky from scoring for the Czech Republic in the 2006 World Cup.

United were relegated from the Championship and Lewis was one of the few bright spots, being elected the club's Player of the Year. His contract was up in July 2007 and he signed for Premiership club Derby County, a move that seemed to revitalise his international career. After a disappointing World Cup many thought his days with the United States were over, but he continued to represent his country during his year at Pride Park, moving beyond the 80-cap mark. He showed he had not lost any of his deadball skills by curling in a free-kick as the States ran out 3–0 winners in Poland in March 2008. He also captained his country again, leading by example by scoring the only goal in a World Cup qualifying win in Barbados. In August 2008, at the age of 34, he was reunited with former national coach Arena at LA Galaxy, where he played alongside former England skipper David Beckham.

PETER LORIMER
(Scotland 1969–75)

Winger
Born: Broughty Ferry, Dundee, 14 December 1946.
Caps: Leeds United 21
Goals: 4

THUNDERBOOTS Peter Lorimer is the only man to have represented Scotland at every level. Leeds United's record goalscorer, whose shooting terrorised goalkeepers throughout the world, played at schoolboy, youth, amateur, Under-23 and full international level. The Dundonian is a Leeds legend, having made his debut as a 15-year-old, and has scored more goals for the club than any other player in his near 20-year career at Elland Road.

Lorimer was a kid in demand, but unfashionable Leeds won the race to sign him, scout John Quinn having identified his talent when watching the youngster play at Stobswell School before Lorimer had gained any representative honours. Revie was so keen to get Lorimer's signature that he was stopped for speeding on his way to Dundee. Lorimer was a boy wonder for Dundee Schools, piling in goals from all angles, earning Under-15 Scotland honours when he was still only 13.

In 1961–62 he had smashed in 176 goals, including a couple as Scotland Schools beat England 4–2, his performance attracting a posse of scouts, but forward-thinking United had already beaten them to the punch. Lorimer was just 15 years and 289 days old when an injury crisis saw Revie give the young Scot his debut in a 1–1 home draw with Southampton on 29 September 1962. He still had not signed professional forms when he was selected by the Scottish FA for an amateur tour party for a tournament in Nairobi, Kenya. His progress was checked by a broken leg, which ruled him out for more than six months, but he worked his way through the juniors and reserves to earn more first-team appearances. He scored

Peter Lorimer.

the first of his 168 League goals by netting the winner against Nottingham Forest on 4 September 1965. That was his breakthrough season, with 16 goals, including a hat-trick in a 6–0 League Cup romp against Bury. He was top scorer in 1967–68 with 30 goals when Leeds won the League Cup, quickly followed by the Fairs Cup, in which he scored four times against Luxembourg amateurs Spora in the first round.

When United won the title in 1968–69 he was not as productive, but the big surprise was that his full international debut did not come until November 1969, when he came on as a substitute for Wolves's Hugh Curran in a dead European Championship rubber against Austria. A goal in each half from Helmut Redl gave the home side a 2–0 win. The following month he scored twice in his first Under-23 game against France, but apart from a couple of Home International games against Wales and Northern Ireland he found himself frozen out of the Scotland squad by the Scottish FA.

The Scots top brass were unhappy that Lorimer had spent part of one summer playing and coaching in South Africa, without telling them, when they wanted him for a tour. It was a political hot potato, and Lorimer found himself banned by the Scottish FA, although the ban was lifted after Tommy Docherty took over team affairs from Bobby Brown. The Doc argued that he needed his best players, like Lorimer, if Scotland were two have any chance of qualifying for the World Cup. The Scottish FA relented and allowed Lorimer to play in the 1972 Home Internationals just after he picked up an FA Cup-winners' medal with Leeds. He responded with the second goal in a 2–0 win against Northern Ireland in Belfast. He then smashed in a thumping drive from distance to see off Wales, but suffered the disappointment of a 1–0 defeat against England at Hampden Park.

Scotland were in a three-nation World Cup qualifying group along with Denmark and Czechoslovakia. They made a flying start, with 'Lash' having an excellent match as Scotland thumped Denmark 4–1 in Copenhagen, and he netted the second goal in the return in Glasgow, when the Scots, who had David Harvey making his international debut, won 2–0; however, that match had a nasty sting in the tail for Lorimer after he was sent off with his man-marker Per Roentved. In his next match he scored an own-goal when the ball glanced off his head past Bobby Clark to set England on their way to a 5–0 Hampden humiliation of Scotland in the Scottish FA centenary game.

The Denmark dismissal ruled Lorimer out of the big showdown with Czechoslovakia, so he was not selected for the summer friendlies against Switzerland and Brazil, leaving him more time to polish his recently acquired second Fairs Cup-winners' medal after Leeds saw off the challenge of Juventus. In the event Scotland, who had been shaken by Docherty's controversial decision to quit as national team boss to take over at Manchester United, beat the Czechs without Lorimer thanks to a winner from his Leeds teammate Joe Jordan.

Willie Ormond was the new man in charge and had no hesitation in taking Lorimer to the Finals in West Germany. It was only the third time that the Scots had qualified for the Finals, and Lorimer and the other Leeds lads in the party went there on a high, having swept to their second League title.

Lorimer potted a 20-yard volley to open the scoring against Zaire, but the Africans did well to keep the score down to 2–0, Jordan heading in the second. Lorimer also hit the bar, but the margin of victory was to prove Scotland's undoing. They played well against Brazil and were possibly worth more than a 0–0 draw, but a 1–1 draw with Yugoslavia saw Ormond's men eliminated on goal difference. Lorimer only featured once for Scotland in 1975, coming on for Celtic's Dixie Dean in a 2–1 defeat against Spain in a European Championship qualifier at Hampden Park. There was also disappointment on the club front as Leeds lost the European Cup Final to Bayern Munich in Paris.

United had recovered wonderfully well from the debacle of Brian Clough's 44 days in charge to have a real tilt at the Continent's top prize. Lorimer scored the crucial away goal in Barcelona in the semi-final and had a volley controversially chalked off in the Final, enabling Munich to recover and snatch a 2–0 win. That was the last of the Finals in which Lorimer, and many of the other great

Peter Lorimer (right) gets Scotland on the move against England. Leeds United teammate Joe Jordan is in the background.

members of Revie's squad were to appear. The squad was starting to break up, and Lorimer's international career was also nearly at an end. He was recalled for the double header against Denmark, with Scotland needing to win both matches to keep their Euro hopes alive. The 1–0 win in Copenhagen was overshadowed by the SFA's suspension of five players, including skipper Billy Bremner, after an incident after the game. The Leeds captain did not play for Scotland again.

The following month Scotland defeated the Danes 3–1 in what was Lorimer's final start for his country. The victory was ultimately hollow, as Spain's draw with Romania eliminated the Scots. Lorimer pulled on the dark blue jersey for the final time on a bitterly cold Hampden night when he came off the bench to replace John Doyle, a speedy winger, who was making his debut in a 1–1 draw against Romania. Doyle joined Celtic shortly afterwards but died at the age of 30 in tragic circumstances when he was electrocuted while working on his new home.

Although international goalkeepers and defensive walls were to be spared Lorimer's rocket-shooting, there were no signs that his club career was coming to an end. He remained at Elland Road until he was 33, by which time the club was on the slide from the heights scaled under Don Revie. He joined Toronto Blizzard in March 1979, but returned to Yorkshire later in the year for a season with York City before going back to Canada as assistant to Johnny Giles at Vancouver Whitecaps.

In winter 1983 Lorimer was back at Elland Road, training in preparation for another season, when news came through that the North American Soccer League had folded. Leeds had been relegated, and new boss Eddie Gray was working on a shoestring budget trying to bring through a talented crop of youngsters including John Sheridan, Denis Irwin, Terry Phelan, Tommy Wright and Scott Sellars. Gray asked Lorimer to help the youngsters on the pitch, and at the age of 36 – older than his manager – he rejoined United.

Veteran skipper Lorimer's influence certainly helped the kids develop, and in that second spell at the club he overhauled John Charles's goalscoring record in the process. The last of his 238 Leeds goals was a late penalty winner against Middlesbrough just after Gray had been sacked. Billy Bremner was installed as the new boss and Lorimer left shortly afterwards. He had a short stint in Israel as player-coach with Hapoel Haifa, then went on to run the Commercial pub in Leeds, becoming a United board member in March 2004, acting as a fans' ambassador. He also worked as an analyser for local radio and remains a regular in the press room at Elland Road, scene of many of his wonder goals. His goal ratio for Scotland did not match his Leeds figures, but he had a rather stop-start international career, suffering from the lack of a consistent run in the side because of suspension and availability, while competition was also hot for the

right-wing berth with the likes of Old Firm duo Willie Henderson and Jimmy Johnstone on the scene.

The record books will show that Peter Lorimer made a massive contribution to Leeds United Football Club – and they are not wrong. It is not just the stats that are impressive but the nature of his goals. Lorimer did not do tap-ins. He was a fearsome striker of the ball, cutting in from the right to drive a missile into the top corner, or crashing in free-kicks or penalties with great power and accuracy. There may have been quicker wingers around, but few as effective. What is often overlooked is the number of games he played for Leeds – just over 700 – a testament to his fitness and durability.

TEDDY LUCIC
(Sweden 1995–2006)
Defender
Born: Biskopsgaard, Gothenburg, 15 April 1973.
Caps: Vasta Frolunda 5, IFK Gothenburg 12, Bologna 7, AIK Solna 23, *Leeds United 3, Bayer Leverkusen 23, Hacken 13. Total: 86
* On loan from Solna

SWEDISH defender Teddy Lucic almost started his international career at Elland Road. He was included in the national squad for the first time for the 1995 Umbro Cup, which was being held in England, and made his debut in a 1–0 defeat against Brazil at Villa Park. Four days later he was in the Swedish side that lined up against England, who

Teddy Lucic.

scrambled a 3–3 draw in Leeds after strikes from David Platt and Darren Anderton in the final two minutes.

Lucic could have played football for any one of three countries, as his father was Croatian and his mother was born in Finland. But it was soon clear he would play for the land of his birth after he starred with IF Lundby in the early 1990s, which led to a move to Vastra Frolunda, and he was included in the 1994 World Cup squad but did not play, having to wait until the following year to make his breakthrough in the Umbro Cup. Elevation to the national side was soon followed by a move to IFK Gothenburg, one of Sweden's major clubs, where he won a League Championship medal in his first season in 1996.

Gothenburg were regular performers in Europe, and Lucic was a regular in the Swedish defence, either at centre-back or full-back. He moved into Serie A with Bologna but only managed nine appearances in two years with the Italian club before returning to Sweden with AIK Solna. When Solna ran into financial problems they had to get some of their major stars, Lucic among them, temporarily off the wage bill. He pitched up at Elland Road on loan in August 2002, but his arrival was delayed as he played a friendly against Russia and was in the Swedish squad that kicked off their Euro 2004 qualifying campaign with a 0–0 draw against Latvia. He was one of several foreign players drafted in on loan by Leeds boss Venables, who had been in charge of England when Lucic made his second international appearance in that six-goal thriller.

At the same time as agreeing to his loan move to Leeds, AIK extended the 29-year-old's contract until November 2004 to avoid losing him on a Bosman. Lucic arrived at Elland Road after playing in all their World Cup games in the Far East earlier in the year, including the 1–1 draw with England in Saitama. Victory over Nigeria and a draw against Argentina saw them top the group and they were expected to progress to the quarter-finals at the expense of Senegal. Henrik Larsson gave Sweden an early lead, but the Africans were level by half-time thanks to Henri Camara, and the same player scored the sudden death golden goal in extra-time to knock out the Scandinavians.

During his 16 games with Leeds, Lucic managed to do something he did not manage in his 86 appearances with Sweden – score a goal. It came in a 3–2 defeat at Chelsea in January 2003 when he bundled in a corner, but he was at Leeds during a turbulent time in their history. With Venables forced to sell top names as the Whites announced huge debts, Leeds struggled in the Premiership and were knocked out of Europe and the FA and League Cups by Malaga and Sheffield United respectively.

No doubt it was a relief for Lucic to get away from Elland Road to play for the national team. He featured in a thrilling friendly against the Czech Republic in Teplice when the Swedes came from 1–0 and 3–2 down to draw 3–3.

After missing the King's Cup tournament in Thailand, which was played during the Swedish League's midwinter

Referee Carlos Simon (Brazil) seems pleased with his decision to send off Teddy Lucic against Germany in the 2006 World Cup. Sweden lost 2–0.

break, he was back for a key Euro qualifier against Hungary at the beginning of April when a Marcus Allback double gave Sweden an excellent away win. Peter Reid had taken over from Venables, but along with another loan international, Spain's Raul Bravo, Lucic was jettisoned after a dire display in a 3–1 defeat at Liverpool. As he was not needed by Leeds he was released to play a friendly against Croatia in Stockholm just before the end of a traumatic season.

Lucic then linked up with German side Bayer Leverkusen for a couple of seasons and played in the 2006 World Cup, featuring in all three group games against England, Paraguay and Trinidad & Tobago. The second-round game against Germany in Munich was a disaster for Sweden. They were 2–0 down inside 12 minutes, then had Lucic sent off for a second bookable offence, and the hosts were able to cruise into the quarter-finals. Lucic returned to Sweden to play for Hacken, with whom he made his last international appearances before joining Elfsborg in 2008.

BILLY McADAMS
(Northern Ireland 1954–62)
Forward
Born: Belfast, 20 January 1934.
Died: Barrow, Cumbria, 13 October 2002.
Caps: Manchester City 5, Bolton Wanders 9, Leeds United 1. Total: 15
Goals: 7

Billy McAdams.

international debut against Wales. His first goal for Northern Ireland came against Scotland in a 2–2 draw at Hampden Park in November 1954, but he suffered a slipped disc in a friendly against Millwall and was ruled out for nearly two years, missing two FA Cup Finals with City. He returned with a goal on his comeback at Luton and was given a hero's welcome on his first game back at Maine Road when he netted the only goal against Leeds on 12 September 1956. The following month he set up Jimmy McIlroy's equaliser as England were held 1–1 at Windsor Park after Stanley Matthews had scored his first international goal in eight years.

When McAdams next faced England again in 1960 he scored twice at Windsor Park, just a few weeks after leaving Manchester City for Bolton Wanderers in a £15,000 transfer. It was a thrilling game, with England flattered by their 5–2 victory thanks to a couple of late goals. McAdams's second goal, a thumping header, was terrific, but 18 days later he topped that with his treble against West Germany in another exciting game in Belfast. Northern Ireland had reached the quarter-finals of the 1958 World Cup and opened their bid for more glory against the Germans, who took a quick lead through Albert Brulls.

McAdams blasted in a centre from Billy Bingham to equalise, and six minutes after the interval Windsor Park went wild as he put the green-shirted Irish in front with a header. But within five minutes Uwe Seeler and Charly Dorfel had wrestled the lead back again. Dorfel killed the game off with his second goal after 80 minutes, but right near the end McAdams completed his treble with a right-foot drive.

McAdams played in the return – a 2–1 defeat in Berlin – and the two other group games against Greece before making a long overdue appearance at Wembley against England. After missing the 1955 and 1956 FA Cup Finals, McAdams was keyed up for the game and went close to giving Ireland the lead. Bobby Charlton put England in front but Ireland, prompted by Danny Blanchflower in his 50th international, always carried a threat and deservedly equalised when McAdams and Manchester United youngster Jimmy Nicholson combined to set up scorer Jimmy McIlroy.

BILLY McADAMS was the first British player to score a hat-trick against West Germany. Geoff Hurst may have famously achieved the feat for England in a World Cup Final and Michael Own bagged a treble in a wonderful 5–1 win in Munich, but the bustling Northern Ireland forward beat them to it. However, it was typical of the bad luck that was to dog McAdams throughout his career that he finished up on the losing side as the Irish lost 4–3 at Windsor Park – a result that ended their hopes of qualifying for the 1962 World Cup. His final international, coming during his brief six-month period with Leeds United, also ended in defeat as Ireland went down 4–0 in Holland in a Rotterdam friendly.

McAdams first started banging in goals at Grosvenor Secondary School in Belfast and was working as an apprentice heating engineer while playing as an amateur with Banbridge Town and Glenavon. He had a three-month trial with Burnley, but could not agree terms and returned to Ireland to turn pro with Distillery. He was still only 19 when he joined Manchester City for £10,000, becoming the first player from the province to move for a five-figure fee. He made his debut in a 2–1 win against Sunderland on 2 January 1954 when the Maine Roaders' winning goal was scored by McAdams's partner at inside-left, Don Revie. The young Irishman scored a hat-trick the following week in a 5–2 mauling of Bradford Park Avenue in the FA Cup, and by the end of the season he had made his

Ticket from Holland versus Northern Ireland in 1962 – Billy McAdams's last international appearance.

Inside a month Don Revie swooped to bring his old Manchester City teammate to Elland Road to boost a shot-shy attack. McAdams was fast, direct and could leather the ball as hard as anyone around, but the move did not really work out. However, McAdams did get on the scoresheet in the final game of the season when Leeds won 3–0 at Newcastle to guarantee their Second Division status. His 15th and final cap – and only one as a Leeds player – came in a one-sided friendly in Rotterdam at the end of the season when a couple of goals by Tonny van der Linden guided Holland to an easy 4–0 win.

Later that summer McAdams was sold by United to Brentford for £8,000, and he later had spells with Queen's Park Rangers and Barrow before settling in Cumbria. He suffered from ME later in his life and died, after a battle against cancer, aged 68 – a sad end for a courageous player.

GARY McALLISTER

(Scotland 1990–99)

Midfield
Born: Newarthill, Motherwell, 25 December 1964.
Caps: Leicester City 3, Leeds United 41, Coventry City 13. Total: 57
Goals: 5

CLASS act Gary McAllister's impeccable midfield credentials saw him captain Leeds United and Scotland. A wonderful passer of the ball, he was a member of the Whites team which won the 1991–92 Championship before succeeding fellow Scot Gordon Strachan as United skipper. He led his country on football's battlefields around the world for four years. Of his 57 caps, 41 were won at Leeds, and he led his country 31 times – a record which puts him among the best in Europe. Only Lucas Radebe, Ian Harte, Gary Kelly and Billy Bremner have won more caps while at Elland Road.

Macca got the ball rolling with his local club, Fir Park Boys, before joining Motherwell in 1981, and it was not long before scouts from England were checking his progress. He was 20 when a £250,000 deal took him to Leicester City in August 1985, and he broke into the national team at the end of 1989–90. He was called up to partner Stuart McCall, son of former Leeds player Andy McCall, against East Germany at Hampden Park, but ended up on the wrong end of a 1–0 scoreline, Thomas Doll getting the decisive goal from the penalty spot.

The following Saturday Leeds fans got their first glimpse of Scotland's latest international in a highly-charged game at Elland Road. Howard Wilkinson's team were wobbling on the run-in to the Second Division title race, with just one win in seven, so victory over Leicester in the penultimate game of the season was vital. Mel Sterland's goal gave United the edge, but McAllister fired in a stunning shot past Mervyn Day via a post to turn up the tension several notches before Strachan blew the roof off Elland Road with a late winner.

The Whites won their final game at Bournemouth to clinch the title and Wilkinson raided Filbert Street for McAllister for £1 million after the midfielder rejected a transfer to Nottingham Forest because he was not impressed by Brian Clough's blunt approach. It was a fantastic piece of business by Wilkinson as McAllister's more subtle skills replaced the more aggressive approach of hard man Vinnie Jones in the middle of the park.

McAllister, Strachan, David Batty and Gary Speed formed a wonderful midfield quartet, which saw United finish fourth on their return to the top flight and the following season they took the big prize for only the third time in the club's history. His form in the First Division made McAllister an automatic choice for Scotland as Andy Roxburgh's men began their bid for the European Championships. He played in a 2–1 win against Romania and then hit what turned out to be the winner against Switzerland as the Scots edged another 2–1 victory.

Both those games were at Hampden, and McAllister enhanced his growing reputation with a mature performance as the Scots drew 1–1 in Bulgaria. They continued to play solid, consistent football, and belief grew when they won a priceless point against Switzerland in Berne. Trailing 2–0, Roxburgh reshuffled his formation immediately after the second Swiss goal by sending on substitute McAllister, and the Leeds man played a key role in the rescue act, which was completed with an Ally McCoist goal seven minutes from time.

Scotland captain Gary McAllister.

Despite a 1–0 defeat in Romania, Scotland eased past San Marino in Glasgow to book their ticket to the Finals in Sweden. Qualification left McAllister to concentrate on United's title battle, and it is a testament to his fitness that he was the only outfield player to play in all 42 League games in that famous season.

Scotland warmed up for Euro '92 with a couple of games in North America, beating the United States 1–0 and Canada 3–1, McAllister scoring twice against the Canadians, against whom Hearts goalkeeper Henry Smith, a former Leeds junior, also made his third and final appearance for Scotland. McAllister headed to Euro '92 walking on air, but Scotland were in a tough group with Holland and Germany, knowing they would probably have to avoid defeat against one or the other to stand a chance of going through. They almost did it in Gothenburg against the Dutch, but their brave effort was ended by Denis Bergkamp's goal on 76 minutes.

Germany, even without broken arm victim Rudi Voller, were just too strong and won 2–0 to eliminate the Scots, who made sure the Tartan Army had something to cheer by winning their final game against the CIS 3–0, McAllister scoring the third goal from the penalty spot. McAllister's stock had risen during the tournament, but Leeds struggled with the mantle of champions the following season. They were well off the pace in the new Premiership and were knocked out of the European Cup by Rangers 4–2 on aggregate, despite taking the lead at Ibrox in the first leg with a stunning McAllister volley after only 69 seconds.

Rangers was the team McAllister had supported as a kid, and he was back at Ibrox as Scotland took on Italy, desperate to get their World Cup qualifying campaign back on track. They had started with a 3–1 defeat in Switzerland followed by a 0–0 home draw with Portugal, but failure to take their chances meant Scotland had to settle for another goalless draw, and hopes of making the Finals were already looking slim. Subsequent results made that fear a reality, but McAllister had the consolation of captaining his country for the first time in a 1–1 draw with Switzerland in Aberdeen on 8 September 1993.

Leeds finished fifth that season, with the remarkably consistent McAllister being an ever-present and lifting the club's Player of the Year award. He had also been handed the captain's armband by new Scotland manager Craig Brown and was to play a huge role in Scotland's qualification for Euro '96. The Championships were being staged in England and every member of the Tartan Army was desperate for their men to set up a cross-border raid into Auld Enemy territory. McAllister's men did not disappoint. They were in a group containing Russia, Finland, Greece, San Marino and the Faroe Isles.

When it came down to the wire Scotland's final three fixtures were all at the newly renovated Hampden Park, and if they won the lot they would be heading to the Finals.

Gary McAllister after scoring for Scotland.

Scotland had lost 1–0 in Greece when key decisions went against them, so revenge was sweet when McCoist came off the bench to score the only goal at Hampden with his first touch. It was a massive win and was followed by a priceless 1–0 win against Finland, which left Scotland the formality of seeing off San Marino, which they did 5–0 amid a carnival atmosphere. The excitement went up several notches as the draw for the Finals put McAllister's men in with England, Holland and Switzerland.

It was a mouthwatering prospect, but first McAllister was hoping to collect some silverware with Leeds United. Wilkinson had gradually restructured the Whites after their 1992 title success, and McAllister was one of the few faces still around to have shared in that Championship glory. Now he was hoping to lead Leeds to more silverware in the League Cup, last won by United in 1968. The addition of the explosive Tony Yeboah had given a new dimension to the Leeds attack, but United were poor in the Final, losing 3–0 to Aston Villa.

Wembley was to blow an ill wind – literally – on McAllister's return to the famous old stadium in the summer. Having opened with a creditable 0–0 draw with Holland at Villa Park, McAllister led out the Scots at Wembley against England. The match lived up to its expectations, fought out at high speed on a warm, but breezy afternoon.

Alan Shearer's header put England ahead, but McAllister was handed the opportunity to put the Scots level when they were awarded a penalty deep into the second half. Up stepped Macca for the pivotal moment of the match, but his shot was blocked by the diving David Seaman – a former United junior before making his name with Arsenal. To rub salt into McAllister's wounds, England broke away and Paul Gascoigne scored a wonderful solo goal to seal a 2–0 win.

Celebrity psychic spoon-bender Uri Geller later claimed he made the ball move as McAllister was about to strike the penalty – whatever the reason, it was a miss that some Scots fans were never going to forgive him for. Scotland won their final game against Switzerland but were denied a place in the quarter-finals on goals scored. The Swiss game was McAllister's 41st and last international as a Leeds player, as he joined Coventry later that summer in a £3 million deal. He continued to lead his country but missed the infamous 'three-second cap' match in Estonia. The World Cup qualifier in Tallin on 9 October 1996 was scheduled to kick-off at 6.45pm, but Scotland were not happy with the temporary floodlights, FIFA officials agreed and on the morning of the game brought the kick-off forward to 3pm. The Estonians said they had insufficient notice and did not turn up. Scotland took the field on their own and formally kicked off before the referee brought an end to the proceedings.

McAllister was serving a one-match ban, but FIFA later ordered the game to be replayed, which it was, in Monaco, and ended 0–0. The upshot was that McAllister was forced to sit out of Scotland's game with Sweden instead, but they still went on to qualify. It was not long before he had to endure an even longer absence from action as he tore a cruciate ligament, which ruled him out of the World Cup Finals. After 16 months out of international action, he led Scotland in a 2–1 defeat at Celtic Park against the Czech Republic in a Euro 2000 qualifier, but was jeered by a group of unforgiving fans throughout, and ironic cheers rang out as he was substituted after 65 minutes.

Not surprisingly the 34-year-old announced his retirement from international football, but went on to enjoy an Indian summer at Liverpool, where he proved that form may be temporary, but class is permanent. In 2000–01 he was at the centre of Liverpool's all-conquering Cup campaign as the Reds won the FA Cup, League Cup, UEFA Cup and Super Cup, his finest moment coming in an astonishing 5–4 victory against Spanish side Alaves in the UEFA Cup, in which he scored a penalty, had a hand in three of Liverpool's other goals and delivered the free-kick which provided the Merseysiders with their golden-goal winner. He was created an MBE in 2001 in recognition of his 20 years in the game and rejoined Coventry as player-manager, quitting in January 2004 to spend more time with his wife, who fought a long battle with cancer until her death in March 2006.

McAllister worked as a thoughtful analyser on television before returning to Elland Road as United's manager in succession to Dennis Wise on 29 January 2008. The Scot modelled Leeds's style of play on his own – a passing game – and they reached the League One Play-off Final. But Wembley was to prove the stadium of pain for McAllister once more, as they lost 1–0 to Doncaster Rovers, his third crushing loss there in 12 years.

United could not continue their improvement, and a string of poor results, including defeat against non-League Histon, saw McAllister axed in January 2009. He made 231 appearances in six years for Leeds, scoring 31 goals, and is regarded as one of the best midfielders the Whites have ever had. Despite his obvious quality, there was always a feeling that some Scots fans did not show the same appreciation for his talents, particularly the vocal minority of Scottish fans who would not forgive him for that 1996 penalty miss, yet it is hard to think that they have had a better midfielder since he retired.

JIM McCABE

(Northern Ireland 1948–53)

Wing-half

Born: Draperstown, Co. Londonderry, 17 September 1918.

Died: Teesside, July 1989

Caps: Leeds United 6

WING-HALF Jim McCabe played six games for Northern Ireland – and tasted defeat in each one. His international appearances were spread over a five-year period and all came while he was at Elland Road. A highly versatile performer, he occupied four different positions in those half-dozen games.

McCabe's family moved to the South Bank area of Middlesbrough when he was a youngster, and he played with Billingham Synthonia Juniors and South Bank East End, joining Middlesbrough in May 1937. Before he could get into the first team, war broke out, and he served in the Green Howards alongside his pal and fellow Boro youngster Wilf Mannion, a hugely talented inside forward who went on to play 26 times for England. McCabe saw action in the Middle East and attained the rank of sergeant. The pair had both grown up in Middlesbrough and were close off the field, McCabe being best man at Mannion's wedding.

McCabe was not in Mannion's class as a footballer – few people were – but he was a strong, durable wing-half who made his long-delayed debut in a 2–2 draw with Liverpool on 4 October 1946. Middlesbrough finished 11th that season, while an ageing Leeds team finished rock-bottom and set about rebuilding the side in Division Two. In November 1947, Leeds had a £15,000 bid for Mannion rejected, but they were more successful four months later when a raid on Ayresome Park saw them sign McCabe for £10,000 plus goalkeeper John Hodgson.

The fee was a record for Boro, and despite dropping down a division McCabe went on to win his first cap in November 1948 against Scotland. He had not missed a Leeds game since his transfer, and his call-up at right-half was reward for his consistent, solid displays. McCabe and Ireland got off to a dream start as two Davy Walsh goals in the opening five minutes stunned Hampden Park, but Jimmy Houliston and Jimmy Mason made it all-square before burly Queen of the South forward Houliston headed a dramatic last-minute winner.

For McCabe it was as close as he got to avoiding defeat in an Irish shirt. Both he and clubmate Davy Cochrane

Jim McCabe proudly wearing a Republic of Ireland cap.

retained their places for the next Home International, a 2–0 defeat against Wales in Belfast. But worse was to follow for the Leeds duo, as they were in the side hammered 9–2 at Maine Road by a rampant England, for whom Manchester United forward Jack Rowley scored four times. McCabe had played left-half in that match, and when he next reappeared in the green of Ireland he was back at right-half, facing Wales, who won 2–1 at Belfast.

With the exciting Danny Blanchflower making the number-four shirt his own for Northern Ireland, McCabe did not get another international chance for two years. With Leeds struggling for goals, they switched the mighty John Charles from defence to attack, with McCabe shuffling across to centre-half. Both moves were successful, and when both were picked for the Northern Ireland versus Wales game at Windsor Park there was the prospect of both being in direct opposition. It did not quite turn out that way, as McCabe filled in at right-back while Charles helped himself to a couple of goals as Wales triumphed 3–2. Both Irish goals were scored by Barnsley's Eddie McMorran, who had a brief and unsuccessful spell with Leeds a couple of years earlier.

McCabe was restored to his more familiar position of centre-half for the next international, a 3–1 loss to Scotland on 3 October. McCabe was past 35 and it was clear his Northern Ireland days were over. At the end of the season he left Leeds after 152 League games to join Peterborough, thus going from the national team to playing Midlands League football in the space of just a few months. After hanging up his boots, McCabe returned to Teesside and worked at ICI Wilton.

JOHN McCLELLAND
(Northern Ireland 1980–90)
Defender
Born: Belfast, 7 December 1955.
Caps: Mansfield Town 6, Glasgow Rangers 26, Watford 20, Leeds United 1. Total: 53
Goals: 1

BIG John McClelland certainly knew his way round Britain – he was the first man to play professionally for clubs in all four of the home nations. His spell at Leeds United saw him win a League Championship medal for the only time in a career that stretched to nearly quarter of a century. During that time he rubbed his square shoulders with some of the world's greatest players and is rated as one of Northern Ireland's all-time greats. He started out with Portadown in his homeland before joining Cardiff City, who released him after only one full game, and he joined non-League Bangor City in North Wales. He had played in both defence and attack, but at Bangor he put his 6ft-plus 13st frame to use strictly as a centre-half to excellent effect. He was a part-timer, working as a theatre orderly in a hospital, when Mansfield Town manager Billy Bingham, the former Northern Ireland ace, spotted McClelland's potential and signed him for £10,000 in May 1978. He was an instant success, becoming the Stags' first-ever international player, making six appearances for Northern Ireland in his three years at Field Mill. A £90,000 bid by Rangers was too much for a club the size of Mansfield to turn down, and McClelland linked up with the Glasgow club.

Scotland and Northern Ireland were both battling it out in group six in a bid to reach the 1982 World Cup Finals and both made it. Scotland had already won the group before Gerry Armstrong's goal gave them victory over Israel in Belfast and a ticket to their first Finals in 24 years as runners-up. The Ulstermen were managed by Bingham – McClelland's former boss at Mansfield – and provided the fairytale of the Finals. Big John played in every minute of Ireland's games in Spain, which started with draws against Yugoslavia and Honduras in Zaragoza. That left the Irish needing to beat hosts Spain in Valencia to top the group, and they put in a brilliant display in a physical battle in a volatile atmosphere. Bingham's men had matched the highly-fancied Spaniards' stride for stride, and went in front just after half-time when goalkeeper Luis Arconada pushed the ball out to Armstrong, who drilled it home.

Northern Ireland's John McClelland, who now hosts tours of Elland Road.

On the hour Mal Donachy was ordered off for retaliation after a foul by full-back Jose Camacho, but McClelland was outstanding as the Irish held firm to go into the next group stage, where they would face Austria and France. Once again the outsiders from Ireland defied the odds in the blistering heat of Madrid to draw 2–2 with Austria thanks to a couple of Billy Hamilton goals. The result eliminated Austria, who had already lost to France, so Northern Ireland had to beat the French to take their place in the semi-finals. It proved a game too far for the Irish, as Les Bleus swept to a thrilling 4–1 victory.

After their heroics in Spain, no one was taking the Irish challenge for European Championship glory lightly, and the feel-good factor continued as they beat champions West Germany home and away in qualification. McClelland also scored his only goal for his country during the campaign in a 2–1 win against Turkey in Belfast. The Irish win in Hamburg had left the Germans needing to beat Albania to qualify on goal difference. The Germans did it, but not with the usual Teutonic efficiency, as Albania were within 10 minutes of earning a 1–1 draw, which would see Ireland through, when full-back Gerhard Strack headed the German winner.

McClelland gained League Cup-winners' medals with Rangers in 1982 and 1983, before joining Graham Taylor's Watford, who were setting the First Division alight. It was while he was at Vicarage Road that Bobby Robson picked him for a star-studded Football League XI to play the Rest of the World at Wembley to mark the League's centenary in 1987. McClelland played the full 90 minutes to keep the likes of Maradona, Platini and Lineker off the scoresheet in a 3–0 League win.

Selection for such a big game was some compensation for not playing in the 1986 World Cup Finals, McClelland's place being taken by the younger Alan McDonald, the Queen's Park Rangers defender. But McClelland, although a non-playing member of the squad, bounced back to regain his place in the Northern Ireland team. He joined Leeds at the age of 33 for £100,000 in summer 1988 and had a frustrating first season at Elland Road. He made his debut on the opening day of the season and suffered as Newcastle striker Micky Quinn scored four goals as the Magpies won 5–2.

McClelland was injured in the game and underwent a heel operation which kept him on the sidelines until the New Year. With Chris Fairclough and Peter Haddock locking down the central defensive positions as the Whites headed the Second Division table, Macca was loaned back to Watford to build up his match fitness. But he only played one senior game back at Vicarage Road before he returned to Leeds. Then, out of the blue, he was named as Northern Ireland's captain for a friendly against Norway in Belfast. Manager Billy Bingham did not want to risk some of his regular players and wanted McClelland's experience to help out a young new-look team. The Leeds man completed the 90 minutes to prove he could still compete at the top level, but Norway scored twice in a four-minute spell to overturn Ireland's lead to win 3–2.

Leeds won the Second Division title, but McClelland did not get a medal as he only played three League games, playing the same number in United's first season back in the top flight. Fairclough was now partnered by Chris Whyte at the back, but McClelland was still around and enjoyed a decent run in the team at the start of the title-winning 1991–92 season, playing enough games to pick up a winners' medal, even though he spent a month on loan at Notts County.

Despite being in the winter of his playing career, he was still surprisingly quick for a big guy with his awkward upright running style eating up the yards. His knowledge of the game was unsurpassed, but time was catching up with him and he took on a player-coach role at St Johnstone, later becoming manager. After that he played at Arbroath, Carrick Rangers, Wycombe and Yeovil before his distinguished career ended when he broke a leg on his only appearance for Darlington. Since then he has worked as a postman and hosts tours of Elland Road and is able to point to his name on the club's international honours board.

STEPHEN McPHAIL
(Republic of Ireland 2000–04)
Midfield
Born: Westminster, London, 9 December 1979.
Caps: Leeds United 10. Total: 10
Goals: 1

WHEN Stephen McPhail first broke into the Leeds United team, manager George Graham hailed him as 'the new

Stephen McPhail.

Liam Brady'. High praise indeed from a man who worked with the top-class Republic of Ireland midfielder in his days as boss of Arsenal. McPhail, not surprisingly, did not live up to such high expectations, but there was no doubting his quality during his time at Elland Road.

The Whites have picked up many a fine young player from across the Irish Sea, and McPhail slotted neatly into that pigeonhole. Although born in London, he was raised in Dublin and came through the Academy ranks at Leeds, being one of the outstanding crop of talent which won the 1997 FA Youth Cup, having turned pro the previous year. He made his United debut as an 18-year-old, coming on as a substitute in a 1–0 defeat at Leicester on 7 February 1998, but it was a cameo appearance at Derby a couple of months later which had Whites' fans purring. Coming off the bench, his first touch was a superb 40-yard pass to set up Jimmy-Floyd Hasselbaink for United's final goal in a 5–0 romp.

Predominately left-footed, he possessed instant control and broad vision and gained more first-team experience when Republic legend David O'Leary took over at Elland Road. He played for the Republic of Ireland side in the World Youth Championships and was soon elevated to the Under-21 team after recovering from a knee ligament injury. His reward was a five-year contract, and the inevitable full international call came when he played against Scotland at the end of the 1999–2000 season. That was the prelude to the Nike Cup in America, McPhail playing in a 1–1 draw with the hosts in Boston before scoring the opening goal in a 2–1 victory against South Africa in New Jersey. Goalscoring was not the most potent weapon in his armoury, and the two goals he had scored for Leeds at that stage had both come in the same match – a 2–0 win at Chelsea which cemented United's place at the top of the Premiership the week before Christmas 1999.

McPhail was still flying high when he made his World Cup qualifying debut, coming on for Kevin Kilbane late on in a 4–0 win against Cyprus in Dublin, which booked Ireland's place in a Play-off with Asian runners-up Iran. McCarthy's men overcame Iran 2–1 on aggregate, but

McPhail did not make the squad for the Finals as injury ruined his 2001–02 season. He was loaned to Millwall but was sent off in his first game for the Lions against Sheffield Wednesday, and after three games returned to Elland Road.

O'Leary lost his job in the summer, and McPhail was hoping to impress new boss Terry Venables. After figuring in the Republic's 3–0 friendly win in Finland, he had a bit of a run in the Leeds team, which was being dismantled because of the club's financial problems. McPhail played a full 90 minutes as the Irish held Greece to a goalless draw in Athens, but his lack of regular first-team football, both under Venables and his successor, Peter Reid, left him on the fringes of the Euro 2004 qualifying games.

The Irishman's career was stuck in limbo, so he linked up with his old mentor Paul Hart, who had guided United to Youth Cup glory in 1997, at Nottingham Forest in Division One. His loan spell looked like being made permanent, but he was recalled by Eddie Gray's who had replaced Reid. Leeds were relegated, but at least McPhail had seen a bit of action with both United and Forest, and that helped keep him in the Republic frame, featuring in three friendlies against Turkey, Canada and Nigeria.

The Nigerian game was played at the Valley, Charlton's home in London, but the Irish crashed to a 3–0 defeat and it was the last time McPhail represented his country. The match also saw Enoch Showunmi, then of Luton and later of Leeds, come on as a late substitute for the Africans. McPhail joined Barnsley on a free in summer 2004, moving to Cardiff two years later. His improved form with the Welsh club saw him captain Ireland B in a 0–0 draw with Scotland B in October 2006, and he skippered the Bluebirds in their 1–0 defeat to Portsmouth in the 2008 FA Cup Final.

One of the most consistent performers in the Championship, McPhail was selected by new Irish manager Giovanni Trappatoni for his first squad for the friendly games against Serbia and Colombia. Although McPhail did not come off the bench in either game, he was part of a 28-man training camp on the Portuguese Algarve and played against local side Lagos on 19 May 2008. The message from Trappatoni was clear – there was still time for the 28-year-old to resurrect his international career.

GORDON McQUEEN
(Scotland 1974 –81)
Centre-half
Born: Kilbirnie, Ayrshire, 26 June 1952.
Caps: Leeds United 17, Manchester United 13. Total 30
Goals: 5

TOWERING Gordon McQueen missed out on the 1978 World Cup Finals after a freak injury in the Home International against Wales. The giant Leeds United centre-half was fully expected to be Scotland's first choice for the tournament when he clattered into a goalpost in a 1–1 draw with Wales at Hampden Park. He damaged his right knee and, with the Finals in Argentina less than a month away, had little chance of recovering in time.

Four years earlier McQueen had been in the squad that went to Germany, but he did not get a game as he was understudy to Jim Holton, the man he eventually replaced in both Manchester United and Scotland teams. At a shade over 6ft 3in, McQueen was near unbeatable in the air and proved devastating at corners and set pieces, weighing in with several vital goals for both club and country. His father, Tom, was a goalkeeper with Hibernian, Berwick Rangers, East Fife and Accrington Stanley, playing in the same team as long-serving Leeds trainer Les Cocker with the latter. Gordon looked poised to inherit his dad's gloves as he was a 'keeper at school, but he made his name as a centre-back with Largs Thistle.

Trials with Liverpool and Glasgow Rangers did not come to anything so he joined St Mirren. With Jack Charlton's career coming to an end, Leeds combed Britain for a suitable young replacement and discovered the 20-year-old blond-haired McQueen giving Scottish League forwards a hard time. For a modest outlay of £30,000 he joined the payroll at Elland Road in September 1972, making his debut in a 3–2 win at Derby the following March. He became an automatic choice the next season as United stormed to the First Division title, making a call-up for the international team a formality. He made his first start a fortnight before the 1974 World Cup when a Scotland side containing five Leeds players – McQueen, skipper Billy Bremner, goalkeeper David Harvey and forwards Joe Jordan and Peter Lorimer – lost 2–1 in Belgium. The quintet were all included in Ally McLeod's squad for Argentina, and only the relative rookie, McQueen, did not get a game.

It was a different story post-tournament when McLeod's first choice centre-half Holton was carried off in a friendly against East Germany, never to play for his country again. By the time he recovered, McQueen had won his second cap against Spain at Hampden, which ended in a 2–1 defeat. Two games into Holton's Manchester United comeback he broke a leg against Sheffield Wednesday, leaving the door open for McQueen to inherit his place in the national team.

McQueen may well have taken Holton's jersey in any event, as he had a magnificent 1974–75 season, particularly in the European Cup, scoring goals in both legs against Ujpest Doza and another in the fog-shrouded 3–0 quarter-final home victory against Anderlecht. His dismissal in the semi-final in Barcelona reduced him to tears, however, as he was suspended from the Final against Bayern Munich in Paris. McQueen was also finding the net for Scotland, as he proved a massive threat when he went up into the opposition box. It was his 43rd-minute header that forced Portugal goalkeeper

Gordon McQueen all set for the 1978 World Cup Finals.

Vitor Damas to parry the ball, and defender Artur Jorge tried to clear the ball but sliced it into his own net for the only goal of the game.

The Leeds player also hit the bar with a header against Wales and was in the team that saw off Northern Ireland 3–0, but was brought down to earth as the Scots were thrashed 5–1 at Wembley. The final game of the season saw Scotland in European qualifying action when captain for the night McQueen salvaged a point in Romania as he hooked home a last-minute shot for a 1–1 draw. Having established himself in the Scotland set-up, McQueen was sidelined for the vast majority of 1975–76 with a pulled muscle and an Achilles tendon injury, missing seven internationals.

McQueen returned for Scotland's World Cup qualifier in a fiery encounter in Prague and was one of four Scots booked in a 2–0 defeat that saw Andy Gray and Czech captain Anton Ondrus sent off. He was also in the scoring groove for Leeds, netting seven League goals in 1976–77, and was one of the stars of the Home Internationals, scoring in the victories against Northern Ireland and England, the latter prompting a mass invasion of the Wembley pitch after the final whistle, with fans ripping up chunks of turf and tearing down the goalposts. There were further scenes of joy for the Tartan Army when McQueen and Scotland beat Wales 2–0 to guarantee their ticket to the World Cup Finals. But the season was to turn on its head for Leeds's outstanding defender. His Leeds career hit

Gordon McQueen.

PAUL MADELEY

(England 1971–77)

Defender / Midfield
Born: Leeds, 20 September 1944.
Caps: Leeds United 24

PAUL MADELEY was a unique one-man team. He filled every outfield position for Leeds United in a career of unparalleled versatility. His astonishing ability to play anywhere was reflected at the highest level as he played in both full-back slots, at centre-half and in midfield in his 24 caps for England. He famously turned down the chance to be in the 1970 World Cup Finals, but Alf Ramsey held no grudges and Madeley's magnificent form simply could not be ignored. He is one of the few Leeds-born players to have represented both his local club and his country, but it was clear from his early days that he was earmarked for football stardom.

While at Parkside Secondary School he was a member of the England Schools squad four times – but never capped – and after four months with Yorkshire League side

Paul Madeley of Leeds United and England.

the skids when he was involved in a bout of fisticuffs with Scotland colleague and goalkeeper David Harvey during an FA Cup third-round tie against Manchester City. The mood darkened as City went 2–0 up midway through the second half, sparking a mass pitch invasion. Mounted police were called in to break up the packs of invaders before referee Colin Seel was able to resume play 15 minutes later.

McQueen requested a transfer and followed Joe Jordan to Manchester United when the clubs agreed a British record fee of £495,000. He was a shoe-in for Scotland in the World Cup Finals, but disaster struck at Hampden when he suffered the knee injury. He still flew to Argentina as a member of the squad, but was not able to play as the Scots failed to get beyond the group stage. McQueen went straight back into the Scotland team after the tournament, scoring a fine diving header in a 3–2 defeat in Austria during McLeod's swansong as manager. He was also on the mark in a 4–0 European Championship victory against Norway in Glasgow at the end of the season. His 30th and final game for Scotland was a 2–0 defeat against Wales in Swansea. A scorer in Manchester United's 3–2 defeat against Arsenal in the 1979 FA Cup Final, he returned to Wembley four years later when the Red Devils beat Brighton to lift the Cup.

McQueen was badly injured at Liverpool in January 1984 and missed the rest of the season and most of 1984–85 before going to Hong Kong to play for the Seiko club. He later managed Airdrie and coached his old club St Mirren and Middlesbrough before becoming a Sky TV pundit. His daughter, Hayley, was a sports presenter with Sky before becoming anchor on MUTV.

Farsley Celtic the Leeds Schools centre-half joined Leeds United as an apprentice professional. With United he won England Youth caps as a stepping stone to his League debut in a 1–0 home victory against Manchester City on 11 January 1964, when Jack Charlton and his usual replacement, Freddie Goodwin, were both injured.

Although he was being groomed as a successor to Charlton, Madeley gained plaudits over the next few seasons for his ability to fill any position. In 1967–68 he scored 10 goals in all competitions and played up front in the League Cup Final victory against Arsenal as new signing Mick Jones was Cup-tied. That was Madeley's first match at Wembley and brought him his first winners' medal – and that was soon followed by another as United beat Ferencvaros in the Fairs Cup Final.

Perhaps the fact he had no regular position to call his own meant he surprisingly never received a call-up for the Under-23 side, but he had been outstanding in a strong FA XI, captained by World Cup-winner Ray Wilson, which won the Expo 1967 tournament in Canada. Madeley's first 'official' senior representative honour did not come until September 1969, when he played at centre-half alongside clubmate Norman Hunter in the Football League's 3–0 win against the League of Ireland at Barnsley.

By that time the Leeds pair had won League Championship medals and were pushing for places in Ramsey's World Cup squad, and three months after that game at Oakwell seven Leeds players – Madeley included for the first time – were named in a 30-strong squad to face Portugal in a friendly at Wembley. The 1969–70 season saw United chasing silverware on three fronts, but they were ultimately to miss out on the League, FA Cup and European Cup in heart breaking fashion. There was also to be a twist in the tail of a gruelling season for Madeley.

Along with Jack Charlton, Allan Clarke, Terry Cooper, Norman Hunter, Mick Jones and Paul Reaney he had been chosen for the 40-strong provisional World Cup squad, but when it was slimmed down to 28 Madeley's name was missing. Then Reaney broke a leg at West Ham, and

Don Revie's good luck telegram to Paul Madeley ahead of the player's England debut against Northern Ireland in 1971.

Madeley was drafted in as his replacement by Ramsey, only for the player to withdraw 24 hours later. He cited exhaustion after playing 58 games for United and said he felt he would not do himself, or England, justice. Arsenal's Bob McNab took Madeley's place in the 28 but did not make the 22 that travelled to Mexico.

The Leeds star recognised that he might have burned his bridges as far as international recognition was concerned, but Ramsey bore no grudges and Madeley was picked for his first England game against Northern Ireland in Belfast on 15 May 1971. His initial job was to mark George Best, but the Manchester United wizard moved to the opposite flank early in the game. It was Best who was involved in a major talking point, flicking the ball away from Gordon Banks and nodding it into the net as the England goalkeeper was about to clear the ball upfield, only for referee Alastair MacKenzie to disallow the goal. To add to Ireland's grievance Leeds striker Clarke looked offside when he scored the game's only goal.

In the summer Madeley scored in the 2–2 draw in Italy against Juventus – the priceless goal going a long way towards helping Leeds lift the Fairs Cup on the away goals ruling after the teams drew 1–1 in the second leg when Madeley was stretchered off with a head wound. After making his England debut at right-back, Madeley was deployed in midfield in his second international as England beat Switzerland 3–2 in a European Championship qualifier in Basle, but he donned the number-two shirt again in the re-match at Wembley when the teams drew 1–1.

England guaranteed their place in the quarter-finals with a 2–0 win in Greece, Madeley providing a sublime through pass for Tottenham's Martin Chivers to wrap up victory in the final minute. To reach the semi-finals England would have to overcome old foes West Germany, and Madeley occupied the right-back slot in both meetings. The first, at Wembley, was dominated by the Germans' sharp counter-attacks, created by their outstanding midfield, and the visitors deserved their 3–1 win with goals from Uli Hoeness, Gunter Netzer (penalty) and Gerd Muller, even though it was 1–1 with six minutes remaining. Germany were happy to defend in the teeming Berlin rain, and the 0–0 draw ended England's interest in the competition. Sandwiched between these two disappointments was one of the highlights of Madeley's career as he had an outstanding game at left-back, covering for broken leg victim Terry Cooper, as Leeds beat Arsenal 1–0 to lift the FA Cup for the only time in the club's history.

Madeley played in the victories against Wales and Scotland to enhance his growing reputation at international level and found himself in yet another position – centre-half – when he lined up on a bitterly cold Glasgow night against Scotland in February 1973 in a game to mark the Scottish FA's centenary celebrations. Bobby Moore was making his 100th appearance for England, and it was the only time that Madeley partnered the inspirational skipper in the heart of the defence. The pair were immaculate on a rock-hard snow-covered surface as England skated to a 5–0 win, with Madeley's clubmate Peter Lorimer scoring an own-goal.

Leeds suffered double disappointment at the end of 1972–73 when they were shocked by Sunderland in the FA Cup Final, then lost the European Cup-winners' Cup Final to AC Milan, when they were victims of a scandalous refereeing performance.

England's post-season games started in Czechoslovakia when a last-minute goal fashioned in Leeds – made by Madeley, scored by Clarke – salvaged a 1–1 draw. But the big game came the following week as Ramsey's men took on Poland in a World Cup qualifier. Madeley retained his right-back spot, but a rare error by Moore contributed to a 2–0 victory for the Poles, and a disappointing England performance was compounded by the dismissal of Alan Ball near the end.

England recovered their poise with a 2–1 friendly win in Russia then lost 2–0 in Italy when Moore made a record-breaking 107th appearance for his country. It was Italy's first-ever win against England. Madeley played in both games and had established himself as the first-choice right-back in Ramsey's eyes. He had little to do as Austria were swept aside 7–0 at Wembley three weeks before the make-or-break World Cup showdown with Poland. Despite dominating from start to finish, the 1–1 draw with the Poles meant England would not be going to the 1974 Finals.

Madeley and England also lost 1–0 at Wembley to Italy a month later in what was Moore's final international and Ramsey's penultimate game in charge. Consolation for Madeley came in the shape of another League Championship medal before manager Don Revie took the England job. It was no surprise that Madeley was on the teamsheet for Revie's first game in charge – a 3–0 European Championship qualifying win against Czechoslovakia, followed the next month by a 0–0 draw with Portugal.

It was Madeley who provided a string of crosses to help Newcastle forward Malcolm Macdonald score all five of the goals England put past Cyprus to consolidate their position at the top of the group, but a damaging 2–1 defeat in Bratislava and a 1–1 in Portugal – when Madeley had a midfield anchor role – saw Revie's men stumble and the Czechs went on to win 3–0 in Cyprus to finish as group winners.

The play-anywhere star missed the Home Internationals and the Bi-centennial tournament in America, but he was recalled at centre-half to partner Liverpool's Phil Thompson as England opened their World Cup campaign with a 4–1 win in Finland in summer 1976. However, Madeley, at 32, was aware his international career was coming to an end.

His final match came against Holland at Wembley in February 1977 when the brilliant Johann Cruyff inspired the Dutch to a 2–0 win. Two years earlier Madeley's superb marking job on Cruyff had been a major factor in Leeds beating Barcelona in the European Cup semi-final, but the three-times European Footballer of the Year was

untouchable against England. Madeley still had lots to offer Leeds, where supporters had named him their Player of the Year in 1975–76, and the loyal one-club man went on to play 725 times for the Whites before retiring in 1980.

In today's transfer market he would have been priceless. Jimmy Armfield once described him as a Rolls-Royce – an uncannily accurate portrait. Madeley was smooth and classy, and had a wonderful engine than would run for endless miles in luxurious style.

RUI MARQUES
(Angola 2006– to date)
Central defender.
Born: Luanda, 3 September 1977.
Caps: Leeds United 14

AFTER two years at Elland Road Rui Marques broke into Angola's World Cup squad before making a League appearance for the Whites. It was certainly a bizarre start to life at Elland Road, where he had arrived with a good pedigree in German and Portuguese football. He had been with Benfica, Ulm, Stuttgart and Maritimo before having trials with several clubs in England prior to the 2004–06 season.

Leeds had just been relegated from the Premiership, and new manager Kevin Blackwell was hurriedly piecing together a new-look squad. Marques signed a deal for the Whites after rejecting offers from Ipswich and Southampton. But the only time the United fans saw him was in a 2–0 League Cup victory against Oldham a year later when he looked uncomfortable at right-back. Seemingly surplus to requirements, he was allowed to jet off to Seoul to make his international debut against South Korea, coming on for the final couple of minutes for defender Antonio Lebo Lebo in a 1–0 defeat.

After landing back in England he was loaned to Hull City, making his League debut in a 1–1 draw at Ipswich in March 2006. That was still his only taste of League football in England when Angola's coach Luis Oliveira Goncalves called him up as a replacement for the injured defender Jacinto in a 30-man training squad ahead of the World Cup. The Palancas Negras – the Black Antelopes – had qualified for the Finals for the first time, while some of Africa's more established football nations missed out on the German jamboree.

Marques had been born in the Angolan capital of Luanda, but at the age of seven he and his family had to flee the country, which was in the grip of civil war. Most of his life had been spent in Portugal, and Angola had been drawn in the same group as the Portuguese, Mexico and Iran in the Finals. After watching from the bench as Angola lost pre-tournament friendlies to Argentina and Turkey 3–0 and 3–2 respectively, he made the cut for the World Cup squad.

Angola were the lowest rated team in the tournament,

Rui Marques.

and their eagerly awaited opening game against their former colonial masters Portugal in Cologne went the way of the Europeans thanks to Pauleta's fourth-minute goal. Marques made his second international appearance when he came on as a substitute against Mexico in Cologne. He replaced Figueiredo with 17 minutes left of a stalemate, but within minutes Andre Makanga was sent off. Marques and his teammates hung on for a goalless draw, which kept their hopes of progress alive.

Substitute Flavio put Angola ahead in their last group game, but Iran's equaliser ended any hopes of the Africans going into the second phase. Once again Marques had come on as a substitute, but it counted for nothing when he reported back to Elland Road for pre-season training. He simply did not get a sniff of a first-team chance under Blackwell, and when Dennis Wise took over in October the new manager told Marques he could leave. Marques told Wise he could not understand why he had been brought to the club if he had never been given a chance and got his head down in training.

New Year's Day 2007 turned out to be a pivotal date in Marques's United career. He made his first Championship start against Coventry and gave an assured performance in a 2–1 victory. That was the start of a belated run in the Leeds side, and although United were relegated Marques signed a new contract at the start of August 2007. His

calm, assured defensive play shone like a beacon as Leeds made a blazing start to life in the third tier of English football for the first time in their history. In January 2008 he linked up with Angola once again for the African Nations Cup Finals. He came on as a sub in midfield in a warm-up game with Egypt in Portugal, which ended 3–3, and started in central defence in a 2–1 defeat in Morocco.

Marques had an excellent tournament, playing in all the games as the Angolans reached the quarter-finals in Ghana after battling through a tough group, which included Tunisia, Senegal and South Africa.

All the Angolan games were in Tamale, and they were looking like getting maximum points in their opener against South Africa on the back of Manucho's 29th-minute goal when Elrio van Heerden struck three minutes from the end. After falling behind against highly rated Senegal, Angola fought back to win 3–1 with Manchester United-bound Manucho scoring twice. Marques impressed again as Angola got the point they needed to go into the last eight in a stalemate with Tunisia, who topped the group on goal difference.

Angola moved on to Kumasi, birthplace of one-time Leeds hero Tony Yeboah, to face Egypt, one of the favourites for the African title. Hosny Abd Rabou fired the North Africans ahead from the penalty spot, but Manucho levelled three minutes later from long range. The Pharaohs regained their lead through Amr Zaki before the interval and held on to win 2–1, then thumped Ivory Coast 4–1 in the semi-finals and edged out Cameroon 1–0 in the Final in Accra.

When Marques returned to Leeds he was working for a new manager, Gary McAllister having replaced Wise, who had left the club for Newcastle United. An injury ruled him out of the Play-offs, and he was badly missed at Wembley as Yorkshire rivals Doncaster Rovers emerged deserved 1–0 winners. It had been a great effort by Leeds to get that far after being deducted 15 points at the start of the season. Marques signed a new two-year contract at the end of the season and headed back to Africa to play in four World Cup qualifiers in June.

Goncalves's side kicked off with a comfortable 3–0 win against Benin in Luanda before coming from behind to beat Niger 2–1 in Niamey. Their third game in a fortnight saw them thumped 3–1 in Uganda, but Marques retained his place for the return in Luanda in which they were held to a goalless draw, which was ultimately to prove very costly for the Black Antelopes.

Goncalves, who fully earned his nickname 'The Professor' for the solid work he had done in getting Angola on football's global map, was replaced by his assistant Mabi de Almeida in October 2008 and Marques missed the subsequent victories against Benin and Niger. It was the unfancied Benin who progressed to the final African group stages.

Marques struggled in his last Angolan outing – a 4–0 defeat against Mali in Paris. That may have signalled the end of his international career, but his experience could be vital as Angola host the 2010 African Nations Cup Finals.

CON MARTIN

(Northern Ireland 1946–50 and Republic of Ireland 1946–56)

Goalkeeper / Defender

Born: Rush, Dublin, 20 March 1923.
Northern Ireland caps: Glentoran 1, Leeds United 3, Aston Villa 2. Total: 6
Republic of Ireland caps: Glentoran 3, Leeds United 3, Aston Villa 24. Total: 30
Republic of Ireland goals: 6

Con Martin international playing card.

CON MARTIN was the Paul Madeley of his day – a super versatile international player. A multi-talented sportsman, he played for both Northern Ireland and the Republic of Ireland, making his debut for the latter as a substitute goalkeeper in Eire's first international after World War Two. He played Gaelic football in his youth, helping Dublin win the Leinster title. At the same time he was also playing soccer for Drumcondra, and when the Gaelic Athletic Association, who had a ban on foreign sports, discovered this the association expelled Martin and withheld his medal. He received it 30 years later when the ban was lifted.

Martin had been introduced to football while serving with the Irish Air Corps and helped the Drums win the FAI Cup and played for a League of Ireland XI against an Irish League XI at right-back in Dublin on 18 March 1946 when the IL lads won 2–1. Just after the game Belfast-based Glentoran bought him out of the Air Corps and Martin found himself in demand by both association. He was one of several players – Leeds's Harry Duggan included – in the immediate post-war era who played for both Northern Ireland and the Republic of Ireland. He turned out for the Republic first in Portugal, when he came on as a substitute for injured Cork United goalkeeper Ted Courtney after half an hour when the Irish were already trailing 3–0. Because of his Gaelic football background, Martin went in goal and impressed the 60,000 Stadium of Light crowd with his assured handling.

Eire lost 3–1, but Martin slipped on the gloves again the following week when a goal from Arsenal's Paddy Sloan gave them a great 1–0 win in Spain, but it was Martin's superb display which was the main talking point. After playing in goal in his first two Republic games, he turned out at centre-half as England marked their first visit to Dublin with a 1–0 win.

Martin's teammate Johnny Carey knew his club Manchester United were on the look out for a goalkeeper, but the rising Glentoran star turned down the Red Devils to join Leeds United as an outfield player in an £8,000 deal in December 1946, a month after playing at right-half in his Northern Ireland debut in a 0–0 draw against Scotland. He endured a torrid Division One debut at left-back as Leeds crashed 6–2 at Sheffield United. That was typical of Leeds's season, as an ageing side failed to win a single away fixture and were relegated.

Spectators, starved of top-class football during the war, packed grounds throughout the country and his first outing for the Republic as a Leeds player saw the game against Spain delayed during the match because the crowd had spilled on to the Dalymount Park pitch. It was 1–1 when Ireland won a free-kick near the touchline, but Kevin O'Flanagan was unable to take it so referee Jack Barrick took the sides off for 25 minutes while the police cleared the touchlines. Martin was at centre-half and did his bit to repel some dangerous Spanish attacks as Ireland won 3–2.

Seven months later Martin was in the Northern Ireland side which beat Scotland 2–0, then found himself marking winger Tom Finney as the North snatched a thrilling last-minute 2–2 draw against England at Goodison Park. Internationals were coming thick and fast for Martin, who retained his right-back place for a 2–0 defeat against Wales in Wrexham in March and at the end of the season he played left-back twice for the Republic as they lost both games of their Iberian tour. They melted away to a 2–0 defeat in the Lisbon heat and lost 2–1 to Spain in Barcelona.

Leeds had endured a disappointing 1947–48 season, labouring to 18th in Division Two, and it was no surprise

Con Martin (far right) gets airborne to help the Republic of Ireland keep Austria at bay in Vienna.

when Martin took the chance to move into the top division with a £10,000 move to Aston Villa, United using the cash to help manager Frank Buckley to rebuild the side. He had played 49 games for Leeds.

Martin became a major star at Villa Park, playing twice more for Northern Ireland and 24 times for the Republic, skippering the side on five occasions. He scored six goals for the RoI including a penalty in their famous 2–0 victory at Goodison Park in 1949, which saw them become the first non-UK side to win on English soil. He was extremely popular at Villa, topping 200 appearances, and although principally a centre-half he did occupy several other positions and in 1951–52 was the goalkeeper for the bulk of the season. During his time at Villa Park it is reckoned he played for five years with a broken nose without realising it. In summer 1956 he returned to Ireland as player-manager of Waterford, later managing Shelbourne and working as assistant manager at Cork Hibernians.

One son, Mick, was a midfielder with the Republic, Manchester United, Newcastle and West Brom; another, Con junior, played for several League of Ireland clubs, as did his son-in-law, Gerry Garvan. Con senior's grandson, Owen Garvan, is a Republic of Ireland Under-21 international with Ipswich Town.

NIGEL MARTYN

(England 1992–2002)

Goalkeeper

Born: St Austell, Cornwall, 11 August 1966.

Caps: Crystal Palace 3, Leeds United 20. Total 23

PERHAPS it is possible to forsee the future by looking at tea leaves at the bottom of a cup. A prediction by a Bristol Rovers tea lady that goalkeeper Nigel Martyn was destined for the top certainly came true. She was on holiday in Cornwall when she spotted Martyn playing for South-Western League side St Blazey and tipped off Pirates manager Gerry Francis, the former England skipper.

Martyn, who was working for a coal merchant while playing part-time football, was invited to Eastville for trials and signed at the start of the 1987–88 season, going straight into the first team.

The tea lady was a good judge. Martyn played every game in 1988–89, conceding just two goals in a 15-match spell midway through the season, which ended with Rovers beaten in the Third Division Play-off Final by Port Vale.

Martyn became the automatic first choice for the England Under-21s, winning 11 caps, and played for England B against Italy at Brighton before becoming Britain's first £1 million goalkeeper when he left Division Three table-toppers Rovers and joined Crystal Palace in November 1989. He ended the season in the FA Cup Final as the Eagles lost to Manchester United after a replay. He spent seven years at Selhurst Park and represented England three times, the first coming in Moscow in April 1992 when he replaced Chris Woods for the final 11 minutes of a 2–2 draw. He played the first half of England's next game, a 1–0 win in Hungary, and completed the full game against Germany in the US Cup in the first game the following season as England played on an indoor pitch, losing 2–1 in Detroit's Pontiac Silverdome.

Surprisingly Martyn, who won the Division One title with Palace in 1994, had not played any more games for England by the time he joined Leeds in summer 1996 for

Nigel Martyn.

£2.25 million – a British record fee for a goalkeeper. Howard Wilkinson wanted someone to replace Arsenal-bound John Lukic and Martyn fitted the bill perfectly. He was already a quality goalkeeper, but at Elland Road he simply got better. His consistency was unmatched, his positional sense was top class, his power and strength saw him dominate his area and, despite his size, he had remarkable reflexes. His inevitable England recall came after 19 clean sheets in 37 games of his first Leeds season, when a South African side containing United teammates Lucas Radebe and Phil Masinga was beaten 2–1 at Old Trafford thanks to Ian Wright's 76th-minute winner.

England were heading to the 1998 World Cup Finals with Leeds Player of the Year Martyn as back-up for David Seaman, and he played in the friendlies against Cameroon, which Glenn Hoddle's men won 2–0, and Chile. Liverpool's 18-year-old wonder kid Michael Owen made his debut in the latter but was upstaged by Marcel Salas whose double gave the South Americans a 2–0 win at Wembley.

In the build-up to the Finals England played in the Hassan II Trophy in Morocco and Martyn starred in a 0–0 draw with Belgium, which went to a penalty shoot-out, the Belgians winning 4–3 after misses by Rob Lee and Les Ferdinand.

Seaman was England's undisputed number one, so the vast majority of the Leeds goalkeeper's games were in friendlies. Martyn shut out the Czechs in a 2–0 win in November 1998, but his return to Wembley three months later saw a different result against France. Former Leeds boss Wilkinson was in temporary charge of the national team, and with the match goalless at the interval brought on Martyn for Seaman, but the United 'keeper had little hope of stopping two Nicholas Anelka strikes which gave Les Bleus victory. The Whites were now in the David O'Leary managerial era, and Martyn was one of the senior players in an exciting young squad that included an up-and-coming young 'keeper in Paul Robinson, whose presence kept Martyn on his toes.

Martyn made back-to-back appearances in the September 1999 European Championship qualifiers as Alan Shearer scored a hat-trick in the 6–0 rout of part-timers Luxembourg, and Leeds teammate David Batty was sent off near the end of a dull 0–0 draw in Poland.

United stormed through to the UEFA Cup semi-finals, with Martyn having one of his best-ever games for Leeds as United held Fabio Capello's Roma side 0–0 in the Olympic Stadium and completed the job in the second leg thanks to Harry Kewell's spectacular second-half strike.

Martyn, 33, was at the peak of his powers, but still had to play second fiddle to Seaman in the England set-up in the Euro 2000 Finals in Holland and Belgium. He was on the bench as England let an early 2–0 lead slip to lose to Portugal in Eindhoven, but Shearer's goal saw off Germany to put Kevin Keegan's men back in the reckoning.

When Seaman was injured in the warm-up just before the kick-off in Charleroi against Romania, Martyn was thrust into action. It was 2–2 with a minute to go when Phil Neville brought down Viorel Moldovan a minute from the end and Iaon Ganea's penalty sent Martyn the wrong way to eliminate England.

The unflappable Martyn was again in tip-top form for United, particularly in the Champions League, although while he was out because of groin injury England Under-21 international Robinson seized his chance in impressive style. After spending some time on the bench Martyn regained his place before the end of the season as United overcame all the odds to reach the Champions League semi-finals. He also came off the bench in Sven-Goran Eriksson's first game in charge of England – a 3–0 win against Spain at Villa Park – when he saved Javi Moreno's late penalty after replacing David James.

Martyn and James also shared goalkeeping duties as Mexico were thumped 4–0 at Derby and Holland emerged 2–0 victors at Tottenham. But when Seaman was ruled out of the key World Cup qualifier against Greece at Old Trafford it was the Leeds man who got the nod. It looked as though it was going to be another big-game disappointment for Martyn until David Beckham's sensational injury-time free-kick snatched a 2–2 draw and the point England needed to make the Finals.

That match was Martyn's last game in a competitive England fixture – his remaining five appearances were all friendlies, including a 2–1 defeat against Italy at Elland Road, and the pre-World Cup matches against Cameroon and South Korea. Eriksson continued his policy of mass substitutions in all these games, and the only match of the five in which Martyn completed a full 90 minutes was a 1–1 draw against Sweden at Old Trafford in November 2001.

Arsenal veteran Seaman played in all England's games as they reached the quarter-finals, where they were knocked out by Ronaldinho's speculative dipping long-range strike. The patient Martyn was in the squad and he was handed the number-13 jersey – an unlucky number which seemed to plague the goalkeeper as he returned to Elland Road.

The new season saw a new manager, Terry Venables, in charge, and his preferred choice was Robinson. Despite playing in every Premiership game the previous season, Martyn did not start a single one in 2002–03. His club and England career had come to a full stop, so it was no surprise when Chelsea and Everton moved for him in summer 2003. He opted to join the Toffees, and it proved a wise choice as he ousted another young England shot-stopper, Richard Wright, from the first team.

Just as he had been at Leeds, Martyn was a huge hit with the fans at Goodison Park, announcing his retirement as he approached his 40th birthday because of an ankle injury. Of his 666 League appearances, 207 had been for Leeds, and many Whites fans believe he is the best goalkeeper to have played for United. The tea lady at Bristol Rovers certainly knew her stuff.

PHIL MASINGA
(South Africa 1992–2001)

Forward

Born: Klerksdorp, Johannesburg, 28 June 1969.
Caps: Mamelodi Sundowns 13, Leeds United 12, St Gallen 1, Salernito 4, Bari 27, Coventry City 1. Total: 58
Goals: 18

STRIKER Phil Masinga was one of South Africa's trailblazers after the country emerged from the era of apartheid. The South African FA were members of FIFA between 1952 and 1976, but had been suspended for the last 12 years of their membership because of the government's stance on race. It was not until 1992 that South African were readmitted to FIFA, and the young Masinga was at the forefront of the return to football's international family. A tall, leggy forward, Masinga began with Jomo Cosmos in Johannesburg before joining Mamelodi Sundowns in 1991. He played in South Africa's first official game of the post-apartheid period, when Cameroon were beaten 1–0 at the King's Park rugby ground in Durban on 7 July 1992 in front of 40,000.

That was the first of three matches against Cameroon in the space of five days and the final game, in Johannesburg, saw Masinga and his cousin, Bennet Masinga, score in a 2–2 draw.

South Africa's first target was to reach the African Nations Finals, but they did not start well as they lost 4–1 in Zimbabwe – Phil scoring the visitors' goal – and he was sent off two minutes from the end of their 1–0 defeat against Zambia. His goals helped the Sundowns win the League Championship in 1993 and the following year he and Kaiser Chiefs defender Lucas Radebe were spotted in international action by scout Geoff Sleight, who alerted Leeds boss Howard Wilkinson. The pair were snapped up for £250,000 and while Radebe went on to be a major player at Elland Road, Masinga, who turned down the chance to sign for Porto to join United, found the going tougher in the long run.

The striker did well in pre-season and was a regular starter in the early months, notching his first goal in a 3–2 home defeat at the hands of Chelsea. That was one of the few games in which he completed 90 minutes as he adjusted to the pace of the Premiership, but this did not stop him performing well on the international stage, scoring winners in African Nations qualifiers against Madagascar and Mauritius.

Masinga's highlights for United that season included a double in a rare 3–1 win at Arsenal and a nine-minute extra-time hat-trick after coming off the bench in an FA Cup replay against Walsall. Although he had to be largely content with a substitute's role with Leeds, he continued to be a regular for his country, and only a late Marcelo Gallardo penalty denied South Africa a famous win against Argentina in a post-season friendly.

The emergence of Tony Yeboah restricted Masinga's appearances for United still further, but he was a key man when South Africa kicked off their bid for the African Nations title on home soil in January 1996. He scored the Bafana Bafana's first goal in their opening group game against Cameroon as a 75,000 Johannesburg crowd celebrated a 3–0 victory. He was in the team that beat Angola 1–0 to book a quarter-final place against Algeria, which saw a late goal by John Moshoeu take South Africa into the last four.

Masinga missed the 3–0 semi-final triumph against Ghana but started the Final against Tunisia. The Leeds striker was withdrawn midway through the second half and it was his replacement, Wolves's Mark Williams, who made an immediate impact with two goals in four minutes to give South Africa their first African title.

Back at Leeds, the addition of Tomas Brolin to the Whites squad made it even harder for Masinga to get a game and, although he scored in a rare start in the 3–0 Coca-Cola Cup semi-final win against Birmingham City he did not make the bench at Wembley against Aston Villa.

With Masinga out of the starting line up, Wilkinson was able to release him for a prestigious friendly against Brazil in Johannesburg in April, in which the world champions came back from 2–0 down to win 3–2 thanks to Bebeto's late penalty.

Phil Masinga.

Immigration authorities ruled that Masinga had not played sufficient first-team football in his two years at Leeds to renew his work permit, so he moved to Swiss club St Gallen. He was only there a few months before moving across the border into Italy to play for Salernitana. It was while he was there that he scored against former Leeds teammate Nigel Martyn in a 2–1 defeat at Old Trafford to set a new South African goal-scoring record, overhauling Donald Wilson's best aggregate which had stood since 1947.

An impressive start with his new club saw him step up to play for Bari for four years, and he continued to make his mark for his country, scoring the winner against Congo which took South Africa to their first World Cup Finals. Before they headed to France, South Africa defended their African Nations crown, and they made a good fist of it. They reached the Final against Egypt with both Masinga and Radebe in the side, but the Pharaohs proved too strong and ran out 2–0 winners.

In the World Cup Finals in France, South Africa lost 3–0 to the host nation in their opening match in Marseille, then Masinga came on for Shaun Bartlett in an explosive 1–1 draw with Denmark. Three players, all second-half substitutes, were dismissed – South Africa's Alfred Phiri and Danish duo Miklos Molnar and Morten Wieghorst. A 2–2 draw with Saudi Arabia, which Masinga missed, saw the Bafana Bafana on the plane home.

Masinga's 50th cap came as a 2–0 win against Mauritius in Durban put South Africa through to the African Nations once more, and his final goal for his country came in another ANC qualifier when Liberia were beaten 2–1.

Despite his goalscoring exploits, he was not popular with a section of Bafana Bafana fans and was booed virtually every time he touched the ball when playing for a Nelson Mandela XI against the World Stars in August 1999. He vowed never to play in front of a home crowd again, but was persuaded by President Mandela himself to reverse his decision.

Masinga had slipped behind Benni McCarthy and Shaun Bartlett, the only men to have bettered his 18 goals for South Africa, in the pecking order, and his last appearance came when he replaced McCarthy during a 3–0 friendly defeat in Sweden in August 2001.

Masinga had left Bari in the summer and had returned to England to play for Coventry City, but before the start of the season he was denied a work permit once again and the move collapsed. He later played for the Al-Wahada club in the United Arab Emirates before returning to his homeland as a coach with PJ Stars. He was appointed a 2010 World Cup ambassador.

DOMINIC MATTEO

(Scotland 2000–02)

Defender

Born: Dumfries, Dumfriesshire, 28 April 1974.

Caps: Leeds United 6

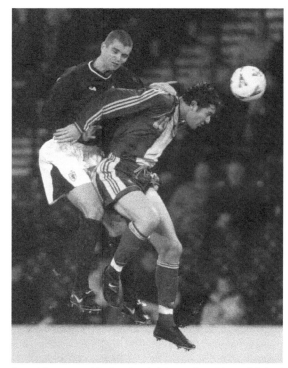

Dom Matteo, on his Scotland debut, wins this aerial duel with Australia's Brett Emerton.

DOMINIC Matteo was a man in demand on the international scene. He was born in Scotland of English parents and Italian grandparents and was eligible to play for all three countries. The utility player actually played senior football for England when at Liverpool before declaring his allegiance to the country of his birth while he was at Leeds. He certainly had one of the most unusual careers at the top level.

Born in Dumfries, he was brought up in Liverpool and was spotted playing for junior side Birkdale United by Kenny Dalglish, who was watching his young son, Paul, in action. Matteo joined Liverpool's School of Excellence as an 11-year-old and worked his way through the ranks, winning England Youth honours, and made his senior debut in a 1–1 draw at Manchester City in October 1993. He won four caps at Under-21 level against France, Belgium, Portugal and Switzerland as he gradually forced his way into the Reds first team as Liverpool made good use of his versatility.

Matteo could play in a variety of defensive positions as well as on the left side of midfield, and was still only 21 when he was a surprise call-up for Glenn Hoddle's 23-man squad for a World Cup qualifier at Wembley. He did not make the bench and two Alan Shearer goals gave England a priceless 2–1 victory against Poland in October 1996.

It was at centre-back that he played for England B in their 2–1 defeat to Chile at the Hawthorns in February 1998, and after nine players withdrew from an experimental Hoddle squad for a friendly in Switzerland the following month Matteo got another call-up, but once again did not play. He eventually settled at left-back at Anfield before Leeds, resurgent under David O'Leary, snapped him up in a £4.75 million transfer in August 2000. A knee injury prevented him making his debut until United pulled off a shock 1–0 Champions League victory against AC Milan at Elland Road with Matteo on the left side of the Leeds midfield.

Matteo was one of the stars of United's run to the semi-finals, scoring in the 6–0 rout of Turkish side Besiktas, but he topped that in the San Siro when his 44th-minute header earned Leeds a point to take them into the money-spinning second phase and cemented his personal place in United folklore.

Shortly before his move from Liverpool he committed his international future to Scotland. Former Leeds star Gary McAllister, a teammate of Matteo at Anfield, helped persuade the Dumfries-born player to throw in his lot with Scotland. That inevitably alerted Scotland manager Craig Brown, and the popular Leeds player found himself singing the *Flower of Scotland* anthem with his Scouse twang as he lined up for his full debut in a 2–0 defeat against Australia at Hampden Park. But that did not deter Sven-Goran Eriksson from asking about Matteo's availability three months later. Because the Aussie match was a friendly it did not preclude Matteo from playing for England.

The Swede's interest was rejected and a few weeks later Matteo played in Scotland's crucial World Cup qualifier against Belgium, which ended any hope England had of luring Matteo to the Three Lions. Two goals from Billy Dodds put the Scots in control, the second coming from the penalty spot after an incident which saw defender Eric Deflandre sent off. With an hour remaining Belgium looked to have no chance, but Marc Wilmots pulled one back on 58 minutes and an injury-time header from Daniel van Buyten went past goalkeeper Neil Sullivan to shatter the Scots, whose qualification hopes lay in tatters.

Four days later Scotland saw off San Marino 4–0 with skipper Colin Hendry scoring twice. The same player elbowed substitute Nicola Albani in the final minute, and although the referee missed the incident Hendry was given a three-match ban. Matteo also played back-to-back World Cup games in September as Scotland were held to a 0–0 stalemate at Hampden by Croatia and were then beaten 2–0 by Belgium in Brussels – a result which all but ended Scotland's qualification hopes.

The Scottish FA appointed Bertie Vogts as Brown's replacement, and Matteo played in the German's first match in charge, when the talented French tore his team apart in Paris. A Scotland side which also included future Leeds men Sullivan in goal and Dougie Freedman as a deep-lying forward were lucky to escape with just a 5–0 beating.

Matteo, who was having recurring problems with his knees, was appointed Leeds captain after Rio Ferdinand's

move to Manchester United and opted to call time on his fledgling Scotland career in February 2003 in an effort to extend his days at club level.

Fans' favourite Matteo played 147 times for Leeds, scoring four goals – none as crucial as his San Siro stunner – before he left Elland Road. He was one of many Leeds players released after relegation in 2004 and joined Blackburn Rovers, moving on to Stoke in January 2007, suffering badly from injuries at both clubs.

ALAN MAYBURY
(Republic of Ireland 1998–2005)
Full-back
Born: Dublin, 8 August 1978.
Caps: Leeds United 2, Heart of Midlothian 7, Leicester City 1. Total: 10

ALAN MAYBURY was only 19 when he won his first cap for the Republic of Ireland. The Leeds United youngster was one of six new faces in an experimental side put out by manager Mick McCarthy for a friendly versus the Czech Republic on a bitterly cold March night in Olomouc in 1998. The defender, who played at right-back behind teammate Gary Kelly, was replaced by Robbie Keane at

Alan Maybury closes in on Czech Republic striker Milan Baros.

half-time in a pre-arranged switch as McCarthy used the game to check out fringe players ahead of the European Championship qualifiers. It was certainly a step up in class for Maybury, as he had only started nine Premiership games for Leeds before he faced a Czech side ranked fifth in the world.

Maybury attended Mount Temple Comprehensive School in Dublin and skippered Ireland's Under-15 and Under-16 sides before joining United in summer 1995 from St Kevin's Boys' Club. Home-sickness and a broken arm blighted his early progress, but he bounced back to make his debut in an injury-ravaged team at Aston Villa in February 1996, although he had to wait eight months before his next first-team appearance, such was the strength of United's squad.

The FA Youth Cup-winner certainly impressed Leeds boss George Graham, and he was handed a four-year contract. A B international appearance against Northern Ireland paved the way for his full debut against the Czechs a fortnight later.

Although he won half a dozen Under-21 caps in the space of 11 months, he could not get in the Leeds team during 1998–99 and was loaned to Reading in March. He was promptly sent off on his debut for the Royals against Manchester City. He returned to Elland Road at the end of the season and won his second cap in a 1–0 defeat against Northern Ireland in Dublin, with the proceeds of the game going to support the victims of the Omagh bombing.

Injury, the purchase of Danny Mills and the continued presence of Gary Kelly blocked his path to the Leeds first team, and he did not kick a ball in anger for them in 1999–2000. He was loaned to Crewe but did get a taste of Champions League football, albeit a painful one, with United.

David O'Leary's high-fliers had already qualified for the quarter-finals when Maybury was drafted in to face Lazio at Elland Road in a dead rubber in March 2001. It was his first Leeds game for three years, and with United leading 3–2 in injury time a dreadful lunge by Czech international Pavel Nedved on Maybury saw the Irish defender carried off. Amazingly the referee gave the Italians the free-kick, and Sinisa Mihajlovic blasted in the equaliser.

Maybury needed regular first-team football, and it was provided by Hearts, whose manager Craig Levein tabled a successful bid at the start of the following season. Maybury helped the Jambos into successive third places in the Scottish Premier League, and his consistent work saw him earn an international recall. He had not played for the Republic for nearly five years but did well in a friendly against the Czech Republic when a last-minute Robbie Keane goal gave the boys in green a 2–1 win. That opened the door for more friendly appearances for Maybury against Poland, Romania, Nigeria, Jamaica and Holland, the latter being a fine 1–0 win in Amsterdam when the mercurial Keane scored the only goal on the stroke of half-time.

Maybury's only tournament action was in a 3–0 World Cup qualifying win against Cyprus when he replaced Manchester United's John O'Shea for the final seven minutes. Not long after that game Levein was appointed Leicester manager and Maybury followed his old boss to the Walkers Stadium in a £100,000 deal in January 2005, winning his final cap in friendly against China in Dublin which the Irish won 1–0 with a Clinton Morrison goal.

Maybury returned to the SPL on loan with Aberdeen in January 2008 but his contract was not renewed by the Foxes at the end of the season. He eventually managed to get fixed up with Colchester United, making his debut where it all started for him – Elland Road – as the Essex side beat Leeds 2–1.

LUBOMIR MICHALIK

(Slovakia 2006–08)
Central-defender
Born: Cadca, Zilina, 13 August 1983.
Caps: Senec 1, Bolton Wanderers 2, *Leeds United 1.
Total: 4
Goals: 2
* On loan from Bolton

GIANT Slovakian defender Lubomir Michalik was hoping a switch to English football would lead to regular appearances for his country. He had already made an instant impact on the international scene with a goal on his debut against the United Arab Emirates just before his move to Premiership club Bolton Wanderers.

The 6ft 4in Michalik began his career with Senec in his homeland and was given his chance by national boss Jan Kocian in a friendly in Abu Dhabi on 10 December 2006. He replaced Pavol Farkas at half-time and eight minutes later headed in a free-kick to help Slovakia to a 2–1 win. The following month he signed a three-and-a-half year deal with Bolton, but manager Sam Allardyce did not think Michalik was quite ready for the Premiership and was happy to loan him to Leeds for a month to gain more experience of the English game.

United were fighting for survival, and Michalik was quick to make an impact helping United shut out Luton in a 1–0 debut win. After 1–1 draws at Leicester and Southend, Michalik was included in the Slovakian squad for a European Championship qualifier against the Republic of Ireland.

Both countries, and the Czech Republic, were scrapping for second spot behind Germany, and the fixture was only the second soccer match played at Dublin's Croke Park following the relaxation of the non-Gaelic sports ban at the stadium while Lansdowne Road was being refurbished. Four days before Slovakia's visit, a Stephen Ireland goal had given the Republic an historic 1–0 win against Wales in a Euro group game in front of a massive crowd. The Slovakia clash also proved a tense affair, settled

Jan Koller, the Czech Republic's giant striker, goes down under a challenge from Lubo Michalik during Slovakia's 3–1 defeat in Prague in a Euro 2008 qualifier.

by Reading striker Kevin Doyle's early goal, but Michalik came off the bench for the final four minutes in the hope that his aerial presence could provide Slovakia with an equaliser, but to the relief of the 71,297 crowd Ireland, managed by Steve Staunton, hung on.

Michalik returned to Elland Road to resume the battle against relegation and his late header against Plymouth earned three priceless points for Dennis Wise's side, but an injury crisis at Bolton saw him recalled to the Reebok Stadium, and he marked his full Premiership debut with a goal in a 2–2 draw at Chelsea.

Leeds, meanwhile, were relegated and, despite being generally confined to Bolton's reserves in 2007–08, Michalik played in the Euro qualifiers against the Czech Republic and San Marino in November. Slovakia lost 3–1 in Prague but eased to a 5–0 win in Serraville when the Wanderers defender scored the opening goal and also picked up a booking.

Wise was anxious to sign Michalik on a permanent basis, and when the Trotters signed Gary Cahill from Aston Villa for £4.5 million the Leeds boss set up Michalik's £500,000 transfer. The deal went through on the final day of the January transfer window, even though Gary McAllister had taken over from Wise, who had left to become Newcastle United's executive director of football.

Michalik went straight into the Leeds team and was a non-playing member of the Slovakia squad that lost 2–1 to Iceland in a friendly in March and played at Wembley in the Division One Play-off Final defeat against Doncaster Rovers.

Under McAllister Michalik improved his groundwork but, despite playing at a lower level, did not reach the heights of the previous season. When Simon Grayson replaced McAllister he brought in Leeds-born Richard Naylor from Ipswich and 25-year-old Michalik found himself out of the picture with Leeds and Slovakia.

LIAM MILLER

(Republic of Ireland 2004–08)
Midfield
Born: Cork, 13 February 1981.
Caps: Celtic 4, Manchester United 8, *Leeds United 1, Sunderland 6, Unattached 1. Total: 20
Goals: 1
* On loan from Manchester United.

LIAM Miller's only goal for his country came while he was on loan with Leeds United. And it was a cracker – a 30-yard drive billowing the back of the Swedish net in a thumping 3–0 win in Dublin. Goals by Damien Duff and Robbie Keane had put the Irish in control of the friendly encounter, but Miller's strike, which sped past goalkeeper Andreas Isaksson on 70 minutes, was the pick of the bunch.

Cork-born Miller attended Coachford College, played junior football with Ballincollig and represented Eire at various levels. He joined Celtic as a youngster, making his SPL debut against Dundee United towards the end of the 1999–2000 season. While at Parkhead he broke into the Republic's Under-21 side and had a six-month loan with Danish side Aarhus.

Miller found himself at the centre of an administrative blunder by the FA of Ireland during their Euro 2004 qualifying campaign. He had been booked in games at home to Switzerland and in Albania, which triggered a one-match ban, but despite being suspended he still

Liam Miller goes shoulder to shoulder with Sweden's Anders Svensson in Dublin. It was in this game that Miller scored his only goal for the Republic of Ireland.

captained the Irish to a 2–1 win against Albania at Dalymount Park. Manager Don Givens was unaware that Miller should not have been included, and UEFA scratched the result and awarded the Albanians a 3–0 win.

Miller was a stylish midfielder who possessed a defence-splitting pass, and his fine performances in the Champions League for Celtic saw him introduced to senior international football when he came on for Gary Doherty against the Czech Republic on 31 March 2004. He played three more friendlies against Poland, Romania and Nigeria before joining Manchester United in the summer.

Although he continued to play more games for Ireland, he did not earn a regular place at Old Trafford and had 10 caps to his name when he joined Leeds on loan in November 2005 for three months, an arrangement which was extended until the end of the Championship season. In his second outing for the Whites he scored the winner at Southampton, where Leeds stormed back from 3–0 down with 19 minutes to play to pull off a sensational 4–3 victory. His only other goal that season came for Ireland when he netted from long range against Sweden.

Miller helped United to the Championship Play-off Final at Cardiff's Millennium Stadium, where they lost 3–0 to Watford. Had United won, it was widely expected that Miller would join Leeds on a permanent basis.

Instead, he joined new Sunderland manager and former Manchester United and Republic teammate Roy Keane at the Stadium of Light, scoring his first goal for the Black Cats in a 3–0 win at Leeds – a result which pushed manager Kevin Blackwell a step closer to the axe.

Miller continued to accrue Irish caps, despite being put on the transfer list by Keane at the end of February 2008 because of poor time-keeping and lack of discipline. Although he was up for sale, he managed a handful of games at the end of the season and played in new Republic boss Giovanni Trapattoni's first game in charge, in which former Leeds junior Andy Keogh scored a last-minute goal to salvage a 1–1 draw with Serbia.

In a bid to revive his club career he dropped back into the Championship with Queen's Park Rangers in January 2009 on a six-month contract. He did not stay on at Loftus Road and trained with Cork City ahead of winning his 20th cap in a friendly against Nigeria at Fulham when he was still without a club.

DANNY MILLS

(England 2001–03)

Full-back
Born: Norwich, Norfolk, 18 May 1977.
Caps: *Leeds United 19. Total: 19
*1 while on loan at Middlesbrough

DANNY MILLS had a storming 2002 World Cup with England. His detractors may have queried his selection, but

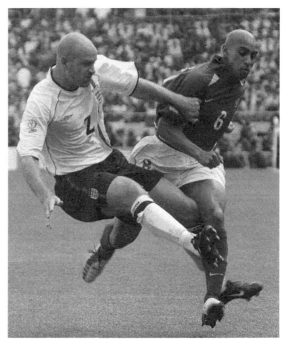

Danny Mills comes out on top against Roberto Carlos during the 2002 England versus Brazil World Cup quarter-final.

the Leeds player was among the most consistent defenders in the tournament.

Manchester United's Gary Neville was a shoe-in for the right-back spot in the World Cup but Mills, relatively untried at international level, was thrust into the spotlight when Neville broke a bone in his foot during the Champions League semi-final clash with Bayer Leverkusen, with the Finals just a few weeks away.

Neville's brother Phil, Manchester United's Wes Brown and the combative Mills were left to battle it out for the position, with the relatively inexperienced Leeds player getting the nod. Many critics felt Sven-Goran Eriksson had made the wrong choice, citing Mills's indiscipline as a black mark, but he hardly put a foot wrong in England's five games in Japan, in which he played every minute.

It was the peak of a career which began with his home-town team, Norwich City, whom he joined after leaving Sprowston High School. He worked through the junior ranks to win England Youth honours and make his League debut on the opening day of the 1995–96 season when a couple of goals by Leeds old boy Jon Newsome helped the Canaries to a 3–1 win at Luton.

Despite red cards against Queen's Park Rangers and West Brom the following season, he was named captain of a Nationwide League Under-21 side managed by Charlton's Alan Curbishley to face their Serie A counterparts from Italy in February 1997.

Curbishley was clearly a big fan of Mills, as the following year a £350,000 transfer took him to the Valley, where he won the first of his 14 Under-21 caps against Sweden. He helped Charlton into the Premiership via the Play-offs after the Addicks' dramatic penalty shoot-out victory over Sunderland.

Charlton were relegated in 1999, and Leeds boss David O'Leary quickly moved for his man, but United's initial bid was knocked back. With injuries and suspensions crippling England, Mills was called into the full England squad for the first time for a European Championship qualifier against Bulgaria, while Leeds and Charlton continued their transfer discussions.

Eventually Leeds had to pay £4.3 million for Mills, whose take-no-prisoners style soon endeared him to the Elland Road faithful. He continued to represent England Under-21s and played his part in United's run to the 2001 Champions League semi-finals. He possessed a crunching tackle, liked to get forward, and his heading ability also saw him cover at centre-back when required. His form was rewarded by his first appearance for the senior England side, coming on for Emile Heskey in a 4–0 thumping of Mexico at Pride Park, Derby. He was one of 10 substitutes used by Eriksson that day as the Swede opted to make multiple changes during games in the build-up to the World Cup Finals.

This meant that many of the fringe players like Mills only got 45 minutes, sometimes less, to show the England boss what they could do with World Cup places up for grabs. Mills played friendlies against Mexico, Holland, Sweden, Italy – at Elland Road – Paraguay, South Korea and Cameroon without starting, or completing, a full game. With key man Gary Neville ruled out of the Finals, Mills and Wes Brown were named in Eriksson's 23-man squad, with Phil Neville left out. Leeds man Mills was handed the number-two shirt for the tournament opener against Sweden.

Although Sol Campbell gave England the lead in Saitama, Niclas Alexandersson equalised, with some observers laying part of the blame at Mills's door. It was Mills's eighth England appearance and the first time he completed the full 90 minutes. He was excellent as David Beckham's penalty sank Argentina in Sapporo and solid as a rock in the stalemate against Nigeria that saw the Three Lions through to the second phase against Denmark. Despite picking up a booking, Mills was once again assured as the Danes were beaten 3–0. The biggest game of his life saw him up against the stars from Brazil, but once again he was not fazed by reputations and was one of England's outstanding performers. When Michael Owen put in-form England ahead it looked as though Mills's World Cup adventure would continue, but Brazil levelled through Rivaldo and Ronaldinho's dipping long-range winner broke English hearts. Although Ronaldinho was red-carded, England did not have the guile in the remaining half-hour to take the game into extra-time.

Mills's stock had risen through the tournament, but he returned to a club who were in financial turmoil. O'Leary

had been replaced by former England boss Terry Venables, but he was forced to sell some star names and Mills was linked with several moves away from Elland Road. However, his battling qualities were just what was required as United successfully staved off relegation with Mills having a fine season.

His consistency ensured he maintained his place in the England squad, although he continued to find himself on and off the pitch as Eriksson continued his policy of multiple replacements. Against Australia at Upton Park, Mills was one of an entire team which came on at half-time, among them Wayne Rooney, who at 17 years 111 days became England's youngest debutant since James Prinsep, of Clapham Rovers, played against Scotland in 1861. That record has since fallen to Arsenal's Theo Walcott, who was 36 days younger when he made his international bow.

FIFA's top man Sepp Blatter felt countries who made such wholesale changes were eroding the value of international football and at a meeting of the International FA Board at Claridge's Hotel in London, a rule was introduced to restrict coaches to six substitutions per match.

One of the features of Mills's England career was that his 19 appearances were all on different grounds. Wembley was being rebuilt and England's home games were being taken round the country like an international roadshow. In summer 2003 Mills played a friendly against Serbia & Montenegro at Leicester before helping England beat Slovakia 2–1 in a European Championship qualifier in Middlesbrough.

Despite being good enough for England, Mills was not picked by Venables's replacement, Peter Reid, for the opening game of the season against Newcastle. Four days after the 2–2 draw with the Magpies, Mills played in England's 3–1 win over Croatia in Ipswich. At the end of the week United and Middlesbrough thrashed out a deal which took Mills to the Riverside on a season-long loan.

Mills's first game in a Boro shirt was against Leeds, who won 3–2 at Boro. But it was a false dawn, for United were relegated at the end of the season, while their England full-back continued to churn out consistent performances for Middlesbrough in his usual combative style, winning a Carling Cup-winners' medal as the Teessiders beat Bolton 2–1 at Cardiff's Millennium Stadium to lift their first major trophy since the Amateur Cup in 1898.

While at Middlesbrough, Mills played his final game for England, coming on at half-time in a 1–1 draw with Portugal on the Algarve, in a match which saw former World Footballer of the Year Figo make his 100th appearance for the hosts and Tottenham's Ledley King score on his debut.

Leeds's relegation meant they simply could not afford to keep Mills, but his free transfer in July 2004 included a clause that United would continue to pay part of his wages. His time at City was not particularly successful and while injured he lost his place to Micah Richards and was loaned out to Hull, Charlton and Derby.

MIKE O'GRADY

(England 1962–69)

Winger

Born: Leeds, 11 October 1942.
Caps: Huddersfield Town 1, Leeds United 1. Total: 2
Goals: 3

TWO England games – spread over six years – and three goals. Those are impressive facts which beg the question – why did Mike O'Grady not play more games for England? One of the answers is injury, which forced him to quit aged 31. Another is Alf Ramsey's preference for playing without wingers – a tactic that helped win the World Cup.

The Leeds-born left-winger burst on the scene as a teenager, winning the first of his caps as a 20-year-old, but he found himself spending too much time on the treatment tables at both Huddersfield and United. The fifth son of a Irishman from County Mayo and a Yorkshire mother, O'Grady attended Corpus Christi School in Leeds, his football talents seeing him represent the city and Yorkshire. But he opted for Leeds Road rather than Elland Road as an amateur in April 1958 and while he was in the juniors at Huddersfield continued to study as a draughtsman. However, manager Bill Shankly, later to achieve great fame at Liverpool, had a future in football mapped out for O'Grady, who turned pro at 17.

Just 10 League games after making his Terriers' debut against Bristol Rovers towards the end of 1959–60 he

Mike O'Grady.

made the first of his three Under-23 appearances against Scotland at Middlesbrough's Ayresome Park. His inside partner was Blackburn's Chris Crowe, the former Leeds player. Denis Law scored the only goal of the game.

Huddersfield were a modest Second Division side, but O'Grady was mixing it with the likes of Bobby Moore, Gordon Banks and George Cohen. He was a Terriers regular for the following two seasons and was a surprise choice by coach Walter Winterbottom for England for the Home International against Northern Ireland at Windsor Park in October 1962.

England were skippered by Jimmy Armfield and, as well as O'Grady from Second Division Huddersfield, Everton centre-half Brian Labone and Bolton forward Freddie Hill were making their debuts. Jimmy Greaves put England ahead, but Armfield put through his own net for the Irish to equalise. O'Grady emerged as the match-winner in the last quarter, converting a fine Greaves pass before firing home a second shortly afterwards. It was a headline-grabbing finale, and 11 days later he made the first of three Football League appearances as the Irish League were beaten 3–1 at Norwich. O'Grady was on the scoresheet for England again as the Under-23 side thrashed Belgium 6–1 at Plymouth a couple of weeks later, and was pencilled in for a second appearance for the senior side against Wales at Wembley in what was Winterbottom's last game in charge, although he had to pull out because of injury. The Huddersfield flyer recovered in time to net another representative goal as the Football League defeated the Italian League 3–2 – John Charles scoring twice for the Italians.

O'Grady, who was fast and direct, was big news, but a back injury saw him in and out of the Huddersfield side, and a bid by his old boss Shankly to take him to Liverpool fell through. Don Revie kept a close eye on proceedings and felt O'Grady would add a bit more zip to his attack, so he brought the Leeds-born player home in a £30,000 deal in October 1965. His debut could not have gone much better as Northampton were thrashed 6–1, and the following week he netted the winner at Stoke. He won his third Under-23 cap the following month when France were beaten 3–0 at Norwich, Sheffield United forward Mick Jones grabbing a couple of the goals.

United finished the season as runners-up and O'Grady must have been in new England manager Alf Ramsey's plans until injury – which led to inconsistent form – struck again. O'Grady managed just 20 League games in the next two years and, after turning down the chance to join Northampton, roared back to his best. United lifted the Fairs Cup, and O'Grady sparkled in United's 1968–69 title-winning season, scoring eight League goals. His fantastic form earned him a recall to the England side for the friendly against France in March 1969, and once again he produced the goods on the big stage, forming a deadly left-sided partnership with clubmate Terry Cooper, who

Mike O'Grady is on target for England on his debut against Northern Ireland.

was making his first England start. O'Grady opened the scoring with a thumping right-foot volley and England took the French apart in the second half on a heavy rain-lashed pitch with a Geoff Hurst hat-trick – which included two penalties – and a solo effort from Francis Lee. O'Grady seemed well placed to make a bid for a World Cup place, but Ramsey, who was formulating his 'wingless wonders' plan, dropped the Leeds flank player and never chose him again.

Further personal disappointment came in the summer when Revie bought Allan Clarke to partner Mick Jones up front and O'Grady found himself out of the team in the subsequent reshuffle. He sought a transfer, to which Revie agreed, sparking outrage from Leeds fans who loved O'Grady's natural attacking instincts. He left Elland Road for Wolves in an £80,000 deal just days after his parting shot – a goal inside 35 seconds in the 10–0 rout of amateurs Lyn Oslo in the European Cup. Knee and Achilles ligament damage restricted his appearances with Wolves and after a loan spell with Birmingham he saw out the end of his career with Rotherham United, retiring in May 1974.

After football he worked for Yorkshire Television's documentary film department. A film of O'Grady's career would be one of peaks and troughs, his fleeting England appearances mixed with long spells of injury.

PAUL OKON

(Australia 1991–2003)

Midfield / Sweeper

Born: Sydney, 5 April 1972.

Caps: Marconi Stallions 1, Club Brugge 3, Lazio 1, Fiorentina 10, Middlesbrough 10, Leeds United 2, Vicenza 1. Total: 28

A MISERABLE season at Elland Road did provide one outstanding highlight for Australian skipper Paul Okon. Away from the derision he received at Leeds, the veteran midfielder led the Socceroos to a famous victory against England. Having beaten the Poms at cricket, rugby union,

rugby league and plenty of other sports, the Aussies finally inflicted a football defeat on England on a memorable night for the Green and Golds at West Ham's Upton Park.

Okon wore the skipper's armband that night as a Harry Kewell-inspired Australia turned over Sven-Goran Eriksson's teams (the Swede fielded an entirely different XI in the second half) 3–1. Ironically, it had been former Lazio coach Eriksson's patience several years earlier which had helped Okon resurrect his career which had begun in a blaze of glory.

Brought up in the Sydney suburb of Bossley Park, the Marconi Stallions player won his first cap aged 18 in February 1991 in a 2–0 friendly defeat of Czechoslovakia in his home city as a substitute. Féted as a star of the future and keen to do well in Europe, he joined Belgian club Brugge and played for Australia in the 1992 Barcelona Olympics, the Olyroos being beaten 1–0 by Ghana in the bronze medal Play-off match in the Nou Camp.

Operating as a sweeper, Okon was outstanding in 1995, winning the Belgian Player of the Year award as Brugge cleaned up the League and Cup double and was named the Oceanian Player of the Year the following season when Brugge retained the Cup. He was ready for a step up, and Lazio boss Dino Zoff flew to Belgium personally to sign Okon, who was regarded by many back home as the best player ever to come out of Australia. His ability to play pin-point passes out from the back made him ideally suited to Serie A, but when Roberto Di Matteo moved from the Rome club to Chelsea, the Aussie found himself operating in midfield. He adapted well until his career was brought to a grinding halt by an injury to his right knee, which doctors were struggling to fix. Lazio's medical team had given up on him, and after being out of action for 18 months the future looked bleak. But Australian physio Kaye MacPherson, aunt of supermodel Elle, successfully nursed him back to something like fitness, and by the time he was ready to play again Eriksson was in charge at Lazio.

The Swede put him back in the team, but in 1999 Okon joined Fiorentina for a season under Giovanni Trappatoni before ending up in the Premiership with Middlesbrough in 2000. He had missed three years of international football, but went on to captain his country in 24 of his 28 appearances, despite struggling to hold down a regular place at the Riverside after Steve McLaren took over from Terry Venables.

Okon had been sat in the stands sidelined when Venables's Australian team let a place in the 1994 World Cup Finals slip through their grasp in a Play-off against Iran, and four years later the Boro anchorman felt the pain on the battlefield as the Aussies lost to Uruguay in another Play-off.

The following summer Okon's move to Leeds seemed to fall under the radar as the media were obsessed with Rio Ferdinand's departure from Elland Road to Manchester United. He had been scratching around in Boro's reserves

Australia skipper Paul Okon battles for possession with Uruguay's Mario Regueiro.

SALOMON OLEMBE
(Cameroon 1997– to date)
Midfield / Full-back
Born: Yaounde, 8 December 1980.
Caps: Nantes 33, Marseille 26, *Leeds United 1, Total: 60
* On loan from Marseille
Goals: 4

and was loaned out to Watford before joining fellow Aussie stars Harry Kewell and Mark Viduka at Leeds on a free. The move saw Okon link up with his former Middlesbrough boss Venables, who knew the player well even though injury had prevented him for playing for El Tel when he was in charge of Australia.

However, hopes that Okon's time at Leeds would be the springboard to the next World Cup did not materialise. Injury ruled him out of action for the first five months of the season, and when he returned Leeds, way above their heads in debt, were struggling to keep afloat in the Premiership. Venables wanted Okon to do a similar job to that of David Batty, but his lack of mobility saw him struggle, although his former boss at Brugge, Frank Farina, reckoned he could still do a job for Australia.

Farina gave Okon the captain's armband for the England match and was rewarded with a solid 90-minute performance, while Kewell and Viduka created havoc up front on an historic night for Australia. Within a few weeks Leeds axed Venables and his replacement, Peter Reid, dropped Okon, who was told he could find a new club. He was still at Elland Road at the start of the next season when he lasted just over an hour as Australia lost 2–1 against the Republic of Ireland in Dublin and days later, he returned to Italian football with Vicenza.

His final international hurrah was back in England on 7 September 2003 at Reading's Madejski Stadium, when he led the Aussies to a 2–1 win against Jamaica. But all those years of injury and spells under the surgeon's knife had taken their toll – after a season playing for Oostende in Belgium and a year in the Cypriot sunshine with Apoel, Okon returned Down Under to play for Newcastle Jets. He retired in June 2007 and became assistant coach at Gold Coast United, taking charge of the Australian Under-18 side in October 2008. Many connected with Soccer Australia believe Okon will one day go on to coach the Socceroos and take them to the heights which he was once tipped to achieve as a player.

EXPERIENCED Cameroon star Salomon Olembe has seen many things on a football pitch in his 10-year international career. But even he was stunned when goalkeeping coach Thomas Nkono was handcuffed by riot police, hauled off the pitch and led away down the player's tunnel before the start of the 2002 African Nations Cup semi-final with host nation Mali. His alleged crime? Using black magic. A policeman had run onto the pitch to pick up an object from where Nkono and Cameroon team boss Winfried Schafer had been standing. Believing it to be a charm which could influence the game, the police slapped Nkono in irons.

The sensational incident prompted Schafer to threaten not to play the game, and it was only when embarrassed Confederation for African Football officials intervened to tell police that if he was not released the match would not go ahead that order was restored. It was certainly a magical match for Olembe – he scored twice in five minutes either side of the interval as holders Cameroon stormed home 3–0. In the Final Cameroon retained their title by beating Senegal 3–2 on penalties after the game finished goalless. Olembe had been a key figure in both tournaments and also figured in two World Cup Finals in a sparkling career that included a season-long loan spell at Elland Road.

Olembe had been a boy star, dazzling with his home-town club Diamant Yaounde before Nantes took him to France as a teenager. His Ligue 1 debut came shortly before his 17th birthday against Marseille – a club he was later to join. But first he enjoyed great success with Nantes, winning his first full cap against Cuba in a tournament in Haiti in October 1997 and the following month coming on as a late substitute at Wembley in a 2–0 loss to England. Rio Ferdinand, who had only just turned 19, made his debut in that match, but was a positive veteran compared to Olembe. At 16 years 342 days, Olembe was the youngest player in any England match since Ireland's Sam Johnston nearly 115 years earlier.

Cameroon, building for the future, had four teenagers in their team – a youth policy which was to bear fruit with their African Nations triumphs and successive appearances in the World Cup Finals. Olembe won two Coupe de France medals in 1999 and 2000 before having a great season as a holding midfielder in Nantes' title-winning side of 2000–01. He was hot property and switched to Marseille in January 2002 just before the African Nations tournament.

Later in the year he played in all three World Cup group games in Japan as they kicked off with a 1–1 draw with the

Saloman Olembe, who made his debut for Cameroon at the age of 16.

Republic of Ireland and beat Saudi Arabia, with star striker Samuel Eto'o scoring the only goal. That set up a make-or-break clash with Germany, who had Carsten Ramelow dismissed five minutes before half-time. The game was still goalless and the odds tilted in the African champions' favour, but Marco Bode put the Germans ahead and when Patrick Suffo was ordered off to make it 10-a-side Germany quickly added another goal through Miroslav Klose to knock out Cameroon.

Olembe did not get the success he had hoped for in the South of France as Marseille suffered from regular changes to the coaching staff that saw him in and out of the side. In an effort to get more game time he agreed to join Leeds, but it was a case of out of the frying pan and into the fire.

Marseille may have been having problems, but Leeds were really going through the mill. Olembe and teammate Cyril Chapuis were among several loan players recruited by Peter Reid just after the start of the 2003–04 season. He came on for his debut during a dreadful 4–0 hammering at Leicester which saw another new recruit, Brazilian World Cup-winner Roque Junior, have a torrid debut. Olembe also featured in the next two games – a home defeat against Birmingham and another 4–0 mauling, this time at Everton. The relegation writing was already on the wall and, after a 6–1 humiliation at Portsmouth, Reid was axed and Olembe barely featured under new boss Eddie Gray. It was no doubt with some relief that Olembe was able to escape to Tunisia in January to be with the Cameroon squad seeking a hat-trick of African Nations titles.

Olembe was no longer a regular for his country, and the only action he tasted was as a substitute in a goalless draw with Egypt in the final group game with the Indomitable Lions already guaranteed a place in the last eight. In the quarter-final Eto'o put Cameroon ahead, but goals by Jay-Jay Okoacha and John Utaka turned the game round for Nigeria and ended Cameroon's reign as champions.

With Leeds's relegation duly confirmed, Olembe returned to Marseille and was loaned out again the following season to Qatar club Al Rayan, winning his place back in the national side. He played in all Cameroon's games in the 2006 African Nations Finals in Egypt, but had been substituted before their quarter-final with Ivory Coast was decided by penalties, which boiled down to a shoot-out between two of the world's great strikers – Eto'o of Barcelona and Chelsea's Didier Drogba. Eto'o missed the 12th Cameroon penalty, but Drogba made no mistake with his to kill off the Lions.

Olembe returned to the Premiership with Wigan in 2007, but saw little action and moved on to Turkish club Kayeriespor before the close of the season keen to resurrect his international career. Olembe, who seems to have been around for ever, will not be 30 until the end of 2010, so he still has time to add to his haul of 60 caps.

ALAN PEACOCK

(England 1962–65)

Centre-forward
Born: Middlesbrough, 29 October 1937.
Caps: Middlesbrough 4, Leeds United 2. Total: 6
Goals: 3

ENGLAND manager Walter Winterbottom described Alan Peacock as 'the finest header of the ball in the country'. Unfortunately for Peacock he was also one of the unluckiest, dodgy knees forcing him to retire prematurely. It was a sad end to a goal-laden career for a six-foot centre-forward in the classic mould – superb in the air, strong and brave. Had he remained healthy he could have challenged Geoff Hurst for a place in the 1966 World Cup team, but instead he was laid up with ligament damage in his right knee while Ramsey's men stormed on to lift the Jules Rimet Trophy. Peacock's England debut had come four years earlier when the tournament was held in Chile, and he was a free-scoring Middlesbrough player.

Peacock joined his local team straight from Lawson Street School and represented England's Youth team in 1955, making his Second Division debut with Boro the same year. He formed a lethal twin attacking spearhead with another Middlesbrough-born youngster, the super-confident Brian Clough. They piled in goals – 262 between

them – from all over the place, but Clough, growing increasingly frustrated at the team's lack of success because of a woeful defence, moved on to Sunderland in 1961. Peacock remained at Boro and continued to thrive, winning a place in the World Cup squad for Chile.

England opened the tournament with Gerry Hitchens of Inter Milan at centre-forward, but a disappointing performance in a 2–1 defeat to Hungary saw him make way for Peacock against Argentina in Rancagua. Peacock, still a Second Division player, made an impressive debut and continually had the beating of his marker, Ruben Navarro, the Argentine skipper, in the air. It was this advantage that paved the way for England's opener as Navarro handled a goal-bound Peacock header on the line, leaving Wolves's Ron Flowers to blast in the penalty.

Peacock retained his place to face Bulgaria, when a dire 0–0 draw was enough to secure a quarter-final meeting with champions Brazil in Vina del Mar. The Boro boy was set to play, but had to pull out at the last minute because of a groin injury. His deputy, Hitchens, got on the scoresheet, but there was no doubting Brazil's superiority as they eased home 3–1.

The injury was typical of Peacock's luck, but back at Ayresome Park he continued to lead the line with great authority and played in the autumn Home Internationals against Northern Ireland and Wales. He set up the second of Mike O'Grady's goals in the 3–1 win in Belfast and

Alan Peacock (left) watches Jimmy Greaves go close to breaking the deadlock against Bulgaria in the 1962 World Cup Finals.

scored twice himself in the 4–0 victory against Wales in front of just 27,500, the smallest crowd ever to see an England international at Wembley.

Now established as England's attack leader, many observers reckoned Peacock would be on the move to a First Division club, with both Everton and Spurs expressing an interest, but when he did leave it was to another Second Division outfit, Leeds United.

After Peacock underwent a cartilage operation on his left knee, Leeds boss Don Revie, himself a Middlesbrough boy, agreed a £50,000 fee for Peacock, rising a further £5,000 should United secure promotion. The Elland Road directors did have to shell out the extra cash, and Peacock was worth it as his eight goals in 14 games took Leeds to the Second Division title. Given Peacock's history of injury it was a gamble, but it paid off in the short term. He had simply carried on where he had left off at Boro – scoring goals. He already had 126 goals in 218 games to his name at Ayresome Park, and all the portents suggested that he would build on those impressive stats with Leeds. But the injury jinx struck again – a right knee injury on a pre-season tour of East Germany led to another operation, and Peacock missed the first two months of the First Division campaign. On his comeback, in a reserve game against Bolton, the knee trouble flared up again and Peacock had to go back on to the operating table. At long last he returned to action in late February and was soon on the goals trail again, yet there were to be no tangible rewards for the frustrated Peacock as he and his Leeds teammates finished runners-up to Manchester United and were beaten in the FA Cup Final by Liverpool.

With full pre-season training under his belt Peacock started 1965–66 in great form, prompting Alf Ramsey to pick him to face Wales at Wembley. Selection, in preference to Sheffield United's young rising star Mick Jones, confirmed that the centre-forward was back at his best and very much in the frame for England's World Cup campaign. However, Peacock struggled to make an impression in Cardiff as the two sides fought out a below-par 0–0 draw – the first time that England had failed to score against the Welsh in 33 years. He missed the following game when Austria became only the third foreign side to win at Wembley with an unexpected 3–2 victory, but he was recalled for the home game with Northern Ireland. This time he played more like his club form, flicking the ball on for Joe Baker to give England the lead, but the team performance was not the best. George Best equalised for Ireland, but Peacock's overhead kick on 73 minutes gave England victory. He thus became the first Leeds player to score for England.

At that stage Peacock was the leading candidate to be England's centre-forward in the World Cup – but once again injury was to thwart him. The tournament was just five months away when he went down in a heap in a 2–0

defeat at Sunderland and was stretchered off. It was further ligament trouble in his right knee, and yet another operation signalled the end of his season.

While Peacock was sidelined, a young forward from West Ham called Geoff Hurst was given his chance by Ramsey, and the rest is history.

Peacock managed a comeback of sorts in 1966–67, but his battered body only managed a handful of games, taking his record to 31 goals in 65 games for Leeds, before starting afresh at Plymouth in October 1967. He only lasted six months in Devon before quitting the game on doctors' advice. He returned to his native Middlesbrough, ran a newsagents business, worked as a matchday host at the Riverside and founded the Middlesbrough Former Players' Association.

NOEL PEYTON
(Republic of Ireland 1956–63)
Inside-forward
Born: Dublin, 4 December 1935.
Caps: Shamrock Rovers 1, Leeds United 5. Total: 6

VICTORIES on the football field against Germany are generally been hard to come by. But darting little inside-forward Noel Peyton was in a winning Republic of Ireland side against the Germans in his first two internationals. The unexpected double was the highlight of Peyton's career, which began with junior club East Wall in the 1950s before he stepped up to the League of Ireland with Shamrock Rovers. He achieved great success with the Hoops, winning a Championship medal in 1957 to add to the FAI Cup-winners' medal he had won the previous year when Shamrock beat Cork Athletic 3–2 in the Final.

Nippy and hard-working, Peyton soon started pushing for international recognition, representing the League of Ireland for the first time in September 1956 when they held a strong Football League team to a 3–3 draw at Dalymount Park after trailing by two goals at the interval.

The Irish selection committee were out in force for both these games, liked what they saw of Peyton and decided to give him his first international start in a relatively inexperienced line up against World Cup holders West Germany in Dublin on 25 November. It was an eagerly-anticipated game and the Irish, featuring three new caps – Drumcondra goalkeeper Alan Kelly and Shamrock duo Peyton and Jimmy McCann – rose to the occasion with a terrific 3–0 win, with all the goals coming in the second half.

A buoyant Peyton was brought down to earth the following week when he played in the LoI's 3–1 defeat against the Scottish League in Glasgow, but his performances were attracting the interest of English clubs, and he enhanced his growing reputation by scoring in a 2–2 draw with the Irish League in Dublin later in the

Noel Peyton.

invaded the pitch after 65 minutes and the referee had to abandon the game.

Peyton made a flying start to his United career, making his debut in a 2–0 win at Bolton – Leeds's first-ever League win at Burnden Park at the 14th time of asking. But injury, coupled with the emergence of Chris Crowe, saw Peyton on the sidelines for much of the 1958–59 season as United, now under the guidance of Bill Lambton, only just managed to avoid the drop.

Jack Taylor took over from Lambton, and Peyton got more games in 1959–60, but he could not prevent relegation. There was some consolation for Peyton at the end of the season – a recall to the Irish side. His second cap, like his first four years earlier, came against West Germany. This time it was in Dusseldorf, where a goal by Derby County's Fionan Fagan on the half-hour stunned 51,000 home fans as the Irish became the first team to win in Germany for three years. The next week Ireland were in Malmo, and when skipper Noel Cantwell hobbled off as Sweden went 3–0 up just before half-time, Peyton was sent on as the experienced West Ham man's replacement.

Peyton was joined in the Republic side in September 1960 by Leeds clubmate Peter Fitzgerald for the first visit to Dublin by a Welsh side, who took their chances to win 3–2 and end Ireland's eight-game unbeaten home run. Peyton had switched to inside-left for that match, and that was the position he occupied for most of the 1960–61 season for Leeds. The only problem was that Manchester United's rising young star Johnny Giles was being utilised in that position by the Irish selectors.

Leeds were gradually being rebuilt by new manager Don Revie, but he stood by Peyton in 1961–62, and the Irishman rewarded his boss with his best season, five goals from 37 Division Two games.

Although he was not first choice at the start of 1962–63, Peyton made his first start in a competitive game for Ireland when they drew 1–1 with Iceland in Reykjavik to seal a place in the second round of the European Championships. Matches were played over two legs, and Eire's 4–2 win in Dublin the previous month meant the Irish could adopt a fairly cautious approach in the return game. As a result it was a poor game, although Peyton had the satisfaction of having a hand in the Republic goal scored by Newcastle's Liam Tuohy.

Although the next Euro game, against Austria, was 12 months away, Ireland only played once more after the Iceland fixture. It was a friendly against Scotland on a scorching hot June day, settled by an early Cantwell goal, but it left Peyton with painful memories. Not only was it his last international appearance, but he also had to go off just before half-time with a nasty head wound. He was replaced by Sunderland's Ambrose Fogarty.

With Elland Road now packed with bright young stars it was time for Peyton to move on, and a few weeks after the Scotland game he joined York City in Division Four for

season. October 1957 proved to be a crucial month in his development. He travelled to Elland Road to lock horns with another Football League XI, which included Leeds United's centre-half Jack Charlton. Peyton gave an assured display as the battling Irish went down 3–1 to earn the approval of watching scouts. Romania sent a B team to the Emerald Isle later in the month to take on the Republic and their Northern counterparts. Peyton played in a 1–1 draw at Dalymount Park, Dublin, against the Romanians, who were then crushed 6–0 by Northern Ireland B in Belfast two days later.

It was now a question of which English club would sign 22-year-old Peyton, and that club turned out to be Leeds, whose £5,000 bid was accepted in January 1958. United boss Raich Carter went to Dublin to watch Peyton in his final game, a crucial 2–1 win against Drumcondra, which produced a near riot as the crowd

£4,000. The Minstermen had a miserable season and had to apply for re-election, and although they improved in 1964–65, injury-hit Peyton hardly played and became player-manager of Barnstaple Town at the end of the campaign. He later returned to Ireland with St Patrick's Athletic, for whom his brother Willie played.

AUBREY POWELL

(Wales 1946–51)

Inside-forward

Born: Lower Cwmtwrch, Glamorgan, 19 April 1918.
Died: Methley, near Leeds, 27 January 2009.
Caps: Leeds United 5, Everton 2, Birmingham City 1.
Total: 8
Goals: 1

BRAVE Aubrey Powell defied medical opinion to forge a wonderful career for both club and country. At 18 he had the world at his feet. The Welsh teenager had broken into Leeds United's team as a right-winger, sparkling on his debut on Christmas Day 1936 as United crushed Middlesbrough 5–0 at Elland Road. It was a dream start for the youngster from Cwm Wanderers who had opted to join Leeds after being on the books of Swansea Town as an amateur. But his football world came to a shattering halt on 20 March 1937 at Preston North End. Just five minutes into the game he was challenged by left-back John Batey and lay in agony on the Deepdale turf. He had suffered a compound fracture of his right leg just above the ankle, with the bone exposed through his skin. It was an horrific injury, and it took nine minutes to carefully get the stricken Powell off the pitch.

While he was taken to Preston Royal Infirmary 10-man Leeds went on to lose 1–0 to a Frank O'Donnell goal, but Powell's future was of greater concern. Doctors said he would never play again, and surgery on the leg left it fractionally shorter than the other. But Powell lived for football and would not be beaten, and with the help of the Leeds backroom staff gradually built up strength in his limbs to return to action.

Sixteen months later he was back in the first team in a 3–0 defeat at Liverpool and he was given a rapturous reception at Elland Road the following week when Leeds slaughtered Leicester City 8–2, Gordon Hodgson becoming the only United player to score five goals in a game.

Manager Billy Hampson had switched Powell to an inside-forward position, where he was able to have a greater influence on games, forming an eye-catching combination with his right-wing partner David Cochrane, another youngster.

While Northern Ireland soon capped Cochrane, Wales had yet to call upon Powell when war broke out. Powell became an army PT instructor, stationed in North

A painting of Aubrey Powell in his Welsh kit.

Yorkshire, Hull and Belgium, but was never far from a football field. He played in four wartime internationals, represented the Army and Northern Command and played for an FA XI in a high-profile game in Belgium. His first international during hostilities was a 1–1 draw with England at Ninian Park, Cardiff, in 1943, and later in the year 80,000 people escaped the worries of war for an afternoon to see England thump Wales 8–3. Powell scored

One of Aubrey Powell's Welsh caps – this one for playing against England.

A selection of Aubrey Powell's Welsh international caps and shirts.

one of the Red Dragons' goals while his namesake, Ivor Powell, the Queen's Park Rangers forward, who later had a spell as coach at Elland Road, broke his collarbone and was replaced by England's Stan Mortensen.

England were a powerful team, but Leeds star Powell lowered their colours with the only goal of the 1945 Victory International at West Bromwich. The dapper Powell was highly thought of and had actually played alongside many of England's all-time greats, including Mortensen, Tommy Lawton, George Hardwick and Joe Mercer, for an FA XI against Belgium in Brussels earlier in the year.

Powell, a fluent Welsh speaker who packed a punch with his shooting, played 126 times for Leeds during the war – a figure only bettered by Gerry Henry – and was 28 when peace-time football resumed in 1946–47. He was actually one of the younger members of the Leeds squad as many of the pre-war players were well into their 30s. The bulk of the team were past their best and despite Powell's best efforts – nine goals from 34 games – were relegated. He won the first of his official caps that season against Scotland at Wrexham when Wales, trailing to a Willie

Aubrey Powell, in his Welsh shirt, with his caps. The clock was presented to him by Cwm Wanderers to mark his international exploits.

Waddell penalty, hit back to win 3–1 with goals from Bryn Jones and Trevor Ford (2). However, England brought Wales down to earth at Maine Road with goals from Wilf Mannion (2) and Lawton earning a 3–0 win, although Powell came close to scoring for Wales with a header.

Relegated Leeds won five of their opening seven Second Division games, with Powell scoring a hat-trick in a 5–0 drubbing against Plymouth, but he was on the end of another 3–0 reverse against England in Cardiff the following month.

Wales may not have been able to match England, but they pulled off a fine 2–1 win against Scotland at Hampden Park after falling behind to an Andy McLaren header. Goals by Trevor Ford and George Lowrie turned the game around as Scotland played out the last few minutes with 10 men after goalkeeper Willie Miller was carried off with a gash to the head.

Wales, well prompted by Powell, built on that result by defeating Northern Ireland 2–0 in Wrexham but Leeds, despite 10 goals by their Welsh star from inside-right, failed to make the expected impact in Division Two, finishing a disappointing 18th. It was obvious Leeds needed to rebuild, and they sold their tricky little dribbler to Everton for £10,000, one of the biggest fees in British football at the time, using the cash to bring in new players. Powell had contributed 25 goals in 119 peacetime games for Leeds.

Powell won two more caps in his two years at Goodison Park against England and Belgium, Trevor Ford scoring a hat-trick against the latter in a 5–1 win. In August 1950 he joined Birmingham for £7,000 and played his final international against Scotland, scoring Wales's goal in a 3–1 defeat at Cardiff when Bobby Collins won his first cap for Scotland. He only managed 15 games for Birmingham before severe arthritis forced him to curtail his career in 1951 at the age of 33. He returned to Leeds to work for a confectionary firm run by his Leeds-born wife's family and also coached Yorkshire League side Leeds Ashley Road in the 1960s.

LUCAS RADEBE

(South Africa 1992–2003)

Defender / Midfield

Born: Diepkloof, Johannesburg, 12 April 1969.
Caps: Kaizer Chiefs 12, Leeds United 58. Total: 70
Goals: 2

HAD the bullet gone a degree to the right Lucas Radebe would probably have spent the rest of his life in a wheelchair. The Kaizer Chiefs star was shot in a Soweto township in 1991, the lead projectile missing his spine by a fraction. The motive for the shooting has never been clear, but it came frightenly close to cutting down a player who was soon to fire his way to glory with South Africa and Leeds United.

Radebe, one of 12 children, had a tough upbringing in the apartheid era but was a bright kid, enjoying his football on dirt pitches with his mates. At 15 he moved out of the more dangerous Soweto area to live in Bophuthatswana – an independent homeland in North West South Africa – and starred as a goalkeeper with ICL Birds United in the local professional League while studying to be a teacher. The athletic Radebe won a gold medal in the Inter-State Games in Port Elizabeth when Bophuthatswana beat South Africa 1–0 in the Final. He

South African captain Lucas Radebe after his final appearance for his country against England in Durban.

combined playing with studying to be a teacher, but after switching from goalkeeper to outfield defence he attracted the attention of Kaizer Chiefs, South Africa's most famous club, gave up his studies and made his debut against Bush Bucks in April 1990.

The Chiefs did the League and Cup double in 1992, and Radebe made his international debut at the end of the season in a three-game series against Cameroon, who were fresh from pushing England hard in the 1990 World Cup quarter-finals, Bobby Robson's men needing extra-time to edge a 3–2 win.

The matches were to mark South Africa's return to the FIFA family after expulsion because of apartheid and were the country's first official internationals for 42 years. The South Africans were dubbed Bafana Bafana – Zulu for 'The Boys' – and the matches were played out against the backdrop of Nelson Mandela's election to power. They were exciting times for South Africa and its footballers, whom Leeds boss Howard Wilkinson felt were worth checking out, particularly the free-scoring Phil Masinga. United scout Geoff Sleight watched an Orlando Pirates versus Kaizer Chiefs game and reported that Masinga looked useful, but Radebe was an even better player.

The Whites recruited the pair for £250,000 each, a South African record, in August 1994, but although Wilkinson knew Masinga was an out-and-out striker, he did not seem to know Radebe's best position – defence or midfield? His first full start, at Queen's Park Rangers, came on the right wing.

Ruptured knee ligaments in March 1995 put Radebe out of action for nearly nine months, but he was desperate to play in the African Nations Finals in his homeland. He had recovered sufficiently to come on as a sub in a 2–0 win at Bolton and persuaded a sceptical Wilkinson to let him go to the Championships – but only after South Africa boss Clive Barker sent team doctor Victor Ramathesele to reassure Leeds that they would only field Radebe if he was fit to play.

Consequently Radebe was eased into the tournament, missing the opening 3–0 win against Cameroon and coming on at the end of the 1–0 victory against Angola, before starting against Egypt. The Leeds player played in a dramatic quarter-final against Algeria when the Bafana Bafana missed a late penalty but still conjured up a winner from Shoes Moshoeu. In the semi-finals, Radebe's superb marking job on Leeds teammate Tony Yeboah laid the platform for a 3–0 win against Ghana.

The Final, against Tunisia in Johannesburg, attracted an 'official' attendance of 80,000, although observers reckon it was nearer 100,000. Wolves's Mark Williams was the hero, coming on as sub to score twice to see the host nation triumph. Radebe returned to Elland Road with renewed confidence, boosted further by an invitation to replace retiring skipper Neil Tovey as his country's skipper. His first match as captain was a 2–1 victory against Zaire in a World Cup qualifier played in neutral Togo because Zaire was plunged into civil war.

Skipper Radebe's next match had massive exposure as he led out South Africa against England at Old Trafford – his country's first game against a European side away from home. The Bafana Bafana gave a good account of themselves, England only clinching a 2–1 win with an Ian Wright goal that had more than a suspicion of handball about it.

It was at Old Trafford earlier that season that Radebe came on as a sub for Leeds against Manchester United and played in goal for most of the game after Mark Beeney had received an early red card. It took a late Roy Keane goal to defeat Radebe, who had already shown Leeds fans his goalkeeping skills a few weeks earlier when he went in the nets for the injured John Lukic at Elland Road with United trailing 1–0 – and that was how it stayed. The Boro game was the first after the Whites lost 3–0 to Aston Villa in the League Cup Final when Radebe played out of position at right-back.

Radebe's defensive skills blossomed at Elland Road under new manager George Graham. The South African was a tremendous reader of the game, his tackling was

Lucas Radebe at full stretch in training with South Africa.

perfectly timed, his work on the ball had improved greatly and Leeds fans had taken him to their hearts.

Inevitably, with the African Championships played every two years in the middle of the English domestic season, the club versus country conflict reared its head, with Graham upset that Radebe was being called up by the South African FA for friendlies and less important tournaments like the Confederations Cup. It was in the latter, against Uruguay in December 1997, that Radebe scored his first goal for his country in a 4–3 defeat that spelled the end of Barker's managerial reign.

The SAFA argued that they were building towards the World Cup in France, for which they had qualified, and also had the defence of the African title to look forward to in Burkina Faso. It added up to a busy 1998 for Radebe, whose team made a spirited defence of their African crown, qualifying for the quarter-finals after coming through a difficult group containing Ivory Coast, Angola and Namibia.

Goals from South Africa's new star striker Benni McCarthy and defender David Nyathi earned a 2–1 win against Morocco to set up a tense semi-final meeting with DR Congo, which also finished 2–1, settled by McCarthy's sudden death goal in extra-time. The Final proved a step too far for Radebe and his men as they lost 2–0 to a slick Egyptian team, but morale was high as the Bafana Bafana prepared for the World Cup under new manager Phillipe Troussier. However, the Frenchman was a strict disciplinarian, and his style did not go down too well with some of his squad. Frustrated at the attitude of some of his party in France, Troussier threatened to quit then sent home Brendan Augustine and the aptly-named Naughty Mokoena for breaking a curfew.

Radebe spent much of the World Cup acting as peacemaker between his manager and his players. Not surprisingly, in their first appearance at the biggest football event on earth South Africa struggled. They were outclassed by the hosts 3–0 and recovered to draw 1–1 with Denmark in Toulouse, but blew hopes of any further progress when they were held 2–2 by Saudi Arabia, a side they were fully expected to beat.

The disappointing showing led to Troussier's exit and the appointment of Trott Moloto, who reappointed Radebe as his skipper. Leadership also came his way at Elland Road as Graham handed him the captain's armband for 1998–99, a position he continued to hold after Graham's departure to Tottenham.

United's new man in charge, David O'Leary, dubbed Radebe 'the Chief', a moniker which the fans embraced as the South African's ever-increasing excellent displays at the back boosted his already high popularity ratings.

Leeds were back in Europe and Radebe was taming some of the Continent's top strikers with performances of calm authority. He even weighed in with a rare late goal to knock Spartak Moscow out of the UEFA Cup, but the club versus country issue would not go away. Radebe was having to serve two masters and in February 1999 played three games in two continents in five days. After playing in United's 2–0 FA Cup replay defeat at Tottenham on a Wednesday, he jetted off to Gabon to help South Africa to a 4–1 win in an African Nations qualifier on Saturday before flying back to England to play in the 2–1 televised Premiership victory at Leicester.

It was a punishing schedule for the South African Sports Star of the Year and Leeds feared it would lead to their skipper's premature burn-out. But one game he was not going to miss was a match against a World Stars XI just three games into the 1999–00 Premiership season. He had been chosen to captain – for the first half only – a Nelson Mandela XI in Johannesburg and he was not going to turn down the honour.

Radebe was certainly racking up the air miles and led his country to their first victory against a European nation when they beat Sweden in Pretoria three months after the Mandela match. Although a milestone game, the SAFA, who had first call on his services, warned their skipper he would have to turn up for the friendly or they would block him from playing against Southampton.

Leeds could do nothing about it, even though they knew Radebe would also be missing for the African Nations Finals later in the season. The Championships were hosted jointly by Ghana and Nigeria and once again the Bafana Bafana were one of the fancied teams. Back in Yorkshire, Leeds were no doubt hoping Radebe's men would make an early exit, but they breezed through their group, beating Gabon, DR Congo and drawing with Algeria to go head-to-head with Ghana in Kumasi. Despite having Barnsley's Eric Tinkler dismissed just after half-time, South Africa won 1–0 to go through against the other joint hosts, Nigeria. The match was held in the Surulere Stadium in Lagos where Nigeria had been unbeaten in two decades, a run they extended with a 2–0 victory.

Frustratingly for Leeds, there was a meaningless third-fourth Play-off game, which the South Africans won on penalties against Tunisia before just 1,000 spectators in Accra. Leeds, with Radebe at the heart of the defence alongside Jonathan Woodgate, were flying high in the Premiership, shaking off their captain's mid-season absence in the African Nations Cup to finish third and qualify for the Champions League. With United going well in Europe there were showdown talks with the SAFA in an effort to cut down on their demands for Radebe, who had just signed a new deal with the club. Things came to a head when, as Leeds were losing to Liverpool in the FA Cup, Radebe was thousands of miles away playing against Burkina Faso.

The Chief's body and mind were starting to feel the effects of his constant globe-trotting. He had been playing non-stop football for two seasons and had returned from the African Championships with a niggling injury.

At last United extracted a degree of flexibility from the SAFA in regard to Radebe, who was beginning to hint at his retirement from international football. He suffered an injury-hit 2000–01 in any case, and his season ended at Sunderland in March with ligament damage to his left knee. He could only look on in frustration as United's young team continued their amazing run in the Champions League semi-finals.

Ironically, having reached an agreement about his international future, Leeds had to do without their captain for the entire 2001–02 season because of his knee trouble, although he recovered sufficiently for South Africa to include him in Jomo Sono's squad for the World Cup in the Far East.

The ever-smiling Leeds skipper made his first tentative steps to recovery when he came on for the second half of a 1–0 friendly victory against Madagascar in Durban at the end of the season. He proved his fitness in the Reunification Cup competition in Hong Kong against Scotland and Turkey before leading South Africa out in their Group B opener against Paraguay.

A late penalty by Quinton Fortune earned the Bafana Bafana a 2–2 draw, and a 1–0 victory against Slovenia in Daegu boosted hopes of further progress. A point against Spain would put South Africa through and twice they fought back from a goal down – Radebe getting the second equaliser – before Real Madrid star Raul earned the Europeans a 3–2 victory.

Once again injuries took their toll in 2002–03, and Radebe called time on his illustrious international career, his swansong game coming against England at King's Park, Durban. It was an eventful game, seen by the SAFA as England's nod of approval towards South Africa's staging of the 2010 World Cup. Gareth Southgate scored after just 35 seconds, Benni McCarthy equalised from the spot, David Beckham went off with a fractured wrist just after the interval and Emile Heskey netted the winner for Sven-Goran Eriksson's team on 64 minutes.

Radebe, South Africa's finest defender, received a rousing reception after the game as he addressed the crowd by microphone to say farewell after a long and proud international career that spanned a decade and 70 caps. He still had unfinished business at Leeds, who were deep in financial debt and starting to struggle on the field. As big name stars were sold off, Radebe remained at Elland Road, but further injuries meant he could only start 11 Premiership games of their 2003–04 relegation season.

He managed even fewer in League One, making just one start – a 0–0 draw at Wolves in August in which he came off after rupturing an Achilles tendon. He did manage to stretch his legs on the international stage once more, playing in the Tsunami Disaster fund-raiser in Barcelona organised by FIFA. But his attempted comeback ended in the reserves at Manchester United shortly afterwards when he damaged medial knee ligaments.

Throughout his time at Leeds he had forged an unbreakable bond with the supporters and he came off the bench for the final game of the season against Rotherham to play in his 200th League game for the club. Almost 38,000 watched his testimonial game at Elland Road when the proceeds were shared between nine charities in Great Britain and Africa.

Charity fundraising was always close to his heart, and he was a deserved winner of a FIFA Fair Play Award for his charity work and fight against racism in football. He always had the personality, bravery and professionalism to bounce back from injuries and never lost sight of the fact that he was lucky to earn a living from football.

A catalogue of injuries in his 11 years at Elland Road meant Radebe's appearance tally was relatively small, but those figures only tell part of the remarkable story of the man whose rose from the townships of Soweto to become a legend in Leeds.

PAUL REANEY
(England 1968–71)
Right-back
Born: Fulham, London, 22 October 1944.
Caps: Leeds United 3. Total: 3

CONSIDERING the brilliant George Best rated Paul Reaney as the toughest full-back he ever faced, it is strange that the Leeds United defender only won three England caps. True, a broken leg just before the 1970 World Cup may have robbed him of more international appearances, but he was largely ignored by Alf Ramsey. Even more baffling was that he did not get a call-up from his old club boss Don Revie when he inherited Ramsey's job in 1974. 'Speedy' Reaney was a fixture in Revie's wonderful team, winning all the major honours United achieved in a glory-laden era. Apart from that period out with his fractured leg, Reaney was there every step of the way, from winning the Second Division title in 1964 to reaching the European Cup Final 11 years later.

Although born in Fulham, Reaney moved with his family to Yorkshire when he was only two weeks old, settling in Leeds where his performances for Cross Green and Leeds Schools attracted the attention of his local club. He was playing for Middleton Parkside and was working as an apprentice car mechanic when he joined United's groundstaff in October 1961. He was one of a crop of outstanding young players and made his senior debut in a 2–0 win at Swansea in September 1962 shortly before his 18th birthday.

Revie was not shy at giving youth a chance, and he was rewarded in Reaney's case with staggering consistency, which saw the right-back play nearly 750 times for United in a 17-year career at Elland Road. His turn of pace, willingness to get into the opposition half and ability to deliver crosses with uncanny accuracy were all eye-catching aspects of his game. But he also mastered the less spectacular

Paul Reaney in action for England on the concrete surface in Malta's National Stadium at Gzira.

arts of defending – tackling, man-marking and positional play. He was also the king of the goalline clearance. On the rare occasions that the opposition managed to outwit the Leeds defence, Reaney would materialise, as if by magic, on the goalline to head or kick clear.

Representative honours soon came Reaney's way. He made his debut for the England Under-23 side in a 2–2 draw in France and went on the end-of-season tour of Hungary, Turkey and Israel, but did not get a game as Sheffield United's Len Badger played in all three games. He faced Scotland, West Germany and Czechoslovakia in 1965 with the Young England team, but the World Cup had come too early for him, with Fulham's outstanding George Cohen and Blackpool veteran Jimmy Armfield the obvious choices for Ramsey. But future Leeds boss Armfield did not play for England after the tournament and injury put an end to Cohen's international days in 1967, leaving the right-back place up for grabs.

Keith Newton (Blackburn), Cyril Knowles (Tottenham) and Tommy Wright (Everton) were all given a go by Ramsey before Reaney, on his way to a League Championship medal, finally got his chance. Even that was at the expense of someone else.

A broken leg left Paul Reaney in hospital and out of the 1970 World Cup reckoning with England.

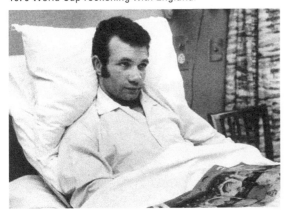

Uncapped clubmate Terry Cooper was set to make his debut at left-back in December 1968 against Bulgaria at Wembley but had to pull out through injury, so Reaney was called into the squad as a replacement. Sir Alf's full-back pairing was Newton and Arsenal's Bob McNab with Reaney on the bench, but he got on for Newton for the last 10 minutes of a 1–1 draw.

It was not the breakthrough Reaney had hoped for, and while Cooper subsequently nailed down the left-back spot in the England team, the tall Newton remained Ramsey's preference at right-back. When Cooper was unavailable or not selected, Newton switched to left-back with Wright, with whom he later played at Everton, taking the number-two shirt.

Twelve months and 10 England games later, Reaney finally got his first England start. It was back at Wembley for a friendly against Portugal. With the World Cup in Mexico just six months away, it was a big opportunity for the Leeds player and his left-back partner, Liverpool's Emlyn Hughes, who was making his second England appearance. Both were solid in a low-key game settled by Jack Charlton's 24th-minute header, although had Francis Lee converted a later penalty it would have been a more realistic scoreline.

Leeds were pushing hard for a European Cup, League and FA Cup treble, and Reaney had already been called into the England squad for Mexico when his world came crashing down on Thursday 2 April at West Ham's Upton Park when he broke a leg. He was out of the rest of the title run-in as Leeds chased Everton, the European Cup semi-finals against Celtic, the FA Cup Final against Chelsea and the World Cup.

It took Reaney 27 weeks of hard labour to work his way back to full fitness. Initially he returned to action too soon, but once he built up strength in his leg he was in the Leeds team again. Not only that, he resumed England duty.

Under the captaincy of Alan Mullery, Ramsey sent out an inexperienced side for a European Championship qualifier in Malta in February 1971. Roy McFarland (Derby), Martin Chivers (Tottenham) and Everton duo Joe Royle and Colin Harvey were all making their debuts, while Reaney was making his first start for England in a competitive game. The narrow pitch was devoid of grass and like concrete under the baking Mediterranean sun, so it was not surprising that both sides struggled in a poor game settled by Martin Peters's shot on 35 minutes.

The next month Reaney was in the Football League representative side that beat the Scottish League 1–0 in Glasgow, and his confidence was boosted further by selection for England's next European game against Greece at Wembley. Injury cost him the chance of playing in that match, and he was never to play for the national team again as Ramsey tried Chris Lawler (Liverpool), Peter Storey (Arsenal) and Leeds clubmate Paul Madeley in the right-back berth.

Reaney was probably at his best as Leeds won the title in 1973–74, but Derby's David Nish became the latest to jump ahead of him in the England queue. Even when Revie was installed as England boss, Reaney's vast big-match experience did not get him a recall – and he was still only 30. The Leeds stalwart, whose appearance record is only bettered by contemporaries Jack Charlton and Billy Bremner, moved on to Bradford City in 1978. He then had a spell in Australia with New South Wales club Newcastle United, being named Australia's Player of the Year before returning to Yorkshire to run coaching courses at schools and holiday camps. Those kids were in good hands as Reaney, noted for his great humour, was a fine teacher. He was not the luckiest player when it came to England games, and there was a sad postscript to his career in 1993 when burglars broke into his home and stole a wall safe containing all his medals, but at least they left his treasured England caps.

PAUL ROBINSON

(England 2003– to date)

Goalkeeper

Born: Beverley, East Yorkshire, 15 October 1979.
Caps: Leeds United 4, Tottenham Hotspur 37. Total: 41

PAUL ROBINSON will be hoping to recapture his best form and a place in England's 2010 World Cup squad. The Beverley-born shot-stopper was outstanding in his early years with Leeds United, breaking into the national team when he was only 23 years old – quite young for a keeper. Eventually he became Sven-Goran Eriksson's first choice and played in the 2006 World Cup until a dip in form in the Euro 2008 qualifiers saw him slip down the pecking order.

Robbo joined United at 16 and was a member of the side that won the FA Youth Cup, but he had to be patient for a first-team slot as the superb Nigel Martyn was at his peak. When Martyn injured a rib in a UEFA Cup game against Roma, Robinson was able to mark his debut by keeping a clean sheet in a 0–0 home draw with Chelsea on 25 October 1998, making a further four appearances that season. He looked ready for the breakthrough, but England man Martyn was an ever-present in the 1999–2000 season, which saw Robinson occupy a place on the bench in every game.

Working hard under goalkeeping coach Steve Sutton, Robinson looked a natural goalkeeper and word had spread beyond Elland Road about his talents. Standing 6ft 4in tall and powerfully built, he proved an outstanding prospect and despite his lack of experience was called in to the full England squad for training by Kevin Keegan ahead of a European Championship qualifying game against Poland.

October 2000 proved a decisive month in Robinson's career. He made his first Under-21 appearance against Denmark at the beginning of the month before coming on for the injured Martyn in a 3–1 Premiership win against Charlton, then kept his nerve as United forced a 0–0 draw in Turkey against Besiktas in the Champions League. Robinson topped that with a magnificent display against Barcelona at Elland Road as a series of stunning saves kept the Catalans at bay until 20 seconds from the end when Rivaldo snatched an equaliser. United's board were sufficiently impressed to get Robinson to sign a five-year contract, and although the fit-again Martyn recaptured his first-team place at the end of January Leeds knew that they had another future England goalkeeper in the shape of Robinson. He became the regular Under-21 stopper in 2001 but could not oust Martyn, who played in every Premiership game in 2001–02. However, he was given his chance by new manager Terry Venables the following campaign and grabbed it with both hands, some heroic performances earning him a place in Sven-Goran Eriksson's squad for the friendly against Australia at Upton Park on 12 February 2003.

England became the first nation ever to change an entire team at half-time, and among those who came on for the first time were Robinson and 17-year-old wonderkid Wayne Rooney. England already trailed 2–0 to Australia, who were inspired by Robinson's Leeds teammate Harry Kewell, when the United 'keeper came on for David James. The match finished in an historic 3–1 win for the Aussies. At the end of the season Robinson, an ever present for Leeds, replaced James again in 2–1 win against South Africa in Durban. The same scenario was repeated the following season in victory against Croatia at Ipswich and defeat at Old Trafford to Denmark. Robinson had played four 'second-half' games for England and, although that first England start was moving ever-closer, Leeds were in financial freefall and were forced to sell their star names.

The hugely-popular Robinson had already sealed his place in Elland Road history by scoring a last-minute headed equaliser against Swindon Town in a League Cup tie. The game was eventually won by Leeds after more

Paul Robinson stretches under the tuition of England goalkeeper coach Ray Clemence (left) and England coach Sven-Goran Eriksson.

heroics by Robinson in the penalty shoot-out; however, the fact that United were severely stretched by Swindon said much about their poor form in 2003–04.

Robinson remained a defiant last line of defence but had little protection from a cobbled-together back line, and when United were relegated it was inevitable he would leave Elland Road. A £1.5 million transfer to Tottenham Hotspur was concluded at the end of the season and before he started a game for his new club, he was in the starting line up to face Iceland at the City of Manchester Stadium in the summer, England coasting to a 6–1 win.

Robinson was understudy to James for the 2004 European Championships, but his form for Tottenham saw him become England's first choice for the World Cup qualifiers. In the Finals in Germany he was reliable as England reached the quarter-finals. He shut out Paraguay, Trinidad & Tobago, Ecuador and Portugal, only to go out to the latter on penalties.

Under Eriksson's replacement, Steve McClaren, Robinson continued as his country's regular goalkeeper for the Euro 2008 qualifiers, but his confidence suffered a massive blow after defeat in Croatia in October 2006. England trailed to an Eduardo Da Silva goal after an hour when eight minutes later Gary Neville sent a backpass towards Robinson. The ball took an unexpected bobble as Robinson shaped to kick the ball clear and it rolled into the net for a freak goal. From that moment on Robinson found his every move come under scrutiny from the media as England's campaign slowly unravelled. His cause was not helped when he made a mistake in a friendly against Germany, who became the first team to beat England at the new Wembley in August 2007.

Although Robinson retained his place for the Euro qualifiers, the end came in the penultimate game in the group – a 2–1 loss to Russia in Moscow – where he pushed a shot into the path of Roman Pavlyuchenko, who netted a 73rd-minute winner. Under pressure McClaren reacted by dropping Robinson for the final game – a must-win match against Croatia at Wembley. In the Spurs man's place came another former Leeds goalie, Scott Carson, for only his second England start. It proved a disastrous choice by McClaren as a clearly nervous Carson, on Liverpool's books, was badly at fault for the first goal as England crashed to a 3–2 defeat and failed to qualify.

Robinson, who won a League Cup-winners' medal with Tottenham in 2008, joined Blackburn Rovers for £3.5 million in the summer of that year, but the switch did not see him regain his England place. McClaren was succeeded by Fabio Capello, who turned to the rejuvenated James as his first choice while Manchester United's Ben Foster and West Ham's Robert Green have also emerged as other contenders. However, Robinson has the edge on experience over their claims and, with James nudging towards 40, the former Leeds man cannot have given up hope of adding to his total of 41 caps.

ROQUE JUNIOR
(Brazil 1999–2005)

Central-defender
Born: Santa Rita do Spaucai, Minas Gerais, 31 August 1976.
Caps: Palmeiras 2, AC Milan 29, *Leeds United 3, Bayer Leverkusen 16. Total: 50
*While on loan from AC Milan
Goals: 2

WORLD Cup-winner Roque Junior endured four months of abject misery at Elland Road. Brought in on loan by Peter Reid to plug the gap in central defence following the sale of Rio Ferdinand and Jonathan Woodgate, the Brazilian simply could not adapt to the pace and physicality of the Premiership. The gap at the back became a gaping hole into which opposition forwards rushed virtually unopposed. In his seven games for United, a staggering 25 goals were conceded. It was a case of Roque by name, rocky by nature. It was a mystery to Leeds fans how a player with such a top-class pedigree could struggle so badly yet was still his country's first-choice centre-back. He began in Brazil with Sao Jose but made his name with Palmeiras, the Sao Paulo-based club, making his international debut in a 2–2 draw with

Roque Junior in action against Germany.

Holland in Amsterdam in October 1999. Roque Junior marked his second appearance, a 7–0 win against Thailand, with a goal, and it was not long before he joined the continuing exodus of top Brazilians to Italy when he joined AC Milan.

Roque's time with the Rossoneri was punctuated by long spells of injury, but he was seen by national coach Wanderley Luxemburgo as a key man in the scrap for World Cup qualification. The Finals without Brazil would be a bit like Punch without Judy, but at one stage that looked a possibility. They finished fourth in the South America group to claim the last automatic qualification to the 2000 Finals, pipping Uruguay on goal difference, so were spared going into a Play-off with Australia.

Midway through the campaign Roque Junior scored a 94th-minute winner against Colombia to earn Brazil three priceless points. Important at the time, it proved absolutely crucial in the great scheme of things because if Colombia had held out both they and Uruguay would have finished above Brazil, who would not have qualified.

The appointment of Phil Scolari turned the tide for Brazil, who won all their group games in Japan against Turkey, China and Belgium before coming from behind to beat England 2–1 in the quarter-final. Ronaldo's goal eliminated Turkey in the semis, and the same player's double against Germany won the Final in Yokohama. It was a triumph that had seemed so unlikely for Brazil just a few months earlier.

Roque Junior played in all six games in the Finals, but in Serie A knocks and niggles continued to frustrate his Milanese employers. A shoulder injury ruled him out for much of 2002–03, but he returned in time to come on as a 70th-minute substitute for Alessandro Costacurta in the all-Italian Champions League Final at Old Trafford. AC and Juventus could not muster a goal between them after two hours, and Milan won the penalty shootout 3–2 on penalties.

Three years earlier Leeds had been dreaming of similar glory – meeting AC Milan and Roque Junior on

the way – in their wonderful run to the Champions League semi-finals. But the bid for unexpected glory came at a very high price and Leeds were having to sell their top stars to keep afloat. They were forced to plunge into the loan market, and Roque Junior was among the men who arrived on a season-long loan in a blaze of publicity.

The World and European champion jetted in to England after helping Brazil beat Ecuador 1–0 in a World Cup qualifier in Manaus and was plunged straight into the Leeds team at Leicester. It was a disaster as the Foxes cruised home 4–0, and the following week the new Brazilian recruit was sent off on his home debut – a 3–2 defeat against Birmingham.

Jet lag could no longer be an excuse, and another 4–0 hiding – this time at Everton – set the relegation alarm bells ringing. Roque Junior took time out with a suspension and an appearance for Brazil in a friendly against Jamaica at Leicester. His return to the Walkers Stadium, scene of his nightmare United debut, was much happier this time as a Roberto Carlos goal gave the South Americans a 1–0 win in November 2005. Briefly it looked as though Roque Junior might have turned the corner when he scored twice – celebrated in manic fashion – against Manchester United in a Coca-Cola Cup tie. But once again the defence imploded and Leeds lost 3–2.

After that it simply got worse as the Whites lost 4–1 at Arsenal and 6–1 at Portsmouth, the Pompey humiliation seeing Reid get the sack. Roque Junior left all the turmoil behind him and flew back to South America for two more World Cup qualifiers.

The first stop was Lima, where Rivaldo's goal was cancelled out by Newcastle's Nolberto Solano to earn Peru a 1–1 draw. Brazil then moved on to Curitiba, where they shared six goals with Uruguay. Kaka and Ronaldo put Brazil 2–0 up inside 28 minutes, but Uruguay roared back to lead with goals from Diego Forlan (2) and Gilberto Silva until another Ronaldo strike four minutes from time salvaged a point for Carlos Alberto's team. He returned to Elland Road carrying an injury, but it was clear new boss Eddie Gray did not want to keep him anyway, and the player returned to his parent club in January and was immediately farmed out to another Italian side, Siena.

Since then Roque Junior played in Germany with Bayer Leverkusen and Duisburg, had a spell in Qatar with Al Rayyan, and then returned home to sign for his old club Palmeiras. During this time he took his number of international appearances to 50 – although that figure does include games against a Catalonia XI and Spanish club side Seville, which the Brazilian FA considered as full internationals. His last match in the canary yellow of his country was in sharp contrast to his stay in Leeds – an 8–0 hammering of the United Arab Emirates in Abu Dhabi in November 2005.

Roque Junior lines up for Brazil against the Republic of Ireland in Dublin. He's on the far left, back row.

LAMINE SAKHO

(Senegal 2004)

Striker

Born: Louga, 28 September 1977.
Caps: *Leeds United 2
* On loan from Marseille

SENEGAL got special dispensation from FIFA to pick Lamine Sakho for their 2004 African Nations Finals squad. The forward was on loan at Leeds from Marseille and had played for the French Under-21 side earlier in his career. FIFA agreed to the switch to Sakho's home nation after the French Football Federation gave up their claim on the player. From the outside it looked as though he was only in manager Guy Stephan's party to make up the numbers, but he did play in the tournament twice – his only games for Senegal.

Sakho, whose father had represented Senegal, left his homeland when he was eight years old and went on to make a name for himself as a bright young forward with Nîmes and Lens.

In summer 1999 he played four times for the French Espoirs' team – the Under-21s – and was in good company, playing alongside the likes of William Gallas, Frederic Kanoute and Willy Sagnol. Sakho maintained the form he had shown in the French League with goals in victories against Iceland and Armenia. He found himself a player in demand, but injuries stalled his career until he joined big guns Marseille in January 2002. He did not make the expected impact at the Stade Vélodrome and after playing in a pre-season tournament in Dublin for Leeds as a trialist was recruited on a season-long loan by United boss Peter Reid.

Sakho arrived with fellow French loanees Zoumana Camara and Didier Domi, as Leeds were deep in debt and unable to splash the cash. In Sakho's case initial impressions were good as he had a lively debut in a 2–2 home draw against Newcastle and was among the scorers as the Whites snatched a last-gasp 3–2 win at Middlesbrough.

United's new front runner had plenty of pace, but games seemed to pass him by, fitness doubts crept in, and after a series of disastrous results Reid was axed. Former United legend Eddie Gray came in and largely swept away the loan men, including Sakho, who was unable to add to his goal at the Riverside.

Senegal had tried to get clearance to play Sakho in the 2002 World Cup, but the move was rejected by FIFA because of his French Under-21 connections. Two years on they tried again and secured his services – as did Mali in the case of Tottenham striker Kanoute.

Leeds were not playing Sakho, so had no objection to him linking up with the Lions of Teranga – the Senegal team's rather exotic nickname. On the back of their quarter-final showing in the World Cup, which included a

Lamine Sakho.

famous group victory against France, Senegal were among the favourites to take the African crown. Sakho joined up with the squad too late to be involved in a pre-tournament friendly against South Africa and missed the opening two group games – a 0–0 draw with Burkina Faso and a 3–0 victory against Kenya. However, he came off the bench in the second half in the 1–1 draw with Mali which saw both countries advance to the last eight.

Surprisingly, Sakho was picked from the start of the quarter-final clash with home nation Tunisia in Rades. The 57,000 crowd created a hostile atmosphere in the 7th November Stadium, but Senegal gave as good as they got, and it was Sakho who almost broke the deadlock with a first-half header which went a fraction over the bar. A ferocious match was decided in Tunisia's favour midway through the second half with a controversial goal by Jawhar Mnari, with Senegal adamant there had been an obvious foul on El-Hadji Diouf in the build-up to the goal. The Senegal delegation stormed on to the pitch to confront referee Ali Busjain, but the United Arab Emirates official stood firm – as did the Tunisian goal.

Play was held up for five minutes and shortly before the end Sakho was replaced by Diomansy Kamara, but by then the game had deteriorated into a kicking match. There was 10 minutes of time added, which saw four bookings, injuries and a series of skirmishes in a game which left a nasty taste in the mouth.

On his return to Elland Road, Sakho managed just one substitute's appearance in a 1–1 draw at Old Trafford before returning to Marseille. Unable to recapture his early career form, he has since had spells with St Etienne and Montpellier before joining Cypriot club Alki Larnaca as a midfielder in August 2008.

JOHN SHERIDAN

(Republic of Ireland 1988–95)
Midfield
Born: Stretford, Manchester, 1 October 1964.
Caps: Leeds United 5, Sheffield Wednesday 29. Total: 34
Goals: 5

COMPETITION for places in the Republic of Ireland midfield was red hot in John Sheridan's day. His contemporaries included Roy Keane (67 appearances), Andy Townsend (70) and Ray Houghton (73), Ronnie Whelan (53) and Kevin Sheedy (46), not to mention all-time record holder Steve Staunton, who made dozens of

John Sheridan.

his 102 appearances on the left of midfield before moving into defence, and Paul McGrath (83), the Manchester United and Aston Villa player, who played as a midfield anchorman before playing at the back. To finish with a tally of 34 is of immense credit to the highly talented Sheridan, whose career took off at Elland Road after he looked to be heading for the scrapheap.

Rejected by Manchester City after being on their books as a schoolboy, he joined Leeds and within six months broke into the first team as an 18-year-old. He had a wonderful repertoire of passing skills, possessed a cracking shot and was a danger from set pieces. He recovered from a broken leg at Barnsley in October 1983 to become a central figure in United's bid to reclaim their place back in English football's top flight.

Sheridan benefited from Jack Charlton's policy of digging up family roots to unearth players born outside Ireland to represent the country. Townsend was born in Kent, but his grandmother hailed from County Kerry, Glasgow-born Houghton's father was Irish and Sheridan hailed from Manchester of Dublin-born parents.

The rising Leeds star played for Eire's Under-21s against England in March 1985 and faced Scotland a couple of years later, but United's involvement in the 1987 Play-offs, coupled with a few injuries, meant Sheridan had to pull out of five Irish squads before he finally made his debut against Romania in March 1988.

Ireland won 2–0, and Sheridan's display saw him keep his place for the following month's friendly against Yugoslavia, which turned out to be anything but friendly. Four Slavs were booked, Marco Elsner was sent off and Walsall's David Kelly was also cautioned for fighting. Sheridan's superbly delivered corners had Yugoslavia in all sorts of trouble as Ireland emerged 2–0 victors again.

The Leeds playmaker's progress continued with his first international goal as Eire's build-up to the European Championships in Germany continued with a 3–1 victory against Poland at Lansdowne Road, Sheridan smashing home the third goal on 40 minutes. Sheridan had played his way into Big Jack's Euro squad and made his fourth successive appearance as Ireland stretched their unbeaten run to 10 games with a 0–0 draw in Norway a couple of weeks before the start of the tournament.

Charlton opted for his more experienced men, and Sheridan did not see any action in Germany as Ireland pulled off a famous victory against England thanks to Houghton's early strike. But a 1–1 draw with the Soviet Union and a late header by Dutch substitute Wim Kieft sent the brave Irish tumbling out.

The 1988–89 season was barely a month old when United sacked manager Billy Bremner, the man who had threatened to resign if his prized midfielder Sheridan was ever sold. Sheridan had scored 27 League goals in the last two seasons, but despite his brilliance it had not been enough to get Leeds out of Division Two. That total did not include a magnificent curling injury-time free-kick in the Play-off Final with Charlton, whose Peter Shirtliff snatched promotion from under United's noses with two late goals.

For a Leeds side who had been beaten in extra-time in the semi-finals of the FA Cup by Coventry it was hard to take, and they could not match those heights in 1987–88. A modest start to the following campaign saw Bremner replaced by Sheffield Wednesday boss Howard Wilkinson.

Sheridan made his competitive debut for the Republic in a 2–0 defeat in Seville as Spain notched a 2–0 World Cup qualifying win and, although he was a regular under Wilkinson, lifting his Leeds appearance tally beyond 250, he did not play for Ireland again that season.

In summer he was sold for £650,000 to Nottingham Forest, who wanted a replacement for the Manchester United-bound Neil Webb, but the deal was agreed while Forest boss Brian Clough was on holiday. On his return, Clough virtually ignored his new acquisition, playing him just once – in a League Cup tie – before the midfielder's three months of misery at the City Ground was ended by Sheffield Wednesday chief Ron Atkinson, who snapped Sheridan up for £500,000. He was an inspired signing, and Sheridan became as popular at Hillsborough as he had at Elland Road, assuring his place in Owls' folklore by scoring a spectacular League Cup Final winner against Manchester United in 1991. Regular football in just over six years with Wednesday also saw him back on the international scene as the Irish were enjoying a golden period under Charlton, but Sheridan had to be patient.

A member of the 1990 World Cup squad, he was confined to bench duty as the Republic squeezed through the group stages before beating Romania 5–4 on penalties in Genoa, David O'Leary memorably striking the spot-kick which put Ireland into the last eight.

Despite not having won a game, the Irish were in the quarter-finals, but were undone by a lone goal from the tournament's star striker 'Toto' Schillaci, who sent hosts Italy marching on. Sheridan's only action in the Finals came in this game as a late substitute for John Aldridge. The competition had elevated the status of the team back home in Ireland, but they failed to qualify for the 1992 European Finals, only for Charlton to get them back on track by taking them to America for the 1994 World Cup Finals.

Sheridan was a regular in the States, playing every minute of their four games, a sensational 1–0 opening group victory against Italy paving the way for a last sixteen showdown with Holland in Orlando. That proved a step too far, as first-half goals by Dennis Bergkamp and Wim Jonk gave Dick Advocaat's side a 2–0 win. The Dutch also put paid to Irish hopes two years later when two Patrick Kluivert goals in a Play-off for the last Euro '96 vacancy at Anfield saw Sheridan and Co. miss out on the Finals. He had probably been at his peak for Ireland in the qualifying campaign, but that game against Holland in Liverpool was his final international.

After a loan spell at Birmingham City he joined Bolton, with whom he won a First Division Championship medal in 1997, and played briefly for Doncaster Rovers before ending his playing career, aged 39, with Oldham, a club he was later to manage. In summer 2009 he was appointed manager of Chesterfield.

ALAN SMITH
(England 2001–07)
Striker
Born: Rothwell, near Leeds, 28 October 1980.
Caps: Leeds United 8, Manchester United 10, Newcastle United 1. Total: 19
Goals: 1

FEISTY home-grown Leeds striker Alan Smith had a rapid elevation to the international ranks. Kevin Keegan gave him his first senior England call-up just two years after he roared onto the Premiership scene by scoring with his first touch in a tremendous 3–1 victory at Anfield.

A former FA School of Excellence player, Smith, who had represented England at various Youth levels, found himself on the bench at Anfield in November 1998 after an England Under-18 tour to the Middle East was postponed. Liverpool were leading through a Robbie Fowler penalty when new Leeds boss David O'Leary sent Smith on for Clyde Wijnhard in the 79th minute. The 18-year-old made an instant scoring impact and lit the touchpaper on an explosive introduction to senior football. Two further goals by Jimmy-Floyd Hasselbaink gave Leeds the points and the feel-good factor flowed into the following week, with Smith scoring in a 4–1 Elland Road demolition of Charlton.

'Smithy' played without fear and got under defenders' skin with his aggressive all-action attitude. Leeds fans loved it – a local lad who was not fazed by big reputations – and it was not long before he was building a reputation of his own.

United finished fourth to qualify for the UEFA Cup for a second successive season and Smith was soon terrorising continental opposition, scoring on his Under-21 debut at Bradford's Valley Parade when Denmark were whipped 4–1. He was still only 19 when he was training with Howard Wilkinson's Under-21 squad at Oulton Hall, near Wakefield, ahead of a game against Georgia, when a call came through from Keegan to join the senior squad for their game in France. Smith did not play in the 1–1 draw in Paris, but had clearly been earmarked for the future.

Sven-Goran Eriksson, who took over as England boss after Keegan quit, was clearly of the same opinion. Although Smith's sheer will-to-win earned him too many red cards, the Swede admired the Leeds striker's battling qualities and his ability to deal with high-pressure games in the Champions League. Smith and Viduka were forming a lethal partnership and the winning goal against Lazio in Rome's Olympic Stadium, which the Australian created

Determination is etched on the face of Leeds United and England striker Alan Smith.

with a sublime backheel for Smith to finish with calm authority, was as good as it gets.

If Smith had shown a cool head in that tense situation, he lost it in the semi-final in Valencia. With United losing 3–0 and on the brink of elimination, Smith was sent off for a late lunge in the dying seconds of injury time. The young striker's detractors believed he needed to get rid of that reckless streak if he wanted to play for England. Sven, though, did not agree with that theory. At the end of the season Smith came on as a substitute in a 4–0 thumping of Mexico in May 2001, but further games off the bench against Greece and Holland were not enough to secure him a place in the 2002 World Cup squad.

For England's first match after the tournament, Eriksson tried out several new faces against Portugal at Villa Park. Smith made his first start for the Three Lions and gave a sparkling display, flying in to score with typical bravery with a near-post header from Leeds colleague Lee Bowyer's cross.

Smith, who had played 10 times for the Under-21s, seemed well equipped for a long run in the senior side and his performance against Portugal drew comparisons with Alan Shearer. But in his next start, a Euro 2004 qualifier against Macedonia in Southampton, the old red mist descended again and he was dismissed for a second bookable offence in injury time in an error-strewn 2–2 draw. It was the seventh sending-off of his career and he was still only 21. He did not play for England again for 16 months, despite a four-goal display against Hapoel Tel Aviv in the UEFA Cup helping to keep him in Eriksson's thoughts. Despite that 4–1 win against the Israelis, Leeds were in freefall on the pitch and financial meltdown off it. Smith, now often utilised as a midfielder by United, gave his all in a hopeless cause as the Whites slid towards inevitable relegation. Substitute appearances in a 1–1 draw in Portugal and a 1–0 defeat in Sweden gave Smith a glimmer of hope of making the 23-man squad for Euro 2004, but he missed out as Eriksson handed the final striking slot to Aston Villa's Darius Vassell.

Relegation meant Smith would inevitably move, but his destination – arch-rivals Manchester United – angered many Leeds followers. For Smith, the £7 million transfer to Old Trafford and the guidance of Sir Alex Ferguson looked the perfect combination to resurrect his England career before the 2006 World Cup.

Things started brightly enough, and Smith transferred his form to England colours, starting a 3–0 victory against Ukraine before being involved in the World Cup qualifiers against Austria, Wales and Azerbaijan.

Ironically, given his past disciplinary record, Smith was sent on as a replacement for Manchester United club-mate Wayne Rooney just before half-time in a friendly against Spain. Rooney, already on a yellow card, was visibly boiling, so Eriksson took him off before he was sent off. It was a bad night all round as England lost 1–0, and the Madrid crowd dealt out severe racial abuse to some of England's black players.

Smith went on England's post-season tour of America, playing the full 90 minutes of the 2–1 win against the United States in Chicago and coming on as a late replacement for hat-trick hero Michael Owen in a 3–2 victory over Colombia in New Jersey.

With Rooney's emergence up front, Ferguson thought Smith would one day succeed Roy Keane in midfield and Smith found himself under fire from some quarters when he turned down the chance to feature in a friendly against Denmark in August 2005, citing lack of match practice, to play for Manchester United reserves. It was a good one to miss – England lost 4–1.

Disaster was lurking round the corner for Smith. He broke a leg and dislocated an ankle in a freak accident while trying to block a Liverpool free-kick in an FA Cup tie in February 2006. It was career-threatening, but Smith fought back and 13 months later played and scored in a 3–1 England B victory against Albania, earning him inclusion in the senior side to face Brazil at Wembley the following week when a last-gasp goal gave the South Americans a 1–1 draw.

Smith made another friendly Wembley appearance – in a 2–1 defeat against Germany – before joining Newcastle for £7 million the following day. His last international appearance came as a substitute in a 1–0 win in Austria when he replaced goalscorer Peter Crouch. As the goals at St James' Park dried up, so did Smith's England appearances. Yet to reach 30 years old, there is time for Smith to reemerge as an international player, but niggling fitness problems and a lack of goals are proving obstacles to that particular dream.

Leeds certainly got the best out of Smith, whose youthful exuberance swept through the corridors of Elland Road and Thorp Arch like a breath of fresh air. He did not get as much game-time as expected at Old Trafford or St James' Park, where injuries have bitten huge chunks out of his career. Of his 19 England matches, he only stayed on the full 90 minutes in two of them, and his lone goal, although a treasured memory, was insufficient to hold down a regular starting place in the national side.

GARY SPEED

(Wales 1990–2004)

Midfield

Born: Mancot, Flintshire, 8 September 1969.
Caps: Leeds United 35, Everton 9, Newcastle United 36, Bolton Wanderers 5. Total: 85
Goals: 7

NO outfield player has represented Wales more times than Gary Speed. Only goalkeeper Neville Southall's 92 appearances tops Speed's wonderful record of longevity for his country. A modern-day legend, he's played more Premiership games than any other player and as he approached the age of 40 was still on the books of Championship side Sheffield United.

It all kicked off at Elland Road with Leeds United, whom he joined straight from Hawarden Grammar School in 1987. A Welsh youth international, he was handed his chance by Howard Wilkinson in the final home game of the 1988–89 season against Oldham after scoring in 12 consecutive Northern Intermediate League games. But his real breakthrough came the following year as United won the Second Division title, playing a major role in the second half of the campaign as Leeds stormed to promotion.

Even though he had still only started one League game, Speed gained a call-up as a non-playing substitute against Holland at Wrexham in October. All reports coming out of Elland Road were of a star in the making and a fortnight after Leeds clinched the title at Bournemouth, Speed made his Under-21 bow in a 2–0 win against Poland, getting his first senior run-out the following day when he came on for Glyn Hodges in a 1–0 win against Costa Rica at Cardiff.

Leeds and Speed took the First Division by storm, scoring past Welsh hero Southall on an opening day 3–2 victory at Everton. United's young Welshman featured in every League game that season, weighing in with seven goals, as Wilko's stormtroopers finished fourth.

Despite his stunning first full season, Speed was eased gradually into the national team by manager Terry Yorath, the former Leeds player. He played in friendlies against Denmark, Republic of Ireland and Iceland as well as making fleeting sub appearances in the Euro 1992 qualifiers against Luxembourg and West Germany – yes, the Berlin Wall was still up when Speedo was an international.

The young Welshman dovetailed perfectly into a formidable all-international midfield featuring the guile of Gordon Strachan, the pin-point passing of Gary McAllister and the drive of David Batty. Speed operated on the left where he showed good footwork, a decent turn of foot and

a sense of timing, which would see him arrive in the box to get on the end of crosses from the right. As Leeds upped their performance level a notch to take the First Division title in 1992, Speed once again featured in every match and his value to Wales was increasing with every match.

Although Wales were just edged out of the Euro Finals, finishing a point behind Germany, Speed was involved in a string of friendlies throughout the season, the highlight a famous victory against Brazil at Cardiff Arms Park when a goal from Dean Saunders gave the Red Dragons their first win against the South American superstars at the seventh time of asking.

Speed also suffered a massive downer when Wales opened their World Cup qualifying bid in Romania at the end of the season. At half-time they trailed 5–0 in Bucharest, but managed to regroup, and they pulled one back through Ian Rush and prevented the Romanians from inflicting further damage. The next fixture offered the principality the perfect opportunity to recover the goal difference, and they thumped the Faeroe Islands 6–0 in Cardiff, Rush scoring an easy hat-trick.

Wales had a decent record on home soil, particularly at the Arms Park, and beat group leaders Belgium 2–0 in March 1993, with Rush getting one of the goals, to surpass the national goalscoring record of 23 held jointly by Ivor Allchurch and Trevor Ford. It was on their travels where Wales dropped points and it was a similar story for Leeds, who suffered a backlash in the defence of their title, failing to win a single away game in the new Premiership. Wales's home form deserted them in their hour of need on 17 November 1993. Victory against Romania in Cardiff, coupled with anything less than a Czech victory in Belgium, would put Wales into the World Cup Finals in the United States.

At half-time Wales trailed after a Gheorghe Hagi shot was misjudged by the usually reliable Southall, but on the hour Speed touched on a Ryan Giggs free-kick for Dean Saunders to stab in from close range. Within 60 seconds Wales were back in the Romanian box, and Speed went

Gary Speed in action for Wales in 1991.

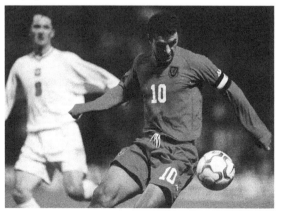

Gary Speed, captain of Wales.

down under a challenge from Dan Petrescu to give Wales a golden chance to seize the lead. Up stepped Swindon Town's Paul Bodin, yet to miss a penalty for Wales, but he smacked his spot-kick against the bar before it was scrambled clear. The visitors made the most of their escape when Florin Raduciou fired home from 10 yards eight minutes from time to silence the raucous crowd and shatter Welsh dreams. To rub salt into their wounds, the game in Brussels ended goalless, so a win for the Red Dragons would have booked that Atlantic crossing. Even worse, at the final whistle a flare fired on to the pitch struck a North Stand spectator in the throat and killed him. A night that had promised so much ended in tragedy.

Speed ended the season by reaching the 25-appearance mark for his country, but he had yet to find the net – a statistic out of kilter with his form at Leeds, where he had hit 10 goals in the season. Wales suffered badly for the next two years, only goal difference keeping them above Albania at the bottom of the Euro '96 qualifying group. They had a batch of horrendous results including a 3–2 defeat in Moldova – despite Speed's first goal for his country – were thrashed 5–0 in Georgia, who did the double by winning in Cardiff, and crashed 3–0 at home to Bulgaria. The Leeds ace played in eight of the 10 qualifiers and provided one of the few chinks of light by scoring the winner against Moldova in Cardiff.

Wales were in need of a shake-up and a major change was also made by Speed when he left Leeds for Everton, the club he had supported as a boy, in summer 1996 for £3.5 million. Elevated to captaincy by both his club and country, Speed seemed set fair, but life at Goodison Park did not work out as he had hoped and after 18 months he moved on to Newcastle United. He was a permanent fixture in the Welsh side, but the team continued to struggle in qualifiers and were badly exposed by Dennis Bergkamp's treble in Eindhoven as they crashed 7–1 to Holland in November 1996 in their biggest World Cup defeat. Later that month Speed scored his first senior hat-trick as Everton routed Southampton by the same score.

Wales got nowhere near qualification again, but if Wales called Speed answered with pride, a virtue his side restored in an amazing 6–4 defeat to Turkey in Istanbul when Bobby Gould's team were on the end of several dubious refereeing decisions.

Speed topped 300 appearances for both Leeds and Newcastle, renewing his midfield partnership with David Batty while on Tyneside. The Welshman now occupied a more central midfield role, but was also sometimes used at left-back by Wales later in his career. Steering clear of major injury was one of the keys to Speed's longevity, but the dream of leading Wales in the Finals of a Championship never materialised. Euro 2000 passed them by, and they only won one qualifier for the 2002 World Cup, but they emerged from the darkness to power out of the blocks in the race to Euro 2004.

Speed led his men to a 2–0 victory in Finland before a memorable night in the Millennium Stadium saw Italy defeated. Speed then scored in both back-to-back victories against Azerbaijan to leave the principality as group leaders at the halfway point. Successive defeats against Italy and Serbia-Montenegro pegged them back and eventually they had to settle for second behind Italy and went into a Play-off with Russia. The difference in size between the two nations is vast, but on the football pitch it was wafer thin. Wales did the hard work by drawing 0–0 in Moscow, but fell at the final hurdle as they could not recover from Vadim Evseev's 23rd-minute goal in Cardiff.

In July 2004 Speed moved on to Bolton, but his evergreen career with Wales kept rolling along. He was 35 and determined to have one last stab at reaching a World Cup Finals. Wales were pitched into a tough group including England and Poland, but began with a useful point in Azerbaijan thanks to a Speed goal. They were held to a draw by nine-man Northern Ireland (Wales also had Robbie Savage dismissed) in Cardiff and lost 2–0 to England. Barring a big improvement, Wales were not going to make it once again.

The end for Speed and Wales came on 13 October 2004 against Poland. With the score at 1–1 Speed was taken off by Mark Hughes with 12 minutes remaining. The old warhorse turned to each side of the Millennium Stadium to wave his farewell, and within six minutes of his leaving the battle Poland had gone 3–1 up. John Hartson pulled one back at the end, but barring a mathematical miracle Wales were already out of the running.

After the game, Speed, bordering on tears, announced his retirement from the international football. The last 44 of his 85 games had seen him wear the captain's armband with enormous pride, but after 15 years at the Welsh coalface it was time to call it a day.

Speed had already taken up some coaching and was widely tipped to replace Hughes, but the FA of Wales did not ask, and he dropped into the Championship to play for ex-Leeds manager Kevin Blackwell at Sheffield United. He had a future coaching position built into his contract with the Bramall Lane club, which looked increasingly like being activated as he underwent surgery on his back in December 2008, ruling him out for the rest of the Blades' season. A move into management beckons, and many media pundits predict he will inherit the Wales job one day and instil his beliefs and work ethic into a new batch of players.

GARY SPRAKE

(Wales 1963–74)

Goalkeeper

Born: Winch Wen, near Swansea, 3 April 1945.

Caps: Leeds United 32, Birmingham City 5. Total: 37

BY HIS own admission Gary Sprake should have played more times for Wales. He estimates that he could have doubled his cap tally had he not been persuaded by Leeds boss Don Revie to pull out of international games with 'injury'. Sprake was caught in the classic club versus country dilemma at a time when United were constantly chasing silverware, while Wales were chasing shadows.

The goalkeeper had his critics outside Elland Road, highlighting a handful of gaffes in key games, but there could be no doubting his quality and, along with Neville Southall and Jack Kelsey, he is up there as Wales's best-ever net-minder. Sprake actually used to live next door but one to Arsenal star Kelsey.

While working behind a superb Leeds defence there were occasions when his concentration did slip, but he was always on the ball when he played for the principality, possibly because their defence was not as good as United's and the need to keep his focus was greater. He joined Leeds as an apprentice in June 1960 and made his debut as a 16-year-old in dramatic fashion. While the first team were down in Southampton preparing for their game at the Dell on 17 March 1962, goalkeeper Tommy Younger, the former Scottish international, fell ill. Just five hours before the kick-off young Sprake was still in his digs in Leeds when he received a message to get down to Hampshire. A taxi whisked him to Manchester Airport, where he caught a flight to Southampton, arriving at the ground just before the start. The game was delayed by 15 minutes, and Sprake

Gary Sprake in high-flying action for Wales.

emerged from the match with much credit despite United's 4–1 defeat.

The following season he became Revie's first-choice 'keeper, and a series of brilliant athletic displays saw him picked by the Welsh FA for an Under-23 game against England at Ashton Gate, Bristol. He had already been told that he would make his senior debut against Scotland the following week if he did well against the English. Sprake thwarted a side featuring future World Cup heroes Geoff Hurst and Martin Peters several times in a 1–1 draw.

Seven days later he made history, becoming Wales's youngest-ever goalkeeper at 18 years 7 months and 17 days when he played in a 2–1 defeat at Hampden Park – a record that remains today. He did well in Glasgow, but was under-par in his next game as Northern Ireland won 3–2 in Swansea. After helping United to the Second Division Championship, Sprake and Wales gained revenge over Scotland with a 3–2 win in Cardiff, but made a disastrous start to their World Cup qualifying campaign when they lost 1–0 and 2–0 in Denmark and Greece respectively.

Leeds were in the title hunt and going well in the FA Cup, while Wales were already anchored at the bottom of their group and still to play favourites the Soviet Union twice. With vital Leeds games on the horizon, Revie told Sprake he could not afford to risk letting him play for Wales and phone calls from Elland Road to the Welsh FA headquarters informing them that Sprake was injured were commonplace. The rising Leeds star missed the next four internationals as Dave Hollins (Newcastle United) and Tony Millington (Crystal Palace) deputised and over the years both players were to benefit from Sprake's absence from the national side.

Wales goalkeeper Gary Sprake is on his guard as George Best gets in a shot for Northern Ireland.

After narrowly missing the double with Leeds, Sprake was back in the Welsh goal for the visit of England to Ninian Park. The future World Cup-winners were always a big draw in the principality, but Wales, fielding six players from outside the top division, matched them stride for stride. Sprake's assured performance in a 0–0 draw meant that England had failed to score against Wales for the first time in 33 years.

Later in the month Sprake returned to Cardiff for the defeat of the USSR 2–1 with goals from Roy Vernon and the veteran Ivor Allchurch, but with European games now added to Leeds's workload Sprake only played once more for his country in the next 12 months. Leeds had fought their way through to the semi-finals of the Fairs Cup against Real Zaragoza, which required a third game after the sides finished level on aggregate. As a result Sprake missed Wales's tour to South America, where they lost to Brazil – twice – and Chile. To make it worse the Spaniards won the deciding game 3–1 at Elland Road. The die had been cast – Leeds were pushing hard for honours on all fronts while Wales had to do without their best goalkeeper.

Having failed to make the World Finals, Wales looked for solace in the European Championships, with the British Championship matches doubling up as the qualifiers. Sprake played in three of the six games as Wales finished well off the pace just above Northern Ireland.

When he did play Sprake was invariably Wales's star performer, operating behind a defence which was largely made up of Second Division players. Many believe he was at his peak as United won the League Cup before a fantastic display in Budapest kept Ferencvaros at bay to see the Whites become the first British side to lift the European Fairs Cup.

Wales only played three matches in 1968, and Sprake did not play in any of them, but with United moving closer towards their first Championship, the Leeds number one made a rare friendly appearance against World Cup runners-up West Germany in Frankfurt. With United out of all the Cups, Revie felt able to declare Sprake fit and the player responded with another top-class display. Wales seemed to be heading for a remarkable 1–0 win on the back of Barrie Jones's first-half goal when legendary marksman Gerd Muller scored with the last kick of the game, although the cross that supplied the opening for Muller had gone out of play.

Sprake was an ever-present as Leeds won the First Division title, letting in just 26 goals – a record at the time – and keeping 24 clean sheets. With the title in the bag, United's international stars got the green light to play in Home Internationals, which were being played in bulk at the end of the season to improve player availability. Sprake suffered a nightmare start to the week and was responsible for two of the goals in a 5–3 mauling by Scotland in Wrexham, but recovered his poise with a great performance at Wembley in midweek. A header by Ron Davies gave the Welsh a half-time lead, but despite Sprake's best efforts England turned it round with a Bobby Charlton piledriver and a 72nd-minute strike by Francis Lee, who had hit the bar with a penalty in the first period.

Sprake completed the week by keeping out Ireland in a dull 0–0 draw in Belfast and took time out from his summer break to star against the Rest of the UK at Cardiff in a game to mark the investiture of the Prince of Wales, Lee scoring the only goal for the combined nations.

Wales's World Cup hopes were already in tatters. They were the whipping boys in a three-team group featuring European champions Italy and East Germany. Sprake had missed the first two matches, which ended in defeat, and was helpless as the Germans won 3–1 in Cardiff and Italy won 4–1 in Rome to leave Wales without a point. Welsh boss Dave Bowen could only field a depleted side, which included a debut for Leeds reserve Terry Yorath, in the Olympic Stadium, but despite a string of fine Sprake saves the Red Dragons could not hold Luigi Riva, the Cagliari star scoring a hat-trick.

Sprake suffered a difficult end to 1969–70. After being at fault for one of Chelsea's goals in the drawn FA Cup Final, he was carried off in the European Cup semi-final after a collision with Celtic's John Hughes. He was still Revie's first choice for the next season, winning a second Fairs Cup medal, and had an outstanding Home Championships as Wales held England and Scotland to goalless draws but went down 1–0 in Belfast to a Bryan Hamilton goal.

Once again Wales had got their European qualification programme off to a poor start, drawing at home with Romania and losing 3–1 to Czechoslovakia at Swansea before a John Toshack goal earned them a win in Finland. The rematch against the Finns was on a bitterly cold Swansea night, and Sprake came off with a knee injury at half-time and was replaced by Millington, who went on to play in the defeats in Czechoslovakia and Romania later that autumn.

At Leeds, Sprake was coming under increasing pressure from long-standing deputy David Harvey. Towards the end of the season the Welshman was dropped by Revie. Harvey did well and kept his place for the FA Cup Final victory against Arsenal.

Sprake's demotion was good news for Wales, and he embarked on his longest run in the national team – seven matches. He figured in all the 1972 Home Internationals and, although he was now playing second fiddle to Harvey, faced England – twice – and Poland in World Cup games. Colin Bell's goal gave England victory in Cardiff, but Wales inflicted a damaging blow in the re-match at Wembley with a deserved 1–1 draw. Goals by Leighton James and Trevor Hockey saw Poland beaten in Cardiff, and the Welsh were still in with a sniff of qualification. But the scent went cold after an arduous 19-hour trip, which included a twice-delayed flight, to Katowice as Poland won 3–0, Wales having midfielder Hockey sent off. The Poles followed up that win with a point at Wembley to sensationally knock England out.

Within weeks of that horror journey behind the Iron Curtain, Sprake drew his Elland Road career to a close. With Harvey installed as number one, he joined Birmingham in a £100,000 deal, thus ending 10 years with Leeds in which he had played more than 500 games, the most ever by a United goalkeeper.

Sprake suffered a broken ankle while at St Andrews but was still able to add five more Welsh caps before illness forced his premature retirement at the age of 30. He has since suffered from life-threatening heart problems, leading to a couple of by-pass operations.

BERT SPROSTON

(England 1936–38)

Right-back

Born: Elworth, Cheshire, 22 June 1914.

Died: Bolton, 27 January 2000.

Caps: Leeds United 8, Tottenham Hotspur 2, Manchester City 1. Total: 11

BERT SPROSTON and his England teammates were used as a political football on England's 1938 continental tour. Opening the three-match programme was a game against Germany, in the grip of Nazi fever, in the Olympic Stadium, Berlin. Europe was on the brink of war, with Adolf Hitler making threatening speeches and Germany's neighbours fearing the imminent threat of invasion. The game, therefore, took on a symbolic significance, being between the strength-through-joy Germans and England, bastion of democracy.

Sproston was an England regular, but nothing could have prepared him for playing in a country run by a dictator who was virtually regarded as a god by his people. In his autobiography *Feet First*, published a decade after the infamous Germany versus England game, Stanley Matthews recalls the fanatical admiration which Hitler inspired. The winger and Sproston were having a cup of tea in a café when there was a rush to the door to see a procession of motorcycles, SS men and two large black limousines.

'Our beloved Führer has just passed by,' said a German customer as he stood to attention. Little did they know it but Sproston, Matthews and the rest of the England lads would have to show the same deference to Hitler before the game got underway two days later.

England were in the dressing room just before the kick-off when an FA official popped his head round the door and instructed the team to give the Nazi salute

The British ambassador to Berlin, Sir Nevile Henderson, foreground, watches the Germany versus England game with Rudolf Hess, Hitler's deputy, two seats away.

Somewhere in this England line up giving the infamous Nazi salute in pre-war Berlin is Leeds United's Bert Sproston.

during the playing of the national anthem. The order was at the behest of Sir Nevile Henderson, the British ambassador to Berlin, who was anxious to avoid inflaming any German sensitivities. The England lads were told that it was not an endorsement of the Nazis, but a courtesy to the host country. Despite initial protests, the players reluctantly agreed to the diplomat's request. Sproston and Co. gave the salute in front of 105,000 swastika-flag waving fans and proceeded to play the Germans off the pitch, winning 6–3.

Oddly, 24 hours later a touring Aston Villa side took on a German Select XI – which included players from annexed Austria – in the same stadium. Once again the FA requested the English side to give the infamous salute before the game, but Villa dug their heels in and refused. During the playing of the anthems they stood to attention with their arms at their sides, while some in the crowd showed their displeasure by booing and whistling. Villa followed England's lead on the pitch, winning 3–2.

Sproston was unquestionably one of the best defenders of the inter-war period. After being rejected by Huddersfield Town, he signed for Leeds from Cheshire club Sandbach Ramblers in May 1933 and eventually succeeded George Milburn at right-back. He was fast, hard tackling, remained cool under pressure, and his excellent distribution put him a class above the usual sturdy club defender.

Bert Sproston takes time out with his England teammates, who watch centre-forward Willie Hall tee-off. Sproston is fourth from the right, with Leeds colleague Wilf Copping second from the right.

Leeds, although an unfashionable club, had some excellent players in the 1930s: Willis Edwards, Ernie Hart and Wilf Copping, and Sproston followed them into the England team, ousting Arsenal's George Male from the right-back position after shining in two Football League representative games against the Scottish League and the Irish League. His first England match, though, was not a success as Wales beat the English for the first time in more than 50 years. His next cap came 12 months later when a debut hat-trick by Chelsea's George Mills helped sink Ireland 5–1 at Windsor Park.

When England took on Wales again at Middlesbrough's Ayresome Park in November 1937 it looked as though they would inflict another defeat on Sproston and England when Eddie Perry put them ahead. But England fought back to win with Stanley Matthews and Willie Hall on the scoresheet.

A Matthews hat-trick – all scored with his left foot – ushered in December as England beat Czechoslovakia 5–4 in a thriller at Tottenham, the club Sproston was to join from Leeds. Sproston was accompanied in the England side by United colleague Eric Stephenson for the next game against Scotland. England were hoping to get a victory under their belts ahead of their forthcoming European tour, but Scotland shut out the England attack for the first time at Wembley and won 1–0 with Tommy Walker's early goal.

In the absence of Sproston and Stephenson, Leeds lost by the same score to Arsenal, who were also affected by international calls, at Elland Road. United finished in a respectable ninth position, but Sproston had no time to put his feet up. More or less as soon as the season finished the England party left by boat for the Hook of Holland and then travelled overland to Berlin, a journey that took two days.

The Germans had been together for 10 days in the Black Forest sharpening up for the big game, but they were utterly outplayed by England, whose goals came from Jackie Robinson (2), Cliff Bastin, Frank Broome, Len Goulden and Matthews.

Having seen off Germany, England were expected to thrash Switzerland in Zurich the following week, but underestimated their opponents, losing 2–1 with Andre

Abegglen scoring the winner with a controversial penalty 17 minutes from the end after German referee Dr Peco Bauwens, resplendent in cycling breeches, ruled that Huddersfield's Alf Young had handled. On their way home, Sproston played his seventh England game of a busy season as France were beaten 4–2, a late Bastin penalty easing the nerves. Leeds supporters were also getting edgy as rumours about Sproston's departure from Elland Road started to circulate.

United were in financial difficulty, and rumour turned to fact as the Leeds board accepted a near-record £9,500 from big-spending Second Division club Tottenham for their star defender. However, Sproston did not settle in London, because the threat of war was becoming an ever-increasing reality. Three months into the new season Spurs got their money back when he returned north to be with his family to play for Manchester City. It was certainly an unusual debut as he travelled to Maine Road with the Tottenham party on Friday, completed his transfer that night and played against his old team the following day, City winning 2–0.

During his short time at Spurs he played twice for England – in a 4–2 defeat against Wales which featured a goal from 19-year-old Everton starlet Tommy Lawton and a 3–0 victory against a Rest of the World side at Wembley in a game which marked the 75th anniversary of the FA. At City Sproston played just one more game for England when Norway were thumped 4–0 at Newcastle, Millwall's Reg Smith marking his debut with a couple of goals. However, he did feature in a couple of wartime internationals as Wales were beaten 3–2 at Wrexham and Scotland were held 1–1 at Hampden Park in front of a 75,000 khaki-clad crowd with British fighters circling overhead to put off any threat of a German attack. Sproston served with the Army during the war, and his football opportunities were limited, but he did play for the Combined Services and managed some guest games with Millwall. On the return to peacetime football he won his only domestic honour, a Division Two Championship medal with Manchester City. Sproston retired in 1950 and was appointed trainer by Bolton Wanderers the following year, enjoying a long association with the Trotters.

ERIC STEPHENSON
(England 1938)
Inside-left
Born: Bexleyheath, Kent, 17 September 1914.
Died: Burma, 8 September 1944.
Caps: Leeds United 2.

BRAVE Eric Stephenson served his country with pride on both the playing field and battlefield. The Leeds United inside-forward was the only contemporary England international player of his day to die while serving in World

LEEDS UNITED A.F.C. LTD.

"At the going down of the sun and in the morning,
we will remember them."

THE LATE
Major JOSEPH ERIC STEPHENSON
2nd K.E.O. GURKHA RIFLES
Killed in Action, 8th September, 1944

Cover from the post-war Leeds United programme against Celtic. Proceeds from the game went to Eric Stephenson's widow.

War Two. Although christened Joseph Eric, he was always known by his second name, possibly to distinguish him from his engineer father, Joseph.

Stephenson's family moved from East London to Leeds when he was young, and he played for Oakwood Stormcocks and Leeds Schools before joining Harrogate, then a Northern League club, in 1931. Although most of his games were in the reserves, the 17-year-old showed sufficient promise to be signed by Leeds on amateur terms, turning pro in September 1934. He made his debut in a 3–1 home win against Portsmouth the following March and scored twice in his next game, a 2–2 draw at Everton.

Despite an impressive start, it was not for a couple of years that he started to play on a more regular basis, being one of the shining lights in 1937–38 as Leeds finished ninth in Division One. He was a small, neat, probing inside-forward, whose main strength was creating chances for others, but his call-up as a replacement for West Ham's Len Goulden for the game at Wembley against Scotland on 9 April 1938 came out of the blue. Also making his debut was Middlesbrough centre-forward Mickey Fenton, while Stephenson's club-mate Bert Sproston was at right-back.

The Scots won 1–0 with a sixth-minute cross-shot from Hearts's Tommy Walker and Stephenson was marked out of

the game in the first-half by Preston's tough-tackling Bill Shankly. But he escaped the clutches of the man who was to gain worldwide fame as a Liverpool manager in the second half. It was through a succession of fine passes from Stephenson to Cliff Bastin that England's best hope of an equaliser lay.

The storm clouds of war were gathering apace when Stephenson won his second cap in a 7–0 demolition of Ireland at Maine Road in November 1938. It was one-way traffic towards Leeds's Irish goalkeeper Jim Twomey, but Stephenson and Millwall's Reg Smith did not see much of the ball on the right. Stanley Matthews and Tottenham's Willie Hall were creating havoc on the other flank, Hall scoring five times, Matthews once and centre-forward Tommy Lawton adding the other.

Stephenson went on England's 1939 continental tour of Italy, Yugoslavia and Romania but did not play. Three games into the next season, the Football League programme was abandoned as the country entered the war and Stephenson, who played 155 games for Leeds, scoring 22 goals, joined up as a physical training instructor with the Army at Aldershot. Organised football did continue, and Stephenson was able to turn out for Leeds while he was based with the Manchester Regiment in Malton, North Yorkshire. He played in representative games for the Army, FA and Football League, and was named as a reserve for the England versus Scotland game at Newcastle in February 1941 in which Fulham full-back Joe Bacuzzi headed into his own goal to give the Scots a 3–2 win.

But Stephenson was soon to leave football way behind him. After taking an Officer Cadet Training Unit course he gained his commission and went to India in 1942. He joined the 2nd King Edward VII Own Gurkha Rifles,

Eric Stephenson (left) and Leeds United teammate Bert Sproston set off from Leeds Station to London ahead of the international against Scotland in 1938.

The full stained-glass window panel to Eric Stephenson at Lidgett Park Methodist Church, Leeds.

known as the Sirmoor Rifles. They were part of a group known as the Chindits, who were formed and trained by Major General Orde Wingate specifically to operate behind enemy lines.

Stephenson, who had risen to the rank of major, was a part of this guerrilla force and was among those who made a famous 350-mile incursion into Japanese-held Burmese territory. It was extremely dangerous jungle warfare in which disease, as well as enemy fire, claimed thousands of

The stained-glass window inscription to Eric Stephenson at Lidgett Park Methodist Church, Leeds.

lives, Stephenson among them. He was killed in action nine days before his 30th birthday and is buried in Taukhyan War Cemetery. His memory is permanently remembered, though, near his Leeds home in Chelwood Drive.

Stephenson was a member of Lidgett Park Methodist Church and was a lieutenant in the 30th Leeds Company Boys' Brigade. His church commissioned a Belfast company to make a stained-glass window of seven lights commemorating four servicemen – Stephenson among them – who lost their lives in World War Two, and three women. The Gurkha Rifles's regimental badge is depicted with the inscription below an image of St Michael: 'He endured hardness as a good soldier of Jesus Christ. Major Joseph Eric Stephenson. Killed in action Burma 1944. This window is a tribute to his memory from his wife and children.'

Leeds United did not forget their man either. On 27 May 1947 a benefit match against Glasgow Celtic was held at Elland Road, attracting 19,000 spectators. The Scottish side won 3–1. Everton's Jock Dodds, guesting for Leeds, scored the United goal, and the proceeds from the game went to Stephenson's widow, Olive, and their children.

BYRON STEVENSON
(Wales 1978–82)
Defender
Born: Llanelli, Camarthenshire, 7 September 1956.
Died: Wales, 6 September 2007.
Caps: Leeds United 11, Birmingham City 4. Total: 15

BYRON STEVENSON felt the full crushing weight of international football authority. The Leeds United defender received an incredible four-and-a-half year European ban after being sent off while playing for Wales in Turkey. Although the suspension was later reduced considerably, the Draconian sentence blighted his Welsh career. Tall and slim, he eventually settled into a defensive role after filling a variety of positions in his 10 years at Elland Road. He joined as an apprentice in April 1972 and was initially groomed as a replacement for Norman Hunter, but made his debut at right-back in a 1–1 draw at Sheffield United on April Fools' Day 1975, shortly before United's European Cup semi-final triumph against Barcelona.

The Welsh Youth international remained on the fringes at Leeds, adding just one more Division One start to his CV before making his first Under-21 appearance in a 0–0 draw with England at Molineux. Two more Under-21 appearances against Scotland followed, but Stevenson had only just had a little run in the Leeds first team at right-back when he made his debut for Wales – at left-back in the final Home International of the season against Northern Ireland. A Nick Deacy penalty gave Wales, who fielded

Byron Stevenson.

three Leeds players – Stevenson, Brian Flynn and Carl Harris – a 1–0 win at Wrexham's Racecourse Ground. The trio returned to the Racecourse Ground in October as Wales, with former United reserve goalkeeper Glan Letheran also on the bench, started their European Championship bid with a crushing 7–0 win against group whipping boys Malta, Chester's Ian Edwards scoring four times.

The following month Wales eked out a narrow 1–0 victory against Turkey thanks to a goal from Deacy to maintain their winning start, but group favourites West Germany put Wales in their place with a 2–0 in Wrexham. Stevenson was on the bench for the German game but was back for the Home Internationals. A John Toshack hat-trick sank Scotland 3–0 in Cardiff, and England were held 0–0 at Wembley, where Stevenson gave one of his best displays for the principality to subdue a home attack which included Lawrie Cunningham of West Brom for the first time.

In Stevenson's five appearances for Wales they had yet to concede a goal, a sequence which was ended when they drew 1–1 in Belfast. Stevenson's performances had cemented his place in the Welsh side and with Liverpool's Joey Jones he had formed a formidable full-back pairing, one that was rarely tested in Valetta as Wales eased past Malta 2–0, despite a Robbie James penalty miss. The victory left Wales with qualification for Euro '80 in Italy in their own hands as they travelled to West Germany and Turkey in an autumn double-header. Mike Smith's team

had done well so far, but their qualification hopes were shattered by a 5–1 thrashing in Cologne as Germany seized control of the group.

Wales knew they still had an outside chance if they could beat Turkey in Izmir, but it proved a disastrous night for Stevenson. Wales had been dominant in the first half, going close several times before the dynamic of the match changed when Stevenson was sent off in the 69th minute. Although the referee did not directly see the incident, the Leeds player allegedly hit Buyak Mustafa, fracturing the Turk's cheekbone. Wales tried to reorganise, but within 10 minutes of going down to 10 men were behind when Onal scored the only goal to send the Ataturk Stadium into a frenzy and their team temporarily to the top of the group.

The repercussions for Stevenson were grave, as he was hit by a massive ban, although it was later reduced on appeal. These must have been dark times for the Welsh defender, as Leeds were also struggling under Jimmy Adamson and fans' unrest was growing at Elland Road. At least he came back from the cold to play for Wales again in the summer after missing the Home Internationals, coming on as substitute for former United star Terry Yorath in Reykjavik and creating a goal for Ian Walsh in a 4–0 World Cup qualifying victory against Iceland. Stevenson did not play for Wales for a further 15 months, until he played in the 2–0 qualifying defeat in Czechoslovakia in September 1981.

With goals hard to come by for a relegation-threatened Leeds, Stevenson was swapped for Birmingham City's flamboyant striker Frank Worthington in March 1982. After just two games with his new club Stevenson played in a 1–1 friendly in Valencia where the Spanish crowd showered the Welsh with oranges, cans and bottles.

A 1–0 defeat against Scotland was a much quieter affair and you could almost hear a pin drop when a paltry 2,315 fans bothered to turn up for Wales's 3–0 win against Northern Ireland at Wrexham – the rest presumably watched the FA Cup Final replay between Spurs and Queen's Park Rangers, which was screened on television at the same time. A week later Stevenson played his last game for Wales when an Ian Rush goal earned a surprise victory against France in Tolouse. At the end of the match Stevenson swapped shirts with the great Michel Platini – not a bad souvenir to sign off a 15-cap career.

In summer 1985 he left St Andrews for a season at Bristol Rovers, where he played in midfield alongside former England captain Gerry Francis. Knee problems prompted Stevenson to give up the full-time game, then he played for Garforth Town in the Northern Counties East League and ran pubs in the Leeds area. He later returned to his native Wales, where he died of throat cancer a day before his 51st birthday. The following Sunday a minute's silence was held at Cardiff's Millennium Stadium before Wales's Euro 2008 qualifier against Germany to mark Stevenson's passing at a tragically early age.

DAVID STEWART

(Scotland 1977)
Goalkeeper
Born: Glasgow, 11 March 1947.
Caps: Leeds United 1

ONE-cap wonder is a much-used cliché – but in David Stewart's case it is true. He had a wonderful match in his one and only appearance for Scotland, saving a penalty and pulling off a series of brilliant saves. Stewart had taken the number-one jersey at Leeds from another Scottish international, David Harvey, when he earned his call-up from Ally McLeod, his one-time boss at Ayr United. Ally's Army were closing in on a place in the 1978 World Cup Finals in Argentina and a friendly in East Germany offered him the perfect opportunity to have a look at Stewart, who was now in the Leeds team on merit ahead of Harvey.

A Scotland team which included regulars Gordon McQueen and Joe Jordan, as well as substitute Arthur Graham, had an uncomfortable night in Berlin against a physical German team. Although Scotland had more of the ball, East Germany created more chances, and only Stewart's heroics kept them at bay until the 66th minute when Helmut Schade grabbed the only goal. The Leeds keeper's work was still not finished for the night as his penalty save 13 minutes later prevented Has-Jurgen Doerner from doubling the lead.

McLeod complained about East Germany's strongarm tactics, but his side got the rub of the green a fortnight later when Scotland clinched their place in the World Cup Finals with a 2–0 win against Wales. Their opening goal, a Don Masson penalty, came after it appeared Joe Jordan, not Welsh defender Dave Jones, had handled in the box. Scotland were literally within touching distance of the Finals. Stewart watched from the bench that night as McLeod had put his regular number one, Alan Rough, back between the posts. The word was that McLeod would take Stewart to Argentina if he was still in the Leeds team at the end of the season. He was not, so McLeod took Jim Blyth (Coventry City) and Bobby Clark (Aberdeen) as the men to back up Partick Thistle's Rough. After that Stewart vanished from the international scene almost as quickly as he had arrived.

Stewart was a relatively late starter in the professional game, giving up his job as an upholsterer and carpet fitter three years after joining Ayr in 1967 from Kilsyth Rangers, with whom he had just won a Scottish Junior Cup medal. He was still a part-timer when he won a Scottish Under-21 cap against Wales at Pittodrie in January 1970. The game ended 1–1, John O'Hare, later to be signed for Leeds by Brian Clough, equalising for the Scots after Shrewsbury's ex-Elland Roader, Dennis Hawkins, had put Wales in front.

With long-serving Gary Sprake leaving United for Birmingham City, Don Revie needed a goalkeeper as

David Stewart, who saved a penalty on his one and only appearance for Scotland.

support for Harvey and felt Stewart, 26, fitted the bill. He had built up plenty of experience at the Somerset Park club and Revie's final signing, a snip at £30,000, proved an inspired one. He bided his time in the reserves but, when Harvey was put out of action after a car crash, Stewart grabbed his chance with both hands. His reflexes were astonishing, and he had an inspired game in the 1975 European Cup semi-final in Barcelona. Oddly enough he had been doing some upholstery work at Glasgow's Central Hotel five years earlier when Leeds checked in ahead of their European Cup semi against Celtic – a remarkable transformation in fortunes. Quiet and unassuming off the pitch, it is often overlooked that he was United's goalkeeper in the Final against Bayern Munich in Paris when he could do little to prevent either of the German side's second-half goals.

Harvey was re-installed as Jimmy Armfield's first choice the following season, but Stewart had forced his way back on merit by the time he got his only call to arms by Scotland. Unable to shift Harvey on a permanent basis, Stewart went to West Brom in November 1978 for £70,000 but did not get a game, so he joined Swansea City; where he took over from former Leeds junior Glan Letheran. After a year playing in Hong Kong, he returned to Swansea and set up in business as a goldsmith. He was certainly pure gold for Scotland that night in Berlin, glittering in his sole senior game for his country.

GORDON STRACHAN

(Scotland 1980–92)

Midfield

Born: Edinburgh, 9 February 1957.
Caps: Aberdeen 28, Manchester United 14, Leeds United 8. Total: 50
Goals: 5

HISTORY seemed to repeat itself when Gordon Strachan earned a recall to the Scotland side after his exploits with Leeds United. It was a case of déjà vu. More than a quarter of a century earlier Bobby Collins, another veteran international, dropped out of the top flight to join the Elland Road payroll. Strachan, like Collins, not only led the Whites back into the top flight as Second Division champions, but regained his rightful place in the national team. Both men, small in size but giants in stature, were at the heart of reviving a club that was threatening to go nowhere.

Strachan was 32 and his best days seemed well behind him when he joined Leeds from cross-Pennine rivals Manchester United for £300,000 in March 1989. He had won a stack of domestic honours – two Scottish titles, three Scottish Cups and a UEFA Cup-winners' Cup with Aberdeen and the 1985 FA Cup with Manchester United – in addition to playing 42 times for his country.

The last of those appearances came a fortnight before he put pen to paper with Leeds, coming on as a substitute for Ian Ferguson in a World Cup qualifier against France in Glasgow. Two strikes from Mo Johnston left the Scots sitting pretty at the top of their group, but Strachan's decision to drop down a division seemed to indicate to Scotland boss Andy Roxburgh that the midfield firefly was ready to exit the international stage. He missed the next five internationals, but was in the starting line up for the first time as a Leeds player in the return against France in the Parc des Princes. Goals by Didier Deschamps, Eric

Scottish terrier Gordon Strachan nips at the heels of the Dutch.

Cantona and an own-goal by Steve Nichol swept the Tartan Army aside and left them needing at least a point from the final game against Norway. They managed it with a 1–1 draw in front of a sellout Hampden Park crowd, but Strachan played no part in the game.

Strachan harboured dreams of playing in a third successive World Cup Finals, but Roxburgh omitted him from the squad to go to Germany. In 1982, as an Aberdeen player, he had played in all three of Scotland's games as they beat New Zealand, lost to Brazil and drew with the USSR. Further disappointment followed four years later when, this time as a Manchester United player, he also played in all the Scots' matches as they were beaten by Denmark and West Germany – against whom he scored a fine goal – before a 0–0 draw against a crude Uruguay side put them on the plane home from Mexico.

It seemed as though Strachan was finished as an international player, but Scotland badly missed his experience as a 1–0 opening defeat to Costa Rica left them an impossible task, with Brazil and Sweden to follow. Leeds fans certainly believe Strachan should have gone to Italia '90 after leading the Whites to the Second Division title. He wore the captain's armband in all of United's 46 League games, netting 16 goals, none as vital as his late winner against Leicester in the penultimate game of the season. His ability and fitness – boosted by a much publicised diet including seaweed tablets and bananas – were unquestioned. When he continued to churn out the same level of performances in the top flight, the clamour for his Scotland return grew louder.

After an absence of 16 months, covering a dozen games, Strachan was back, playing a full 90 minutes in a 1–0 loss against the USSR in Glasgow three days before his 34th birthday. His performance confirmed he had a role to play in Scotland's quest to reach the European Championships and he played in the qualifier against Bulgaria in which a John Collins goal salvaged a 1–1 draw at Hampden.

Leeds were one of the surprise packages of the First Division, finishing fourth, with their inspirational skipper named the Football Writers' Footballer of the Year, 11 years after winning the Scottish version. There was one further accolade in store for the little dynamo: he was named captain of Scotland for the first time, marking the occasion with a 63rd-minute penalty against San Marino to break the deadlock. Gordon Durie added a second goal to ensure Strachan got off to a winning start.

Despite a long-term back injury, Strachan upped his game as Leeds won the 1991–92 First Division title and continued to captain Scotland as they pushed on to qualify for Euro '92, which was being held in Sweden. His final game was a friendly against Finland at Hampden Park on 25 March 1992, his 50th appearance for his country, a landmark which earned him entry in to the Scottish FA's Hall of Fame. Sadly, Hampden was near-deserted as less

Gordon Strachan.

The Strachan playing dynasty has been continued by his son Gavin, who played under his dad at Coventry and has since played for various other clubs, including Notts County in 2008–09. It was an uphill battle at Coventry, and Strachan was sacked in September 2001, taking over at Southampton, whom he took to the 2003 FA Cup Final before resigning the following February to take a break from football and spend more time with his family. He took up television punditry and was a big hit, combining shrewd tactical awareness with humour, but the lure of matchdays was growing. After Berti Vogts resigned as Scotland's coach Strachan was linked with the job, but the post went to Walter Smith.

Strachan was back in mainstream football when he was appointed manager of Celtic and, after a dreadful start, led them to three successive titles, a Scottish Cup and two Scottish League Cups. It would be a brave man who would bet against him being Scotland's manager one day.

FRANK STRANDLI
(Norway 1992–99)
Striker
Born: Kristiansand, Vest-Agder, 16 May 1972.
Caps: IK Start 6, Leeds United 2, Lillestrom 13, Panathinaikos 1, Aalborg 2. Total: 24
Goals: 3

than 10,000 witnessed a low-key 1–1 draw and a symbolic changing of the guard. Strachan, 35, came off after 65 minutes and was replaced by clubmate Gary McAllister, the man who would replace him as skipper of both Leeds and Scotland.

Shortly after hoisting the League Championship aloft, Strachan called time on his illustrious international career, but was far from finished with football, and football was far from finished with him. Wilkinson recognised that he had to use Strachan more sparingly in 1992–93, particularly as Leeds were involved in the European Cup, but United struggled to wear the crown of champions with any confidence. Strachan, made an OBE in the New Year's Honours List, continued to defy time to remain a major influence at the club, pushing his Leeds appearances beyond the 200 barrier.

Wilkinson described Strachan as the best value-for-money signing he ever made. A fantastic example to younger players with his extraordinary fitness, the Scot had a wonderfully sharp football brain, instant control, dribbling skills, a powerful shot, inch-perfect delivery from set pieces, and a will to win tempered by cheeky humour. Many tipped Strachan as the man to replace Wilkinson at Elland Road, but the wee man extended his playing career still further by joining Coventry City in March 1995, becoming the Sky Blues' player-manager 20 months later and finally ending an extraordinary 26-year playing career which had started with Dundee.

NORWEGIAN international Frank Strandli lived out every Leeds United fan's dream – getting to play for the club. A member of the Norwegian branch of the Leeds United Supporters' Club, he secured a move to Elland Road. United were champions when the 20-year-old made his switch from IK Start in January 1993 for £250,000, almost a year to the day Howard Wilkinson signed Eric Cantona. Unfortunately, despite a promising start the Scandinavian could not match the exploits of the charismatic French star. After his scoring debut against Middlesbrough, Wilkinson said of Strandli: 'He found it hectic. He will have to adjust or go under.' Sadly, he sank like a stone.

Strandli certainly had all the right credentials. He had won Under-18 and Under-21 caps in abundance and had broken into the national side when he was 19 in games against Egypt, Bermuda and the Faroe Islands. His senior appearances for Norway had risen to six, with games against Scotland, Holland and China, when Wilkinson finally got his man. The Leeds boss had originally wanted to sign him in October 1992, but Strandli had difficulties in obtaining a work permit while he completed his national service with the Norwegian Army. His Premiership debut could not have gone much better. After about an hour without really looking like breaking down Middlesbrough's defence Wilkinson replaced Rod Wallace with his new acquisition, and it took the Norwegian just 11

Frank Strandli in action for Norway.

JIM TWOMEY
(Northern Ireland 1938)
Goalkeeper
Born: Newry, Co. Down, 13 April 1914.
Died: Leeds, 9 November 1984.
Caps: Leeds United 2

minutes to score with a left-foot finish six yards out. That paved the way for a 3–0 win – including a rare David Batty goal – that hadn't really looked on the cards.

Hopes that Wilkinson had unearthed a goalscoring gem did not materialise. Strandli, who looked as though he needed to shed a few pounds, could not adapt to the pace of the English game and only managed one more goal for the Whites. Despite failing to make an impact at Leeds, national coach Egil Olsen still believed he could do a job for Norway. In January 1994 he was languishing in United's reserves when he joined the Norway squad in Phoenix, Arizona, for their game against the United States. The long flight was worth it as Strandli scored his first international goal, just before half-time, but the States hit back to win 2–1, Cobi Jones scoring a last-minute winner.

Three months later Strandli played the full 90 minutes of a 0–0 draw with Portugal in Oslo, but lack of first-team action at Leeds meant he was not to play for his country again for more than two years. He went back to Norway on loan at Brann Bergen before signing for Lillestrom in 1995 when he rediscovered sufficient form to win his place back in the Norway team, scoring on his return against Azerbaijan in a 5–0 World Cup qualifying win in Oslo. Strandli became the regular strike partner for Tore Andre Flo, who played for Leeds near the end of his career, during the campaign.

Unbeaten Norway, with Strandli playing in all eight games, topped their group, but a lack of goals saw the man Lillestrom fans dubbed 'the Pit Bull', fail to make Olsen's squad for the Finals. He did net in a 3–3 friendly draw with France in February 1998 and played in a pre-tournament game against Denmark, but had fallen behind the likes of Ole Gunnar Solskjaer and Werden Bremen's Harvard Flo in the pecking order.

Strandli had a brief spell in Greece with Panathinaikos, with whom he played Champions League football, including a 2–1 defeat at Wembley against Arsenal, which attracted a 73,455 crowd. He then moved to Denmark to play for Aalborg, helping them win the Superligaen in 1999, but a succession of injuries, including a recurring groin problem, forced him to quit in February 2008 at the age of 28.

GOALKEEPER Jim Twomey was still a Leeds United reserve when he made his Northern Ireland debut; however, his fine display against Wales changed all that as he finally clinched his place in the Leeds first team after three months of Central League football.

Twomey was a skilful boxer and Gaelic footballer as a youngster, but he opted for football as his main sport. His excellent handling made him a natural goalkeeper, and by the age of 15 he had made his debut for local club Newry Town. His big breakthrough came in 1937 when he was chosen to represent the Irish League against the Scottish League at Glentoran's Oval ground in September. The Scots won 3–2 but, with the Irish selectors looking for a replacement for the legendary Elisha Scott, Twomey did his chances of full international recognition no harm.

Belfast Celtic's Tommy Breen was regarded as Everton hero Scott's natural replacement, and had just boosted his profile by joining Manchester United, but now Twomey had staked his claim. The Newry man retained his place in

Ireland goalkeeper Jim Twomey.

Jim Twomey covers his post.

the Irish League side to face the Football League at Blackpool on 6 October 1937. Many scouts beat a path to Bloomfield Road, where the FL's strong line up, which included Leeds full-back Bert Sproston, won 3–0. The margin of victory would have been much greater but for Twomey.

English clubs were soon in touch with Newry, where Twomey was playing as a part-timer while working as a woodworking machinist. Leeds manager Billy Hampson beat off the opposition, and in December Twomey joined the paid ranks at Elland Road. Initially he had to play second fiddle to Reg Savage, but his breakthrough came in dramatic fashion in March 1938. On Saturday 12 March Twomey was playing for the reserves at Blackpool while the first team were losing 2–0 against Leicester. Four days later he was in Belfast making his Ireland debut against Wales. Once again he rose to the occasion, keeping a clean sheet as Ireland won 1–0 with a goal from Chelsea's Joe Bambrick.

On his return to Elland Road Twomey was told he would make his first-team debut on Saturday – 16 March – which also happened to be at Blackpool. The Lancashire seaside town was proving to be a bit of an attraction for Twomey, who, although United were thumped 5–2, kept his Leeds place for the rest of the season. He was the first choice throughout the following campaign, which included his second appearance for Ireland.

Breen was unfit to face England at Maine Road in November 1938, so Twomey was called in. It proved a harrowing experience as the Leeds goalkeeper was left with little protection as Stanley Matthews and Willie Hall ran riot on the left flank. Tommy Lawton put England ahead on early on before Tottenham's Hall scored a three-and-a-half minute hat-trick as the Irish found themselves 4–0 down after 40 minutes. Hall added two more after half-time to become the first man to score five in a game for England. Tormentor-in-chief Matthews, who regarded his performance as just about his best ever, scored the final goal of a 7–0 rout, running half the length of the field before slipping the ball past Twomey.

The declaration of war meant that Twomey's hopes of further international action were over and he returned home to Newry, playing for Linfield in the 1944 Irish Cup Final defeat at the hands of Belfast Celtic. After the war he resumed his career with Leeds, with whom he played a handful of wartime games, and took his final appearance total with the club to 111 before becoming Halifax Town's trainer-coach in 1949. He also did some part-time scouting for Leeds and worked in an office while living in Beeston, near Elland Road.

A founder member of the Leeds United Ex-Players' Association, he was a tireless worker for charity. Modest and generous to a fault, he sold his Irish international caps at auction and the proceeds helped swell funds for a kidney machine unit.

MARK VIDUKA
(Australia 1994– to date)
Striker
Born: Melbourne, New South Wales, 9 October 1975.
Caps: Melbourne Knights 2, Dynamo Zagreb 12, Glasgow Celtic 4, Leeds United 7, Middlesbrough 16, Newcastle United 4. Total: 45
Goals: 11

NO SOONER had Mark Viduka arrived at Elland Road then he was off on long-term duty with Australia in the Olympic Games. Leeds's new £6 million summer signing from Celtic had played just three Premiership games when he flew home in the quest for medals. Soccer Australia usually fielded an Under-23 side in their Olympic matches, but, frustratingly for Leeds, he was included as an over-age player to boost his country's medal hopes on home soil. Leeds had to comply with the release of Viduka, who was a veteran of the 1996 Olympic team, and reserve goalkeeper Danny Milosevic. Both played in the tournament opener against a strong side from Italy, whose Inter Milan midfielder Andrea Pirlo scored a late winner to send the 93,000-plus Melbourne crowd home disappointed.

A 3–2 defeat against Nigeria and a 1–1 draw with Honduras was bad news for the locals, but good tidings for Leeds – the Aussies were out and Viduka was on his way back to Yorkshire. The big striker with the delicate touch had been considered hot property back home since bursting on the scene with Melbourne Knights, with whom he won the Australian title in 1995. He scored 32 goals in just 24 appearances for the Australian Under-20 side and almost netted a goal a game in his 18 outings for the Olympic/Under-23 team.

At 18 he made his full international debut in a 1–0 win against South Africa in Adelaide in June 1994. It was clear that to develop his game he had to leave Australia and he signed for Croatian club Dynamo Zagreb. The cash from the transfer was used to build a stand at Knights' Stadium, and it was duly named after him. It was not long before

Mark Viduka wheels away in triumph after scoring for Australia against the Republic of Ireland.

Viduka, who is of Croatian and Ukrainian descent, was making a name for himself in Europe, helping the renamed Croatia Zagreb to three successive League and cup doubles.

It was new Australian coach Terry Venables, the future Leeds boss, who had a good, long look at Viduka in 1997. He gave the striker his first start for three years as Australia won 1–0 in Macedonia to give the Aussies their first victory on European soil in 20 years. Viduka played for Venables 10 times in 1997, but the year ended in disappointment for the powerful forward, whose early red card in a Continental Cup game against Brazil in Saudi Arabia paved the way for a crushing 6–0 defeat.

In December 1998 Viduka joined Celtic for £3.5 million and scored 27 goals in his first full season, earning the Scottish Player of the Year award. Just before the 2000–01 season got underway, Leeds snapped him up after unravelling a vast amount of red tape. Despite playing in Scotland for 18 months, he was denied a work permit by the Department of Employment because he had not played enough international matches in the past two years to qualify. Leeds appealed, pointing out that no European-based Australian players had played in any of their country's four competitive matches during the two-year period as they were against minnows like the Cook Islands and Tahiti. Viduka got his permit, but Leeds had to wait until his return from the Olympics before he got into overdrive, finishing the season as top scorer with 17 Premiership goals, including four in a sensational 4–3 win against Liverpool and four more in the Champions League campaign.

Leeds and other European clubs were unhappy when their Australian-based players were called up for a friendly against France in Melbourne in November 2001. The Aussies saw the match as a vital warm-up game ahead of their World Cup Play-off double header against Uruguay. Frank Farina's team did well to hold France 1–1 and nine days later gained a vital edge against the South Americans thanks to Kevin Muscat's penalty. But the dreams of Viduka, Harry Kewell and Co. evaporated in Montevideo as Uruguay swept Australia aside 3–0 to book a place in the Finals.

Although never a prolific scorer for his country, Viduka was seen as a main man in Australia's progress and the usual club versus country issue continually reared its head. In fact, in his four years as a Leeds player he only pulled on the Aussie shirt seven times – and four of those were in Europe. He played in the famous Australian 3–1 victory against England at Upton Park in 2003 and was on target in the next match as the Aussies lost 2–1 to the Republic of Ireland at Lansdowne Road. The big Leeds man poked his side ahead from close range, but the Irish, using the game as a warm-up match before their European qualifier against Russia, hit back to win 2–1 with late goals from John O'Shea and Clinton Morrison, both set up by Ian Harte.

Kewell, Liverpool's new signing from Leeds, had to pull out shortly before the kick-off with Achilles tendon trouble, but he linked up with great effect with Viduka as Australia beat Jamaica 2–1 at Reading the next month. With Leeds under massive financial pressure, it was clear Viduka would soon be joining Kewell on the way out of Elland Road. The striker had netted 20 Premiership goals in 2002–03 – 14 coming in the final 10 games – to keep the Whites up. He could not repeat the miracle the following season, picking up red cards against Leicester and Bolton in the run-in, as United slipped into the Championship. Viduka did take time out from United's struggles to put in another fine display as Australia beat South Africa at Leicester at the end of March.

In the summer he joined Middlesbrough for £4.5 million, helping Boro to the UEFA Cup Final, where they lost to Seville, and three years later joined Newcastle, where he struggled with injuries. After leaving Elland Road Viduka was made Australia's captain and flourished under Guus Hiddink's coaching, leading the Socceroos to the 2006 World Cup Finals in Germany, where they went out to 10-man Italy in the second round. After Marco Materazzi's dismissal, the Aussies had the numerical advantage as the stalemate was approaching extra-time, but they conceded a last-minute penalty which substitute Francesco Totti put away.

Viduka considered international retirement, but opted to play on as Australia were included in the Asian Cup for the first time. The Australians were regarded as one of the favourites for the competition, held in 2007, but were beaten on penalties by Japan in a penalty shootout.

RUSSELL WAINSCOAT
(England 1929)
Born: East Retford, Nottinghamshire, 28 July 1898.
Died: Worthing, Sussex, July 1967.
Caps: Leeds United 1

RUSSELL WAINSCOAT'S only England appearance came in a celebrated and controversial game against Scotland.

The noise that greeted the only goal, scored direct from a corner in the final minute, is reckoned to have been the origin of the famous 'Hampden Roar'. But that was only half the story of a windswept Glasgow afternoon which saw England's hopes of sharing the Home International Championship blown away.

The stylish inside-forward had burst on the scene with Barnsley, scoring a hat-trick on his debut against Fulham in March 1920 and moving to Middlesbrough for £4,000, but

Russell Wainscoat.

he was sold to Leeds for half that price in March 1925. It was not long before he was knocking on the England door, going on an FA tour of Canada in 1926 and scoring five times in a game against Thunder Bay. Wainscoat was hailed by Leeds followers as the best player in his position in the country, with his close ball control, dribbling and powerful shooting marking him out as a player of class. His own personal highlight was four goals in a 6–3 win against West Ham in the penultimate game of the season, but it was not sufficient to prevent Leeds from relegation. He was outstanding as United came straight back up and maintained that form back in the top flight with a string of superb performances, which earned him selection for an England trial match against The Rest at Hillsborough, and he did not disappoint in a 4–3 victory.

Both 30-year-old Wainscoat and Leeds teammate Willis Edwards were picked for the game at Hampden Park on 13 April 1929, which would determine the destination of the Home Championship. Interest in the game was huge, with 110,512 packing newly-expanded Hampden's steep terracing, and the match threw up two major incidents.

In the 25th minute England claimed a penalty after a shot had been blocked. Scotland goalkeeper Jack Harkness seized the ball, ran a few yards, and cleared. Referee Arnold Josephs blew to penalise Harkness under a new law relating to the goalkeeper not being permitted to carry the ball more than four steps without bouncing the ball on the ground. Josephs awarded an indirect free-kick on the six-yard line in the middle of the area. Amid farcical scenes, all the Scots outfield players lined up behind the ball rather than on their own goalline. When the confusion was finally sorted out, Leeds man Wainscoat stood over the ball with only Harkness in his sights and the rest of the players behind him. As the free-kick was indirect, he could not shoot at goal, so he passed the ball sideways, prompting a mad charge for the leather, which was won by Scottish skipper Jimmy McMullen, who booted it out for a corner.

The incident livened up a relatively low-key affair, but Wainscoat came close to breaking the deadlock when he headed a cross from Jack Bruton, of Burnley, just over the bar. England were handed a huge advantage for the entire second half when Scotland's Huddersfield Town star Alex Jackson dislocated an elbow in a collision with Ernie Blenkinsop. But England could not make it count, and the match was drifting towards a 0–0 draw with both teams looking set to share the Championship when Aberdeen winger Alec Cheyne won a corner at the death. He swept it into the penalty area, where a sudden gust of wind altered the trajectory of the ball and it flew into the corner of the net past goalkeeper Jack Hacking. The roar which greeted the goal and the final whistle was deafening. The crowd had witnessed a remarkable finale – and probably the first international goal to be scored directly from a corner, as a rule allowing such an eventuality had only been introduced two years earlier.

Wainscoat never played for England again, a fate shared by four of his teammates that day – Bruton, Hacking and Bolton duo Jimmy Seddon and Harry Nuttall. He had two more excellent seasons with Leeds, finishing with 87 goals in 215 League appearances, before moving to Hull, helping the Tigers to the 1933 Division Three North title before retiring the following year. A superb all-round sportsman, he also played Yorkshire Council cricket for Barnsley.

JASON WILCOX

(England 1996–2000)
Winger
Born: Farnworth, Lancashire, 15 July 1971.
Caps: Blackburn Rovers 2, Leeds United 1. Total: 3

JASON WILCOX got to grips with football after representing England at judo. The black belt was tipped as Olympic potential as a youngster and was selected for his country, but he eventually opted to take up a career in football. The decision paid dividends as he was capped three times by three different England managers, the last coming shortly after he joined Leeds United. His father wrote to several Lancashire clubs in an effort to get young Wilcox a trial, and Blackburn Rovers signed him on associate schoolboy forms in June 1986. The winger went through the club's academy ranks and turned professional three years later. He made his debut in April 1990, but it was not until 1991–92 that he began to hold down a first-team place on a regular basis, playing on the right flank, while former Leeds man Scott Sellars twinkled on the left. Sellars moved to Newcastle at the end of the season and Wilcox switched wings, with Stuart Ripley coming into the team on the right.

The two widemen formed a devastating partnership, providing Alan Shearer plenty of ammunition with their pace and skill. After overcoming Legionnaire's Disease, which threatened his career for a time, Wilcox came back stronger than ever and was called up for an England training squad in 1994. The Three Lions were due to play Germany on 20 April – Hitler's birthday – but the FA called the game off after receiving police intelligence that big demonstrations were planned.

England coach Venables still went ahead with his 24-man get-together, which also included Norwich City's Chris Sutton for the first time. Sutton joined Wilcox and Shearer at Blackburn in the summer and Rovers swept to the Premiership title in 1995. Injury delayed Wilcox's England debut until May 1996 when he played the full 90 minutes of a comfortable 3–0 Wembley win against Hungary. He also played in an England B victory in Hong Kong at the end of the month, but it was not enough to win a place in Venables's Euro '96 squad.

Despite another B appearance in a 2–1 defeat against Chile, it was nearly three years before he gained another

England's Jason Wilcox looks for a route round an Argentina defender at Wembley.

England chance when former Leeds hero Howard Wilkinson, filling in after the FA terminated Glenn Hoddle's contract, picked Wilcox in the squad to face France. By the time the Blackburn man got on four minutes from the end, Nicolas Anelka's double had already wrapped up an easy Wembley victory. Later that year Wilcox severed his 13-year association with Rovers and joined Leeds in a £3 million deal. United were one of the teams of the moment, with David O'Leary's side playing some outstanding attacking football.

Wilcox slotted into his new surroundings pretty quickly and a man-of-the-match performance, and a goal, in a 2–1 win at Sunderland in January 2000 in front of new England boss Kevin Keegan, probably clinched his place in the side against Argentina the following month. The 0–0 draw before a near 75,000 crowd was overshadowed by the death on the same day of the legendary Sir Stanley Matthews, 85. There was a silent tribute to the great man, but the two teams could not produce a performance to lighten a dark day.

Keegan played Wilcox as a left wing-back in that match, but a knee injury denied the new Leeds man a place in the Euro 2000 squad. Indeed, injury was to blight much of the rest of Wilcox's stay at Elland Road, as he had to watch much of the thrilling run to the Champions League semis on the sidelines after being a key man in helping United reach the last four of the UEFA Cup the previous season.

From a frontline player with England aspirations, he slipped to the fringes at Leeds, and when the Whites were relegated in 2004 joined Leicester City on a free. His luck with injuries did not change, and after suffering a cruciate ligament injury he moved to Blackpool, where he ended his career in 2006, setting up his own judo schools in Lancashire.

HAROLD WILLIAMS

(Wales 1949–50)

Winger

Born: Briton Ferry, near Neath, 17 June 1924.
Caps: Newport County 2, Leeds United 2. Total: 4

CREAM rises to the top, and that was certainly the case for Harold Williams, the flying milkman. A power-packed pocket-sized winger of blurring speed, he gave Leeds United fantastic service and was unlucky not to win more than four Welsh caps. He was signed by Major Frank Buckley after starring for Newport County in a shock 3–1 FA Cup win at Elland Road, part-timer Williams having risen early in the morning to do his milk round.

A former Briton Ferry Schools captain, he played with his local club in Wales before being rejected by Swansea Town after trials. Although he was quick and was an exciting dribbler, the Swans management felt that at 5ft 4in and weighing less than nine stone, Williams did not have the physique to cope with professional football. During the war, Williams served on Royal Navy destroyer escorts in the Atlantic, but his football skills saw him make guest appearances in Ireland with Belfast Celtic and Cliftonville. At the end of the war he resumed playing with Briton Ferry, but it was not long before he joined the paid ranks at Newport, reportedly being signed by manager Tom Bromilow while Williams was on his milk round with his horse and cart.

Newport finished bottom of Division Two in Williams's first season, and County struggled for the next couple of Division Three (South) seasons before grabbing national headlines with FA Cup victories against Leeds and Huddersfield. In the fifth round, County pushed Portsmouth all the way before losing 3–2 at Fratton Park to the team who were to be crowned Division One champions at the end of the season.

The star of Newport's giant-killing run was Williams, the little man in size five boots, whose displays earned him his first international appearance a month after the Portsmouth match. Williams showed he was no flash in the pan as Wales triumphed 3–0 in Belfast with goals from George Edwards and Trevor Ford. At the end of the season he went on Wales's three-game European tour, playing in a 4–0 defeat against Switzerland, inspired by two-goal winger Jaques Fatton, in Berne.

Inevitably there was a rush to sign 25-year-old Williams, and the race was won by Leeds manager Major Frank Buckley, whose £3,000 cash offer, plus defender Roly Depear, was accepted by Newport. Williams was a great signing for Leeds. He could play on either wing and his tiny feet possessed a powerful shot. He had little difficulty in adapting to life in Division Two and some of his FA Cup magic rubbed off on the club as they reached the

Harold Williams wearing one of his Wales caps.

sixth round in his first season at Elland Road. Four days after he and 18-year-old wonder kid John Charles put up a heroic display at Arsenal, who snatched a semi-final place with a Reg Lewis goal, the pair lined up against Northern Ireland at Wrexham. Most eyes were on debut boy Charles, but it was Williams who had the better game and retained his place for the next international against Scotland. This time he was joined in the side by former Leeds man Aubrey Powell, then with Birmingham, and it proved to be the final international for both men. Powell scored Wales's goal, but they were eclipsed by a fine display from Scotland, who had a player making his debut with the same physical stature as Williams – Bobby Collins. The Scots won 3–1 with goals from Lawrie Reilly (2) and Billy Liddell.

Williams was facing stiff competition from Leicester City's Mal Griffiths, whom the Welsh selectors went with for the next four games, three of which were won against Ireland, Portugal and Switzerland. The emergence of Newcastle's Billy Foulkes saw Williams slip further down the international pecking order and his Wales days were effectively ended when he broke a leg on 22 November 1952 in a 2–2 draw at Everton.

Williams fought back to help United to promotion in 1955–56, but did not play in the top flight for Leeds and returned to Somerton Park. His departure from Newport had been completed seven years earlier on his milk round; now the paperwork for his return to Somerton Park was completed in the County chairman's bedroom. The club secretary was in hospital so the chairman, who was ill in bed, countersigned the transfer forms.

Williams was only back in Wales for four months before he moved back to Yorkshire with Bradford Park Avenue, where injury ended his career. A keen Leeds United follower, Williams ran a pub near Elland Road and later at Gildersome.

JONATHAN WOODGATE

(England 1999– to date)
Centre-back
Born: Middlesbrough, 22 January 1980.
Caps: Leeds United 4, Newcastle United 1, *Real Madrid 1, Tottenham Hotspur 2. Total: 8
* While on loan to Middlesbrough

FROZEN out of international football for the best part of two years, Jonathan Woodgate's England career has been a spluttering affair. At 19 he looked destined for a long run in the team, then the infamous court case involving teammate Lee Bowyer put his England career on hold, followed by an injury and a disastrous spell with Real Madrid. It all added up to eight caps spread over a 10-year period – a poor return for a player of great ability. Perhaps it was a case of too much, too young. A schoolboy player on Middlesbrough's books, he joined Leeds at 16 and was a member of the 1997 FA Youth Cup-winning side. One of David O'Leary's first moves when he inherited the Elland Road hot-seat was to promote the commanding young defender to the first team.

Woodgate made his Premiership debut in a 1–1 draw in October 1998 at Nottingham Forest, where his coolness under pressure was a feature of a game which saw Leeds reduced to 100 men after the first-half dismissal of Danny Granville. O'Leary, himself a top-notch centre-back with Arsenal and the Republic of Ireland, kept Woodgate in the team, and he continued to earn rave reviews. Leeds clearly had a young diamond, but even the most ardent of United fans were stunned when he was called up to train with the full England squad in March ahead of Kevin Keegan's first game in charge – a Euro qualifier against Poland. He was then in the England squad to face Hungary the following month before Keegan thrust him into the side to face Bulgaria in Sofia in the summer.

Woodgate had played just 25 Premiership games and had not even made an Under-21 appearance when Keegan fast-tracked him into the key European Championship qualifier. He did not disappoint in a 1–1 draw, although he was withdrawn after 65 minutes after Bulgarian substitute Martin Petrov was sent off because England, needing victory, opted to sacrifice a defender. The ploy did not work; the Three Lions looked short of ideas, and Woodgate's performance was one of the few crumbs of

Jonathan Woodgate in action during his England debut in Bulgaria.

comfort. Two days later he signed a new four-year contract with Leeds and confirmed his arrival as a senior player with a fine performance as the Under-21s beat Argentina 1–0 at Craven Cottage.

England did eventually scrape into the Euro 2000 Finals, but Woodgate was not part of the squad, as both he and Bowyer had been suspended from international football. Both men were facing trial for causing grievous bodily harm and affray after an attack on a student in Leeds city centre – charges both players denied.

While Bowyer seemed to thrive on the pitch during the court case, Woodgate looked stressed and sustained a heel injury against Middlesbrough, which took him out of the first-team firing line. He was out for eight months, during which the initial trial collapsed, but in the retrial at Hull Crown Court he was acquitted of grievous bodily harm, but found guilty of affray, for which he received 100 hours community service. Bowyer was cleared of both charges.

England coach Sven-Goran Eriksson felt it was too soon to pick Woodgate for the 2002 World Cup, but played him in a 1–1 friendly draw with Portugal at Villa Park – three years and three months after his first cap. That was just a warm-up for the autumn European qualifiers against Slovakia and Macedonia. Woodgate was solid alongside Gareth Southgate as England won 2–1 in Slovakia, but England struggled to a 2–2 draw with Macedonia, the dropped points being compounded by the dismissal of Leeds striker Alan Smith.

It was looking as though Woodgate could put his off-the-field troubles behind him, but as Leeds's massive debts began to mount the commanding centre-back joined the Elland Road exodus and was sold to Newcastle for £9 million. He soon won his fifth cap – a 1–0 defeat in Sweden when he was replaced by Southgate at half-time – but once again injury struck, ruling him out of the European Championships in Portugal.

There were genuine concerns about his long-term fitness after a nagging thigh problem, which made Real Madrid's £13.4 million swoop for him in August 2004 even more astonishing. He missed the entire La Liga season because of injury and hadn't played for 17 months when he made a disastrous debut in Spain against Atletico Bilbao, scoring an own-goal before being sent off.

Woodgate seemed miles away from an England recall while he was in Spain and his hopes of international football became even more distant when coach Fabio Capello arrived at the Bernabeu and signed Italy's World Cup-winning skipper Fabio Cannavaro as his key defender.

'Woody' knew he needed to move if he was to resurrect his career and, after only 14 appearances for the Spanish giants, he was loaned to his home-town club, Middlesbrough, where he was made captain. Boro boss Gareth Southgate, who had played alongside Woodgate for England, believed the new, mature, Woodgate should get an England recall. That wish came true against Spain at Old Trafford. He resumed the defensive partnership with Rio Ferdinand that they had briefly enjoyed at Leeds, but Spain took the honours 1–0. That pairing could have been the dream ticket for Leeds United – and England – but Woodgate's injury troubles restricted the number of times they played alongside each other.

Woodgate's move to Middlesbrough became permanent, and he responded with a series of commanding displays. Fifteen months back on Teesside ended abruptly as he joined Tottenham for £7 million. In only his fifth game for Spurs he scored the goal which won the 2008 Carling Cup as they beat Chelsea 2–1 in extra-time. Since then he has played twice more for England against Trinidad & Tobago and the Czech Republic, as he battles for more England opportunities under Capello, the man from whom he escaped at Real Madrid.

NIGEL WORTHINGTON

(Northern Ireland 1984–97)

Left-back / Midfield

Born: Ballymena, Co. Antrim, 4 November 1961.
Caps: Sheffield Wednesday 50, Leeds United 14, Stoke City 2. Total: 66

MODEL professional Nigel Worthington has emerged as one of Northern Ireland's most influential characters. He is their current manager and played for his country for 13 years, two of them while he was at Leeds United, slipping under the radar almost unnoticed when he arrived at

Nigel Worthington.

Elland Road. He was already in the autumn of his career when he was recruited by Howard Wilkinson, who was a huge admirer of low-profile Worthington's unflinching reliability.

Worthington made his name with his local club, Ballymena United, where he won 14 caps at Under-18 level. His big breakthrough came in 1981 when he won Irish and Ulster Cup-winners medals, was named Ulster Young Footballer of the Year and played for the Irish League in their 1–0 defeat in Dublin against the League of Ireland. Talent-spotting young Notts County manager Howard Wilkinson signed Worthington for £100,000 in July 1981 and that was the start of a great partnership between the two, which extended into management.

When Wilko took the Sheffield Wednesday job in June 1983 he signed Worthington again eight months later and the move to a bigger club opened the door to international football. Worthington made his international debut in a 1–1 draw in Swansea against Wales in May 1984, his country's final game in the last-ever Home International Championship. The point Northern Ireland gained was enough for the province to win and keep the trophy.

Worthington became an integral part of the Northern Ireland set-up for the next 12 years, the highlight being the 1986 World Cup Finals in Mexico. The previous tournament, at which the Irish were the surprise package, had come too early for Worthington, but he was in the starting line up for the 1–1 draw with Algeria and a 2–1 loss to Spain, but missed the final group game against Brazil, a 3–0 defeat in retiring goalkeeper Pat Jennings's last international appearance.

Initially, Worthington was a left-sided midfielder, but he settled into the left-back spot with Wednesday, with whom he won the League Cup and gained promotion in 1991.

Solid and utterly reliable, he was Northern Ireland's first choice for virtually a decade as they battled, without success, to qualify for more World Cups and the European Championships, with Worthington taking the captain's armband on several occasions. He was 33 when he rejected a new contract at Hillsborough to link up with Wilkinson for a third time at Leeds in summer 1994. He was seen as cover for Tony Dorigo, but the Aussie suffered knee and hamstring problems so Worthington ended up playing a good half of the season.

The Irish had just started their bid to make it to Euro '96, and Worthington's first Northern Ireland outing as a Leeds player was a 2–1 defeat at Portugal in Belfast, but they made up lost ground by winning 2–1 in Austria in October 1994. The recovery was short-lived as Worthington and the North were crushed 4–0 at Windsor Park by their rivals from across the border. The Ulster team's topsy-turvy campaign continued when they drew the rematch in Dublin to prevent the Republic going to the top of the group, then won in Latvia with an Iain Dowie penalty. With two qualification places up for grabs, Northern Ireland were still in the mix as they flew across the Atlantic to take part in the Canada Cup competition in the summer. Worthington came on as a sub in a 2–0 defeat to the hosts in Edmonton and was restored to the starting line up by manager Bryan Hamilton for the next game, a 2–1 defeat in Chile.

After that short break, Northern Ireland returned to Belfast to face Latvia at Windsor Park and knew victory would keep them in the qualification hunt. Everything was going according to plan when Crystal Palace striker Dowie opened the scoring, but the men from the Baltic hit back to win 2–1 to deliver a real hammer blow. It was a result that was to come back and haunt Hamilton's squad in the final analysis. Although Worthington was now largely confined to the bench at Elland Road, he was still Northern Ireland's first-choice left-back and helped tame the attacking talents of runaway group leaders Portugal in a 1–1 draw in Oporto. A routine 4–0 win in Liechtenstein kept Northern Ireland's slim qualification hopes alive as they, the Republic and Austria went into the final round of fixtures all in with a chance, although in the North's case it was largely down to maths.

The best the three countries could hope for was a place in the Play-offs as Portugal had already qualified. A big Northern Irish win against Austria in Belfast, coupled with a hefty defeat of the Republic in Portugal, could still put Worthington and the North into the Play-offs – and the miracle almost happened. The Republic crashed 3–0 in Lisbon, while Northern Ireland enjoyed a remarkable 5–3 victory against the Austrians, leaving both Irish teams on 17 points. However, it was Eire who clung on to second spot on goal difference – just one goal.

Euro '96 in England would have been a fitting finale for Worthington, who had played in all his country's qualifiers, but it was not to be. The season was to end in climactic fashion for the veteran Ulsterman. He did play in friendlies against Norway, Sweden and Germany as those countries warmed up for the Finals, but he was left on the bench at Wembley as Leeds crashed 3–0 to Aston Villa in the League Cup Final, even though Dorigo was absent, the left-back slot going to Lucas Radebe.

In the summer the 34-year-old joined Stoke, where he played twice more for his country to take his total of international appearances to 66, which leaves him in Northern Ireland's all-time top 10. He then entered management with Blackpool, Norwich and Leicester before being appointed to the top job by his country with Glynn Snodin as his assistant. (see International Managers)

TONY YEBOAH
(Ghana 1985–97)
Striker
Born: New Tafo Krofrom, Kumasi, 6 June 1966.
Caps: Okwahu United, Saarbrucken, Eintracht Frankfurt, Leeds United 17, Hamburg, Al Hittad. Total: 59
Goals: 26

BLACK Stars striker Tony Yeboah shone brightly at Elland Road, lighting up matches with goal-grabbing exploits. His father, Mike, was a player with Kumasi Highlanders, and young Yeboah played for several clubs in Ghana before shining with Kumasi Cornerstones, which led to him being invited to train with the national team, the Black Stars, in 1984 when he was 18. A move to Okwahu United saw him break into the international set-up and a man-of-the-match performance in a World Cup qualifier against Zambia triggered a move to German second division club Saarbrucken.

In 1990 he joined Eintracht Frankfurt, where he spent four explosive years, twice topping the Bundesliga goal charts. But the arrival of Jupp Heynkes as coach unsettled Yeboah and fellow African star player Jay Jay Okocha, Nigeria's captain. In January 1995, Yeboah arrived at Elland Road on a short-term contract. Yeboah did have a reputation for being a feisty character, and was once involved in a much-publicised row with Ghana's best player Abedi Pele over the captaincy of the country, but none of that concerned Leeds boss Howard Wilkinson, who was in no doubt he had pulled off a major coup. After spending a month getting Yeboah up to match fitness, he unleashed him on unsuspecting Premiership defences. The star of Ghana responded with 13 goals from just 16 starts, giving United fans a genuine goalscoring hero to cheer.

Fresh from scoring the winner at Newcastle United in April, the rejuvenated Yeboah reported for African Nations Cup duty against Niger in Accra and netted the only goal of the game, although the result was later annulled as Niger withdrew from the competition.

Ghana sharpshooter Tony Yeboah.

Getting Yeboah on an extended contract was Wilkinson's priority in the summer and a record £3.4 million deal was sealed. Was his previous season's form a flash in the pan? No chance. Yeboah picked up where he left off, with his wrecking-ball shooting sending shivers down the defensive spine of the opposition.

Not only was he a great goalscorer, but a scorer of great goals. His thunderous volley against Liverpool was voted Leeds United's best-ever goal, but his stunning effort against Wimbledon and his hat-trick bender against Monaco were not far behind – all achieved in the opening weeks of the season. The only downside for Leeds followers was that Yeboah would be missing during the African Nations Cup Finals in January along with South African duo Lucas Radebe and Phil Masinga. As part of the build-up Yeboah was released for a friendly against Egypt in December during a week of internationals, but on his return from Cairo just a day before United's game at Sheffield Wednesday, Wilkinson made a rare error of judgement. He opted to play him at Hillsborough, but he looked jaded and was substituted as United crashed 6–2.

It was only a temporary blip, however, as Yeboah was on target as United beat Manchester United 3–1 at Elland Road the following weekend. Suitably refreshed, he flew back to Ghana to play in pre-tournament games against

Saudi Arabia and Zimbabwe before kicking-off their African Nations Cup campaign in South Africa against Ivory Coast. The two countries had met six months earlier in the qualifiers when Ghana won 2–0, Yeboah getting one of the goals. History repeated itself in Port Elizabeth as Ghana won by the same scoreline, with the Leeds striker scoring the opening goal in spectacular fashion when he converted a Sam Johnson cross.

Victories against Tunisia and Mozambique ensured Ghana, one of the favourites, finished top of the group and earned a quarter-final shot at Zaire. Once again Yeboah proved his value with the only goal. The semis pitched the Black Stars against hosts South Africa in Johannesburg, and Yeboah found himself marked out of the game by his Leeds teammate Lucas Radebe. After Yeboah missed an early chance, the Bafana Bafana went on to dominate, winning 3–0.

Yeboah had played in all five of Ghana's matches, but was rested from the third-fourth Play-off defeat against Zambia and returned to Elland Road, where he scored in both legs of the Coca-Cola Cup semi-finals against Birmingham City to fire the Whites to their first Wembley Final for 23 years. It proved a dreadful anticlimax, as Yeboah was starved of possession in a 3–0 defeat and his mood could not have brightened when he badly damaged his knee playing for Ghana in a prestige friendly in Brazil. Although he scored his usual goal, the Africans were crushed 8–2 and United's star man subsequently missed the next nine months because of the injury.

By the time the African sharpshooter was ready to play again, a new man was in charge – George Graham. The Scot was unable to call upon Yeboah until the final game of 1997, a 1–0 loss at Manchester United, where the fans' favourite, back after nine months out, lasted 70 minutes before coming off with hamstring trouble, causing him to miss the New Year's Day defeat at Newcastle United.

Leeds badly needed Yeboah's goals to light up a dull season, but behind the scenes tension between Graham and Yeboah was building. Soon a war of words was fought out on the back pages as Yeboah flew 4,000 miles to Ghana to face Morocco in a World Cup qualifier. Graham was furious that the player was not fit enough to play for Leeds, but was happy to turn out for Ghana. Yeboah responded that he needed matches to get fit, and playing for his country was one way of achieving that. The Morocco game ended at 2–2, Yeboah being substituted by Luton Town's Kim Grant. He also played in an African Nations Cup qualifier against Zimbabwe a fortnight later, which saw the rift between the player and his manager widen.

Matters between two strong characters came to a head at the end of March in explosive style. Yeboah had been put back in the team by Graham, who took him off during a 1–0 defeat at Tottenham, prompting Yeboah to throw his shirt at the Leeds bench and head straight down the tunnel, never to pull on a United top again.

For the next game, at Sheffield Wednesday, Yeboah said he had a hamstring injury, yet within days he was playing in another World Cup qualifier as Ghana drew 1–1 in Sierra Leone. The Black Stars seemed to be heading for victory when the hosts levelled with a controversial late penalty. After the game a frustrated Yeboah, who was substituted, delivered a verbal volley to assistant coach Sam Arday and was promptly dropped by Dutch coach Rinus Israel for the next game against Gabon in Accra.

A fallen idol, Yeboah moved back to Germany shortly after the start of the following season when a £1 million deal took him to Hamburg, where he became embroiled in a lengthy tax evasion case, which was finally settled out of court, before winding down his career in Qatar. He retired from the international scene in 1999 with 26 goals in 59 games, and now runs a string of hotels back home.

TERRY YORATH

(Wales 1969–81)
Midfield
Born: Cardiff, 27 March 1950.
Caps Leeds United 28, Coventry City 20, Tottenham Hotspur 8, Vancouver Whitecaps 3. Total: 59
Goals: 2

VENERABLE West Germany manager Helmut Schoen hailed Welsh skipper Terry Yorath as a great leader. The man who lifted the 1974 World Cup was no mean judge of a footballer, and his assessment of Yorath was spot-on. The man who started his career with Leeds United played 59 times for Wales, 42 of them as captain, and under his management the Red Dragons came desperately close to qualifying for the World Cup Finals. He's been one of the principality's most influential figures since World War Two, yet only became a footballer by chance.

Like many Welsh kids he was schooled as a rugby union player and had trials as a scrum-half with Cardiff Schools. One day he went to see his brother Dai play football for Cardiff Schools against Rhondda Valley Boys, but the Cardiff lads were a player short, so Yorath was pressed into action, borrowed a pair of boots, did well and was asked the join the squad. He won four Welsh Schools caps as a left-winger and was spotted by Leeds United's top scout in Wales, Jack Pickard, the man who recruited John Charles. Despite offers from clubs nearer to home – his home-town Cardiff and both Bristol clubs – he took the plunge at Leeds, signing as an apprentice in 1965.

The Revie revolution was gathering speed at Elland Road, and breaking in to the first team was tough. Such was the quality at Revie's disposal that Yorath had played only one First Division game at the end of the 1967–68 season, when a scratch Leeds side lost 3–0 at Burnley, before making his international debut in a 4–1 defeat in Italy.

Terry Yorath captained Wales in 42 games.

Established in the Wales Under-23 side when he was only 17, he played in all the 1971 and 1972 Home Internationals yet was still only on the fringes at Leeds. By the time he made his 11th appearance for Wales, against Scotland in May 1973, he had still only played four full games for Leeds. Not surprisingly for a man who shared his digs with Norman Hunter, Yorath was a hard-tackling, aggressive player whose will to win always impressed Welsh manager Dave Bowen, who had no reservations about making a Leeds reserve a vital part of his squad. Yorath's patience finally paid off as he played in the majority of the matches in the 1973–74 Championship-winning season and played in the European Cup Final. By then he was at the forefront of Wales's bid to reach the Finals of the World Cup and the European Championships. Their three-team World Cup group was famously won by Poland at England's expense, but the point Yorath and his men extracted from a 1–1 draw at Wembley was equally as damaging.

The Welsh, galvanised by Yorath's drive and determination, had a pretty good team in the mid-1970s when they made Mike Smith their full-time manager. They were the only British team to reach the quarter-finals of the 1976 European Championships, from which they made a bitter and controversial exit at Cardiff. The qualifiers started with a 2–1 defeat in Austria, but a 2–0 home win against Hungary and a 5–0 thumping of Luxembourg, Wales's biggest win against foreign opposition, which featured Yorath's first international goal, got Wales back on an even keel. They then became the first side to win a competitive match in Hungary, before making it four wins on the bounce with victory in Luxembourg. Wales were now in charge of the group and it was not a position they would relinquish, wrapping up a place in the last eight by beating Austria with a goal from 33-year-old Arfon Griffiths on his home ground of Wrexham. It was Wales's finest moment since their 1958 World Cup heroics.

Left to fly the flag for Britain, Wales faced Yugoslavia over two legs for a place in the last four. Manager Smith opted for containment in Zagreb, playing John Toshack as a lone striker, but the swift-moving Slavs tore up the script after just 45 seconds when Yorath slipped on the wet turf and Momcilo Vukotic scored. Danilo Popivoda added another goal in the second half, leaving Wales to make up a 2–0 deficit at Ninian Park.

Wales remained upbeat despite defeat, but their task became nigh-on impossible when Yugoslavia scored a controversial opening goal in a highly-charged game in Cardiff. Villain of the piece as far as Wales were concerned was East German referee Rudi Glöckner. He allowed Yugoslavia to take a free-kick inside their own territory with the ball still rolling. Wales's defence was caught out, and Malcolm Page collided with Popivoda in the box. Glöckner, still struggling to keep up with play, pointed to the spot and Josip Katalinski rammed home the penalty.

Just before the interval Ian Evans pulled one back to give Wales hope and fire up the atmosphere a few more degrees. It reached boiling point during a bad-tempered second half when Glöckner disallowed an overhead kick goal by John Mahoney for dangerous play. The crowd erupted, beer cans were thrown on to the field, some supporters confronted Yugoslavia goalkeeper Enver Maric and the under-fire referee took the teams off for five minutes while order was restored.

After play resumed Glöckner disallowed, correctly, a Toshack score, but he soothed the crowd's ire by giving Wales a penalty. Up stepped Yorath and shot tamely at Maric – 'It was the worst penalty kick I've ever seen,' admitted the crestfallen skipper. It ended 1–1 and Wales were out, with Glöckner needing a police escort to get off the pitch. It was Yorath's last international as a Leeds player. Although he never gave anything less than 100 per cent, he was not a terrace favourite at Elland Road, where a section of fans gave him the bird. The time had come to move on and he joined Coventry City for £135,000. He wore the captain's armband at Highfield Road and continued to lead Wales, who proved their exploits in the European Championships had been no fluke with more good results in 1977. These included a 3–0 beating of newly-crowned European champions Czechoslovakia and a 1–0 win against England, when a Leighton James penalty gave Wales their first victory on English soil for 42 years. Wales could have won the British title outright, but were held 1–1 in Belfast in what was distinguished referee Jack Taylor's final game, the official receiving Yorath's shirt at the final whistle as a memento. Welsh hopes of reaching their first World Cup Finals for 20 years were shattered when they lost to Scotland 2–0 at Anfield, where they literally suffered at the hands of Joe Jordan when the former Leeds striker's handball was interpreted as a penalty against Wales.

Tottenham boss Keith Burkinshaw was a big admirer of Yorath's defensive midfield qualities and signed him for £300,000 in August 1979 to win the ball for the likes of Glenn Hoddle, Ossie Ardiles and Ricky Villa. It was a role he relished, and he continued to play regularly for Wales, making his 50th international against Turkey in November 1979 when Byron Stevenson was sent off in a 1–0 defeat in Izmir.

In February 1981 he crossed the Atlantic to play for Vancouver Whitecaps, managed by former Leeds hero Johnny Giles, who had also recruited other United stars of old, Peter Lorimer, David Harvey and Ray Hankin. Yorath's commitments in Canada threw up a few availability problems for Wales boss Mike England, but in Yorath's first game since joining the American Soccer League he scored the final goal in a 3–1 friendly win against the Republic of Ireland at Tolka Park. He played twice more in World Cup qualifiers against Turkey and the Soviet Union before his international career was brought to a close; however, he still had a lot more to offer Wales as he entered management and went on to take his country desperately close to the place in the World Cup Finals they had craved for decades (See International Managers).

Note: Leeds United's own international honours board includes the name of Australian goalkeeper Danny Milosevic, but he did not play a full international for his cuntry. He did play in the Olympic Games for Australia in 2000, but such matches are not considered as full internationals by Soccer Australia. Milosevic did not play a first-team game for Leeds.

Leeds City Internationals

JOE ENRIGHT

(Ireland 1912)
Inside-left
Born: Athlone 1890.
Caps: Leeds City 1

HISTORY has not been kind in summing up Joe Enright's international career. The *Yorkshire Post* certainly pulled no punches in describing the Leeds City forward as 'the greatest failure on the Irish side' in his only game against Scotland in March 1912. He and Leeds teammate Joe Moran were making their international debuts in an under-strength Irish side, and Scotland were soon fully in command, winning 4–1 with goals from Watty Aikenhead (2), Billy Reid and Bobby Walker.

Enright was immediately discarded by the selectors, but of the clutch of Irish players recruited by Leeds

Joe Enright.

manager Frank Scott Walford, Enright was among the most successful. He was a bit of a teenage star with Shelbourne, playing twice for the Irish League in October 1909 when they were outclassed by the Football League 8–1 at Oldham and lost 2–0 in Glasgow to the Scottish League. He moved to Leeds in summer 1910 and initially he did well at Elland Road, reaching double figures in the scoring charts in his first two seasons to earn his Ireland call-up. Enright did not feature as much after Herbert Chapman took over from Scott Walford and was transferred to Newport County for £50. That was a big fee in those days, as the rest of the County team had only cost £45.

At the end of the season he linked up with Scott Walford again by signing for Coventry and scored four goals in their 10–1 thrashing of Newport in November 1914. During World War One he served with the Army in the Royal Army Ordnance Corps until 1919 and guested on a regular basis for his home-town club, Athlone.

JOE MORAN

(Ireland 1912)
Wing-half
Born: Dublin, 9 February, year not known.
Caps: Leeds City 1

LIKE clubmate Joe Enright, Joe Moran found international football a step too far. The Leeds City duo only played against Scotland in 1912 because the Irish FA was in dispute with several of its own clubs and failed to get Everton and Bradford City to release four players. Moran was a replacement for Val Harris, the experienced Everton player. Thus it was a patched-up Irish side that took the field in front of 12,000 spectators at Windsor Park, while elsewhere in Belfast a further 10,000 watched a rival match organised by the Irish clubs who had boycotted the Ireland versus Scotland fixture.

Moran 'plodded along gamely', said the *Yorkshire Post* of the Dublin-born forward's contribution in a one-sided 4–1 defeat in which Scotland's bricklayer goalkeeper Jimmy Brownlie touched the ball just once in the second half. Moran had been a member of the Shelbourne side that reached three Irish Cup Finals, and finished runners-up in the Irish League in 1907. A consistent half-back, he played in a 2–0 Irish League defeat at the hands of the Scottish League in October 1909.

In summer 1911, after winning a United Ireland Cup medal when the Shels beat Bohemians, he joined the large posse of Irish players at Elland Road. City were run on a tight budget and for two years had a policy of picking up

Joe Moran.

relatively cheap recruits from the Emerald Isle with Moran, Enright, Mick Foley, Billy Gillespie, Alec Creighton and goalkeeper Leslie Murphy among them. Moran stayed a couple of seasons at Elland Road before, it is believed, he returned to Ireland.

RICHARD MORRIS
(Wales 1902–08)
Inside-forward
Born: Newtown, Montgomeryshire, 25 April 1883.
Caps: Newtown 1, Druids 2, Liverpool 5, Leeds City 1, Grimsby Town 1, Plymouth Argyle 1. Total: 11
Goals: 1

MUCH-TRAVELLED Dickie Morris was the first Leeds player to earn international honours. The inside-forward had already represented his country eight times when he arrived at Elland Road from Liverpool in summer 1905 shortly after City's election to the Football League.

A veteran of the Boer War, Morris played for Newtown, with whom he made his international debut on the left wing in a 3–0 defeat against Ireland at Cardiff in February 1902. Shortly afterwards he had a brief spell with Ruabon-based Druids, winning a second cap when Wales held England 0–0 at Wrexham thanks to a penalty save from

Dickie Morris, Leeds City's first international player.

goalkeeper Dickie Roose. He was in the team that slumped 5–1 to Scotland at Greenock just three weeks before the Ibrox Disaster claimed the lives of 26 people at the Scotland versus England game. He played in five successive internationals while at Liverpool with his high speed dribbling proving effective and was one of the biggest pre-season signings for the newly-elected City club.

Morris's lone Wales appearance while a City player produced one of the principality's finest results to date. The previous season, inspired by the great wing wizard Billy Meredith, they had beaten Scotland for the first time after 30 years of trying. But few gave the Welsh any hope of repeating the feat when they tackled the Scots at Tynecastle 12 months later, because Manchester City star Meredith was serving a suspension for allegedly bribing an Aston Villa player to lose a match.

Dickie Morris, second from right, front row, lines up for Wales before the 1907 international against Ireland.

The Welsh selectors were also without several other regulars but the stand-ins, some drawn from League clubs' reserve sides, did their country proud. Meredith's replacement, Lot Jones, opened the scoring when goalkeeper Jimmy Raeside allowed a shot to slip through his hands. Another Jones, Stoke reserve John, who had come in for Notts County's Arthur Green, added another to give Wales a 2–0 win and surprise back-to-back victories against the Scots.

Morris spent only one season at Leeds, moving on to Grimsby Town, where he scored one of the goals in a 3–2 win against Ireland in 1907, which helped Wales win the Home International crown for the first time. Once again he moved on in the summer, joining Plymouth where, as he had at Leeds, he became their first international player when he won his final cap in 1908 – a 1–0 defeat to Ireland in Aberdare.

BILLY SCOTT

(Ireland 1903–13)
Goalkeeper
Born: Belfast, 1 January 1883.
Died: Liverpool, 16 August 1936.
Caps: Everton 21, Leeds City 3. Total: 24

FOOTBALL hooliganism is not a modern trait. Leeds City's star goalkeeper Billy Scott witnessed a near-riot in his final international with Ireland which saw an opposition player arrested and another attacked. The extraordinary scenes that followed Scotland's 2–1 win at Dublin's Dalymount Park remain some of the most shocking ever seen in football.

Scott and his brother, Elisha, are rated Ireland's best pre-war goalkeepers. Between them they played 56 times for their country – Billy making 25 appearances, several as captain, and his younger brother 31. The final three of Billy's games were as a Leeds player and included the infamous Scotland clash and Ireland's first-ever victory against England. He started his career as an amateur with Cliftonville but made his name at Linfield, with whom he

won an Irish League and Cup double in 1902 and 1904. Inter-League and full international honours soon followed before a high-profile transfer to Everton, where he made more than 250 League appearances and won an FA Cup-winners' medal in 1906 when the Goodison Park side beat Newcastle United 1–0 in the Final at Crystal Palace.

Utterly reliable, several eyebrows were raised when Herbert Chapman signed him for Leeds City in a controversial transfer. Chapman agreed to pay Scott a full year's salary of £208 from June 1912 to the following April. That was effectively two months extra wages and above the allowed £4 a week. As a result Leeds were fined and Scott ordered to repay the extra cash.

Scott's last international before he joined Leeds saw him on the receiving end of a 6–1 thrashing by England, but there was no way the Irish selectors were going to drop him. In those days the only Irish internationals were in the British Championship and Scott retained his place for the 1913 Home Internationals. It started with a 1–0 defeat on Distillery's ground against a Welsh side including four new

Irish goalkeeper Billy Scott.

W. SCOTT (Goal)
IRELAND.

caps, one of whom, Wrexham's James Roberts, scored the only goal after five minutes. On the same day, Leeds City, with Tony Hogg replacing Scott in between the uprights, beat Bradford City 2–0 in an Elland Road mudbath.

Hogg kept his place, but Scott still played in Ireland's next game, an historic 2–1 win against England. It was the first time Ireland had beaten England in 32 attempts, and the sequence looked set to be extended at Windsor Park when Charlie Buchan put the visitors ahead. With Ireland's inside-left Jim Macauley limping, it looked odds on England would win, but Scott kept them at bay with some great saves. Former Leeds forward Billy Gillespie, now knocking in goals at Sheffield United, scored twice to earn Ireland a wonderful win. While Scott was lapping up the plaudits, Leeds had lost 6–0 at Stockport the same afternoon and the Irishman won his City place back. However, nothing would have prepared him for the events that were about to unfold in Dublin the following month.

Despite dominating for long periods, Ireland lost 2–1 to Scotland but the crowd were incensed that English referee Arthur Adams had allowed Alec Bennett's winning goal to stand as the Rangers man looked offside. At the final whistle, several Scottish players tried to grab the ball as a souvenir, Sheffield Wednesday's George Robertson emerging with the leather, only to have it knocked out of his hands by a spectator, Patrick Gartland. It was picked up by Ireland's American-born player Billy Andrews, but in the struggle that followed Gartland was knocked over. Rumour quickly spread that Robertson had broken Gartland's leg, and a furious mob gathered outside the Scottish dressing room, smashing windows. The Scots were locked in for more than an hour and Robertson, a school teacher by profession, was arrested and taken to a police station. The Irish FA, keen to diffuse the situation, agreed to pay the costs of the injured Gartland, who dropped the charges against Robertson, who was released. But the Irish mob continued to vent their fury and followed the Scottish party back to their hotel, where Swindon full-back Jock Walker was attacked outside.

It was an extraordinary end to Scott's fine international career, and a couple of seasons later his brother Elisha, whom Billy had recommended to Everton, became his long-term successor in the Irish team.

Internationals Before Joining Leeds United

MANSOUR ASSOUMANI
(Mali)

Defender

Caps: Montpellier 1

Tall French-born defender Mansour Assoumani had one appearance for the Mali national team to his name when he joined United on a one-month contract. The former Montpellier player, whose parents originate from the Coromos, played once for Leeds, in a 3–1 defeat at MK Dons in December 2008, Gary McAllister's last game in charge. He later joined Wrexham.

HUGH BAIRD
(Scotland 1956)

Centre-forward

Caps: Airdrie 1

Free-scoring forward Hugh Baird made his sole appearance for Scotland in a 1–1 draw with Austria in front of 90,000 at Hampden in 1956. The following summer Leeds bought him from Airdrie for £12,000, but 16 months later he was back in Scotland with Aberdeen. Until the 1970s the SFA only awarded caps for matches in the Home Championships, and it was 50 years after the Austrian game that he actually received his cap.

NICK BARMBY
(England 1988–95)

Midfield / Forward

Caps: Tottenham Hotspur 2, Middlesbrough 8, Everton 5, Liverpool 8. Total 23

Goals: 4

Nick Barmby played in England's famous 5–1 win in Germany barely a year before joining Leeds for an injury-hit spell in August 2002. He became the first graduate from the FA National School to make a senior England appearance when he made his debut in a 0–0 draw with Uruguay.

JIM BEGLIN
(Republic of Ireland 1984–87)

Full-back

Caps: Liverpool 15

Jim Beglin, a member of United's 1990 Division Two Championship-winning squad, also played in a B international when the Republic beat England 4–1 at Cork while he was a Leeds player. Of his 15 caps, five were World Cup qualifiers in 1985.

NATHAN BLAKE
(Wales 1994–2004)

Forward

Caps: Sheffield United 5, Bolton Wanderers 5, Blackburn Rovers 12, Wolverhampton Wanderers 7. Total: 29

Goals: 4

A big, strong, powerful forward, Nathan Blake's international career lasted 10 years – considerably longer than his spell on loan at Leeds from Leicester. He scored on his second appearance – a 2–1 win at Coventry – but came off in the next, an FA Cup defeat at the Hawthorns, with a ruptured hamstring and did not play League football again.

TOMAS BROLIN
(Sweden 1990–95)

Forward

Caps: Norkopping 5, Parma 42. Total: 47

Goals: 26

Regarded as a figure of fun while at Leeds, the overweight version of Tomas Brolin, who had continual run-ins with George Graham, was nothing like the razor-sharp striker worshipped in Sweden. He did not look back after netting twice on his international debut against Wales in April 1990. He played in the 1990 and 1994 World Cups, the Swedes finishing third in the latter, and in the 1992 European Championships he scored in a win against England as Sweden went on to reach the semi-finals. Brolin broke a foot against Hungary in November 1994 and was never the same player again.

GEORGE BROWN
(England 1926–32)

Centre-forward

Caps: Huddersfield Town 8, Aston Villa 1. Total: 9

Goals: 5

Three times a Championship-winner with Huddersfield Town, George Brown was 32 when he joined Leeds in September 1935. He scored eight minutes into his England debut in a 3–3 draw with Ireland and hit doubles against Belgium (9–1) and France (6–0) in 1927. He was top scorer in his only season at Leeds in 1935–36.

KENNY BURNS
(Scotland 1974–81)

Central-defender

Caps: Birmingham City 8, Nottingham Forest 12. Total: 20

Goals: 1

Burns started life as a striker but developed into a rock-hard defender during the Clough-Taylor years at Nottingham Forest. After being named Footballer of the Year in 1978, Kenny Burns played in the World Cup Finals against Peru and Iran in Argentina. He alternated between defence and midfield during United's 1981–82 relegation season. Burns's sole Scotland goal came in a 3–0 win against East Germany in a 1974 friendly at Hampden.

PAUL BUTLER
(Republic of Ireland 2000)
Central-defender
Caps: Sunderland 1
Paul Butler qualified to play for the Republic because his wife was Irish, and his only game saw him up against enormous Czech striker Jan Koller. Ireland trailed 2–0 at the interval thanks to two Koller goals, Butler was substituted at the interval and Ireland won 3–2. He captained United for two seasons after their relegation from the Premiership.

ZOUMANA CAMARA
(France 2001)
Central-defender
Caps: Marseille 1
One of several French loan men to arrive at Elland Road as the club started to slide out of the Premiership, Lens defender Zoumana Camara played once for France in a 1–0 Confederations Cup defeat to Australia in June 2001.

STEPHEN CRAINEY
(Scotland 2002–04)
Left-back
Caps: Celtic 4, Southampton 2. Total: 6
Crainey played in Bertie Vogts first game in charge as Scotland manager – a 5–0 thumping by France in Paris. He only avoided defeat once as a Scotland player, and that was in a 2–2 draw with the Faroe Islands. He endured a tough time with injuries and lack of confidence at Leeds but has shaped well at Blackpool.

KEN De MANGE
(Republic of Ireland 1987–88)
Midfield
Caps: Liverpool 1, Hull City 1. Total 2
International honours bypassed Ken De Mange in his six-month stay at Elland Road. He arrived from Liverpool without any League experience but had already won an Eire cap in a famous 1–0 win against Brazil in Dublin when he replaced skipper Mick McCarthy for the final half-hour. His other Irish outing was also off the bench, in a 4–0 win against Tunisia, after he left Leeds.

BRIAN DEANE
(England 1991)
Forward
Caps: Sheffield United 2
Both muscular striker Brian Deane's England games came on tour in back-to-back games against New Zealand, which were won 1–0 and 2–0. He came on at half-time in the first and came off at the interval in the second. He had two spells with Leeds – July 1993 to July 1997 and July 2004 to March 2005, scoring 45 goals.

UGO EHIOGU
(England 1996–2002)
Central-defender
Caps: Aston Villa 1, Middlesbrough 3. Total: 4
All defender Ugo Ehioghu's international appearances were as a substitute. The first came in a 3–0 win in China as a replacement for Tony Adams. He then had to wait nearly five years for his next, against Spain. The last came at Elland Road in a 2–1 defeat to Italy. Ehiogu, who had a couple of months on loan at Leeds from Middlesbrough in 2006–07, also made 21 appearances at Under-21 level and won an England B cap.

TORE ANDRE FLO
(Norway 1995–2004)
Forward
Caps: Tromso 4, SK Brann 13, Chelsea 38, Glasgow Rangers 8, Sunderland 6, Siena 8. Total: 76
Goals: 23
Tore Andre Flo's 23 goals make him Norway's joint fourth-highest scorer along with Ole Gunnar Solskjaer. Excellent in the air and a sure touch on the ground, he made his international debut in a 0–0 draw with England in October 1995 in Oslo. He opened his scoring account in a 3–2 defeat against Trinidad & Tobago the following month. Nicknamed 'Flonaldo' by Norwegian fans, he scored in a 2–1 win over World Cup holders Brazil as they reached the second round in 1998. He turned up at Leeds in January 2007 but announced his retirement 14 months later. The following year he made a comeback with MK Dons. His brother Jostein, and cousin, Harvard Flo, also played for Norway.

HAYDEN FOXE
(Australia 1998–2003)
Central-defender
Caps: Arminia Belefield 1, Sanfrecce Hiroshima 8, West Ham United 5, Portsmouth 1. Total: 15
Goals: 2
Big Hayden Foxe was a member of the Socceroos 1996 and 2000 Olympic squads. His full debut came in a 0–0 draw with

the US in San Jose in November 1998. After playing in Germany and Japan, he made his way to England to play for West Ham and Portsmouth, suffering a two-year injury nightmare at Pompey before pitching up at Elland Road on a five-month contract. His Aussie goals came in victories against Fiji (2–0) and an 11–0 crushing of Samoa in 2001, both at Coffs Harbour.

DOUGIE FREEDMAN

(Scotland 2001–02)

Forward

Caps: Crystal Palace 2

Goals: 1

Vital goals from former Scotland international striker Dougie Freedman helped take Leeds to Wembley for the 2008 League One Play-offs. He was brought in by fellow Scot Gary McAllister on loan from Crystal Palace and was a key man as United finished the season strongly. Freedman was handed his first international start by Craig Brown, responding with a goal in a 2–1 win against Latvia in a World Cup qualifier. He also played in Bertie Vogts' first game in charge – a 5–0 thumping in France.

COLIN GRAINGER

(England 1956–57)

Winger

Caps: Sheffield United 6, Sunderland 1. Total: 7

Goals: 3

Two goals on his England debut in a 4–2 triumph against Brazil in front of 100,000 fans – what a start to international football for Colin Grainger. The match – in which John Atyeo and Roger Byrne both missed penalties – was reckoned to be one of the greatest ever seen beneath the Twin Towers and included a goal for 41-year-old Stanley Matthews. Grainger, not surprisingly, could not top it, although a goal in Berlin in a 3–1 win against world champions West Germany came close. After starring with Sheffield United and Sunderland, his time at Leeds was disrupted by a cartilage operation in 1961. Known as the 'Singing Winger', crooner Grainger's cousin Dennis played for Leeds while his nephew, Ed Holliday, also played for England.

MICHAEL GRAY

(England 1999)

Left-back

Caps: Sunderland 3

Michael Gray's three England appearances came in a six-week period against Hungary, Sweden and Bulgaria – all draws. The goalless affair against the Swedes at Wembley saw Manchester United's Paul Scholes become the first player sent off while playing for England at home. Gray had two loan spells with Leeds in 2005 and 2007 while registered with Blackburn.

JOEL GRIFFITHS

(Australia 2005–08)

Winger

Caps: Neuchatel Xamax 1, Newcastle Jets 2. Total: 3

Goals: 1

Joel Griffiths hoped his move to Leeds United would help him force his way into the Socceroos 2006 World Cup squad. He had been playing in Switzerland with Neuchatel Xamax and had made his Aussie debut in October 2005, scoring in a 5–0 win against Jamaica at Craven Cottage. But he made just two substitute appearances with the Whites and did not make the Australian party for the Finals, despite being in the squad for the Play-offs with Uruguay. He returned Down Under and was a big hit with Newcastle Jets, winning two further caps against Kuwait and Ghana. His twin brother Adam and younger brother Ryan, have also played for Australia.

STEVE GUPPY

(England 1999)

Left-winger

Caps: Leicester City 1

England boss Kevin Keegan briefly turned to Leicester City's Steve Guppy to solve a left-side attacking conundrum. The experiment lasted just one game, a 2–1 win against Belgium at the Stadium of Light. The former Port Vale and Glasgow Celtic man also made just one start for Leeds, scoring and conceding a penalty against Nottingham Forest at Elland Road.

MARK HATELEY

(England 1984–92)

Forward

Caps: Portsmouth 4, AC Milan 20, AC Monaco 7, Glasgow Rangers 1. Total: 32

Goals: 9

Mark Hateley burst onto the international scene with a thumping headed goal on his full debut in a sensational 2–0 win in Brazil. A huge transfer to AC Milan followed, and his goals helped England to the 1986 World Cup Finals in which he started the group games against Portugal and Morocco. He arrived at Leeds, aged 34, on a month's loan in August 1996, figured in half a dozen games, did not score and went back to parent club Queen's Park Rangers.

DANNY HAY

(New Zealand 1998–2007)

Central-defender

Caps: Perth Glory 16, Walsall 5, Auckland Kingz 1, Perth Glory 10, Waitakere United 2. Total: 34

Goals: 2

Man mountain Danny Hay should have felt at home in the Leeds United strip as he had been a regular with the All Whites – New Zealand's national team. A £200,000 squad man, he rarely played for Leeds and did not get his place in the Kiwi side back after he joined Walsall in 2002. He captained New Zealand to their first international win on European soil in May 2006 when they beat Georgia 3–1 in Germany. Another highlight was scoring the only goal in the Oceania Cup semi-final in 1998. In 2007 he retired from international football in order to pursue a teaching career.

STEVE HODGE
(England 1986–91)
Midfield
Caps: Aston Villa 11, Tottenham Hotspur 4, Nottingham Forest 9. Total: 24
Steve Hodge played in the 1986 World Cup, including the famous 'Hand of God' quarter-final against Argentina. After the final whistle he swapped shirts with match-winner Diego Maradona and has since loaned the top to the National Football Museum in Preston. Signed by Leeds for £900,000 from Forest, he did not command a regular place because of injury and left for Queen's Park Rangers in 1994. He also won eight Under-21 caps.

GORDON HODGSON
(England 1930–1931)
Centre-forward
Caps: Liverpool 3
Goals: 1
Powerhouse Gordon Hodgson was born in South Africa and won amateur caps for that country. A major star on a tour of England in 1924–25, he signed for Liverpool and set seasonal and aggregate scoring records until they were broken by Roger Hunt. He was the only forward not to score on his England debut, a 5–1 win against Ireland at Bramall Lane in 1930, but netted in the next, a 4–0 win against Wales in Wrexham. He played for Leeds for a couple of seasons before World War Two and was on the coaching staff before becoming Port Vale's manager.

SETH JOHNSON
(England 2000)
Midfield
Caps: Derby County 1
Caretaker manager Peter Taylor handed Seth Johnson 18 minutes of senior international football when he came on for Gareth Barry in a 1–0 friendly defeat in Turin, where Gennaro Gattuso's goal gave Italy a 1–0 win in November 2000. Johnson had been a regular in Taylor's Under-21 team, but his time at Leeds was bedevilled by a succession

of injuries and had little chance to live up to his £7 million transfer from Derby, where he returned on a free.

JOCK MacDOUGALL
(Scotland)
Centre-half
Caps: Airdrie 1
A rock in the heart of Airdrie's defence as they won the 1924 Scottish Cup, Jock MacDougall was hardly tested in his only international. The Scots thumped Ireland 4–0 at Ibrox in February 1926, Hughie Gallacher scoring a hat-trick. Despite top form at Sunderland, from whom he joined Leeds in November 1934, MacDougall was never called upon by Scotland again. His younger brother Jimmy, a Liverpool inside-forward, played for Scotland twice.

ALBERT McINROY
(England 1926)
Goalkeeper
Caps: Sunderland 1
Albert McInroy picked the ball out of the net just five minutes into his England debut. He was beaten by former Leeds City man Billy Gillespie, for whom it was a record-breaking 13th goal for Ireland. The game, at Anfield, finished 3–3. McInroy, who won an FA Cup-winners' medal with Newcastle, was 34 when he joined Leeds for a couple of seasons in 1935.

EDDIE McMORRAN
(Northern Ireland 1946–57)
Centre-forward
Caps: Belfast Celtic 1, Barnsley 9, Doncaster Rovers 5
Total: 15
Goals: 4
Former blacksmith Eddie McMorran was Northern Ireland's regular number nine in the early 1950s. He actually won his first cap while with Belfast Celtic in a 7–2 whipping by England in the first Home International game after the war. Unsuccessful spells with Manchester City and Leeds (January 1949 – July 1950) passed without further international call-ups, but he rediscovered his goal touch at Barnsley and scored on his return to the Irish team in 1950 with their goal in a 4–1 defeat against England. He also scored twice as Northern Ireland lost 3–2 to Wales in 1953, and his final games came in World Cup qualifiers against Italy and Portugal.

JOHN O'HARE
(Scotland 1970–72)
Forward
Caps: Derby County 13
Goals: 5

A Brian Clough signing, bustling forward John O'Hare did not stay long at Leeds and went on to enjoy great success with 'Old Big 'Ead' at Nottingham Forest; however, all his games for Scotland were when he was with Cloughie at Derby, scoring winners against Northern Ireland and Denmark in his early games. His goals also helped the Scots beat Belgium and Portugal in European Championship qualifiers and Peru in a friendly.

JOHN OSTER
(Wales 1998–2004)
Winger
Caps: Everton 3, Sunderland 10. Total: 13
John Oster won his first cap in 1998 without kicking a ball. The Everton winger came on as a very late substitute against Belgium, and the final whistle came before he got a touch. He faced Brazil and Jamaica later the same year before being sent off in successive Under-21 matches against Italy. He left Goodison Park for Sunderland, where he was in and out of the team and had spells out on loan, including one at Leeds. Kevin Blackwell sent Oster back to the Black Cats in disgrace after he was found guilty of a breach of discipline at United's Christmas party in 2004, the year of his last appearance for Wales against Northern Ireland in 2004.

CARLTON PALMER
(England 1992–93)
Midfield
Caps: Sheffield Wednesday 18
Goals: 1
Carlton Palmer's telescopic legs ate up the England midfield during Graham Taylor's reign. His only goal came in 6–0 romp against San Marino – a match best remembered, or forgotten, for David Platt's last-minute penalty miss, which would have seen him join Willie Hall and Malcolm MacDonald as the only men to score five in a game for England. Palmer played exactly 100 League games for Leeds.

DEREK PARLANE
(Scotland 1973–77)
Centre-forward
Caps: Glasgow Rangers 12
Goal: 1
Derek Parlane scored heaps of goals for Rangers, but he could not replicate that record with either Leeds or Scotland. His only international strike was the last goal in a 3–0 win against Northern Ireland at Hampden in 1975. He also won five Under-23 caps and one at Under-21 level.

MICHAEL RICKETTS
(England 2002)
Forward
Caps: Bolton Wanderers 1
A stack of goals for Bolton earned Michael Ricketts an England cap and a big money move to Middlesbrough. He was given 45 minutes in the Amsterdam Arena by Sven-Goran Eriksson in a 1–1 draw with Holland before being replaced by Kevin Phillips. That proved the peak of his career, which included a brief, unproductive, spell at Leeds in 2004–05.

DAVID ROBERTSON
(Scotland 1992–94)
Left-back
Caps: Glasgow Rangers 3
George Graham signing David Robertson struggled to settle at Elland Road with injury leading to a lack of confidence. The left-back made his international debut for Andy Roxburgh when an Ally McCoist goal saw off Northern Ireland at Hampden Park in February 1992. He also played in a World Cup qualifier against Switzerland and a friendly against Holland.

DAVID ROCASTLE
(England 1988–92)
Midfield
Caps: Arsenal 14
A silky smooth midfielder with Arsenal, Rocastle's England debut came in September 1988 when Neil Webb's goal beat Denmark at Wembley. He played in several qualifiers for the 1990 World Cup but did not make Bobby Robson's final squad of 22. He had a dreadful 16 months at Leeds after a £2 million switch from Highbury, suffering from a lack of form and fitness. 'Rocky' died of cancer, aged just 33, in March 2001.

IAN RUSH
(Wales 1980–96)
Forward
Caps: Liverpool 32, Juventus 6, Liverpool 35. Total: 73
Goals: 28
Wales's record goalscorer, Ian Rush scored 346 goals in two spells with Liverpool, whom he joined from Chester as an 18-year-old. He was still a reserve at Anfield when he made his Wales debut against Scotland in May 1980. Although his extraordinary predatory instincts could give Wales a vital edge in games, they were not expected to win, and he never played in the Finals of a major international tournament. He did score some memorable victories for the principality, none more so than the Euro

'92 qualifying win against Germany. Signed in the winter of his career by Leeds boss Howard Wilkinson, Rush found himself stuck on the right of midfield after George Graham took over from Wilko. In 2007 Rush was appointed Elite Performance Director for the Welsh Football Trust, a part-time role in which he will help develop the next generation of Welsh players.

ARMANDO SA

(Mozambique 2002–06)

Defender

Caps: Benfica, Villareal, Espanyol. Total: 21

Versatile defender Armando Sa had a decent pedigree in Portugal and Spain before being signed on loan for Leeds by Dennis Wise. Mozambique produced the great Eusebio, but he played on the world stage with Portugal and recent sides from the island have struggled to make an impact in both World Cup and African Nationals qualifiers. Russian coach Victor Bondarenko did get them to the 2003 World Cup Play-offs, but they lost both matches to Guinea with Sa playing in each game.

LEE SHARPE

(England 1991–93)

Winger

Caps: Manchester United 8

England were struggling against the Republic of Ireland in a European Championship qualifier at Wembley in March 1991 when manager Graham Taylor binned the wing-back system at half-time and brought on winger Lee Sharpe for his debut. The game finished 1–1 and Sharpe did not get another chance until two years later as a sub in a 2–0 World Cup qualifying win in Turkey. He figured in four games in the ill-fated pre-tournament campaign and also made eight Under-21 appearances. Howard Wilkinson's last signing for Leeds, he did not fit in with George Graham's plans in an injury-hit time at Elland Road.

ENOCH SHOWUNMI

(Nigeria 2004)

Forward

Caps: Luton Town 2

Born in Kilburn, London, of Nigerian parents, towering striker Enoch Showunmi went from playing with non-League Willesden Constantine in the Middlesex County League to international football in a few months. The Luton striker played a couple of games in the Unity Cup competition in London, featuring against the Republic of Ireland and Jamaica in May 2004. A former advertising body double for French international Patrick Viera, he joined Leeds in August 2008 from Bristol City, but a blood clot on a lung ended his season at Christmas.

ERIC SMITH

(Scotland 1959)

Wing-half

Caps: Glasgow Celtic 2

With Dave Mackay around, Eric Smith did not get many opportunities with Scotland. He did, however, go on the 1959 summer tour when he played in a 1–0 win in Holland and a 1–0 defeat in Portugal. He also played in a 3–3 tour opener in Aarhus against Jutland, which is regarded as an unofficial international. He joined Leeds the following year, moving back to Scotland with Greenock Morton, where he started a successful coaching career, which included a stint under Don Revie in the Middle East.

SAM SODJE

(Nigeria 2005–06)

Central-defender

Caps: Brentford 1, Reading 1, unattached 1. Total: 3

Sam Sodje will not forget his Nigerian debut in a hurry. At late notice the Nigerian FA arranged a friendly in Bucharest on 16 November 2005, but did not give several of their top players sufficient time to get clearance from their clubs to play. The game was arranged, called off, then given the go-ahead. Consequently, just four hours before the kick-off the Super Eagles squad arrived with just six players, no manager and no kit. The game was put back two hours while the NFA recruited Nigerian-born players based in Romania and the game went ahead – a further 20 minutes late. Sodje had been starring with Brentford at the time, and picked up an injury during the Romanian game, but was forced to play on because of a lack of substitutes. In the circumstances Nigeria did well to only lose 3–0. Sodje's bandana-wearing brother Efe, also a defender, played for Nigeria in the 2002 World Cup. Sodje went to Leeds on loan at the end of 2008–09 and helped the Whites reach the League One Play-offs before returning to his parent club. He was then released just days before making his third appearance for Nigeria in a 1–1 draw with the Republic of Ireland at Fulham.

MEL STERLAND

(England 1988)

Right-back

Caps: Sheffield Wednesday 1

Dubbed 'Zico' by Sheffield Wednesday fans, Mel Sterland's coveted England cap came in a friendly against Saudi Arabia in Riyadh in November 1988. Ex-Leeds junior David Seaman and his Arsenal teammates Michael Thomas, Brian Marwood and Alan Smith also made their debuts in an experimental England side. Sterland won Division One and Two titles with Leeds. He also won seven Under-21 caps.

STEVE STONE

(England 1995–96)

Midfield

Caps: Nottingham Forest 9

Goals: 2

Injury forced right-side midfielder Steve Stone to end his career at Leeds, where he only managed a handful of appearances. At his peak he was an industrious and intelligent player, making his debut as a substitute for Dennis Wise in a 0–0 draw in Norway in October 1995. The Forest man scored in each of his next two games – a 3–1 win against Switzerland and a 1–1 draw with Portugal – both at Wembley. A member of Terry Venables's Euro '96 squad, he came off the bench to face Switzerland and Scotland in the group stages and Spain in the quarter-finals.

NEIL SULLIVAN

(Scotland 1997–2003)

Goalkeeper

Caps: Wimbledon 16, Tottenham Hotspur 12. Total: 28

Extremely consistent at Leeds, Neil Sullivan made his Scotland debut in a 1–0 defeat to Wales at Rugby Park, Kilmarnock. He was the regular 'keeper for the Euro 2000 campaign, which ended with a 2–1 aggregate defeat against England in a Play-off. He also played in several 2002 World Cup qualifiers, making his last appearance in a 2–0 friendly defeat against the Republic of Ireland in February 2003 when he was replaced by Dunfermline's Paul Gallacher at half-time. His Championship form with Leeds earned him a recall to the Scotland squad the following year, but he did not get to play.

PAUL TELFER

(Scotland 2000)

Defender

Caps: Coventry City 1

A nephew of former Scotland player Eamonn Bannon, Paul Telfer won three Under-21 caps and represented his country once in a 2–0 defeat against France in March 2000 at Hampden Park when he was substituted after 67 minutes. He came out of retirement in August 2008 to play under Gary McAllister's management at Leeds.

MICKEY THOMAS

(Wales 1977–86)

Midfield

Caps: Wrexham 11, Manchester United 13, Everton 1, Brighton & Hove Albion 5, Stoke City 10, Chelsea 9, West Bromwich Albion 2. Total: 51

Goals: 4

Much-travelled energetic midfielder Mickey Thomas was a Wales regular for the best part of a decade, making his debut in a 2–0 defeat against West Germany. One of his finest performances came when Wales thrashed England 4–1 at the Racecourse Ground, scoring the equaliser to set his side on their first home win against the Three Lions for 25 years. No stranger to controversy off the field, Thomas prided himself on his fitness, and the only major injury he sustained was with Leeds, where he managed just three starts in the 1989–90 Division Two title-winning season.

ALAN THOMPSON

(England 2004)

Midfield

Caps: Glasgow Celtic 1

Alan Thompson was one of many players Sven-Goran Eriksson tried to solve a thorny problem on the left of England's midfield. In Tommo's case the try-out lasted an hour, after which he was replaced by Emile Heskey in a 1–0 defeat in Gothenburg in March 2004. The match was to mark the centenary of the Swedish FA and was England's 11th game without a win against the Scandinavians. A former England Youth and Under-21 international, he shone with Newcastle, Bolton, Villa and Celtic, and his class was evident in his short injury-hit time at Elland Road, which saw him named captain. He filled in for one game as Dennis Wise's assistant after Gus Poyet's move to Tottenham.

TOM TOWNSLEY

(Scotland 1925)

Centre-half

Caps: Falkirk 1

Tom Townsley captained Scotland on his only appearance. He kept the Welsh forwards off the scoresheet at Ninian Park at the end of October 1925, although it was made easier after Welsh captain Fred Keenor dislocated a knee in the second minute. John 'Tokey' Duncan, Adam McLean and Willie Clunas ended the resistance with goals in the final 15 minutes of a 3–0 win. Townsley was great at Leeds, making 167 appearances after his move from Falkirk.

BOBBY TURNBULL

(England 1919)

Right-winger

Caps: Bradford Park Avenue 1

Middlesbrough-born right winger Bobby Turnbull dazzled with Leeds's neighbours Bradford Park Avenue for almost seven years. He earned one cap against Ireland in 1919 when Jack Cock gave England the lead after just 30 seconds, but had to settle for a 1–1 Windsor Park draw. He also played in three Victory internationals, scoring in a 2–2 draw with Scotland at Goodison Park. Turnbull also toured South Africa with the FA the following year, playing in all three Test matches. Although not capped during his six seasons at Leeds, he did tour South Africa again in 1929, playing twice more in 'Tests'.

DAVID WHITE

(England 1992)

Winger

Caps: Manchester City 1

David White had a great chance to make a name for himself on his England debut against Spain in Santander in September 1992. The Manchester City man was clean through on goal after just two minutes, missed, and Gregorio Fonseca netted the only goal 10 minutes later. White, who also represented his country at Youth, Under-21 and B level, had two frustrating years at Elland Road battling against ankle problems.

JOCK WHITE

(Scotland 1922–23)

Inside-forward

Caps: Albion Rovers 1, Heart of Midlothian 1. Total: 2

Snow and sleet turned Wrexham's Racecourse Ground into a snow-covered ice rink for Jock White's Scotland debut against Wales. He was one of seven new caps who emerged from the blizzard defeated 2–1. The following year his second appearance came in a 1–0 win in Ireland. Considering his fantastic goalscoring record with Hearts, it is surprising he did not play more for Scotland. Leeds paid a huge £5,600 fee for White, who scored 38 goals in 108 games before returning to Hearts in 1930. His brother-in-law, Andy Anderson, also played for Scotland and Hearts.

KEN WILLINGHAM

(England 1937–39)

Right-half

Caps: Huddersfield Town 12

Goal: 1

Ken Willingham stood shoulder-to-shoulder with Wilf Copping on his England debut –no wonder the amateurs of Finland never got a look-in. England cruised to an 8–0 win in Helsinki, Willingham joining the attack to score on 77 minutes. Sterner tests followed, but the stylish Willingham always rose to the occasion, even keeping the Continent's best off the scoresheet as England beat the Rest of Europe 3–0 at Highbury in 1938. He saw out his career with Leeds after the war and had a couple of seasons on the coaching staff before taking up a similar post with Halifax. A Football League representative six times, he was a wonderful all-round sportsman, having also run for England schools and played shinty at international level.

FRANK WORTHINGTON

(England 1974)

Forward

Caps: Leicester City 8

Goals: 2

Extraordinary entertainer Frank Worthington came to the fore with England in Joe Mercer's caretaker reign following the sacking of Sir Alf Ramsey. Jovial Joe went for flair in his line ups, and the cavalier Worthington was certainly in that category. Wonderfully gifted, he made an instant impact by coming on for another Mercer maverick, Stan Bowles, to enable England to beat Northern Ireland 1–0. Worthington scored on his third outing, a bruising 2–2 draw with Argentina at Wembley, and also hit the only goal in Bulgaria on a three-game Eastern European tour. New boss Don Revie kept faith with Worthington for his first game in charge, a Euro qualifier against Czechoslovakia, and dropped him to the bench for the next game against Portugal before leaving him out of the action altogether after that. At Leeds his goals were not quite enough to prevent United from relegation in 1982.

TOMMY YOUNGER

(Scotland 1955–58)

Goalkeeper

Caps: Hibernian 8, Liverpool 16. Total: 24

After Scotland's 7–2 defeat at Wembley Tommy Younger replaced Aberdeen's Fred Martin in goal, playing in the next 24 matches, the last four as captain. He led the Scots in the 1958 World Cup in Sweden when they drew 1–1 with Yugoslavia and lost 3–2 to Paraguay, in what was his final international. Big, strong and brave, Younger was only on the losing side with Scotland six times. He saw out his career in a short spell at Elland Road, returning to Scotland, where he ran a successful vending machine business, became a director at his old club, Hibs, and was appointed president of the Scottish FA in 1983. He was still in that post when he died in January 1954.

Note: Centre-forward Frank McKenna won three England amateur caps and also represented Great Britain in an Olympic Games preliminary round match against Bulgaria. Other Leeds first-teamers to make amateur appearances for their country also include Billy Hudson (Wales) and Peter Lorimer (Scotland).

Note: Leeds signed Patrick Kisnorbo, an Australian international defender, from Leicester City in July 2009. The Melbourne-born player has won 14 full caps, the first against Vancouver in July 2002. His last match for the Aussies was a 3–1 defeat to Iraq in July 2007. Four days after his United debut against Exeter City on the opening day of the 2009–10 season he made his 15th appearance for the Aussies when he featured in a 3–0 win against the Republic of Ireland in Limerick.

Internationals After Leaving Leeds United

SCOTT CARSON

(England 2007– to date)

Goalkeeper

Caps: Liverpool 3

Senior international football may have come a bit too early for Scott Carson. Developed at Leeds, where he made just two Premiership starts, he was sold to Liverpool for £750,000 in January 2005 during the Whites' crippling financial crisis. He has since had long loan spells with a string of clubs and made his England debut against Austria in a friendly in Vienna in November 2007. Five days later Steve McClaren gave Carson his first competitive game in a European qualifier at Wembley, making a high-profile error in a damaging 3–2 defeat. Fabio Capello used Carson as a second-half replacement for David James in a 2–1 win in Germany in November 2008. The 'keeper has played for England B twice and the Under-21s 29 times, eight as a Leeds player.

TOM CASEY

(Northern Ireland 1955–58)

Wing-half

Caps: Newcastle United 10, Portsmouth 2. Total: 12

Goals: 2

A small non-stop midfield dynamo, Tom Casey moved from amateur football with Irish League club Bangor to the professional game with Leeds as a 19-year-old. The move came too early for him, but he did well at Bournemouth to earn a transfer to Newcastle, with whom he made his international debut against Wales in April 1955 when deputised for Bertie Peacock. He covered for Glasgow Celtic man Peacock several times and played three times in Northern Ireland's successful 1958 World Cup qualifying campaign, scoring in a 3–0 victory against Portugal in Belfast. He played twice in the Finals, in attack against West Germany and France. After the tournament he joined Portsmouth and kept his place up front for the first international of the season, scoring in a 3–3 draw with England in October 1958 when he shoulder-charged goalkeeper Colin McDonald over the line. Later that month Casey reverted back to his usual wing-half role, but the Irish were overwhelmed 6–2 by Spain in Madrid, Barcelona's Juston Tejada Martinez scoring four. It was Casey's last international outing. After his playing days were over he managed and coached extensively, including a spell with the Northern Ireland youth team. He died in Nailsea, Somerset, on 11 January 2009 at the age of 78.

CHRIS CROWE

(England 1962)

Winger

Caps: Wolverhampton Wanderers 1

England Youth star Chris Crowe was one of the few Leeds bright lights in the late 1950s, winning Under-23 caps against France and Scotland. He was sold to Blackburn before United were relegated and won a couple more Under-23 outings before joining Wolves, where he was elevated to full international status. His chance came against France at Hillsborough in October 1962 when manager Walter Winterbottom gambled on introducing four new caps – Crowe, Mike Hellawell (Birmingham City), Ray Charnley (Blackpool) and Crowe's Wolves teammate Alan Hinton – for a European Nations first-round match. It backfired, as England needed a controversial Ron Flowers penalty to nick a 1–1 draw, and the second leg produced a 5–2 French victory. Newcastle-born Crowe had represented Scotland Schools when his family lived in Edinburgh.

WARREN FEENEY

(Northern Ireland 2002– to date)

Forward

Caps: Bournemouth 3, Luton Town 15, Cardiff City 14. Total: 32

Goals: 5

United Youth player Warren Feeney was released without playing for the first team and joined Bournemouth on a free in 2001. He got his career going with the Cherries and has since played for Stockport, Luton and Cardiff, making his Northern Ireland debut against Liechtenstein in March 2002. The bulk of the hard-working Feeney's appearances have been as a substitute, but he contributed his most important goal to date with the winner in a 3–2 World Cup qualifying victory against Poland on 28 March 2009. His father Warren senior (Glentoran) and grandfather Jim (Linfield and Swansea) both played for Ireland.

JOHN JOE FLOOD

(Republic of Ireland 1926–31)

Inside-forward

Caps: Shamrock Rovers 5

Goals: 4

John Joe Flood had an eventful time in the early days of Republic of Ireland football. He and Italian goalkeeper Giovanni de Pra were both knocked out in a collision in the

Republic's first-ever international on 21 March 1926. He scored a hat-trick in his second outing, a 4–0 win against Belgium in Dublin. Flood was also on target as the Irish beat the same opposition 3–1 in Brussels in 1930. He captained the Irish side against Spain in his penultimate match. Flood and Bob Fullam both joined Leeds from Shamrock Rovers in 1923, but only Fullam played in the first team, and Flood returned to Ireland. Flood had a second go in England with Crystal Palace during 1926–27.

CALEB FOLAN
(Republic of Ireland 2008– to date)
Forward
Caps: Hull City 4
Republic of Ireland boss Steve Staunton invoked the 'granny rule' to acquire the services of Leeds-born striker Caleb Folan for the Euro 2008 qualifying campaign. The Wigan striker, whose grandparents came from Ireland, was issued a passport at the last minute, but injury prevented him from playing in the campaign and also ruled him out of friendlies with Ecuador and Bolivia. Staunton's replacement, Giovanni Trappatoni, sent on Folan as an injury-time sub for Kevin Doyle in a World Cup qualifier against Cyprus and handed him his first start in a 3–2 friendly defeat against Poland at Croke Park in November 2008. Folan had been a Leeds United trainee in the late 1990s, but did not make the first team. He joined Chesterfield, then Wigan, before becoming Hull City's first £1 million player in August 2007.

BOB FULLAM
(Republic of Ireland 1926–27)
Inside-forward
Caps: Shamrock Rovers 2
Goals: 1
Former docker Bob Fullam is credited with scoring the Republic of Ireland's first international goal in a 2–1 defeat at the hands of Italy B in Dublin on 27 April 1927. The previous year he and former Leeds reserve teammate John Joe Flood played in Turin in Ireland's first international match. He is regarded as one of Shamrock Rovers's most influential players of the inter-war years and also had a spell in the US, having a major hand in forming the Philadelphia Celtic club. He later coached Shamrock.

ANDY GRAY
(Scotland 2003)
Forward
Caps: Bradford City 2
The 18-year-old's performance at Wembley in the 3–0 defeat by Aston Villa in the 1996 League Cup Final was one of the few bright spots for Leeds. He did not really push on

from that performance and joined Nottingham Forest the following year, later playing for Bradford City, where he gained two Scotland caps. He came on in a European Championship qualifier in Kaunas in April 2002 shortly after Lithuania scored their match-winning penalty. The following month he came on for the last 30 minutes of a 1–1 draw with New Zealand at Hampden Park. A player in demand, big fees have since taken him to Sheffield United, Sunderland, Burnley and Charlton. His dad, Frank, and uncle, Eddie, both played for Leeds and Scotland.

PHIL HUGHES
(Northern Ireland 1986–87)
Goalkeeper
Caps: Bury 3
Phil Hughes opted to join Leeds after being released from Manchester United as a teenager. The former Northern Ireland Youth international managed a handful of games as cover for David Harvey before joining Bury. He went to the 1986 World Cup Finals, but did not play for his country until after the tournament, when the great Pat Jennings retired. Hughes played in Northern Ireland's first game after the tournament, a 3–0 defeat against England at Wembley in a European Championship qualifier. He kept a clean sheet against Turkey the following month and his final game came in a 1–1 draw with Israel.

WILLIE HUMPHRIES
(Northern Ireland 1962–65)
Winger
Caps: Ards 1, Coventry City 13. Total: 14
Goals: 1
Little Billy Humphries emerged as a speedy international winger a couple of years after leaving Elland Road. United snapped him up from Ards in September 1958, but he did not really settle and returned to the Irish club 14 months later. His first cap came in a 4–0 defeat against Wales in April 1962, and it was not long before he joined Coventry City, where he spent three productive years. He established himself on the Irish right wing and scored in their first European Championship game, a 2–0 win against Poland. He later played for Swansea before returning to Ards for a third time, playing until just short of his 40th birthday. He also won three amateur caps for Ireland.

DENIS IRWIN
(Republic of Ireland 1990–99)
Full-back
Caps: Manchester United 56
Goals: 4
Compact full-back Denis was definitely one that Leeds allowed to get away. He had developed as a youngster

under Eddie Gray's stewardship but was sold by Billy Bremner to Oldham in May 1986 for £60,000. The Latics sold him on to Manchester United for a profit in the region of £560,000 in 1990, and he became a cornerstone of the Old Trafford defence for the next dozen years. He made his debut for the Republic within months of his move to Manchester, playing in a 1–0 win against Morocco. That made him the first Irish player to be honoured at school, Youth, Under-21 and full level. Irwin became an instant regular for Eire for the next nine years, playing in the 1994 World Cup Finals. A dead ball specialist, he netted his first international goals against the United States and Belgium from free-kicks, and the last two with penalties against Croatia and Paraguay. Even when young rising Leeds United star Gary Kelly arrived on the scene at right-back, manager Jack Charlton ensured he kept Irwin in the team by moving him to the opposite flank. Cool, calm and collected, Irwin's last game came in a 0–0 draw in Turkey – a result which knocked the Republic out of the European Championship Play-offs – announcing his retirement after the match.

VINNIE JONES
(Wales 1994–97)
Midfield
Caps: Wimbledon 9
By and large controversial hard man Vinnie Jones kept out of trouble in his one season with Leeds, the Division Two title-winning campaign of 1989–90. Yet it took 'Psycho' just four games of his international career to get sent off – against Georgia in June 1995. The tough midfielder was in his second spell with Wimbledon when he was dismissed after 25 minutes for trampling on Mikhail Kavelashvili, and the Georgians went on to win the Euro qualifier 1–0, while Jones missed the rest of Wales's ill-fated campaign. Despite the red card, Jones did captain his adopted country, qualifying via his grandparents' birth in Ruthin, after a vote among Bobby Gould's squad. There was never any doubting Jones's commitment to Wales – he even had a red dragon tattooed on his chest. Since retiring in 1999 he has forged a successful career as an actor in America and remains one of the most popular players to have pulled on a Leeds shirt.

ANDY KEOGH
(Republic of Ireland 2007 – to date)
Forward
Caps: Wolverhampton Wanderers 11
Goals: 1
Andy Keogh was at Leeds United during Peter Ridsdale's big-spending era which saw the likes of Mark Viduka, Alan Smith, Harry Kewell, Robbie Fowler and Robbie Keane barring his way to the first team. The Republic

Under-19 player's only action was as a sub in a 2–1 Carling Cup defeat at Portsmouth in October 2004. Sold to Scunthorpe, his goals earned him a £600,000 move to Wolves. His Eire debut came in May 2007 when he was one of seven new starters who drew 1–1 with Ecuador in New York, Keogh having got his chance when another former Leeds junior, Caleb Folan, pulled out of the squad. His only international goal came in Giovanni Trappatoni's first game as Ireland's boss – an explosive last-minute shot which salvaged a 1–1 draw with Serbia at Croke Park.

JIM LANGLEY
(England 1958)
Left-back
Caps: Fulham 3
Londoner Jim Langley spent the 1952–53 season with United but blossomed on his return south, winning England B caps against West Germany, Yugoslavia and Scotland. After playing in all four 'Test' matches against South Africa on the FA's 1956 summer tour he joined Fulham where he formed a strong full-back partnership with George Cohen. Langley made his England debut at the same time as 19-year-old Bobby Charlton, just two months after the Munich Air Disaster, in a 4–0 hammering of the Scots in front of 130,000 at Hampden. In the next match England beat Portugal 2–1, but Langley missed a 70th-minute penalty, his shot striking an upright. Four days later, just a month before the start of the World Cup Finals, England melted in the Belgrade heat to a 5–0 caning by Yugoslavia, whose winger Alexandar Petakovic, the man being marked by Langley, scored a hat-trick. The performance saw Langley lose his expected World Cup squad place to Bolton's Tommy Banks.

AARON LENNON
(England 2006– to date)
Winger
Caps: Tottenham Hotspur 11
Leeds-born Aaron Lennon's rapid rise to England stardom has come as no surprise to any Whites fans who saw him dazzle at Elland Road as a youngster before his £1 million sale to Tottenham in July 2005. He shot through the Under-19, Under-21 and England B ranks to make his debut as a substitute in a 6–0 romp against Jamaica when Peter Crouch scored a hat-trick at Old Trafford in June 2006. He made the World Cup squad, coming off the bench against Trinidad & Tobago, Ecuador and, in the quarter-finals, Portugal. Lennon, blessed with incredible pace, is regarded as a successor to the right-flank berth occupied by David Beckham and figured in European qualifiers in Steve McClaren's reign before being given his chance by Fabio Capello.

TERRY PHELAN

(Republic of Ireland 1991–2000)

Full-back

Caps: Wimbledon 8, Manchester City 19, Chelsea 8, Everton 3, Fulham 4. Total: 42

Like fellow Irish international full-back Denis Irwin, Terry Phelan was released prematurely by Leeds boss Billy Bremner in 1986. Manchester-born, he qualified to wear the green shirt as his mother came from County Sligo and Phelan was capped at Youth, Under-21, Under-23 and B levels, becoming the world's most expensive defender when Manchester City signed him from Wimbledon for £2.5 million in September 1992. A lightning-quick left-back, he played in the 1994 World Cup Finals in the US, and his number of appearances is impressive considering he had versatile full-backs Denis Irwin, Gary Kelly, Steve Staunton and Jeff Kenna as competition.

ALEX SABELLA

(Argentina 1983)

Midfield

Caps: Estudiantes 4

After failing to sign teenager Diego Maradona, Sheffield United netted fellow Argentinian Alex Sabella instead. He moved to Leeds for £400,000 in 1980 but returned home after relegation to sign for Estudiantes. He made four appearances for the national team in the 1983 Copa America, including a victory against Brazil, but did not make manager Carlos Bilardo's squad for the 1986 World Cup. After retirement, Sabella became a coach, but he has worked mostly as assistant to Daniel Passarella. The pair coached the Argentina national team from 1994–98 and Uruguay from 1999–2000. They also teamed up at Italian club Parma, Mexican side Monterrey, Brazilian outfit Corinthians and River Plate of Argentina. Sabella was appointed coach of Estudiantes in March 2009.

JOHN SCALES

(England 1995)

Central-defender

Caps: Liverpool 3

Harrogate-born Scales left Leeds in 1985 after failing to make the first team, but became established at Bristol Rovers, triggering a move to Wimbledon's 'Crazy Gang'. The central defender joined Liverpool for £3.5 million and made three England appearances in the Umbro Cup against Japan, Sweden and Brazil. He seemed set to rejoin Leeds in 1996 but opted to sign for Tottenham, where his time was blighted by injury.

DAVID SEAMAN

(England 1988–2002)

Goalkeeper

Caps: Queen's Park Rangers 3, Arsenal 72. Total: 75

When young Seaman was at Elland Road he had the consistent John Lukic in front of him, so Eddie Gray sold the teenager to Peterborough in August 1982 for £4,000. Rotherham-born Seaman had no first-team experience but soon made his mark at Peterborough, earning a £100,000 move to Birmingham, where he won 10 Under-21 caps. In 1986 he played at Queen's Park Rangers on their infamous plastic pitch and was chosen for his England debut by Bobby Robson – a 1–1 draw against Saudi Arabia in November 1988. Seaman was being coached by former Arsenal and Scotland 'keeper Bob Wilson and in 1990 moved to Highbury, where he was to play for 13 years, winning a pile of honours. At Arsenal he took over between the posts from Lukic, the man whose form had barred his way at Elland Road eight years earlier. Seaman was chosen as the third goalkeeper for the 1990 World Cup behind Peter Shilton and Chris Woods, but had to pull out because of injury. Seaman was outstanding for Arsenal but was overlooked for the Euro '92 squad by Graham Taylor, who opted for Woods and Nigel Martyn, then a Crystal Palace player. It was only when Terry Venables took control of England selection that Seaman became the first choice. He was one of the stars of Euro '96, thanks to his penalty-saving heroics. He stopped a Gary McAllister spot-kick in the 2–0 group win against Scotland, and his save from Miguel Angel Nadal in the penalty shoot-out against Spain clinched England a place in the semi-finals, where the Three Lions lost 6–5 on penalties to Germany. Seaman played in the 1998 World Cup and Euro 2000 and made his 50th international appearance against Hungary in April 1999. Although he had lost some of his early athleticism, he was Sven-Goran Eriksson's number one for the 2002 World Cup, playing in every game, but shouldered responsibility for Ronaldinho's free-kick winner for Brazil in the quarter-finals. A couple of games later he struggled in a 2–2 European Championship qualifying draw at Southampton, which proved to be the last game of a wonderful international career.

HENRY SMITH

(Scotland 1988–92)

Goalkeeper

Caps: Heart of Midlothian 3

Like fellow goalkeeper Seaman, Lanarkshire-born Smith did not play senior football for the Whites but managed nearly 500 games for Hearts, winning three caps against Saudi Arabia, Northern Ireland and Canada. He was also in the Euro '92 squad as back-up to Andy Goram. He was Jimmy Adamson's first signing for Leeds, joining from Winterton Rangers in October 1978, but could not dislodge John Lukic or David Harvey. The nearest he got to first-team action was on the bench for a UEFA Cup tie against Romanian side Craiova.

PAUL WILLIAMS
(Northern Ireland 1991)
Forward / Defender
Caps: West Bromwich Albion 1

Son of Belfast-born Nobel Peace Prize winner Betty Williams, Paul signed for Leeds in the late 1970s and won international Youth honours, but did not make the first team. He played for numerous clubs after that with his only Northern Ireland senior appearance coming while he was at West Brom. Although the cap is treasured, the result was not – an embarrassing 1–1 draw with the Faroes in May 1991.

Note: Both Ken De Mange (Republic of Ireland) and Danny Hay (New Zealand) played for their countries before and after their time at Leeds United, but they were not honoured while at Elland Road.

Internationals Before Joining Leeds City

GEORGE LAW

(Scotland 1910)

Left-back

Caps: Rangers 3

All George Law's Scotland appearances came in the Home Internationals when he was a left-back with Rangers, from whom he joined Leeds in July 1912. Scotland beat England 2–0 in front of 111,000 at Hampden to clinch the title.

EVELYN LINTOTT

(England 1908–09)

Centre-half

Caps: Queen's Park Rangers 3, Bradford City 4. Total: 7

Evelyn Lintott combined teaching with football throughout his career. He won five amateur international caps and seven for the full senior England side. He joined City in June 1912 from the Paraders. A lieutenant in the 15th Battalion West Yorkshire Regiment (Prince of Wales Own), he died in the Battle of the Somme on 1 July 1916, aged 32.

HAYDEN PRICE

(Wales 1907–09)

Half-back

Caps: Aston Villa 1, Burton United 1, Wrexham 3. Total: 5

Hayden Price's first Welsh cap was won while he played with Aston Villa, usually in the reserves or third team. He played for City in 1909–10 and was later secretary/manager of Walsall and manager of Grimsby Town.

JIMMY SPEIRS

(Scotland 1908)

Inside-forward

Caps: Glasgow Rangers 1

Like Lintott, Jimmy Speirs died in World War One, cut down at Ypres on 20 August 1917. His sole cap was won in a 2–1 win against Wales at Dens Park, Dundee, in 1908. He skippered Bradford City's 1911 FA Cup-winning side when he headed the goal to beat Newcastle. Speirs joined Leeds for £1,400 in 1913.

Note: Distinguished journalist and author Ivan Sharpe won a gold medal with the Great Britain football team in the 1912 Olympics in Sweden. Although the team represented Britain, it was made up of entirely English players and wore the England strip. He won 12 amateur caps and had a full international trial when he was with Derby County in 1912. Sharpe joined City the following year and also returned to Leeds in November 1920 to play for United.

Internationals After Leaving Leeds City

MICK FOLEY
(Republic of Ireland 1926)
Half-back
Caps: Shelbourne 1
Signed from Shelbourne in 1910 as a teenager, Mick Foley made 133 first-team appearances in 10 years with City before returning to the Shels. At the age of 34 he captained the Republic of Ireland in their first international, a 3–0 defeat against Italy in Turin on 21 March 1926. It was his only international appearance.

BILLY GILLESPIE
(Northern Ireland 1913–30)
Forward
Caps: Sheffield United 25
Goals: 13
Young Billy Gillespie's chances at Leeds were few and far between after joining from Derry Celtic. He joined Sheffield United in December 1912 and became a Blades and Ireland legend, spending 17 seasons at Bramall Lane. He became an instant hero in his homeland, scoring both goals on his international debut as Ireland beat England for the first time, 2–1. He managed Derry City from 1932 to 1948.

BILLY HALLIGAN
(Northern Ireland 1911–12)
Inside-forward
Caps: Derby County 1, Wolverhampton Wanderers 1.
Total: 2
Goals: 1

Another of Frank Scott Walford's recruits from across the Irish Sea, former Distillery inside-forward Billy Halligan spent nine months at Elland Road before joining Derby for £400 in February 1910. He won his first cap with Derby, scoring in a 2–1 defeat against Wales. His second, and last, Irish appearance came in a 6–1 hammering by England when he was a Wolves player.

BILLY KIRTON
(England 1921)
Centre-forward
Caps: Aston Villa 1
Goals: 1
Slick centre-forward Billy Kirton was sold to Aston Villa for £500 in the infamous Leeds City auction after the club were chucked out of the Football League. He made 261 appearances for Villa, scoring the winning goal in the 1920 FA Cup Final against Huddersfield Town. He was also on the mark on his only England appearance – a 1–1 draw with Ireland in October 1921.

HARRY MILLERSHIP
(Wales 1920 – 1921)
Right-back
Caps: Rotherham County 6
Another of the auctioned men, Chirk-born Harry Millership fetched £1,000 and was on his way to Rotherham County, where he won six Welsh caps in the 1920 and 1921 Home Championships.

Leeds United's International Managers

This section covers players, managers and backroom staff of Leeds United who have worked as international managers.

GEORGE AINSLEY

(Ghana 1958–59, Pakistan 1961–62, Israel 1964)

GLOBE-TROTTING George Ainsley spread the football gospel throughout the world in a long and varied coaching career. The South Shields-born inside-forward played for Sunderland and Bolton before joining Leeds in December 1936. Together with clubmate Ken Gadsby, he went on an FA tour of South Africa and appears to have been bitten by the travel bug. On that trip three 'Test' matches were played and the United duo both played in the last one, a 2–1 win in Johannesburg.

After serving in the RAF, Ainsley rejoined Leeds after the war before finishing his playing days in May 1949. He coached Cambridge University in the 1950s and became an FA staff coach, a post that took him to Wiesbaden in Germany to instruct the US Armed Forces team.

The FA were always keen to promote the game abroad and at the end of the 1957–58 season a representative squad, including Leeds full-back Grenville Hair, played a seven-game tour of Nigeria and Ghana, the latter having

George Ainsley.

just gained independence from Britain when it was known as Gold Coast. They were among the stronger of the African football nations, and it was around this time that Ainsley coached Ghana, who played Nigeria annually for the Jalco Cup, which had been donated by the Nigerian firm of Joe Allen and Co.

Next stop for Ainsley was Pakistan, whom he steered to the Final of the Merdeka Tournament in Malaya in which they lost 2–1 to Indonesia in the Final. He moved on to South Africa in November 1962 to coach club side Highland Park in Johannesburg before taking up the position of Israel's national coach towards the end of 1963. His task was to get the Israelis to the Final of the Olympic tournament which was being held in Tokyo. Ainsley got off to a great start with a 1–0 in Saigon against South Vietnam, but the tables were turned as the Vietnamese won 2–0 in front of 40,000 fans in Tel-Aviv to go through to the Final Play-off with South Korea for a place in Japan.

After the best part of 10 years travelling the world, Ainsley returned to England and managed Workington from July 1965 to November 1966.

JACK CHARLTON

(Republic of Ireland 1986–95)

ACCORDING to urban legend, Jack Charlton will never have to buy a pint of Guinness in Ireland. Fans of the Republic would be fighting to get to the bar to buy a drop of the black stuff for 'Saint' Jack, the man who led the country to the uncharted territory of two World Cups and a European Championship. His managerial career was a success almost from the moment he retired from Leeds United and walked into the job as Middlesbrough's manager. He became Manager of the Year in his first season after Boro won the Second Division by a 15-point margin.

In 1977 he took over at Hillsborough, taking Sheffield Wednesday up to Division Two. After a break from the game he had a brief spell as caretaker manager at Boro before replacing Arthur Cox at Newcastle. When some of the Geordie fans booed him during a pre-season friendly in 1985, Charlton, a son of Ashington, opted to quit. He was the surprise choice of the FA of Ireland, who had been expected to give the job to former Liverpool manager Bob Paisley. Instead, World Cup-winner Jack was unveiled in February 1986 and immediately set about the task of moulding a talented group of individuals into a team. He had the likes of Liam Brady, Mark Lawrenson and Ronnie Whelan at his disposal and got off to fine start, winning Eire's first piece of silverware in a

Republic of Ireland boss Jack Charlton addresses the media during the 1990 World Cup Finals.

In the sizzling heat of Orlando, Ireland lost 2–1 to Mexico – a match which saw Charlton berate officials for not allowing players to take on water. A goalless draw with Norway in the final group game saw Ireland progress, but Holland proved too strong and won 2–0 to make the quarter-finals.

The next target was Euro '96, with Charlton eyeing a return to Wembley, scene of his and England's greatest triumph 30 years earlier. It proved beyond Big Jack and his team as they dropped valuable points against Northern Ireland, Austria and Liechtenstein. That put them into a Play-off with Holland, who won 2–0, prompting Charlton and his right-hand man, Maurice Setters, to quit after 10 brilliant years in charge.

Fans often disregard FIFA's official rankings, but Charlton's achievement of lifting Ireland to an all-time high of sixth – above Brazil – cannot be underestimated. His record of 47 wins, 30 draws and just 17 defeats from 94 matches says it all.

JOHNNY GILES
(Republic of Ireland 1973–80)

HOTLY tipped as Don Revie's successor, Johnny Giles did taste managerial success, but not with Leeds United.

On getting the England job in 1974, Revie suggested to the Leeds board that they go for Giles; instead they went for Brian Clough and 44 days of utter turmoil. The Irish midfield star left Elland Road for West Brom the following year and as player-manager took the Baggies into the First Division in his first season in command.

Johnny Giles while manager of the Republic of Ireland.

triangular tournament in Reykjavik with victories against hosts Iceland and Czechoslovakia.

Charlton used the second-generation rule to increase his pool of players and adopted a simple, but highly effective, direct style of play which took the Republic to the 1988 European Championships in West Germany. It was a member of Ireland's extended family – Scots-born Ray Houghton – who scored the goal which beat England 1–0 in the opening game in Stuttgart. A 1–1 draw with the Soviet Union and an undeserved defeat to a late Dutch goal eliminated the Irish, but they had made their mark.

Football fever swept through Ireland as they qualified for the 1990 World Cup Finals for the first time. Charlton's boys did not disappoint, but it was tense stuff, drawing with England, Holland and Egypt to squeeze through their group. In the last sixteen, their game with Romania went down to penalties, David O'Leary memorably thumping home the winning kick after Packie Bonner's save from Daniel Timofte.

In the quarters, the Republic gave as good as they got against hosts Italy before losing 1–0 to a Toto Schillaci goal. The Irish party returned home as heroes, an estimated 500,000 people flooding the streets of Dublin to catch a glimpse of the boys in green. Charlton worked the magic once more as Ireland qualified for the 1994 World Cup in the United States, where they gained revenge over Italy in their opening game with a 2–1 win.

Giles had been the Republic of Ireland's player-manager since October 1973, making an immediate impression as his side beat Poland 1–0 in Dublin just four days after the Poles' remarkable 1–1 draw had knocked England out of the World Cup.

Until Giles's appointment, Irish football had been run in a relaxed fashion, but he instilled greater professionalism in both his squad and the organisational set-up. Traditionally, Ireland's best players played in England and often they would play for their clubs on a Saturday afternoon, catch the night ferry to Dublin and play for Ireland on a Sunday afternoon. This inevitably led to many player withdrawals, so Giles got the FAI to play their internationals in midweek at the same time as England were playing. It was a simple change of policy but one which helped the Irish cause, particularly on their home turf of Dublin.

After finishing bottom of their 1972 European Championship qualification group, Ireland improved considerably under Giles four years later, finishing just a point behind the Soviet Union, a dropped point in Turkey costing them the chance of progress. The men in the shamrock shirts were no longer a pushover and Giles gave debuts to men of the quality of David O'Leary, Liam Brady, Frank Stapleton and Mark Lawrenson. While they regularly picked up points at home, they were not helped by some poor refereeing on their travels, notably in Bulgaria in a World Cup qualifier in June 1977 when they had an obvious penalty rejected, a goal disallowed and countless minor infringements punished.

Giles continued playing until May 1979, when he won his 39th cap against West Germany, but he could not quite make the breakthrough to a major tournament, missing out on Euro '80. Feeling he had taken Eire as far as he could, he resigned in March 1980 shortly after the opening game of the 1982 World Cup qualifiers – a narrow 3–2 win against Cyprus in Nicosia.

Midway through his Ireland reign, he left West Brom to play for, and manage, Dublin-based Shamrock Rovers, but three years after giving up the national job he moved to Canada to manage Vancouver Whitecaps in the North American Soccer League for three seasons. He returned to England to manage West Brom for a second time, finishing in 1985. He has since been a highly respected pundit in the media.

PETER REID
(Thailand 2008– to date)

PETER REID managed to pull Leeds United clear of the Premiership relegation zone after he was appointed in March 2003. But he was swimming against a financial tide which threatened to become a tsunami that would engulf the club. While other clubs were spending millions, Reid

After leaving Leeds, Peter Reid became manager of Thailand.

had to dabble in the loan market, but his recruits were poor and after a 6–1 hammering at Portsmouth he was axed after eight months in charge. He re-entered management with Coventry City at the end of the season, but left the club by mutual consent in January 2005.

After being out of management for nearly four years, Reid landed the post of manager of Thailand in September 2008. He signed a four-year contract with the specific target of building a side capable of qualifying for the 2014 World Cup Finals. He soon made a good impression, winning the three-team T&T Cup competition in Vietnam, a tournament which also included North Korea, in March 2009.

The former England midfielder, capped 13 times, had enjoyed great playing success with Bolton and Everton, being named the 1985 Footballer of the Year. He started his managerial career with Manchester City before having six games in charge of the England Under-21s and taking Sunderland to the 1996 First Division Championship.

DON REVIE
(England 1974–77, United Arab Emirates 1977–80)

A BRILLIANT playing strategist, Don Revie was a fairly straightforward choice for the FA after his glorious 13-year reign at Elland Road. He was the favourite to succeed World Cup-winner Sir Alf Ramsey and, after Joe Mercer's spell as caretaker, the Leeds United man was installed as the national team boss at the age of 47.

A fine inside-forward, the Middlesbrough-born Revie won six caps as a player with Manchester City and after a spell as player-manager steered Leeds into uncharted trophy-winning territory – two League titles, an FA Cup,

England's Don Revie slots the ball home against Scotland at Wembley in 1955.

a League Cup, two Fairs Cups and numerous near misses. His position as Leeds United's greatest manager remains unchallenged.

Before Revie arrived Leeds were a mundane, under-achieving club, but he transformed them into one of the best in the world. Initially the football was tough and uncompromising, but in the 1970s his squad produced some wonderful performances. Unfortunately, he could not replicate what he had achieved in his later years at Elland Road with England. Although he got off to a good start with a 3–0 win against Czechoslovakia in a European Championship qualifier at Wembley, his reign was marred by constant changes in team selection.

At Leeds, Revie always knew which men to pick for the task in hand, but with England he seemed fazed by the sheer number of choices open to him. His early results were good, including five-goal returns against Scotland and Cyprus, Newcastle striker Malcolm Macdonald getting them all in the latter, but a series of negative performances followed and England failed to reach the European Finals as the Czechs topped the group.

Don Revie on the eve of his first game in charge of England against Czechoslovakia with his skipper Emlyn Hughes, of Liverpool.

Revie's honeymoon period was over, and his critics were sharpening their knives. It was already clear that qualification for the 1978 World Cup Finals had to be achieved or Revie would be out. With Italy, Finland and Luxembourg in the group, it was clear that the hopes of Lancaster Gate rested on the outcome of the games against the Italians. After beating Finland twice, England were comprehensively outplayed in Rome, losing 2–0, and the press poured scorn on Revie's tactics. Predictably, England swept Luxembourg aside at Wembley, but Revie did not see the job through.

After a poor showing in the Home Internationals, Revie could see the writing was already etched large on the wall. He missed the opening game of the three-match summer tour to South America, leaving his faithful Leeds lieutenant, trainer Les Cocker, to oversee a 0–0 draw with Brazil in Rio. Revie had said he had another match to watch, but, as it later transpired, he had flown to Dubai to pave the way for being installed as manager of the United Arab Emirates.

Revie joined the England party for the draws with Argentina and Uruguay, but before the next Euro games with Luxembourg and Italy he quit to take up his £350,000 a year contract with the UAE. The fallout from his walk out was huge. FA chairman Sir Harold Thompson slapped a 10-year ban on Revie for bringing the game into disrepute. The former Leeds boss successfully sued the FA in December 1979, but it was a hollow victory as the judge, Justice Cantley, criticised aspects of Revie's character.

Although 'The Don's' actions failed to dim the affection in which he was held at Elland Road, he was hammered mercilessly by the media. His popularity may have plunged among England fans, but in the UAE he was lauded for the three years' work he did as coach. The Gulf nation had only been members of FIFA for two years, and Revie put much of the infrastructure in place for future UAE coaches, like Brazilian duo Carlos Alberto and Mario Zagallo, to build on.

In May 1980 Revie took over club side Al Nasr and four years later he was appointed manager of Cairo club Al Ahli, before returning to England to briefly take up a consultancy role at his beloved Leeds United, where the old standing Spion Kop was renamed the Revie Stand in 1994. A road close to the ground is also named after him. Revie revealed in 1988 that he was suffering from the incurable motor-neurone disease and he died on 26 May 1989 at Murrayfield Hospital, Edinburgh.

STEVE STAUNTON
(Republic of Ireland 2006–07)

FORMER Republic of Ireland player and manager Steve Staunton spent 11 months at Elland Road as Gary McAllister's assistant. But the combination failed to fire consistently as United found themselves off the pace in League One and the pair were axed in December 2008. It

Republic of Ireland boss Steve Staunton.

further behind in the group and were booed off Croke Park after labouring to a 1–1 draw with Cyprus, a result which confirmed they would not be going to the Finals. Shortly afterwards, Staunton's 21-month reign was ended by the FAI, who installed experienced Giovanni Trappatoni as their new man in charge.

JOCK STEIN
(Scotland 1965 and 1978–85)

LIKE Brian Clough, Jock Stein spent 44 days as manager of Leeds United. But unlike the volatile Clough, the players were not happy to see the back of the popular Scot. The big man was a legend at Celtic, winning many honours, the pinnacle being when he became the first manager in Britain to win the European Cup. He was awarded the CBE in 1970 but was out of the game for 10 months after a serious car injury in 1975, followed by a

Jock Stein spent only 44 days at Leeds before leaving to manage Scotland.

was quite a fall from grace for Staunton, who just 14 months earlier was in charge of the Republic of Ireland, whom he had served brilliantly on the field.

The Drogheda-born left-sided player made a record 102 appearances for Eire, having double spells with Liverpool and Aston Villa before finishing his career with Coventry and Walsall. A veteran of the 1990, 1994 and 2000 World Cups, he is the only player to figure in all 13 games Ireland have played in the Finals, skippering them in Japan after Roy Keane's dramatic departure. He was doubling up as assistant coach at the Bescot Stadium when he was made the Republic's manager in January 2006. Although Staunton was a bit of a surprise appointment, he made a flying start with a 4–0 friendly win against Tunisia. He appointed Aston Villa's reserve-team coach and former teammate Kevin McDonald as his coach, and engaged veteran Bobby Robson as international consultant. The new regime built on that Tunisian result with a superb display to thrash Sweden 3–0, but it did not take long for the honeymoon to end. His first competitive match ended in a 1–0 defeat against Germany when he was sent off for kicking a water bottle onto the pitch in frustration. The second Euro 2008 qualifier was even worse as Ireland lost 5–2 to Cyprus in Nicosia, and they only just avoided disaster in San Marino when they scraped a 2–1 win with an injury-time goal from Manchester City's Stephen Ireland.

Successive victories against Wales and Slovakia bought Staunton time, but it proved a false dawn as they fell heart attack and several major operations. He was moved upstairs by Celtic, but Stein, a former Celtic defender, missed the day-to-day cut and thrust of football management and agreed a three-year contract with Leeds in August 1978. However, he did not sign the contract and, after Ally McLeod departed the Scotland job, the SFA came calling and Stein took charge of his country's team for a second time.

Stein had a short spell in charge on a part-time basis between May and December 1965 and ran Scotland's Under-23 side 10 years later while in charge at Celtic, where his European experience made him the obvious choice to build a squad capable of reaching the 1982 World Cup Finals. Big Jock, who did not play for Scotland, gradually overhauled McLeod's squad during their European Championship campaign with World Cup qualification as his priority. Their group included Portugal, Northern Ireland, Sweden and Israel, but they came through it, sealing their place in the Finals in Spain with a draw in Belfast with a game to spare.

Stein's team kicked off their bid for glory with a 5–2 win against New Zealand in Malaga, but they were brought down to earth by Brazil, who scored some stunning goals in a 4–1 victory in Seville. Back in Malaga, Scotland's defensive errors were punished by the USSR, whose 2–2 draw and better goal difference was enough to send Scotland home. Stein remained in charge but could not get Scotland to their first Euro Finals, so once again the World Cup was the target.

It was nerve-shreddingly tight, with Scotland needing a point from their final game in Cardiff to secure a Play-off place at least. They did it with a controversial 80th-minute penalty by Davie Cooper, which cancelled out Mark Hughes's early strike. Stein collapsed at the final whistle and died in the Ninian Park medical room shortly afterwards. He was 62.

Stein's assistant, Alex Ferguson, took temporary charge and a 2–0 aggregate victory against Australia put the Scots into the Finals, where they lost to Denmark and West Germany and drew a bruising goalless battle with Uruguay. After his death Stein was voted Scotland's greatest manager and inducted into the Scottish Sports Hall of Fame.

TERRY VENABLES
(England 1994–96, Australia 1996–97)

THE much-heralded Terry Venables spent just eight turbulent months in charge of Leeds United. He had walked into a financial minefield at Elland Road in 2002 and soon found top players like Rio Ferdinand were being sold to reduce the club's multi-million pound debt. Relations with chairman Peter Ridsdale finally reached breaking point and Venables, forced to work on a modest

Terry Venables, in his role as England manager.

budget, was sacked in March 2003 as the Whites were sliding towards relegation.

In his heyday Venables had been a forward-thinking coach who was much in demand, rising to lead England to the semi-finals of Euro '96. The former Chelsea, Tottenham and England player cut his managerial teeth with Crystal Palace and Queen's Park Rangers before landing the coaching post at Barcelona. Dubbed 'El Tel', he took the Catalan giants to the La Liga title in his first season, followed by a European Cup Final appearance. Returning to London, he won the FA Cup with Tottenham in 1991 and in January 1994 was appointed England manager despite some members of the FA having reservations about his business dealings. He had replaced the much-maligned Graham Taylor after the former Aston Villa man's failure to lead England to the 1994 World Cup Finals. Venables's target, therefore, was Euro '96, a competition which England were hosting. As such, Venables only had a succession of friendlies and the Umbro

Terry Venables, who had a brief spell in charge of Australia.

Trophy, also held in England, to work with up to the start of the competition.

Performances were fairly ordinary, and the tabloid press had a feeding frenzy when Paul Gascoigne, among others, became involved in high jinks at altitude as England flew back from a couple of games in the Far East just a fortnight before the start of Euro '96. England had not played a competitive – if that is the right word – game since beating San Marino 7–1 over two years earlier. The lack of tournament time showed in an opening 1–1 draw with Switzerland, but the peroxide-blond Gazza lit up Wembley with a wonder goal to seal a 2–0 win against the Scots. It got even better with an Alan Shearer double as Holland were eclipsed 4–1 in one of England's best post-war performances.

After that it was a tale of penalties. After luckily holding Spain 0–0 in the quarters they won the shoot-out, only to lose on the dreaded spot-kicks in the semi-finals against Germany after playing well enough to win in normal time. Gareth Southgate's saved penalty at 5–5 was the final kick of the Venables era, but the Londoner re-emerged on the international scene in November when he was unveiled as Australia's manager. His brief was simple – get the Socceroos to the World Cup Finals. He steered the Aussies to the Final of the 1997 Confederations Cup, where they lost to Brazil and, as expected, swept through the weak Oceania group to set up a Play-off against Iran for a place in the World Finals. They drew 1–1 in Teheran and were 2–0 up in the second leg when Iran scored two late goals to snatch the big prize on aggregate. It cost Venables his job, and after spells at Crystal Palace and Middlesbrough he landed at Elland Road.

Since then he has worked as assistant to England manager Steve McClaren, but the duo were sacked two days after England failed to qualify for the 2008 European Championships.

HOWARD WILKINSON
(England 1999 and 2000)

UNITED'S 'Sergeant Wilko' drilled discipline into his Leeds team and structure into an ailing club, winning the First and Second Division titles with the Whites. He had done well in his previous jobs at Notts County and Sheffield Wednesday, but was at the peak of his managerial powers at Elland Road and remains the last English manager to have won England's top-flight League, back in 1992.

Four months after being axed by Leeds, Wilkinson was hired by the FA to become its technical director, overseeing coaching and other training programmes at all levels of the game. It seemed a job highly suited to Wilkinson, who was a broad thinker about the game, and it was under his guidance that the FA began the National Football Centre project.

Howard Wilkinson, who has been the temporary manager of England twice.

During his time in this role, Glenn Hoddle was sacked as England manager, and Wilkinson was put in temporary charge, overseeing the 2–0 defeat by France at Wembley on 10 February 1999 when two second-half goals from Nicholas Anelka gave Les Blues a deserved victory. Hoddle was replaced by Kevin Keegan, and Wilkinson took over the Under-21 job from Peter Taylor, but he lost three of the six matches he was in charge and resigned in June 2001 to be replaced by David Platt.

When Keegan quit after England lost a World Cup qualifier to Germany on 7 October 2000, Under-21 boss Wilkinson took on the caretaker role once again for the 0–0 draw with Finland in Helsinki four days later. Taylor was then in charge for one match – a 1–0 friendly defeat in Italy – before Sven-Goran Eriksson was unveiled as the new permanent manager.

In 2002 Wilkinson re-entered club management at Sunderland in partnership with Steve Cotterill, but the duo failed and with the Black Cats rock-bottom of the Premiership they were sacked in May 2003. Since then Wilkinson has had a brief spell in China with Shanghai Shenhua, coached at Leicester City and Notts County, and joined Sheffield Wednesday, the club he supported as a boy, as technical director in January 2009. He is also chairman of the League Managers' Association.

NIGEL WORTHINGTON
(Northern Ireland 2008– to date)

CURRENT Northern Ireland manager Nigel Worthington is spearheading his country's campaign to reach the 2010 World Cup Finals. A long-standing, reliable full-back, the former Leeds United player had clearly learned much of the art of management from his mentor Howard Wilkinson. He played for Wilko at Notts County and Sheffield Wednesday and entered management as player-manager at Blackpool in 1997–98, but after two and a half seasons in charge resigned.

Northern Ireland boss Nigel Worthington.

against Georgia in Belfast produced the extraordinary scenario of all-time leading goal scorer David Healy netting at both ends. The Irish finished behind Spain and Sweden in their Euro group, but in front of Denmark, and the work Worthington had put in saw the IFA hand him a two-year contract with World Cup qualification in mind. Initial results look as though it was a smart decision. With three games remaining, Northern Ireland topped the group and, although others have games in hand, qualification was a possibility, with trips to Poland and the Czech Republic to come, as well as a home game against the biggest threat, Slovakia.

Northern Ireland are unbeaten in their last nine qualifiers in Belfast, a sequence which Worthington has helped mastermind. In March 2009 a 3–2 win against Poland and a 1–0 victory against Slovenia in the space of four days at Windsor Park put them in with a chance of making the Finals for the first time since 1986, when Worthington was a member of the squad.

TERRY YORATH
(Wales 1988–93, Lebanon 1995–97)

AFTER taking Wales to within a penalty-kick from World Cup qualification, Terry Yorath was controversially sacked. Wales achieved some great results under the guidance of Yorath, who for several years worked for his country on a part-time basis while still being involved in club management. Fans were so angry about his treatment that they chanted his name in support during the first international home match after his departure – a friendly against Norway at Ninian Park. John Toshack had been appointed as technical director to replace Yorath, but such was the backing for the former Leeds and Wales captain that he quit after a month.

After a spell as player/assistant coach at Bradford City, Yorath first entered management with Swansea City in July 1986, initially doubling up as a player. It was while he was with the Swans that he was appointed manager of Wales in April 1988 on a part-time basis, and he juggled both jobs with some success, gaining Swansea promotion to Division Three in 1988. He left the Vetch Field club in February 1989 to manage Bradford City and to be closer to his family. That did not go down well with the Welsh club, who embarked on a £400,000 law suit to block the move, before an injunction was finally lifted. After a year at Valley Parade he returned to Swansea but could not achieve his previous success and in March 1991 left to concentrate on managing Wales. His first game in charge of the principality had seen them lose a friendly 4–1 in Sweden, but he soon made his mark with a 3–2 win in Malta followed by a tremendous 1–0 victory in Italy thanks to a goal from master marksman Ian Rush, who was then plying his trade with Juventus.

After working as Wilkinson's assistant with the England Under-21 team, he joined Norwich City as assistant manager to former Northern Ireland teammate Bryan Hamilton, who had been Northern Ireland's manager from 1994 to 1997. Hamilton quit the Canaries in December 2000 and Worthington took charge, saving the club from relegation and steering them to the Play-offs in 2002 before winning the First Division the following season.

Instantly relegated from the Premiership, Norwich were not able to bounce back, and Worthington lost his job in September 2006, but re-emerged as caretaker manager at relegation-threatened Leicester City and, despite keeping the Foxes in the Championship, did not get the full-time job. In June 2007 he was taken on by the Irish FA on a short-term contract until the end of the Euro 2008 qualifying tournament in November, with former Leeds man Glynn Snodin as his assistant. Worthington's first competitive game in charge saw Liechtenstein beaten 3–1 at Windsor Park, but their hopes of progress were shattered by successive self-inflicted defeats on the road. In Latvia they went down to Chris Baird's own-goal, while Keith Gillespie put into his own net to hand Iceland a last-minute 2–1 win.

Own-goalitis also spread to friendlies as Manchester United defender Johnny Evans scored at the wrong end to see Bulgaria win 1–0 in Belfast, and even a 4–1 victory

In Rush, Mark Hughes, Dean Saunders and goalkeeper Neville Southall, Wales had some excellent players at their disposal, but the squad lacked depth and inevitably finished behind Holland and West Germany in the bid to reach Italia '90. But Yorath's men were heading in the right direction, and another strike by Rush earned Wales one of their greatest victories in June 1991. His 60th-minute goal beat world champions West Germany and sent a 38,000 Cardiff Arms park crowd wild as Yorath's men headed their European Championship qualifying group at the half-way stage. It was Germany's first defeat in 16 matches, a sequence stretching 16 months.

The result only galvanised Germany, who won all their remaining games, including a 4–1 thumping of Wales, to pip the Red Dragons by a point. Despite that disappointment, the emergence of Leeds's Gary Speed and Manchester United man Ryan Giggs meant Wales could no longer be regarded as pushovers in international competition. Yorath could even add victory over Brazil to his CV, a 1–0 win at Cardiff coming just three months after the triumph against West Germany.

Qualification for the World Cup in 1994 rested on the outcome of the final group game against Romania in Cardiff. Victory would put Wales through, and at 1–1 they were awarded a penalty,. Paul Bodin missed, Wales went on to lose 2–1 and Yorath's 41-match reign was brought to an end by the FAW. After a short time with Cardiff City,

Yorath was appointed national team coach of war-torn Lebanon in June 1995. He was based in Beirut, battered and blasted by rocket-fire, travelled everywhere with a bodyguard and used a translator from Moscow to get across his instructions. Because of the heat, training was done in the evenings, sometimes in the Bekha Valley, close to armed insurgents' training camps. Death and destruction were part of daily life.

Despite all these hurdles, Yorath won his first six games in charge as he prepared the team for the Arab games, including victories against Slovakia, Georgia and Ecuador. Under Yorath's leadership Lebanon rose 60 places in the FIFA rankings to go higher than Wales, who had gone into freefall since his sacking. He left the Middle East in 1997, coaching at Huddersfield Town and Bradford City before becoming Paul Jewell's assistant at Sheffield Wednesday. He was manager in 2001 but resigned the following year. He returned to football in 2008 as director of football with Ryman League side Margate, where his brother Dai and nephew Dean had both played, and was appointed manager for the rest of the season in November.

Yorath was hit hard in 1992 when his 15-year-old-son, Daniel, who was about to start a career with Leeds United, collapsed and died while playing football with his dad in their garden. Daniel had an undetected heart condition. One of Yorath's daughters is television sports presenter Gabby Logan.

Leeds United Managers Who Played For England

FOUR Leeds United managers who also played for England, but not for United, are covered in this section.

JIMMY ARMFIELD

(1959–66)
Right-back
Caps: Blackpool 43

ALTHOUGH he never managed England, 'Gentleman' Jimmy Armfield has been a highly influential figure with the FA. He had a major say in the appointments of Terry Venables and Glenn Hoddle to the England position as the FA's headhunter. The pipe-smoking Armfield did a tremendous job of picking up the pieces at Elland Road after Brian Clough's shock tenure. He achieved something the great Don Revie could not do – he got Leeds United to the European Cup Final.

Armfield had been a wonderful one-club servant with Blackpool and played 43 times for England as an overlapping right-back, making his international debut in a 2–0 win against Brazil in front of 120,000 fans packed into Rio's huge Maracana Stadium.

Acclaimed as the best player in his position in the 1962

Jimmy Armfield leads England out against the Rest of the World at Wembley in 1963.

World Cup, Armfield played in 31 successive internationals and captained England in 15 matches, including his final appearance, a 3–0 win in Finland just a few weeks before the start of the 1966 World Cup. Injury saw the 30-year-old lose his place in the side to Fulham's George Cohen, and although he was a member of the squad he did not play. Armfield retired in 1971 after 17 years with Blackpool and became manager at Bolton Wanderers, taking them to the 1973 Division Three Championship.

After the Clough turmoil, Leeds needed a safe pair of hands on the tiller, and Armfield proved an excellent choice as the experienced squad pulled together to put in some brilliant displays in Europe, only to fail at the final hurdle against Bayern Munich. Rioting by Leeds fans in Paris that night saw the club banned from European competition for four years, a sentence halved after Armfield's articulate representations to UEFA.

Armfield and his assistant, Don Howe, another former England man, gradually rebuilt the ageing Leeds squad, but success did not come quickly enough for the Leeds board, who axed the pair in July 1978. He has worked as a highly respected analyst in the media since then, particularly as a radio summariser. The FA tapped into his knowledge when they appointed him as a consultant. In his role he recommended Venables for the job in 1994 and Hoddle two years later.

In 2000 Armfield was awarded an OBE for his services to football and was awarded a place in the football Hall of Fame at the National Football Museum in Preston in 2008 – a year after he revealed he was receiving treatment for cancer. Amazingly modest, Armfield has never been a man to seek the headlines, but he ranks as one of the all-time great men of football.

FRANK BUCKLEY

(1914)
Centre-half
Caps: Derby County 1

CHARISMATIC Frank Buckley was noted for his eccentric training methods during his five years as manager of Leeds United. Dancing to music coming over the PA system, a mechanical kicking machine and the use of 'monkey-gland' treatment were all designed to improve his players' balance, sharpen their reflexes and concentrate the mind. But former Army man Major Buckley was no quack. He was a highly respected authoritarian manager who reached

Leeds United manager and England player Frank Buckley.

ONE of England's greatest inside-forwards, the grandly named Horatio Stratton Carter took over from Major Frank Buckley at Leeds. As a player he was a class act, winning 13 caps and making a further 17 wartime and Victory appearances when many observes felt he was at his peak as a player.

A schoolboy international at 13, Carter started with his local club Sunderland, with whom he won a League Championship and an FA Cup. The 'Silver-haired Maestro' made his England debut in front of 92,963 fans against Scotland at Wembley. England, who had Ernie Hart and Wilf Copping in defence, won 3–0.

Carter was up and running. He scored his first goal in his fourth game, a 3–1 win against Ireland at Stoke, and netted the final goal in a 6–2 thrashing of Hungary in the penultimate international before the war. He and Stanley Matthews were the jewels in England's wartime crown, and Carter also struck up a memorable combination with Northern Ireland international Peter Doherty at Derby, where he won another FA Cup medal. For a couple of years after the war Carter continued to pull the strings for England, including two goals as Holland were crushed 8–2 at Huddersfield. In his 13 England matches Carter only appeared on the losing side once – his last appearance, a 1–0 defeat in Switzerland, coming in May 1947 when he was 34.

Carter subsequently replaced Major Buckley at Hull, taking the Tigers to the Division Three (North) title in 1949. He opted out of football to run a sweet shop, but was lured out of retirement to play for Cork Athletic in Ireland before his managerial appointment at Leeds in May 1953. Building his side round the magnificent John Charles, Carter guided United up to Division One in 1956, but his five-year contract was not renewed when it came up for renewal two years later. He later managed

the pinnacle of his playing career with selection for England against Ireland in 1914. The match, at Middlesbrough's Ayresome Park, did not go according to plan as Ireland won 3–0, former Leeds City man Billy Gillespie getting one of the goals.

Centre-half Buckley, who played for Aston Villa, Brighton, Manchester United, Manchester City, Birmingham, Derby County and Bradford City, was an all-action character. He fought in the Boer War and World War One, joining the 17th Middlesex Regiment as an officer, reaching the rank of major. He commanded the 'Footballers' Battalion', made up of soccer professionals, and was badly wounded in the Battle of the Somme in August 1916.

After the war, he managed Norwich and Blackpool, before taking over at Wolves, where he developed an outstanding youth policy. He was then in charge of Notts County and Hull City before arriving at Elland Road in May 1948, aged 64. His brother, Chris 'Ticker' Buckley was both a player and chairman at Aston Villa.

RAICH CARTER
(1934–47)
Inside-forward
Caps: Sunderland 6, Derby County 7. Total: 13
Goals: 7

Raich Carter in action for England against Scotland.

Mansfield and Middlesbrough, but it will always be as a player that he will be best remembered.

Carter was an outstanding all-round sportsman and played cricket for Durham against Australia in 1934 and played three times for Derbyshire.

DENNIS WISE

(1991–2000)
Midfield
Caps: Chelsea 21
Goals: 1

LIFE was never dull with firebrand Dennis Wise around. A former member of Wimbledon's 'Crazy Gang', who stunned Liverpool to lift the FA Cup in 1988, he enjoyed a brilliant career in Chelsea's midfield, where his combative approach earned him plenty of run-ins with authority, while he was also involved in several unsavoury incidents off the field. Those scrapes tended to overshadow the fact that he was an outstanding leader for Chelsea, skippering the London club in the FA Cup triumphs of 1997 and 2000 and the League Cup and UEFA Cup-winners' Cup double in 1998.

Wise was a surprise selection by Graham Taylor for a European Championship qualifier against Turkey in Izmir in May 1991, but he proved his value with the only goal of the game, bundled in after 32 minutes. It was to be his only goal in 21 England appearances, and, despite his fiery reputation, he picked up just one booking while wearing a Three Lions shirt.

Most of his appearances came for Graham Taylor and Kevin Keegan, but his last was for caretaker manager Howard Wilkinson, the former Leeds boss, against Finland in 2000. Wise also played three times for England B and once for the Under-21s.

After a brief time at Leicester he became Millwall's player-manager, taking the Lions to the 2004 FA Cup Final, but he resigned the following year and played for Southampton, where he was caretaker manager for a short time, and Coventry.

Wise was named Swindon's manager in May 2006, with his former Chelsea teammate Gus Poyet as his assistant, but within four months the pair had been installed as the Leeds United managerial team. The move to Elland Road reunited them with Ken Bates, the former Chelsea chairman.

Although Wise could not stop Leeds from sliding in to League One, he did a remarkable job at the start of the following season, which United kicked off with a handicap of 15 deducted points. Unable to sign any new players until the question of the Whites' future was resolved, Wise paid some members of the squad out of his own pocket.

Leeds won their opening seven games, but following Poyet's departure to Tottenham as coach United began to stumble, and Wise quit the club in January 2008 to become Newcastle's executive director of football, a position he gave up in April 2009.

Dennis Wise at an England training session.

International Miscellany

This section covers former Leeds managers, backroom staff and non-international Leeds players who have contributed to international football.

JIMMY ADAMSON
(England)

HAD Jimmy Adamson said 'yes' to the FA he could have been the man in charge of England for the 1966 World Cup Finals instead of Alf Ramsey. He was the international committee's first choice after Walter Winterbottom resigned after the 1962 Finals in Chile.

Burnley's long-serving half-back and captain Adamson, the reigning Footballer of the Year, never won an England cap but was a member of the playing party in South America and also acted as Winterbottom's assistant. The 33-year-old, a fully qualified FA coach, took charge of training while Winterbottom looked after tactics in South America. The FA's mandarins were impressed with Adamson's work and offered him the England job, but he

Jimmy Adamson.

Jimmy Adamson, far right, puts the 1962 England World Cup squad through their paces.

turned it down, stating that he did not have sufficient experience to do the role justice. He went on to join the Turf Moor coaching staff, taking over as manager from Harry Potts in 1970, a post he held until January 1976. After a spell in Holland, Adamson replaced Leeds's FA Cup conquerer Bob Stokoe at Sunderland, from whom he joined Leeds in 1978 after Jock Stein's departure.

Adamson took Leeds into Europe, but his success was short-lived, performances deteriorated, and he resigned amid fans' unrest in 1980. He never worked in football again.

ROY AITKEN
(Scotland)

A FORMER Celtic captain, the midfielder played 57 times for Scotland. He also played for Newcastle United, St Mirren and Aberdeen, managing the latter to the 1995 Scottish League Cup. He became a coach at Leeds United in 1999 under David O'Leary and was widely praised for his work. In June 2003 he linked up with O'Leary again, at Aston Villa, and took charge of three pre-season games in 2006 after the Irish manager left by mutual consent. In January 2007 he was named as one of Alex McLeish's assistants with the Scottish national team and followed McLeish, newly appointed boss at Birmingham, to be the Blues' first-team coach.

LES COCKER
(England)

AMAZINGLY Sir Alf Ramsey never received a medal for winning the World Cup, and neither did his right-hand men Harold Shepherson and Leeds United's own Les Cocker. Only the teams which played on the day gained medals

Scotland's Roy Aitken.

England and Leeds United trainer Les Cocker.

while the trio – along with non-playing squad members like Norman Hunter – left the stadium empty-handed. After a long campaign, FIFA eventually relented and the squad and backroom boys received their medals in 2009.

Cocker was a journeyman forward with his native Stockport and Accrington Stanley, being appointed assistant trainer at Peel Park in 1957 before working with Luton Town in a similar position. One of the first fully-qualified FA coaches, Cocker studied anatomy and physiology, his work attracting the attention of England manager Walter Winterbottom. He was made trainer to the England Under-23 team against Israel at Elland Road in November 1961, a year after joining Leeds United.

Cocker became Don Revie's faithful lieutenant at Leeds, but also helped prepare the England squad for the 1962 World Cup in Chile and was retained, with Middlesbrough's Harold Shepherdson, when Ramsey replaced Winterbottom. The trio were at the hub of the 1966 triumph and the tournament in Mexico four years later.

Four weeks after Revie was appointed England manager in 1975, Cocker left Leeds to become the national team's trainer and Revie's assistant. Cocker even took charge of the England team for the opening game of their South American tour against Brazil, while Revie was away checking on players, but the former Leeds boss was actually negotiating his exit to the Middle East.

When Revie quit, Cocker became trainer-coach at Doncaster Rovers, linking up with former United hero Billy Bremner, the man in charge at Belle Vue. It was during one of Donny's coaching sessions that Cocker collapsed and died on 4 October 1977, aged just 53.

DON HOWE
(England)

FORMER England defender Don Howe spent a couple of seasons at Leeds United as Jimmy Armfield's assistant. He arrived after the 1975 European Cup Final, having already managed West Bromwich Albion and Turkish club Galatasaray after being assistant to Bertie Mee's double-winning Arsenal side of 1971. Howe played 23 times for England and featured in the 1958 World Cup when he was a West Brom player.

In August 1977 he returned to one of his former clubs, Arsenal, as head coach and four years later worked under Ron Greenwood with the England team, his services being retained by another Baggies old boy, Bobby Robson, when he took charge of the national side. After working in club management with Arsenal, Queen's Park Rangers and Coventry, he returned to the England fold as assistant manager to Terry Venables, helping the team to the Euro '96 semi-finals. Since then he has worked as Arsenal's youth-team manager and came out of retirement to work with the FA of Ireland as part of the panel which selected Giovanni Trapattoni as Eire's boss in 2008.

Don Howe, right, with England manager Bobby Robson.

BRIAN KIDD
(England)

BRIAN KIDD endured a rather uneasy relationship with some Leeds United supporters after he was elevated to first-team coach by David O'Leary. The former Manchester United forward made two England appearances against Northern Ireland and Ecuador, scoring in a 2–0 win against the South Americans after coming off the bench. Kidd also played for Arsenal, Manchester City and Bolton Wanderers, as well as a few clubs in the United States. He cut his managerial teeth at Barrow and Preston before re-joining Manchester United as youth-team coach in 1988, moving up to be Alex Ferguson's assistant for

Brian Kidd directing operations at an England training session.

seven years in 1991. Another crack at management with Blackburn Rovers failed – they were relegated just four years after winning the Premiership – but in May 2000 he joined the Whites as youth coach. Ten months later he was promoted to assistant manager, above Eddie Gray, by O'Leary. But United's form dipped and many fans blamed Kidd, who remained at the club to work with Terry Venables after O'Leary's dismissal. The managerial merry-go-round continued, and when Peter Reid entered the fray Kidd departed in May 2003, just three months after being named as England's part-time assistant coach by Sven-Goran Eriksson. Just weeks before Euro 2004 Kidd had to give up the role because he was receiving treatment for prostate cancer, from which he has been given the all-clear.

Always in demand, Kidd then worked with Bryan Robson and Neil Warnock at Sheffield United before becoming assistant manager to Leeds old boy Paul Hart, Portsmouth's caretaker manager in February 2009.

SYD OWEN
(England)

WHILE Les Cocker whipped Don Revie's men into tip-top physical condition, former England centre-half Syd Owen honed their individual skills. Birmingham-born Owen spent nearly all his playing career at Luton Town, where he was captain for nine years, being named Footballer of the Year in 1959, making his final appearance, aged 36, in that year's FA Cup Final defeat against Nottingham Forest. He had toured with the FA to Australia, South Africa, Rhodesia and the West Indies and found himself flung into the international side at the age of 31.

Centre-half had been a problem position for England for some seasons, and Owen was the latest to be thrown into the mix as the 1954 World Cup approached. He certainly had a baptism of fire, playing in a brief two-game continental tour just prior to the tournament in Switzerland.

England kicked-off with a 1–0 defeat against Yugoslavia, Rajko Mitic scoring three minutes from the end, but it had been mainly one-way traffic towards the England goal from start to finish, and Owen did well under pressure. Critics, however, reckoned it was one of the weakest England squads for many years, and their fears were compounded a week later by the 'Mighty Magyars'. Six months earlier Hungary had destroyed England 6–3 at Wembley, and many doubted the wisdom of playing them again in their own backyard just before the World Cup. The FA ploughed on with the fixture, but Owen and Co. were destroyed 7–1 in Budapest, a result which remains England's biggest defeat.

Owen kept his place for the World Cup opener against Belgium in Basle but struggled in a 4–4 draw, a last-minute Jimmy Dickinson own-goal denying England victory.

Syd Owen, right, cannot prevent Hungary scoring one of their seven goals in Budapest in 1954.

Owen finished the game limping, so the selection committee switched Billy Wright to centre-half and brought in Bill McGarry for his debut against hosts Switzerland. England won 2–0, Wright stayed at centre-half for the next five years, and Owen's brief international career was over.

Owen had qualified as an FA coach in 1952 and after quitting as a player was appointed Luton's manager, a position he held until April 1960. Three months later he arrived at Elland Road as coach and, together with Cocker and Revie's assistant Maurice Lindley, the 'masterspy' scout who complied the Leeds manager's famous dossiers on the opposition, formed a formidable backroom staff.

After 22 years at Elland Road, Owen quit because the club could not promise him a written contract. He then worked for Manchester United but returned to Leeds, at manager Eddie Gray's request, in October 1982. Owen died in January 1999.

IVOR POWELL
(Wales)
SOMEWHERE in the *Guinness Book of Records* you'll find the name of Ivor Powell – at over 90 years old, the oldest working football coach. Born in July 1915, the Welsh

Ivor Powell in Wales kit.

international's amazing 55-year coaching career included nearly four years with Leeds United in the 1950s. As a player he served Queen's Park Rangers, Aston Villa, Port Vale and Bradford City as a wing-half, winning eight Welsh caps, plus four more in wartime. It was during a game with England at Wembley in September 1943 that he broke a collarbone and was replaced by England's Stan Mortensen.

A PT instructor with the RAF based in Blackpool, he became firm friends with the legendary Stanley Matthews, the wing wizard being best man at Powell's wedding. A £17,500 fee, a record for a half-back, saw him move from Queen's Park Rangers to Villa in 1948 before player-manager spells with Port Vale and Bradford City. Injury ended his playing days at Valley Parade, but he stayed on as manager, although was dismissed in February 1955 after a string of poor results.

After running a pub in Manningham, Powell joined the Leeds coaching staff in July 1956 after United's promotion to Division One. The experienced Powell's work did not go unnoticed, and he was lured back into management by Carlisle United in May 1960, a position he held for three years. He was appointed manager at Bath City in 1964 and coached PAOK in Greece before returning to Bath to work with the university's football team, now known as Team Bath. He has worked with the students for more than 30 years, was inducted into the Welsh Sports Hall of Fame in 2004 and made an MBE four years later, receiving his honour from the Queen shortly before his 92nd birthday. He still works as assistant coach at Team Bath, of whom he is president.

Ivor Powell still going strong as coach to Team Bath.

Gus Poyet.

GUS POYET
(Uruguay)

FORMER Uruguayan international Gus Poyet provided the sharp wit and banter in his double act with Dennis Wise at Leeds. Although he was only at Elland Road a year as assistant to his old Chelsea teammate, he impressed with his work on the training field. He was still fit and even played in a couple of friendlies during a club break in Cyprus.

Wise and Poyet had arrived from Swindon Town, and although they could not prevent United's relegation to League One, they quickly pulled the ailing team together. It was only after Poyet's departure to Tottenham, another of his former clubs, as first-team coach, that United's results deteriorated. He helped Spurs win the Carling Cup, but when Spanish manager Juan Ramos was axed in October 2008 after a woeful start to the season, Poyet left White Hart Lane too.

A wonderful attacking midfield player, Poyet made his name in Spain with Real Zaragoza, skippering them to 1995 European Cup-winners' Cup glory against Arsenal before coming to England. He played 26 times for Uruguay, helping them win the Copa America in 1995 when he was named the tournament's top player. Poyet's international debut came in 1993 in a 2–1 win against Peru, and he skippered the side twice in 1995 against Colombia and the United States.

GLYNN SNODIN
(Northern Ireland)

NORTHERN IRELAND boss Nigel Worthington appointed Glynn Snodin as his assistant manager when he took on the job in summer 2008. The Doncaster-born midfielder was a popular player with Leeds between 1987 and 1992, although his time at Elland Road was hit by a bad bout of glandular fever. He is credited by some with inventing the 'Leeds salute', much used by fans, after scoring a goal at Plymouth. He topped 600 games in a career which took in Barnsley, Sheffield Wednesday, Doncaster Rovers and Hearts before embarking on a highly successful coaching career with Charlton,

Glynn Snodin with his Northern Ireland boss Nigel Worthington.

ANDY WATSON
(Scotland)

SIGNED by Eddie Gray in 1983, Andy Watson struggled to adapt to the pace of the English game. The former Hibernian midfielder returned to Edinburgh to play for Hearts before rejoining the Hibees, but was forced to quit at 29 with a knee injury. The Scottish Under-23 international then embarked on a long partnership with Alex McLeish, working as his assistant at Motherwell, Hibs and Rangers before taking over the fortunes of the Scottish national side in January 2007. Roy Aitken was also part of McLeish's backroom staff. After coming close to taking Scotland to the 2008 European Championship Finals, they resigned to take over at Birmingham City.

SAM WEAVER
(England)

MUCH has been made by the modern media of long throws into the box as a new attacking weapon. But England international and Leeds United assistant trainer Sam Weaver was an exponent of the art well before World War Two.

A Newcastle United FA Cup-winner in 1932, the wing-half won his three England caps while at St James' Park. He later played for Chelsea and Stockport County before guesting for Leeds during the war. He was assistant trainer at Elland Road from summer 1947 until June 1949 when

Southampton and West Ham. He rejoined Leeds in February 2009 and combines his work with his role as former Leeds man Worthington's assistant.

Glynn's younger brother, Ian, captained United, and while Ian was at Everton was called up by England to play Greece in February 1989, but he withdrew because of injury and never got another chance.

Andy Watson.

Sam Weaver demonstrates his prodigious long throw.

he was appointed Millwall's trainer, a role he held until January 1954. He also played county cricket for Somerset and was masseur to Derbyshire CC.

DAVE WILLIAMS
(Wales)

FORMER Welsh international Dave Williams was drafted in to join the Leeds United coaching staff in summer 1995 by Howard Wilkinson.

Vastly experienced, he had already been assistant manager and caretaker manager of Wales, for whom he played five times as a busy Norwich City midfielder, all his caps coming after he turned 30. He took temporary charge of Wales in a 2–1 defeat against Yugoslavia in March 1988 following the departure of Mike England and the appointment of former Leeds star Terry Yorath.

A former Norwich City assistant manager, Williams was in charge of the reserve team at Elland Road before coaching the Manchester United youth team until July 2002. In January 2005, the Welsh FA gave him a new role looking after their Under-21, Under-19 and Under-17 teams under former Leeds hero Brian Flynn.

David Williams.

International Appearances

Appearances given here refer to caps won while with Leeds, including those on loan from other clubs. The figures in brackets after results are goals scored by the player in that match. Before 1924 there was only one Ireland team, then the Republic of Ireland began separate matches.

Attendances have been obtained from contemporary sources, newspapers, handbooks and various websites of countries' Football Associations and the RSSSF (Rec.Sport Soccer Statistics Foundation).

In the key to games, it should be noted that the current European Championship was called the European Nations Cup from 1958 to 1966 when a knockout format was used.

The details provided go up to the end of June 2009.

Key: ANF – African Nations Finals, ACQ – African Nations Qualifier, CC – Confederations Cup, ECC – England Challenge Cup, ECF – European Nations/European Championship Finals, ENQ – European Nations/European Championship Qualifier, F – Friendly, HC – Home Championship, IC – Independence Cup, KC – Kirin Cup, OG – Olympic Games, TT – Toulon Tournament, WCF – World Cup Finals, WCQ – World Cup Qualifier, USBT – USA Bicentennial Tournament, USC – US Cup

Leeds United Full Internationals

ANGOLA
Rui Marques

1 March 2006	F	South Korea (sub)	Seoul	0–1	63,255
2 June 2006	WCF	Iran (sub)	Leipzig	1–1	38,000
16 June 2006	WCF	Mexico (sub)	Hanover	0–0	43,000
13 January 2008	F	Egypt (sub)	Alvercera	3–3	7,705
17 January 2008	F	Morocco	Rabat	1–2	25,000
23 January 2008	ANF	South Africa	Tamale	1–1	15,000
27 January 2008	ANF	Senegal	Tamale	3–1	10,000
31 January 2008	ANF	Tunisia	Tamale	0–0	10,000
4 February 2008	ANF	Egypt	Kumasi	2–1	40,000
1 June 2008	WCQ	Benin	Luanda	3–0	6,000
8 June 2008	WCQ	Niger	Niamey	2–1	23,000
14 June 2008	WCQ	Uganda	Kampala	1–3	20,000
23 June 2008	WCQ	Uganda	Luanda	0–0	16,000
11 February 2009	F	Mali	Paris	0–4	–

AUSTRALIA
Jacob Burns

15 November 2000	F	Scotland (sub)	Hampden Park	2–0	30,985
28 February 2001	F	Colombia	Bogata	2–3	2,071

Harry Kewell

24 April 1996	F	Chile	Antofagasta	0–3	30,000
9 October 1996	F	Saudi Arabia	Riyadh	0–0	–
1 October 1997	F	Tunisia (as sub)	Tunis	3–0	20,000
22 November 1997	WCQ	Iran	Tehran	1–1 (1)	128,000
29 November 1997	WCQ	Iran	Melbourne	2–2 (1)	85,022
16 December 1997	CC	Saudi Arabia	Riyadh	0–1	20,000
19 December 1997	CC	Uruguay	Riyadh	1–0 (1)	22,000
21 December 1997	CC	Brazil	Riyadh	0–6	65,000
23 February 2000	F	Hungary	Budapest	3–0	14,000
11 November 2001	F	France	Melbourne	1–1	53,228
20 November 2001	WCQ	Uruguay	Melbourne	1–0	84,656

Date	Comp	Opponent	Venue	Score	Attendance
25 November 2001	WCQ	Uruguay	Montevideo	0–3	62,000
12 February 2003	F	England	Upton Park	3–1 (1)	34,590

Neil Kilkenny

Date	Comp	Opponent	Venue	Score	Attendance
22 June 2008	F	China	Sydney	0–1	70,054

Paul Okon

Date	Comp	Opponent	Venue	Score	Attendance
12 February 2003	F	England	Upton Park	3–1	34,590
19 August 2003	F	Republic of Ireland	Dublin	1–2	37,200

Mark Viduka

Date	Comp	Opponent	Venue	Score	Attendance
11 November 2001	F	France	Melbourne	1–1	53,228
20 November 2001	WCQ	Uruguay	Melbourne	1–0	84,656
25 November 2001	WCQ	Uruguay	Montevideo	0–3	62,000
12 February 2003	F	England	Upton Park	3–1	34,590
19 August 2003	F	Republic of Ireland	Dublin	1–2 (1)	37,200
7 September 2003	F	Jamaica	Reading	2–1	8,050
30 March 2004	F	South Africa	Loftus Road	1–0	16,108

AUSTRIA
Martin Hiden

Date	Comp	Opponent	Venue	Score	Attendance
25 March 1998	F	Hungary	Vienna	2–3	21,000
24 April 1998	F	USA	Vienna	0–3	17,000
27 May 1998	F	Tunisia (sub)	Vienna	2–1	12,000
19 August 1998	F	France (sub)	Vienna	2–2	44,000
5 September 1998	ECQ	Israel (sub)	Vienna	1–1	20,000
10 October 1998	ECQ	Cyprus	Larnaca	3–0	10,000
14 October 1998	ECQ	San Marino	Serravalle	4–1 (1)	1,218

BRAZIL
Roque Junior

Date	Comp	Opponent	Venue	Score	Attendance
12 October 2003	F	Jamaica	Leicester	1–0	32,000
16 November 2003	WCQ	Peru	Lima	1–1	80,000
19 November 2003	WCQ	Uruguay	Curitiba	3–3	30,000

All on loan from AC Milan

BULGARIA
Radostin Kishishev

Date	Comp	Opponent	Venue	Score	Attendance
28 March 2007	ECQ	Albania	Sofia	0–0	25,000

On loan from Leicester City

CAMEROON
Salomon Olembe

Date	Comp	Opponent	Venue	Score	Attendance
3 February 2004	ANF	Egypt (sub)	Monastir	0–0	20,000

On loan from Marseille

DR CONGO
Tresor Kandol

Date	Comp	Opponent	Venue	Score	Attendance
20 August 2008	F	Togo	Dreux	2–1	1,000

On loan at Millwall

ENGLAND
Peter Barnes

Date	Comp	Opponent	Venue	Score	Attendance
9 September 1981	WCQ	Norway (sub)	Oslo	1–2	22,000
25 May 1982	F	Holland (sub)	Wembley	2–0	69,000

David Batty

Date	Comp	Opponent	Venue	Score	Attendance
21 May 1991	ECC	USSR (sub)	Wembley	3–1	23,798

25 May 1991	ECC	Argentina	Wembley	2–2	44,497
1 June 1991	F	Australia	Sydney	1–0	36,827
3 June 1991	F	New Zealand	Auckland	1–0	17,500
12 June 1991	F	Malaysia	Kuala Lumpur	4–2	41,248
11 September 1991	F	Germany	Wembley	0–1	59,493
16 October 1991	ECQ	Turkey	Wembley	1–0	50,896
12 May 1992	F	Hungary (sub)	Budapest	1–0	12,500
14 June 1992	ECF	France	Malmo	0–0	26,535
17 June 1992	ECF	Sweden	Solna	1–2	30,126
14 October 1992	WCQ	Norway	Wembley	1–1	51,441
17 February 1993	WCQ	San Marino	Wembley	6–0	51,154
9 June 1993	WCQ	United States	Boston	0–2	37,652
13 June 1993	F	Brazil	Washington	1–1	54,118
28 April 1999	F	Hungary	Budapest	1–1	20,000
5 June 1999	ECQ	Sweden	Wembley	0–0	75,824
9 June 1999	ECQ	Bulgaria	Sofia	1–1	22,000
4 September 1999	ECQ	Luxembourg	Wembley	6–0	68,772
8 September 1999	ECQ	Poland	Warsaw	0–0	17,000

Lee Bowyer

7 September 2002	F	Portugal	Villa Park	1–1	40,058

Jack Charlton

10 April 1965	HC	Scotland	Wembley	2–2	98,199
5 May 1965	F	Hungary	Wembley	1–0	52,000
9 May 1965	F	Yugoslavia	Belgrade	1–1	60,000
12 May 1965	F	West Germany	Nuremburg	1–0	67,000
16 May 1965	F	Sweden	Gothenburg	2–1	18,000
2 October 1965	HC	Wales	Cardiff	0–0	30,000
20 October 1965	F	Austria	Wembley	2–3	65,000
10 November 1965	HC	Northern Ireland	Wembley	2–1	71,000
8 December 1965	F	Spain	Madrid	2–0	25,000
5 January 1966	F	Poland	Goodison Park	1–1	47,750
23 February 1966	F	West Germany	Wembley	1–0	75,000
2 April 1966	HC	Scotland	Hampden Park	4–3	133,000
4 May 1966	F	Yugoslavia	Wembley	2–0	54,000
26 June 1966	F	Finland	Helsinki	3–0 (1)	10,500
3 July 1966	F	Denmark	Copenhagen	2–0 (1)	32,000
5 July 1966	F	Poland	Chorzow	1–0	70,000
11 July 1966	WCF	Uruguay	Wembley	0–0	87,148
16 July 1966	WCF	Mexico	Wembley	2–0	92,570
20 July 1966	WCF	France	Wembley	2–0	98,270
23 July 1966	WCF	Argentina	Wembley	1–0	90,584
26 July 1966	WCF	Portugal	Wembley	2–1	94,493
30 July 1966	WCF	West Germany	Wembley	4–3 aet	96,924
22 October 1966	HC/ECQ	Northern Ireland	Belfast	2–0	45,000
2 November 1966	F	Czechoslvakia	Wembley	0–0	75,000
16 November 1966	HC/ECQ	Wales	Wembley	5–1 (1)	76,000
15 April 1967	HC/ECQ	Scotland	Wembley	2–3 (1)	99,063
21 October 1967	HC/ECQ	Wales	Cardiff	3–0	45,000
3 April 1968	ECF	Spain	Wembley	1–0	100,000
15 January 1969	F	Romania	Wembley	1–1 (1)	77,000
12 March 1969	F	France	Wembley	5–0	83,000
7 May 1969	HC	Wales	Wembley	2–1	72,000
5 November 1969	F	Holland	Amsterdam	1–0	40,000
10 December 1969	F	Portugal	Wembley	1–0 (1)	100,000
14 January 1970	F	Holland	Wembley	0–0	75,000
11 June 1970	WCF	Czechoslovakia	Guadalajara	1–0	49,000

Trevor Cherry

24 March 1976	F	Wales	Wrexham	2–1	21,000
15 May 1976	HC	Scotland (sub)	Hampden Park	1–2	85,165
23 May 1976	USBT	Brazil	Los Angeles	1–0	32,495
13 June 1976	WCQ	Finland	Helskini	4–1	24,500
8 September 1976	F	Republic of Ireland	Wembley	1–1	51,000
17 November 1976	WCQ	Italy	Rome	0–2	70,750
30 March 1977	WCQ	Luxembourg	Wembley	5–0	78,000
28 May 1977	HC	Northern Ireland	Belfast	2–1	34,000
4 June 1977	HC	Scotland (sub)	Wembley	1–2	100,000
8 June 1977	F	Brazil	Rio de Janeiro	0–0	77,000
12 June 1977	F	Argentina	Buenos Aires	1–1	60,000
15 June 1977	F	Uruguay	Montevideo	0–0	36,000
7 September 1977	F	Switzerland	Wembley	0–0	43,000
12 October 1977	WCQ	Luxembourg	Luxembourg	2–0	9,250
16 November 1977	WCQ	Italy	Wembley	2–0	92,000
19 April 1978	F	Brazil	Wembley	1–1	92,000
13 May 1978	HC	Wales	Cardiff	3–1	17,750
29 November 1978	F	Czechoslovakia	Wembley	1–0	92,000
23 May 1979	HC	Wales	Wembley	0–0	70,250
10 June 1979	F	Sweden	Solna	0–0	35,691
6 February 1980	ECQ	Republic of Ireland	Wembley	2–0	90,250
13 May 1980	F	Argentina (sub)	Wembley	3–1	90,000
17 May 1980	HC	Wales	Wrexham	4–1	24,250
20 May 1980	HC	Northern Ireland	Wembley	1–1	32,000
24 May 1980	HC	Scotland	Hampden Park	2–0	85,000
31 May 1980	F	Australia	Sydney	2–1	26,750
18 June 1980	ECF	Spain (sub)	Naples	1–2	14,500

Allan Clarke

11 June 1970	WCF	Czechoslovakia	Guadalajara	1–0 (1p)	49,000
12 November 1970	F	East Germany	Wembley	3–1 (1)	93,000
12 May 1971	ECQ	Malta	Wembley	5–0 (1p)	36,000
15 May 1971	HC	Northern Ireland	Belfast	1–0 (1)	33,500
19 May 1971	HC	Wales (sub)	Wembley	0–0	70,000
22 May 1971	HC	Scotland (sub)	Wembley	3–1	91,469
14 February 1973	F	Scotland	Hampden Park	5–0 (2)	48,470
15 May 1973	HC	Wales	Wembley	3–0	39,000
19 May 1973	HC	Scotland	Wembley	1–0	95,950
27 May 1973	F	Czechoslavakia	Prague	1–1 (1)	25,000
6 June 1973	WCQ	Poland	Chorzow	0–2	118,000
10 June 1973	F	USSR	Moscow	2–1	85,000
14 June 1973	F	Italy	Turin	0–2	52,000
26 September 1973	F	Austria	Wembley	7–0 (2)	48,000
17 October 1973	WCQ	Poland	Wembley	1–1 (1p)	100,000
14 November 1973	F	Italy	Wembley	0–2	95,000
20 November 1974	ECQ	Portugal	Wembley	0–0	70,750
30 October 1975	ECQ	Czechoslovakia	Bratislava	1–2	45,000
19 November 1975	ECQ	Portugal (sub)	Lisbon	1–1	30,000

Terry Cooper

12 March 1969	F	France	Wembley	5–0	83,000
7 May 1969	HC	Wales	Wembley	2–1	72,000
10 May 1969	HC	Scotland	Wembley	4–1	89,902
1 June 1969	F	Mexico	Mexico City	0–0	105,000
14 January 1970	F	Holland	Wembley	0–0	75,000
25 February 1970	F	Belgium	Brussels	3–1	20,500
21 May 1970	F	Colombia	Bogata	4–0	28,000

24 May 1970	F	Ecuador	Quito	2–0	22,250
2 June 1970	WCF	Romania	Guadalajara	1–0	50,000
7 June 1970	WCF	Brazil	Guadalajara	0–1	66,750
11 June 1970	WCF	Czechoslovakia	Guadalajara	1–0	49,000
14 June 1970	WCF	West Germany	Leon	2–3 aet	23,250
25 November 1970	F	East Germany	Wembley	3–1	93,000
12 May 1971	ECQ	Malta	Wembley	5–0	36,500
15 May 1971	HC	Northern Ireland	Belfast	1–0	33,500
19 May 1971	HC	Wales	Wembley	0–0	70,000
22 May 1971	HC	Scotland	Wembley	3–1	91,469
13 October 1971	ECQ	Switzerland	Basle	3–2	58,000
10 November 1971	ECQ	Switzerland	Wembley	1–1	98,000
20 November 1974	ECQ	Portugal	Wembley	0–0	70,750

Wilf Copping

13 May 1933	F	Italy	Rome	1–1	50,000
20 May 1933	F	Switzerland	Berne	4–0	26,000
14 October 1933	HC	Ireland	Belfast	3–0	35,000
15 November 1933	HC	Wales	Newcastle	1–2	12,000
6 December 1933	F	France	Tottenham	4–1	17,097
14 April 1934	HC	Scotland	Wembley	3–0	92,963
24 May 1939	F	Romania	Bucharest	2–0	40,000

Tony Currie

19 April 1978	F	Brazil	Wembley	1–1	92,000
13 May 1978	HC	Wales (sub)	Cardiff	3–1 (1)	17,750
16 May 1978	HC	Northern Ireland	Wembley	1–0	48,000
20 May 1978	HC	Scotland	Hampden Park	0–1	90,000
24 May 1987	F	Hungary (sub)	Wembley	4–1 (1)	74,000
29 November 1978	F	Czechoslovakia	Wembley	1–0	92,000
7 February 1979	ECQ	Northern Ireland	Wembley	4–0	92,000
19 May 1979	HC	Northern Ireland	Belfast	2–0	34,000
23 May 1979	HC	Wales	Wembley	0–0	70,250
10 June 1979	F	Sweden	Solna	0–0	35,691

Tony Dorigo

11 September 1991	F	Germany	Wembley	0–1	59,493
25 March 1992	F	Czechoslovakia (sub)	Prague	2–2	12,320
12 May 1992	F	Hungary	Budapest	1–0	12,500
17 May 1992	F	Brazil	Wembley	1–1	53,428
17 February 1993	WCQ	San Marino	Wembley	6–0	51,154
29 May 1993	WCQ	Poland	Katowice	1–1	60,000
9 June 1993	USC	USA	Boston	0–2	37,652
13 June 1993	USC	Brazil	Washington	1–1	54,118
13 October 1993	WCQ	Holland	Rotterdam	0–2	48,000

Willis Edwards

1 March 1926	HC	Wales	Crystal Palace	3–1	23,000
17 April 1926	HC	Scotland	Old Trafford	0–1	49,429
20 October 1926	HC	Ireland	Anfield	3–3	20,000
14 February 1927	HC	Wales	Wrexham	3–3	16,910
2 April 1927	HC	Scotland	Hampden Park	2–1	111,214
11 May 1927	F	Belgium	Brussels	9–1	35,000
21 May 1927	F	Luxembourg	Esch	5–2	5,000
26 May 1927	F	France	Colombes	6–0	25,000
31 March 1928	HC	Scotland	Wembley	1–5	80,868
17 May 1928	F	France	Colombes	5–1	40,000
19 May 1928	F	Belgium	Antwerp	3–1	25,000

22 October 1928	HC	Ireland	Goodison Park	2–1	34,000
17 November 1928	HC	Wales	Swansea	3–2	14,000
13 April 1929	HC	Scotland	Hampden Park	0–1	110,512
19 October 1929	HC	Ireland	Belfast	3–0	37,000
20 November 1929	HC	Wales	Stamford Bridge	6–0	32,945

Rio Ferdinand

28 February 2001	F	Spain	Villa Park	3–0	42,129
24 March 2001	WCQ	Finland	Anfield	2–1	44,262
28 March 2001	WCQ	Albania	Tirana	3–1	18,000
25 May 2001	F	Mexico	Derby	4–0	33,597
6 June 2001	WCQ	Greece	Athens	2–0	46,000
1 September 2001	WCQ	Germany	Munich	5–1	63,000
5 September 2001	WCQ	Albania	Newcastle	2–0	51,046
6 October 2001	WCQ	Greece	Old Trafford	2–2	66,009
10 November 2001	F	Sweden	Old Trafford	1–1	64,413
13 February 2002	F	Holland	Amsterdam	1–1	48,500
21 May 2002	F	South Korea	Seoguipo	1–1	39,876
26 May 2002	F	Cameroon	Kobe	2–2	42,000
2 June 2002	WCF	Sweden	Saitama	1–1	52,271
7 June 2002	WCF	Argentina	Sapporo	1–0	35,927
12 June 2002	WCF	Nigeria	Osaka	0–0	44,864
15 June 2002	WCF	Denmark	Niigata	3–0	40,582
21 June 2002	WCF	Brazil	Shizuoka	1–2	47,436

Robbie Fowler

27 March 2002	F	Italy (sub)	Leeds	1–2 (1)	36,635
17 April 2002	F	Paraguay (sub)	Anfield	4–0	42,713
26 May 2002	F	Cameroon (sub)	Kobe	2–2 (1)	42,000
15 June 2002	WCF	Denmark (sub)	Niigata	3–0	40,582

Billy Furness

13 May 1933	F	Italy	Rome	1–1	50,000

Brian Greenhoff

31 May 1980	F	Australia (sub)	Sydney	2–1	26,750

Ernie Hart

17 November 1928	HC	Wales	Swansea	3–2	14,000
19 October 1929	HC	Ireland	Belfast	3–0	37,000
20 November 1929	HC	Wales	Stamford Bridge	6–0	32,945
7 December 1932	F	Austria	Stamford Bridge	4–3	42,000
1 April 1933	HC	Scotland	Hampden Park	1–2	134,710
14 April 1933	HC	Scotland	Wembley	3–0	92,363
10 May 1934	F	Hungary	Budapest	1–2	40,000
16 May 1934	F	Czechoslovakia	Prague	1–2	40,000

Norman Hunter

8 December 1965	F	Spain (sub)	Madrid	2–0	25,000
23 February 1966	F	West Germany	Wembley	1–0	75,000
4 May 1966	F	Yugoslavia	Wembley	2–0	54,000
26 June 1966	F	Finland	Helsinki	3–0	10,500
27 May 1967	F	Austria	Vienna	1–0	85,000
8 May 1968	ECQ	Spain	Madrid	2–1 (1)	120,000
22 May 1968	F	Sweden	Wembley	3–1	72,500
1 June 1968	F	West Germany	Hanover	0–1	79,250
5 June 1968	ECF	Yugoslavia	Florence	0–1	40,000
8 June 1968	ECF	USSR	Rome	2–0	80,000

15 January 1969	F	Romania	Wembley	1–1	77,000
7 May 1979	HC	Wales	Wembley	2–1	72,000
14 January 1970	F	Holland	Wembley	0–0	75,000
14 June 1970	WCF	West Germany (sub)	Leon	2–3 aet	23,250
3 February 1971	ECQ	Malta	Ta'qali	1–0	20,000
29 April 1972	ECF	West Germany	Wembley	1–3	95,000
13 May 1972	ECF	West Germany	Berlin	0–0	75,000
20 May 1972	HC	Wales	Cardiff	3–0	33,000
23 May 1972	HC	Northern Ireland	Wembley	0–1	43,000
27 May 1972	HC	Scotland	Hampden Park	1–0	119,325
15 November 1972	WCQ	Wales	Cardiff	1–0	39,000
24 January 1973	WCQ	Wales	Wembley	1–1 (1)	73,000
10 June 1973	F	USSR (sub)	Moscow	2–1	85,000
26 September 1973	F	Austria	Wembley	7–0	48,000
17 October 1973	WCQ	Poland	Wembley	1–1	100,000
15 May 1974	HC	Northern Ireland (sub)	Wembley	1–0	47,000
18 May 1974	HC	Scotland	Hampden Park	0–2	94,487
30 October 1974	ECQ	Czechoslovakia	Wembley	3–0	85,000

Mick Jones

14 January 1970	F	Holland	Wembley	0–0	75,000

Paul Madeley

15 May 1971	HC	Northern Ireland	Belfast	1–0	33,500
13 October 1971	ECQ	Switzerland	Basle	3–2	58,000
10 November 1971	ECQ	Switzerland	Wembley	1–1	98,000
1 December 1971	ECQ	Greece	Pireus	2–0	42,000
29 April 1972	ECF	West Germany	Wembley	2–3	95,000
13 May 1972	ECF	West Germany	Berlin	0–0	75,000
20 May 1972	HC	Wales	Cardiff	3–0	33,000
27 May 1972	HC	Scotland	Hampden Park	1–0	119,325
14 February 1973	F	Scotland	Hampden Park	5–0	48,470
27 May 1973	F	Czechoslovakia	Prague	1–1	25,000
6 June 1973	WCQ	Poland	Chorzow	0–2	118,000
10 June 1973	F	USSR	Moscow	2–1	85,000
14 June 1973	F	Italy	Turin	0–2	52,000
26 September 1973	F	Austria	Wembley	7–0	48,000
17 October 1973	WCQ	Poland	Wembley	1–1	100,000
14 November 1973	F	Italy	Wembley	0–1	95,000
30 October 1974	ENQ	Czechoslovakia	Wembley	3–0	85,000
20 November 1974	ENQ	Portugal	Wembley	0–0	70,750
16 April 1975	ENQ	Cyprus	Wembley	5–0	65,000
30 October 1975	ENQ	Czechoslovakia	Bratislava	1–2	30,000
19 November 1975	ENQ	Portugal	Lisbon	1–1	40,000
13 June 1976	ENQ	Finland	Helsinki	4–1	24,500
8 September 1976	F	Republic of Ireland	Wembley	1–1	51,000
9 February 1977	F	Holland	Wembley	0–2	90,000

Nigel Martyn

24 May 1997	F	South Africa	Old Trafford	2–1	52,676
15 November 1997	F	Cameroon	Wembley	2–0	46,176
11 February 1998	F	Chile	Wembley	0–2	65,228
29 May 1998	F	Belgium	Casablanca	0–0	25,000
18 November 1998	F	Czech Republic	Wembley	2–0	38,535
10 February 1999	F	France (sub)	Wembley	0–2	74,111
4 September 1999	ECQ	Luxembourg	Wembley	6–0	68,772
8 September 1999	ECQ	Poland	Warsaw	0–0	17,000
10 October 1999	F	Belgium (sub)	Sunderland	2–1	40,897

31 May 2000	F	Ukraine	Wembley	2–0	55,975
20 June 2000	ECF	Romania	Charleroi	2–3	30,000
28 February 2001	F	Spain (sub)	Villa Park	3–0	42,129
25 May 2001	F	Mexico	Derby	4–0	33,597
15 August 2001	F	Holland	Tottenham	0–2	35,238
6 October 2001	WCQ	Greece	Old Trafford	1–1	66,009
10 November 2001	F	Sweden	Old Trafford	1–1	64,413
13 February 2002	F	Holland	Amsterdam	1–1	48,500
27 March 2002	F	Italy	Elland Road	1–2	36,635
21 May 2002	F	South Korea	Seoguipo	1–1	39,876
26 May 2002	F	Cameroon	Kobe	2–2	42,000

Danny Mills

25 May 2001	F	Mexico (sub)	Derby	4–0	33,597
15 August 2001	F	Holland (sub)	Tottenham	0–2	35,238
10 November 2001	F	Sweden (sub)	Old Trafford	1–1	64,413
27 March 2002	F	Italy	Elland Road	1–2	36,635
17 April 2002	F	Paraguay (sub)	Anfield	4–0	42,713
21 May 2002	F	South Korea	Seoguipo	1–1	39,876
26 May 2002	F	Cameroon (sub)	Kobe	2–2	42,000
2 June 2003	WCF	Sweden	Saitana	1–1	52,271
7 June 2003	WCF	Argentina	Sapporo	1–0	35,927
12 June 2003	WCF	Nigeria	Osaka	0–0	44,864
15 June 2003	WCF	Denmark	Niigata	3–0	40,582
21 June 2003	WCF	Brazil	Shizuoka	1–2	47,436
7 September 2003	F	Portugal	Villa Park	1–1	40,058
12 February 2003	F	Australia (sub)	West Ham	1–3	34,590
22 May 2003	F	South Africa	Durban	2–1	48,000
3 June 2003	F	Serbia Montenegro	Leicester	2–1	30,900
11 June 2003	F	Slovakia	Middlesbrough	2–1	35,000
20 August 2003	F	Croatia (sub)	Ipswich	3–1	28,700
18 February 2003+	F	Portugal (sub)	Faro	1–1	27,000

+ On loan at Middlesbrough

Mike O'Grady

12 March 1969	F	France	Wembley	5–0 (1)	83,000

Alan Peacock

2 October 1965	HC	Wales	Cardiff	0–0	30,000
10 November 1965	HC	Northern Ireland	Wembley	2–1 (1)	71,000

Paul Reaney

11 December 1968	F	Bulgaria (sub)	Wembley	1–1	80,000
10 December 1969	F	Portugal	Wembley	1–0	100,000
3 February 1971	ECQ	Malta	Ta'quali	1–0	20,000

Paul Robinson

12 February 2003	F	Australia (sub)	West Ham	1–3	34,590
22 May 2003	F	South Africa (sub)	Durban	2–1	48,000
20 August 2003	F	Croatia (sub)	Ipswich	3–1	28,700
16 November 2003	F	Denmark (sub)	Old Trafford	2–3	64,159

Alan Smith

25 May 2001	F	Mexico (sub)	Derby	4–0	33,597
6 June 2001	WCQ	Greece (sub)	Athens	2–0	46,000
15 August 2001	F	Holland (sub)	Tottenham	0–2	35,238
7 September 2002	F	Portugal	Villa Park	1–1 (1)	40,058
12 October 2002	ECQ	Slovakia (sub)	Bratislava	2–1	30,000

16 October 2002	ECQ	Macedonia	Southampton	2–2	32,095
18 February 2003	F	Portugal (sub)	Faro	1–1	27,000
31 March 2003	F	Sweden (sub)	Gothenburg	0–1	40,464

Bert Sproston

17 October 1936	HC	Wales	Cardiff	1–2	40,000
23 October 1937	HC	Ireland	Belfast	5–1	40,000
17 November 1937	HC	Wales	Middlesbrough	2–1	30,608
1 December 1937	F	Czechoslovakia	Tottenham	5–4	35,000
9 April 1938	HC	Scotland	Wembley	0–1	93,267
14 May 1938	F	Germany	Berlin	6–3	105,000
21 May 1938	F	Switzerland	Zurich	1–2	25,000
26 May 1938	F	France	Paris	4–2	55,000

Eric Stephenson

9 April 1938	HC	Scotland	Wembley	0–1	93,267
16 November 1938	HC	Ireland	Old Trafford	7–0	40,386

Russell Wainscoat

13 April 1929	HC	Scotland	Hampden Park	0–1	110,512

Jason Wilcox

23 February 2000	F	Argentina	Wembley	0–0	74,008

Jonathan Woodgate

9 June 1999	ECQ	Bulgaria	Sofia	1–1	22,000
7 September 2002	F	Portugal (sub)	Villa Park	1–1	40,058
12 October 2002	ECQ	Slovakia	Bratislava	2–1	30,000
16 October 2002	ECQ	Macedonia	Southampton	2–2	32,095

FRANCE
Eric Cantona

19 February 1992	F	England	Wembley	0–2	58,723
25 March 1992	F	Belgium	Paris	3–3	25,000
27 May 1992	F	Switzerland	Lausanne	2–1	21,000
5 June 1992	F	Holland	Lens	1–1	40,000
10 June 1992	ECF	Sweden	Stockholm	1–1	29,860
14 June 1992	ECF	England	Malmo	0–0	26,535
17 June 1992	ECF	Denmark	Malmo	1–2	25,763
14 October 1992	WCQ	Austria	Paris	2–0 (1)	39,186
14 November 1992	WCQ	Finland	Paris	2–1 (1)	30,000

Olivier Dacourt

30 May 2001	CC	South Korea (sub)	Taegu	5–0	61,500
1 June 2001	CC	Australia	Taegu	1–0	44,000
3 June 2001	CC	Mexico (sub)	Ulsan	4–0	28,000
16 October 2002	ECQ	Malta (sub)	Valletta	4–0	10,000
30 April 2003	F	Egypt	Paris	5–0	54,554

GHANA
Tony Yeboah

23 April 1995*	ANQ	Niger	Accra	1–0 (1)	40,000
25 May 1995	F	Norway	Oslo	2–3	8,312
1 July 1995	F	Ivory Coast	Abidjan	0–2	—
30 July 1995	ANQ	Congo	Brazzaville	2–0	21,000
12 November 1995	F	Sierra Leone	Accra	2–0	—
14 December 1995	F	Egypt	Cairo	2–1	15,000

5 January 1996	F	Saudi Arabia	Jeddah	1–1	20,000
9 January 1996	F	Zimbabwe	Harare	1–1	—
14 January 1996	ANF	Ivory Coast	Port Elizabeth	2–0 (1)	8,000
19 January 1996	ANF	Tunisia	Port Elizabeth	2–1	1,000
25 January 1996	ACF	Mozambique	Bloemfontein	2–0	3,500
28 January 1996	ACF	Zaire	Port Elizabeth	1–0 (1)	8,000
31 January 1996	ACF	South Africa	Johannesburg	0–3	80,000
27 March 1996	F	Brazil	Sao Joue de Rio Preto	2–8 (1)	20,000
6 January 1997	F	Togo	Lome	0–4	—
12 January 1997	WCQ	Morocco	Kumasi	2–2	45,000
26 January 1997	ANQ	Zimbabwe	Harare	0–0	45,000
5 April 1997	WCQ	Sierra Leone	Freetown	1–1	70,000

*This match was later annulled as Niger withdrew from the competition.

HOLLAND
Jimmy-Floyd Hasselbaink
27 May 1998	F	Cameroon	Arnhem	0–0	24,000
1 June 1998	F	Paraguay	Eindhoven	5–1 (1)	21,000
5 June 1998	F	Nigeria	Amsterdam	5–1 (1)	44,500
13 June 1998	WCF	Belgium	St Denis	0–0	75,000
25 June 1998	WCF	Mexico	St Etienne	2–2	35,000

ICELAND
Gylfi Einarsson
26 March 2005	WCQ	Croatia	Zagreb	0–4	17,912
30 March 2005	F	Italy	Padova	0–0	16,687
4 June 2005	WCQ	Hungary	Reykjavik	2–3	4,613
18 August 2005	F	South Africa (sub)	Reykjavik	4–1	3,302
3 September 2005	WCQ	Croatia	Reykjavik	1–3	5,520
7 October 2005	F	Poland	Warsaw	2–3	7,500
12 October 2005	WCQ	Sweden (sub)	Solna	1–3	33,000
28 February 2006	F	Trinidad & Tobago (sub)	Loftus Road	0–2	7,890

NORTHERN IRELAND
Bobby Browne
19 October 1935	HC	England	Belfast	1–3	40,000
11 March 1936	HC	Wales	Belfast	3–2	20,000
23 October 1937	HC	England	Belfast	1–5	40,000
16 March 1938	HC	Wales	Belfast	1–0	15,000
8 October 1938	HC	Scotland	Belfast	0–2	40,000
16 November 1938	HC	England	Maine Road	0–7	40,386

David Cochrane
16 November 1938	HC	England	Maine Road	0–7	40,386
15 March 1939	HC	Wales	Wrexham	1–3	24,000
28 September 1946	HC	England	Belfast	2–7	57,000
27 November 1946	HC	Scotland	Hampden Park	0–0	98,776
16 April 1947	HC	Wales	Belfast	2–1	43,000
4 October 1947	HC	Scotland	Belfast	2–0	52,000
5 November 1947	HC	England	Goodison Park	2–2	68,000
10 March 1948	HC	Wales	Wrexham	0–2	33,160
17 November 1948	HC	Scotland	Hampden Park	2–3	100,000
9 March 1949	HC	Wales	Belfast	0–2	—
1 October 1949	HC	Scotland	Belfast	2–8	50,000
16 November 1949	HC	England	Maine Road	2–9	70,000

Wilbur Cush

4 December 1957	F	Italy	Belfast	2–2 (2)	50,000
15 January 1958	WCQ	Italy	Belfast	2–1 (1)	60,000
16 April 1958	HC	Wales	Cardiff	1–1	38,000
8 June 1958	WCF	Czechoslovakia	Halmstad	1–0 (1)	10,647
11 June 1958	WCF	Argentina	Halmstad	1–3	14,174
15 June 1958	WCF	West Germany	Malmo	2–2	21,990
17 June 1958	WCF	Czechoslovakia	Malmo	2–1	6,196
19 June 1958	WCF	France	Norrkopping	0–4	11,800
4 October 1958	HC	England	Belfast	3–3 (1)	58,000
15 October 1958	F	Spain	Madrid	2–6	–
5 November 1958	HC	Scotland	Hampden Park	2–2	72,732
22 April 1959	HC	Wales	Belfast	4–1	35,000
3 October 1959	HC	Scotland	Belfast	0–4	56,000
18 November 1959	HC	England	Wembley	1–2	60,000
6 April 1960	HC	Wales	Wrexham	2–3	16,500

Harry Duggan

19 October 1929	HC	England	Belfast	0–3	37,000
20 October 1930	HC	England	Bramall Lane	1–5	30,000
22 April 1931	HC	Wales	Wrexham	2–3	11,693
17 October 1932	HC	England	Blackpool	0–1	23,000
14 October 1933	HC	England	Belfast	0–3	35,000
20 October 1934	HC	Scotland	Belfast	2–1	39,752
27 March 1935	HC	Wales	Wrexham	1–3	17,000
13 November 1935	HC	Scotland	Tynecastle	1–2	30,000

David Healy

9 February 2005	F	Canada	Belfast	0–1	11,156
26 March 2005	WCQ	England	Old Trafford	0–4	65,239
30 March 2005	WCQ	Poland	Warsaw	0–1	25,000
4 June 2005	F	Germany	Belfast	1–4(1p)	14,000
17 August 2005	F	Malta	Valetta	1–1 (1)	1,850
3 September 2005	WCQ	Azerbaijan	Belfast	2–0	11,909
7 September 2005	WCQ	England	Belfast	1–0 (1)	14,000
8 October 2005	WCQ	Wales	Belfast	2–3	14,000
12 October 2005	WCQ	Austria	Vienna	0–2	20,000
1 March 2006	F	Estonia	Belfast	1–0	14,000
16 August 2006	F	Finland	Helsinki	2–1 (1)	12,500
2 September 2006	ECQ	Iceland	Belfast	0–3	14,500
6 September 2006	ECQ	Spain	Belfast	3–2 (3)	14,500
7 October 2006	ECQ	Denmark	Copenhagen	0–0	41,482
11 October 2006	ECQ	Latvia	Belfast	1–0 (1)	14,500
24 March 2007	ECQ	Liechtenstein	Vaduz	4–1 (3)	4,340
28 March 2007	ECQ	Sweden	Belfast	2–1 (2)	14,500

Billy McAdams

9 May 1962	F	Holland	Rotterdam	0–4	30,000

Jim McCabe

17 November 1948	HC	Scotland	Hampden Park	2–3	100,000
9 March 1949	HC	Wales	Belfast	0–2	–
16 November 1949	HC	England	Maine Road	2–9	70,000
7 March 1951	HC	Wales	Belfast	1–2	12,000
15 April 1953	HC	Wales	Belfast	2–3	45,000
3 October 1953	HC	Scotland	Belfast	2–0	58,248

John McClelland

27 March 1990	F	Norway	Belfast	2–3	3,500

Con Martin

4 October 1947	HC	Scotland	Belfast	2–0	52,000
5 November 1947	HC	England	Goodison Park	2–2	68,000
10 March 1948	HC	Wales	Wrexham	0–2	33,160

Jim Twomey

16 March 1938	HC	Wales	Belfast	1–0	15,000
16 November 1938	HC	England	Maine Road	0–7	40,386

Nigel Worthington

7 September 1994	ECQ	Portugal	Belfast	1–2	6,000
12 October 1994	ECQ	Austria	Vienna	2–1	26,000
16 November 1994	ECQ	Republic of Ireland	Belfast	0–4	10,336
29 March 1995	ECQ	Republic of Ireland	Dublin	1–1	32,200
26 April 1995	ECQ	Latvia	Riga	1–0	1,560
22 May 1995	F	Canada	Edmondton	0–0	12,112
26 May 1995	F	Chile	Edmondton	1–2	6,124
7 June 1995	ECQ	Latvia	Belfast	1–2	6,000
3 September 1995	ECQ	Portugal	Porto	1–1	50,000
11 October 1995	ECQ	Liechtenstein	Eschen	4–0	1,100
15 November 1995	ECQ	Austria	Belfast	5–2	8,000
27 March 1996	F	Norway	Belfast	0–2	5,343
24 April 1996	F	Sweden	Belfast	1–2	5,666
29 May 1996	F	Germany	Belfast	1–1	11,770

NORWAY
Eirik Bakke

23 February 1999	F	Turkey (sub)	Istanbul	2–0	7,000
27 February 2000	F	Slovakia	Oslo	2–0	16,518
3 June 2000	F	Italy	Oslo	1–0	25,248
13 June 2000	ECF	Spain	Rotterdam	1–0	50,000
18 June 2000	ECF	Yugoslavia	Liege	0–1	24,000
21 June 2000	ECF	Slovenia	Arnhem	0–0	22,000
7 October 2000	WCQ	Wales	Cardiff	1–1	55,000
11 October 2000	WCQ	Ukraine	Oslo	0–1	23,612
28 February 2001	F	Northern Ireland	Belfast	4–0	7,502
25 April 2001	F	Bulgaria	Oslo	2–1	6,211
2 June 2001	WCQ	Ukraine	Kiev	0–0	45,000
6 June 2001	WCQ	Belarus	Oslo	1–1	17,164
6 October 2001	WCQ	Armenia	Yerevan	4–1	12,000
17 April 2002	F	Sweden (sub)	Oslo	0–0	20.759
14 May 2002	F	Japan	Oslo	3–0	8,348
21 August 2002	F	Holland	Oslo	0–1	15,356
7 September 2002	ECQ	Denmark	Oslo	2–2	25,114
12 October 2002	ECQ	Romania	Bucharest	1–0	20,000
16 October 2002	ECQ	Bosnia-Herzegovina	Oslo	2–0	24,169
2 April 2003	ECQ	Luxembourg	Luxembourg	2–0	3,000
22 May 2003	F	Finland	Oslo	2–0	13,436
7 June 2003	ECQ	Denmark	Copenhagen	0–1	41,824
11 June 2003	ECQ	Romania	Oslo	1–1	24,890

Alf–Inge Haaland

20 August 1997	WCQ	Finland (sub)	Helsinki	4–0	35,520
25 August 1997	F	France	Marseilles	3–3	55,000
10 September 1997	WCQ	Switzerland (sub)	Oslo	5–0	22,603

25 March 1998	F	Belgium (sub)	Brussels	2–2	13,371
27 May 1998	F	Saudi Arabia	Molde	6–0	13,114
10 October 1998	ECQ	Slovenia	Ljubljana	2–1	6,200
14 October 1998	ECQ	Albania	Oslo	2–2	17,770
18 November 1998	F	Egypt	Cairo	1–1	25,000
28 April 1998	ECQ	Georgia	Tbilisi	4–1	20,000
5 June 1998	ECQ	Albania	Tirana	2–1	6,211

Gunnar Halle

30 April 1997	WCQ	Finland (sub)	Oslo	1–1	22,287
30 May 1997	F	Brazil (sub)	Oslo	4–2	21,799
20 July 1997	F	Iceland	Reykjavik	1–0	7,500
20 August 1997	WCQ	Finland	Helsinki	4–0	35,520
6 September 1997	WCQ	Azerbajdjan (sub)	Baku	1–0	10,000
10 September 1997	WCQ	Switzerland	Oslo	5–0	22,603
25 March 1998	F	Belgium	Brussels	2–2	13,371
20 May 1998	F	Mexico	Oslo	5–2	16,274
16 June 1998	WCF	Scotland	Bordeaux	1–1	30,236
27 March 1999	ECQ	Greece (sub)	Athens	2–0	50,000
20 May 1999	F	Jamaica	Oslo	6–0	9,630

Frank Strandli

15 January 1994	F	USA	Phoenix	1–0 (1)	20,000
20 April 1994	F	Portugal	Oslo	0–0	17,509

REPUBLIC OF IRELAND
Jeff Chandler

26 September 1979	F	Czechoslovakia (sub)	Prague	1–4	12,000
29 October 1979	F	USA	Dublin	3–2	17,000

Jonathan Douglas

7 October 2006	ECQ	Cyprus (sub)	Nicosia	2–5	12,000
11 October 2006	ECQ	Czech Republic	Dublin	1–0	35,500
15 November 2006	ECQ	San Marino (sub)	Dublin	5–0	34,018
24 March 2007	ECQ	Wales	Dublin	1–0	72,539
8 September 2007	ECQ	Slovakia (sub)	Bratislava	2–2	12,360

Harry Duggan

27 April 1927	F	Italy B	Dublin	1–2	20,000
11 May 1930	F	Belgium	Brussels	3–1	15,000
3 May 1936	F	Hungary	Budapest	3–3	20,000
9 May 1936	F	Luxembourg	Luxembourg	5–1	8,000

Peter Fitzgerald

28 September 1960	F	Wales	Dublin	2–3	20,000
6 November 1960	F	Norway	Dublin	3–1 (2)	26,000
7 May 1961	WCQ	Scotland	Dublin	0–3	36,000

Johnny Giles

23 September 1963	ECQ	Austria	Vienna	0–0	26,800
13 October 1963	ECQ	Austria	Dublin	3–2	40,000
11 March 1964	ECQ	Spain	Seville	1–5	27,200
8 April 1964	ECQ	Spain	Dublin	0–2	38,100
10 May 1964	F	Poland	Cracow	1–3	60,000
13 May 1964	F	Norway	Oslo	4–1 (1)	14,354
24 May 1964	F	England	Dublin	1–3	40,000
5 May 1965	WCQ	Spain	Dublin	1–0	40,772
27 October 1965	WCQ	Spain	Seville	1–4	29,452

10 November 1965	WCQ	Spain	Paris	0–1	35,731
22 May 1966	F	Austria	Vienna	0–1	33,000
25 May 1966	F	Belgium	Liege	3–2	3,000
23 October 1966	ECQ	Spain	Dublin	0–0	37,000
16 November 1966	ECQ	Turkey	Dublin	2–1	20,000
22 February 1967	ECQ	Turkey	Ankara	1–2	35,000
10 November 1968	F	Austria	Dublin	2–2	18,000
4 December 1968	WCQ	Denmark*	Dublin	1–1 (1p)	23,000
4 May 1969	WCQ	Czechoslovakia	Dublin	1–2	32,002
21 September 1969	F	Scotland	Dublin	1–1	27,000
6 May 1970	F	Poland	Poznan	1–2	35,000
9 May 1970	F	West Germany	Berlin	1–2	60,000
10 May 1971	ECQ	Italy	Dublin	1–2	25,000
15 November 1972	WCQ	France	Dublin	2–1	30,000
13 May 1973	WCQ	USSR	Moscow	0–1	70,000
5 May 1974	F	Brazil	Rio de Janiero	1–2	74,696
8 May 1974	F	Uruguay	Montevideo	0–2	40,000
12 May 1974	F	Chile	Santiago	2–1	—
30 October 1974	WCQ	USSR	Dublin	3–0	35,000
20 November 1974	ECQ	Turkey	Izmir	1–1	67,000
10 May 1975	ECQ	Switzerland	Dublin	2–1	50,000
18 May 1975	ECQ	USSR	Kiev	1–2	100,000
21 May 1975	ECQ	Switzerland	Berne	0–1	20,000

*Abandoned after 50 minutes because of fog. Caps were still awarded.

Ian Harte

2 June 1996	F	Croatia (sub)	Dublin	2–2	29,100
4 June 1996	F	Holland	Rotterdam	1–3	15,002
9 June 1996	USC	Mexico	New Jersey	2–2	25,332
15 June 1996	USC	Bolivia	New Jersey	3–0 (1)	14,624
31 August 1996	WCQ	Liechtenstein	Eschen	5–0 (1)	4,000
9 October 1996	WCQ	Macedonia	Dublin	3–0	31,671
10 November 1996	WCQ	Iceland (sub)	Dublin	0–0	33,869
11 February 1997	F	Wales	Cardiff	0–0	7,000
2 April 1997	WCQ	Macedonia (sub)	Skopje	3–0	8,000
30 April 1997	WCQ	Romania	Bucharest	0–1	21,500
21 May 1997	WCQ	Liechtenstein	Dublin	5–0	28,575
20 August 1997	WCQ	Lithuania	Dublin	0–0	32,600
6 September 1997	WCQ	Iceland	Reykjavik	4–2	5,000
10 September 1997	WCQ	Lithuania	Vilnius	2–1	7,000
29 October 1997	WCQ	Belgium	Dublin	1–1	32,305
16 November 1997	WCQ	Belgium	Brussels	1–2	38,000
22 April 1998	F	Argentina	Dublin	0–2	38,000
23 May 1998	F	Mexico	Dublin	0–0	25,500
10 February 1999	F	Paraguay	Dublin	2–0 (1)	27,600
4 September 1999	ECQ	Croatia (sub)	Zagreb	0–1	25,000
8 September 1999	ECQ	Malta (sub)	Valletta	3–2	6,200
23 February 2000	F	Czech Republic	Dublin	3–2	30,543
2 September 2000	WCQ	Holland	Amsterdam	2–2	50,000
7 October 2000	WCQ	Portugal	Lisbon	1–1	65,000
11 October 2000	WCQ	Estonia	Dublin	2–0	34,562
15 November 2000	F	Finland	Dublin	3–0	22,368
24 March 2001	WCQ	Cyprus	Nicosia	4–0 (1)	13,000
28 March 2001	WCQ	Andorra	Barcelona	3–0 (1p)	5,000
25 April 2001	WCQ	Andorra	Dublin	3–1	30,000
2 June 2001	WCQ	Portugal	Dublin	1–1	34,000
6 June 2001	WCQ	Estonia	Tallin	2–0	9,000
15 August 2001	F	Croatia	Dublin	2–2	27,000

1 September 2001	WCQ	Holland	Dublin	1–0	49,000
6 October 2001	WCQ	Cyprus	Dublin	4–0 (1)	35,000
10 November 2001	WCQPO	Iran	Dublin	2–0 (1p)	35,000
15 November 2001	WCQPO	Iran	Teheran	0–1	110,000
13 February 2002	F	Russia	Dublin	2–0	44,000
27 March 2002	F	Denmark	Dublin	3–0 (1)	42,000
17 April 2002	F	United States	Dublin	2–1	39,000
16 May 2002	F	Nigeria	Dublin	1–2	42,652
1 June 2002	WCF	Cameroon	Niigata	1–1	33,679
5 June 2002	WCF	Germany	Ibaraki	1–1	35,854
11 June 2002	WCF	Saudi Arabia	Yokohama	3–0	65,320
16 June 2002	WCF	Spain	Suwon	1–1*	38,926
21 August 2002	F	Finland	Helsinki	3–0	12,225
7 September 2002	ECQ	Russia	Moscow	2–4	23,000
16 October 2002	ECQ	Switzerland	Dublin	1–2	40,000
12 February 2003	F	Scotland	Glasgow	2–0	33,337
20 April 2003	F	Norway	Dublin	1–0	32,643
19 August 2003	F	Australia (sub)	Dublin	2–1	37,200
6 September 2003	ECQ	Russia (sub)	Dublin	1–1	36,000
9 September 2003	F	Turkey	Dublin	2–2	27,000
11 October 2003	ECQ	Switzerland	Basle	0–2	31,006
18 November 2003	F	Canada (sub)	Dublin	3–0	23,253
31 March 2004	F	Czech Republic	Dublin	2–1 (1)	42,000
28 April 2004	F	Poland	Bydoszcz	0–0	18,000

*Spain won 3–2 on penalties

Robbie Keane

24 March 2001+	WCQ	Cyprus	Nicosia	4–0	13,000
28 March 2001+	WCQ	Andorra	Barcelona	3–0	5,000
2 June 2001+	WCQ	Portugal	Dublin	1–1	34,000
15 August 2001	F	Croatia	Dublin	2–2	27,000
1 September 2001	WCQ	Holland	Dublin	1–0	49,000
10 November 2001	WCQPO	Iran	Dublin	2–0 (1)	35,000
15 November 2001	WCQPO	Iran	Teheran	0–1	110,000
13 February 2002	F	Russia	Dublin	2–0 (1)	44,000
27 March 2002	F	Denmark	Dublin	3–0 (1)	42,000
17 April 2002	F	United States	Dublin	2–1	39,000
16 May 2002	F	Nigeria	Dublin	1–2	42,652
1 June 2002	WCF	Cameroon	Niigata	1–1	33,679
5 June 2002	WCF	Germany	Ibaraki	1–1 (1)	35,854
11 June 2002	WCF	Saudi Arabia	Yokohama	3–0 (1)	65,320
16 June 2002	WCF	Spain	Suwon	1–1*(1p)	38,926
21 August 2002	F	Finland	Helsinki	3–0 (1)	12,225

+ On loan from Inter Milan
*Spain won 3–2 on penalties

Gary Kelly

23 March 1994	F	Russia	Dublin	0–0	34,000
20 April 1994	F	Holland	Tilburg	1–0	30,000
24 May 1994	F	Bolivia (sub)	Dublin	1–0	32,500
29 May 1994	F	Germany (sub)	Hanover	2–0 (1)	50,000
5 June 1994	F	Czech Republic	Dublin	1–3	43,465
28 June 1994	WCF	Norway	New York	0–0	76,332
4 July 1994	WCF	Holland	Orlando	0–2	61,355
7 September 1994	ECQ	Latvia	Riga	3–0	2,200
12 October 1994	ECQ	Liechtenstein	Dublin	4–0	32,980
16 November 1994	ECQ	Northern Ireland	Belfast	4–0	10,336
29 March 1995	ECQ	Northern Ireland	Dublin	1–1	32,500

26 April 1995	ECQ	Portugal	Dublin	1–0	33,000
3 June 1995	ECQ	Liechtenstein	Eschen	0–0	4,500
11 June 1995	ECQ	Austria	Dublin	1–3	33,000
6 September 1995	ECQ	Austria	Vienna	1–3	24,000
11 October 1995	ECQ	Latvia	Dublin	2–1	33,000
15 November 1995	ECQ	Portugal	Lisbon	0–3	80,000
13 December 1995	ECQ	Holland	Anfield	0–2	40,000
19 February 1997	F	Wales (sub)	Cardiff	0–0	7,000
30 April 1997	WCQ	Romania	Bucharest	0–1	21,500
21 May 1997	WCQ	Liechtenstein	Dublin	5–0	28,575
6 September 1997	WCQ	Iceland	Reykjavik	4–2	5,500
10 September 1997	WCQ	Lithuania	Vilnius	2–1	7,000
29 October 1997	WCQPO	Belgium	Dublin	1–1	32,305
15 November 1997	WCQPO	Belgium	Brussels	1–2	38,000
25 March 1998	F	Czech Republic	Olomouc	1–2	9,405
22 April 1998	F	Argentina	Dublin	0–2	38,500
23 May 1998	F	Mexico	Dublin	0–0	8,500
4 September 1999	ECQ	Croatia	Zagreb	0–1	25,000
9 October 1999	ECQ	Macedonia	Skopje	1–1	4,500
23 February 2000	F	Czech Republic	Dublin	3–2	30,543
2 September 2000	WCQ	Holland (sub)	Amsterdam	2–2	50,000
15 November 2000	F	Finland	Dublin	3–0	22,368
24 March 2001	WCQ	Cyprus	Nicosia	4–0 (1)	13,000
28 March 2001	WCQ	Andorra	Barcelona	3–0	5,000
25 April 2001	WCQ	Andorra	Dublin	3–1	34,000
2 June 2001	WCQ	Portugal	Dublin	1–1	34,000
6 June 2001	WCQ	Estonia	Tallin	2–0	9.000
15 August 2001	F	Croatia	Dublin	2–2	27,000
1 September 2001	WCQ	Holland	Dublin	1–0	49,000
10 November 2001	WCQP	Iran (sub)	Dubin	2–0	35,000
15 November 2001	WCQP	Iran (sub)	Tehran	0–1	110,000
13 February 2002	F	Russia	Dublin	2–0	44,000
27 March 2002	F	Denmark	Dublin	3–0	42,000
17 April 2002	F	USA (sub)	Dublin	2–1	39,000
16 May 2002	F	Nigeria (sub)	Dublin	1–2	42,652
1 June 2002	WCF	Cameroon	Niigata	1–1	33,679
5 June 2002	WCF	Germany	Ibaraki	1–1	35,854
11 June 2002	WCF	Saudi Arabia	Yokohama	3–0	65,320
16 June 2002	WCF	Spain	Suwon	1–1 (aet)*	38,926
21 August 2002	F	Finland	Helsinki	3–0	12,225
16 October 2002	ECQ	Switzerland	Dublin	1–2	40,000

*Spain won 3–2 on penalties

Stephen McPhail

30 May 2000	F	Scotland	Dublin	1–2	30,213
6 June 2000	NC	USA	Boston	1–1	16,319
11 June 2000	NC	South Africa	New Jersey	2–1 (1)	45,008
15 August 2001	F	Croatia (sub)	Dublin	2–2	27,000
6 October 2001	WCQ	Cyprus (sub)	Dublin	4–0	35,000
21 August 2002	F	Finland (sub)	Helsinki	3–0	12,225
20 November 2002	F	Greece	Athens	0–0	5,500
9 September 2003	F	Turkey (sub)	Dublin	2–2	27,000
18 November 2003	F	Canada (sub)	Dublin	3–0	23,253
29 May 2004	F	Nigeria	Charlton	0–3	7,438

Con Martin

2 March 1947	F	Spain	Dublin	3–2	42,102
23 May 1948	F	Portugal	Lisbon	0–2	50,000
30 May 1948	F	Spain	Barcelona	1–2	65,000

Alan Maybury

25 March 1998	F	Czech Republic	Olomouc	1–2	9,405
29 May 1999	F	Northern Ireland	Dublin	0–1	12,100

Noel Peyton

11 May 1960	F	West Germany	Dusseldorf	1–0	51,000
18 May 1960	F	Sweden	Malmo	1–4	31,339
28 September 1960	F	Wales	Dublin	2–3	20,000
2 September 1962	ECQ	Iceland	Reykjavik	1–1	9,100
9 June 1963	F	Scotland	Dublin	1–0	26,000

John Sheridan

23 March 1988	F	Romania	Dublin	2–0	15,000
27 April 1988	F	Yugoslavia	Dublin	2–0	12,000
22 May 1988	F	Poland	Dublin	3–1 (1)	18,500
1 June 1988	F	Norway (sub)	Oslo	0–0	9,494
16 November 1988	WCQ	Spain	Seville	0–2	50,000

SCOTLAND
Willie Bell

18 June 1966	F	Portugal	Hampden Park	0–1	24,000
25 June 1966	F	Brazil	Hampden Park	1–1	74,933

Billy Bremner

8 May 1965	F	Spain	Hampden Park	0–0	60,146
13 October 1965	WCQ	Poland	Hampden Park	1–2	107,580
9 November 1965	WCQ	Italy	Hampden Park	1–0	100,393
7 December 1965	WCQ	Italy	Naples	0–3	79,000
2 April 1966	ENQ	England	Hampden Park	3–4	134,000
18 June 1966	F	Portugal	Hampden Park	0–1	24,000
25 June 1966	F	Brazil	Hampden Park	1–1	74,933
22 October 1966	ECQ	Wales	Cardiff	1–1	32,500
16 November 1966	HC	Northern Ireland	Hampden Park	2–1	45,281
15 April 1967	ECQ	England	Wembley	3–2	99,063
22 November 1967	HC	Wales	Hampden Park	3–2	57,472
24 February 1968	ECQ	England	Hampden Park	1–1	134,000
16 October 1968	F	Denmark	Copenhagen	1–0	12,000
6 November 1968	WCQ	Austria	Hampden Park	2–1 (1)	80,856
11 December 1968	WCQ	Cyprus	Nicosia	5–0	10,000
16 April 1969	WCQ	West Germany	Hampden Park	1–1	115,000
3 May 1969	HC	Wales	Wrexham	5–3 (1)	18,765
6 May 1969	HC	Northern Ireland	Hampden Park	1–1	7,483
10 May 1969	HC	England	Wembley	1–4	89,902
17 May 1969	WCQ	Cyprus	Hampden Park	8–0	39,095
21 September 1969	F	Republic of Ireland	Dublin	1–1	30,000
22 October 1969	WCQ	West Germany	Hamburg	2–3	72,000
5 November 1970	WCQ	Austria	Vienna	0–2	11,000
15 May 1971	HC	Wales	Cardiff	0–0	19,068
22 May 1971	HC	England	Wembley	1–3	91,469
13 October 1971	ECQ	Portugal	Hampden Park	2–1	58,612
10 Nov 1971	ECQ	Belgium	Aberdeen	1–0	36,500
1 December 1971	F	Holland	Amsterdam	1–2	18,000
20 May 1972	HC	Northern Ireland	Hampden Park	2–0	39,710
24 May 1972	HC	Wales	Hampden Park	1–0	21,332
27 May 1972	HC	England	Hampden Park	0–1	119,325
29 June 1972	IC	Yugoslavia	Belo Horizonte	2–2	4,000
2 July 1972	IC	Portugal	Porto Alegre	0–0	15,000
5 July 1972	IC	Brazil	Rio de Janeiro	0–1	130,000

18 October 1972	WCQ	Denmark	Copenhagen	4–1	31,000
15 November 1972	WCQ	Denmark	Hampden Park	2–0	47,109
14 February 1973	F	England	Hampden Park	0–5	48,470
16 May 1973	HC	Northern Ireland (sub)	Hampden Park	1–2	39,018
19 May 1973	HC	England	Wembley	0–1	95,950
22 June 1973	F	Switzerland	Berne	0–1	10,000
30 June 1973	F	Brazil	Hampden Park	0–1	70,000
26 September 1973	WCQ	Czechoslovakia	Hampden Park	2–1	100,000
14 November 1973	F	West Germany	Hampden Park	1–1	58,235
11 May 1974	HC	Northern Ireland	Hampden Park	0–1	53,775
14 May 1974	HC	Wales	Hampden Park	2–0	41,969
18 May 1974	HC	England	Hampden Park	2–0	94,487
1 June 1974	F	Belgium	Bruges	1–2	12,000
6 June 1974	F	Norway	Oslo	2–1	18,432
14 June 1974	WCF	Zaire	Dortmund	2–0	30,000
18 June 1974	WCF	Brazil	Frankfurt	0–0	62,000
22 June 1974	WCF	Yugoslavia	Frankfurt	1–1	56,000
20 November 1974	ECQ	Spain	Hampden Park	1–2 (1)	92,100
5 February 1975	ECQ	Spain	Valencia	1–1	60,000
3 September 1975	ECQ	Denmark	Copenhagen	1–0	40,300

Stephen Caldwell

18 February 2004	F	Wales	Cardiff	0–4	47,124
30 May 2004	F	Trinidad & Tobago (sub)	Edinburgh	4–1	16,187

On loan from Sunderland

Bobby Collins

10 April 1965	HC	England	Wembley	2–2	98,199
8 May 1965	F	Spain	Hampden Park	0–0	60,146
23 May 1965	WCQ	Poland	Chorzow	1–1	95,000

Arthur Graham

7 September 1977	F	East Germany (sub)	Berlin	0–1	50,000
20 September 1978	ECQ	Austria (sub)	Vienna	2–3	71,500
25 October 1978	ECQ	Norway	Hampden Park	3–2	65,372
19 May 1979	HC	Wales	Cardiff	0–3	20,371
22 May 1979	HC	Northern Ireland	Hampden Park	1–0 (1)	28,524
26 May 1979	HC	England	Wembley	1–3	100,000
2 June 1979	F	Argentina	Hampden Park	1–3 (1)	61,918
7 June 1979	ECQ	Norway	Oslo	4–0	17,269
17 October 1979	ECQ	Austria	Hampden Park	1–1	72,700
16 May 1981	HC	Wales	Swansea	0–2	18,935

Eddie Gray

10 May 1969	HC	England	Wembley	1–4	89,902
17 May 1969	WCQ	Cyprus	Hampden Park	8–0 (1)	39,095
22 October 1969	WCQ	West Germany	Hamburg	2–3	72,000
5 November 1969	WCQ	Austria	Vienna	0–2	11,000
15 May 1971	HC	Wales	Cardiff	0–0	19,068
18 May 1971	HC	Northern Ireland	Hampden Park	0–1	31,643
10 November 1971	ECQ	Belgium	Aberdeen	1–0	36,500
1 December 1971	F	Holland	Amsterdam	1–2	18,000
6 May 1976	HC	Wales	Hampden Park	3–1 (1)	25,000
15 May 1976	HC	England	Hampden Park	2–1	85,165
8 September 1976	F	Finland	Hampden Park	6–0 (1)	16,338
17 November 1976	WCQ	Wales	Hampden Park	1–0	63,233

Frank Gray

7 April 1976	F	Switzerland	Hampden Park	1–0	15,531
25 October 1978	ECQ	Norway	Hampden Park	3–2	65,372
29 November 1978	ECQ	Portugal	Lisbon	0–1	70,000
19 May 1979	HC	Wales	Cardiff	0–3	20,371
22 May 1979	HC	Northern Ireland	Hampden Park	1–0	28,524
26 May 1979	HC	England	Wembley	1–3	100,000
2 June 1979	F	Argentina (sub)	Hampden Park	1–3	61,918
19 May 1981	HC	Northern Ireland	Hampden Park	2–0	22,448
23 May 1981	HC	England	Wembley	1–0	90,000
9 September 1981	WCQ	Sweden	Hampden Park	2–0	81,511
18 November 1981	WCQ	Portugal	Lisbon	1–2	25,000
24 February 1982	F	Spain	Valencia	0–3	30,000
23 March 1982	F	Holland	Hampden Park	2–1 (1)	71,000
24 May 1982	HC	Wales	Hampden Park	1–0	25,284
15 June 1982	WCF	New Zealand	Malaga	5–2	20,000
18 June 1982	WCF	Brazil	Seville	1–4	47,379
22 June 1982	WCF	USSR	Malaga	2–2	45,000
13 October 1982	ECQ	East Germany	Hampden Park	2–0	40,355
17 November 1982	ECQ	Switzerland	Berne	0–2	26,000
15 December 1982	ECQ	Belgium	Brussels	2–3	48,877
30 March 1983	ECQ	Switzerland	Hampden Park	2–2	36,923
28 May 1984	HC	Wales	Cardiff	2–0	14,100
1 June 1983	HC	England	Wembley	0–2	84,000
12 June 1983	F	Canada	Vancouver	2–0	15,000

David Harvey

15 November 1972	WCQ	Denmark	Hampden Park	2–0	47,109
26 September 1972	WCQ	Czechoslovakia	Bratislava	0–1	15,500
14 November 1973	F	West Germany	Hampden Park	1–1	58,235
11 May 1974	HC	Northern Ireland	Hampden Park	0–1	53,775
14 May 1974	HC	Wales	Hampden Park	2–0	41,969
18 May 1974	HC	England	Hampden Park	2–0	94,487
1 June 1974	F	Belgium	Bruges	1–2	12,000
14 June 1974	WCF	Zaire	Dortmund	2–0	30,000
18 June 1974	WCF	Brazil	Frankfurt	0–0	62,000
22 June 1974	WCF	Yugoslavia	Frankfurt	1–1	56,000
30 October 1974	F	East Germany	Hampden Park	3–0	39,445
20 November 1974	ECQ	Spain	Hampden Park	1–2	92,100
5 February 1975	ECQ	Spain	Valencia	1–1	60,000
3 September 1975	ECQ	Denmark	Copenhagen	1–0	40,300
29 October 1975	ECQ	Denmark	Hampden Park	3–1	48,021
8 September 1976	F	Finland	Hampden Park	6–0	16,338

David Hopkin

7 September 1997	WCQ	Belarus	Aberdeen	4–1 (2)	12,000
12 November 1997	F	France (sub)	St Etienne	1–2	19,514
31 March 1999	ECQ	Czech Republic	Glasgow	1–2	44,513
4 September 1999	ECQ	Bosnia	Sarajevo	1–2	26,000
5 October 1999	ECQ	Bosnia	Glasgow	1–0	30,574

Joe Jordan

19 May 1973	EC	England (sub)	Wembley	0–1	95,950
22 May 1973	F	Switzerland	Berne	0–1	10,000
30 June 1973	F	Brazil	Hampden Park	0–1	70,000
26 September 1973	WCQ	Czechoslovakia (sub)	Hampden Park	2–1 (1)	100,000
17 October 1973	WCQ	Czechoslovakia	Bratislava	0–1	15,000
14 November 1973	F	West Germany (sub)	Hampden Park	1–1	58,235

11 May 1974	HC	Northern Ireland (sub)	Hampden Park	0–1	53,775
14 May 1974	HC	Wales	Hampden Park	2–0	41,969
18 May 1974	HC	England	Hampden Park	2–0 (1)	94,487
1 June 1974	F	Belgium	Bruges	1–2	12,000
6 June 1974	F	Norway	Oslo	2–1 (1)	18,432
14 June 1974	WCF	Zaire	Dortmund	2–0 (1)	30,000
18 June 1974	WCF	Brazil	Frankfurt	0–0	62,000
22 June 1974	WCF	Yugoslavia	Frankfurt	1–1 (1)	56,000
30 October 1974	F	East Germany	Hampden Park	3–0	39,445
20 November 1974	ECQ	Spain	Hampden Park	1–2	92,100
5 February 1975	ECQ	Spain	Valencia	1–1 (1)	60,000
6 May 1976	HC	Wales	Hampden Park	3–1	25,000
8 May 1976	HC	Northern Ireland	Hampden Park	3–0	49,897
15 May 1976	HC	England	Hampden Park	2–1	85,165
13 October 1976	WCQ	Czechoslovakia	Prague	0–2	38,000
17 November 1976	WCQ	Wales	Hampden Park	1–0	63,233
1 June 1977	HC	Northern Ireland	Hampden Park	3–0	44,699
4 June 1977	HC	England	Wembley	2–1	98,108
7 September 1977	F	East Germany	Berlin	0–1	50,000
21 September 1977	WCQ	Czechoslovakia	Hampden Park	3–1 (1)	85,000
12 October 1977	WCQ	Wales	Anfield	2–0	50,800

Peter Lorimer

5 November 1969	WCQ	Austria (sub)	Vienna	0–2	11,000
15 May 1971	HC	Wales	Cardiff	0–0	19,068
18 May 1971	HC	Northern Ireland	Hampden Park	0–1	31,643
20 May 1972	HC	Northern Ireland (sub)	Hampden Park	2–0 (1)	39,710
24 May 1972	HC	Wales	Hampden Park	1–0 (1)	21,332
27 May 1972	HC	England	Hampden Park	0–1	119,325
18 October 1972	WCQ	Denmark	Copenhagen	4–1	31,000
15 November 1972	WCQ	Denmark	Hampden Park	2–0 (1)	47,109
14 February 1973	F	England	Hampden Park	0–5	48,470
19 May 1973	HC	England	Wembley	0–1	95,950
14 November 1973	F	West Germany (sub)	Hampden Park	1–1	58,235
18 May 1974	HC	England	Hampden Park	2–0	94,487
1 June 1974	F	Belgium	Bruges	1–2	12,000
6 June 1974	F	Norway	Oslo	2–1	18,432
14 June 1974	WCF	Zaire	Dortmund	2–0 (1)	30,000
18 June 1974	WCF	Brazil	Frankfurt	0–0	62,000
22 June 1974	WCF	Yugoslavia	Frankfurt	1–1	56,000
20 November 1974	ECQ	Spain (sub)	Hampden Park	1–2	92,100
3 September 1975	ECQ	Denmark	Copenhagen	1–0	40,300
29 October 1975	ECQ	Denmark	Hampden Park	3–1	48,021
17 December 1975	ECQ	Romania	Hampden Park	1–1	11,375

Dominic Matteo

15 November 2000	F	Australia	Hampden Park	0–2	30,985
24 March 2001	WCQ	Belgium	Hampden Park	2–2	37,480
28 March 2001	WCQ	San Marino	Hampden Park	4–0	27,313
1 September 2001	WCQ	Croatia	Hampden Park	0–0	47,384
5 September 2001	WCQ	Belgium	Brussels	0–2	48,500
27 March 2002	F	France	Paris	0–4	80,000

Gary McAllister

12 September 1990	ECQ	Romania	Hampden Park	2–1	12,081
17 October 1990	ECQ	Switzerland	Hampden Park	2–1 (1)	20,740
14 November 1990	ECQ	Bulgaria	Sofia	1–1	40,000
6 February 1991	F	USSR (sub)	Hampden Park	0–1	20,763

1 May 1991	ECQ	San Marino	Serravalle	2–0	3,412
11 September 1991	ECQ	Switzerland (sub)	Berne	2–2	48,000
13 November 1991	ECQ	San Marino	Hampden Park	4–0	35,170
19 February 1992		Northern Ireland	Hampden Park	1–0	13,650
25 March 1992	F	Finland (sub)	Hampden Park	1–1	9,275
17 May 1992	F	USA	Denver	1–0	24,157
21 May 1992	F	Canada	Toronto	3–1 (2,1p)	10,872
3 June 1992	F	Norway	Oslo	0–0	8,786
12 June 1992	ECF	Holland	Gothenburg	0–1	35,720
15 June 1992	ECF	Germany	Norrkopping	0–2	17,638
18 June 1992	ECF	CIS	Norrkopping	3–0 (1p)	14,660
9 September 1992	WCQ	Switzerland	Berne	1–3	10,000
14 October 1992	WCQ	Portugal	Ibrox Park	0–0	22,583
18 Nov1992	WCQ	Italy	Ibrox Park	0–0	33,029
17 February 1993	WCQ	Malta	Ibrox Park	3–0	35,490
8 September 1993	WCQ	Switzerland	Aberdeen	1–1	24,000
13 October 1993	WCQ	Italy	Rome	1–3	61,178
17 November 1993	WCQ	Malta	Taq'uali	2–0	8,000
23 March 1994	F	Holland	Hampden Park	0–1	36,809
20 April 1994	F	Austria	Vienna	2–1	35,000
27 May 1994	F	Holland	Utrecht	1–3	17,500
7 September 1994	ECQ	Finland	Helsinki	2–0	12,845
16 November 1994	ECQ	Russia	Hampden Park	1–1	31,254
18 December 1994	ECQ	Greece	Athens	0–1	20,310
29 March 1995	ECQ	Russia	Moscow	0–0	25,000
26 April 1995	ECQ	San Marino	Serraville	2–0	2,738
16 August 1995	ECQ	Greece	Hampden Park	1–0	34,910
6 September 1995	ECQ	Finland	Hampden Park	1–0	35,505
11 October 1995	F	Sweden	Stockholm	0–2	19,121
15 November 1995	ECQ	San Marino	Hampden Park	5–0	30,306
27 March 1996	F	Australia	Hampden Park	1–0	20,608
24 April 1996	F	Denmark	Copenhagen	0–2	23,031
26 May 1996	F	USA (sub)	New Britain	1–2	8,526
30 May 1996	F	Colombia	Miami	0–1	5,000
10 June 1996	ECF	Holland	Villa Park	0–0	34,363
15 June 1996	ECF	England	Wembley	0–2	76,864
18 June 1996	ECF	Switzerland	Holland	1–0	34,926

Gordon McQueen

1 June 1974	F	Belgium	Bruges	1–2	12,000
20 November 1974	ECQ	Spain	Hampden Park	3–0	39,445
5 February 1975	ENQ	Spain	Valencia	1–1	60,000
13 May 1975	F	Portugal	Hampden Park	1–0	34,307
17 May 1975	HC	Wales	Cardiff	2–2	23,509
20 May 1975	HC	Northern Ireland	Hampden Park	3–0	64,696
24 May 1975	HC	England	Wembley	1–5	98,241
1 June 1975	ENQ	Romania	Bucharest	1–1 (1)	80,000
3 September 1975	ENQ	Denmark	Copenhagen	1–0	40,300
13 October 1976	WCQ	Czechoslovakia	Prague	0–2	38,000
17 November 1976	WCQ	Wales	Hampden Park	1–0	62,233
28 May 1977	HC	Wales	Wrexham	0–0	14,468
1 June 1977	HC	Northern Ireland	Hampden Park	3–0 (1)	44,699
4 June 1977	HC	England	Wembley	2–1 (1)	98,103
7 September 1977	F	East Germany	Berlin	0–1	50,000
21 September 1977	WCQ	Czechoslovakia	Hampden Park	3–1	85,000
12 October 1977	WCQ	Wales	Anfield	2–0	50,800

David Stewart
7 September 1977	F	East Germany	Berlin	0–1	50,000

Gordon Strachan
11 October 1989	WCQ	France	Paris	0–3	25,000
6 February 1991	F	USSR	Hampden Park	0–1	20,763
27 March 1991	ECQ	Bulgaria	Hampden Park	1–1	33,119
1 May 1991	ECQ	San Marino	Serravalle	2–0 (1p)	3,512
11 September 1991	ECQ	Switzerland	Berne	2–2	48,000
16 October 1991	ECQ	Romania	Bucharest	0–1	30,000
19 February 1992	F	Northern Ireland	Hampden Park	1–0	13,650
25 March 1992	F	Finland	Hampden Park	1–1	9,275

SENEGAL
Lamine Sakho
2 February 2004	ANF	Mali (sub)	Tunis	1–1	7,500
7 February 2004	ANF	Tunisia	Rades	0–1	57,000

On loan from Marseille

SLOVAKIA
Lubomir Michalik
28 March 2007*	ECQ	Republic of Ireland (sub)	Dublin	0–1	71,297

*On loan from Bolton Wanderers

SOUTH AFRICA
Phil Masinga
4 September 1994	ANQ	Madagascar	Antananarivo	1–0 (1)	35,000
15 October 1994	ANQ	Mauritius	Mabopane	1–0 (1)	20,000
13 November 1994	ANQ	Zambia	Lusaka	1–1	40,000
13 May 1995	F	Argentina	Johannesburg	1–1	45,000
15 December 1995	F	Germany	Johannesburg	0–0	27,500
13 January 1996	ANF	Cameroon	Johannesburg	3–0 (1)	80,000
20 January 1996	ANF	Angola	Johannesburg	1–0	60,000
24 January 1996	ANF	Egypt	Johannesburg	0–1	40,000
27 January 1996	ANF	Algeria	Johannesburg	2–1	30,000
4 February 1996	ANF	Tunisia	Johannesburg	2–0	80,000
24 April 1996	F	Brazil	Johannesburg	2–3 (1)	80,000
1 June 1996	WCQ	Malawi	Blantyre	1–0	55,000

Lucas Radebe
4 September 1994	ANQ	Madagascar	Antananarivo	1–0	35,000
15 October 1994	ANQ	Mauritius	Mabopane	1–0	20,000
13 November 1994	ANQ	Zambia	Lusaka	1–1	40,000
20 January 1996	ANF	Angola	Johannesburg	1–0	60,000
24 January 1996	ANF	Egypt	Johannesburg	0–1	40,000
27 January 1996	ANF	Algeria	Johannesburg	2–1	30,000
21 January 1996	ANF	Ghana	Johannesburg	3–0	70,000
3 February 1996	ANF	Tunisia	Johannesburg	2–0	80,000
24 April 1996	F	Brazil	Johannesburg	2–3	80,000
1 June 1996	WCQ	Malawi	Blantyre	1–0	55,000
15 June 1996	WCQ	Malawi	Johannesburg	3–0	30,000
9 November 1996	WCQ	Zaire	Johannesburg	1–0	55,000
11 January 1997	WCQ	Zambia	Lusaka	0–0	27,500
6 April 1997	WCQ	Congo	Pointe Noire	0–2	10,000
27 April 1997	WCQ	Zaire	Lome	2–1	7,000
24 May 1997	F	England	Manchester	1–2	52,676
4 June 1997	F	Holland	Johannesburg	0–2	35,000
8 June 1997	WCQ	Zambia	Johannesburg	3–0	73,000

16 August 1997	WCQ	Congo	Johannesburg	1–0	95,000
11 October 1997	F	France	Lens	1–2	29,677
17 November 1997	F	Germany	Dusseldorf	0–3	27,000
7 December 1997	F	Brazil	Johannesburg	1–2	40,000
17 December 1997	CC	Uruguay	Riyadh	3–4 (1)	15,000
8 February 1998	ANF	Angola	Bobo–Dioulasso	0–0	20,000
11 February 1998	ANF	Ivory Coast	Bobo–Dioulasso	1–1	10.000
16 February 1998	ANF	Namibia	Bobo–Dioulasso	4–1	500
22 February 1998	ANF	Morocco	Ouagadougou	2–1	20,000
25 February 1998	ANF	DR Congo	Ouagadougou	2–1	40,000
28 February 1998	ANF	Egypt	Ouagadougou	0–2	40,000
20 May 1998	F	Zambia	Johannesburg	1–1	25,000
25 May 1998	F	Argentina	Buenos Aires	0–2	40,000
6 June 1998	F	Iceland	Baiersbroon, Germany	1–1	1,500
12 June 1998	WCF	France	Marseilles	0–3	55,000
18 June 1998	WCF	Denmark	Toulouse	1–1	33,500
24 June 1998	WCF	Saudi Arabia	Bordeaux	2–2	31,800
3 October 1998	ANQ	Angola	Johannesburg	1–0	20,000
23 January 1999	ANQ	Mauritius	Curepipe	1–1	2,385
27 February 1999	ANQ	Gabon	Pretoria	4–1	50,000
10 April 1999	ANQ	Gabon	Libreville	0–1	40,000
28 April 1999	F	Denmark	Copenhagen	1–1	17,592
5 June 1999	ANQ	Mauritius	Durban	2–0	40,000
16 June 1999	F	Zimbabwe	Johannesburg	0–1	40,000
27 November 1999	F	Sweden	Pretoria	1–0	28,000
23 January 2000	ANF	Gabon	Kumasi, Ghana	3–1	20,000
27 January 2000	ANF	DR Congo	Kumasi, Ghana	1–0	3,500
2 February 2000	ANF	Algeria	Kumasi, Ghana	1–1	2,000
6 February 2000	ANF	Ghana	Kumasi, Ghana	0–1	50,000
10 February 2000	ANF	Nigeria	Lagos, Ghana	0–2	40,000
12 February 2000	ANF	Tunisia	Accra, Ghana	2–2*	3,000
13 January 2001	ANQ	Liberia	Johannesburg	2–1	10,000
27 January 2001	WCQ	Burkino Faso	Rustenburg	1–0	25,000
12 May 2002	F	Madagascar	Durban	1–0	35,000
20 May 2002	RC	Scotland	Hong Kong	2–0	5,000
22 May 2002	RC	Turkey	Hong Kong	2–0	10,000
2 June 2002	WCF	Paraguay	Busan, Korea	2–2	25,000
8 June 2002	WCF	Slovenia	Daegu, Korea	1–0	47,000
12 June 2002	WCF	Spain	Daejeon, Korea	2–3 (1)	31,000
22 May 2003	F	England	Durban	1–2	48,000

* After extra-time, South Africa won 4–3 on penalties

SPAIN
Raul Bravo
2 April 2003	ECQ	Armenia	Amilivia	3–0	13,500

On loan from Real Madrid

SWEDEN
Teddy Lucic
20 November 2002	F	Czech Republic	Teplice	3–3	10,238
2 April 2003	ECQ	Hungary	Budapest	2–1	28,000
30 April 2003	F	Croatia	Stockholm	1–2	15,109

On loan from AIK Solna

WALES
Mark Aizlewood
18 February 1987	F	USSR	Swansea	0–0	17,617
1 April 1987	ECQ	Finland (sub)	Wrexham	4–0	7,696

9 September 1987	ECQ	Denmark (sub)	Cardiff	1–0	20,535
27 April 1988	F	Sweden	Stockholm	1–4	11,656
1 June 1988	F	Malta	Valletta	3–2	7,000
4 June 1988	F	Italy	Brescia	1–0	21,000
14 September 1988	WCQ	Holland	Amsterdam	0–1	58,000
26 April 1989	F	Sweden (sub)	Wrexham	0–2	8,000
31 May 1989	WCQ	West Germany	Cardiff	0–0	25,000

John Charles

8 March 1950	HC	Northern Ireland	Wrexham	0–0	33,000
16 May 1951	F	Switzerland	Wrexham	3–2	28,000
15 April 1953	HC	Northern Ireland	Belfast	3–2 (2)	45,000
14 May 1953	F	France	Paris	1–6	33,020
21 May 1953	F	Yugoslavia	Belgrade	2–5	55,000
10 October 1953	HC	England	Cardiff	1–4	61,000
4 November 1953	HC	Scotland	Hampden Park	3–3 (2)	71,378
21 March 1954	HC	Northern Ireland	Wrexham	1–2 (1)	32,187
9 May 1954	F	Austria	Vienna	0–2	58,000
22 September 1954	F	Yugoslavia	Cardiff	1–3	48,000
16 October 1954	HC	Scotland	Cardiff	0–1	60,000
10 November 1954	HC	England	Wembley	2–3 (2)	91,112
20 April 1955	HC	Northern Ireland	Belfast	3–2 (3)	30,000
22 October 1955	HC	England	Cardiff	2–1	60,000
9 November 1955	HC	Scotland	Hampden Park	0–2	53,887
23 November 1955	ECQ	Austria	Wrexham	1–2	23,000
11 April 1956	HC	Northern Ireland	Cardiff	1–1	45,000
20 October 1956	HC	Scotland	Cardiff	2–2	60,000
14 November 1956	HC	England	Wembley	1–3 (1)	93,796
10 April 1957	HC	Northern Ireland	Belfast	0–0	30,000
20 October 1962	HC	Scotland	Cardiff	2–3 (1)	50,000

Alan Curtis

23 May 1979	HC	England	Wembley	0–0	70,250
25 May 1979	HC	Wales	Belfast	1–1	6,500
2 June 1979	ECQ	Malta	Valetta	2–0	9,000
11 September 1979	F	Republic of Ireland	Swansea	2–1 (1)	6,825
17 October 1979	ECQ	West Germany	Cologne	1–5 (1)	60,000
21 November 1979	ECQ	Turkey	Izmir	0–1	50,000

Brian Flynn

16 November 1977	WCQ	Czechoslovakia	Prague	0–1	20,000
14 December 1977	F	West Germany	Dortmund	1–1	53,000
18 April 1978	F	Iran (sub)	Tehran	1–0	45,000
13 May 1978	HC	England	Cardiff	1–3	17,698
17 May 1978	HC	Scotland	Hampden Park	1–1	70,241
19 May 1978	HC	Northern Ireland	Wrexham	1–0	9,077
25 October 1978	ECQ	Malta	Wrexham	7–0 (1)	11,475
29 November 1978	ECQ	Turkey	Wrexham	1–0	11,800
19 May 1979	HC	Scotland	Cardiff	3–0	20,371
23 May 1979	HC	England	Wembley	0–0	75,000
25 May 1979	HC	Northern Ireland	Belfast	1–1	6,500
2 June 1979	ECQ	Malta	Valetta	2–0 (1)	9,000
11 September 1979	F	Republic of Ireland	Swansea	2–1	6,825
17 October 1979	ECQ	West Germany	Cologne	1–5 (1)	60,000
17 May 1980	HC	England	Wrexham	4–1	24,236
21 May 1980	HC	Scotland	Hampden Park	0–1	24,236
23 May 1980	HC	Northern Ireland	Cardiff	0–1	12,913
2 June 1980	WCQ	Iceland	Reykjavik	4–0 (1p)	10,254

15 October 1980	WCQ	Turkey	Cardiff	4–0 (1)	11,770
19 November 1980	WCQ	Czechoslovakia	Cardiff	1–0	20,175
24 February 1980	F	Republic of Ireland	Cardiff	3–1	15,000
25 March 1981	WCQ	Turkey	Ankara	1–0	35,000
16 May 1981	HC	Scotland	Swansea	2–0	18,985
20 May 1981	HC	England	Wembley	0–0	34,250
30 May 1981	WCQ	USSR	Wrexham	0–0	29,366
9 September 1981	WCQ	Czechoslovakia	Prague	0–2	41,500
18 November 1981	WCQ	USSR	Tibilisi	0–3	80,000
27 April 1982	HC	England	Cardiff	0–1	23,000
24 April 1982	HC	Scotland	Hampden Park	0–1	25,284
27 May 1982	HC	Northern Ireland	Wrexham	3–0	2,315
2 June 1982	F	France	Toulouse	1–0	35,000
22 September 1982	ECQ	Norway	Swansea	1–0	5,000

Carl Harris

24 March 1976	F	England	Wrexham	1–2	21,000
6 May 1976	HC	Scotland	Hampden Park	1–3	35,000
14 Dec 1977	F	West Germany	Dortmund	1–1	53,000
18 April 1978	F	Iran (sub)	Teheran	1–0	45,000
13 May 1978	HC	England	Cardiff	1–3	17,698
17 May 1978	HC	Scotland	Hampden Park	1–1	70,241
19 May 1978	HC	Northern Ireland	Wrexham	1–0	9,077
25 October 1978	ECQ	Malta	Wrexham	7–0 (1)	11,475
29 Nov 1978	ECQ	Turkey	Wrexham	1–0	11,800
2 May 1979	ECQ	West Germany	Wrexham	0–2	26,900
23 May 1979	HC	England	Wembley	0–0	70,250
2 June 1979	ECQ	Malta	Valetta	2–0	9,000
23 May 1980	HC	Northern Ireland (sub)	Cardiff	0–1	12,913
2 June 1980	WCQ	Iceland (sub)	Reykjavik	4–0	10,254
15 October 1980	WCQ	Turkey	Cardiff	4–0	11,770
19 November 1980	WCQ	Czechoslovakia (sub)	Cardiff	1–0	20,175
24 February 1980	F	Republic of Ireland	Cardiff	3–1	15,000
25 March 1981	WCQ	Turkey	Ankara	1–0 (1)	35,000
16 May 1981	HC	Scotland	Swansea	2–0	18,985
20 May 1981	HC	England	Wembley	0–0	34,250
30 May 1981	WCQ	USSR	Wrexham	0–0	29,366
9 September 1981	WCQ	Czechoslovakia	Prague	0–2	41,500
7 October 1981	WCQ	Iceland	Swansea	2–2	20,000
27 April 1982	HC	England	Cardiff	0–1	50,000

Matthew Jones

9 October 1999	ECQ	Switzerland (sub)	Wrexham	0–2	5,064
23 February 2000	F	Qatar	Doha	1–0	2,000
23 May 2000	F	Brazil	Cardiff	0–3	72,500
2 June 2000	F	Portugal	Chaves	0–3	11,000
11 October 2000	WCQ	Poland (sub)	Warsaw	0–0	14,000

Aubrey Powell

19 October 1946	HC	Scotland	Wrexham	3–1	29,568
13 November 1946	HC	England	Maine Road	0–3	59,250
18 October 1947	HC	England	Cardiff	0–3	55,000
12 November 1947	HC	Scotland	Hampden Park	2–1	88,000
10 March 1948	HC	Northern Ireland	Wrexham	2–0	33,160

Gary Speed

20 May 1990	F	Costa Rica (sub)	Cardiff	1–0	5,977
11 September 1990	F	Denmark	Copenhagen	0–1	8,700

14 November 1990	ECQ	Luxembourg (sub)	Luxembourg	1–0	6,800
6 February 1990	F	Republic of Ireland (sub)	Wrexham	0–3	9,168
1 May 1991	F	Iceland	Cardiff	1–0	3,656
5 June 1991	ECQ	Germany (sub)	Cardiff	1–0	38,000
11 September 1991	F	Brazil	Cardiff	1–0	20,000
16 October 1991	ECQ	Germany (sub)	Nuremburg	1–4	46,000
13 November 1991	ECQ	Luxembourg	Cardiff	1–0	20,000
19 February 1992	F	Republic of Ireland	Dublin	1–0	15,100
20 May 1992	WCQ	Romania	Bucharest	1–5	23,000
30 May 1992	F	Holland	Utrecht	0–4	20,000
3 June 1992	KC	Argentina	Tokyo	0–1	31,000
7 June 1992	KC	Japan	Matsuyama	1–0	30,000
9 September 1992	WCQ	Faeroes	Cardiff	6–0	6,000
14 October 1992	WCQ	Cyprus	Limassol	1–0	15,000
18 November 1992	WCQ	Belgium	Brussels	0–2	21,000
17 February 1993	F	Republic of Ireland	Dublin	1–2	9,500
31 March 1993	WCQ	Belgium	Cardiff	2–0	27,002
6 June 1993	WCQ	Faroe Islands (sub)	Toftir	3–0	4,209
8 September 1993	WCQ	RCS (as sub)	Cardiff	2–2	37,558
13 October 1993	WCQ	Cyprus	Cardiff	2–0	10,000
17 November 1993	WCQ	Romania	Cardiff	1–2	40,000
9 Ma 1994	F	Norway	Cardiff	1–3	10,000
20 April 1994	F	Sweden	Wrexham	0–2	4,694
7 September 1994	ECQ	Albania	Cardiff	2–0	15,791
12 October 1994	ECQ	Moldova	Kishinev	2–3 (1)	12,000
16 November 1994	ECQ	Georgia	Tblisi	0–5	45,000
14 December 1994	ECQ	Bulgaria	Cardiff	0–3	20,000
29 March 1995	ECQ	Bulgaria	Sofia	1–3	60,000
26 April 1995	ECQ	Germany	Dussledorf	1–1	45,000
6 Sept1995	ECQ	Moldova	Cardiff	1–0 (1)	5,000
1 October 1995	ECQ	Germany	Cardiff	1–2	25,000
15 November 1995	ECQ	Albania	Tirana	1–1	6,000
24 January 1996	F	Italy	Terni	0–3	20,000
24 April 1996	F	Switzerland (sub)	Lugano	0–2	8,000

Gary Sprake

20 November 1963	HC	Scotland	Hampden Park	1–2	56,067
15 April 1964	HC	Northern Ireland	Swansea	2–3	10,434
3 October 1964	HC	Scotland	Cardiff	3–2	50,000
21 October 1964	WCQ	Denmark	Copenhagen	0–1	30,000
9 December 1964	WCQ	Greece	Athens	0–2	26,000
2 October 1965	HC	England	Cardiff	0–0	30,000
27 October 1965	WCQ	USSR	Cardiff	2–1	34,521
30 March 1966	HC	Northern Ireland	Cardiff	1–4	12,860
22 October 1966	HC	Scotland	Cardiff	1–1	32,500
21 October 1967	HC	England	Cardiff	0–3	45,000
22 November 1967	HC	Scotland	Hampden Park	2–3	57,472
26 March 1969	F	West Germany	Frankfurt	1–1	40,000
3 May 1969	HC	Scotland	Wrexham	3–5	18,765
7 May 1969	HC	England	Wembley	1–2	70,000
10 May 1969	HC	Northern Ireland	Belfast	0–0	12,500
28 July 1969	F	Rest of UK	Cardiff	0–1	14,000
22 October 1969	WCQ	East Germany	Cardiff	1–3	22,409
4 November 1969	WCQ	Italy	Rome	1–4	90,000
11 November 1969	ECQ	Romania	Cardiff	0–0	29,000
15 May 1971	HC	Scotland	Cardiff	0–0	19,068
18 May 1971	HC	England	Wembley	0–0	85,000
22 May 1971	HC	Northern Ireland	Belfast	0–1	22,000

13 October 1971	ECQ	Finland	Swansea	3–0	10,301
20 May 1972	HC	England	Cardiff	0–3	34,000
24 May 1972	HC	Scotland	Hampden Park	0–1	21,332
27 May 1972	HC	Northern Ireland	Wrexham	0–0	15,647
15 November 1972	WCQ	England	Cardiff	0–1	36,384
24 January 1973	WCQ	England	Wembley	1–1	62,000
28 March 1973	WCQ	Poland	Cardiff	2–0	12,000
12 May 1973	HC	Scotland	Wrexham	0–2	17,765
19 May 1973	HC	Northern Ireland	Anfield	0–1	4,946
26 September 1973	WCQ	Poland	Anfield	0–3	120,000

Byron Stevenson

19 May 1978	HC	Northern Ireland	Wrexham	1–0	9,077
25 October 1978	ECQ	Malta	Wrexham	7–0	11,475
29 November 1978	ECQ	Turkey	Wrexham	1–0	11,800
19 May 1979	HC	Scotland	Cardiff	3–0	20,371
23 May 1979	HC	England	Wembley	0–0	75,000
25 May 1979	HC	Northern Ireland	Belfast	1–1	6,500
2 June 1979	ECQ	Malta	Valetta	2–0	9,000
17 October 1979	ECQ	West Germany	Cologne	1–5	60,000
21 November 1979	ECQ	Turkey	Izmir	0–1	50,000
2 June 1980	WCQ	Iceland (sub)	Reykjavik	4–0	10,254
9 September 1981	WCQ	Czechoslovakia	Prague	0–2	41,500

Harold Williams

8 March 1950	HC	Northern Ireland	Wrexham	0–0	33,000
21 October 1950	HC	Scotland	Cardiff	1–3	60,000
8 March 1950	HC	Northern Ireland	Wrexham	0–0	33,000
21 October 1950	HC	Scotland	Cardiff	1–3	60,000

Terry Yorath

4 November 1969	WCQ	Italy	Rome	1–4	90,000
15 May 1971	HC	Scotland	Cardiff	0–0	19,068
18 May 1971	HC	England	Wembley	0–0	85,000
22 May 1971	HC	Northern Ireland	Belfast	0–1	22,000
27 October 1971	ECQ	Czechoslovakia	Prague	0–1	32,000
20 May 1972	HC	England	Cardiff	0–3	34,000
24 May 1972	HC	Scotland	Hampden Park	0–1	21,332
27 May 1972	HC	Northern Ireland	Wrexham	0–0	15,647
24 January 1973	WCQ	England	Wembley	1–1	62,000
28 March 1973	WCQ	Poland	Cardiff	2–0	12,000
12 May 1973	HC	Scotland	Wrexham	0–2	17,765
26 September 1973	WCQ	Poland	Chorzow	0–3	120,000
11 May 1974	HC	England	Cardiff	0–2	26,000
14 May 1974	HC	Scotland	Hampden Park	0–2	41,969
18 May 1974	HC	Northern Ireland	Wrexham	1–0	9,311
14 September 1974	ECQ	Austria	Vienna	1–2	34,000
30 October 1974	ECQ	Hungary	Cardiff	2–0	8,445
20 November 1974	ECQ	Luxembourg	Swansea	5–0 (1)	10,530
16 April 1975	ECQ	Hungary	Budapest	2–1	30,000
1 May 1975	ECQ	Luxembourg	Luxembourg	3–1	5,000
17 May 1975	HC	Scotland	Cardiff	2–2	23,509
19 November 1975	ECQ	Austria	Wrexham	1–0	28,182
24 March 1976	F	England	Wrexham	1–2	20,987
24 April 1976	ECF	Yugoslavia	Zagreb	0–2	55,000
6 May 1976	HC	Scotland	Hampden Park	1–3	25,000
8 May 1976	HC	England	Cardiff	0–1	24,500
14 May 1976	HC	Northern Ireland	Swansea	1–0	10,000
22 May 1976	ECF	Yugoslavia	Cardiff	1–1	30,000

UNITED STATES OF AMERICA
Eddie Lewis

17 August 2005	WCQ	Trinidad & Tobago	East Hartford	1–0	25,488
3 September 2005	WCQ	Mexico	Ohio	2–0	24,685
8 October 2005	WCQ	Costa Rica	San Jose	0–3	30,000
1 March 2006	F	Poland	Kaiserslautern	1–0	13,395
26 May 2006	F	Venezuela (sub)	Cleveland	2–0	29,745
28 May 2006	F	Latvia	East Hartford	1–0	24,636
12 June 2006	WCF	Czech Republic	Gelsenkirchen	0–3	52,000
22 June 2006	WCF	Ghana	Nuremburg	1–2	41,000

B INTERNATIONALS
AUSTRALIA
Harry Kewell

12 June 1999	World Stars	Sydney	3–2	88,101

ENGLAND
David Batty

14 November 1989	Italy	Brighton	1–0	16,125
12 December 1989	Yugoslavia	Millwall	2–1	8,231
27 March 1990	Republic of Ireland	Cork	1–4	10,000
27 April 1991	Iceland	Watford	1–0	3,814
24 March 1992	Czechoslovakia	Budejovice	1–0	6,000

Lee Chapman

27 April 1991	Iceland	Watford	1–0	3,814

Jack Charlton

20 May 1970	Colombia	Bogata	1–0	28,000
24 May 1970	Deportiva Universidad	Quito	4–1	22,250

Allan Clarke

20 May 1970	Colombia	Bogata	1–0	28,000
24 May 1970	Deportiva Universidad	Quito	4–1	22,250

Tony Dorigo

18 February 1992	France	Loftus Road	3–0	4,827
24 March 1992	Czechoslovakia (sub)	Budejovice	1–0	6,000

Norman Hunter

20 May 1970	Colombia	Bogata	1–0	28,000
24 May 1970	Deportiva Universidad	Quito	4–1	22,250

John Lukic

11 December 1990	Algeria (sub)	Algiers	0–0	1,000

Mel Sterland

12 December 1989	Yugoslavia (sub)	Millwall	2–1	8,231
11 December 1990	Algeria	Algiers	0–0	1,000

REPUBLIC OF IRELAND
Jim Beglin

27 March 1990	England	Cork	4–1	10,000

Alan Maybury

11 March 1998	Northern Ireland	Dublin	0–1	10,200

SCOTLAND
David Hopkin

21 April 1998	Norway U23	Tynecastle	1–2	7,845

WALES
Matthew Jones

24 March 1998	Scotland	Cumbernauld	0–4	5,989

UNDER-23 INTERNATIONALS
AUSTRALIA
Neil Kilkenny

27 June 2008		Chile (sub)	Darwin	3–4	1,404
29 June 2008		Chile	Darwin	1–1	1,780
20 July 2008		China	Changchung	0–1	10,000
24 July 2008		Japan (sub)	Kobe	1–2	17,185
31 July 2008		South Korea (sub)	Seoul	0–1	20,533
10 August 2008	OG	Argentina	Shanghai	0–1	38,182

ENGLAND
Chris Crowe

11 November 1959	France	Sunderland	2–0 (1)	26,495
2 March 1960	Scotland	Hampden Park	4–4	25,000

Norman Hunter

4 November 1964	Wales	Wrexham	3–2	15,193
25 November 1964	Romania	Coventry	5–0	27,476
24 February 1965	Scotland	Aberdeen	0–0	25,000

Mike O'Grady

3 November 1965	France	Norwich	3–0	20,203

Paul Reaney

8 April 1964	France	Rouen	2–2	15,000
24 February 1965	Scotland	Aberdeen	0–0	25,000
25 May 1965	West Germany	Frieburg	0–1	15,000
29 May 1965	Czechoslovakia	Liberec	0–0	6,000

REPUBLIC OF IRELAND
John Sheridan

11 April 1989	Northern Ireland	Dublin	3–0 (1p)	3,200

SCOTLAND
Billy Bremner

24 May 1964	France	Nantes	2–0	1,000
2 December 1964	Wales	Kilmarnock	3–0 (1)	6,000
24 February 1965	England	Aberdeen	0–0	25,000

Eddie Gray

30 November 1966	Wales	Wrexham	6–0 (2)	5,341
1 March 1967	England	Newcastle	3–1	22,097

Frank Gray

13 March 1974		England	Newcastle	0–2	4,511
2 September 1975	ECQ	Denmark	Frederikshavn	1–0	6,000
28 October 1975	ECQ	Denmark	Edinburgh	4–1	16,500
16 December 1975	ECQ	Romania	Falkirk	4–0	8,000
24 March 1975	ECQ	Holland	Edinburgh	2–0*	32,593

*After extra-time. Holland won 4–3 on penalties. The first leg finished 2–0 to Holland in Breda.

Joe Jordan

24 March 1975	ECQ	Holland	Edinburgh	2–0*	32,593

*After extra-time. Holland won 4–3 on penalties. the first leg finished 2–0 to Holland in Breda.

Peter Lorimer

3 December 1969	France	Hampden Park	4–0 (2)	5,004
14 January 1970	Wales	Aberdeen	1–1	14,500

WALES
Carl Harris

4 February 1976	Scotland	Wrexham	2–3	2,222

Denis Hawkins

30 November 1966	Scotland	Wrexham	0–6	5,341
22 February 1967	Northern Ireland	Belfast	1–2*	8,000
1 November 1967	England	Swansea	1–2	14,928
20 March 1968	Northern Ireland	Cardiff	0–1	2,669
2 October 1968	England	Wrexham	1–3	11,084

*Abandoned after 73 minutes, ground waterlogged.

Glan Letheran

4 February 1976	Scotland	Wrexham	2–3	2,222

Gary Sprake

13 November 1963	England	Bristol	1–1	16,841
4 December 1963	Scotland	Wrexham	3–1	10,716
5 February 1964	Northern Ireland	Belfast	3–3	18,000
4 November 1964	England	Wrexham	3–2	15,193
10 February 1965	Northern Ireland	Cardiff	2–2	6,000

Terry Yorath

2 October 1968	England	Wrexham	1–3	11,084
1 October 1969	England	Bristol	0–2	22,286
14 January 1970	Scotland	Aberdeen	1–1	14,500
2 December 1970	England	Wrexham	0–0	16,367
5 January 1972	England	Swindon	0–2	18,028
26 January 1972	Scotland	Aberdeen	0–2	15,000
29 November 1972	England	Swansea	0–3	6,414

UNDER-21 INTERNATIONALS
(1976 to date)
ENGLAND
David Batty

28 May 1988	F	Switzerland (sub)	Lausanne	1–1	1,000
7 February 1989	F	Greece (sub)	Patras	0–1	2,000
5 June 1989	TT	Bulgaria	Toulon	2–3	1,000
7 June 1989	TT	Senegal	Toulon	6–1 (1)	1,000
9 June 1989	TT	Republic of Ireland	Toulon	0–0	1,000
11 June 1989	TT	USA	Toulon	0–2	1,000
10 October 1989	ECQ	Poland	Jastrzbruj	3–1	5,000

Lee Bowyer

31 August 1996	ECQ	Moldova	Chisinau	2–0	850
12 February 1997	ECQ	Italy	Bristol	1–0	13,850
1 April 1997	F	Switzerland	Swindon	0–0	10,167
29 April 1997	ECQ	Georgia	Charlton	0–0	12,714
9 September 1997	ECQ	Moldova	Wycombe	1–0	5,534
9 February 1998	F	France	Derby	2–1	32,865

26 March 1998	EC	Poland	Southampton	5–0	15,202
8 October 1999	F	Denmark	Bradford	4–1 (1)	15,220
22 February 2000	F	Argentina	Fulham	1–0	15,748

Michael Bridges
| 8 October 1999 | F | Denmark | Bradford | 4–1 | 15,220 |

Andy Couzens
8 June 1995	TT	Malaysia (sub)	Toulon	2–0	700
10 June 1995	TT	Angola	Toulon	1–0	250
12 June 1995	TT	France (sub)	Toulon	0–2	650

Fabian Delph
| 18 November 2008 | F | Czech Republic (sub) | Bramall Lane | 2–0 | 18,735 |

Mark Ford
| 23 April 1996 | F | Croatia | Sunderland | 0–1 | 4,376 |
| 31 August 1996 | ECQ | Moldova | Chisinau | 2–0 | 850 |

Seth Johnson
| 16 April 2002 | F | Portugal | Stoke | 0–1 | 28,000 |

Matthew Kilgallon
30 March 2004	F	Sweden (sub)	Kristiansand	2–2	7,320
17 August 2005	F	Ukraine	Middlesbrough	3–1	5,658
7 September 2005	ECQ	Poland (sub)	Rybnik	3–1	3,000
12 October 2005	ECQ	Azerbaijan (sub)	Baku	0–0	1,500
14 November 2006	F	Holland	Alkmaar	1–0	15,000

John Lukic
9 September 1980	F	Norway	Southampton	3–0	6,973
14 October 1980	ECQ	Romania	Ploesti	0–4	10,000
25 February 1980	F	Republic of Ireland	Anfield	1–0	5,882
28 April 1981	ECQ	Romania	Swindon	3–0	8,739
31 May 1981	ECQ	Switzerland	Neuchatel	0–0	1,500
5 June 1981	ECQ	Hungary	Keszthely	2–1	8,000
17 November 1981	ECQ	Hungary	Nottingham	2–0	8,734

Danny Mills
3 September 1999	ECQ	Luxembourg	Reading	5–0	18,094
7 September 1999	ECQ	Poland	Plock	1–3 (1)	1,500
8 October 1999	F	Denmark	Bradford	4–1 (1)	15,220
22 February 2000	F	Argentina	Fulham	1–0	15,748
29 March 2000	ECQ	Yugoslavia (sub)	Barcelona	3–0	1,000
27 May 2000	ECF	Italy	Bratislava	0–2	1,000
29 May 2000	ECF	Turkey	Bratislava	6–0 (1)	250
1 June 2000	ECF	Slovenia	Bratislava	0–2	9,113

James Milner
| 30 March 2004 | F | Sweden (sub) | Kristiansand | 2–2 | 7,320 |

Paul Robinson
8 October 2000	F	Denmark	Bradford	4–1	15,220
31 August 2001	F	Georgia	Middlesbrough	6–1	5,103
6 October 2001	ECQ	Germany	Derby	1–1	30,155
10 October 2001	ECQ	Finland	Valkeakoski	2–2	1,426
27 February 2001	F	Spain	Birmingham	0–4	13,761
12 February 2002	F	Slovenia	Nova Gorica	1–0	350

Date	Comp	Opponent	Venue	Score	Attendance
26 March 2002	F	Italy	Bradford	1–1	21,642
16 April 2002	F	Portugal	Stoke	0–1	28,000
17 May 2002	ECF	Switzerland	Zurich	2–1	16,000
20 May 2002	ECF	Italy	Basle	1–2	12,980
22 May 2002	ECF	Portugal	Zurich	1–3	10,000

Alan Smith

Date	Comp	Opponent	Venue	Score	Attendance
8 October 1999	F	Denmark	Bradford	4–1 (1)	15,220
22 February 2000	F	Argentina (sub)	Fulham	1–0	15,748
6 October 2001	ECQ	Germany	Derby	1–1	30,155
10 October 2001	ECQ	Finland	Valkeaksoski	2–2 (1)	1,426
27 February 2001	F	Spain	Birmingham	0–4	17.176
26 March 2002	F	Italy	Bradford	1–1	21,642
16 April 2002	F	Portugal	Stoke	0–1	28,000
17 May 2002	ECF	Switzerland	Zurich	2–1	16,000
20 May 2002	ECF	Italy	Basle	1–2	12,980
22 May 2002	ECF	Portugal	Zurich	1–3	10,000

Noel Whelan

Date	Comp	Opponent	Venue	Score	Attendance
11 October 1994	F	Austria (sub)	Kapfenburg	3–1	2,800
15 November 1994	F	Republic of Ireland	Newcastle	1–0 (1)	25,863

Jonathan Woodgate

Date	Comp	Opponent	Venue	Score	Attendance
22 February 2000	F	Argentina	Fulham	1–0	15,748

NORTHERN IRELAND
Wes Boyle

Date	Comp	Opponent	Venue	Score	Attendance
21 April 1998	ECQ	Switzerland (sub)	Lurgan	2–1	300
20 May 1998	TT/ECQ	Scotland (sub)	Toulon	1–1	500
23 March 2001	ECQ	Czech Republic (sub)	Ballymena	0–2	1,411
27 March 2001	ECQ	Bulgaria	Vratsa	0–2	3,400
1 June 2001	ECQ	Bulgaria (sub)	Belfast	1–1	769
5 June 2001	ECQ	Czech Republic	Prague	0–4	–
5 October 2002	ECQ	Malta	Ta'quali	2–2 (1)	–

Gary O'Hara

Date	Comp	Opponent	Venue	Score	Attendance
22 March 1994	F	Romania	Belfast	0–0	–

NORWAY
Frank Strandli

Date	Comp	Opponent	Venue	Score	Attendance
27 April 1993	ECQ	Turkey (sub)	Honefoss	5–2 (1)	4,000
1 June 1993	ECQ	England	Stavanger	1–1	6,840
8 June 1993	ECQ	Holland	Utrecht	1–2	1,500
21 September 1993	ECQ	Polan	Stavanger	3–1	2,395
12 October 1993	ECQ	Poland	Pitka	0–2	10,000
9 November 1993	ECQ	Turkey	Istanbul	1–3 (1)	–

SCOTLAND
David McNiven

Date	Comp	Opponent	Venue	Score	Attendance
12 October 1976	ECQ	Czechoslovakia	Pilsen	0–0	3,000
9 February 1977	F	Wales (sub)	Edinburgh	3–2 (1)	4,538
30 March 1978	ECQ	Switzerland (sub)	Berne	0–2	500

Alan Martin

Date	Comp	Opponent	Venue	Score	Attendance
18 November 2008	F	Northern Ireland	Hamilton	1–3	2,149
28 March 2009	ECQ	Albania	Elbasan	1–0	1,600

On loan at Barrow

WALES

Steve Balcombe

24 February 1982	F	France (sub)	Troyes	0–0	4,811

Kevin Evans

4 June 1999	ENQ	Italy (sub)	Paolo Mazza	2–6	7,000
8 June 199	ENQ	Denmark	Wrexham	1–2 (1)	881

Glan Letheran

15 December 1976	F	England	Wolverhampton	0–0	4,389
9 February 1977	F	Scotland	Edinburgh	2–3	4,538

Matthew Jones

10 October 1997	ENQ	Belgium	Mouscron	0–1	500
4 September 1998	ENQ	Italy	Wrexham	1–2	1,375
9 October 1998	ENQ	Denmark	Odense	2–2	947
13 October 1998	ENQ	Belarus	Barry	0–0	326
30 March 1999	ENQ	Switzerland	Winterthur	0–1	1,050
4 June 1999	ENQ	Italy	Paolo Mazza	2–6 (1)	7,000
8 October 1999	ENQ	Switzerland	Newtown	0–0	1,050

Gary Speed

19 May 1990	F	Poland	Merthyr	2–0	1,785
5 December 1990	F	England	Tranmere	0–0	6,288
30 May 1991	F	Poland	Warsaw	2–0 (2)	–

Byron Stevenson

15 December 1976	F	England	Wolverhampton	0–0	4,389
9 February 1977	F	Scotland	Edinburgh	2–3	4,538
8 February 1978	F	Scotland	Chester	1–0	2,454

Gwyn Thomas

15 December 1976	F	England	Wolverhampton	0–0	4,389
6 February 1979	F	England	Swansea	0–1	5,642
20 September 1979	ECQ	Norway	Frederikstad	3–2	1,051

REPUBLIC OF IRELAND

Len Curtis

24 March 1992	F	Switzerland	Dublin	1–1	1,500
25 May 1992	ECQ	Albania	Dublin	3–1	1,200

Ian Harte

23 March 1996	F	Russia	Drogheda	0–1	2,500
30 May 1996	F	Norway	Drogheda	1–1	500

Gary Kelly

17 November 1992	ECQ	Spain (sub)	Jerez	1–2	12,000
9 March 1993	ECQ	Germany	Dublin	0–1	–
23 March 1993	ECQ	Germany	Baunatal	0–8	–
26 May 1993	ECQ	Albania	Tirana	1–1	–
12 October 1993	ECQ	Spain	Drogheda	0–2	500

Stephen McPhail

13 October 1998	ENQ	Malta (sub)	Arklow	2–1	4,500
31 May 1999	F	Scotland	Elgin	0–1	3,816
2 June 1999	F	Northern Ireland (sub)	Inverness	1–0	605
8 June 1999	ENQ	Macedonia	Galway	0–0*	2,000
31 August 1999	ENQ	Yugoslavia	Dublin	0–2	740

3 September 1999	ENQ	Croatia	Zagreb	1–5	1,103
31 August 2001	ENQ	Holland	Waterford	1–0	–

* UEFA awarded the Republic of Ireland a 3–0 win as Macedonia fielded a suspended player

Alan Maybury

10 October 1998	ENQ	Romania	Drogheda	0–2	1,250
27 April 1999	ENQ	Sweden	Birr Town	0–3	1,800
31 May 1999	F	Scotland	Elgin	0–1	3,816
2 June 1999	F	Northern Ireland (sub)	Inverness	1–0	605
31 August 1999	ENQ	Yugoslavia	Dublin	0–2	740
7 September 1999	ENQ	Malta	Ta'Quali	3–1	1,158

Tony O'Dowd

30 May 1990	F	Malta (as sub)	Valetta	1–1	–
16 October 1990	ECQ	Turkey	Dublin	3–2	3,500
13 November 1990	ECQ	England	Cork	0–3	3,000

John Sheridan

25 March 1985	F	England	Portsmouth	2–3	5,489
17 February 1987	ECQ	Scotland	Edinburgh	1–4	4,136

Curtis and O'Dowd did not play first-team football for Leeds United

UNOFFICIAL INTERNATIONALS
(Including wartime and Victory games)

ALL IRELAND
Johnny Giles

4 July 1973		Brazil	Dublin	3–4	34,000

This match, at Lansdowne Road, was regarded as a full international by the Brazilian FA, but not the Irish.

ENGLAND
Jack Charlton

4 June 1969		Mexico XI	Guadalajara	4–0	45,000

This game was played as part of England's 1970 World cup warm–up programme.

Trevor Cherry

31 May 1976		Team America	Philadelphia	3–1	16,231

This game was played as part of the United States Bicentennial Tournament.

Terry Cooper

17 May 1967		Young England	Highbury	1–4	20,077

Wilf Copping

13 April 1939		Wales	Wembley	0–1	40,000

Paul Reaney

17 May 1967		Young England	Highbury	1–4	20,077

FA OF IRELAND XI
Johnny Giles

5 January 1972		West German Olympic XI	Dublin	3–0	–

GREAT BRITAIN
John Charles

13 August 1955		Rest of Europe	Belfast	1–4	60,000

Played at Windsor Park to mark the 75th anniversary of the Irish FA.

IRELAND
David Cochrane

9 September 1944	Combined Services	Belfast	4–8	49,875

IRELAND/WALES
John Charles

14 May 1956	England/Scotland	Dublin	3–3	—

IRISH FREE STATE
Harry Duggan

6 May 1936	Rhineland	Cologne	1–4	—

The Irish international side were touring Germany and played a German international side which was chosen from players from the Rhineland only, so it has never been included by the Republic in official records.

REST OF UK

Billy Bremner, Jack Charlton and Terry Cooper all played for the Rest of the United Kingdom versus Wales at Ninian Park on 28 July 1969 in a game to mark the investiture of Charles, the Prince of Wales. The Rest won 1–0 in front of 13,605 fans with money raised from the game going to the Aberfan Disaster Fund. Gary Sprake was in goal for Wales (see below).

SCOTLAND
Billy Bremner

24 February 1964	Scottish League	Glasgow	3–1	12,000

Peter Lorimer

27 January 1971	Celtic/Rangers XI	Hampden Park	2–1 (1)	81,405

This game was played to raise funds for the Ibrox Park Disaster.

WALES
Aubrey Powell

8 May 1943	England	Cardiff	1–1	25,000
25 September 1943	England	Wembley	3–8 (1)	80,000
20 October 1945	England	West Bromwich	1–0 (1)	56,000
4 May 1946	Northern Ireland	Cardiff	0–1	45,000

Gary Sprake

28 July 1969	Rest of UK	Cardiff	0–1	13,605

WORLD STARS
Lucas Radebe

12 June 1999	Australia	Sydney	2–3	88,101

YOUNG ENGLAND
Norman Hunter

17 May 1967	England	Highbury	4–1	20,077

Paul Reaney

13 May 1966	England	Stamford Bridge	4–1	18,274

OTHER INTERNATIONAL MATCHES
AUSTRALIAN OLYMPIC TEAM
Danny Milosevic

6 September 2000	F	Kuwait	Melbourne	3–0	x

8 September 2000	F	South Africa	Melbourne	1–0	—
13 September 2000	OG	Italy	Melbourne	0–1	93,252
16 September 2000	OG	Nigeria	Sydney	2–3	38,080
19 September 2000	OG	Honduras	Sydney	1–2	37,788

x Played behind closed doors

Mark Viduka

13 September 2000	OG	Italy	Melbourne	0–1	93,252
16 September 2000	OG	Nigeria	Sydney	2–3	38,080
19 September 2000	OG	Honduras	Sydney	1–2	37,788

INTERNATIONAL TRIALS MATCHES
ENGLAND
Matches involving Leeds players were England versus The Rest, and Possibles versus Probables

Wilf Copping

| 22 March 1933 | England | Portsmouth | 5–1 | 15,103 |
| 21 March 1934 | The Rest | Sunderland | 1–7 | 13,500 |

Willis Edwards

16 February 1926	The Rest	Newcastle	3–4	15,000
17 January 1927	The Rest	Stamford Bridge	7–3	11,473
7 February 1927	The Rest	Bolton	2–3	14,000
23 February 1928	The Rest	West Bromwich	5–1	10,355
8 Feb 1928	The Rest	Middlesbrough	8–3	18,431
4 February 1929	The Rest	Hillsborough	4–3	17,400
11 March 1929	The Rest	Tottenham	1–2	16,000
12 March 1930	The Rest	Anfield	1–6	12,000

Billy Furness

| 21 March 1934 | The Rest | Sunderland | 1–7 | 13,500 |

Ernie Hart

4 February 1929	The Rest	Hillsborough	4–3	17,400
11 March 1929	The Rest	Tottenham	1–2	16,000
21 March 1934	The Rest	Sunderland	1–7	13,500

Bert Sproston

| 13 October 1937 | Possibles | Goodison Park | 1–1 | 7,000 |

Russell Wainscoat

| 4 February 1929 | The Rest | Hillsborough | 4–3 | 17,400 |

SCOTLAND
Anglo Scots versus Scots
Tom Jennings

| 13 March 1928 | Scots | Partick | 1–1 (1) | 6,000 |

ASSORTED REPRESENTATIVE MATCHES
YORKSHIRE
Both Willis Edwards and Russell Wainscoat played for Yorkshire against Lancashire on 27 April 1925 at Turf Moor, Burnley, Yorkshire winning 4–3 in front of 6,000 fans. The match was a benefit game for the dependents of Jack Howarth, a Burnley player, and was used by the Football League to experiment with a new offside law.

FA XI
Jack Charlton

| 18 October 1961 | British Army | Sunderland | 1–2 | — |

Willis Edwards

10 October 1928	Lancashire	Bolton	5–6	8,000

Russell Wainscoat

10 Oct1928	Lancashire (sub)	Bolton	5–6	8,000

IRISH NATIONAL LOTTERY XI

Both Gordon Strachan and Gordon McAllister played for the Irish National Lottery XI against a Republic of Ireland XI at Dublin on 11 May 1994, the Republic winning 5–1 in front of 42,630 fans.

COMMON MARKET CELEBRATION MATCH

Johnny Giles, Norman Hunter and Peter Lorimer all played for The Three against The Six in a match at Wembley to mark the entry of the United Kingdom, Republic of Ireland and Denmark (The Three) to the existing Common Market (The Six) comprising players from Belgium, France, Holland, Italy, Luxembourg and West Germany. The Three won 2–0 in front of 36,500 fans.

FOOTBALL LEAGUE REPRESENTATIVES

Although not international games, Football League representative games were often used as trial matches ahead of international fixtures.

Jack Charlton

9 October 1957	League of Ireland	Elland Road	3–1	13,000
17 March 1965	Scottish League	Hampden Park	2–2 (1)	38,409
27 October 1965	League of Ireland	Hull	5–0 (1)	28,283
16 March 1966	Scottish League	Newcastle	1–3	32,900
21 September 1966	Irish League	Plymouth	12–0	35,458
27 September 1966	Belgian League	Brussels	2–2	35,000

Trevor Cherry

17 March 1976	Scottish League	Hampden Park	1–0 (1)	8,874

Wilf Copping

4 October 1933	Irish League	Preston	4–0	14,400
10 February 1934	Scottish League	Hampden Park	2–2	59,000

Willis Edwards

13 March 1926	Scottish League	Hampden Park	2–0	49,000
9 October 1926	Irish League	Belfast	6–1	14,000
19 March 1927	Scottish League	Leicester	2–2	26,000
21 September 1927	Irish League	Newcastle	9–1	1,122
10 March 1928	Scottish League	Hampden Park	6–2	60,000
22 September 1928	Irish League	Belfast	5–0	15,000
7 November 1928	Scottish League	Villa Park	2–1	25,000
25 September 1928	Irish League	Goodison Park	7–2	18,000
2 November 1929	Scottish League	Hampden Park	1–2	40,000
23 September 1931	Irish League	Blackpool	3–0	15,233
7 November 1931	Scottish League	Hampden Park	3–4	51,000

Ernie Hart

7 November 1928	Scottish League	Villa Park	2–1	25,000
25 September 1928	Irish League	Goodison Park	7–2	18,000
2 November 1929	Scottish League	Hampden Park	1–2	40,000

Norman Hunter

28 October 1964	Irish League	Belfast	4–0	20,000
17 March 1965	Scottish League	Hampden Park	2–2	38,409
27 October 1965	League of Ireland	Hull	5–0	28,283
16 March 1966	Scottish League	Newcastle	1–3	32,900

27 September 1967	Belgian League	Brussels	2–2	35,000
10 September 1969	League of Ireland	Barnsley	3–0	11,939

Paul Madeley

10 September 1969	League of Ireland	Barnsley	3–0	11,939

Paul Reaney

16 March 1966	Scottish League	Newcastle	1–3	32,900
10 September 1969	League of Ireland	Barnsley	3–0	11,939
17 March 1971	Scottish League	Hampden Park	1–0	17,657

Bert Sproston

22 September 1937	Scottish League	Hampden Park	1–0	40,000
6 October 1937	Irish League	Blackpool	3–0	14,700

FA TOURS
George Ainsley

1 July 1939	South Africa	Johannesburg	2–1	17,000

Ken Gadsby

1 July 1939	South Africa	Johannesburg	2–1	17,000

Grenville Hair

13 May 1961	Malaya	Kuala Lumpur	4–2	20,000
17 May 1961	Singapore	Singapore	9–0	14,294
21 May 1961	Hong Kong	Hong Kong	4–2	–
23 May 1961	Combined Chinese XI	Hong Kong	3–0	20,000
5 June 1961	New Zealand	Wellington	8–0	–
10 June 1961	New Zealand	Auckland	6–1	–

Also to Bermuda and West Indies 1955, Ghana and Nigeria 1958, Malaysia, Hong Kong

Ernie Hart

15 June 1929	South Africa	Durban	3–2 (1)	12,000
13 July 1929	South Africa	Johannesburg	2–1	–
17 July 1929	South Africa	Cape Town	3–2	–

Norman Hunter

3 June 1967	Leon (Mexico)	Montreal	3–0	–
9 June 1967	First Vienna (Austria)	Montreal	2–1	–
11 June 1967	Borussia Dortmund (Germany)	Montreal	3–2 (1)	22,467

Paul Madeley

3 June 1967	Leon (Mexico)	Montreal	3–0	–
9 June 1967	First Vienna (Austria)	Montreal	2–1	–
11 June 1967	Borussia Dortmund (Germany)	Montreal	3–2 (1)	22,467

Bobby Turnbull

13 July 1929	South Africa	Johannesburg	2–1	–
17 July 1929	South Africa	Cape Town	3–2	–

Russell Wainscoat
to Canada 1926

Ernie Hart played for the Professionals against Amateurs at Millwall on 7 October 1929. The Professionals won 3–0.

George Ainsley played for the English Professional Trainers against Norway in Oslo on 2 August 1946. The trainers, drawn from players who were coaching in Norway in summer 1946, won 1–0 in front of a 25,000 crowd.

LEEDS CITY
FULL INTERNATIONALS

WALES
Dickie Morris

3 March 1906	HC	Scotland	Edinburgh	2–0	25,000

IRELAND
Joe Enright

16 March 1912	HC	Scotland	Belfast	1–4	12,000

Joe Moran

16 March 1912	HC	Scotland	Belfast	1–4	12,000

Billy Scott

18 January 1913	HC	Wales	Belfast	0–1	20,000
15 February 1913	HC	England	Belfast	2–1	20,000
15 March 1913	HC	Scotland	Dublin	1–2	12,000

AMATEUR INTERNATIONALS
ENGLAND
Ivan Sharpe

7 February 1914	F	Wales	Plymouth	9–1 (1)	–
24 February 1914	F	Belgium	Brussels	8–1 (2)	–
5 June 1914	F	Denmark	Copenhagen	0–8	–
10 June 1914	OG	Sweden	Stockholm	5–1 (1)	–
12 June 1914	OG	Sweden	Stockholm	5–0	–

AMATEUR REPRESENTATIVE GAMES
Ivan Sharpe

6 October 1913 for Amateurs versus Professionals	Millwall	2–7	20,000

List of Caps and Scorers

International Caps With Leeds United

58 — Lucas Radebe (South Africa)

56 — Ian Harte (Republic of Ireland)

54 — Billy Bremner (Scotland)

52 — Gary Kelly (Republic of Ireland)

41 — Gary McAllister (Scotland)

36 — Gary Speed (Wales)

35 — Jack Charlton (England)

32 — Brian Flynn (Wales), Johnny Giles (Republic of Ireland), Gary Sprake (Wales)

28 — Norman Hunter (England), Terry Yorath (Wales)

27 — Trevor Cherry (England), Joe Jordan (Scotland)

24 — Frank Gray (Scotland), Carl Harris (Wales), Paul Madeley (England)

23 — Eirik Bakke (Norway)

21 — John Charles (Wales), Peter Lorimer (Scotland)

20 — Terry Cooper (England), Nigel Martyn (England)

19 — David Batty (England), Allan Clarke (England), Danny Mills (England)

18 — Tony Yeboah (Ghana)

17 — Rio Ferdinand (England), David Healey (Northern Ireland), Gordon McQueen (Scotland)

16 — Willis Edwards (England), David Harvey (Scotland), Robbie Keane (Republic of Ireland)

15 — Wilbur Cush (Northern Ireland)

14 — Rui Marques (Angola), Nigel Worthington (Northern Ireland)

13 — Harry Kewell (Australia)

12 — David Cochrane (Northern Ireland), Eddie Gray (Scotland), Phil Masinga (South Africa)

11 — Gunnar Halle (Norway), Byron Stevenson (Wales)

10 — Tony Currie (England), Arthur Graham (Scotland), Alf-Inge Haaland (Norway), Stephen McPhail (Republic of Ireland)

 9 — Mark Aizlewood (Wales), Eric Cantona (France), Tony Dorigo (England)

 8 — Harry Duggan (Northern Ireland), Gylfi Einarsson (Iceland), Ernie Hart (England), Eddie Lewis (United States of America), Alan Smith (England), Bert Sproston (England), Gordon Strachan (Scotland)

 7 — Wilf Copping (England), Martin Hiden (Austria), Mark Viduka (Australia)

 6 — Bobby Browne (Northern Ireland), Alan Curtis (Wales), Jim McCabe (Northern Ireland), Dominic Matteo (Scotland)

 5 — Olivier Dacourt (France), Jonathan Douglas (Republic of Ireland), Jimmy-Floyd Hasselbaink (Holland), David Hopkin (Scotland), Matthew Jones (Wales), Aubrey Powell (Wales), Noel Peyton (Republic of Ireland), John Sheridan (Republic of Ireland)

 4 — Harry Duggan (Republic of Ireland), Robbie Fowler (England), Paul Robinson (England), Harold Williams (Wales), Jonathan Woodgate (England)

 3 — Bobby Collins (Scotland), Peter Fitzgerald (Republic of Ireland), *Teddy Lucic (Sweden), Con Martin (Northern Ireland), Con Martin (Republic of Ireland), Paul Reaney (England), *Roque Junior (Brazil)

 2 — Peter Barnes (England), Willie Bell (Scotland), Jacob Burns (Australia), *Stephen Caldwell (Scotland), Jeff Chandler (Republic of Ireland), Alan Maybury (Republic of Ireland), Paul Okon (Australia), Alan Peacock (England), *Lamine Sakho (Senegal), Eric Stephenson (England), Frank Strandli (Norway), Jim Twomey (Northern Ireland)

 1 — Lee Bowyer (England), *Raul Bravo (Spain), Billy Furness (England), Brian Greenhoff (England), Mick Jones (England), Tresor Kandol (DR Congo), Neil Kilkenny (Australia), *Radostin Kishishev (Bulgaria), Billy McAdams (Northern Ireland), John McClelland (Northern Ireland), Lubomir Michalik (Slovakia), Mike O'Grady (England), *Salomon Olembe (Cameroon), David Stewart (Scotland), Russell Wainscoat (England), Jason Wilcox (England)

* Appearances while on loan with Leeds United

Note: Harry Duggan and Con Martin were dual Irish internationals, playing 12 and six times respectively for their countries.

International Goals With Leeds United

13 – David Healy (Northern Ireland)

12 – John Charles (Wales)

10 – Allan Clarke (England)

9 – Ian Harte (Republic of Ireland)

7 – Robbie Keane (Republic of Ireland), Joe Jordan (Scotland)

6 – Jack Charlton (England)

5 – Wilbur Cush (Northern Ireland), Brian Flynn (Wales), Tony Yeboah (Ghana)

4 – Harry Kewell (Australia), Gary McAllister (Scotland), Phil Masinga (South Africa), Peter Lorimer (Scotland)

3 – Billy Bremner (Scotland), Eddie Gray (Scotland), Jimmy-Floyd Hasselbaink (Holland), Gordon McQueen (Scotland)

2 – Eric Cantona (France), Tony Currie (England), Alan Curtis (Wales), Peter Fitzgerald (Republic of Ireland), Robbie Fowler (England), Johnny Giles (Republic of Ireland), Arthur Graham (Scotland), Carl Harris (Wales), David Hopkin (Scotland), Norman Hunter (England), Gary Kelly (Republic of Ireland), Lucas Radebe (South Africa), Gary Speed (Wales)

1 – Frank Gray (Scotland), Martin Hiden (Austria), Stephen McPhail (Republic of Ireland), Mike O'Grady (England), Alan Peacock (England), John Sheridan (Republic of Ireland), Alan Smith (England), Gordon Strachan (Scotland), Frank Strandli (Norway), Mark Viduka (Australia), Terry Yorath (Wales)

International Appearances With Leeds City

3 – Billy Scott (Northern Ireland)

1 – Joe Enright (Northern Ireland), Joe Moran (Northern Ireland), Dickie Morris (Wales)

Order of International Debuts

1 March 1926	Willis Edwards (England) versus Wales
27 April 1927	+Harry Duggan (Republic of Ireland) versus Italy B
17 November 1928	Ernie Hart (England) versus Wales
13 April 1929	Russell Wainscoat (England) versus Scotland
19 October 1929	+Harry Duggan (Northern Ireland) versus England
13 May 1933	Wilf Copping (England) versus Italy
13 May 1933	Billy Furness (England) versus Italy
19 October 1935	Bobby Browne (Northern Ireland) versus England
17 October 1936	Bert Sproston (England) versus Wales
16 March 1938	Jim Twomey (Northern Ireland) versus Wales
9 April 1938	Eric Stephenson (England) versus Scotland
16 November 1938	David Cochrane (Northern Ireland) versus England
19 October 1946	Aubrey Powell (Wales) versus Scotland
2 March 1947	+Con Martin (Republic of Ireland) versus Spain
4 October 1947	+Con Martin (Northern Ireland) versus Scotland
17 November 1948	Jim McCabe (Northern Ireland) versus Scotland
8 March 1950	John Charles (Wales) versus Northern Ireland
8 March 1950	Harold Williams (Wales) versus Northern Ireland
4 December 1957	Wilbur Cush (Northern Ireland) versus Italy
11 May 1960	Noel Peyton (Republic of Ireland) versus West Germany
28 September 1960	Peter Fitzgerald (Republic of Ireland) versus Wales
9 May 1962	Billy McAdams (Northern Ireland) versus Holland
23 September 1963	Johnny Giles (Republic of Ireland) versus Austria
20 November 1963	Gary Sprake (Wales) versus Scotland
10 April 1965	Bobby Collins (Scotland) versus England
8 May 1965	Billy Bremner (Scotland) versus Spain
2 October 1965	Alan Peacock (England) versus Wales
8 December 1965	Norman Hunter (England) versus Spain (sub)
18 June 1966	Willie Bell (Scotland) versus Portugal
11 December 1968	Paul Reaney (England) versus Bulgaria (sub)
12 March 1969	Terry Cooper (England) versus France
10 April 1965	Jack Charlton (England) versus Scotland)
12 March 1969	Mike O'Grady (England) versus France
10 May 1969	Eddie Gray (Scotland) versus England
4 November 1969	Terry Yorath (Wales) versus Italy
5 November 1973	Peter Lorimer (Scotland) versus Austria (sub)
14 January 1970	Mick Jones (England) versus Holland
11 June 1970	Allan Clarke (England) versus Czechoslovakia
15 May 1971	Paul Madeley (England) versus Northern Ireland
15 November 1972	David Harvey (Scotland) versus Denmark
19 May 1973	Joe Jordan (Scotland) versus England
1 June 1974	Gordon McQueen (Scotland) versus Belgium
24 March 1976	Trevor Cherry (England) versus Wales
24 March 1976	Carl Harris (Wales) versus England
7 April 1976	Frank Gray (Scotland) versus Switzerland

7 September 1977	Arthur Graham (Scotland) versus East Germany (sub)
7 September 1977	David Stewart (Scotland) versus East Germany
16 November 1977	Brian Flynn (Wales) versus Czechoslovakia
19 April 1978	Tony Currie (England) versus Brazil
19 May 1978	Byron Stevenson (Wales) versus Northern Ireland
23 May 1979	Alan Curtis (Wales) versus England
26 September 1979	Jeff Chandler (Republic of Ireland) versus Czechoslovakia (sub)
31 May 1980	Brian Greenhoff (England) versus Australia (sub)
9 September 1981	Peter Barnes (England) versus Norway (sub)
18 February 1987	Mark Aizlewood (Wales) versus USSR
23 March 1988	John Sheridan (Republic of Ireland) versus Romania
11 October 1989	Gordon Strachan (Scotland) versus France
27 March 1990	John McClelland (Northern Ireland) versus Norway
20 May 1990	Gary Speed (Wales) versus Costa Rica (sub)
12 September 1990	Gary McAllister (Scotland) versus Romania
21 May 1991	David Batty (England) versus USSR (sub)
11 September 1991	Tony Dorigo (England) versus Germany
19 February 1992	Eric Cantona (France) versus England
15 January 1994	Frank Strandli (Norway) versus USA
23 March 1994	Gary Kelly (Republic of Ireland) versus Russia
4 September 1994	Phil Masinga (South Africa) versus Madagascar
4 September 1994	Lucas Radebe (South Africa) versus Madagascar
7 September 1994	Nigel Worthington (Northern Ireland) versus Portugal
23 April 1995	Tony Yeboah (Ghana) versus Niger
24 April 1996	Harry Kewell (Australia) versus Chile
2 June 1996	Ian Harte (Republic of Ireland) versus Croatia (sub)
30 April 1997	Gunnar Halle (Norway) versus Finland (sub)
24 May 1997	Nigel Martyn (England) versus South Africa)
20 August 1997	Alf-Inge Haaland (Norway) versus Finland (sub)
7 September 1997	David Hopkin (Scotland) versus Belarus
25 March 1998	Martin Hiden (Austria) versus Hungary
25 March 1998	Alan Maybury (Republic of Ireland) versus Czech Republic
24 May 1998	Jimmy-Floyd Hasselbaink (Holland) versus Lausanne Sport
23 February 1999	Eirik Bakke (Norway) versus Turkey (sub)
9 October 1999	Matthew Jones (Wales) versus Switzerland (sub)
9 June 1999	Jonathan Woodgate (England) versus Bulgaria
23 February 2000	Jason Wilcox (England) versus Argentina
30 May 2000	Stephen McPhail (Republic of Ireland) versus Scotland
15 November 2000	Jacob Burns (Australia) versus Scotland (sub)
15 November 2000	Dominic Matteo (Scotland) versus Australia
28 February 2001	Rio Ferdinand (England) versus Spain
24 March 2001	Robbie Keane (Republic of Ireland) versus Cyprus
25 May 2001	Danny Mills (England) versus Mexico (sub)
25 May 2001	Alan Smith (England) versus Mexico
30 May 2001	Olivier Dacourt (France) versus South Korea (sub)
11 November 2001	Mark Viduka (Australia) versus France
27 March 2002	Robbie Fowler (England) versus Italy (sub)
7 September 2002	Lee Bowyer (England) versus Portugal
20 November 2002	*Teddy Lucic (Sweden) versus Czech Republic
12 February 2003	Paul Okon (Australia) versus England

12 February 2003	Paul Robinson (England) versus Australia
2 April 2003	*Raul Bravo (Spain) versus Armenia
12 October 2003	*Roque Junior (Brazil) versus Jamaica
2 February 2004	*Lamine Sakho (Senegal) versus Mali (sub)
3 February 2004	*Salomon Olembe (Cameroon) versus Egypt (sub)
18 February 2004	*Stephen Caldwell (Scotland) versus Wales
9 February 2005	David Healy (Northern Ireland) versus Canada
26 March 2005	Gylfi Einarsson (Iceland) versus Croatia
17 August 2005	Eddie Lewis (USA) versus Trinidad & Tobago
1 March 2006	Rui Marques (Angola) versus South Korea (sub)
7 October 2006	Jonathan Douglas (Republic of Ireland) versus Cyprus (sub)
28 March 2007	*Radostin Kishishev (Bulgaria) versus Albania
28 March 2007	*Lubomir Michalik (Slovakia) versus Republic of Ireland (sub)
22 June 2008	Neil Kilkenny (Australia) versus China
20 August 2008	*Tresor Kandol (DR Congo) versus Togo
12 August 2009	Patrick Kisnorbo (Australia) versus Republic of Ireland

* Appeared while on loan, or a Leeds player on loan at another club
+ Dual Irish international

ORDER OF INTERNATIONAL DEBUTS WITH LEEDS CITY

3 March 1906	Dickie Morris (Wales) versus Scotland
16 March 1912	Joe Enright (Northern Ireland) versus Scotland
16 March 1912	Joe Moran (Northern Ireland) versus Scotland
18 January 1913	Billy Scott (Northern Ireland) versus Wales

International Matches at Elland Road

Full Internationals

8 June 1995
Umbro Cup
England 3 *(Sheringham 44, Platt 88, Anderton 89)*
Sweden 3 *(Mild 11, 37, K. Andersson 46)*

ELLAND Road had been selected as one of the stadia for Euro '96, so this Umbro Cup game was a trial run for the organisers. The construction of the new 17,000 £5.5 million East Stand had helped Leeds to become one of the hosts for the Championships. The game was the first full England international held outside Wembley since a 1–1 draw with Poland at Goodison Park on 5 January 1966.

England were outplayed by the Swedes for large parts of the game, but rescued a draw with late goals by David Platt and Darren Anderton. England had beaten Japan 2–1 in their opening game, but lost 2–1 to tournament winners Brazil in the final game at Wembley. Former Leeds junior John Scales and future United player Nick Barmby got on as subs, while Teddy Lucic, a future loanee, played for Sweden.

England versus Sweden 1995.

England: Tim Flowers (Blackburn Rovers), Warren Barton (Newcastle United), Colin Cooper (Nottingham Forest), Gary Pallister (Manchester United) [sub John Scales (Tottenham Hotspur) 80 mins], Graeme Le Saux (Blackburn Rovers), Darren Anderton (Tottenham Hotspur), David Platt (Sampdoria), John Barnes (Liverpool) [sub Paul Gascoigne (Lazio) 63 mins], Peter Beardsley (Newcastle United) [sub Nick Barmby (Tottenham Hotspur) 63 mins], Teddy Sheringham (Tottenham Hotspur), Alan Shearer (Blackburn Rovers).
Manager: Terry Venables
Sweden: Thomas Ravelli (IFK Gothenburg), Gary Sundren (AIK Stockholm), Pontus Kamark (IFK Gothenburg), Joachim

Autographed and framed England and Sweden shirts at Elland Road from the 1995 Umbro Cup game.

Bjorklund (IFK Gotheburg), Teddy Lucic (Vasta Frolunda), Niclas Alexandersson (Halmstads), Hakan Mild (Servette), Magnus Erlingmark (IFK Gothenburg) [sub Ola Andersson (AIK Stockholm) 88 mins], Niklas Gudmundsson (Halmstads), Kennet Andersson (Caen) [sub Dick Lidman (AIK Stockholm) 84 mins)], Henrik Larsson (Feyenoord)
Manager: Tommy Svensson
Referee: Leslie Mottram (Scotland) **Attendance:** 32,008

9 June 1996
European Championship Finals, Group B
Bulgaria 1 *(Stoitchkov 65 pen)*
Spain 1 *(Alfonso 74)*

Euro '96 programme.

THIS game opened Group B with Romania taking on France in Newcastle the following day. All the action came in an explosive second half in which Bulgaria's star striker Hristo Stoichkov was outstanding. He had already gone close several times before putting his team ahead from the spot after strike partner Emil Kostadinov had been fouled. Seven minutes later defender Petar Houbtchev was sent off and shortly afterwards substitute Alfonso Perez flicked in the equaliser.

More drama followed as Antonio Pizzi was sent off on 75 minutes for hacking down Radostin Kishishev, who was to have two loan spells with Leeds a decade later.

Bulgaria: Borislav Mihaylov (Reading), Radostin Kishishev (Neftochemik Burgas), Petar Houbtchev (SV Hamburg), Trifon Ivanov (Rapid Vienna), Ilian Kiriakov (Aberdeen) [sub Tzanko Tzvetanov (Waldhof Mannheim) 72 mins], Yordan Letchkov (SV Hamburg), Zlatko Yankov (KFC Uerdingen), Krassimir Balakov (VfB Stuttgart), Emil Kostadinov (Bayern Munich) [sub Ivailo Iordanov (Sporting Lisbon) 73 mins], Hristo Stoichkov (Parma), Luboslav Penev (Real Madrid) [sub Daniel Borimov (1860 Munich) 78 mins]
Manager: Dimitar Penev
Spain: Andoni Zubizaretta (Valencia), Alberto Belsue (Real Zaragosa), Aberlardo Fernandez (Barcelona), Sergi (Barcelona), Jose Luis Perez Caminero (Atletico Madrid) [sub Donato Gama (Deportivo La Coruna) 82 mins], Guillermo Amor (Barcelona) [sub Alfonso Perez (Real Betis) 72 mins], Fernando Hierro (Real Madrid), Luis Enrique (Real Madrid), Julen Guerrero (Athletic Bilbao) [sub Jose Emilio Amavisca (Real Madrid) 51 mins], Juan Antonio Pizzi (CD Tenerife)
Manager: Javier Clemente
Referee: Piero Ceccarini (Italy) **Attendance:** 24,006

15 June 1996
European Championship Finals, Group B
France 1 *(Djorkaeff 48)*
Spain 1 *(Caminero 85)*

TWO of the tournament's heavyweights went head to head protecting long unbeaten runs – France 24 matches and Spain 17. In a low-key cautious affair in front of the group's largest attendance, the Spanish came within five minutes of seeing their record ended. Youri Djorkaeff, whose father Jean played against England in the 1966 World Cup, shot France ahead just after half-time. Near the end Julio Salina laid the ball back for Jose Luis Caminero to knock in the point-saver. France went on to beat Romania 3–1 and top the group.

France: Bernard Lama (Paris St Germain), Jocelyn Angloma (Torino) [sub Alain Roche (Paris St Germain) 65 mins], Laurent Blanc (Auxerre), Marcel Desailly (AC Milan), Bixente Lizarazu (Bordeaux), Christian Karembeu (Sampdoria), Didier Deschamps (Juventus), Vincent Guerin (Paris St Germain) [sub Lilian Thuram (Monaco) 81 mins], Youri Djorkaeff (Paris St Germain), Zinedine Zidane (Bordeaux), Patrice Loko (Paris St Germain) [sub Christophe Dugarry (Bordeaux) 74 mins]
Manager: Aime Jacquet
Spain: Andoni Zubizaretta (Valencia), Jorge Otero (Valencia) [sub Francisco Kiko (Atletico Madrid) 59 mins], Juan Manuel Lopez (Atletico Madrid), Aberlardo Fernandez (Barcelona), Sergi Barjuan (Barcelona), Rafael Alkorta (Real Madrid),

Fernando Hierro (Real Madrid), Jose Emilio Amavisca (Real Madrid), Luis Enrique (Real Madrid) [sub Javier Manjarin (Deportivo La Coruna) 55 mins], Jose Luis Perez Caminero (Atletico Madrid), Alfonso Perez (Real Betis) [sub Julio Salinas (Sporting Gijon) 83 mins]
Manager: Javier Clemente
Referee: Vadim Zhuk (Bulgaria) **Attendance:** 35,626

18 June 1996
European Championship Finals, Group B
Romania 1 *(Radiciou 29)*
Spain 2 *(Manjarin 11, Amor 84)*

SUBSTITUTE Guillermo Amor headed a late goal to book Spain's place in the quarter-finals, but there was a hint of controversy about it. Romania defender Daniel Prodan was lying injured in the area, playing Sergi Barjuan onside, and the Barcelona man's cross was touched back by Alfonso Perez for Amor to score.

Javier Manjarin had given Spain an early lead but Gheorghe Hagi, winning his 100th cap, fashioned the equaliser for Florin Radiciou, but it was Spain who marched on to a quarter-final showdown with Terry Venables's England.

Romania: Florin Prunea (Dinamo Bucharest), Anton Dobos (Steaua Bucharest), Daniel Prodan (Steaua Bucharest) [sub Ioan Lupescu (Bayer Leverkusen) 86 mins], Tibor Selymes (Cercle Bruges), Dan Petrescu (Chelsea), Ovidiu Stinga (UD Salamanca), Gheorghe Popescu (Barcelona), Gheorghe Hagi (Barcelona), Constantin Galaca (Steaua Bucharest), Florin Radiciou (Espanyol) [sub Ion Vladoiu (Steaua Bucharest) 77 mins], Adrian Ilie (Steaua Bucharest) [sub Dorinel Munteanu (Cologne) 66 mins]
Manager: Angel Iordanescu
Spain: Andoni Zubizaretta (Valencia), Juan Manuel Lopez (Atletico Madrid), Aberlardo Fernandez (Barcelona) [sub Guillermo Amor (Barcelona) 64 mins], Rafael Alkorta (Real Madrid), Sergi Barjuan (Barcelona), Miguel Nadal (Barcelona), Fernando Hierro (Real Madrid), Javier Manjarin (Deportivo La Coruna), Fransisco Kiko (Atletico Madrid), Jose Emilio Amavisca (Real Madrid) [sub Julen Guerrero (Athletic Bilbao) 72 mins], J.A. Pizzi (CD Tenerife) [sub Alfonso Perez (Real Betis) 57 mins]
Manager: Javier Clemente
Referee: Ahmet Cakar (Turkey) **Attendance:** 32,719

27 March 2002
Friendly International
England 1 *(Fowler 63)*
Italy 2 *(Montella 67, 90 pen)*

THIS was a big night for footballer-spotting anoraks. No less than 41 players featured on the Elland Road turf as two of Europe's big guns met in a pre-World Cup friendly. Sven-Goran Eriksson changed his entire England team, while his opposite number Giovanni Trappatoni made eight substitutions.

As a spectacle it was a poor game, but Leeds's recently acquired goal-poacher Robbie Fowler gave England the lead, but Italy were level soon afterwards through Vincent Montella, who scored a last-minute penalty winner after Massimo Maccarone was brought down by David James. Maccarone had played – and scored – in the 1–1 Under-21 meeting between the two countries at Valley Parade the previous night.

England versus Italy 2002.

England: Nigel Martyn (Leeds United) [sub David James (West Ham United) HT], Danny Mills (Leeds United) [sub Phil Neville (Manchester United) HT], Sol Campbell (Arsenal) [sub Ledley King (Tottenham Hotspur) HT], Gareth Southgate (Middlesbrough) [sub Ugo Ehiogu (Middlesbrough) HT], Wayne Bridge (Southampton) [sub Gary Neville (Manchester United) 87 mins], David Beckham (Manchester United) [sub Danny Murphy (Liverpool) HT] , Nicky Butt (Manchester United) [sub Owen Hargreaves (Bayern Munich) HT], Trevor Sinclair (West Ham United) [sub Teddy Sheringham (Tottenham Hotspur) 70 mins], Emile Heskey (Liverpool) [sub Robbie Fowler (Leeds United) HT], Michael Owen (Liverpool) [sub Darius Vassell (Aston Villa) HT]
Manager: Sven-Goran Eriksson

Italy: Gianluigi Buffon (Juventus), Gianluca Zambrotta (Juventus), Fabio Cannavaro (Parma), Alessandro Nesta (Lazio) [sub Daniele Adani (Fiorentina) 82 mins], Marco Materazzi (Inter Milan) [sub Mark Iuliano (Juventus) 57 mins], Christian Panucci (Roma) [sub Francesco Coco (Barcelona) 74 mins], Christiano Zanetti (Inter Milan) [sub Demetrio Albertini (AC Milan) 57 mins], Roberto Di Baggio (InterMilan) [sub Gennaro Gattuso (AC Milan) 57 mins], Marco Delvecchio (Roma) [sub Massimo Maccarone (Empoli) 74 mins], Francesco Totti (Roma) [sub Vincent Montella (Roma) HT], Christiano Doni (Atalanta) [sub Damiano Tomassi (Roma) HT]
Manager: Giovanni Trapattoni
Referee: Herbert Fandel (Germany) Attendance: 36,635

England Trials

22 January 1906
The North 0
The South 2 (Day 75, Woodward 78)

DESPITE fielding the first £1,000 footballer, Middlesbrough's Alf Common, The North came off second best to The South. Several of the South's gentleman players were drawn from the amateur ranks including cricketers Stan Harris (Surrey, Gloucestershire and Sussex), Gilbert Vassell (Somerset) and Sammy Day (Kent). Of the 22 players on view at Elland Road, 10 went on to play in the following month's 5–0 win against Ireland in Belfast.

The North: Nat Robinson (Birmingham), Bob Crompton (Blackburn Rovers), Tommy Rodway (Preston North End), Ben Warren (Derby County), Colin Veitch (Newcastle United), Jimmy Bradley (Liverpool), Dickie Bond (Preston North End), Alf Common (Middlesbrough), Arthur Brown (Sheffield United), Joe Bache (Aston Villa), Albert Gosnell (Newcastle United).
The South: James Ashcroft (Woolwich Arsenal), Archie Cross (Woolwich Arsenal), Tom Riley (Brentford), Pat Collins (Fulham), Walter Bull (Tottenham Hotspur), Kelly Houlker (Southampton), Gilbert Vassall (Old Carthusians), Sammy Day (Old Malvernians), Vivian Woodward (Tottenham Hotspur), Stanley Harris (Old Westminsters), Gordon Wright (Cambridge University)
Referee: E. Case (Birkenhead) Attendance: 7,000

19 February 1923
England versus The North
Cancelled because of snow.

21 January 1924
The North 5 (Jack 35, 38, Stephenson 2, Bradford 43, Seymour 50)
The South 1 (Haines 85)

NORTHERN clubs dominated the 1923–24 First Division, and their strength was reflected in this comfortable victory against the amateurs of the South. Star of the show was inside-forward Clem Stephenson of Huddersfield Town, who went on to win the title. His performance earned him his sole England cap the following month when Wales pulled off a shock 2–1 win at Ewood Park, Blackburn. None of the South trialists appeared in that match. Stephenson had played regularly for Leeds City during World War One.

The FA reallocated the game to Elland Road after the previous year's fixture was snowed off. The low crowd is attributed to a rail strike and incessant drizzle.

The North: Ronnie Sewell (Blackburn Rovers), Warney Cresswell (Sunderland), Sam Wadsworth (Huddersfield Town), Fred Kean (Sheffield Wednesday), James Seddon (Bolton Wanderers), Percy Barton (Birmingham), Sam Chedgzoy (Everton), David Jack (Bolton Wanderers), Joe Bradford (Birmingham), Clem Stephenson (Huddersfield Town), Stan Seymour (Newcastle United)
The South: Ben Howard Baker (Corinthians), Tom Parker (Southampton), Alfred Bower (Corinthians), Bert Smith (Tottenham Hotspur), Claude Ashton (Corinthians), Tommy Meehan (Chelsea), Dr Jimmy Paterson (Arsenal), Stanley Earle (Clapton), Willie Haines (Portsmouth), Jack Elkes (Tottenham Hotspur), Jackie Hegan (Corinthians)
Referee: E. Farrar (Leeds) Attendance: 4,496

Under-23 Internationals

9 November 1961
England 7 *(Byrne 15, 70, F Hill 18, 53, Farmer 40, S Hill 74, Harris 86)*
Israel 1 *(Levi 8)*

Under-23 International Football

ENGLAND
versus
ISRAEL

ELLAND ROAD GROUND
LEEDS

Thursday, 9th November, 1961
Kick-off 7.30 p.m.

. . . . .

Official Programme . . . Price 6d.

England Under-23 versus Israel, 1961.

ENGLAND fell behind to an early goal by Shlomo Levi but overran the Israelis. They peppered Hapoel Tel Aviv goalkeeper Yaacov Hodorov to make it 3–1 at half-time and put four past his replacement, Yair Nosowski in the second half. Of the England players, the peerless Bobby Moore went on to skipper England to their 1966 World Cup triumph. England manager Walter Winterbottom watched the game, having presided over the Football League side which lost to the Italian League 2–0 at Old Trafford the previous night.

England: Gordon West (Blackpool), Joe Kirkup (West Ham United), Bobby Moore (West Ham United), Brian Labone (Everton), Gordon Jones (Middlesbrough), Alan Deakin (Aston Villa), Steve Hill (Blackpool), Johnny Byrne (Crystal Palace), Ted Farmer (Wolverhampton Wanderers), Freddie Hill (Bolton Wanderers), Gordon Harris (Burnley)
Manager: Walter Winterbottom
Israel: Yaacob Hodorov (Hapoel Tel Aviv) [sub Yair Nosowski (Hapoel Kfar-Saba) HT], Eliezer Aharonov (Maccabi Petah-Tikva) [sub Yaacob Grundman (Bnei-Yehuda Tel-Aviv) 38], Zvi Tendler (Hapoel Haifa), Shalom Peterburg (Hapoel Petah-Tikva), Amatsia Levkovih (Hapoel Tel Aviv), Gidon Tish (Hapoel Tel Avv), Avraham Menchel (Maccabi Haifa), Nahum Stelmach (Hapoel Petah-Tikva), Rehavia Rosenboim (Hapoel Tel Aviv), Shlomo Levy (Hapoel Haifa), Reuven Yang (Hapoel Haifa).
Manager: Gyula Mandi
Referee: Menahem Askenazi (Israel) **Attendance:** 12,419

7 April 1965
England 0
Czechoslovakia 0

ALF Ramsey did not get many clues for the World Cup as the Young Lions drew a blank with Czechoslovakia in front of a poor Elland Road attendance. The best player, Alan Ball, was making his fourth Under-23 appearance, and he was the only one of the team to play in the following year's glorious victory against West Germany. Mick Jones, of course, was later to join Leeds for £100,000, while Martin Chivers came close to a last-minute winner.

England: Bill Glazier (Coventry City), Len Badger (Sheffield United), Tommy Smith (Liverpool), Vic Mobley (Sheffield Wednesday), Bobby Thomson (Wolverhampton Wanderers), Henry Newton (Nottingham Forest), Bert Murray (Chelsea), Martin Chivers (Southampton), Mick Jones (Sheffield United), Alan Ball (Blackpool), George Armstrong (Arsenal)
Manager: Alf Ramsey
Czechoslovakia: Alexandr Vencel (Slovan Bratislava), Miroslav Camarada (Dukla Prague), Vladimir Taborsky (Sparta Prague), Vaclav Migas (Dukla Slany), Karel Knesl (Dukla Prague), Ivan Hrdlicka (Slovan Bratislava), Frantisek Vesely (Slavia Prague), Stanislav Strunc (Sparta Plzen), Eduard Gaborik (Slovan Bratislava), Miroslav Rodr (Dukla Prague), Dusan Kabat (Dukla Prague)
Manager: Jira Vaclav
Referee: Henri Faucheux (France) **Attendance:** 8,533

Under-21 International

European Championship, Group 6
7 October 2005
England 1 *(Cole 18)*
Austria 2 *(Janko 56, 76)*

MARKO Janko's second-half double proved extremely damaging to England's hopes of reaching the European Championship Finals in Portugal. They missed the chance to go top of the group, which was won by Germany, leaving second-placed England to go into a Play-off with France, which they lost on aggregate.

The England side included three former Leeds players – Scott Carson, James Milner and Aaron Lennon – who all went on to win full international honours.

England: Scott Carson (Liverpool), Steven Taylor (Newcastle United), Leighton Baines (Wigan Athletic), Michael Dawson (Tottenham Hotspur), Anton Ferdinand (West Ham United) [sub Ryan Taylor (Wigan Athletic) 71 mins], Tom Huddlestone (Tottenham Hotspur), James Milner (Newcastle United), Tom Soares (Crystal Palace) [Luke Moore (Aston Villa) 61 mins], Carlton Cole (Chelsea) [sub Cameron Jerome (Cardiff City) 87 mins], Jerome Thomas (Charlton Athletic), Aaron Lennon (Tottenham Hotspur)
Manager: Peter Taylor
Austria: Ramazan Ozcan (Austria Lustenau), Mario Sonnleitner (Grazer AK), Dennis Mimm (Wacker Innsbruck), Markus Berger (SV Ried), Alexander Pollhuber (Red Bull Saltzburg), Florian Metz (Austria Vienna), Besian Idrizaj (Liverpool) [sub Philipp Weissenberger (SC Schwanestadt) 67 mins], Gyorgy Garics (Rapid Vienna), Zlatko Junzovic (Grazer AK), Andreas Holzl (Wacker Innsbruk), Marco Janko (SV Saltzburg) [sub Lukas Mossner (SV Mattersburg) 90 mins]
Manager: Willibald Rutternsteiner
Referee: Joeni Van de Velde (Belgium) **Attendance:** 28,030

Amateur Internationals

20 November 1909
England 4 *(Owen 2, Woodward 44, J. Wright og 75, Jordan 88)*
Ireland 4 *(Robertson 5, 82, McDonnell 15, Hooper 20)*

THIS was the first full international match staged at Elland Road – and it turned out to be a real thriller. Ireland had not beaten England at football at either professional or amateur level, but came mighty close at Leeds, leading 3–1 with 15 minutes remaining. They were denied by West Brom's Billy Jordan, who equalised just before the end. Oxford University graduate Jordan had been ordained into the church two years earlier. Receipts for the match were £198 1s 3d.

England: R.G. Brener (Darlington), W.S. Corbett (Birmingham), A.E. Scother (Oxford City), F. Fayers (Watford), F.W. Chapman (South Nottingham), J.E. Olley (Clapton), A. Berry (Fulham), V.J. Woodward (Chelmsford), W.C. Jordan (West Bromwich Albion), A.S. Owen (Leicester Fosse), E.W. Williams (Portsmouth)
Ireland: F. McKee (Cliftonville), P. McCann (Belfast Celtic), P.J. Thunder (Bohemians), J. Wright (Cliftonville), D. Martin (Cliftonville), L. Donnelly (Distillery), J. Wright (Distillery), J. Robertson (Cliftonville), J. McDonnell (Bohemians), Dr W.F. Hooper (Bohemians), F. Thompson (Cliftonville)
Referee: A.A. Jackson (Scotland) **Attendance:** 8,000

16 March 1929
England 3 *(Ashton 28, Kail 67, 85)*
Scotland 1 *(Gates og 51)*

SCOTLAND included eight players from Glasgow club Queen's Park in their line up but were not match for the individual skill and strength of the England players. Edgar Kail, who won three full England caps, was a thorn in the Scots' side and richly deserved his two goals. Chartered accountant Claude Ashton, also capped by the full England side, scored the opener.

On the same day Scotland's rugby union players beat England 12–6 at Murrayfield to retain the Calcutta Cup.
England: B. Howard Baker (Corinthians), F.J. Gregory (Millwall), E.H. Gates (London Corinthians), C.E. Glenister (Navy), A.H. Chadder (Corinthians), J.G. Knight (Casuals), L. Morrish (Dulwich Hamlet), E. Kail (Dulwich Hamlet), C.T. Ashton (Corinthians), A.G. Doggart (Corinthians), K.E. Hogan (Army)
Scotland: R.L. Small (St Bernards), W.O. Walker (Queen's Park), W. Wiseman (Queen's Park), J. McDonald (Queen's Park), R. Gillespie (Queen's Park), W.S. King (Queen's Park), I. McDonald (Murrayfield Amateurs), W.S. Chalmers (Queen's Park), D. McLelland (Queen's Park), J.R. Russell (Edinburgh University), W.G. Nicholson (Queen's Park)
Referee: G.D. Nunnery (Shropshire) **Attendance:** 15,571

26 March 1958
England 1 *(Bradley 6)*
France 1 *(Christobal pen 24)*

ENGLAND'S scorer, schoolteacher Warren Bradley, was signed for Manchester United by Matt Busby after the Munich Air Disaster. A small, tough little winger, he went on to win three full England caps to add to the 11 he won as an amateur.

Only a brilliant display by goalkeeper Mike Pinner enabled England to escape with a draw. A solicitor, he played for Pegasus, whose players were graduates drawn from the universities of Oxford and Cambridge. Pinner played 52 times for the England amateur team.
England: M.J. Pinner (Pegasus), J. Dougall (Pegasus), J.H. Valentine (Loughborough College), R. Vowells (Corinthians Casuals), S. Prince (Walthamstow Avenue), H. Dodkins (Ilford), W. Bradley (Bishop Auckland), D. Bumpstead (Tooting and Mitcham), G. Mortimore (Woking), G. Hamm (Woking), A.M. Peel (Sheffield University)
France: R. Cesaire (VS Quevilly), B. Rodzik (Stade de Rheims), F. Phillipe (AS Brest), M. Christobal (St Etienne), G. Lelong (VS Quevilly), R Monnet (Olympic Lyonaisse), R. Hauser (FC Mulhouse), M. Mouchel (AS Cherbourg), J.L. Bettenfield (AAJ Sainte Fountaine), J. Buron (Dieppe), M. Longle (SCO Angers)
Referee: H. Anderson (Denmark) **Attendance:** 6,000

Rugby League Internationals at Elland Road

Many games of rugby league have been staged at Elland Road, which was used by the RFL for various Cup Finals and semi-finals. Hunslet Hawks shared the ground with Leeds United in the mid-1980s after their home, the nearby greyhound stadium, had been demolished. Considerably larger crowds, though, were attracted by the following international matches, which included New Zealand's shock 24–0 victory against Australia in the 2005 Tri-Nations Final.

9 November 1985	Great Britain 6	New Zealand 6	Att: 22,209
8 November 1985	Great Britain 4	Australia 34	Att: 30,808
10 November 1990	Great Britain 0	Australia 14	Att: 32,500
20 November 1994	Great Britain 4	Australia 23	Att: 39,468
27 November 2004	Great Britain 4	Australia 44	Att: 39,120
26 November 2005	Australia 0	New Zealand 24	Att: 26,534

Footnote: South Africa's rugby union Springboks also played at Elland Road when 14,471 saw them beat The North 19–3 in a representative game on 10 November 1992.

International Speedway at Elland Road

Leeds Lions speedway team raced at Fullerton Park, Elland Road, between 1928 and 1938 and were Northern League champions in 1929. Fullerton Park was for many years the Leeds United training ground opposite the main stadium and is now used as a car park. Two international speedway meetings have been held at Fullerton Park.

| 12 July 1930 | Unofficial Test match | England 29 | Australia 13 |
| 13 August 1938 | Division Two international | England 30 | Dominions 77 |